THE
COMPLETE
ELVIS

EDITED BY MARTIN TORGOFF

ART DIRECTION BY ED CARAEFF

Virgin

L O N D O N

ACKNOWLEDGMENTS

A great many people provided indispensable assistance in putting this book together, as researchers, sources of information, contributors of illustrations, editorial assistants, and just plain old good friends. They are: Jacki and Julie Moline, Carol Ash, Merry Aronson, Pat Rainer, Gay McRae, Stanley Booth, Jerry Schilling, Joan Deary and Sym Meyers of RCA, David Dalton, Ruth Landa, Linda Ray Pratt, Patti Carr Black of the Mississippi State Historical Museum, William Ferris of the Southern Culture Center, Michael Gross, John Walker, Stephanie Chernikowski, and, of course, Kathy Cunningham (my birdie).

Also thanks to Greil Marcus for his patience and to Bill Whitehead, his editor at Dutton, for his helpful suggestions about the excerpts of *Mystery Train*.

And now for the people at Delilah, that rapidly expanding fiefdom of pop publishing, a word of thanks: to Stephanie Bennett, the Publisher and Queen Bee; to Jeannie Sakol, the Editorial Grand Vizier; and to Madeleine Morel, Publicity Director. Special Thanks to Karen Moline, their indefatigable Managing Editor (whose harried disposition is only surpassed by her intelligence and beauty), and to Ed Caraeff, Designer Extraordinaire, Virginia Rubel, Trevor Calender, Una Fahy and Production Manager Richard Schatzberg.

Printed in the United States of America

First published in Great Britain in 1982 by Virgin Books.
61-63 Portobello Road, London W11 3D.

First published in the United States in 1982 by
Delilah Communications, Ltd.

UK distribution by Phin Publishing Ltd.,
Phin House, Cheltenham, Glos.

ISBN: 0 907080 30 8

Book and cover design by Ed Caraeff

THE COMPLETE ELVIS

CONTENTS

EDITOR'S NOTE

This book was originally conceived as a work that would blend some of the latest writing about Elvis Presley with a few of the classics published over the years, topped off by a compendium of useful information about him—a handbook-guidebook, if you will. Of course, as any Elvis fan will be quick to tell you, no single book about Elvis will *ever* be truly "complete": Elvis was too grandiose a figure for that, with far too many levels and aspects; it would take a multi-volume set of books, a veritable encyclopedia, to ever render Elvis complete. But this book *is* complete in that it contains so many different perspectives by fans, critics, journalists, scholars, — that it spans the spectrum of viewpoint. The book is also "complete" in that it makes an attempt to distill an ever-growing body of information down to the barest kernels while still maintaining a comprehensive scope. *The Complete Elvis*, then, is really a complete potpourri, designed to entertain, inform, provoke, and to stand as a handy reference work.

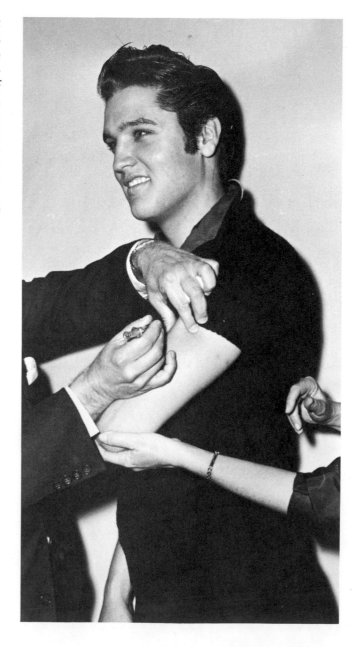

Part One is an anthology of writings. "Anagrams" is a short but sharply observed meditation about Elvis and his continuing impact by Glenn O'Brien, music columnist for *Interview* magazine. "After the Flood: Elvis and His Literary Legacy" takes on the huge body of books and articles that has emerged over the years as seen through the eyes of the author (yours truly) of an "inside" account of Elvis' life; it is not a formal study, but rather an informal guide that attempts to highlight many of the paradoxes and ironies about Elvis' literature.

The following two articles are both by Stanley Booth, a well-known Memphis-based journalist. "A Hound Dog, To A Manor Born," the first piece, is a classic look at Elvis' fifties origins as sharply contrasted with the Elvis of the late sixties (it was first published in *Esquire* magazine in 1968, the year before Elvis' comeback).

"The King Is Dead! Hang the Doctor!" is a penetrating look at the trials (literally and figuratively) and tribulations of Dr. George Nichopoulos—or "Dr. Nick," as Elvis' personal physician is now known throughout the world. Despite his vilification by media and fans in the wake of Elvis' death, the article confronts the entire issue of Elvis' health and the moral ambiguities of his prescription drug problem from Dr. Nick's side. It is not meant as an apologia for Dr. Nick's mistakes, but a useful glance at a man trapped helplessly in the whirlpool of media madness following Elvis' death.

The next piece is an essay by Linda Ray Pratt, a professor of English at the University of Lincoln, Nebraska, originally published by the *Southern Quarterly* and by the University Press of Mississippi in *Elvis: Images and Fancies* (1979). "Elvis Or the Ironies of a Southern Identity" is an excellent example of the kind of scholarly writing being inspired by Elvis at many universities. It is followed by "The Bootleg Elvis," John Walker's lighthearted examination of some of the more bizarre offerings from the hundreds of bootleg albums.

In a section called "Three Fan-atics," we have the feelings and memories of three female Elvis fans of completely different ages and backgrounds. Karen Moline's "A Letter To Elvis" is a breathless and unabashed query about the role of women in Elvis' life; "A Real Gone Cat" by Stephanie Chernikowski is a personal flashback from the night of Elvis' death to the author's adolescence in Beaumont, Texas; and in "More Notes of a Fan-atic," Memphis' own Gay McRae, one of the true Keepers of the Flame among Elvis' fans, simply writes about her lifelong obsession.

Then, in "Elvis In Hollywood," Bill Reed looks into Elvis' love/hate relationship with Tinseltown, the site that housed some of his strongest dreams and fantasies and came to embody some of his most frustrating professional failures.

Finally, two pieces of original fiction complete the anthology. "Two Fantasies" contains two starkly different imaginings: Lenny Kaye's "If Elvis Had Lived"; and "Graceland Uber Alles," from the perfervid brain of Lester Bangs, an imaginary encounter in a hotel room between Elvis Presley and Bob Dylan(!). No doubt we will see many more short stories, plays, screenplays and novels about Elvis in the coming years.

The second part of the book is devoted to references and contains basic information about Elvis, his life, music, films, and people, places, and things. Again, it is a guidebook, not an encyclopedia of trivia. The "Elvis A–Z" originated with Elvis' British fan club. (As everybody knows, Elvis' British fans have always been among the most dedicated in the world.) It was started by the late Albert Hand, the Derby printer who became the editor of the *Elvis Monthly*, and was revised on several different occasions: once by Tim Saville and Ian Bailaye (edited by Todd Slaughter); recently by Ann Nixon; and here in America for this publication, where it has been re-organized and Americanized while retaining the flavor and enthusiasm of the British fans. With the RCA albums, the American catalogue numbers (matrix) have been substituted for the British, but for individual songs, all numbers have been left off. Instead, the song entries have been rewritten to include songwriter, a brief description, date and place of recording, approximate date of release (in the U.S.), the various LP's or EP's it appears on over the years, and the live versions. The more popular bootleg albums are listed individually. A comprehensive international bibliography follows the "A–Z" references.

Martin Torgoff
New York
October, 1981

ANAGRAMS   BY GLENN O'BRIEN

VEILS

In 1984 it will be thirty years since Elvis did it. *Did it!* What? It: ie. his thing, a thing which is still working its magic. What Elvis did was magic. He did a thing that launched a million things. Magic is the art of pure influence—the power of the will to move wills. Helen of Troy launched a thousand ships they say, but Elvis launched a million hips, and a million guitars, a million acts, a million songs.

What was it that Elvis willed? There are a lot of answers to that question, but the most obvious may be the best. First of all Elvis willed his stardom. In a very short time he transformed himself from a singing truck-driver to an idol of unequalled magnetism: *A Flaming Star.*

Elvis' personal transformation to stardom is one of the most contagious parts of his personality. Everyone moved by Elvis was moved to some degree toward stardom. "Every man and every woman is a star," asserted the notorious magician Aleister Crowley, as one of the principles of his magic; and it was to the star in every man and woman that Elvis addressed himself.

And how did he send himself? Well, as mage Crowley put it, "Sex is the most powerful tool available to the magician." And if Elvis didn't know what tool he was using at first, it couldn't have taken him long to figure it out.

Elvis was called "The King" early on. The title came naturally; he reached the top and stayed there, virtually unchallenged. Now he's gone but still King—"the King is dead, long live the King."

What made Elvis the King and what keeps him there is a tremendous individuality. He was quintessentially unique—alone in any crowd. When Elvis drove girls wild he did it alone. It wasn't his band, it wasn't the music; it was his person, his presence, his imperturbable solitude. No one is as alone as a king—he has no peers. A king is always surrounded by his household and his court, but he is always isolated by his position.

That's the way it was with Elvis. In a group of superstars he was alone; hanging out with his ever-present entourage he was alone. Like most kings Elvis probably longed for some real company but his position made it impossible. And as with conventional monarchs it was perhaps this irrevocable solitude that appealed to the masses. Elvis' solitude, his loneliness could be appreciated by the masses of fans. Ordinary nobles, ordinary celebrities are never alone, but a king, an Elvis somehow shares the loneliness of the crowd.

So when Elvis sang as a lonely man he was heroically authentic—his loneliness was true—and so he sang for every loner, every ego in a sea of egos.

It wasn't until Beatlemania that any power came along that equalled Elvis' cult of personality. But the Beatles were not "The King." It took four of them to generate the excitement of Elvis. Their effect was similar, but it wasn't the same. The fab four were sexual nobles, pop oligarchs, but not kings.

It is said that Elvis was depressed by the mass hysteria generated by the Beatles. Jealous, maybe, but not simple jealousy. A king must always be on guard against usurpers. But Elvis' personality never had to fear a single rival. This new kind of mass hysteria was something else though. His rival was not a man but a band. He wasn't really in competition, but how does a man compete with a group.

Perhaps it wasn't simple jealousy that the Beatles evoked in Elvis, but a sort of abstract fear, a fear that the whole world was changing into a place without kings. Perhaps somewhere deep in Elvis' heart he felt that the individual that he symbolized was losing out to a new system of corporate identities.

Perhaps Elvis felt the fear not of the king losing his throne to another king, but to a mob, or to an oligarchy. One man might never displace him, but a group of men might make up a "corporate person" that would threaten not just him but everything he stands for—the heroic individual.

As a great king perhaps he didn't fear for his kingdom but for kingship itself.

Elvis was a sex star. He didn't have to study it. He knew it—a twitch of the hips brought screams to throats of a thousand girls, and tears to their eyes. Elvis knew what it was that interested these young women. He didn't need a theory.

Opposite: Return to Memphis, 1960.

But if he'd wanted one he could have found a heavy. Wilhelm Reich, the great outlaw psychologist, might have had a field day explaining Elvis if he had taken time out from his busy work schedule to notice. According to Reich the principal organizing tool of the superstate is sexual repression. Nowhere in Reich's tomes *The Mass Psychology of Fascism* or *The Function of the Orgasm*, et al., is Elvis mentioned. But the enormous response to Elvis was perhaps the greatest proof of Reich's theories—proof of the existence of an enormous, er-uh reservoir of quite untapped sexual energy. Elvis knew how to tap it, but he only gave it a slight tap. Enough of a tap, however, to let you know it was very much there.

In fact it would seem that few knew what an enormous reservoir of latent sex was out there until Elvis started them screaming.

Elvis must have known that he had magic, a ritual kind of magic. Perhaps he never thought of himself as a fertility god. Maybe he never thought of himself as a return to the original idea of a "King" in an age without kings. But maybe he did.

EVILS
★ ★ ★ ★ ★ ★ ★ ★ ★ ★ ★ ★ ★ ★ ★ ★

Elvis was a natural. He didn't really have to work for it; *he was it*. But what he was he must have only begun to understand later.

When his magic really started to work Elvis must have been as surprised as everybody else. And he must have been surprised at both sides of the reaction—the screaming, weeping girls tearing at his clothes and the hellfire and brimstone preachers railing against his influence.

Like anybody else Elvis could be good and could be bad, but he must have been surprised at just how good and how bad he was seen to be. His biggest job must have been getting along with his image, from the beginning to the end. It must have been amusing at first, to see how bad they thought he was, and how wonderful. But when he did get the idea he had to go along with it.

The Shangri-La's defined Elvis' cosmic position, and that of his historical co-workers (like James Dean, Marlon Brando, Gene Vincent, etc.) in their song "The Leader of the Pack:" *Is he bad?* asks one girl. *Well*, coos another, *He's good bad, but not evil*.

Elvis must have realized early on that he stood for "good bad but not evil." And then he must have realized that it wasn't an easy thing to stand up for.

Such questions of morality are everpresent, but also ever-mobile. Morality is like climate—it looks permanent but it's very subject to change. Morals were one

Elvis, Lizabeth Scott and the grave of Deke Rivers in *Loving You* (1957).

thing when Elvis came in and something else entirely
when he went out, but in a way he was always on top or
on the bottom of the situation.

Like beauty good and bad are in the eyes of the be-
holders. When there's a major split among the behold-
ing masses somebody always steps up to take the heat

At the beginning Elvis was the prime target for the
"moral majority" of the day. But because Elvis started
out with assurance and massive approval he knew he
wasn't bad. He didn't have to take a middle of the road
position. He was no Pat Boone. But neither was he a
James Dean. Elvis knew he was good, so he was free to
be "bad."

Elvis was a love object—he knew it and he knew that
love wasn't bad and therefore he wasn't either. This is
the actual plotline of numerous Elvis flicks, and of his
life too. Elvis was a natural, and he knew that natural
had to be good. *Roustabout* is a good model of Elvis'
moral dilemma. In this flick he's a good boy who looks
"bad;" riding a cycle in leathers he's the target of the
spontaneous moral outrage of a protective father,
guarding his girl from flirtation. But this merely spurs
Elvis on to show that he's a good boy down deep—a
natural man who knows the real meaning of love.

But in the process Elvis has to overcome the tempta-
tions of his image. And this was a big part of the real life
Elvis process too. Elvis the gospel singer was not exactly
doing penance for his bad-boy sexual image, but he was
trying hard to show that there were two sides to this
solid gold coin. Elvis, "crying in the chapel" was crying
not just for himself but for the world of images, moral
abstractions, black and white.

The "good bad but not evil" have a hard time of it.
But, natch, the rewards are great. Still, sometimes it's
hard to live to be able to collect. The great wildmen of
rock have often taken the rap, taken the dive for moral
traditions. It's all in the game, of course, but the rules
are up for grabs and sometimes it's played for keeps.

LEVIS
* * * * * * * * * * * * * * * *

The history of pop music is the history of the next-
big-thing. In many cultures it is possible for music to
remain unchanged in form for hundreds, even
thousands of years; but here in techno-culture music
and the other arts reflect the basic doctrine of progress.
General Electric could have summed up the culture
scene just as aptly as it's own business with it's motto:
"Progress is our most important product."

In the fine arts it's been one ism after another. In
music it's been trend upon trend. The pop scene has all
the militant impermanence of *Vogue* and enformes it
with the dogmatism of Darwinism.

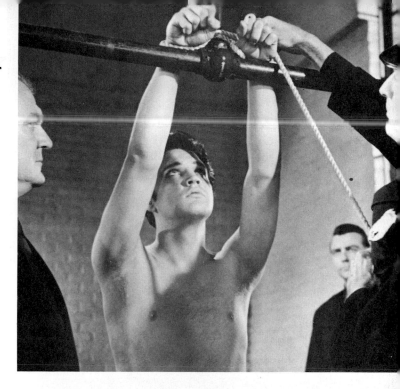

Jailhouse Rock (1957).

But after Beatlemania, after the British Invasion, folk rock, after the summer of Love and acid rock, after glitter, heavy metal, bubblegum, after punk and new wave and no wave, before and after it all there is still Elvis—the only permanent standard of the "rock age," the only icon with a modern classicism.

St. Mark's Place in New York's East Village has seen the history of pop trends in-depth: the depths of acid rock, the bottomless pits of punk rock. And here, at a major vortex of Pop relativity where trends begin their radiant broadcast, the trends also end. Here, in the center, it's dead while it's still very much alive as it moves from Kansas into Oklahoma, like an extinguished star whose light still reaches Earth. But dead as the center may be, that's where the serious pop zombies are found too. So after a trend is dead all over, strange anthropological fashion finds remain, somehow holding on to the source, the center, where the big pop bang happened.

Hippies may be long gone elsewhere, but they still move down St. Marks' like day-glo ghosts. And while in London and Peoria the punks have gone new wave and then something else too, already hard core 1977 punks are holding the fort in a time warp.

But even stranger, perhaps, especially to the tourists' eyes are these unbelievable visions of the fifties moving past the herds of punks and held-over hippies, striding past with some spirit in their step like they didn't even see these old/new trendies. From their threads you'd take them for remnants of the punks parents' generation of trendies, but one look at their faces and you know that they are about a generation junior to the fading hippies. These are the neo-rockabillies. Young enough to be punks, they have somehow failed to comprehend the cult of progress.

For rockabillies, old or new, progress does not exist, 1956 has never been improved upon. They are not unaware of what has passed for progress since then, they have simply rejected it. For them the music did not improve, the clothes did not improve, neither did the hairdos or the automobiles. Of course they are not the only pop atavism in town—there are neo-mods, punks as post-industrial rockers, hippies and heavy metal suggest pre-agricultural Europeans, but these other trends are still more trendy than rockabilly. Neo-rockabilly acknowledged the cyclical nature of fashion and then steps right outside it. Trends may come and go but their idea is when you see one that looks best, why not stick with it?

That's the idea anyway. In practice neo-rockabilly is a bit like neo-classicism through the ages—it takes the original forms and ideas to wilder lengths than the original practitioners. But, as rockabilly was always a sort of disciplined wildness or an undisciplined regimen, it could only live today as something more than a wax works replica, if it were more extreme. So the pompadours may be taller, the fabrics might be glossier, the upright bassist might twirl the thing more than Bill

Another cinematic triumph.

Haley, but maybe it's because they have to add a little wildness to make up for their extra restraint. Rockabillies, as aesthetic throwbacks, are basically conservatives in their art, so a bit of baroque keeps them from becoming stodgy wildmen.

Of course another reason why rockabillies are a bit more extreme these days is that the world has been made safe for rockabilly. In 1956 such a hairdo might get one into trouble, today extra inches are needed to keep it on the interesting side of safe.

Elvis was not the only great star of the original rockabilly scene—but he made way for the others. He made the world safe—almost—for Jerry Lee Lewis. He brought rockabilly fashion into fashion.

Before Mr. Presley arrived country was country and city was city and it looked like that ole twain never was about to meet. At first Elvis might have been called a hick, but then it became obvious that a certain kind of hick might be a very exciting thing to be. There's that classic Elvis movie scene that happened more than once in which Elvis steals the hearts etc. of the sophisticated "frat cats" girlfriends. He might have to leave the stage fighting, but Elvis showed everybody that society is "negotiable."

Elvis made the rural man into a sex symbol—almost for the first time. (Sure there was Gary Cooper, et al. but they wore a 'hayseed' veneer—Elvis was authentic.) Still Elvis was no country bumpkin. He had the energy of the "natural" man but he also had the subtlety and sophistication formerly associated only with urbanity. Today we have a cult of the urban cowboy—a citified person trying to "get back" to the country energy and values. But that old rockabilly idol, Elvis and his compatriots, that was the best of both worlds all in one. His clothes might look wild, he might buck like a bronco, but ladies just scratch the surface and you'll know you just scratched a wildlife gentleman.

VILES

Elvis on the floor—his body reaches room temperature. Him dead. After half a lifetime of taking drugs, drugs took him. The first reports said it was a heart attack, but the drugs would no longer be denied. Soon Elvis' pharmaceutical shopping list was world news, a veritable pharmacornucopia—the King was into everything—up, down and sideways. But even the most obvious and undeniable evidence of drug abuse—death—could do no more than slightly tarnish the King's reputation for clean living. Elvis' body might have OD'd but his soul was still clean.

Sure, many of the greatest names in rock and roll heaven ascended there by exceeding the therapeutic dose. But Elvis, even blue in the face, was no dope addict, no dirty junkie. Elvis did not take dope. Elvis took medicine. If he were just another rock doper he would have taken heroin, not codeine; cocaine, not dexidrene. Elvis was into medicine, not dope. He took what was prescribed; it came from the drugstore.

It might be argued that heavy medicine users like Elvis and Howard Hughes preferred the drugstore item to more exotic, contraband brands out of sheer paranoia. You don't get busted for Codeine Tylenol #4 with your name on the bottle. But I don't think that's the story. I think Elvis (and Hughes) took prescription drugs to escape the idea of being a drug addict. It was an essential rationale. "I may be a very sick man," it goes, "but I am not a criminal. I'm not the enemy of society. I AM SOCIETY."

Few Americans can appear at the gates of the White House unexpected, demand an audience with the President and get it. Even his cabinet often found President Nixon inaccessible. But not Elvis. Elvis just shows up at the gate one day and asks to see President Nixon. In minutes there they are—the King and the Emperor—face to face. If only the tape machine had rolled through that appointment. (Did it?) What prompted Presley to drop in on Nixon was the singer's desire to lend his hand to the President's recently declared "war on drugs." Elvis left the White House with his very own Drug Enforcement Agency badge.

This event was mind-blowing at the time—but post-mortem it is considerably more marvelous. Elvis had been on drugs for years by that time. Still, there are many unanswered questions regarding that bizarre summit. Such as "Why?!" And "Was he on or off?"

There are a few schools of thought on the first problem. 1) Elvis was paranoid about his drug habits and hoped that by joining the war on drugs he would escape scrutiny, perhaps even believing that the DEA badge might come in handy some day. 2) Having suffered for his drug habits Elvis sincerely hoped that his condemnation of drugs would spare others what he had gone through. 3) Both of the above.

As to the "on or off" question—it seems more ironic to imagine Elvis rapping with Dick and getting his narc badge pinned while raging on speed, but "on or off" Elvis' motives might have been exactly the same.

You might call Elvis' endorsement of the war on drugs hypocrisy—but I think it was hypocrisy of a high minded sort. He realized that there were two Elvises—a philosophical *Double Trouble*—there was the flesh and blood Elvis who could only hurt himself and then there was the Divine Elvis, the Platonic Elvis who could not be hurt but who could hurt millions. "If you can't be good," the Platonic Elvis might have said, "be a good example."

The King's office.

LIVES
★ ★ ★ ★ ★ ★ ★ ★ ★ ★ ★ ★ ★ ★ ★

No matter what bag they're in now, one thing shared by most of the successful pop musicians today is

the role Elvis played in shaping their careers and their music. They might be playing funk, heavy metal or new wave music, but Elvis was what inspired them to pick up a guitar and play.

August Darnell is descended from Africans and Germans; he grew up in the Bronx and his first musical turn-on was listening to his father's calypso records. But what first inspired the performer in him was Elvis. Today August's hit group is named Kid Creole and the Coconuts, and August himself is Kid Creole, inspired by Elvis' film *King Creole*. Elvis was white by blood, but he had "soul." It has been said that Elvis' success was a result of his making black music safe for white audiences, but it runs deeper than that. Elvis was King Creole—his music was black and white, the best of both worlds and accessible to people of any bloodline. The fact is that Elvis turned everybody on.

In 1979 Walter Steding, the wild and wily violinist of the New York new wave scene, released a nutty but very dynamic and exciting version of "Hound Dog" featuring Robert Fripp, the eminent guitarist of King Crimson, Bowie, Eno, etc. Walter Steding and Robert Fripp played together many times but their performances on this record are particularly incredible, cosmically berserk. This was the record which turned Walter on to rock and roll at the age of three, and this was the first song that Robert ever played on guitar.

Elvis Costello named himself the same way a Latin American mother might name her baby boy Jesus—he might not be the real Jesus come back but at least some of the magic might rub off.

Mr. Costello's Elvis is a statement of classicism. Hot on the Achillean heels of punk rockers he came into the public eye as a conservative, not an extremist. But where the Rockabillies might be seen as the John Birchers of pop music aesthetics, Costello was more just-right-of-center. His music was new-ish and old-ish. He recognized the Pat Boone—Sid Vicious dialectic for what it is—what it is. A bit, how you say, *recherche*, but now what ain't? (Answer: something but not much.)

Elvis, alive or dead, is a true muse. He inspires thousands of musicians, performers, and actors. He has probably been the subject of more paintings, collages and prints than any other personage. The Elvis image was especially popular—appropriately—among Pop artists. Ray Johnson's Elvis was among the first to use a photo image. In the early seventies Andy Warhol's giant multiple images of a pistol packing Elvis sold at Parke-Bernet Galleries for the highest price ever paid for a Pop painting. It may be that Elvis had the most expensive and most moneymaking image of them all. It was hard to keep up; impossible to let down. Elvis was bigger than life and finally that might have killed him. But the image, "his thing," burns on. Elvis—Him dead—long live The King.

AFTER THE FLOOD:
ELVIS AND HIS LITERARY LEGACY
BY MARTIN TORGOFF

If his innermost heart could have been laid open, there would have been discovered that dream of undying fame; which, dream as it is, is more powerful than a thousand realities.

—Nathaniel Hawthorne, *Fanshawe*

The legend of Elvis Presley, like Paul Bunyan or Johnny Appleseed, has long since passed into the public domain. The amount of literature available on him rivals Lindbergh, Houdini, Valentino, and the Kennedys all put together. Indeed, while the average child in our classroom will probably never remember the names of the first American astronauts to walk the moon, that child will recognize Elvis' face, a few of his more celebrated songs, and know at least the rudiments of his story, for such is the power of the folk hero and the nature of popular culture in our times. Four years after his death, our attention still shifts from one posthumous saga to another—from Dr. Nichopolous and the prescription drug scandal to the litigation in the Memphis Probate Court, where the Presley estate and Colonel Tom Parker are wrangling over Elvis' millions—and the books just keep coming. And yet, in our continuing passion to find out more about this man and assess his enduring legacy, future generations will face snarling problems of historiography and biographical veracity in separating fact from fiction, myth from reality, truth from legend.

It is perfectly appropriate, of course, that the literature about Elvis Presley would be as astonishingly vast and diversified in scope, as full of irony, paradox, and contradiction as the man himself: it ranges from the profound to the profane, stretching from the pinnacles of genuine literary achievement to the glossy superficiality of commercial exploitation, often within the same volume. Elvis continues to fascinate and confound not only his public but a host of writers by his very magnitude as a figure in American life. Hence, by attempting to debunk his myths and reach the 'truth' about him, we invariably succeed in mythologizing him further; and by setting out to revel in the most archetypal of those myths, we reveal important truths not only about Elvis, but about ourselves.

How is it possible, after all, *not* to mythologize a figure who so completely and publically lived out his myths and dreams? No matter how painstaking we try to be in portraying Elvis with sobriety and objectivity—no matter how thorough in research and analysis we are or how careful in the selection of words and images—he tugs relentlessly at our heartstrings, engaging our emotions as surely as he did while singing a song. Any writer who looks hard at Elvis and his legacy is forever in danger of romanticizing him by virtue of the simple fact that Elvis *himself* was so sensational and his story so inherently dramatic.

The Elvis literature today is comprised primarily of writing by fans, promotional materials, straight journalism covering his life and career, formal biography, film and music criticism and reportage, "inspirational" books, serious socio-cultural analyses of his "phenomenon," and "insider's" accounts of his life in the form of memoirs and informal biographies. Each genre of writing contains splendid examples of highly inspired prose as well as the worst drivel imaginable—and *all* occupy a rightful place in the ever-expanding pantheon.

Of all the genres, perhaps the most revealing and misleading are the numerous "insider's" accounts that have emerged since his death. Because Elvis never told his entire story in the form of an autobiography, those around him—family, friends, associates—have told the story for him, often in conflicting versions. Around the time of his discharge from the Army in 1960, Elvis stopped granting interviews to journalists and talking to his public. Thus, an impenetrable wall was constructed around him by his manager and entourage, and for two solid decades (except for a few brief press conferences on important occasions like his wedding and Las Vegas opening), Colonel Tom Parker, to a degree that was unprecedented if not downright frightening in the annals of show business, controlled what the public saw, read and even *thought* about Elvis. When he died, the walls came tumbling down, unleashing an avalanche of books containing torrents of anecdotes, opinions, impressions, revelations, reminiscences, confessions. Each book claimed Elvis as its own, each was packaged by its publisher with corresponding hype pronouncing the publication as *best, first, last,* and *final.*

There were, naturally, valuable and lasting glimpses of Elvis to be gleaned from the flood; on the other hand, many of those who had become the sources for these books had vested interests (other than the purely financial, which are the easiest to comprehend) in their portrayals of Elvis. Their motivations ran the gamut from the purest and most blind expressions of love, loy-

alty, and respect to the premeditated iconoclasm growing out of a need for personal revenge; from setting the record straight to keeping the myths eternally intact; from self-destruction to self-aggrandizement. Certainly the more interesting combine all of the above.

It is well-nigh impossible to make sense of this mountain of material without being able to sift and weigh comparatively to judge the merit of each source, and quite difficult to do so without understanding the nature of the relationship between source and subject. What further complicates this evaluation is that fact that Elvis, for a variety of reasons such as personal insecurities and the jealousies around him, parceled himself out to those around him, giving them different roles to play at different times for different reasons. Like many things in his life, those around him were very neatly compartmentalized—and within the various compartments, he was like a chameleon, depending on his mood at the moment. The logical results are the anomalies and glaring inconsistencies in their stories.

Many Elvis fans maintain that all of these words are ultimately worthless and disposable—the majority of the books, say purists and diehards, belong in the trashcans along with Elvis' empty Pepsi bottles—which leaves us, of course, with nothing but his music, the films, tens of thousands of photographs, and our own subjective experience. Indeed, there has always been something oddly convincing about the argument that the *only* reliable and important truths about Elvis Presley are contained within these things *in and of themselves*, and everything else is a needless and oftentimes fraudulent dilution of the Real Thing. . .

You want to "know" about Elvis? Just listen to "Mystery Train," "Hound Dog," "It's Now Or Never," "Guitar Man," "Polk Salad Annie," "Softly As I Leave You." Watch *King Creole, Blue Hawaii, That's The Way It Is*. Journey through a photo-retrospective of his life and witness his image transmute from wide-eyed youth to bloated, glassy-eyed middle age. Some of the most evocative writing about Elvis has come precisely from writers who have interpreted these subjective truths and cast them against the larger truths of American culture, for which Elvis has long since become a universally accepted paradigm.

I have always believed that no matter how seemingly banal or questionable in taste, all of the books, articles, trivia, esoterica—indeed the entire range of Presleyanna from tee shirts to cocktail swizzle sticks (yes, even Elvis' empty Pepsi bottles)—belong in the story. Both writer and reader/fan, within the frenzy to publish and buy after Elvis' death, have been guilty of certain misdemeanors against the truth: the writer by succumbing to commercial pressures to sensationalize and reveal; the consumers for creating so bullish a market for ever more books and then, despite their obvious hunger and fascination, obstinately clinging to the most candied notions about their idol despite whatever unpalatable truths are revealed in the books. Never, in fact, has so avid a book-buying public been more resentful of the very books it devours.

Of course, the skepticism of the Elvis fan about the latest Elvis book is very well-founded. Rarely has a public been more willingly and successfully manipulated with commercial product than have Elvis' fans by Colonel Parker; and rarely has a public been forced to choose between such black or white editions of a star, between the scurrilous gossip of the cheapest tabloids or the official version immaculately conceived and cranked out by the Colonel's myth-making machinery.

Because Elvis' celebrity was originally rooted in adversity, at a time when he was being villified as the Corrupter of Young America, the role as Keepers of the Faith is a natural one for his fans to play—they know people will say or print *anything* about Elvis, do anything to make a buck. And, to prove them right, no sooner does some whacko assert that Elvis never really died but was abducted by a UFO than a story is printed by the *Enquirer* offering incontrovertible proof and a publisher is ready with an advance. The printing of these stories (I invented this one but there have been *worse*) in the trashy tabloids (the *Star, Globe, Enquirer*) is more than a living testament to the sometimes lunatic nature of the Elvis phenomenon: what it really underscores to us is that Elvis Presley was far too important to be left to the cretinous mentality of these publications.

Similarly, Elvis has also become fair game for anyone seeking to appropriate the vehicle of his legend for their own ideological purposes. Various "inspirational" books have appeared, written around a particular thesis about the meaning of his life and death, in which the prime motivation of the author is neither the creativity of the endeavor, the enshrinement of his myths nor the arrival of the royalty statement, but the propagation of their own beliefs. They range from the most well-meaning and sanctimonious of evangelical Christians to patriots and rednecks; from the charlatans of psychic mumbo-jumbo to the crackpots of spiritualism. Obviously, these books also have their place, but as they continue to emerge and provoke astonishment, one begins to appreciate even more the writings about Elvis which are truly incisive, original, and responsible.

I was not of the Elvis Generation. In 1952, the year I was born, Elvis was languishing in relative obscurity at Humes High, growing his sideburns; his family was residing at the low rent project called the Lauderdale Courts at 185 Winchester Street in Memphis, living slightly above the poverty line thanks to Vernon Presley's paycheck from the United Paint Company and whatever else Gladys and Elvis could muster in. When most people north of the Mason-Dixon line began hearing about Elvis in 1956-57, I was hearing about

Captain Kangaroo. Twenty-two years later, I wrote a book about him.

Bits and pieces of him float to the surface of my childhood memories—a few photos, a passage from "Hound Dog," some of the Elvis junk—but he never really registered until I was taken to see G.I. Blues. Elvis was out of the Army and my sister and cousins (all older) were making a big deal about it. The scene I remember most vividly came at the end when Elvis, who looked great in his uniform (soldiers and ballplayers were my real heroes), sang "Didja Ever" in front of the Stars 'N Stripes.

I remained largely oblivious to Elvis as I grew up during the sixties, not because I didn't like him, but because he wasn't a part of what was happening around me: I could have told you anything you wanted to know about Dylan, Lennon, or Janis, but very little about the Hillbilly Cat; Woodstock and the Fillmore East were much closer to my personal experience than Elvis' Las Vegas Comeback. It wasn't until my passion for music had reached the kind of epidemic proportions which warranted an investigation of the roots of rock and blues that I discovered Elvis and began to comprehend his contribution. By that time, fortunately, the vanguard of the first generation of serious rock critics and historians were publishing their work in magazines like Rolling Stone. Slowly but surely, my Elvis Consciousness was raised by the likes of Greil Marcus, Peter Guralnick and others who had cared enough to apply their talents and energies to those stellar musicians who had weaved the musical spells which had transformed American music and popular culture.

I'm thankful today that I had the chance to see Elvis perform, if only once; being a sucker for spectacle, I couldn't resist his Madison Square Garden appearance in 1972. The experience made me aware of how complex Elvis and his image really were-there was, as the song goes, much more to the picture than meets the eye—and it wasn't Elvis rocking out with his Golden Oldie medleys that provided this realization; rather, it was Elvis standing up there and singing, of all things, "The Impossible Dream."

"Didja Ever" from G.I. Blues (1960).

The first time that I became truly curious about Elvis as a "person" came four years later, in 1976, one year before his death. I was working as an editor for a publishing house by that time and was offered the American rights to an illustrated biography of Elvis, which the company I worked for subsequently published as *The Illustrated Elvis* in the United States. The text of the book, which became a best-seller after Elvis' death, was an exercise in rhapsodic adulation ("He sees them. He grins at them. It is all they need. They prostrate themselves before him. . ." etc.); the photos were what captivated me, particularly one single image at the back of the book, a much-reproduced shot which has since become a metaphor for all that was private and myster-

ious about Elvis at the time. Elvis is leaving the church after Sonny West's wedding in 1970, dressed completely in black except for a white tie and carnation, wearing what appears to be a holster with dangling chains around his waist. The moon-faced gentleman who appears over his right shoulder was Marty Lacker, ex-Memphis Mafioso; and in Elvis' right hand, for some unfathomable reason, is a flashlight (it is *broad daylight*). The expression on his face is a sphynx-like smirk which seems to say: *I know somethin' ain't nobody else knows.* Gee, who *is* this guy anyway, I kept wondering. What's he really *like*?

The year after Elvis' death, I had a rare chance to find out. By that time I was free-lancing as a writer. When I was asked to fly to Memphis and interview Dee Presley and her three sons for a book, it was time to find out everything I possibly could about Elvis Presley, to read, in preparation, everything I could get my hands on.

Thankfully, there was a solid biography. With the publication of *Elvis* by Jerry Hopkins in 1971, every Elvis writer had a reliable signpost along the highway. Working without the official sanction of the Presley camp, Hopkins, like a bloodhound hard on the trail of a fugitive, returned to Tupelo and picked up Elvis' scent and followed it everywhere he could, talking to everybody along the way who would talk back and tracing Elvis' life from birth to re-emergence as a live performer. The research was scrupulous, the tone of the writing affably grabbing, and the analyses well-balanced. By the time Hopkins started his research, Elvis had become more guarded about his private life than ever before, so the book is naturally more effective as an in-depth, step-by-step history of his career than a portrait of a private man; but thanks to extensive interviews and an excellent ear, his insights into Elvis' character were right on target. As samples, witness the transition of the Elvis portrayed in the following two passages, the first Elvis the Young Rocker, the second the Hollywood Elvis of the late sixties.

Famous Flashlight shot.

It seemed somehow that all this energy was but a prelude to what came on stage. Just as there is today—in Last Vegas, primarily—little introduction to Elvis' performance, there was little then. It was possible someone would introduce him, but likely as not Scotty and Bill and D. J. would be set up, having provided the backup music for another singer on the show. Then Elvis would come out and go right into one of his ballads. Draped in black slacks with a pink stripe down the sides, a pink shirt with the collar turned up catching the ends of his longish hair, and a pink sport jacket with big black teardrops on the front and back, he *was* the Hillbilly Cat, he *was* the King of Western Bop. He leaned forward, legs braced, guitar hung around his neck, hands clutching the stand microphone. He looked at the girls in the front row with lidded eyes, eyebrows forming a loving and woeful arch. During the song's instrumental break he gave them that lopsided grin and maybe twitched one leg. Once.

The next song might be a rocker, giving Elvis a

chance to show the folks what they'd come to see. Now both legs were twitching—jerking and snapping back into that original braced position. It's not likely Elvis was thinking of the pentecostal preachers of his Tupelo childhood at moments like this, but it was apparent he hadn't forgotten them. All he'd done was translate hellfire and damnation into "Good Rockin' Tonight." His arms flailed the inexpensive guitar, pounding the wood on the afterbeat and snapping strings as if they were made of cooked spaghetti. From one song right into another, most of them already recorded for Sun or soon to be released. Country songs. With a beat. The girls began to squirm and move; it was music that made their behinds itch.

Twelve or thirteen years later:

> Over the years Elvis had received so many awards he had no trouble filling the fifty-foot trophy room in Graceland's south wing. Most of these had come for his (1) Americanism, (2) charity, (3) humanity, or (4) all the above. The only negative note was in winning the Sour Apple Award (along with Natalie Wood) for being least cooperative with the Hollywood press corps.
> He was a millionaire possessed of unfailing politeness and an unimpeachable love of God, mother and country and had a beautiful, gracious Southern *pregnant* wife.
> He began appearing on the best-dressed lists.
> Album titles of the movie period: *Something for Everybody* (1961), *Elvis for Everyone* (1965).
> Even Hedda Hopper, who slapped Elvis around verbally in the fifties, loved him in the sixties, devoting several Sunday columns to saying how swell a fella he'd become.
> Says a movie executive who worked closely with the Presley camp for several years: "The Colonel didn't want Elvis to come out sounding like Jesus. It's pretty bland. But everybody assumed that's what the Colonel wanted, and that's exactly what he sounded like, and maybe that's what he had become."
> Elvis Presley once may have represented some sort of threat to the American Way, but now he was a part of the Establishment—the All American Boy. Compared to Elvis, Jack Armstrong was a Communist.

After a particularly graphic chapter on Elvis' Las Vegas engagements of 1969-1970, the book closes with the making of Elvis' concert documentaries, thus leaving a considerable time gap between then and August 16, 1977, a period which Hopkins would later cover in his sequel, *The Final Years.*

Along with this biography was a growing body of first-rate reportage and criticism by rock journalists that included work by Stanley Booth (anthologized in this volume), and writings by Robert Christgau, Jon Landau, and Nik Cohn. Also, during the late sixties and seventies, Peter Guralnick was taking the journeys back in time to locate and rediscover the founding fathers of rock, blues, and country which would result in the publication of his two extraordinary books—*Feel Like Going Home: Portraits in Blues and Rock 'n Roll* (1971), and *Lost Highway: Journeys and Arrivals of American Musicians* (1981).

But on the whole, the good articles about Elvis in even the more prestigious magazines were few and far between, which made the true gems, like David Dalton's review of Elvis' Las Vegas opening the pages of *Rolling Stone,* all the more enjoyable and valuable:

> Elvis was supernatural, his own resurrection, at the Showroom Internationale in Las Vegas last August. Everyone complained that Las Vegas was a bad choice, but you only have to look at the old color publicity photos of Elvis to know why it was the only possible place for him to make his debut after nine years of hibernation: The iconic, frontal image, completely symmetrical, stares out of the glossy blue background. The glaring eyes, the surly mouth, the texture of the face completely airbrushed out, the hair jet black with blue metallic streaks—these are superhuman attributes. It is the disembodied face of Krishna, Christ, Mao, where the image dominates the reality. The adherence to this formula has been so dogmatic that until recently you were in danger of a lawsuit from the Colonel if you used a photo of Elvis that was not the officially sanctioned publicity handout. . .
> Even Elvis seemed to find his reincarnation hard to believe. Mumbling, "Whass that, whass that?" He suddenly interrupted one of his long monologues like a speed flash—"Oh, it's okay, it's me, it's me!" And it *was* hard to believe as the curtain finally went up for the third time on Elvis. His head hung down, legs braced for his defiant stance and an acoustic guitar symbollically slung around his neck.
> *Waaal, it's one for the money, two for the show,*
> *Three to get ready, now go cat go . . .*
> Wham! Right into "Blue Suede Shoes" before you have time to take in the whole scene. You are out of control, breathlessly slippin' and slidin' backwards, faster and faster into the past. An incredible rush, and it flashes at you all the faster because Elvis is singing it at almost twice the speed of the old single, so that it lasts in all about a minute and a quarter. As soon as it's over he tears into another hard rocker from his first RCA album:
> *Well, said I got a woman way 'cross town*
> *She's good to me, oh yeah . . .*
> and the Sweet Inspirations echo "she's good to me," pumping back that gospel rhythm like a piston.
> He pauses a moment and for the first time you can take everything in. Elvis is wearing a blue karate jump suit with a long karate belt. His bell bottoms have bright red satin vents and he's wearing a red and white scarf around his neck. His black pointed boots have studs on the toes and heels. His hair is cut in a short Beatle fringe at the front but he's still wearing the Presley sideburns. Behind him is a six-piece band from Memphis and behind them a twenty-five piece orchestra silhouetted by glowing backdrop lighting that oozes through a syrupy range of chartreuse, cerise and aquamarine. To his right are the Sweet Inspirations, a soul group that preceded him with some insipid versions of show tunes. Behind them, Elvis' own backup group, the Imperials, neatly dressed in blazers.
> Elvis speaks. "Viva Las Vegas," he says, laughing; "no, man, that's one number I ain't gonna do"—unexpectedly revealing his attitude to the twelve years of schlock movies. "Welcome to the Showroom Internationale, ladies and gentlemen. This is somethin' else, ain't it? Lookin' 'round at all them decorations, funky

angels hangin' from the ceilin'...tell ya there ain't nothin' like a funky angel, boy." Presiding over the gigantic dining room and its 2,000 paying guests are a giant 20–foot pair of papier mache statues representing Marie Antoinette and Louis XVI, holding a lace handkerchief the size of a tablecloth, and from the ceiling hang a pair of gargantuan cherubs exchanging a length of cream satin material. Above the stage there's a dumpy coat of arms, strictly from Walt Disney. Funky.

"Well, here we go again," says Elvis as he leans into a classic Presley *contraposto*. He's putting himself on. Elvis imitating Elvis. He holds it until everybody catches on and laughs.

"*uhuhmmmmmmmmm, uhuhmmmmmmmmm, uhuhmmmmmmmmm...*"

Funky, indeed. The article describes the rest of the performance in the same colorful detail, giving us what remains as one of the best impressions of Elvis onstage anywhere, past or present.

Finally, in 1975, two years before Elvis Presley's last gasp (or what he called the King's "ascension" in a letter recently), came *Mystery Train*, Greil Marcus's grand opus on America and rock n' roll, which reached its thematic, aesthetic, and emotional crescendo in a final chapter entitled: "Elvis: Presliad," a *tour de force* which has yet to be equaled in the annals of rock/literary writing. The truly amazing thing about "Elvis: Presliad," aside from the scope and intensity of the writing, is that Marcus, in one bold stroke, managed to assure Elvis his rightful place not only as a musical and cultural force of major proportions, but as a figure worthy of the most sustained literary endeavors by serious writers.

Standing at that heady juncture where Elvis' most vital music meets head on with its indigenous cultural currents and historical traditions, Marcus used Elvis' Sun recordings as springboards, making each song an epiphany of something past, something happening as a promise fulfilled, or something for the future. Although there are many brilliant moments about other musicians and performers in the book, Elvis, for good reason, is the only one who allows him the vantage point to sum up his thesis and pan the *entire* horizon, cutting back and forth in time, place, and meaning; and by doing so say as much if not more about "America" as "Elvis." What makes it all so much fun and quite moving is the sheer weight of Marcus' knowledge, the sharp edges of his insights, and the degree to which he *cares* about it all. And somehow, through the alchemical power of his prose, Elvis comes vibrantly alive not only as artist, but as just about everything else: Southern boy, dreamer, idol, myth, American institution. Here, then, several choice moments from the lives of Elvis Presley and Greil Marcus. The first is a short take called "The Rockabilly Moment."

There are four of them in the little studio: Bill Black, the bass player; Scotty Moore, the guitarist; in the back, Sam Phillips, the producer; and the sexy

young kid thumping his guitar as he sings, Elvis Presley, just nineteen. 1954.

The kid with the guitar is...unusual; but they've been trying to put something on the tape Sam keeps running back—a ballad, a hillbilly song, anything—and so far, well, it just doesn't get it.

The four men cool it for a moment, frustrated. They share a feeling they could pull something off if they hit it right, but it's been a while, and that feeling is slipping away, as it always does. They talk music, blues, Crudup, ever hear that, who you kiddin' man, dig this. The kid pulls his guitar up, clowns a bit. He throws himself at a song. *That's all right, mama, that's all right*...eat shit. He doesn't say that, naturally, but that's what he's found in the tune; his voice slides over the lines as the two musicians come in behind him, Scotty picking up the melody and the bass-man slapping away at his axe with a drumstick. Phillips hears it, likes it, and makes up his mind.

All right, you got something. Do it again, I'll get it down. Just like that, don't mess with it. Keep it simple.

They cut the song fast, put down their instruments, vaguely embarrassed at how far they went into the music. Sam plays back the tape. Man, they'll run us outta town when they hear it, Scotty says; Elvis sings along with himself, joshing his performance. They all wonder, but not too much.

They leave, but Sam Phillips is perplexed. Who is gonna play this crazy record? White jocks won't touch it 'cause it's nigger music and colored will pass 'cause it's hillbilly. It sounds good, it sounds sweet, but maybe it's just...too weird? The hell with it.

Simple, huh? The moment would resurface, of course, in scores of Elvis books to follow, but never with the same understated impact, set so effectively against the tapestry of its musical milieu.

And while you're at it, put this one on your turntable—Elvis' 1968 *NBC-TV Special*. First, he sets us up, peeling away at Elvis layer by layer—

There is a sense in which virtually his whole career has been a throwaway, straight from that time when he knew he had it made and that the future was his. You can hear that distance, that refusal to really commit himself, in his best music and his worst; if the throwaway is the source of what is pointless about Elvis, it is also at the heart of much of what is exciting and charismatic. It may be that he never took *any* of it seriously, just did his job and did it well, trying to enjoy himself and stay sane—save for those first Tennessee records, and that night, late in 1968, when his comeback was uncertain and he put a searing, desperate kind of life into a few songs that cannot be found in any of his other music.

—until he gets to the very core of the moment:

It was a staggering moment. A Christmas TV special had been decided on; a final dispute between Colonel Parker (he wanted twenty Christmas songs and a tuxedo) and producer Steve Binder (he wanted a tough, fast, sexy show) had been settled; with Elvis' help, Binder won. So there Elvis was, standing in an auditorium facing television cameras and a live audience for the first time in nearly a decade, finally stepping out from behind the wall of retainers and sycophants he had paid to hide him. And everyone was watching. . .

Sitting on the stage in black leather, surrounded by friends and a rough little combo, the crowd buzzing, he sang and talked and joked, and all the resentments he had hidden over the years began to pour out. He had always said yes, but this time, he was saying no—not without humor, but almost with a wry bit of guilt, as if he had betrayed his talent and himself. "Been a long time, baby." He told the audience about a time back in 1955, when cops in Florida had forced him to sing without moving; the story was hilarious, but there was something in his voice that made very clear how much it had hurt. He jibed at the Beatles, denying that the heroes who had replaced him had produced anything he could not match, and then he proved it. After all this time he wanted more than safety; he and the men around him were nervous, full of adventure.

"I'd like to do my favorite Christmas song," Elvis drawls—squeals of familiarity from the crowd, the girls in the front rows doing their job, imitating themselves or their images of the past, fading into an undertone of giggles as the music begins. Elvis sings "Blue Christmas," a classically styled rhythm and blues, very even, all its tension implied: a good choice. He sings it low and throaty, snapping the strings on his guitar until one of his pals cries, "Play it dirty! Play it dirty!"—on a Christmas song! All right! But this is re-creation, the past in the present, an attempt to see if Elvis can go as far as he once did. Within those limits it works, it is beautiful. The song ends with appropriate, and calculated, screams. . .

It was the finest music of his life. If ever there was music that bleeds, this was it. Nothing came easy that night, and he gave everything he had—more than anyone knew was there.

Granted, this is one of the most dramatic moments of the essay, but the writing retains this virtuosity when the author guides us down the pathways of country or blues or discusses the elements of community and alienation in Southern culture. Indeed, the essay itself is like a piece of music, its many themes (like the "throwaway") harmonically sustained until the *Finale*, which hits like a fully strummed major chord.

These days, Elvis is always singing. In his stage-show documentary, *Elvis on Tour,* we see him singing to himself, in limousines, backstage, running, walking, standing still, as his servant fits his cape to his shoulders, as he waits for his cue. He sings gospel music, mostly; in his private musical world, there is no distance at all from his deepest roots. Just as that personal culture of the Sun records was long ago blown up into something too big for Elvis to keep as his own, so the shared culture of country religion is now his private space within the greater America of which he has become a part.

And on stage? Well, there are those moments when Elvis Presley breaks through the public world he has made for himself, and only a fool or a liar would deny their power. Something entirely his, driven by two decades of history and myth, all live-in-person, is transformed into an energy that is ecstatic—that is, to use the word in its old sense, illuminating. The overstated grandeur is suddenly authentic, and Elvis brings a thrill different from and far beyond anything else in

★ ★

our culture; like an old Phil Spector record, he matches, for an instant, the bigness, the intensity, and the unpredictability of America itself.

One can only wonder if anybody ever brought these words to Elvis Presley's attention before he died. It's doubtful—Elvis was probably too buried in his books on theology, metaphysics and thanatology—and he may not have agreed or even understood the point had he read the piece, but it might have done his heart a world of good. What *is* certain is that the majority of Elvis's fans didn't read the essay either (the book's audience was the younger, more rock-oriented afficionado). What the fans were reading was May Mann's *Elvis and the Colonel (The Private Elvis)* which appeared that same year—a far cry indeed from the Alpine peaks of *Mystery Train*.

During his Hollywood years, May Mann, columnist for the *Hollywood Reporter,* was one of the few writers ever granted "access" to Elvis by the Colonel for interviews. "Access" meant visiting Elvis occasionally at his dressing rooms on movie sets, where Elvis would give her a kiss and she would swoon and ask him a few inane questions. The book was one endless paean to Elvis Presley's perfection, filled with such apocryphal information as the kinds of flowers Elvis gave the many starlets he dated. Naturally, it sold like hotcakes, revealing a ready-made market for the kind of fanzine quickie paperbacks and "scrapbooks" which would abound in years to come, no matter how smarmy or superficial the contents or slapdash the production.

Likewise, *Elvis in Hollywood* (1975) and *The Boy Who Dared To Rock: The Definitive Elvis* (1977), both by Paul Lichter, were quite popular with the fans. As the self-proclaimed "Elvisologist" who edits and publishes the *Memphis Flash* newsletter, and owns and operates the Elvis Unique Record Club, Lichter is primarily a merchandiser, not a writer. He obviously knows a great deal *about* Elvis and even met him backstage, but he knew no more about what Elvis was really *like* than May Mann, and his books are even more sycophantic. Still, being the canny businessman, he knew enough to pack his books full of useful details, summaries, discographies, and lists, thereby creating a substantial product and making them useful additions to any Elvis library, despite the annoying sense of self-importance he displays ("By this time, Paul has become accustomed to being introduced as the man who knows more about Elvis Presley than anybody else on earth," the "About Paul Lichter" section at the end of his second book modestly informs us).

And this was the State of the Art before the bombshell of *Elvis: What Happened?*—or what has since become known, simply, as the infamous "bodyguard book." Originating from the mouths and memories of three canned bodyguards—the villainous trio of Red West, Sonny West, and Dave Hebler—*Elvis: What Happened?* was "told to" a hardboiled Australian writer named Steve Dunleavy and bankrolled by Rupert Murdoch's World News Corporation, publisher of the *National Star.* In the opening scene, which had all the trappings of a cheap gangster movie, Elvis wakes up in his Las Vegas suite in a drug-hazed rage and, like some bloodthirsty Don, decides to have Mike Stone, the man who ostensibly "stole" his wife, "wasted." For Elvis's fans, it was as if *Pearl Harbor* had been bombed all over again!—nothing would ever be the same. *Extraextrareadallaboutit,* the copy on the back of the book screams—

> A DEVOTED SON, A GENEROUS
> FRIEND. A MODEL ARMY RECRUIT.
> A GIFTED ENTERTAINER. A
> BELOVED HERO TO MILLIONS.
> THIS IS THE ELVIS PRESLEY THE
> WORLD KNOWS—AND CHERISHES.
> BROODING. VIOLENT. OBSESSED
> WITH DEATH.
> STRUNG OUT. SEXUALLY DRIVEN.
> THIS IS THE OTHER SIDE OF ELVIS—
> ACCORDING TO THREE MEN WHO
> LIVED WITH HIM THROUGH IT
> ALL—A MAN WHO...

—and we are duly informed of the beautiful young fan Elvis "charms" into joining him on a drug binge that turns her into a vegetable, as well as other shockers about him, all listed neatly (uppers, downers)... Finally this tidbit: "Hurls a pool cue at a party guest who interrupts his game, injuring her breast..." That was only the beginning. Yes, folks, there was violence...obsessions with guns and death...*sex* and *drugs*...all of it slickly packaged with ruthless sensationalism and pawned off as a Last Ditch Attempt To Save Elvis From

Himself. Then came August 16, 1977 and suddenly there were two million copies in print and the book, which had appeared only weeks before the death (installments had been serialized in the *Star*) became one of the final chapters of a sad story. In the wake of Elvis' death, it was disowned by its authors, damned and disbelieved by the fans, and devoured everywhere. Unfortunately, there were truths contained within its dark pages, but very little compassion; and the endeavor smacked of naked and vicious exploitation. Never had so beloved a public figure been so brutally trashed. To Elvis fans a sacred place had been violated; it was a scandal far worse than Watergate. The Great Debate: was Elvis Presley saint or sinner?

What made the book both compelling and insupportable was the fact that it *is* indeed the first look into Elvis' private life, albeit with all the subtlety and style of a peep show on 42nd Street. The discrepancies between the Elvis who was the apple of May Mann's eye and what we are told in *Elvis: What Happened?* are outlandish. Witness:

> Elvis was certainly not on dope. He never has, nor will be. His mother so ingrained in him the logic of a clean mind, clean body, good health, honesty, and integrity.
>
> *—Elvis and the Colonel*

By 1971, Elvis was a changed guy. He was no longer

the shy, fun-loving kid from Memphis. No, he was just living for himself and all that damned junk. He was like a walking drugstore.

—Elvis: What Happened?

It would be myopic to dismiss the entire contents of the book as valueless because of the less-than-wholesome motivations of the authors, who were all (as they admit) seething at their firing. Their "execution," as they called it, was attributed to one of Elvis' "whims." In fact, I would later learn that they were the most troublesome members of the entourage.

In the book, Elvis comes through when Dunleavy feels no need to overdramatize (when the material is neither sordid nor lurid, but simple, banal

The demonic three (l. to r.): Dave Hebler, Red West and Sonny West.

descriptions). Here, for instance, is a telling passage from Red's now-famous recounting of the time he saved Elvis' neck in the bathroom of Humes High in 1952:

> "The place was full of smoke, you could hardly see in front of you for all the smoke," Red recounts. "But I could see far enough to notice that old 'E' was in a whole heap of trouble again. About four or five guys had him in there, and they were holding him and pushing him up against the wall and then grabbing him from behind. They were yelling and laughing and wising off at him and his hair. They decided they were gonna cut his hair.
>
> "Now a smart guy usually keeps his nose out of other people's business. I knew the guys who were has-

sling Elvis. They were on the football squad. I suppose they got this haircutting business from old Coach Boyce. The guys who were giving Elvis a hard time were not really bad guys, just a bit noisy and stuff. But when I saw Elvis' face, it just triggered something inside of me. I mean were were just kids and they weren't gonna kill him or anything, but there was that look of real fear on his face. He was looking like a frightened little animal and I just couldn't stand seeing it. When you're very poor, you tend to let everyone look after their own troubles, but that face of Elvis', I can see it to this day. And I saw that face like that many times later, and it always had the same effect on me. Just churned something up inside of me. It's a child's face and it asks for help."

The theme of Elvis as perpetual "little boy," who never matured emotionally but became a millionaire and thus could indulge all of his childhood fantasies and tastes, repeats itself in this book and in countless others.

> The morning after the decision was made Presley mounted his small bulldozer, but it was obvious that it couldn't do the job, so he hired a full-size construction bulldozer. Red recalls: "I got in the little one and Elvis got atop of the big one. He put a football helmet on for protection. I remember this day because Vernon Presley was sitting on the porch in a rocking chair dozing off. Elvis starts up the bulldozer and yells out to Vernon, 'You better move, Daddy.' Vernon asks why and Elvis says, 'Because I'm going to knock the goddamn house down.' Once again, Vernon gives one of those looks like 'Oh, Lordie,' but he doesn't say anything; he knows too well for that now, so he just gets up and Elvis starts roaring away. We also lit the house and it was blazing like hell and he just bores into it, destroys it. At one time I was in the little bulldozer and he was in the big one, and I look behind and the sonofabitch is pushing me into the burning house while I'm on this little bulldozer. He was laughing his ass off. He was having a great time.
>
> "Anyway, in less than an hour we have just knocked the whole superstructure down to where it drops right into the basement and it's burning up a storm. As the thing is going up in smoke, we hear a fire engine, and the next thing, this fireman sticks his head over the fence and asks what in hell's name we think we're doing.
>
> "Elvis looks up at him with a look on his face which says it was a damn fool question to ask and says, 'We're burning down a house.' And the guy says, 'How did you do that?' and Elvis says, 'With a damn match.'

How different things might have been had the co-authors kept to the track of this type of material rather than playing up Elvis' "dark side"—the book wouldn't have been as controversial, but it might have easily topped the best-seller lists and saved many people much anguish, including Elvis Presley. But the whole *point* of the book was to shock, and the vendetta warranted the most tactless of disclosures, and not only about drugs. Red on the break-up of Elvis and Priscilla:

> Red recalls: "We weren't there, of course, but it appears she told him between shows at the Hilton. Pris-

cilla and the wives—my wife, Pat, was there—were having dinner at Leonardo's, the Italian restaurant at the Hilton. I was with 'E' up in his room. He just told me, 'Go down and get Priscilla.' I went down and told her Elvis wanted to see her. Whatever happened up there, Priscilla later told my wife, Pat, that he made love to her—very forcefully. He took her right on the spot when he knew another man was in the picture."

Vignettes like this, for their crass invasion and exploitation of what must have been one of the most sensitive and private moments in Elvis' life, were what made the book so unforgivable. The release of such material, had I been Elvis Presley, would have mortified me far more than banner headlines about my drug habits across the front page of the *New York Times*.

Apparently, Elvis felt the same way. As soon as he learned about the book's preparation and contents through lawyers and private investigators (like John O'Grady of Los Angeles), his life was pervaded by nightmarish anxieties about its publication and how it might affect his family and reputation, and he tried through intermediaries to settle with his disgruntled ex-bodyguards. However, by that time it was too late; contracts had been signed and emotions too seared for the trio to back off. When Elvis made a phone call to Red one morning in a belated attempt to clear the air, the conversation was recorded, and its transcript concludes the book. If, indeed, the nine pages are accurate, they manage to say more about Elvis and his life than all previous 324. "I think I'd become a dollar sign," Elvis says of Hebler. "In the process he lost sight of Elvis . . . I'd become an object, not a person. I'm not that sign, not that image, I'm myself." He briefly mentions the folly of the racketball venture, his intestinal problems and his weird liquid diet, his fears for his father's health after his heart attack; all in a breath, he talks of loneliness, numerology, pressures, peppering everything with references to songs. "I got a daughter and a life," he says of himself, despite what we know about the boredom, loneliness, and gloom. "What profiteth a man who gains the world but loses his soul? I love to sing . . . since I was two years old." And there we have it.

Elvis offers to help Red and his family, but it's too late—he seems to realize it himself, and the fact that a once-trusted ex-employee is recording his conversation for publication is certainly an indication of it. Ten months later, Elvis was dead, and the flood began in earnest.

On a balmy night in April of 1978, Dee Presley picked me up at the Memphis airport in a white Eldorado convertible about the length of two city blocks, and what became immediately apparent to me as we drove through the streets and people gaped at her was that here, in this world, this woman was a celebrity simply because she had once been married to the father of the King.

Facts: Dee Elliot Stanley met Vernon Presley in Germany while Elvis was stationed at Friedberg. After a rather torrid affair, Dee left her non-com husband, took her three young boys and married Vernon in 1960. They divorced seventeen years later. Her marriage to Vernon had been tempestuous and her relationship with her famous stepson an exercize in cordialty and distance. Her three sons, however, ages only six, five, and four at the time of the marriage, were a different story. Billy, Rick, and David were roughly my age and had all grown up to work for Elvis. David and Rick were among the last to see him alive.

What made the Stanley boys unique was that having grown up around Elvis, he had become their role model. Elvis wasn't simply a combination of "boss" and friend like the others in his entourage, but a big brother and surrogate father. Hence, for better or worse, they had soaked up his character like three hungry sponges, picking up even his trademark mannerisms. Billy Smith, Elvis' younger cousin, also was influenced by Elvis in this manner. The boys were like living extensions of Elvis—missing only the looks and talent—and together they embodied all the best and worst of his world. They understood a great deal about him and his make-up but their knowledge and familiarity, though first-hand, could not have been nearly as complete as somebody like Joe Esposito (who extended much farther back into Elvis' past and occupied

a far more crucial place in his life); and yet their connection with him had been so elemental and emotional that Elvis was illuminated for me simply by being *around* them. Contained within their experience was the essence of Elvis' life and the depth of his tragedy, but in order to communicate that experience I would have

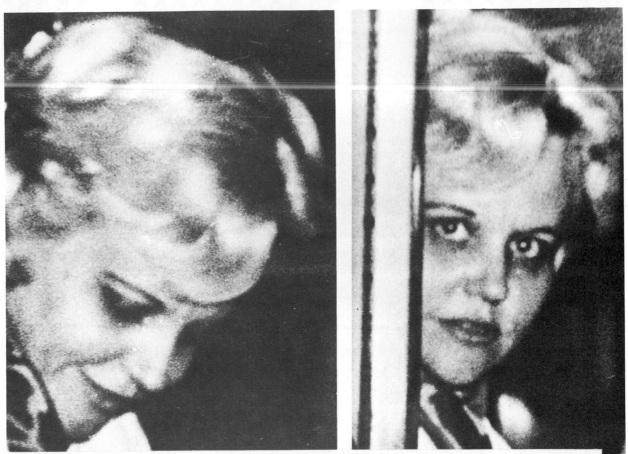

MPP3/11MEMPHIS:Who is this mystery blonde? She arrived by train with Vernon Presley, father of rock n' roll singer Elvis. She has been referred to as "Dee." Neither father nor son Elvis wanted to identify her. Blonde has been houseguest at the Presley mansion, but nobody seems to know who she is. Do you? UNITED PRESS INTERNATIONAL TELEPHOTO

Dee Presley.

to make them all equal partners in the story, a risky proposition because Elvis' story was of paramount importance to the reader.

When the interview period was over, I knew that I had more than enough for a vivid and well-balanced portrait: I was sitting on what we in the profession call a "whale of a story" filled with the kind of triumphs and human frailties that every writer dreams about—and I was filled with anxieties. I had come to respect and care very much about these people—they *trusted* me—the last thing I wanted was to betray that trust by allowing their lives to be trivialized or sensationalized into an *Elvis: What Happened?* I was determined to make the drugs and sex a responsible *part* of the story rather than the story itself—but the power of the marketplace can easily exert a strong influence on the editing process of a manuscript within the publishing house.

It was both exciting and disconcerting to be writing an "inside" book on a subject that was breaking all around me. Simple deduction of what I had learned from the boys combined with several visits to a well-known pathologist led me to believe that the circumstances and causes of death and the resulting conclusions of Dr. Francisco were extremely murky and confusing; and knowing about Dr. Nick and the drugs long before Geraldo Rivera, I realized that it was only a matter of time before he would be publicly flayed for something that he ultimately had little control over. Yes, Dr. Nick had over-prescribed "medication" because Elvis Presley, for many tragic and complicated reasons, had become a drug addict in his final years, but Dr. Nick was the only one of his doctors who had really tried to *help* Elvis. In the end, he had been as powerless as anybody else to make a difference in Elvis' life— and his medical degree only made him more vulnerable.

And then the other books were pumped out, one after the other. The first was *My Life With Elvis* (1978) by Becky Yancey (with Cliff Linedecker), one of the Graceland secretaries, a book that closely followed the prescription for the fan book by offering heaping handfuls of little details about Elvis' pets and expenses and impressions of life around the mansion, but the closest the book came to anything off the beaten path were some catty revelations about how much Linda Thompson had spent on her wardrobe when she was Elvis' girlfriend (Becky, you see, saw the bills) and Ann-Margret's code name ("Bunny") for leaving phone messages so that Priscilla wouldn't know.

It was only the tip of the iceberg: virtually everybody around Graceland, with the exceptions of Vernon Presley, Priscilla, Joe Esposito, Jerry Schilling, and (so far) Colonel Parker was working on something about Elvis—and these were precisely the people who, as major characters in his story, *should* have been writing books, because they could have told us the most. In rapid succession, the books appeared: *A Presley Speaks* by Uncle Vester (with Deda Bonura), a home-spun and simple book about the god-fearing Presley family and life at the front gate; *The Graceland Gates* by Harold Lloyd, or Elvis' cousin's version of Uncle Vester's book. Then came *Inside Elvis* by Ed Parker, Elvis' karate instructor and companion-bodyguard, which got much closer to what it was like hanging out with Elvis Presley but was careful to pander to the tastes of his most loyal fans by staying well away from anything sticky.

The personal accounts continued with *Elvis: Portrait of a Friend* by Marty Lacker, Patsy Lacker, and Leslie S. Smith. The book, which came even closer to the vein of Elvis' character, was divided in three parts, one for the perspective of each co-author. Lacker's section was most interesting, as much for what wasn't said as what was. As Elvis' former personal bookkeeper and one of the co-best men at his wedding, Lacker had been a "Mafia member" during the Sixties but ceased working for Elvis (or was abandoned) when his personal life became a problem (due to his too-ardent adoption of Elvis' lifestyle, including his use of medications). Still, considering that Elvis treated him rather shabbily at times, his section of the book is remarkably free of invective (save for Vernon Presley's anti-Semitic outburst against Lacker's mother). The same, however, cannot be said of the section devoted to his wife, Patsy "Wife Was a Four Letter Word" Lacker, who was deeply resentful of the way Marty just took off for California once he had tasted the High Life with Elvis, leaving Patsy and child back in Memphis. She used the occasion for a tart-tongued tirade about what was wrong with the life at Graceland, who was nice and who wasn't, etc. (One of the emerging characteristics of these books is that the authors all feel the need to pass judgements about each other, and do so brazenly). In the final section, the writer takes it upon himself to overgeneralize about Elvis' drug problems and Dr. Nick's complicity, with titles like "The Doctor as Pusher" (and whatever Smith doesn't know he goes to Sonny West to find out).

What made the book interesting were several passages that are excellent examples of the kind of mythopoeic anecdotes which were becoming characteristic of these memoirs, which take Elvis' most legendary stories and wave them like the American flag. What follows is certainly one of the classics.

> We went to one of the poorest neighborhoods in Memphis. It was really bad. We couldn't understand how people were living like that and yet, most of us had begun our lives in little better surroundings.
>
> I went to the door to be sure we were at the right place and an old man let me in. It was probably the poorest place I've ever seen. There were newspapers keeping the wind from coming in the windows and there was an old coal stove in the middle of the floor. Now this was in the city, not out in the country. It was a shack, not a house.
>
> The old man didn't understand why I was there and I had to explain three or four times. I'm not too sure he understood even then, but I knew I was in the right house when I saw the old lady sitting on a

wooden chair in the other room. I told the man I would be right back.

Outside, I told Elvis the old lady was in the house and the other guys assembled the chair. Elvis carried it into the house and Priscilla and I followed along with the others.

Tears came to all our eyes at the sight of these old people amidst such poverty. Elvis went to the old woman and said, "Hello, I came to give you this chair as a gift for Christmas."

She didn't seem to understand why this white man had come to her house to give her a new wheelchair. She kept looking at it and at him as he showed her how it should be operated. Suddenly she seemed to realize it was really for her and she tried her best to get off the chair she was on and into the new one, but she was unable to do so. Elvis gently picked her up and placed her in the new chair.

The tears were flowing from her old eyes as she cried, "Praise God! God bless you! God bless you! God be praised! God bless you!"

She held Elvis and Priscilla and their tears mixed with hers. Priscilla was on one side and Elvis on the other, sharing with this old woman a moment of happy sadness. There was no member of the tough Memphis Mafia in the room that night who didn't succumb to the emotion. Each of us went over and put our arms around the old lady and clasped the old man's feeble hand. We loved the old couple, we loved Priscilla and we loved each other but most of all we loved Elvis and the sincerity with which he gave his true gift, himself.

Such is the stuff of the Elvis legend. Whether they evoke Elvis as Good Samaritan or King, whether he is giving away a dozen Cadillacs with the wave of a hand or shooting out a television set, exploding in anger or laughing with glee, they all provide the writer with a built-in opportunity to milk these recollections for maximum mileage. In the same vein, Elvis' reaction to first hearing "The Green, Green Grass of Home" during a trip home from California made him stop at phones along the way to call his friend George Klein at the radio station in Memphis to request that the song be replayed over and over again. When he returns to Graceland, his emotional reaction to the song results in this:

When we arrived at Graceland, all of our wives and girlfriends were there and, with the excitement of the homecoming, I forgot the song and my spirits began to lift. I went to find Elvis to see if he needed anything special before I called it a day.

As I went into the hall, I saw Elvis kneeling on the floor crying. I mean really sobbing. He was suffering as I had never before seen. One of the other guys was there with him, and alarmed, I said, "Elvis, what's the matter? What's the matter?" I was certain that he was sick or had been hurt.

He looked at me with tears streaming down his face and slowly choked out, "Marty, when I came in the door, I saw my mother."

"What do you mean, Elvis?" I asked.

"I saw her, man. She was standing there. I saw her."

His emotion and suffering got to me and I began to feel tears in my own eyes. I tried to comfort him. "Elvis, she's always here. As long as you are here, she

will be here too."

Finally, he gained control of himself, got up, hugged me and went to his room.

We didn't see him for about a week. He stayed in his private quarters.

Similar images resurface in *The Truth About Elvis* by Jess Stearn with Larry Geller, but the book is more interesting for the simple reason that Elvis' relationship with Geller, his long-time beautician and "spiritual advisor," was much more provocative, centering around some of the primary interests in Elvis' life.

In all his giving, the greatest gift that Elvis gave was himself.

He was besieged every day of his life with every imaginable request. He received five thousand letters a week, and most of them wanted something. The letters were handled by Vernon and his staff, in an office behind Graceland. Knowing Elvis' desire to please, his father kept all but the most imperative messages from him.

One day, he approached Elvis with a grave face. A nine-year-old girl lay dying of an incurable disease in a Memphis hospital. As a last wish, she had expressed a desire to see Elvis.

Elvis was about to leave for Hollywood to start a picture when Vernon told him of the girl's dying wish.

He didn't hesitate a second. He turned to the aides, helping with his luggage.

"Hold everything," he said. "I've got to see that little girl."

A few minutes later, he was on his way to the hospital. The child was waiting. She gave him a wan smile, and tried to sit up. Elvis reached down, and took her to his breast, kissing her on the forehead.

"You'll be all right," he said. "God will watch over you."

Two weeks later, Larry walked into Elvis' Bel-Air den, and saw that Elvis had been crying.

"That little girl died yesterday. The poor thing, she was so frail and so sweet, so young. She wanted very much to live."

He gave Larry a piercing glance. "Can we meditate together? It may help us to understand."

His spirits were restored. "You know, Larry," he said, "the greatest gift God has for us is the gift of life. And who is to say when it ends. Didn't Jesus say that He was the Resurrection and the Life and that whosoever believed in Him shall never die?"

Such heartrending examples of Elvis' generosity and spiritual conscience are a mainstay of this book, whose authors, being more than familiar with the use of the Zen koan, offer anecdotes that combine analyses of some of the more paradoxical elements in Elvis' character combined with the small but telling moments that bring them sharply into focus. And we are left to digest them.

He was more complex than he realized. He knew the heights of exaltation and the depths of despair at almost the same moment. He would hide himself from the outside world, then launch a tour across the country, with great visibility. He had an artist's appreciation of his own value, but he was essentially humble. One day, he stepped into an elevator in Las Vegas and a youthful admirer raved, "You're the greatest, Elvis, you're the King."

Elvis smiled.

"I may be in the wings," he said, "but I'm not on the throne. There is only one King." He pointed to the sky.

Fortunately, the books was not without its humor as well, a fact that made it all the more authentic, for Elvis was a man who loved to see the funny side of a situation.

> Usually, Vernon and his staff handled the letters. But, periodically, Elvis would take a stack of mail, and go over it, opening the envelopes himself. One night he got Larry to help him. Larry saw him wince as he pulled out a message, written on a scroll of toilet paper. It had every vulgarity known to man on it, and some neither had heard of. There was no mistaking the intention. The writer had enclosed a snapshot of herself in the nude, showing a middle-aged woman with very few graces. Elvis stared for a moment, then shook his head, mournfully:
>
> "God have mercy on the poor thing, she's as ugly as sin, and she's advertising yet."

But Elvis really springs to life in this book during those moments when his humor mixes naturally with the pathos of his loneliness or pain, which produces a bittersweet ambience that comes closer to the true texture of his life than anything else.

> Sometimes his giving backfired. One night in Las Vegas, the entourage brought up a few girls to Elvis' suite. Elvis gravitated, naturally, to a Southern girl with a sweet, innocent face and a honeyed drawl. He was between girl friends at this time and he was ready. The young lady accepted with alacrity Elvis' invitation to stay over. The next day, bowled over by her beauty and charm, he had a local agency deliver her a ten-thousand-dollar sportscar. He laughed gaily, as she drove off into the sunset.
>
> "See you later," she cried.
>
> That evening, Elvis was still rhapsodizing about his new lady love. But as he looked at the entourage, he was struck by the awkward silence.
>
> "What's wrong?" he asked.
>
> One of the security guards stood up with a long face. "Elvis, I hate to tell you this." He looked at him uncomfortably. "But that girl's a hooker, Elvis. We just found out an hour ago."
>
> Elvis' face dropped, and he closed his eyes.
>
> "Maybe," the guard said, "you can get the car back."
>
> Elvis recovered quickly. He looked around, half-sheepishly. "I suppose I could stop payment on the check, but what the hell, hookers need cars, too."

Also notable in the book are discussions of Elvis' interests in religion and other subjects, many of which were shared by Larry, who brought him the books he read. However, the guru-student relationship that Larry supposedly shared with Elvis also results in the book's major drawback: the pretentious tone of the conversational exchange between Larry and Elvis often makes it read like an amateurish version of *Siddhartha*, with the omniscient sage Larry patiently explaining and enlightening his wide-eyed disciple Elvis. Still, *The Truth About Elvis*, for the most part, works admirably.

Other surprises continued to emerge from the flood of fact books, quiz books, recycled biographies, and photo books that poured onto the market, and when they did their obvious superiority made them seem like pearls amidst the chaff. One was Al Wertheimer's *Elvis '56: In the Beginning*, a display of Elvis through the 1956 wave of television, recording, and concert appearances that was rapidly bringing him to the attention of the world and radically altering his life. We see him exactly as he was before his mother died, when he could still walk out in broad daylight alone (and not be ripped to shreds by fans), frozen forever young in time, in a natural state of pristine youth and power. The text of the book, by Wertheimer with Gregory Martinelli, is every bit as good as the photographs and remarkably precise in its rendering of detail and impression. Here is Elvis, for instance, in the RCA Studios in New York, through take after take of "Hound Dog."

> Take eighteen. Elvis closed his eyes, took a deep breath and grated into the microphone, grabbing the lyric and spiking it with a nastiness that made it bite. Scotty's guitar found its edge and Bill's bass surged with the momentum they had been missing. By the end of the take, the Jordanaires thought they had it.
>
> Elvis wanted to try it again. At take twenty-six, Steve thought they had it. Elvis still thought he could do it a little better. Four takes later, Steve called over the PA, "Okay, Elvis. I think we got it." They had engaged the law of diminishing returns. Mistakes were creeping in. Elvis rubbed his face, swept back his hair and resigned. "I hope so, Mr. Sholes."
>
> The working relationship at this session was a departure from what I had seen at other recording sessions. Other artists I had covered were directed by a producer. He was the man in charge, and often the atmosphere was formal and businesslike. With Elvis the mood was casual, relaxed, joking. Steve did not dictate, he managed. And though Elvis was not a forward, take-charge character, he was clearly the one who had to be pleased. When it concerned his music, no one was more serious.
>
> The recording had taken over two hours and without the air conditioner turned on (the mikes would have picked up the noise), the air in the room hung low and close. The double doors were opened, admitting cool air, the noise of vending machines and visitors with glowing compliments. Elvis combed his hair, drank the Coke offered by Junior and shrugged in reply to comments about how good the music was. Steve trod lightly: "Elvis, you ready to hear a playback?" As if bad news never had good timing, he said, "Now's as good a time as any."
>
> Elvis sat cross-legged on the floor in front of the speaker. The engineer announced the take over the PA and let the tape roll. Elvis winced, chewed his fingernails and looked at the floor. At the end of the first playback, he looked like he didn't know whether it was a good take or not. Steve called for take eighteen.

Elvis pulled up a folding chair, draped his arms across its back and stared blankly at the floor. As his voice pierced the speaker grille, everyone waited for his reaction. Then, as if he had received a telegram bearing news that, yes, there's good rockin' tonight, he popped his head up and cracked a smile. Take eighteen was a contender.

The engineer racked take twenty-eight. Elvis left his chair and crouched on the floor, as if listening in a different position was like looking at a subject from a different angle. Again he went into deep concentration, absorbed and motionless. For someone who had to wring the music from his body, he sure took it back lying down. At the end of the song, he slowly rose from his crouch and turned to us with a wide grin, and said "This is the one."

Even if these passages aren't perfectly factual, their value is obvious; Wertheimer was *there*. Also priceless are the photos and recollections of Elvis and his family at 1034 Audubon Drive in Memphis, and little moments like this from Elvis' stay in New York.

The Warwick Hotel had been built to celebrate an earlier era, but it was now suffering from fatigue. Dim lights preserved its fading floral carpets and mottled walls. Room 527 wasn't a suite, but a simple spacious room with a large mirror hanging over a studio couch. Elvis flopped down on the couch, grabbed a fistful of letters from a cardboard box and began reading. After finishing each letter he tore it into small pieces. The remains were deposited on the coffee table next to a collection of aspirin, stomach and cold remedies and a copy of *The Loves of Liberace*. This routine continued until he rolled onto the pile of letters on the couch and stared at the ceiling. I asked:

"What do you think of the big city?"

"I don't really care too much for the big city."

"Well, do you feel more comfortable down South, down in Memphis?"

"Yeah, a lot more comfortable. People understand me better down there."

He tore up a few more letters, settled down with a cushion and dozed off. I had never covered a subject who fell asleep in front of my camera, but I had my assignment. I took a few more pictures, and when I sat down in one of the soft, thick chairs, I followed his example.

The buzz of an electric shaver woke me up. Elvis was in the bathroom. I tried to figure out a discreet way to take his picture when I decided upon the direct approach. I asked if I could come in and take some pictures. He said, "Sure, why not?"

With one white towel around his hips and another slung over his shoulder, Elvis elevated wet combing to an art, examining each angle with the scrutiny of a portrait artist. He was the perfect subject for a photographer, unafraid and uncaring, oblivious to the invasion of my camera.

It all makes you gasp with delight when you pause for a moment to realize that books like Hans Holzer's *Elvis Presley Speaks*, in which the King holds court from the afterlife through the unsuspecting body of a New Jersey housewife, appeared at approximately the same time.

Also reassuring was the appearance in the bookstores of *The Final Years*, Jerry Hopkins's sequel to *Elvis*, a level-headed, well-researched, and surprisingly dispassionate work filled with colorful summations about Elvis' decline like the following.

There was so much he had to face, continually, good and bad, from his fans: The supernova caused by all the Instamatics when he walked on stage; the interminable fan magazine covers, and worse, the supermarket tabloids, prying into his personal life; the consistency with which his albums sold, even when there were no hit singles and the albums themselves were weak; the complete and utter devotion that lapped at his ankles from all those who surrounded him. There were fan clubs in dozens of countries; some were so loyal they chartered planes to come see him in Las Vegas and look at his Memphis home. The mail was enormous. Every time he appeared in public, women of nearly all ages threw themselves at him and showered the stage with room keys, underwear, and folded notes with their names and addresses, for when he came to their town.

Elvis had every damned thing he wanted. Over the years he had owned every kind of transportation, from horses, golf carts, motorcycles, sports cars, and limousines, to pickup trucks, tractors, motor homes, yachts, and airplanes. He'd had spacious homes in three cities, duplicate wardrobes in each of them. He had a faithful, loving girlfriend (Linda) and whenever he wanted someone else for a night or two, he had people on the payroll who went out and got them for him. On a whim he could meet a U.S. President.

Anything he wanted to eat, he could eat, any time he wanted it. Fried banana sandwiches for breakfast! Baconburgers by the sack at midnight! Ice cream, a spoon served with a quart. When he wanted to go shopping, stores and automobile agencies fell all over themselves to open at two and three A.M.

And Elvis hung in there—bloated and sometimes whacked out of his mind on prescription chemicals, but able to "maintain" nearly all the time, able to get out there and give the customers a show.

For those of us who had awaited the book with expectations of something definitive, it was a bit of a letdown. The reason for this was less Hopkins' fault than the situation following Elvis' death: the major characters around Elvis once again did not grant him interviews because they had either clammed up or were writing books of their own! Once again he found himself on the outside, and whatever important interviews he did secure were, on the surface, safe. But, undaunted, he constructed by his mural of Elvis' decline and fall; and even if he ended up not knowing more than the rest of us, the book is indispensable.

Also significant was the publication of a slim volume called *Elvis: Images and Fancies* by the University of Mississippi Press, which marked the first formal contribution of the American intelligentsia to the Elvis phenomenon. Edited by Jac L. Tharpe, the book blended literate essays by fans like Gay McRae with several substantial essays by scholars, some already with grants to study Elvis and his role in American culture. Notable among the essays were "Elvis or the Ironies of a Southern Identity" by Linda Ray Pratt of the University of Lincoln-Nebraska (anthologized in this volume); and

Van K. Brock's "Images of Elvis, the South, and America." The spirit of Greil Marcus is readily discernible in these writings, which derive from some of the issues raised by "Elvis: Presliad." (I wonder how aware Greil might have been of the seeds he was planting by invoking Melville and W.J. Cash's *The Mind of the South* in the same breath with Elvis Presley). This, then, from Van Brock:

> One way of understanding Presley's career is to see him as a man trying to transcend his roots, while affirming them, to weave together the complex, conflicting and tortuous strands of identity that are a part of every Southerner—racial, regional, national and human—and perhaps of every American. No Southerner, at least, can make a complete integration of self without coming to terms with the anomaly he

is to the world and with the awareness that his identity group has compromised or been compromised by another identity group, leaving a gulf between his and another culture, both of which are part of the complex constituency of his whole identity. However they relate to the reality, all Southerners must come to terms with two racial identities, if they are to come to terms with themselves. If Presley happened on this originally by accident, courtesy of Sam Phillips of Sun Records, if at first it made him uncomfortable, it is to his credit that he accepted the necessity. If he sought to integrate the several cultures that nourished him and sometimes sought to honor them individually, as Greil Marcus points out in *Mystery Train*, it should be seen as to some degree a healthy phenomenon for himself and the cultures. If the mirror he held to American culture was warped at times, it still reflected; and an important question is who or how many have held a clearer mirror to it. And if one does not believe that mimesis is the only purpose of the artist, I cannot doubt that, for Presley, whatever his motives (patriotism, narcissism, profit) —and they may have been very complex—that was a large part of his sense of his purpose as an artist.

And, later:

> He seemed to come from the lowest caste in the South, the lowest region of the nation, white blues and black blues sliding in and out of each other, and his voice rose out of the diaphragm of a writhing torso to recreate the myth of America in visual image as well as sound. And the fact that he "made it" gave pride and hope to those who felt repressed, but whose lives seemed relatively futureless, although they were still suspended at what should have been the point of boundless possibility. His realization of that boundless possibility gave substance to their vague fantasies and dreams. Many tried to follow his example and a few succeeded. But for most, to the extent that he mattered to them, their following meant that he would live their lives for them; they would share vicariously the wealth and power and fame they would never have except through him.

Both the mass media and the scholarly community were realizing that the Elvis fans, who had always been an important element in his story, were no longer simply a "public" or a "market" or the curious onlookers at the Graceland wall, but the living manifestation of his

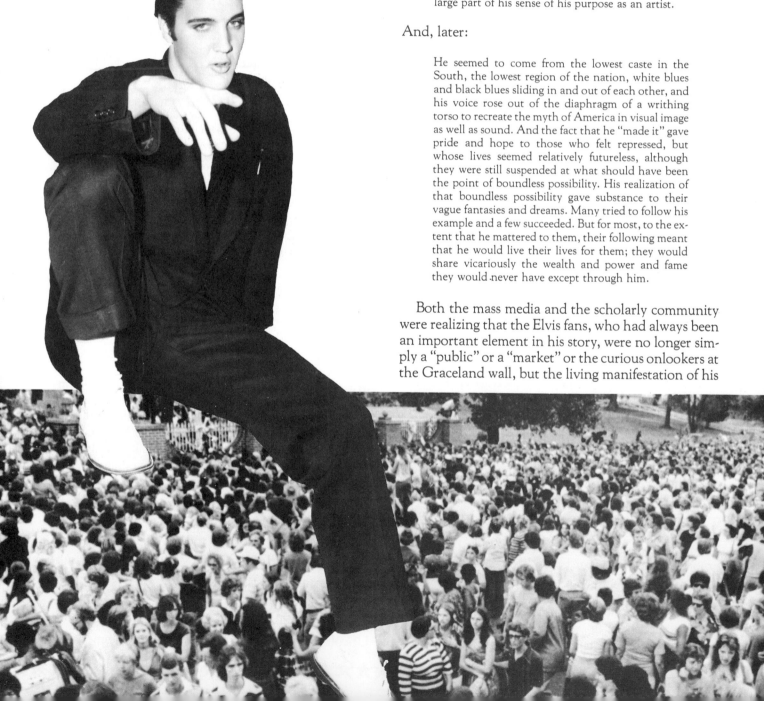

"phenomenon." Yes, the fans had become the legitimate turf of journalists, sociologists, musicologists, cultural historians, their writings to be included in the publications of university presses as well as fan letters. "There is a general misconception that only undereducated women on a low socioeconomic level constitute the Elvis Presley audience," writes Patsy G. Hammontree in "Audience Amplitude: The Cultural Phenomenon of Elvis Presley."

> Rather, his audience is comprised of an incredibly variegated group of people from all economic and social levels. Chronologically, the spectrum stretches from age five to eighty-five. And large numbers of men—including construction workers and physicians—admire Elvis. It is virtually impossible to draw a "profile" of THE Elvis Presley fan because of such diversity, a factor which also precludes any standardized label being applicable to the mass audience. Elvis's popularity was international. He had millions of followers in both Europe and Asia. There are Presley fans even in the Middle East. Someone said boys and girls were wearing Elvis Presley T-shirts in the jungles of Thailand. The diversity of even a sampling attests to the Presley cultural phenomenon. In truth, the man takes on mythic and archetypal dimensions such that for some of his fans only Christ is greater.

The inclusion of scholarly work to the body of Elvis literature signaled no end to the personal books, and even Elvis' nurse chimed in with *I Called Him Babe*, by Marion J. Cocke.

At first glance, Mrs. Cocke's book doesn't seem illuminating or noteworthy, and many fans reacted as if just another person had jumped on the bandwagon to promote themselves and make a few dollars (while in fact, she donated her royalties to charities). But her book has its valuable moments and serves to shed light on Elvis' health problems, bringing us into the emergency room at Baptist Memorial at the precise moment when the reality of Elvis Presley's death becomes official:

> When I got in the room, John Quartermous was doing cardio-pulmonary resuscitation. The room was full, and Dr. Nick was there. He just looked at me, as did John. I read what was in their faces because I couldn't really see Elvis. Owen Taylor, one of the residents, knew that I always took care of Elvis, so he came around the room, stood beside me, and put his arm around me. He asked if I was sure I wanted to stay in there. I said yes, so he just held on tighter and held me up. I reached out and touched one of the interns on the arm and moved him aside so I could see Elvis. When I did, my knees got weak, and Owen held on tighter. I said, "Please stop." It was evident that the soul of this boy had long since left his body, and I could not bear to see them continue. John looked over at Dr. Nick. He told him to hold up on the CPR, and when he saw that there was absolutely no complex on the EKG he agreed that they would stop. He came over and hugged me and we both went out.
>
> My boy was gone . . . .

Finally, we even received a rare look into that mystery of mysteries, Colonel Thomas A. Parker himself, in *Up and Down With Elvis Presley*. Written by *Houston Post* columnist Marge Crumbaker with Gabe Tucker (it never becomes exactly clear *who* Gabe Tucker is: we know he's a part-time associate and sidekick of the old Colonel's from the good ole days, but more than being his cigar smoking buddy, we really don't get the *connection*), the book paints the Colonel as being the real hero of the story. Elvis is almost beside the point here and is tossed off as a minor character, as nothing more than a talented hick. If the book is reliable (and one can *never* be sure), there is much interesting material. Here, according to the authors, is the real reason behind the unprecedented press blackout imposed by the Colonel.

> Something happened shortly after Elvis had resumed civilian life which prompted the Colonel to stop all contact between his star and the media. Elvis had made a disastrous gaffe when a member of the press asked him whether he planned to marry.
> Elvis' reply was: "Why buy a cow when you can get free milk?"
> Parker immediately called an end to all interviews, even with disc jockeys. The Colonel told his people that he was afraid such uncontrolled statements would alienate the Presley fans, but to the star, he gave another explanation: "Holding interviews with only a select few is making us enemies with all the rest. It isn't fair to designate a handful of people and have you talk only to them. See my point?"
> "Sure," Elvis said. "I didn't like giving interviews anyway."
> The blackout had an added advantage; now the element of mystery was added to the Presley legend.

"Disastrous gaffe"? If the anecdote is true, it certainly isn't hard to understand why Elvis never appeared on *The Tonight Show*! God only knows what damaging and self-incriminating things he might have uttered. And here, according to the authors, is the real reason why Elvis never fulfilled his much-vaunted promise to tour abroad.

> Some of the Colonel's reasons for keeping Elvis confined to dates played within the United States boundaries were personal, but some of them stemmed from a very valid fear: the Colonel was onto Elvis' use of dope, and he knew other members of the Memphis Mafia were into it. Passing through customs might have revealed the drugs and tarnished the Elvis image. The Colonel was convinced that if Elvis' drug use were to become public knowledge, it would be the end of everything they'd both worked so hard to achieve.

And now, given this disclosure, I find myself unable to resist raising a simple question that has long troubled me. If the Colonel knew about Elvis' drug dependence and his deteriorating condition (and there is every indication he did); and if he really loved and respected Elvis as he always claimed, then how in heaven's name could he have (in good conscience) continued to book him where he would be seen *in public*; how could he have allowed Elvis, knowing how bad he looked, to sign a contract with CBS to appear on *national television*?

A plausible explanation is that Elvis, given his grandiose spending habits, needed the money; but what is also likely is that the Colonel knew that with Red and Sonny's book coming out, the ballgame was up, and that it was only a matter of time before Elvis Presley met his maker. Witness his reported response to the death of "his boy."

> The Colonel and Esposito consoled one another briefly, then the Colonel thanked Esposito and hung up. He sagged back into his chair and remained motionless for several moments. Then he made up his mind to direct his efforts toward the management of salvaging the reputation of his star. There'd be no display of grief from him, because he intended spending all of his energies on carrying the legend of Elvis forward. Leave the grief to others. The Colonel had work to do.
>
> He called Vernon Presley. "Vernon, I know this is the worst possible time in our lives, and no one will ever replace Elvis. But you must not fail now, Vernon. There are thousands of unknown people out there who'll move in right now and take advantage of Elvis's life, of his fame. We must protect it not just for ourselves, but for Elvis' child Lisa Marie and for his estate. We must move immediately to make sure that outsiders cannot exploit the name of Elvis Presley."
>
> Vernon agreed. The Colonel continued. "We can mourn," he said evenly, "but a prolonged and inactive period of grief over Elvis will prove disastrous for you, for his daughter, for his estate, for his legend. I suggest we move immediately to protect the Elvis image from exploitation by outsiders."

I can't think of anything more damning in the entire body of Elvis literature—and that includes every lurid revelation about him in any book—than these several cold-blooded paragraphs. If all the Colonel could manage at this moment is a sucked-in breath and a whisper of "Oh, God," before his mind turned to Harry Geisler and Factors Inc., to marketing Elvis' name on tee shirts, then Elvis Presley's life must have been sadder than anybody ever imagined. Ironically, the Colonel's concerns for the Presley estate have culminated in a lawsuit: at the time of this writing, he is being sued for fraud by the very estate he sought to protect. Indeed, if Elvis' public needs the next in a line of scapegoats now that Dr. Nick has been summarily chastised, the Colonel just might fit the bill.

As for my own book, I knew that I hadn't written the Great American Elvis Book, but I still felt strongly that it deserved a place on the top shelf along with a few others. The manuscript, delivered in the spring of 1979 was long and unwieldy. My editor, habituated to the hard requirements of mass market publishing, started red-penciling it with a ruthless vigor that left me reeling. We fought over every deletion, we compromised: what emerged was more readable and better paced, but the complexion of the book had been altered in that the gossip and anecdotal elements of the book were now showcased over the analytical and factual because "that's what people want to read." The writing was left intact, but by submitting the work to the normal modern process that takes words and "packages" them into a "product," I had lost control over its proportional contents. The book that emerged was in no way "sensationalized"; it was, however, "commercialized," and in this case the differential between the original and what would be published was in what was left *unsaid*, not in what was said.

I began to consider to what degree *other* Elvis books had been affected by the editorial process, how what had been communicated about the man was either gussied up or watered down, and the implications of this were driven home to me in symbolic terms on the afternoon I was shown the design for the book cover. Because the book concentrates on Elvis' last years, the publisher wanted a strong image from that period on the cover and purchased a stage shot from Harry Siskind, who had covered Elvis on tour during his last year. The shot was familiar and immediately recognizable: Elvis is grinning slyly, pointing offstage, the guitar slung around his neck. But the photo had been doctored by the art department to make it look better for the consumer: the puffiness in his face and body had been airbrushed out, which made him look surreal, artificial, like a facsimile of himself. I'll never forget sitting there, both amused and horrified, thinking that Elvis had had a face lift in 1975 and wore girdles onstage; and that the Colonel had always doctored photos for the very same reasons: to feed the legend, to sell the product.

How far had we all come from the Real Thing? And what was the Real Thing to begin with?

Don't get me wrong: I was as proud of the book as I was critical. I include the following passage from the day of the funeral not because it's the best writing in the book, but because it perhaps comes closest to what I had set out to do. It forms the end of the chapter entitled "Mother and Child Reunion."

> For those who knew Elvis Presley during his life and attended his funeral, the uniform impression seemed to be that an aura of peace seemed to surround him in death, of that sublime release he had sought in life that now seemed spread over him pleasantly, the way night befalls a countryside in summertime after a day of hot, blanching sunshine. In his face, at least, there wasn't a trace of the tempest that had been his life.
>
> The organist started playing "Danny Boy," a song that Elvis loved to play when he felt like sitting at home, warming up his voice by entertaining his friends. The rendition was slow and mournful, like a funeral dirge, as everybody sat, lost in his own private thoughts, communing with his own private memories and meanings. Rick sat, lost, momentarily pulled away from his private pain by the spectacle of it all. Rex Humbard spoke first, but the only thing he could hear were sobs, his mother's from one side and Vernon Presley's from another, rising above the

Col. Parker inspects souvenirs, 1978.

the one woman from Elvis' Hollywood past who simply couldn't stay away, who had to come, and he wondered about that compulsion and what she was feeling. Then there was Linda, who had loved Elvis as much as any woman in his life. If only Elvis had stayed with her, he thought, maybe he would still be alive. He resolved to seek her out after the funeral and tell her how much Elvis had said he really loved her. Colonel Tom Parker was impassively quiet, almost expressionless. What would the Colonel do now? Then Rick looked at the guys who comprised the TCB entourage. They were probably taking it hardest because their lives, which had revolved completely around Elvis', would be most changed. Poor Charlie Hodge, he thought, looking at him; now there's a guy who's known nothing but Elvis Presley for twenty years. He really felt for Charlie. At least he and his brothers were still young men, but Charlie? What in blazes would he do now? God. Then Jackie Kahane spoke briefly—a man who had always tried to make Elvis laugh. At the end of the shows it was always Jackie who'd had to deliver the disappointing news to the assembled multitudes that "Ladies and gentlemen, Elvis has left the building." Elvis could always ask him for the right words in the event of a special occasion on tour, but on the occasion of Elvis' funeral Jackie could only see fit to make the same simple announcement. "Ladies and gentlemen . . . Elvis has left us now . . . but he will go on in the hearts and minds of those who loved him. . . ." Words simply failed, in the end. There would always be something ineffable about Elvis Presley, it seemed, something beyond words. And then Rick heard Vernon Presley, broken, sighing aloud. "Oh, sonny . . . just thank God there is a Lord," and he thought that maybe that was the only meaning, the only explanation.

words. To him they seemed more expressive of what was really going on there, more literate somehow than the words. Then C.W. Bradley delivered the main eulogy. He spoke of his first encounter with Elvis Presley—how impressed he had been by his humility, how speechlessly excited and overcome his daughter had been to meet him—and of the long friendship he had enjoyed with Vernon and Dee . . . and it went on eloquently until he got to the part about the brevity of life, of its transience and meaninglessness in the face of the larger truths of God, and that's when Rick began to look around the room and wonder what it all meant. This life. That life. Elvis' life. What his death said about the world that we live in. The words were beautiful but they failed to reach him; he was too lost in himself, in his own emptiness, in the panorama of the room . . . twenty years of a life to digest, accumulated in that single room, focused on that coffin. Stories about him, the music he created, moments of magnificence, entertainers, friends, enemies, girls he had dated, families he had known, his wife, his daughter, right there, in his music room, in his own home . . . wow, he thought, it was *wild*. He glanced around the room at various people whose lives were so entwined with Elvis' and wondered what they were thinking and feeling. He looked at Joe Esposito, who had been such a pillar of emotional fortitude and responsibility those two days, whom Rick had always looked up to and loved. Suddenly Joe's features seemed to be sagging under the weight of his now emerging emotions; he looked as if he had aged ten years during those two days. Rick looked at Ann-Margret, beautiful, sexy; she was

Looking back, it perhaps seems a bit mawkish and sentimental; but this, within the experience of these people, is what Elvis Presley was all about.

By the time *Publisher's Weekly* panned the book in the fall of 1979, I was back living in New York. "Torgoff even sees fit to inform us about the state of Dee's uterus," read the review. General verdict: not worth the paper it's printed on. Of course, I *had* written about Dee's uterus, but with a purpose: I had wanted to illustrate how insecure she had felt upon first marrying Vernon Presley and moving to Graceland; and how she had sought to establish her presence by bearing child to the clan like a Queen in days of old, but needed an operation because her uterus had become distended from the births of her three children.

And then, as I was contemplating suicide or at least flight to Alaska, the excerpt came out in the *Ladies Home Journal*: yes, they took *only* the sex and drugs. I spent an entire day consuming Jack Daniels and crying on my girlfriend's shoulder. "You better become more thick-skinned about this whole thing," she said, "otherwise I have a feeling you're in for a *lot* of trouble."

The climate was ripe for publication by the time the book appeared in January of 1980: Kurt Russell had scored as "Elvis" on ABC and Geraldo Rivera had put Dr. Nick on the hot seat in Memphis. Accordingly, the publishers threw a big to-do for the family and press at Hisae's. The family made the local talk show rounds, which culminated with an appearance on the *Tomorrow Show*. By that time Rick Stanley had become an ordained minister, and when Tom Snyder would ask a question about Elvis' drug intake, Rick would talk about Jesus. In the following weeks, the book took off in the bookstores.

And me? I guess I got what I wanted: an experience. The reviews were supportive, which helped. *Penthouse* even raved that it was 'the best and truest look at the private life of the most famous man of the Twentieth Century.' They weren't all roses, however. 'While we're at it, let's not forget Martin Torgoff, the young New York-based ghostwriter of the Stanley's *Elvis: We Love You Tender*,' wrote Michael Gordon in the *Star* of Anniston, Alabama. 'It's not easy paying the bills in the Big Apple these days. So what you do is write a book, any book, and plaster Elvis' name on the cover.' I found this particularly ironic, considering that by the time of the publication party, I was so broke that all I could think about was the free grub.

And then I was vindicated forever by Bob Hilburn, pop critic of the *Los Angeles Times*. In a full page review that faulted my writing style and carped about my analyses, he delivered the goods: "Nothing," he wrote, "has told his downfall as convincingly—or as compassionately—as this book." Somebody had noticed.

The book gradually receded into the past and has long since blended into the fray, although the experience of it has turned me into a zealous fan, a hopeless junkie, reading everything that comes out. The Next Big Thing will be Albert Goldman's *Elvis*, a big money bio done with the co-operation of Lamar Fike. Now, if anybody has a bone to pick with Elvis, it's Lamar: for twenty years, he was Elvis Presley's whipping boy. "He even gets the *Colonel*," Rick Stanley told me in a hushed voice the last time I saw him, as if to infer that a sacrosanct bastion had finally been assaulted. "Well, like what?" I asked. "What will be in it?" And he replied, "All of the stories we never would have told you in a million years. The ones you wouldn't have wanted to print anyway . . ."

Folks, the results are in, all 591 pages. With his hefty advance and three years to research and write, Albert Goldman certainly had enough time to produce the long-awaited "definitive" work. He's obviously read everything and conducted scads of interviews (he lists about 150) and the acknowledgments page lists everybody except, yep, you guessed it: Vernon Presley (who passed away in 1979), Priscilla, Lisa Marie, Joe Esposito, Billy Smith, Sam Phillips, and, of course, the old Colonel. (Some would contend that no definitive work on Elvis could ever be produced without hearing from these people.) Still, the book is glutted with valuable and hitherto unavailable information (the Presley genealogy and family history) and filled with well-drawn moments (the Beatles visit to Elvis' Hollywood manse in 1965 and his standoffish reaction). In a particularly remarkable and satisfying chapter, the colorful and corpulent Colonel is once-and-for-all unmasked as the Dutchman Andreas Cornelius van Kuijk (!) and portrayed throughout the book as the money-sucking manipulator he probably is. Richly researched and detailed, comprehensive in scope, and written in the high-powered pop-prose that characterized his earlier books like *Ladies and Gentlemen Lenny Bruce!* (another junkie), Goldman's *Elvis* is nonetheless fatally flawed. It is not merely a "warts-and-all" biography: the author feels compelled to magnify each individual hair growing out of every unsightly blemish. Goldman is not content to detail the horrific amounts of narcotics shot into Elvis' body—he must show us their deleterious effects on his sphincter muscles and gives us Elvis diapered, rolling in his own defecation. Not a pretty picture.

Now it isn't so much of *what* Goldman says that is so disturbing (these things, after all, happened; they are a legitimate part of Elvis' tragedy) as *how* he says it: he condescends, oftentimes with a glibness or flippancy that makes you want to throttle him. And if some writers have been guilty of over-romanticizing Elvis (myself included), Goldman, no mere iconoclast, is guilty of exactly the opposite: he is so busy demythologizing Elvis, so busy substituting Fact over Myth, so intent on his psychosexual interpretations and character dissections, that the magic of the man is utterly obscured, if not entirely discounted. There is no law stipulating that a biographer must like or even respect his subject, but Goldman doesn't appear to be all that *interested*. Elvis is brutish, pitiful, always immature, bizarre, paranoid, schizophrenic, and voraciously self-destructive, but mostly he is just plain *dumb* (a word Goldman uses often)—a dumb, unwashed, mislead, scared, tacky kid crying for his mama, hopelessly lost on a rollercoaster he could never control—and *we* are made to feel dumb by ever having been interested and moved by him in the first place. Perhaps we've become cushioned to the shocks, to the obligatory lurid revelations about Elvis' Dark Side—but this is something else: an uppercut directly to the soft underbelly of what this man represented to so many. And for all of his hard work and literary razzle-dazzle, Goldman comes off as a carrion bird pecking at the remains of a rotting corpse. If this is the price we must pay to learn the "truth" about Elvis Presley, then bring back May Mann.

No matter, you see. In the long run, Goldman's book, like the rest, will represent only one more speck in the incredible mosaic of Elvis Presley's literary legacy. One day, when all the participants in Elvis' drama are dead and gone, and when the machinations of the writers and publishers are no longer a factor, a canny biographer (the one who will write the first truly "definitive" work) will come along. And, poring over all of these documents and artifacts with a mixture of gratitude, fury, bemused bafflement and relentless objectivity, the writer will divine the essential Elvis and tell his story as it has never been told before.

A HOUND DOG,
TO THE MANOR BORN
BY STANLEY BOOTH

Between Memphis and Walls (you turn right a bit past a big sign saying *Church of God, Pastor C.B. Brantley,* DRINK DR. PEPPER), there is a small ranch, a hundred and sixty green and gently rolling acres, a prettier spread than you'd expect to see in the poor, bleak land of North Mississippi. The owner, at thirty-three, has been a millionaire for more than a decade. He has other, more elegant homesteads, but these days he prefers the ranch. Behind the formidable chain-link fence and the eight-foot picket walls that hide his neat red-brick house, he finds a degree of privacy to share with his pretty new wife. The privacy is also shared by twenty-two purebred horses, counting colts, and nine hired hands, counting guards. (There were twelve hands, but the number was reduced recently, so the story goes around the ranch, at the request of the owner's wife.) Then, too, there are the continual visitors—the ones who are allowed inside (some driving Cadillacs given them by the owner as Christmas or birthday presents) and the ones who must stay outside, peering over or through the fences. At times, such as when the owner is out riding, the roadside is solidly lined with sight-seeing cars. Privacy—the privacy in which to enjoy his leisure time—is extremely valuable to the ranch's young owner, especially since he works less than half the year. Taxes would make more work pointless; his annual income is about five million dollars.

And yet, not too many years ago, he was living in a Federal low-rent housing project, working as a truck-driver, movie usher, sometimes forced to sell his blood at ten dollars a pint. Elvis Presley, a Great American Success Story.

By the ranch's main gate, in an air-conditioned hut, sits Elvis' Uncle Travis, a small, grinning man, with hair as black and skin as dark as an Indian's. A straw cowboy hat rests on his knee. He wears black Western pants and a white shirt with *E.P.* monogrammed in black Gothic script across the front. Travis likes to reminisce about the girls he has captured and ejected from his nephew's premises. "I dragged one out from under the old pink Cadillac. She must of heard me comin' and hid under there, and all I saw was her feet stickin' out. I said, 'Come on out of there,' and she didn't move, so I reached down, took ahold of her feet, and pulled. She had a coat of motor oil a inch thick." Travis belches.

"How do they get in?"

"Slip in. Jump a fence just like a billygoat. If they can't climb over, they'll crawl under. If the gate ain't locked they'll drive right through. I had a carload slip past me up at Graceland. Hell, I didn't even go after them, I just locked the damn gate. They made the circle in front of the house, come back down the drive, and when they seen they couldn't get out, the one drivin' says, 'Please op'n the gate.' I told her 'Yes, ma'am, soon's the sheriff got there.' Made out like I was real hot, you know. She says, 'Please don't call the sheriff, my mama will kill me.' I said, 'Not till you get out of jail, I don't reckon.' She like to died. Then I started laughin', and they seen it was all right, and asked me if they could come back after while and talk. So I told them yeah, but while they was gone I got to thinkin', Why'd they have to leave, why couldn't they just stay and talk? But one of they mamas came back with them, and she told on them. I'd scared her daughter so bad she'd peed her pants."

Travis pitches his head back and laughs, displaying a strong white set of uppers. Parked in the drive is a shiny red Ford Ranchero with his name, T.J. Smith, on one door under the ranch's Circle G brand, actually a flying Circle G. I ask what the "G" stands for.

"Could be Graceland," Travis says, "or it could be his mother's name. He meant it to stand for her name." Travis' expression becomes serious when he speaks of Elvis' dead mother, his own sister. "He still keeps that old pink Cadillac he bought for her. Don't never drive it, just keeps it as a keepsake. He's got all the cars he needs. Had a Rolls-Royce up on blocks four or five years. Bought a hundred thousand dollars' worth of trucks and trailers right after he got this place. Money ain't nothing to him. Ole boy from Hernando was down here the other evenin', workin' on the fence, and Elvis drove down in one of his new pickups to take a look. Feller says, 'Shore do like that truck. Always wanted me one of them.' So Elvis says, 'You got a dollar?' Feller says, 'Yeah, I got one,' and gives it to Elvis. 'It's your truck,' Elvis says."

Next Travis tells how Priscilla, the new wife, likes Elvis to take her for rides in one of his souped-up go-karts (top speed, more than a hundred miles an hour) around the driveway at Graceland, tantalizing the squealing girls outside the fence.

Then he spits. "I sit down here, keepin' people out, seven in the mornin' till six in the evenin', five days a week, and I'm about wore out. I think I'll go in the hospital for two or three weeks, take me a rest."

"Maybe you could get a television set to watch while you're working," I suggest.

"Yeah, I believe I will get me one. Either that, or some funny books."

Just outside the gate, in a rented green Impala, are two girls who have come, so they tell me, all the way from New Zealand. "Is he home?" they ask.

"Who?"

One sneers, one ignores. "Did you talk to him? What did he say?"

I look away, trying to select a representative quote. On the roof of the house across the road a man is kneeling behind a camera, snapping pictures of the Circle G. "Let's ride up to Rosemark tomorrow and look at that mare," I tell the girls.

"Pardon?"

"That's what he said."

"What, is *that* all?"

"You should have been here yesterday. He said, 'Would somebody please bring me a Pepsi?'" Pepsi-Cola, I would have explained to the girls, is Elvis' favorite drink, just as his favorite snack is peanut-butter-and-mashed-banana sandwiches; but the Impala roars away, leaving a cloud of dust to settle on my shoes.

Sometime ago, before I saw for myself what Elvis is like, I asked a mutual acquaintance about him. "He's all right," I was told. "Pretty interesting guy to talk to."

"Really. What's the most interesting thing he's ever said to you?"

My friend sat and thought, pulling the hair on his chin. Finally he said, "Well, once he told me, 'Like your beard. How long'd it take you to grow it?' I said it took about three months, and he said, 'I'd like to grow me one sometime, but I don't think I could get away with it. Y'know?' And he sort of winked."

Another friend, whose relation to the Presley household was for a time unique, told me that Elvis is a very straight guy, who uses neither grass nor acid. In Hollywood, Elvis never goes to nightclubs or premieres. Except for work, he hardly leaves his Bel-Air mansion. "He's afraid he wouldn't know how to act," says one of his oldest friends. "And he wouldn't."

Even in Memphis, his recreational activities have been, for a millionaire, unpretentious. In the early days at Graceland (the large, white-columned estate, rather like an antebellum funeral parlor, which Elvis bought in 1957), the big kick was roller skating. After a local rink closed for the evening, Presley and his entourage would come in, skate, eat hot dogs and drink Pepsi-Cola till dawn. When skating palled, Elvis started renting the entire Fairgrounds amusement park, where he and his friends could ride the Tilt-a-Whirl, Ferris wheel, roller coaster, Dodgem cars (Elvis' favorite), and eat hot dogs and drink Pepsis till dawn. Until quite recently, Presley has been in the habit of hiring a local movie theater (the Memphian) and showing rented movies, emphasizing the films of actresses he has dated.

The Memphian has no hot-dog facilities, but provides plenty of popcorn and, of course, Pepsis. Now that he is married and an expectant father, he does not get out so much at night, but the daytime is as glamorous, as exciting as ever.

On a day not long ago, when Presley happened to be staying at Graceland, the house was crowded with friends and friends of friends, all waiting for old El to wake up, come downstairs, and turn them on with his presence. People were wandering from room to room, looking for action, and there was little to be found. In the basement, a large, divided room with gold records hung in frames around the walls, creating a sort of halo effect, they were shooting pool or lounging under the Pepsi-Cola signs at the soda fountain. (When Elvis likes something, he *really* likes it.) In the living room boys and girls were sprawled, nearly unconscious with boredom, over the long white couches, among the deep snowy drifts of rug. One girl was standing by the enormous picture window, absently pushing one button, then another, activating an electrical traverse rod, opening and closing the red velvet drapes. On a table beside the fireplace of smoky molded glass, a pink ceramic elephant was sniffing the artificial roses. Nearby, in the music room, a thin, dark-haired boy who had been lying on the cloth-of-gold couch, watching Joel McCrea on the early movie, snapped the remote-control switch, turning off the ivory television set. He yawned, stretched, went to the white, gilt-trimmed piano, sat down on the matching stool and began to play. He was not bad, playing a kind of limp, melancholy boogie, and soon there was an audience facing him, their backs to the door.

Then, all at once, through the use of perceptions which could only be described as extrasensory, everyone in the room knew that Elvis was there. And, stranger still, nobody moved. Everyone kept his cool. Out of the corner of one's eye Presley could be seen, leaning against the doorway, looking like Lash La Rue in boots, black Levis and a black silk shirt.

The piano player's back stiffens, but he is into the bag and has to boogie his way out. "What is this, amateur night?" someone mutters. Finally—it cannot have been more than a minute—the music stops. Everyone turns toward the door. Well I'll be damn. It's Elvis. What say, boy? Elvis smiles, but does not speak. In his arms he is cradling a big blue model airplane.

A few minutes later, the word—the sensation—having passed through the house, the entire company is out on the lawn, where Presley is trying to start the plane. About half the group has graduated into the currently fashionable Western clothing, and the rest are wearing the traditional pool-hustler's silks. They all watch intently as Elvis, kneeling over the plane, tries for the tenth time to make the tiny engine turn over; when it sputters and dies a groan, as of one voice, rises from the crowd.

Elvis stands, mops his brow (though of course he is not perspiring), takes a thin cigar from his shirt pocket

With Library Workers

and peels away the cellophane wrapping. When he puts the cigar between his teeth a wall of flame erupts before him. Momentarily startled, he peers into the blaze of matches and lighters offered by willing hands. With a nod he designates one of the crowd, who steps forward, shaking, ignites the cigar, and then, his moment of glory, of service to the King at an end, he retires into anonymity. "Thank ya very much," says Elvis.

They begin to seem quite insane, the meek circle proffering worship and lights, the young ladies trembling under Cadillacs, the tourists outside, standing on the roofs of cars, waiting to be blessed by even a glimpse of this young god, this slightly plump idol, whose face grows more babyish with each passing year.

But one exaggerates. They are not insane, only mistaken, believing their dumpling god to be Elvis Presley. He is not. One remembers—indeed, one could hardly forget—Elvis Presley.

The time is the early fifties, and the scene is dull. Dwight Eisenhower is President, Perry Como is the leading pop singer. The world has changed (it changed in 1945), but the change is not yet evident. Allen Ginsberg is a market researcher for a San Francisco securities company. William Burroughs is in New Orleans, cooking down codeine cough syrup. Malcolm X, paroled from Massachusetts' Charlestown Prison, is working in a Detroit furniture store. Stokely Carmichael is skinny, insolent, and eleven years old.

It is, let us say, 1953. Fred Zinnemann rehashes the past with *From Here to Eternity*, and Laslo Benedek gives us, in *The Wild One*, a taste of the future. This is a movie with good guys and bad guys, and the good guys are the ones who roar on motorcycles into a town which is small, quiet, typically American and proceed to take it apart. Their leader, Marlon Brando, will be called an anti-hero. But there is no need for the prefix. He is a new, really contemporary hero: the outcast.

Soon James Dean repeats the theme with even greater success. But Dean's career was absurdly short. "You know he was dead before you knew who he was," someone said. The outcasts of America were left without a leader.

Then, one Saturday night early in 1956 on a television variety program, a white singer drawls at the camera: "Ladies and gentlemen, I'd like to do a song now, that tells a little story, that really makes a lot of sense—*Awopbopaloobop—alopbamboom! Tutti-frutti! All rootie! Tutti-frutti! All rootie!*"

L.C. Humes High: school days.   Graduation photo 1953 (age 18).

Though nearly all significant popular music was produced by Negroes, a white rhythm-and-blues singer was not entirely new phenomenon. Bill Haley and the Comets had succeeded with such songs as "Shake, Rattle and Roll," and "Rock Around the Clock." But the pudgy Haley, in his red-plaid dinner jacket, did not project much personal appeal. This other fellow was something else.

He was not quite a hillbilly, not yet a drugstore cowboy. He was a Southern—in that word's meaning of the combination of rebellion and slow, sweet charm—version of the character Brando created in *The Wild One*. Southern high-school girls, the "nice" ones, called these boys hoods. You saw them lounging on the hot concrete of a gas station on a Saturday afternoon, or coming out of a poolroom at three o'clock of a Monday afternoon, stopping for a second on the sidewalk as if they were looking for someone who was looking for a fight. You even see their sullen faces, with a toughness lanky enough to just miss being delicate, looking back at you out of old photographs of the Confederate Army. They were not named Tab or Rock, nor even Jim, Bill, Bob. They all had names like Leroy, Floyd, Elvis. All outcasts, with their contemporary costumes of duck-ass haircuts, greasy Levis, motorcycle boots, T-shirts for day and black leather jackets for evening wear. Even their unfashionably long sideburns (Elvis' were *furry*) expressed contempt for the American dream they were too poor to be part of.

No one writing about Presley should forget the daring it took to be one of these boys, and to sing. A "hood" might become a mechanic or a house painter or a busdriver or even a cop, but nobody would expect him to be a singer. If he tried it at all, he would have to have some of his own crowd playing with him; he'd have to sing some old songs his own people had sung before him; and he would have to sing them in his own way, regardless of what people might say about him.

"Mama, do you think I'm vulgar on the stage?"

"Son, you're not vulgar, but you're puttin' too much into your singin'. Keep that up and you won't live to be thirty."

"I can't help it, Mama. I just have to jump around when I sing. But it ain't vulgar. It's just the way I feel. I don't feel sexy when I'm singin'. If that was true, I'd be in some kinda institution as some kinda sex maniac."

These days, when asked about the development of his career, Elvis either ignores the question or refers it to "my manager." Generally speaking his manager is the person standing closest to him at the time. This is often Alan Fortas, officially the ranch foreman, a young man only slightly less stocky than a bull, with a history of hostility to reporters. When The Beatles visited Elvis in Hollywood, Fortas, not troubling to remember their names, addressed each of them as, "Hey, Beatle!" They always answered, too; nobody wants to displease Alan.

A more voluble source of information is Dewey Phillips. During Elvis' early career Phillips was

Memphis, 1955.

Sam Phillips, then and now.

Dewey, Wink Martindale and Elvis on WHBQ-TV's *Dance Party,* 1956.

Dewey Phillips.

probably as close to him as anyone except his mother, Gladys. Now retired, Phillips was then one of the most popular and influential disc jockeys in the nation. He still speaks the same hillbilly jive he used as a broadcaster.

"Nobody was picking up on the ole boy back then. He was a real bashful kid, but he liked to hang around music. They'd chased him away from the switchboard at WMPS, and he'd come hang around Q. That's WHBQ, where I was doing my show, *Red Hot and Blue*, every night. Weekends, he'd come down to Sun Records—he'd cut that record, 'My Happiness,' for his mother, paid four dollars for it himself—and Sam Phillips, president of Sun, finally gave him a session. Tried to record a ballad, but he couldn't cut it. Sam got Bill Black, the piano player, and Scotty Moore, the guitarist, to see if they could work anything out with him.

"After a lot of tries, Elvis, Bill and Scotty fixed up a couple of old songs, 'That's All Right, Mama,' and 'Blue of Kentucky' so they sounded a little different. When Elvis began to cut loose with 'That's All Right,' Sam came down and recorded these sonofaguns. One night I played the record thirty times. Fifteen times each side. When the phone calls and telegrams started to come in, I got hold of Elvis' daddy, Vernon. He said Elvis was at a movie, down at Suzore's number-two theater. 'Get him over here,' I said. And before long Elvis came running in. 'Sit down, I'm gone interview you,' I said. He said, 'Mr. Phillips, I don't know nothing about being interviewed.' 'Just don't say nothing dirty,' I told him.

"He sat down, and I said I'd let him know when we were ready to start. I had a couple of records cued up, and while they played we talked. I asked him where he went to high school, and he said 'Humes.' I wanted to get that out, because a lot of people listening had thought he was colored. Finally I said, 'All right, Elvis, thank you very much.' 'Aren't you gone interview me?' he asked. 'I already have,' I said. 'The mike's been open the whole time.' He broke out in a cold sweat."

According to Phillips, Elvis at this time considered himself a country singer. "Sam used to get him, Roy Orbison, Jerry Lee Lewis and Johnny Cash down at Sun and play Big Bill Broonzy and Arthur Crudup records for them, trying to get them on the blues thing, because he felt like that was going to be hot. One of Elvis' first public appearances was at a hillbilly jamboree at the downtown auditorium. Webb Pierce was there, and Carl Smith, Minnie Pearl, a whole houseful of hillbillies. Elvis was nervous, said he wanted me with him. But Sam and I were out at my house, drinking beer, or we had something going, and I missed the afternoon show. Elvis came looking for me, mad as hell. I asked him what he'd sung and he said, '"Old Shep" and "That's How My Heartaches Begin."' What happened? 'Nothing.'

"So that night I went along with him and told him to open with 'Good Rockin' Tonight' and not to sing any hillbilly songs. I introduced him and stayed onstage while he sang. He went into 'Good Rockin',' started to shake, and the place just blew apart. He was nobody, didn't even have his name on the posters, but the people wouldn't let him leave. When we finally went off we walked past Webb Pierce, who had been waiting in the wings to go on. I smiled at him and he said, 'You son of a bitch.'"

The sales of Elvis' records enabled him to get more bookings, and Dewey Phillips bought him an old Lincoln sedan for $450 so he could play out-of-town jobs. Appearing in Nashville at a convention of the Country and Western Disc Jockeys' Association, he was seen, "discovered," by talent scouts for RCA Victor. In a moviehouse matinee in Texarkana, he was discovered by Thomas Andrew Parker, a latter-day Barnum out of W. C. Fields by William Burroughs. A carnival orphan, he had worked in his uncle's "Great Parker Pony Circus," dipped candied apples, shaved ice

didn't know anything about managing. Then Colonel Parker came to town. He knew what he was doing. He didn't talk to Elvis. He went out to the house and told Gladys what he could do for the boy. That Parker is a shrewd moo-foo, man."

Elvis' first appearances on network television, on the Tommy and Jimmy Dorsey show in January and February 1956, changed him from a regional phenomenon into a national sensation. This might not have happened, the American public might simply have shuddered and turned away, had there not been a new group among them: teen-agers, the enemy within. When the older generation, repelled by Presley's lean, mean, sexy image, attacked him from pulpits and editorial columns, banned him from radio stations, the teen-agers liked him more than ever, and went out and bought his records. Entrepreneurs could not afford to ignore Presley. As one radio producer asked, How can you argue with the country's number-one recording

for snow cones, operated merry-go-rounds, even put in a stretch as dog-catcher in Tampa, Florida.

Astute techniques in these businesses had enabled Parker to rise in the world to a position of some prestige. The title "Colonel" had been conferred upon him by, as he put it, "a few governors." He was managing the careers of such big name country entertainers as Hank Snow and Eddy Arnold. But in all his years as a promoter, he had never found so promotable a commodity as Presley.

He had seen Elvis at, for his purposes, just the right time. The demand for Elvis' records prompted RCA to offer $35,000 for Presley, lock, stock, and tapes. Sam Phillips accepted.

"Elvis knew he was going big time," Dewey Phillips remembers, "and he needed a manager. That was late spring of '55. He was the hottest thing in show business, and still just a scared kid. He had got his mother and daddy a nice house, they had three Cadillacs, and no phone. He asked me to be his manager. I told him I

star? Reluctantly, almost unwillingly, show business accepted Elvis. Ed Sullivan, who only a couple of months before had condemned Presley as being "unfit for a family audience," now was obliged to pay him $50,000 for three brief appearances. However, Elvis was photographed only from the waist up, and his material was diluted by the addition of a ballad, "Love Me Tender," which oozed syrup.

Such attempts to make Elvis appear respectable were very offensive to the good ole boys back in Memphis. Steve Allen, involved in a ratings battle with Sullivan, booked Presley, but assured the audience that they would see only "clean family entertainment." Elvis appeared and sang, standing still, wearing white tie and tails, with top hat and cane, but without a guitar. Just after the show went off the air, Dewey Phillips' telephone rang. "Hello, you bastard," Dewey said.

"How'd you know it was me?" asked Elvis.

"You better call home and get straight, boy. What you doing in that monkey suit? Where's your guitar?"

Countryside near Tupelo, Lee County, 1937.

Tupelo Community Swimming Pool. 1937.

MAR 1959

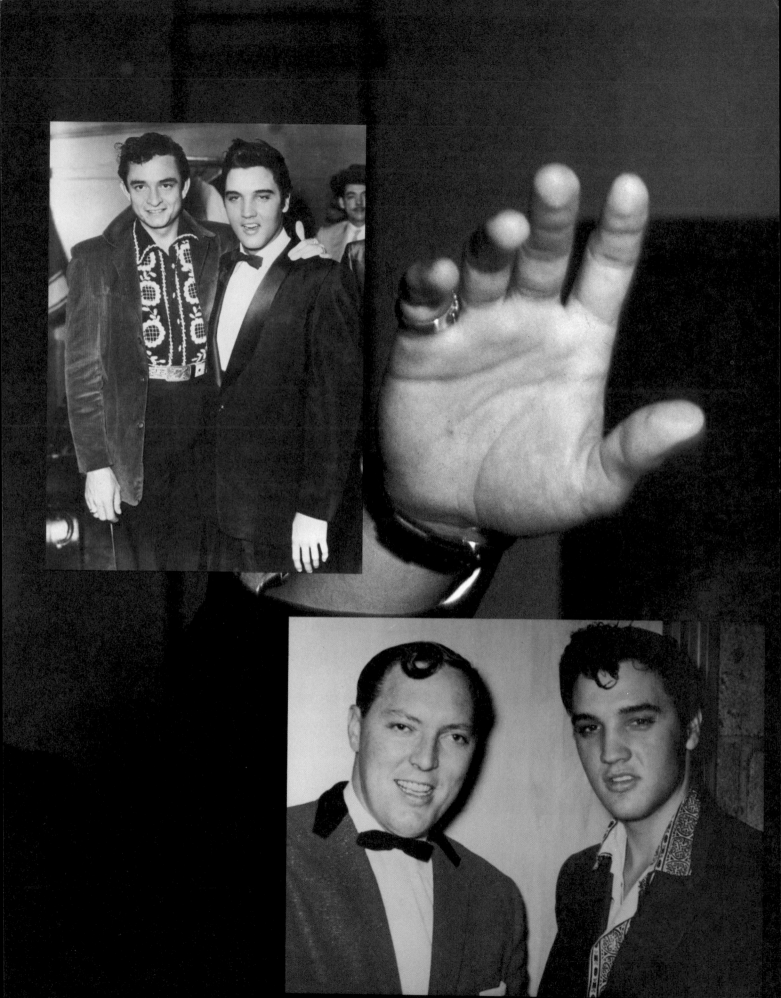

So when Elvis made his next hometown appearance (it was on July 4, 1956) he reassured his people. The occasion was a charity benefit and Colonel Parker had turned down paying engagements so that Elvis could be part of the show. His was the closing spot, and he was preceded by more than a hundred performers, including the orchestras of Bob Morris and Aaron Bluestein, the Admiral's Band of Navy Memphis, a barbershop quartette called the Confederates, Charlotte Morgan's dancing Dixie Dolls, and innumerable singers, by no means the least of which was one Helen Putnam, founder of Fat Girls Anonymous, who dedicated *A Good Man Is Hard to Find* to Elvis.

After nearly three hours, with the audience so bored that it was on the point of having a religious experience, Dewey Phillips, who was master of ceremonies, said, "All right. Here he is," and there he was, his hair hanging over his forehead, a wad of gum in his jaw. He wore a black suit, black shoes, black shirt, red tie, and red socks, clothes with so much drape and flash that they created a new sartorial category, somewhere on the other side of corny. He sang all the old songs in the old way, from "That's All Right" to "Blue Suede Shoes" to "Heartbreak Hotel." He sang until he was dripping with sweat, and when at last he spoke, his words were a promise to his friends, a gift of defiance to his enemies: "I just want to tell y'awl not to worry—them people in New York and Hollywood are not gone change me none."

Then his voice became a growl, an act of rebellion: *You ain't nothin' but a houn' dog*, he sang, and proceeded to have sexual intercourse with the microphone.

> They told me you was high class
> Well, that was just a lie—

If the police had not been there, forming a blue wall around the stage, the audience might have eaten Elvis' body in a Eucharistic frenzy. They were his and he was theirs, their leader: it was an incandescent moment.

And at the same time it was a climactic one. For as he stood there singing defiance at his natural enemies, those with power, prestige, money, the Humes High hood, the motorcycle jockey, was gone, and in his place there was a star, with power, prestige, money. A few months from now at about three o'clock one morning, he would be standing with one of his hired companions outside the Strand Theatre on Main Street in Memphis when a couple of his high-school classmates would drive past, not going much of anywhere, just dragging Main. They would slow their car as they came alongside the Strand; they would see it was Elvis; and then, without a word, they would drive on. "A few years ago," Elvis said, "they would have spoken to me."

Elvis had tried to go on being himself. When Paramount offered him a movie contract with a clause forbidding him to ride motorcycles, he said, "I'd rather not make movies." They let him keep his motorcycles. All that was really necessary was that he stop doing his

Tampa, Fla., 1955.

Jailhouse Rock.

thing and start doing theirs. His thing was "Mystery Train," "Milkcow Blues Boogie." Theirs was "Love Me Tender," "Loving You," "Jailhouse Rock," "King Creole."

Then he was drafted. The Army cut his hair, took away his fancy clothes, and Elvis let them. His country had served him well and he was willing to serve his country. He is nothing if not fair-minded.

While he was stationed in Fort Hood, Texas, Elvis moved his parents to a rented house in the nearby town of Killeen. His mother, who had been doing poorly for more than a year, worsened, and on August 8, 1958, Elvis put her on a train to Methodist Hospital in Memphis. The prognosis was grave and Elvis requested the customary special leave.

It was refused. When the doctors, at Elvis' request, advised his command of the seriousness of his mother's illness, they were told in effect, "If it were anybody else, there'd be no problem. It's standard procedure. But if we let Presley go everybody will yell special privilege."

Days passed while Gladys Presley sank lower and lower. In spite of constant urging from Elvis and his doctors, the leave still was not granted. Finally, on the

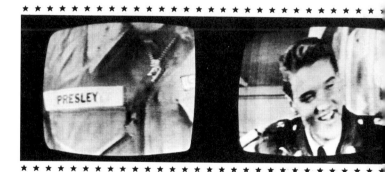

morning of August 12, Elvis decided that he had had enough. "If I don't get a pass by two o'clock this afternoon," he told the doctors, "I'll be home tonight."

The doctors reasoned with him, urged him to remember that he set an example for millions of other boys. But Elvis had made up his mind. A Humes High boy can be pushed only so far. The doctors could only advise the command of Elvis' plans.

So naturally, the pass came through. The Army is not that dumb. Elvis had the same rights as any other American boy.

Back in Memphis Elvis fought his way through the crowds of newsmen outside the hospital. He was in his mother's room for only a few minutes; then he came out, walked down the hall to an empty waiting room, sank into a chair and cried.

His mother had been the one, perhaps the only one, who had told him throughout his life that even though he came from poor country people, he was just as good as anyone. His success had not surprised her, nor had it changed her. Shortly after Gladys Presley was buried, her husband and son were standing on the magnificent front steps at Graceland. "Look, Daddy," Elvis sobbed, pointing to the chickens his mother had kept on the lawn of the hundred-thousand-dollar mansion. "Mama won't never feed them chickens no more."

He has never really gotten over his mother's death. He treasured for many years and may still have, in his office at Graceland, a lighted, fully decorated, artificial Christmas tree, souvenir of the last Christmas the family spent together. He had the tree cared for all the time he was in Germany, where the Army had put him safely away.

Elvis liked Germany and both he and his father found wives there. When his tour of duty was ended, he came out with sergeant's stripes. The whole thing was fictionally celebrated in *G.I. Blues*, a happy movie with a multi-million-dollar gross. One Elvis Presley film followed another: *Flaming Star, Wild in the Country, Blue Hawaii, Girls! Girls! Girls!, Kid Galahad, Follow that Dream, It Happened at the World's Fair, Fun in Acapulco, Viva Las Vegas, Kissin' Cousins, Roustabout, Girl Happy, Tickle Me, Harem Scarem, Frankie and Johnny, Paradise Hawaiian Style, Spinout, Easy Come, Easy Go, Double Trouble, Speedway, Clambake.* They all have two things in common: none lost money, none is contingent at any point upon reality.

But this is not quite true; there is one reality which they reflect. In *Fun in Acapulco*, which played on television recently, Elvis walks into a bar which is full of Mexicans, all of whom have good teeth. A mariachi band is playing. Elvis comes in on the chorus, and carries away the verse. Everyone applauds. The men smile and the girls turn on to him. They all think he's a hell of a fellow. One expects that at any moment he may produce a model plane and lead them out onto the lawn.

Elvis has fulfilled the American dream: he is young, rich, famous, adored. Hardly a day passes in Memphis without a politician wanting to name something after him. So far nothing has been found worthy of the honor. Presley has become a young man of whom his city and his country can be truly proud.

And he may not even know whether he misses the old days, the old Elvis. At Graceland, through the powder-white living room, past the gilded piano, there is a door that looks out onto the swimming pool. If you had been standing there on a recent afternoon, you would have seen Elvis, all alone for a change, riding his motorcycle around the pool, around and around and around.

THE KING IS DEAD!
HANG THE DOCTOR!
BY STANLEY BOOTH

As Dr. Nick and I drove out of Memphis, we passed one of the green and white traffic signs with a guitar pointing the way to Graceland and the likeness, sideburns clearly outlined, of Elvis Presley. Dr. Nick, driving a yellow Cadillac that Presley had given him, looked out at the cold spring rain. "For a long time," he said, "I didn't realize the full extent of the part I was playing in this thing."

We were going to Anniston, Alabama, to spend a few days with Dr. Nick's mother. It was the first chance we had found to talk since the Tennessee State Medical Examiners' hearing, several weeks earlier, where Dr. Nick had been charged with misprescribing to twenty patients, including Elvis Presley.

"One day Father Vieron came to my office," Dr. Nick said. The Reverend Nicholas Vieron, priest of the Greek Orthodox church attended by Dr. Nick and his family, has known Dr. Nick for twenty-five years. "He told me that he thought I was doing myself an injustice, I was doing my practice an injustice, my patients, my family, by being gone so much. That Elvis could have any doctor he wanted and didn't really need me all the time. That I shouldn't devote so much time to him. 'Why do you need to be there? Why can't it be somebody else on some of these tours that you go on?'"

"I gave it some serious thought. This was in 1975. The tours had changed, they'd really gotten laborious. It used to be that after a performance, Elvis enjoyed having some of the fans who would hang around the hotel come up and talk to him, just to get a feeling of people in that area and what they thought of the show and to feed his ego some. This would take two or three hours. I thought it was good for him, because it occupied his time, kept him happier. But some of the bodyguards resented it, because it meant that they had to stay on duty. If he'd get ready for bed, go on and have his supper, then they could go on out to the bar and do their thing.

"So, somehow we got away from doing that, and it really got to be a drag, because a lot of that responsibility after the show—who's going to be with him and talk to him for two or three hours—a lot of times would fall on me. And this was day and night after night. My nights were just horrible. I would go to bed when he'd go to bed, and then he might sleep two or three hours and wake up wide awake, and I'd have to go in and try to get him back to sleep. Then he might sleep two or three more hours, or he might sleep four or five hours. But the average was he'd sleep two or three hours and wake up, two or three hours and wake up. It was hard for me to fit into that schedule. On a tour, I had very little time when I could go and do anything. If he woke up and I wasn't there, he'd go bananas. It got to the point where I was working eighteen or twenty hours a day, sleeping in cat naps.

"It was also causing me an awful hassle at the office. The other doctors were bitching about me being on a constant vacation. How could I expect to come home and want time off? I'd have to work double, I'd have to make up the night calls I missed. And yet it was the same sons of bitches that would derive the benefit from it. The money I got from Elvis went to them, went into office practice. I had a hell of a time with all this.

"So when Father Vieron came in that day, I'd already given it a lot of thought. But Elvis had problems when I didn't go and he'd carry somebody else. There were a couple of tours, one Vegas tour and maybe a couple of other tours, where the shows didn't go too well because he was oversedated. A lot of times when the other doctors would go, it would be hard for them to keep the medicine with them. He always wanted to keep something there by his bed in case he'd wake up. He'd wake up and think he wasn't going back to sleep. He'd be half asleep, and he'd reach over and take whatever was there. Maybe three or four or five sleeping pills. The next day, try to get him up, no way to get him up. There were several times when he was a robot onstage. He'd done these songs so many times, a lot of people didn't realize it, but hell, he might not wake up till halfway through the show or after the show was over. Tell him things that he did, and he just wouldn't remember. After having gone through a few experiences with that, and some really bad ones, it was the consensus of the Colonel and the promoters that things were under better control when Elvis was with me than when he was with some other people. That they'd rather have me on the tours, and it got down to the fact that they weren't going to have any more tours at all if I wasn't going.

"I thought, 'Is it really my place to look at the business aspect of this relationship? Is it really my place to worry about what his promoters and business people are worried about, like, "Is he going to be able to make the next show? Are we going to have to cancel it? Is he going to be too groggy to do the show?"' It was a dilemma for me. It felt like this was going beyond the boundaries of doctoring, and yet it wasn't, because his welfare, his health, were involved, and it's hard to separate that aspect of it from the business aspect.

"But the kicker, my turn-on, was crowds. People would say, 'Don't you get tired of seeing the same damn show over and over again? How can you sit through the same songs all the time?' You don't hear half the songs. But you're watching these thousands of people who are mesmerized by this human being up there, and watching their expressions, their jumping up and down. The real feeling of accomplishment comes from knowing that he was able to do so much for so many. People would carry away something that would last them for weeks and months, for a lifetime."

But at the Medical Examiners' hearing, when asked what he would do if he ever again found himself in a situation like that of being Elvis Presley's physician, Dr. Nick said, "I'd get out of it, if I had the option."

Near Corinth, Mississippi, about a hundred miles from Memphis, we stopped for gasoline. With his fluorescent mane, olive complexion, and distinctive, rugged features, Dr. Nick is easy to recognize. It occured to me that being in Mississippi this year with Dr. Nick could resemble being there some years ago with Dr. Martin Luther King. Dr. Nick has received many threats of violence, and a bullet thought to have been intended for him struck a doctor who was sitting behind him at the Liberty Bowl football game in Memphis on Thanksgiving Day 1978, even before he had been accused in print and on television of killing Elvis Presley.

It had been raining off and on all morning. It would soon be eleven o'clock, but it still seemed early, like a winter morning just before sunrise. We bought soft drinks in cans and drove on, the wipers pushing up dirty trickles of mist.

Before we left Memphis, Dr. Nick had said, "Ask me anything." I asked him how he got to know Elvis Presley. He remembered the first time he treated Presley, who was at the time newly married and staying at his ranch near Walls, Mississippi. On a Saturday afternoon early in 1967, George Klein, a friend of Presley whose fiancee, a nurse, worked for Dr. Nick, called Dr. Nick to the ranch to attend Presley. "He had a movie to start Monday, and he'd been real active the last couple of days riding his horses," Dr. Nick said. "The movie was going to have a lot of action in it, and he was having a difficult time walking because of the saddle sores and blisters he had received. He thought that there might be some way that he could get an immediate cure so he could go on out there. I don't know if he thought I was a faith healer, or what."

Dr. Nick convinced Presley to postpone making the movie for a few days and helped him to notify Colonel Parker and the film company of the delay. Then Dr. Nick left, but he was called back to the ranch twice that afternoon, once to answer a question of Presley's "that he could have asked me over the telephone," and once

again even though Presley "didn't have any problem. He just wanted to talk. I don't remember what the talk was about. That was the first encounter. I didn't realize at that encounter that this was the way he was. That this was going to be a way of life. But it was typical of him; throughout our relationship, there would be times that he could handle something over the telephone, but he'd rather for you to come out and talk to him about it. He'd want me to fly out to California. He'd make up some ridiculous problem. There wasn't anything wrong, he just wanted somebody else to talk to.

"Things got a lot easier for me when he moved to Memphis. After his first major illness, he felt more secure here from a medical standpoint than he did seeing different people on the west coast. His first major illness was that an acupuncturist out there was not giving him acupuncture. He'd have a syringe with Novocain, Demerol, and Cortisone that he would inject, and he'd tell Elvis this was acupuncture. We discovered this when we had to put Elvis in the hospital in '73. We almost lost him then.

"From that time till the time he died, except for a few skirmishes we had, he became very dependent on my opinion. He wouldn't feel like he was show-ready unless he was involved in a certain program. We'd start going through the routine of what we needed to do about his weight, what we needed to do to build up his endurance. We needed to be sure that he'd seen his dentist, that he'd gotten his ingrown toenails clipped so he didn't get in trouble onstage. We had to be sure we had things like a nasal douche, a little glass cup that we'd put salt water in to clean out his sinuses. We had Ace bandages and adhesive tape in case he pulled a groin muscle. He was always having trouble with a sprained ankle, and we took ankle corsets, made sure we had two or three. Sometimes he'd be on such a strict diet that somebody would go to these hotels a day or two ahead of time and prepare his special diet food for him. On a couple of tours he didn't eat anything but diet jelly. He'd get the hots about something like that, some fad. At the time, it was terrible. We wanted him to lose weight, but he's got to have the energy to perform, and it's hard to build up physical endurance without eating properly.

"Actually we had better control over his diet on the road than we did at home. At home we had the problem of everybody mothering him—scared if they don't carry up a dozen ham and biscuits, fix six eggs and a pound of bacon, that the poor little boy won't get enough to eat or else he's gonna get mad at them and they're gonna get fired because they didn't fix the usual thing. A lot of times I'd go by at mealtimes just to eat part of his food, so he wouldn't eat too much.

"When he started spending nearly all of his time here, it was sort of a daily thing. On the way home, I'd stop by and see how he was and kill two or three hours there, then get my ass chewed out when I got home. Where had I been?"

"What made you inclined to stop by there on a daily basis?"

"He'd get his feelings hurt if I didn't. I just enjoyed talking to him. I'd get busy and say I'll go by there tomorrow instead of today, and then tomorrow I'd be busy too and still wouldn't go by there, and the next thing I knew I'd get flak, like, 'Why are you mad at Elvis?' People that he liked, he just liked to be around them, and if you weren't around him, he'd want to know why you weren't.

"We'd usually have sort of a family gathering, have supper all together and break bread. His father would be around, Priscilla was around for a while, some of the guys who were working there. Then that was put to a halt. I'm not sure whether it was Priscilla's doing or a joint thing between Priscilla and Mr. Presley. A lot of guys would go there just to freeload, and Priscilla was into this thing that she wanted some privacy with him. She didn't want to have somebody around every minute of the day. But he couldn't be satisfied unless he had five or ten people around all the time."

"How did he take Priscilla's leaving? Was he crushed by it?"

"He was hurt I think mainly because of the circumstances. That she got involved with her karate instructor, and he's the one who pushed her into that. I think he was more mad at Mike Stone than at Priscilla. He thought that they were friends and that Mike stabbed him in the back. Yet on the other hand he was gone so much of the time touring, he was with other women, and he had such a guilty conscience about being gone so much and doing so many things that he was doing, that he encouraged her to get involved with other activities and other people. That way he wouldn't feel so guilty.

"He seemed to have to have female companionship. Not on a sexual basis, just female companionship. Because he missed his mother so much—because of his not having that relationship, mother to son, he enjoyed relationships like the one with Mrs. Cocke, the nurse. It was a kind of maternal relationship."

"Did Elvis get along with his father?"

"He had a lot of respect for his father. He and his father didn't see eye to eye about a lot of business things that they did together. He kind of let his father run his business, give him something to do. Elvis was always spending more than he was taking in, and it was always driving his father crazy. If Elvis spent all the money in his bank account, he figured he could do another tour and make more.

"I remember one time that we were talking about how rough our parents had it back in the Depression, how they had a hard time making ends meet. We talked about the number of hours our parents worked, and how little they got out of it, and he told this story about his daddy. Once when they were living in Mississippi, they'd gone without food for a couple of days, and Vernon went to some grocery store or food market and stole some food, and he got caught and went to jail for several days. Elvis made me promise that I'd never say anything about that. He said, 'Nobody knows about this. I don't want anybody ever to know this, it would really hurt my daddy if people knew.' Right after Elvis died, it was in one of those damn—*Midnite*, or the *Enquirer*—a lead story, 'Elvis' Father in Jail.' That was when everybody was selling everything they could get."

"When you met Elvis, he was already depending on sleeping pills to go to sleep?"

"Since he started in the movie business, he was taking at least two or three sleeping pills, sedatives, nearly every night. Take it on down to the last few years, on the road, it was so important to him to get rest and sleep so he could be perfect for the next day. He felt like people had to travel so far and pay so much money to see his shows, he wanted everything to be perfect."

"Did the problem you had controlling the amount of medication Elvis took worsen as time went on?"

"No, it never really worsened, in the sense that there was a perpetual problem of taking more and more all the time. It was an episodic thing. There were times when he'd get by with almost nothing, times when he'd take a normal amount, other times that he'd take more—I'm talking about sleep medicines or tranquilizers—depending on what he was going through. There were times when he wanted to sit up and just read. He wouldn't take anything for sleep. He'd sit up and read for two or three days and not take any kind of medicine other than maybe a decongestant or his vitamins. This to me is not an addict.

"They talk about the importance of records of what was done, when the same person was doing the same thing day in and day out. You know this one person as well as you know yourself. You know what you've been through with him. You know if he's having a bad night, if the speakers were bad and he's upset about it, or some song didn't go off right, or the guitar player's string broke, or something created in his mind a bad show. It was always worse in his mind than it was in anybody else's. He was such a perfectionist that I would know when it was going to be hard for him to sleep and hard for me to sleep because I'd be busy all night long trying to get him to sleep. Instead of seeing him every three or four hours, I'm going to be in there every two hours. There have been many nights when I fell asleep across the foot of the bed waiting for him to go to sleep."

"He was seriously against coke, grass, things like that?"

"I don't think I ever saw anybody using drugs on the plane or in the hotel— smoking grass, snorting, or anything. He just wouldn't have it around him, especially when we were working. If he even heard of somebody that was doing something, he'd eat 'em out."

"Do you think he was happy, in the sense of being satisfied with where he had been and where he was going, when you knew him?"

"I think he was happy, up to that point, but he had greater expectations— things that he wanted to accomplish. He in no way had fulfilled his hunger for either knowledge or improving himself as a performer in films or on the stage as a singer. He had a lot that he hadn't touched.

"He had some problems with his health. His blood pressure was a little elevated. He was most of the time overweight, he had problems with his colon that contributed somewhat to his protruding abdomen, he had some liver problems we thought were related to his Tylenol intake. He had some back problems and neck problems. He was a compulsive water drinker. He had to have a gallon of ice water with him all the time. A lot of his puffiness was—he'd take in more than he could get rid of. I never could figure out why he drank so much water. It's a psychological hangup for some people. A psychiatrist could tell you about it.

"He liked the short cuts to everything. He always thought there had to be a quicker way to do everything than the logical, practical way. He was talking one time about how nice it would be if he could go to sleep for a few days and then wake up and lose all his excess weight. He said, 'Why don't you do that? Just keep me asleep for a week or two weeks or something, and let me lose some weight, and then wake me up?' I said, 'It's just not practical, Elvis. Your bowels still have to function, this has to go on, that has to go on. We can't do that.'

"So he goes out to Vegas and talks Dr. Gahnin into doing it. He was out there three weeks, kept him knocked out asleep, had him on some sort of papaya juice diet, and he came back all bloated up, he was taking in more drinking papaya juice than he was taking in on a normal diet. That really clobbered his colon. You need physical activity for your colon to function properly. His was already non-functioning because of his laxative abuse, and all he did was sleep for three weeks."

"Why would he abuse laxatives?"

"He abused laxatives because he stayed so constipated. A lot of things contributed to it. Finally his colon, just like a muscle that you don't use, lost its ability to contract. The normal colon is about this big around," Dr. Nick said, gesturing with his doubled fists together. "Elvis' colon was about the size of your leg. You can imagine how much stuff was in it. Whether it was gas or water or shit or whatever, it occupied space. He thought he had control over things. He thought when he'd lose control that he could regain it any time he wanted to."

"Did you try to get him to be easier on himself, more natural?"

"We talked about it many times, and he'd try something else, follow some other routine until the newness wore off, and then he'd go right back to the same old routine that he'd always done."

"Was his death totally unexpected to you? Did you have any kind of previous indication?"

"No, his death was completely unexpected. Several of us had seen Elvis close to death's door before. We always worried about it. In town, one of the aides was supposed to sleep upstairs in the room next to his in case he got up in the middle of the night, so they could go in and check on him. But unfortunately, the night of his death, the aide was Ricky Stanley, and he was drugged out on something and instead of being upstairs he was downstairs. That morning, Elvis had called down to Ricky to go get him something, he had trouble going to sleep, but they couldn't get Ricky up. Elvis' aunt and the maids had gone down to try to get Ricky up, and he's completely in another world. So Elvis called my office, eight o'clock in the morning, and I wasn't there yet. But Tish Henley, the nurse who lived at Graceland, was there, and Elvis talked to her. Tish told her husband where there were a couple of sleeping pills, to put them in an envelope and give them to Elvis' aunt, and Elvis sent his aunt over to Tish's house, and she carried them back over there to him.

"At the time when I was trying to resuscitate Elvis, in the ambulance, I was so out of it, what was going on—I should have realized that he'd been dead for several hours at that time. Except that when I got there, Joe Esposito told me that Elvis had breathed. If he had just breathed, then there might still be some hope. What had happened was that when they moved Elvis, turned him over, he sort of sighed. He had fallen straight forward like he was kneeling on the floor, but with his head down."

According to the police report, Elvis Presley was found at about 2:30 P.M. on August 16, 1977, face down on the red shag carpet of his bathroom floor, "slumped over in front of the commode. . . . his arms and legs were stiff, and there was a discoloration in his face." The bathroom adjoined Presley's bedroom in the white-columned mansion at Graceland, the thirteen-acre estate in Whitehaven, Tennessee, where he had spent most of his life since the early days of the career that had taken him out of poverty and made him the highest paid entertainer and possibly the most famous human being of his time.

A Memphis Fire Department ambulance and Dr. Nick were called. Dr. Nick arrived and boarded the ambulance as it was leaving Graceland to take Presley to Baptist Memorial Hospital, ten minutes away in Memphis. On the way there and in the emergency room, cardio-pulmonary resuscitation attempts were made without effect. At 3:30 P.M., Dr. Nick pronounced Elvis Presley dead.

In the state of Tennessee, when someone is found dead, the local medical examiner must investigate. Dr. Jerry Francisco, the Shelby County (Memphis) Medical Examiner, was informed of Presley's death by Dr. Eric Muirhead, chief pathologist at Baptist Hospital. Dr. Nick had returned to Graceland and received consent for an autopsy from Elvis' father, Vernon Presley. The fact of Elvis Presley's death had been made public, and a crowd had gathered at Baptist Hospital, creating a traffic jam outside the emergency room. Francisco agreed that the autopsy should be performed at the Baptist Hospital morgue rather than across the street at the Medical Examiner's morgue.

The preliminary, or gross, autopsy was completed before eight o'clock that night. In a press conference afterwards, Dr. Francisco made the "provisional diagnosis" that Presley had died of cardiac arrhythmia: his heart had lost its regular beat and then stopped. To determine the precise cause of the attack, Francisco said, "may take several days, it may take several weeks. It may never be discovered." Francisco also said that the preliminary autopsy had revealed no evidence of drug abuse. The Medical Examiner's office reported to the Homicide Division of the Memphis Police Department that Presley had died a natural death.

A few days before, a book had appeared, titled Elvis: What Happened? Written by three former bodyguards of Presley and a writer for the tabloid press, the book told of Presley's desire to have his wife's lover killed, described his "fascination with human corpses," and called him "a walking drugstore." The book also told of Presley's "having a fit of the giggles" at the 1964 funeral of Memphis radio announcer Dewey Phillips, causing some people to doubt its overall accuracy, since Phillips died in 1968. Still, Presley's sudden death, coming at the same time as the allegations of his drug abuse, caused many to speculate, in spite of the Medical Examiner's statements, that he had died from a drug overdose.

On October 21, 1977, Dr. Francisco, after having reviewed Presley's complete autopsy report and other data including reports from four toxicology laboratories, issued his final opinion. Francisco said that Presley died of hypertensive heart disease resulting in cardiac arrhythmia, and that the death had not been caused by drugs. The next day, the Memphis Commercial Appeal carried a story listing ten drugs said to have been found in autopsy samples of Presley's blood at Bio-Science Laboratories in Van Nuys, California. The story was titled, "Near Toxic Level of Drugs Reported in Presley's Blood."

For over twenty years, Elvis Presley had been famous, but he had not been well known. The details of his private life, of passionate interest to many, were known to very few. These few—the "Memphis Mafia," employees who were friends or relatives of Presley—had surrounded him during his life, basking in the warm glow of his affection and generosity, guarding his privacy with almost total silence. Elvis: What Happened?, the three fired bodyguards' lament, had broken the stillness, but with Presley's death and the revelation that he had left almost his entire estate to his daughter, there were among the Mafia few indeed who did not take part in a Babel of Elvis memories. Almost everyone had a story to tell or at least a book to sell.

The books included My Life with Elvis, by a secretary; A Presley Speaks, by an uncle; The Life of Elvis, by a cousin; I Called Him Babe, by a nurse; Elvis, We Love You Tender, by Presley's stepmother and -brothers; Inside Elvis, by a karate instructor, and Elvis: Portrait of a Friend, by one of Elvis' numerous best

March 24, 1958: Gladys and Vernon see Elvis off to Fort Chaffee.

friends. The movies would come later.

The books told and retold the story of Elvis Aron Presley, the Depression-born son of a Mississippi sharecropper Vernon, who, with his eighth-grade education, misspelled the Biblical name Aaron on his son's birth certificate. Elvis' twin brother, Jesse Garon, born dead, was much discussed, and to it many attributed the unusual affection between Elvis and his mother, the former Gladys Smith, whose actual middle name was Love. "She worshipped that child," a friend was often quoted, "from the day he was borned to the day she died."

The little shotgun house, built by his father and grandfather, where Elvis was born; the single room where Elvis and his family first lived in Memphis; the housing project where they lived during Elvis' years as an outsider at Humes High School; all have become standard parts of the legend. So have the Crown Electric Company, where Elvis worked for forty dollars a week after his graduation from school, and the Sun Recording Company, where Elvis paid four dollars to record on an acetate disc two songs, "My Happiness" and "That's When Your Heartaches Begin," as a present for his mother. Sam Phillips, the owner of Sun, heard Elvis, gave him the chance to make a record for release, and the rest is history, the kind of history that sells.

The first Elvis Presley record was released in 1954; his first movies were released in 1957; the next year, as the career for which she alone had prepared her son was just getting started, Gladys Presley died. Though Elvis made three films a year for ten years after her death, he did not appear in public concert again for over twelve years. He kept for the rest of his life a pink Cadillac that he bought for his mother and kept for many years the tree from their last Christmas together.

There are some interesting photographs of Elvis and Gladys— one of Elvis kissing Gladys while holding a pair of jockey shorts to her bosom, another showing Elvis holding Gladys' head, a handful of her hair, looking into her eyes, curling his lip in a smile, but not a smile, an *earnest* look . . .

What must Elvis have seen, looking into Gladys' eyes? God visited Gladys Presley with the mysteries of birth and death, and the life of Elvis was the result, the realization, of her awe-filled vision. It was her image of him, idealized beyond reason, that the public—his public—accepted.

> He is dressed like a prince, the diamonds glitter, the cape waves; he is tall and athletic, and in the cunning play of lights (all that pale blue and crimson) he seems as unreal as the ghost of a Greek god, the original perfect male. Who cares if he's made up? if the lights are deceiving? if the tune of "Thus Spake Zarathustra" makes you fall for the trick? The fact remains that he *is*, that he floats through countless dreams, and that whatever he was, or wherever he is going, he is now, at this moment, the living symbol of freedom and light.
>
> —W.A. Harbinson, *The Illustrated Elvis*

Elvis was buried—after ghouls tried to steal his body from the mausoleum where it was first interred—at

Graceland beside his mother. "What has died," stated one of the hundreds of editorials about the death of Elvis Presley, "is the adolescence of an entire generation. It is the memory of several million people's first intimation of freedom that was in the white hearse."

The anniversary of his death promises to become a holiday like Christmas or the Fourth of July, when each year more Elvis products are served up. One year after Presley's death, a Canadian writer, in a piece called "The Last Days of Elvis," listed eleven drugs found in Presley's body by the University of Utah Center for Human Toxicology and quoted a pharmaceutical guide regarding contraindications and the dangers of drug interactions. The story contained allegations of a conspiracy of silence including the Memphis police, the *Commercial Appeal*, and Presley's doctors, none of whom were named.

About a year later, the book *Elvis: Portrait of a Friend* was published. It was produced by an ex-employee of Presley named Marty Lacker and his wife Patsy with the help of an editor of veterinary publications. The book contained chapter titles like "The Doctor as Pusher" and "Prescription for Death" and left no doubt that the death-dealing doctor was Dr. Nick.

George Constantine Nichopoulos was born in 1927 in Ridgway, Pennsylvania. His parents, Constantine George (Gus) and Persephone Nichopoulos, both came from villages in Greece. At sixteen or seventeen, Gus came to New York City and worked as a bus boy. In 1925, on a six-month return visit to Greece, he met and became engaged to Persephone Bobotsiares. In January, 1927, after working with a cousin in a restaurant in Ridgway and saving his money, Gus married Persephone in Greece and brought her to Pennsylvania, where, in October, their son was born.

In 1928, with the help of Persephone's brother in Greenville, South Carolina, Gus started running a restaurant in Anniston, Alabama. When he retired, more than forty years later, Anniston celebrated Gus Nichopoulos Day. There are not many Greeks in Anniston, a handsome town of about 45,000 people, on rolling hills in eastern Alabama, and the Nichopoulos family was in many ways exemplary. Since Anniston has no Greek Orthodox church, the Nichopouloses regularly attended a local Episcopal church. Gus, who died in June, 1979, had been a Shriner, a 32nd Degree Mason, an Elk, a Rotarian, a State Farm Valued Customer, a greatly beloved citizen. Persephone still lives in the white frame house where she and Gus reared their son, who came to be called Nick, and his sister Vangie, six years younger.

Nick walked a few blocks to the Woodstock Grammar School and then to Anniston High School. His parents allowed him to play football only if he studied music, and there are photographs of him standing on the front lawn at home, wearing short pants, holding his violin under his chin. He is a dark, serious, little boy. From the time Nick was quite small,

he worked in his parents' restaurant. He was a first-string fullback and halfback on the Anniston Bulldogs football team. He became an Eagle Scout. He couldn't decide whether he wanted to be a priest, own a restaurant, or be a doctor.

In 1946, Nick graduated from high school and joined the Army, which put him to work for eighteen months in a hospital in Munich. When he got out of the Army, he entered the pre-medical course of study at the University of the South in Sewannee, Tennessee, graduating in 1951. That fall, he entered medical school at Vanderbilt University but left after one year to study for a Ph.D. at the University of Tennessee in Memphis. While going to school in Memphis, Nick met Edna Sanidas, whose father also owned a restaurant. Nick and Edna were married in 1954. The next year, their son Dean was born. In 1956, Nick went back to Vanderbilt Medical School, and in 1959 he graduated with an M.D. degree.

In 1963, after serving his internship at St. Thomas' Hospital in Nashville, Dr. Nick brought his family (now there were also two daughters, Chrissie and Elaine) to Memphis and started working in a partnership called the Medical Group. He had worked there four years when he met Elvis Presley.

After he pronounced Presley dead, Dr. Nick stepped out of the emergency room into the room where Presley employees Billy Smith, Joe Esposito, Charlie Hodge, David Stanley, and Al Strada were waiting. Billy, Presley's cousin, had been as close to Presley as any friend Presley ever had. "Dr. Nick started to speak to me and he couldn't talk," Billy told me at the Medical Examiner's hearing. "That's how much Elvis' death hurt him. Dr. Nick loved Elvis. He did everything he could to help Elvis. How can anyone think Dr. Nick would hurt Elvis?"

Ten days after Presley died, the *Commercial Appeal* published an exclusive interview with Dr. Nick. In it Dr. Nick said, "I spent many hours a day thinking about different things to do to help him . . . It's going to take some time to lose some of those thoughts and I think everybody's lost . . . We keep thinking that he's here someplace. It's hard to accept."

A year later, Dr. Nick talked briefly about Presley on a local television show, but otherwise he said no more. While friends and relatives of Presley, no longer on his payroll, signed contracts for books and movies, Dr. Nick, almost alone, kept silent. Priscilla did not speak, but she had been left well off by the divorce. There had been around Elvis Presley a hierarchy of silence, and Dr. Nick was very near its top.

Meanwhile the Elvis memories, finding an audience, began to resemble the music business, sometimes described as a self-devouring organism that vomits itself back up. In New York City, Charles Thompson, a Memphis-born television producer, was reading about Presley. *20/20*, the ABC television news program for which Thompson works, was new and had to have some hot stories if it were to compete with its opposite considered most important, he refused to take even antihistamines, saying, "This one's on my own."

On "The Elvis Cover-Up" program, Geraldo Rivera had accused Dr. Nick of prescribing five thousand drug doses to Presley in the last six months of his life. The Board's revised list of charges made it twelve thousand drug doses in Presley's last eighteen months. Perhaps the single most important point in Dr. Nick's testimony was his statement that the drugs were not for Presley alone but for the entire company, as many as a hundred people, who worked with Presley on the road. Presley appeared with a male vocal group, a female vocal group, a rock and roll rhythm section, and a large orchestra with strings. Dr. Nick, after learning from a few tours' experience what he was likely to need, came prepared to care for everyone from the equipment handlers to the flute player, including the record producer with the transplanted kidney.

"I carried three suitcases full of equipment," Dr. Nick said. "I had everything you'd expect to find in a pharmacy—all kinds of antibiotics for people who were allergic to penicillin, I had expectorants, I had decongestants, I had just what you can imagine you'd use every day in your office. I carried a laryngoscope, I carried some long forceps in case he aspirated, I carried these little bags for breathing, I carried suture material, adhesive tapes, splints, everything that you would expect a first aid stand to have someplace, plus what a physician would have."

The suitcases were kept locked and in Dr. Nick's possession. When he was away, a nurse kept the suitcases and dispensed drugs only according to Dr. Nick's specific orders. Twice during the last six months of Presley's life, Dr. Nick's car was broken into, and drugs for tours were stolen and had to be replaced. The Memphis Police Department had been notified both times.

The drugs were bought in Elvis Presley's name because otherwise Vernon Presley, his son's bookkeeper, wouldn't have paid for them. A long-time acquaintance of the Presleys has said, "Vernon would cringe when somebody spent money. You could actually see him cringe." Dr. Nick wrote prescriptions in his own name before a vacation trip to Hawaii with Presley, some of his associates, and their families because "I knew that if I had charged him for the medication that I was taking along, his father would blow a gasket." Presley gave away fleets of cars, fortunes in jewelry, houses, hundreds of thousands of dollars, but his father could never stop pinching pennies. It was all part of the unique dilemma of being Elvis Presley's physician.

Dr. Nick acknowledged the absence of written records of Presley's treatment, saying, "The reason some of these things were not kept in the office and some of them were not written down someplace else was that people were always perusing his charts. It was difficult to have any confidentiality with his records, whether it be in my office or the hospital or wherever. I certainly wish now there were records. That would certainly be helpful. I think that if he hadn't died, the end result as far as his improvement during this period of time is answer in itself."

Dr. Nick said that he had received with Presley's help a bank loan to pay for his house, and that he was repaying the loan with interest. He had never charged Presley for visits to Graceland. Speaking of the *per diem* fee Presley paid the Medical Group for Dr. Nick's time on the road, Dr. Nick said, with cold understatement, "It's difficult to pay for services that last eighteen hours a day."

"My objective was to help him," Dr. Nick said, "because I thought that he helped so many people—not physically helped people, or monetarily helped people, but—to keep him rolling and to go to his show and see what reward all these people got out of his shows—it's an experience that you'd have to go through, it's like having your first child."

In spite of Dr. Nick's talk of rewards, the state's firm assumption seemed to be that Presley was, as Geraldo Rivera had suggested on *20/20*, "just another victim of self-destructive over-indulgence" who had "followed in the melancholy rock and roll tradition of Janis Joplin, Jimi Hendrix, and Jim Morrison." The idea of Presley following in the tradition of Joplin, Hendrix, and Morrison is one that defies chronology, sociology, musical history, and common sense, but neither "The Elvis Cover-Up" nor the hearing was designed for the purpose of furthering common sense.

On the second day of Dr. Nick's testimony, there was a bomb threat. Dr. Nick's years of effort to help Elvis Presley had earned him threats and accusations, cost him many thousands of dollars in legal fees, and brought shame to his family. "You killed Elvis!" people driving past Dr. Nick's house yell at him, or his wife, or his children.

The Medical Examiners didn't appear to sleep while he testified, as some of them seemed to do at times when other witnesses testified, but Dr. Nick's testimony had the effect of making the witnesses for his defense anti-climactic.

The first of the three doctors who were the state's expert witnesses was a pharmacologist who had never treated any patients; the next said that drug addiction should be cured in two or three weeks, and the last testified that he refused to treat patients who smoke. None of them had any firsthand knowledge of Dr. Nick's patients. Each of the experts perused the charges, saying where he thought Dr. Nick had gone wrong.

Then the defense began. It was late Wednesday afternoon. The party had been going on for three days. There was time this afternoon for the defense to present only two witnesses. Both were ex-girl friends, one of Presley, the other of Presley employee Joe Esposito. Both were good-looking, and though they verified important matters—Dr. Nick's treating Presley with placebos and intercepting drugs from other physicians—they seemed to be comic relief.

On Thursday the defense called sixteen witnesses.

Among them were doctors, members of the Presley staff, Health Related Boards investigators, a coordinator from the Medical Group, and a patient. The patient, a department store executive, told how Dr. Nick helped him overcome the addiction to narcotics he developed while hospitalized for months following an automobile accident. The coordinator testified that the Medical Group had fifteen thousand patients, thirty-five hundred of whom were Dr. Nick's. The twenty patients listed in the charges represented one half of one per cent of Dr. Nick's patients. By choosing at random and comparing six of Dr. Nick's full working days at the Medical Group, it was shown that he prescribed controlled substances to only one out of every twenty patients.

The Health Boards investigators admitted meeting and exchanging information with the 20/20 staff before the charges were delivered to Dr. Nick. One of the investigators testified that the recommendation for the state to file charges against Dr. Nick was made without consulting even one licensed physician. Later, James Cole would admit that he gave the investigators the tip on the Presley "drug death" in the first place.

The Presley employees testified that Dr. Nick cared for all the people who worked with Presley, not just Presley himself. They verified that Dr. Nick gave Presley no medication in an uncontrolled manner, that Presley at times left town to get drugs he couldn't get from Dr. Nick, and that Dr. Nick had instructed them to intercept all drugs coming to Presley from other sources.

Dr. Nick had testified that in 1975 he had arranged for a nurse to live at Graceland "so we could better control and dispense medications." The nurse, Tish Henley, testified that she often took away from Presley medications that did not come from Dr. Nick, and that she sometimes, under Dr. Nick's orders, gave Presley placebos. At no time was dispensing drugs left up to her discretion. After tours, she said, copious amounts of leftover drugs were destroyed.

Some doctors to whom Dr. Nick had referred Presley testified that Presley had showed no signs of narcotic or hypnotic abuse. Dr. Nick was said to show a remarkable interest in patients he referred to other doctors. Dr. Lawrence Wruble, a gastro-intestinal specialist, said that at one point he and Dr. Nick had told Presley to stop doing two shows a night in Las Vegas or they would stop being his doctors, and from that time Presley did only one show. Wruble spoke highly of Dr. Nick's care and concern for Presley. Dr. Walter Hoffman, a cardiologist at the Medical Group who has known Dr. Nick since he was a graduate student, said that Dr. Nick has a unique quality of being "more empathetic than any practitioner I have ever known."

During the hearing's first days, the audience had been divided between Dr. Nick's supporters and detractors. By Thursday afternoon, the troops were tired. Some of us had settled down to being simply reporters with battle fatigue. When the hearing stopped for the day, I had a question for Geraldo Rivera, who was sitting amidst his crew beside an empty seat in the Chamber. After "The Elvis Cover-Up" story, Rivera had done a follow-up in which he said that if Presley's autopsy report were released, the information in it—

"'. . . would send at least one doctor to jail,' yeah, I remember," he said.

"Were you talking about Dr. Nick?"

"Yes, but I didn't understand. I didn't know about all his other patients. I didn't believe Elvis was getting drugs in the mail. I'm beginning to see another side of Dr. Nick. He was definitely no scriptwriter. He made mistakes with Elvis, but I think he's a good man. I just feel bad about his family. I see them looking at me, and I can tell what they're thinking."

"It's obvious they hate your guts," I said pleasantly.

On Friday morning, Dr. Jerry Francisco, the Shelby County Medical Examiner, took the stand and repeated his conclusion that Elvis Presley died of cardiac arrhythmia brought on by high blood pressure and hardening of the arteries. Presley's heart had been twice the normal size for a man of his age and weight, his coronary arteries had been occluded, and he had a long history of hypertension.

Dr. Francisco said that the amounts of drugs in Presley's body did not, even in combination, indicate the likelihood of a drug overdose. The circumstances of his death also indicated that drugs were not at fault. If Presley had taken an oral overdose of drugs shortly after 8:00 A.M. on the day he died, he might have been in a coma by 2:30 P.M., the time he was found, but he would hardly have been stiff and blue, dead for several hours. The typical victim of an oral drug overdose dies a lingering death in a comfortable position, not pitched forward on a bathroom floor.

Dr. Francisco was followed by Dr. Bryan Finkle, an English toxicologist, now Director of the University of Utah Center for Human Toxicology. Dr. Finkle, who has worked in forensic toxicology at New Scotland Yard, testified that the concentration of drugs found in Presley's body was not sufficient to affect Presley's respiration or the amount of oxygen in his blood. Dr. Finkle said that although he had been quoted on "The Elvis Cover-Up" program as saying that drugs may have made "a significant contribution" to Presley's death, he had not been informed, when a member of the 20/20 staff telephoned him, that he was being interviewed or that his statements "would be construed in such a fashion."

Dr. David Stafford, a toxicologist at the University of Tennessee Center for the Health Sciences, said that he had tested Presley's autopsy samples for thirty or forty drugs and had found nothing consistent with the diagnosis of a toxic drug dose.

The last defense witness, not a doctor, testified that Dr. Nick, by caring enough to seek an opinion from a second surgeon, had saved the leg of his old maid aunt.

After lunch on the last day of testimony, portions of

number, CBS television's popular *Sixty Minutes*.

Thompson had worked as a field producer at CBS, leaving when ABC beckoned partly because he and CBS had not seen eye to eye on a story about Billy Carter's supposed violations of federal energy regulations. Thompson had wanted to do the story, but the powers at CBS had thought there was no story, or none worth putting on television. It wasn't Thompson's first such disagreement with an employer. In 1970, when Thompson was working for a television station in Jacksonville, Florida, he did a story on pollution that accused the station itself of polluting and got himself fired.

Thompson had graduated from high school in Memphis, studied journalism at Memphis State University, worked at the *Commercial Appeal*. In the middle nineteen-sixties, Thompson did two tours with the Navy in Vietnam, serving as liaison with the Marines, calling in air strikes. He saw a good bit of action, and when he came back home had troubling nightmares of mangled bodies, burning children, and seemed to see the dark side of issues.

When Thompson learned, the day it happened, that Presley had died, he expected, so he said later, that "by night they would say it was drugs." He was surprised when they didn't, but when he read the Elvis books, among them Marty Lacker's accusation of Dr. Nick, his expectations were at last fulfilled. Thompson's reportorial sixth sense told him, This is Good, this is a Story. King Dies of Drugs from Court Physician is *Good*. The King Is Dead! Hang the Doctor! Still, Thompson admits that he came to Memphis for "a top-to-bottom investigation on Elvis" with nothing more than a hunch. "I didn't have *anything*," he has said.

In looking through the Presley file at the *Commercial Appeal*, Thompson came upon the Bio-Science toxicology report which had been quoted in the "Near Toxic" story. Thompson says that he showed the report to a doctor at Baptist Hospital, who said, according to Thompson, "Jesus Christ, it's obvious. The son of a bitch died of drugs."

At least one doctor at Baptist Hospital says that Thompson showed him the report. He told Thompson that in his opinion, Presley's drug problems had been primarily with laxatives and steroids. The doctor advised Thompson, should he have questions about Presley and drugs, to call Dr. Nick. In July of 1979, by his own count, Thompson tried three times to question Dr. Nick, who would not talk to him. Armed with that fact and the toxicology report, Thompson told the doctor who had suggested that he talk with Dr. Nick: "I think I've got a homicide."

Thompson brought James Cole, his brother-in-law, who like Thompson had worked for the *Commercial Appeal*, in to help research the story. Cole learned that a routine audit of prescription records in Memphis was going to be conducted by the Tennessee Healing Arts Board and telephoned the Board's office in Nashville, the state capitol, "to find out what was going on." He talked with Jack Fosbinder, the Board's chief investigator, who told him that an audit of the first six months of 1979 was in progress. Cole told Fosbinder, so he has said, "We suspect Elvis may have died a drug death. Maybe you should look back into 1977."

In August of 1979, after Charles Thompson's three failed attempts, Thompson's New York colleague, ABC television news performer Geraldo Rivera, came to Memphis to talk to Dr. Nick and failed six times. The *20/20* team had no such trouble talking with the state Health Related Boards' investigators. On September 6, Thompson, Rivera, and Cole came to Dr. Nick's office after a meeting with the investigators, who had told them that Dr. Nick was about to have formal charges brought against him. On this, his seventh try, Rivera succeeded.

In the interview, Rivera asked Dr. Nick various questions about Presley, leading up to the big charge: "The records indicate that, especially in the last year of his life, you prescribed certain medications to Elvis Presley in quite extraordinarily large amounts. Why?"

"I can't comment on that," Dr. Nick said, "and I don't believe that it's true."

"The records we have, Doctor—and I'll say this as gently as I possibly can—indicate that from January 20, 1977 until August 16, 1977, the day he died, you prescribed to Elvis Presley, and the prescriptions were all signed by you— over five thousand schedule two narcotics and/or amphetamines. That comes out to something like twenty-five per day."

"I don't believe that."

"Well, is it something that you'd like to refresh your recollection on, or is it something you deny?"

"I deny it."

While all this television business was happening, I knew nothing about it. I had my own worries. They led me to Dr. Nick. On March 24, 1978, I had fallen from a granite boulder on a north Georgia mountainside, breaking my back, bruising my brain, learning more about pain than I cared to know, finally developing a drug dependence only slightly less grand than that of the late (and no wonder) Howard Hughes.

After a year I tried to stop taking the drugs my doctors prescribed. I tried twice and twice had *grand mal* seizures, full-scale epileptic brain-fries, blind, rigid, foaming at the mouth, fighting off unseen enemies, screaming, turning into a hydrophobic wolf. A neurologist tested the electrical impulses emanating from my head, told me they were abnormal, and advised me to have my brain injected with radioactive dyes, which I declined to do.

About this time, I was at a friend's house and happened to mention that one night soon I was going to be dead before I was asleep. My friend, a patient of Dr. Nick, advised me to make an appointment to see him. On July 5, 1979, I told Dr. Nick all the above.

"This is interesting," he said, "but what do you want from me?"

"I've been given this room full of drugs," I said. "I

don't want to go on taking drugs and I don't want to be epileptic. What are my chances?"

I filled a bottle, bled, coughed, inhaled, exhaled, held still, bent over, dressed, and waited, sitting on a metal table in a cold little room. Dr. Nick came in, shook his head and said, "Looks like you've lived through a nightmare."

I've survived, I thought. It was news to me. Dr. Nick sent me into his office to wait for him. On the wall beside the door there was a large photograph of Elvis Presley, signed and with the inscription, "To my good friend and physician, Dr. Nick." The office was thick with things that were obviously gifts from Dr. Nick's patients. Among them were many small frog figures, so that the office looked like a Greek gift shop being taken over by swamp life.

Dr. Nick came in. We talked about diet and exercise. I hadn't drunk a glass of milk in years and hadn't exercised since running for a helicopter at Altamont. I

maintain professional standards in the state, examine the practices of other doctors— but he didn't seem terribly worried. I kept telling him that if there was another side to his story, he'd better tell it.

"The lawyers don't want the Medical Examiners to get the idea that we want to try this thing in the media," Dr. Nick said. His accusers had no such reluctance.

On January 13, 1980, Dr. Nick's hearing before the Board of Medical Examiners began. Because of Tennessee's "sunshine law" requiring that proceedings of this kind be held in public, the hearing took place in the five hundred-seat City Council Chamber in the Memphis City Hall. Public interest in the case was believed to be great, and attendance was expected to be heavy, but it had not been thought necessary to hire the Mid-South Coliseum.

Whatever else the hearing may have been, it was a physical ordeal. The weather was seasonable for

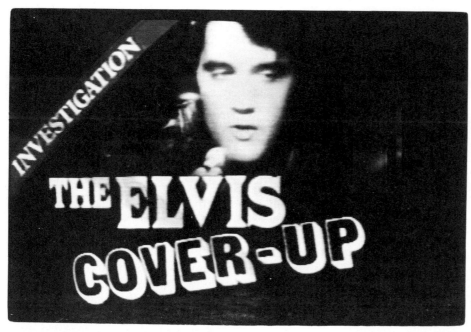

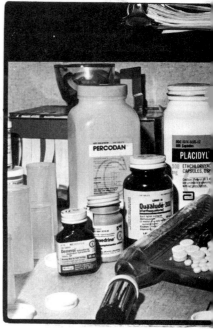

mentioned that I had worried my family, and Dr. Nick said he would call and reassure them. He gave me no drugs, sent me to no specialists, but he let me know that I was going to be all right. I was a bit dazed, trying to get used to the idea.

On September 13, 1979, the ABC television network presented the *20/20* show titled "The Elvis Cover-Up." One of its most characteristic touches was an interview with a retired pharmacist from Baptist Hospital, where Presley's stepbrother, Ricky Stanley, picked up a prescription of Dilaudid for Presley from Dr. Nick the night before Presley died. The pharmacist said that having sold Presley the fatal dose weighed mightily on his conscience. No one bothered to tell the man that no Dilaudid was found in Presley's body.

After "The Elvis Cover-Up" was shown, I saw Dr. Nick socially two or three times. He had been presented with a list of charges by the Board of Medical Examiners— not pathologists but doctors who, to help

January, cold and sometimes wet. The sessions lasted from Monday through Saturday, starting each morning at 8:30 and adjourning usually ten hours later.

The audience, smaller than anticipated, averaged about a hundred people. It included Elvis fans of many descriptions, from old ladies in E.P. baseball jackets to a pair of effete, young, male twins who had come from Ohio to see Dr. Nick swing. Also in the audience were Dr. Nick's immediate family and many of his friends, among them his priest, Fr. Vieron. There were reporters, print and broadcast, local and international, and the photographers were like ants at a picnic. ABC television's numerous lights, cameras, sound recorders, and crew, including Charles Thompson, James Cole, and Geraldo Rivera, were a constant presence, on hand to take postcards of the hanging.

Behind the Chamber's wooden railing sat the state's attorneys and interrogators, Dr. Nick and his lawyers, the five Medical Examiners, and the referee, or hearing officer. Police in plain clothes stood against the rear wall, staring at the audience.

The start of the hearing was delayed by the glare of the television lights. As the Medical Examiners shielded their eyes, the hearing officer insisted that the lights be moved: "We're going to be here for a week, and we can't have everybody go blind."

The charges against Dr. Nick were: first, gross incompetence, ignorance, or negligence; second, unprofessional, dishonorable, or unethical conduct; and last, dispensing, prescribing, or distributing controlled substances "not in good faith" to relieve suffering or to effect a cure. On the first day of the hearing, the state's attorneys called ten of the twenty patients of Dr. Nick listed in the charges to testify. Tennessee has no statute protecting the privacy of exchanges between doctors and patients; Dr. Nick's patients had to testify or go to jail. The patients—among them an investment banker, a record promoter, a landscape gardener, a restaurant

statute prevented the state from calling Dr. Nick. The first day ended with Dr. Nick's lawyers intending to seek a ruling on the question in chancery court.

But on Tuesday, the second morning of the hearing, the defense relented. A chancery court suit might take years; so Dr. Nick, wanting to settle the larger issue, took the stand. He discussed his prescribing practices, talking about each patient in the charges. Count number fifteen, Elvis Presley, received the most attention.

Responding to questions from the state's attorneys and the Medical Examiners, Dr. Nick described the progress of his relationship with Elvis Presley. He told of his efforts, with the help of Memphis alcohol and drug abuse specialists David Knott and Robert Fink, to save Presley's life and restore him to health after his nearly fatal overmedication by the fake acupuncturist in Los Angeles. After Presley learned that Drs. Knott and Fink, who had been called in by Dr. Nick, were

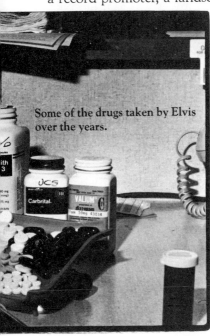

Some of the drugs taken by Elvis over the years.

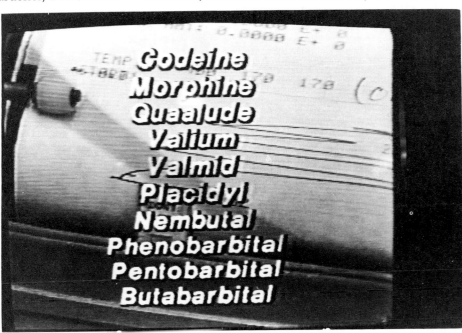

Codeine
Morphine
Quaalude
Valium
Valmid
Placidyl
Nembutal
Phenobarbital
Pentobarbital
Butabarbital

cashier, a doctor's wife, and two ex-heroin addicts— were questioned before the public and the press concerning their most intimate problems, which included alcoholism, insomnia, divorces, abortions, obesity, cancer, and bereavement. After each patient's name in the charges there was a list of prescriptions from Dr. Nick, each list showing a decline in the amount of medicine prescribed. Contrary to the usual pattern in malpractice by over-prescribing, Dr. Nick made no charges for prescriptions and saw his patients often, giving frequent physical examinations. Every patient who testified praised Dr. Nick.

After the patients had testified, the state called Dr. Nick himself to the witness stand. His lawyers insisted that he should not be forced to testify for his accusers; that he would take the stand and submit to cross-examination, but as a part of his defense, not the state's prosecution. The hearing officer took the position that the hearing was not a criminal court, and that no

psychiatrists, he refused to see them.

Keeping drugs from other doctors away from Presley was a continuing problem, Dr. Nick said. He attempted to consult with other doctors who saw Presley, "trying to get some continuity in his treatment," but Presley, without telling Dr. Nick, saw doctors in other towns, some of whom sent him medications by mail. Presley employees were instructed by Dr. Nick to turn over to him all medicines from other doctors so they could be discarded or replaced with placebos.

In 1973, following Presley's "acupuncture" treatments, Dr. Nick said, "I thought he was addicted. I do not think he was an addict." Although he made extensive use of placebos in treating Presley, Dr. Nick said, Presley "had a lot of chronic problems . . . degenerative changes in his back and in his neck . . . that you couldn't treat with placebos." Still, there were times when Presley could not be persuaded to take any medicine at all. Before a Las Vegas opening that Presley

"The Elvis Cover-Up" program were shown to the Examiners, and the lawyers for both sides made their closing statements. The defense said that the collaboration between ABC television and the state's investigators concerning Dr. Nick "allowed the media to punish him unmercifully— without any justice— from September 13, 1979, through January 18, 1980." It was pointed out that Dr. Nick profited from no one's drug dependence, that even patients who took advantage of his trust to obtain drugs had, over the length of time in the charges, been withdrawn from drugs. Dr. Nick had at times, for a variety of reasons, kept incomplete records, but that situation had been corrected before the charges against him had been filed. Dr. Nick, the defense said, "is a fine, compassionate, sensitive physician" who said to his patients, "'I'm going to help you. Remember I'm not perfect, but I'm going to exercise my judgment,' and that is what he did."

The prosecution said that regardless of Dr. Nick's good faith and intentions, we live by standards, and Dr. Nick had violated the standards of his profession. He prescribed too many drugs, in inappropriate amounts, for too long a time. The Examiners were called on to revoke Dr. Nick's license "until such time as the Board can be sure that his practice is consistent with good medical practice."

On Saturday, January 19, 1980, the Board voted on the charges against Dr. Nick. Of the first two charges— gross incompetence, ignorance, or negligence; unprofessional, dishonorable, or unethical conduct—the Board unanimously found Dr. Nick innocent. But he had violated certain relatively minor regulations. He had discarded, without keeping records, drugs whose fate must be recorded. He had also allowed certain patients to receive too many drugs, even though in the long run he had withdrawn his patients from drugs. The Medical Examiners found Dr. Nick guilty on ten of the charges of improper prescribing in the complaint.

One patient to whom Dr. Nick was found guilty of improper prescribing was Elvis Presley. However, one of the Examiners said that the guilty verdict was only for faulty record-keeping and commented that he had found "no evidence that Dr. Nichopoulos was negligent in his care of this patient." Another of the Examiners said, "I think we have to consider the extraordinary circumstances under which he was operating. He was under the gun. I think he exercised considerable restraint in trying to control the medication. There are very extenuating circumstances, and I certainly agree that there was no involvement by Dr. Nichopoulos in any way in the death of Elvis Presley."

The Board suspended for three months Dr. Nick's license to practice medicine, and he was put on probation for three years. The sentence, after "The Elvis Cover-Up" allegations, seemed to some people absurdly light. To others, it seemed unnecessary chastisement of an excellent physician.

At least, Dr. Nick thought, he had run the gauntlet, it was over. He had told what he had done, the Medical Examiners had made their ruling, and it was a relief to have the matter settled at last.

So Dr. Nick thought until he realized that the matter wasn't settled at all. No one had gone to great lengths in reporting the testimonies of Dr. Nick or the witnesses for his defense, but in March, 1980, *Memphis*, the local slick-paper magazine, published an article called "The Elvis Expose: How ABC Unearthed the Story, the *Real* Story." It said that Dr. Nick at the hearing had described Presley as a "ranting drug addict." Without irony it quoted Charles Thompson as saying, "They haven't said anything that disagrees with our first report ('The Elvis Cover-Up') last September." It took no notice at all of the testimonies that the drugs Dr. Nick ordered in Presley's name were not all for him. This is not surprising, since the writer of the article, Tom Martin, a Federal Express employee who writes in his spare time, attended the hearing only on Friday and Saturday mornings and was not present to hear any of the other testimony. It was as if Dr. Nick and the other defense witnesses had never spoken.

The article described matter-of-factly Thompson's personal inclination to believe that Presley died of drugs, James Cole's telling the Health Related Boards' chief investigator about Presley's "drug death," and presented the ABC team in much the same light that they, in one of their various motions to have Presley's autopsy report released, had shone on themselves: ". . . we think that we behaved toward Dr. Nick with the highest courtesy and consideration. We are confident of the truth, honesty, and fairness of what we have broadcast and believe there are no grounds for charges of unfairness, false portrayal, prejudice, exploitation, or sensationalism."

Except for the Greek newspapers, calendars, and bric-a-brac, Dr. Nick's mother's house in Anniston, Alabama, is exactly like my grandparents' old house in south Georgia, down to the African violets in the breakfast room. Being there is like my idea of Greek Orthodox Heaven: nobody forces you to do anything, and there is so much delicious Greek food that you don't have a chance to get hungry.

We arrived on a Friday; Saturday afternoon we took a break from Mrs. Nichopoulos' wonderful cooking and ate sandwiches from Anniston's Golden Rule Barbecue. After lunch we went to the Highland Cemetery to visit the grave of Dr. Nick's father, who died in June, 1979, before "The Elvis Cover-Up" scandal broke. Dr. Nick had told me that one strong bond between him and Presley had been the respect they both had for their parents. I was sure Dr. Nick was glad that his father hadn't died suffering with him the humiliations of the last year.

Later, in the late afternoon at the house Dr. Nick had left to find his future, he reminisced further about the days when he had spent so much time taking care of Presley: "I'd spend two or three hours a night taking care of his eyes. Elvis had glaucoma. He used to dye his eyelashes, and I think that may have had something to

do with it. And he'd get these bacterial infections on his skin—you know, Elvis didn't bathe."

"No," I said, "I didn't."

"He'd take sponge baths, but he wouldn't get wet. He took these pills from Sweden that are supposed to purify your body."

I remembered Billy Smith, Presley's cousin, testifying at the hearing that on the morning of the day Presley died, after they had played racquetball, Presley had cleaned up, and Smith had dried his hair. It was nothing unusual to Presley or to Billy Smith, but I wondered whether many people would ever understand the strange life of Elvis Presley, the sharecropper's millionaire son, the Pauper who became the Prince. He may have been uneducated, he may have been uncultured, his favorite food may have been Pepsi-Cola and peanut butter and mashed banana sandwiches, but he was still the King, and the King didn't open jars, or dry his own hair, or take baths like the common folk. Not even Mick Jagger keeps a cousin on hand to dry his hair, but Mick Jagger's mother never worshipped him or cared for him as lovingly as Gladys Presley had cared for Elvis.

Elvis had been the King, and now he was just a dead junkie, and to many people, the fault was all Dr. Nick's.

The next day, when we left for Memphis, it was misting in Anniston, with just a few raindrops. As we drove, the rain stopped, the afternoon grew warm, the sky was clear and blue. We opened the sun roof and listened to tapes of Elvis singing. Then the weather changed again, and by the time we reached Memphis it was cold, and the sky was overcast, gray and bleak.

On May 16, 1980, the Shelby County Grand Jury indicted Dr. Nick on fourteen counts of illegally prescribing. Each count is punishable by a prison sentence of two to ten years and a fine of as much as $20,000. Dr. Nick is free on bond and awaiting trial.

A local official, a friend of both Presley and Dr. Nick, told me, "They'll ruin him. It's not that they *could* do it; they're *doing* it. The prosecutors don't care what good he's done. They'll put him in jail if they can, and if they can't, they'll bankrupt him. They'll get him on a technicality or keep indicting him on slightly different charges until they break him."

"It's like a medieval ducking trail by ordeal," said a doctor who also knew both Presley and Dr. Nick. "If Dr. Nick drowns, he's innocent."

ELVIS OR THE IRONIES OF A SOUTHERN IDENTITY
BY LINDA RAY PRATT

Elvis was the most popular entertainer in the world, but nowhere as popular as in his native South. In the last years of his career, his audience in other parts of the country was generally centered in the original "fifties" fans whose youth and music were defined by Elvis, and in the lower or working class people who saw in Elvis some glamorized image of their own values. In the South, however, the pattern of Elvis' popularity tended to cut across age barriers and class lines which were themselves a less recognizable thing in a region in which almost no one is more than a generation or two away from poverty, and where "class" in small communities might have more to do with family and past status than with money. Among Southern youth, Elvis was not a relic from a musical past; he was still one of the vital forces behind a Southern rock, which though different now from his, still echoes the rhythms which his music had fused out of the region. His numerous concerts in the South could not exhaust the potential audience. At his death, leading politicians and ministers from the South joined the people on the street in eulogizing him. Local radio and television stations ran their own specials in addition to the syndicated or national programs. Halftime ceremonies at the Liberty Bowl were in tribute to him. When someone commented on national TV that the Presleys were "white trash," it was a regional slur, not just a personal one. The white South expressed love, grief, and praise for Elvis from all age groups at virtually every level of the social, intellectual, and economic structures.

The phenomenon of such widespread sectional regard and emotional intensity went beyond the South's usual pride in the success of "one of our own." The emotion became more puzzling if one listened to some of the reasons offered to explain it: Elvis loved his mother; Elvis' heart was broken; Elvis loved Jesus; Elvis was the American Dream. Such reasons for loving and mourning Elvis seemed strange because, on the surface at least, they were so tangential to Elvis himself or to the musical or cultural impact he unquestionably did have. How, in the face of his vitality and defiance of convention, could one love Elvis because he loved Jesus? And how, in a man expressing nothing if not undisguised sexuality, could one love Elvis because he was so good to his mother? But people, especially those beyond the age group of his original teen fans, often did say such things. Merle Haggard's "From Graceland to the Promised Land," with its emphasis on Elvis' mother's death and his faith in Jesus, is, after all, the perfect Southern folk song about Elvis. The South's involvement with Elvis is sincere, but most of the expressed reasons for it do not reach very far, and some of them seem patently false. They are the myths sent up to justify the emotion and to obscure its source. The emotions spring from associations with a reality the South collectively prefers to conceal and yet constantly experiences. The paradox of Elvis was that he was able simultaneously to reveal the reality of the modern South while concealing it in a myth of the American Dream. He was at once both "King" and outsider.

The myth of Elvis which the South voices is in part very familiar. He is the sharecropper's son who made millions, the Horatio Alger story in drawl. Almost everyone who knew him assured us that, despite the money and fame, "he never changed" (no one remarks how tragic such a static condition would be, were it possible). He never got over his mother's death (in 1958); he was humble and polite; he doted on his little girl; he loved his home town; he never forgot where he came from. He had wealth, yes; but in the tradition of those who love Jesus, he was uncomfortable with riches when others were poor and so gave millions of dollars away to the less fortunate. The American success story turned to altruism. Even his money was not tainted, just dollars freely given in exchange for entertainment so good it always seemed a bargain. Unlike some others whose success was a ticket out of the South and into the broader, happier American identity, Elvis remained in Memphis. His regional loyalty when he could have lived anywhere deeply complimented the South. Graceland was a new image of the Southern plantation, this time free from associations with slavery and a guilt-ridden past. The very gates had musical notes on them. He was a good boy and a good ole boy. Elvis himself seemed to believe this vision; certainly he played to it in his "family" movies, his sacred music, and in his "American Trilogy" dominated by "Dixie." It was a sentimental myth, but, then, W.J. Cash has called Southerners "the most sentimental people in history" (*The Mind of the South*, p. 130).

Elvis' fame initially grew out of an image in opposition to the one the myth attempts to disguise. He was scandalous, sexual, defiant of all authority. He was preached against from the pulpit as an immoral force. In a blackboard jungle, he was the juvenile delinquent. On the streets, he was a hood. Socially, he was a "greaser." Economically, he was "poor white," a gentler rendition of "white trash." Maybe he loved Jesus, but even his Christmas songs could be dirty. In songs like "Santa Claus Is Back In Town" he played with the conventions of Christmas music in order to startle and subvert.

This image of Elvis, the rocker with "a dirty, dirty feeling," "born standing up and talking back," never fully disappeared. His last few movies, like a lot of the lyrics he improvised in concert, were sprinkled with off-color jokes and plays on words. His 1976 image was as excessive and extravagant as his 1956 image, though not in the same ways. The violence still flowed out of the karate movements, the sexuality in such songs as "Burning Love." In concert, his emotional passion sometimes transfigured such schmaltzy songs of lost love and broken hearts as "Hurt" or "You Gave Me a Mountain" into rich autobiographical moments. Even the obscene subversion of Christmas showed up again in "Merry Christmas, Baby."

The Elvis of the sentimental myth would never have changed musical or cultural history, but the authentic Elvis who did so  was transformed into a legend obscuring what the man, the music, or the image really meant. Although some elements of the myth were commonly associated with Elvis throughout the country, in the South—particularly the white South—the myth was insisted upon and pushed to its extremes. The question is why. Jimmy Carter loves his mother and Jesus, too, but the South has not rewarded him with uncritical devotion. The real Elvis, both early and late, might have been severely criticized, but even his drug-involved death is called a "heart attack," the ten drugs the autopsy found in his body merely the "prescription medicines" of a sick and heartbroken man who kept pushing himself because he did not want to disappoint the fans. Those who have argued that people projected onto Elvis anything they liked because his image was essentially vacuous are mistaken; if anything, the image is too rich in suggestion to be acknowledged fully or directly.

Some critics attribute the sentimental myth of Elvis to the cleverness of Colonel Parker and the cooperation of Elvis himself. To do so is to oversimplify a complex phenomenon and to mislead a generation's genuine mythmaking as merely another shrewd "sell" campaign. For anyone less significant than Elvis, the path that Colonel Parker apparently advised by way of numbingly stupid movies and empty music would have been the path to sure oblivion. The 1968 Black Leather television special saved Elvis from that, but allegedly against the advice of Parker who wanted the show to be all Christmas music. Elvis, pursued by the myth and under pressure to confirm it, kept to himself and never told the public anything. The Colonel was smart enough to promote the myth, but it was the authentic handiwork of a society that needed a legend to justify the identification it felt with such a figure. After Elvis died, the Brentwood, Tennessee, Historical Society even supplied the Presley genealogy. The family was, of course, completely respectable, producing "renowned professors, doctors, judges, ministers" in every generation until poverty overcame them during Reconstruction.

C. Vann Woodward has said that the South's experience is atypical of the American experience, that where the rest of America has known innocence, success, affluence, and an abstract and disconnected sense of place, the South has known guilt, poverty, failure, and a concrete sense of roots and place ("The Search for Southern Identity" in *The Burden of Southern History*). These myths collide in Elvis. His American success story was always acted out within its Southern limitations. No matter how successful Elvis became in terms of fame and money, he remained fundamentally disreputable in the minds of many Americans. Elvis had rooms full of gold records earned by million-copy sales, but his best rock and roll records were not formally honored by the people who control, if not the public taste, the rewarding of the public taste. Perhaps this is always the fate of innovators; awards are created long after the form is created. His movies made millions but could not be defended on artistic grounds. *The New York Times* view of his fans was "the men favoring leisure suits and sideburns, the women beehive hairdos, purple eyelids and tight stretch pants" (*New York Times* story by Wayne King, 8 Jan. 1978). Molly Ivins, trying to explain in *The New York Times* the crush of people and "genuine emotion" in Memphis when Elvis died would conclude, "It is not required that love be in impeccable taste." Later, in the year after his death, Mike Royko would sarcastically suggest that Elvis' body and effects be sent to Egypt in exchange for the King Tut exhibit. ("So in terms of sheer popularity, no other American dead body can stand up to Presley's.") The 'Doonesbury" cartoon strip would see fit to run a two-weeks sequence in which "Boopsie" would go visit Elvis' grave. Her boyfriend puts her down with, "2,000,000 necrophiliacs can't be wrong." Elvis' sheer commercial value commanded respect, but no amount of success could dispel the aura of strangeness about him. He remained an outsider in the American culture that adopted his music, his long hair, his unconventional clothes, and his freedom of sexual movement.

Although he was the world's most popular entertainer, to like Elvis a lot was suspect, a lapse of taste. It put one in beehives and leisure suits, in company with "necrophiliacs" and other weird sorts. The inability of Elvis to transcend his lack of reputability despite a history-making success story confirms the Southern sense that the world outside thinks Southerners are freaks, illiterates, Snopeses, sexual perverts, lynchers. I cannot call this sense a Southern "paranoia" because ten years outside the South has all too often confirmed the frequency with which non-Southerners express such views. Not even the presidency would free LBJ and Jimmy Carter from such ridicule. At the very moment in which Southerners proclaim most vehemently the specialness of Elvis, the greatness of his success, they understand it to mean that no Southern success story can ever be sufficient to satisfy a suspicious America.

Tupelo Railway Station, 1937.

And Elvis was truly different, in all those tacky Southern ways one is supposed to rise above with money and sophistication. He was a pork chops and brown gravy man. He liked peanut butter and banana sandwiches. He had too many cars, and they were too pink. He liked guns, and capes, and a Venus de Milo water fountain in the entry at Graceland. I once heard about 1958 that he had painted the ceiling at Graceland dark blue with little silver stars that twinkled in the dark. His taste never improved, and he never recanted anything. He was the sharecropper's son in the big house, and it always showed.

Compounding his case was the fact that Elvis didn't always appear fully white. Not sounding white was his first problem, and white radio stations were initially reluctant to play his records. Not to be clearly white was dangerous because it undermined the black-white rigidities of a segregated society, and to blur those definitions was to reveal the falseness at the core of segregation. Racial ambiguity is both the internal moral condemnation and the social destruction of a racist society which can only pretend to justify itself by abiding by its own taboos. Yet all Southerners know, despite the sternest Jim Crow laws, that more than two hundred years of racial mixing has left many a Southerner racially ambiguous. White Southerners admit only the reality of blacks who have some white blood, but, of course, the knife cuts both ways. Joe Christmas and Charles Bon. Desiree's Baby. In most pictures, Elvis might resemble a blue-eyed Adonis, but in some of those early black and white photographs, his eyes sultry, nostrils flared, lips sullen, he looked just that—black and white. And he dressed like blacks. His early wardrobe came from Lansky Brothers in Memphis. Maybe truck drivers wore greasy hair and long sideburns, but only the blacks were wearing zoot zuits and pegged pants with pink darts in them. Country singers might sequin cactus and saddles on satin shirts, Marty Robbins would put a pink carnation on a white sport coat, and Johnny Cash would be the man in black. Only Elvis would wear a pink sport coat with a black velvet collar. "The Memphis Flash," he was sometimes called.

The music was the obvious racial ambiguity. Elvis' use of black styles and black music angered many Southern blacks who resented the success he won with

With George Wallace.

Tupelo, Mississippi, March, 1936.

"Jitterbugging": Clarkesdale, Mississippi, 1939.

music that black artists had originated but could not sell beyond the "race record" market of a segregated commercial world. In interviews today, these black blues musicians usually say that Elvis stole everything from them, an understandable complaint but one that nevertheless ignores his fusion of black music with white country to create a genuinely new sound. He was the Hillbilly Cat singing "Blue Moon of Kentucky" and "That's All Right (Mama)." Elvis' role in fusing the native music of poor Southern whites and poor Southern blacks into rock and roll is the best known aspect of his career and his greatest accomplishment.

Students of rock always stress this early music, but the sentimental myth gives it less attention, though the records always sold better in the South than in any other region. The music in the myth is more often the love ballads and the Protestant hymns. Yet the music that was in reality most important to Southerners was the music most closely tied to Southern origins. Elvis himself seemed to understand this; compare, for example, his 1974 concert album from Memphis's Mid-South Coliseum (the "Graceland" album) with any other concert album. The music I remember hearing most was music like "Mystery Train," "One Night," "Lawdy Miss Clawdy," "Heartbreak Hotel," "Peace in the Valley," "Blue Christmas," and "American Trilogy." For Southerners, this fusion of "Dixie," "All My Trials," and "The Battle Hymn of the Republic" has nothing to do with the rest of America, although its popularity around the country suggests that other Americans do relate it to their own history. The trilogy seems to capture Southern history through the changes of the civil rights movement and the awareness of black suffering which had hitherto largely been excluded from popular white images of Southern history. The piece could not have emerged before the seventies because only then had the "marching" brought a glimmer of hope. Even Elvis could not have sung this trilogy in New York's Madison Square Garden before there was some reason for pride and hope in the South. Elvis was right to make the song his; it is an appropriate musical history from one whose music moved always in the fused racial experiences of the region's oppressed. Rock and roll, taking inside it rhythm and blues and country, was the rhythm of Southern life, Southern problems, and Southern hopes. It is not coincidence

that rock and roll emerged almost simultaneously with the civil rights movement, that both challenged the existing authority, and that both were forces for "integration."

The most stunning quality about Elvis and the music was the sexuality, yet the sentimental myth veers away from this disturbing complexity into the harmlessly romantic. Elvis might be "nice looking" or "cute" or perhaps "sexy," but not sexual. The sexuality he projected was complicated because it combined characteristics and appeals traditionally associated with both males and females. On one hand, he projected masculine aggression and an image of abandoned pleasure, illicit thrills, back alley liaisons and, on the other hand, a quality of tenderness, vulnerability, and romantic emotion. Andy Warhol captured something of this diversified sexuality in his portrait of Elvis, caught in a threatening stance with a gun in his hand but with the face softened in tone and line. The image made Elvis the perfect lover by combining the most appealing of male and female characteristics and satisfying both the physical desire for sensual excitement and the emotional need for loving tenderness. The music echoed the physical pleasure in rhythm and the emotional need in lyrics that said "Love Me," "Love Me Tender," "Don't," "I Want You I Need You I Love You," and "Don't Be Cruel." Unlike many later rock stars whose music would voice an assault on women, Elvis' music usually portrayed an emotional vulnerability to what women could do *to* him, as well as what he could do *for* them. When the public's notion of his heartbroken private life confirmed this sense of vulnerability, the image took on renewed power. Despite the evidence in the music or the long hair and lashes and full, rounded features, most Elvis fans would deny that his appeal is vaguely androgynous. Many male and female fans talk about Elvis as an ideal male image but would probably find it threatening to traditions of sexual identity to admit that the ideal male figure might indeed combine traditional male characteristics with some which are freely admitted only in women. In the South where sex roles are bound up with the remnants of a chivalric "way of life," open sexuality was allowable only in the "mysterious" lives of blacks, and permissible sexual traits in whites were rigidly categorized by sex. But the image of Elvis goes behind these stereotypes to some ideal of sexuality that combines the most attractive elements in each of them.

Women's sexual imaginations of Elvis have rarely been openly expressed, in part because women weren't supposed to have any explicit sexual fantasies and in part because those who did were perhaps least likely, because of the cultural and regional prohibitions, to admit them. Despite the mass of published material about Elvis, almost nothing of a serious nature by women has been printed. One remarkable exception is a short story by Julie Hecht, "I Want You I Need You I Love You" in *Harper's* (May 1978). Hecht's story makes the only serious effort I have seen to reveal those characteristics which gave Elvis' sexual appeal such complexity and power. The woman in the story remembers first imagining his kiss when she was twelve and didn't know what came after the kiss. Twenty years later in her fantasy of August 1977, she is able to "save" Elvis' life by getting him on a good health food diet. They become "best of friends," and she has her moment of tenderness: "I did get to touch him. I touched his hands, I touched his face, we hugged, we kissed, I kissed his hands, I kissed his face, I touched his face, I touched his arms, I touched his eyes, I touched his hair, I saw his smile, I heard his voice, I saw him move, I heard him laugh, I heard him sing" (*Harper's*, p. 67). This passage illustrates the obsessive physical attraction that combined with the illusion that Elvis was really sweet, tender, and in need of loving care. Seeing or hearing Elvis was never enough; one had to try to touch him. In life, such fans tore at his clothes and his person; in death, they visit his grave. Does any woman really care whether or not Elvis loved his mother or Jesus? But I never met a female fan who did not detest Priscilla. "Somebody ought to put a bullet through her," a pleasant faced middle-aged saleswoman in a bookstore once told me.

Elvis said he grew sideburns because he wanted to look like truck drivers, and many such men would later want to look like him. One important element in Elvis' sexual appeal for men seemed to be the acting out of the role of the "hood" who got the girl, won the fight, and rose above all the economic powerlessness of real hoods. Men who because of class and economic binds knew their own limitations seemed especially attracted to this aspect of the image. They wore their hair like his, affected his mannerisms, sang with his records. Men too sophisticated to betray themselves in such overt ways betrayed themselves in other ways. I remember a highly educated man rhapsodizing about how phallic the black leather suit was that Elvis wore in his 1968 television appearance. When Elvis aged and put on weight, men were his cruelest detractors. They seemed to take his appearance as a personal offense.

Beyond the money, the power, the fame, there was always at some level this aspect of Elvis, the American Dream in its Southern variation. Like other great Southern artists, Elvis revealed those characteristics of our culture which we know better than outsiders to be part of the truth. In Elvis was also the South that is bizarre, or violent, or darkly mysterious, the South called the grotesque in Faulkner or O'Connor. Perhaps this is why a book like *Elvis: What Happened?* could not damage the appeal. The hidden terrors, pain, and excesses of the private life which the book reveals, despite its mean-spirited distortions, only make the image more compelling in its familiarity. Even his drug problem had a familiar Southern accent—prescription medicines, cough syrups, diet pills.

Elvis' South is not the old cotton South of poor but genteel aristocrats. His Mississippi is not that of Natchez. Elvis is the Mississippi of pulpwood, sharecroppers, small merchants. His Memphis had nothing to do with riverboats or the fabled Beale Street. Elvis' Memphis was the post-World War II city of urban sprawl, racial antagonism, industrial blight, slums, Humes High. He walked the real Beale Street. Despite Graceland, and "Dixie" in Madison Square Garden, Elvis was the antithesis of the Rhett and Scarlett South. But no one living in the South today ever knew the Rhett and Scarlett South. Southerners themselves go to Natchez as to a tourist attraction. Elvis' South was the one that most Southerners really experience, the South where not even the interstate can conceal the poverty, where industrial affluence threatens the land and air which have been so much a part of our lives, where racial violence touches deep inside the home, where even our successes cannot overcome the long reputation of our failures. Even Graceland is not really beautiful. Squeezed in on all sides by the sprawl of gas stations, banks, shopping plazas, and funeral homes, Elvis' beloved home is an image of the South that has been "new" now for over fifty years.

Elvis evoked the South of modern reality with a fidelity he could not himself escape. The South rewarded him with its most cherished myths, but Elvis' tragedy was that he got caught in the contradictions. We only wanted to be able to claim that he was a good boy who loved Jesus. He apparently needed to become that, to live out the mythic expectations. He hungered for approval. The problem was that most of what Elvis really was could never be so transmogrified. He *was* the king of rock and roll, but he was uncomfortable with what the title implied. Linda Thompson has said that in his later years he hated hard rock. The further he moved from the conventions of the romantic myth, the more he proclaimed them. The more drugs he used, the more he supported law and order. When the counter culture he helped to usher in became widespread, he thought of helping the FBI as an undercover agent. How could he not be schizophrenic at the end, balancing the rock myth he created, the sentimental myth he adopted, and the emotional needs that made him like anyone else? He was destroyed by having to be what he was and wanting to be what he thought he ought to be. The Jesus-loving boy singing dirty Christ-

Elvis and his entourage ("Memphis Mafia") receive official police badges from the Memphis Police Department.

mas songs. "One Night" and "How Great Thou Art."

After Elvis died, it was necessary to deify him. It isn't after all, very becoming to grieve for a rock idol who died, as *The New York Times* once put it, "puffy and drug-wasted." But saying what and why one grieved was difficult. The South has had a lot of practice mythologizing painful and ambiguous experiences into glamorous and noble abstractions. So it was from Graceland to the Promised Land. Rex Humbard told us that Elvis found peace in Jesus, and Billy Graham assured us that Elvis was in Heaven. Billy was even looking forward to visiting him there. A disc jockey playing "How Great Thou Art" reflects at the end of the record, "And he certainly was." In Tupelo the Elvis Presley Memorial Foundation is building a $125,000 Chapel of Inspiration in his memory. Memphis will put a 50-ton bronze statue on a river bluff. Priscilla wants their daughter to remember, most of all, his humbleness. He loved his Jesus, his daughter, his lost wife. He loved his daddy. He loved the South. He was a great humanitarian. "God saw that he needed some rest and called him home to be with Him," the tombstone reads. Maybe all of this is even true. The apotheosis of Elvis demands such perfection because his death confirmed the tragic frailty, the violence, the intellectual poverty, the extravagance of emotion, the loneliness, the suffering, the sense of loss. Almost everything about his death, including the enterprising cousin who sold the casket pictures to *National Enquirer*, dismays, but nothing can detract from Elvis himself. Even this way, he is as familiar as next door, last year, the town before.

Greil Marcus wrote in his book *Mystery Train: Images of America in Rock 'n' Roll Music* that Elvis created a beautiful illusion, a fantasy that shut nothing out. The opposite was true. The fascination was the reality always showing through the illusion—the illusion of wealth and the psyche of poverty; the illusion of success and the pinch of ridicule; the illusion of invincibility and the tragedy of frailty; the illusion of complete control and the reality of inner chaos. In Faulkner's *Absalom, Absalom!* Shreve thinks that Quentin hates the South. He does not understand that Quentin is too caught in it ever to have thought of such a question, just as Elvis was and just as we were in Elvis. Elvis had all the freedom the world can offer and could escape nothing. What chance that the South could escape him, reflecting it as he did?

Southerners do not love the old Confederacy because it was a noble ideal, but because the suffering of the past occasioned by it has formed our hearts and souls, both good and evil. But we celebrate the past with cheap flags, cliche slogans, decorative license plates, decaled ash trays, and a glorious myth of a Southern "way of life" no one today ever lived. And Southerners do not love Elvis because he loved Jesus or anyone else. The Elvis trinkets, his picture on waste cans or paperweights or T-shirts or glowing in the dark from a special frame, all pay the same kind of homage as the trinkets in worship of the past. People outside the Elvis phenomenon may think such commercialization demeans the idol and the idolater. But for those who have habitually disguised the reality of their culture from even themselves, it is hard to show candidly what and why one loves. In impeccable taste. By the most sentimental people in history.

THE BOOTLEG ELVIS
BY JOHN WALKER

First you hear a kind of tinkling sound, not unlike a miniature babbling brook. Then a low roar, like Niagara Falls from the inside of a barrel. And that sound fades, to be replaced by a faint mechanical clicking. The clicking comes to an abrupt halt, drowned out by a deep voice that says, very clearly and very loudly, *"Yow!"*

There is a flurry of footsteps. A fist knocks politely on a metal door, and a different voice, higher and more heavily accented, says, "Ev'y thing okay in there?"

A metal bolt snaps and the first voice speaks again. "Ah put a *nick* in mah dick!"

Raucous laughter bounces off the tile surroundings and a faint third voice hoots, "Call Dr. Nick!"

A fourth voice barks, "Yessir! Yessir!"

There follows another blast of snorting and cackling which slowly fades into a dull hiss.

And that's the "A-Side" of a little platter called "Powder Room Only." The other side consists of a conversation between Col. Tom Parker and an unidentified man who wants to enter the Men's Room. The Colonel patiently explains that Elvis simply cannot urinate in the presence of strangers and tells the man to come back in an hour.

"**W**here can I *get* this record?", you might ask. Where indeed? Not at your local Disc-O-Mat, that's for damn sure. We're talking "Bootlegs" here, those vinyl outlaws that say more about an artist's popularity by their mere existence than all the gold records in the world. And Elvis Presley's name is on *hundreds* of them.

Now, the *appeal* of bootlegs is obvious. First off, they usually press less than a thousand copies of each title, so it gives you the opportunity to own something that almost no one else has. On the other hand, it's probably something that no one else particularly *wants*, either. With Elvis, though, the range of product is phenomenal. Live recordings of everything from the "Louisiana Hayride" to Elvis' unintentionally final performance in Indianapolis. Studio out-takes filched from the RCA vaults. Press conferences, phone interviews, TV appearances, you name it, someone taped it. Granted, there's some very strange stuff on the market, but certainly no stranger than, say, a record of an Elvis performance with the *songs* edited out, leaving nothing but Elvis' between-song rambling. And *that* record was released by RCA: *Having Fun With Elvis On Stage*, they called it. If that's their idea of fun, then surely they'd appreciate a record of Elvis ducking a phone call, which, in comparison, doesn't really seem all that weird. You might not want to play it at a party, but what the hell, it's something to have.

What follows is a random sampling of what's available under better counters.

"Hysterical fun with Elvis in the studio as he laughs his way through the studio session— trying to get a good take on a song he obviously finds amusing."— catalogue description of *A Dog's Life*. Well, after a build-up like that, the record itself is kind of a let-down. As any casual Elvis fan knows, it didn't take a hell of a lot to amuse The King. Hell, Elvis cracking up in the studio ain't strange, it's *traditional*. Well, hee hee hee, most of the record is pretty straight stuff like "My Way" and "Rock-A-Hula Baby." However, there *is* a great picture of Elvis biting a dog on the cover.

Records like *A Dog's Life* are pretty ubiquitous. Most of them, unfortunately, are pretty El Blando. However, if we back-track a few years, we hit a vein of historical importance.

When Elvis was still under the guiding thumb of Sam Phillips, the Sun studios served as sort of a clubhouse for Elvis and his rockabilly compatriots. Phillips was also one for just letting the tape roll, and some of the most sought-after bootlegs ever came out of these sessions.

Good Rocking Tonight is, like Col. Tom, allegedly Dutch in origin. This would seem to be borne out by the thoughtfully restored "g" in "Rocking." Though the real highlight of this mixed bag is an amphetamine-fueled argument between Jerry Lee Lewis and Sam Phillips regarding The Devil's place in rock music, there is one full side of Elvis making the transit from Country-Western to Rockabilly. Apparently, the flash of a red "Recording" light was never just cause to cease the incessant yakking that seemed to seep onto all these Sun recordings. Mr. Sam frequently makes his opinions known from his seat behind the control panel, and during the second or third false start of a song called "I'll Never Let You Go, Little Darlin'," someone even calls Elvis a nigger.

The hot item of hot items, however, is the legendary "Million Dollar Quartet" session which recently surfaced in a flurry of mystery. While the existence of these tapes has been known for some time, legal wrangles have kept them out of the paws of collectors. Until now. Sort of. See, everybody and his mother claimed ownership of the property, which boasted Elvis, Jerry Lee Lewis, Carl Perkins, and, *maybe*, Johnny Cash, and last I heard, some judge ruled that since Carl Perkins

paid for the original session, then if Carl wanted to make a goddamn May-pole out of the master tape, well, that's Carl's prerogative. So there.

Of course, legality has never been a strong factor governing the release of a bootleg, so what we have here is barely a half-hour's worth of a much lengthier session.

Here's the thing: on the cover, it says "Million Dollar Quartet." There's a big picture of the four of them hunched over a piano. All four names are listed *tres* prominently. You've got liner notes that gush awe at the fact that these four Collassi of Memphis actually achieved this cosmic union, etc. etc. etc. Then, down around the second paragraph, someone gets around to admitting that Johnny Cash isn't actually *on* this record. Which would make it the $750,000 Trio wouldn't it? Well, wouldn't it?

In the end, you get mostly Elvis, Carl, and Jerry Lee harmonizing the hell out of a hymnal, and just futzing around in general. P.S. They claim that The Man In Black probably showed up later on.

A major source of bootleg material used to be the audio portion of Elvis' TV appearances. Of course, now that just about everybody but the RCA Victor dog owns a VTR, a true fanatic might poo-poo these pictureless transcriptions. However, it can't be denied that there is some amazingly bizarre stuff available in this format.

T.V. Guide Presents Elvis takes its name from one of the first big Elvis collector's items, a "Promotional-Only" disc on which Elvis sullenly repudiates random subject matter. However, most of the material consists of Elvis' rare TV appearances. Without the visuals, these tapes have a fairly surreal quality, and when you add the fact that Elvis' various TV hosts tended to treat him like Frances The Talking Mule, you're guaranteed an aural potpourri that probably does more to explain why Elvis went crazy than a hundred copies of *Elvis: What Happened?*.

First off is Elvis' *Steve Allen Show* appearance. After performing a couple of numbers dressed, apparently, in formal evening wear, Elvis trades in his tails for a cowboy suit. Why? All the better to perform comedy, my dear, which Elvis does indeed in the heady company of Mr. Allen, Imogene Coca, and Andy Griffith. The finale is a "Yippie-yi-yo-ki-yay"-type number which concludes with Elvis grumbling *I got a horse and I got a gun / and I'm goin' out and have some fun / I'm a'warnin' you, Galoot, don't step on my blue suede boot.*

Then there's the *Frank Sinatra Timex Special*, where Elvis has to fend off not only Frankie, but the entire Rat Pack as well. After enduring a lot of "sideburn" jokes, Elvis duets with Frank on a medley of "Witchcraft" and "Love Me Tender," two songs which blend about as well as you would expect. The segment ends with Sinatra warning Elvis to keep his paws off his daughter Nancy "on account'a she's spoken for."

Now, here's what Elvis would've called the "Hy"-point of the album (and actually gotten away with it)—a segment of a show called "Hy Gardner Calling." Hy Gardner had a telephone, a split-screen set up, and seemed compelled to ask his guests questions of the "Have You Stopped Beating Your Wife?" variety.

The interview proceeds, everything is going along o.k. . . . well, maybe El sounds a trifle put-out, but does well enough considering that by that point he must have had the Bell Tel. logo permanently ground into his ear. Then Hy's voice crackles evily over the wire, you know, he's just got a couple of things he'd kind of like to clear up. . . .

"What about the rumor that you once shot your mother?" What the . . . ! Elvis lets out a long nervous giggle. Elvis figures that that one takes the cake.

> Hy: "Where'd that one come from? Do you have any idea?"
> Elvis: (Abruptly) "I have no idea, I can't imagine. When you mentioned it to me it was the first time I ever heard it."
> Hy: "Is that right? . . . Well, there's another one too you may never have heard before—several newspaper stories hinted that you smoked marijuana in order to work yourself into a frenzy while singing. What about that?"

Elvis groans loudly and Hy lets him off the hook. Of course, now we all know that Elvis, like Lenny Bruce, considered marijuana a "schluffy" high. And, of course, that's the kind of stuff that might make you shoot your mama.

The last item in the audio-video category is a strange little artifact called *Elvis Presley—Forever Young, Forever Beautiful*.

Actually, the word "strange" just doesn't do this record justice. Inspiredly perverse. That's more like it. What else can you say about a recording that consists mainly of Elvis hogging the piano at a party and singing a song called "Happy, Happy Birthday Baby" six times in a row? Well, he doesn't actually *sing* it every time. Sometimes he gets his hosts to put on a *record* of his girl-friend Anita Wood singing *her* version of it and Elvis sort of *moans* along with it. However, since the phono-graph is somewhere in the far reaches of microphone range, you get a balance of about 10% record, 90% Elvis. Moaning. Real loud.

But maybe I'm not giving the whole picture. "Spend an intimate evening," the liner notes read, "with Elvis, his girlfriend Anita Wood, the Fadal family, Eddie, his lovely wife LaNelle, and their children Janice Lyn and Dana. . . . You will hear Elvis, the perfectionist, as he strives to hit the perfect note on "Happy, Happy Birth-day Baby." You will listen along with Elvis as he learns the song "Tomorrow Night." "A Closer Walk With Thee" will bring a tear to your eye and joy to your heart everytime you hear it." Well, it certainly brought a tear to the eye of one of the wee Fadals, who, ob-viously getting the short shrift on attention in the pres-ence of The King, wails lustily in the background throughout most of the record.

And, don't forget, some people actually own all this on *video tape*! According to an Elvis afficianado of my acquaintance, the video is particularly neat because you see Elvis makin' out with Anita Wood. That Elvis!

Now let's take a little commercial break in the form of a United Press News item thoughtfully included on an LP called *PRESLEYMANIA, VOL. 1*. While a hot sax wails "Heartbreak Hotel" in the background, an announcer who sounds suspiciously like Jack Webb reads off a list of available Presley paraphernalia as if it were a compilation of heinous crimes they'd managed to pin on Elvis.

"Elvis Presley, possibly the hottest name in the record field today and one of filmdom's greatest new sensations seems to be the most desired name in a number of other fields as well. Firms throughout the country have been *begging* for licenses to use the Presley name on their products, and, to date, he is identified with the following:

"T-Shirts, knit pajamas, pencils, purses, wallets, denims, gold-plated adjustable rings, socks, necklaces, pins, guitars, shoes, charm bracelets, handkerchiefs, buttons, scarves, skirts, jackets, hats, *binders* (Good lord!), stuffed *hound dogs* (Choke!), wrist-watches, deco-rative pillows, mirrors, key chains, mittens, scrap books, diaries, photo albums, plaster *busts*, book-ends, shirts, talking records (Prophetic, huh?), fan magazines, *molded* plastic painted *figurines* (Now come on!), 8 × 10 *luminous* pictures, bermuda shorts, capri and *torea-dor* pants (The nerve!), games, lipsticks, co-lognes and trading . . ."

It cuts off there, but I figure the last word was either *cards* or *posts*.

Poor Elvis. As you might have guessed, a lot of people use to just *get* on him, and, in response, Elvis felt compelled to periodically explain himself. And then put it out as a record.

The Truth About Me is a "re-issue" of one of those little flimsy cardboard tear-outs that came, according to the label, with a 1956 fan magazine, and, boy, is it depressing. It sounds like Elvis making a drunken 3 a.m. phone call to a buddy and getting one of those penny-arcade Record-Your-Voice booths by mistake. Through a combination of ham-fisted tape editing and general incoherency, Elvis just *lurches* without pause through a catalogue of subjects that seem to have been weighing heavily on his mind.

While a syrupy string rendition of "Love Me Tender" bleats in the background, you get a classic

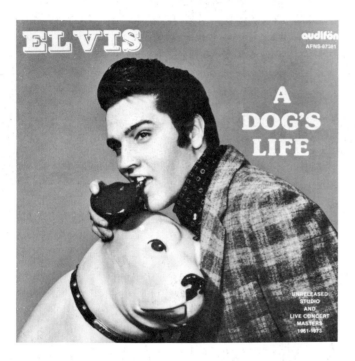

summation of the trauma of being Elvis.

"Hi, this is Elvis Presley. I guess the first thing people want to know is why I can't stand still while I'm singin'. Some people tap their feet, some people snap their fingers, and some people just sway back and forth. I just sort of do'em all together, I guess . . . singin' rhythm and blues really knocks it out. I watch my audience and listen to'em and I know that we're all getting something out of our system and none of us knows what it is. The important thing is, we're gettin' rid of it an' nobody's gettin' hurt. I s'pose you know I've got a lot of cars . . . people have written about it in the papers and a lot of them ask, uh, *write* and ask me why. Well, when I was driving a truck, every time a big shiny car'd go by, it started me sorta day-dreamin'. I always felt that someday, somehow, somethin' would happen to change everything and I'd day-dream about how that would be. The first car I ever bought was the most beautiful

car I've ever seen. It was a second hand, but I parked it outside my hotel the day I got it and set up all night just lookin' at it and the next day, well, the thing caught fire and burned up . . . on the road. And a lot of the mail I get, people ask questions 'bout the kinda things I do, an' that sorta stuff. Well, I don't smoke, I don't drink an' I love to go to movies. Maybe someday I'm gonna have a home and a family on my own an' I'm not gonna budge on'em. I was an only child, but maybe my kids won't be. I s'pose this kinda talk raises another question . . . Am I in love. No, I thought I been in love, but I guess I wasn't . . . it just passed over . . . I guess I haven't met the girl yet, but I will, and I hope it won't be too long 'cause I get lonesome sometimes . . . I get lonesome right in the middle of a crowd . . . I really feel that with her, whoever she may be, I won't be lonesome no matter where I am . . . Well, thanks for letting me talk to you an' sorta get things off my chest . . . I want to thank my loyal fans who watched my performances and then became friends of mine. I sure appreciate you listenin' to my RCA Victor Records and I'd like to thank all the disc-jockeys for playin 'em. Bye-bye." Bye, El.

At last we come to the grand pinnacle of Elvis bootleg-iana, *Elvis Talks Back*. The title is misleading. In fact, sometimes Elvis doesn't even talk at all, as you'll soon see.

Side One consists of a press conference held in Vancouver with a d.j. named Red Robinson and is, as these things go, pretty run-of-the-mill. Side Two, however, contains a couple of masterpieces.

It's always a great thrill when two giants of the entertainment industry come together, and somebody obviously figured they had another King Kong vs. Godzilla on their hands when they set up the historic meeting of Elvis and . . . Peter Noone (!!!), A.K.A. "Herman" of "Herman's Hermits" fame.

Surrounded by his cronies, Elvis has a good old time with young 'erman, though you can't help but wonder if perhaps they weren't just shoved into a giant coffee can by a fifty-foot third grader. Herman, all full of piss and vinegar, asks a series of scintillating questions along the lines of the following:

> *Herman:* "When are you coming to England?
> *Elvis:* Comin' to *where*? Oh, 'scuse me, comin' to England? (listlessly) I don't know . . . maybe in a year or so. . . ."

Herman astutely points out that, despite all the grand hoopla that accompanies every rumor of an impending visit to the U.K., ol' El never quite seems to make it over. "Well," says Elvis mechanically, "Col. Parker has a bad back and so forth." (*Now* it dawns on me where this record gets its title!)

"Yessir, yessir!", hoots the Colonel enthusiastically.

To put it politely, the talk goes on in this vein for quite some time. Herman manages to button-hole Elvis into admitting that "Herman's Hermits" is one of his favorite groups. Then, amidst all the forced camaraderie provided by Elvis' portable human laugh-track,

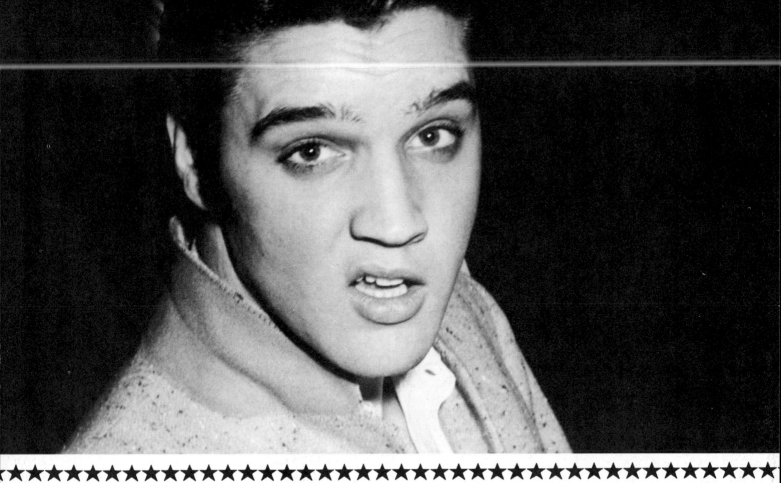

★★

poor Herman gets . . . the creeps.

A bit nervously, Herman points out, "Everybody's . . . *laughing* around here . . . The *sun*, is it?"

Elvis: (tightly) "Yeah, it's the sun. It gits to your head after a while. . . ."

Caught up in a whirlwind of free-association, Herman asks, "What happens every time it rains?"

"We stop and come inside," says Elvis with barely concealed contempt. Turning to Tom Moffet, the fifty-foot-third-grader KPOI d.j. running the show, Elvis sums it all up.

"Tom," says Elvis sarcastically, "This is probably the best interview you've ever had."

After a work-out like that, Elvis needs a little rest. Even on his own bootleg. So it's only fitting that Elvis' wrassle with Peter Noone be followed by a *real* heavyweight bout: Colonel Parker vs. Red Robinson.

Y'all remember Red. He m.c.'d the big show in Vancouver in 1957. And now he'd like to just say "Hi" to Elvis. . . .

Col. Parker: "Gosh, I wish you'd have called about *ten minutes* ago. He *just* left."

The next sound you hear is Red Robinson kicking himself. Then the Colonel rubs it in a little. "He *just* walked out of here." Meanwhile, you can practically hear Elvis eating a sandwich in the background.

Red: "All I wanted to know, you know, if we could get two minutes of 'Howdy' or something. . . ."

Col. Parker: : Well, you can get a few 'Yessirs' and 'Nosirs' from *me*."

Red laughs humorlessly. He and the Colonel engage in a little mutual ass-kissing and, next thing you know, Red is down on his knees. "Is there any chance at all in the next *year* that we might get a minute and a half with Elvis on the phone?"

Now, I forgot to mention, one thing that *really* impresses the Colonel is good manners.

"Well," says Col. Tom, "I'll tell ya, you're very nice about asking 'in the next *year*', so I'm askin' if it's possible in the next *five* years?" For a minute and a half of "Howdy."

Well, I shouldn't have to tell you. . . . The punchline is, as a consolation prize, Red is offered—so help me—a copy of the "Elvis meets Peter Noone" tape. Oh, joy.

"I think," counsels the Colonel, "that tape will hold you for *a long time*. That's a *funny* one."

Ann-Margret

Tuesday We

A LETTER TO ELVIS

BY KAREN MOLINE

Dear Elvis:

There were always women in your life but I wasn't one of them. I'm just one of the millions, the fans, the expectant sobbing screaming mass of women that wanted you and held every breath that you sang deep in their hearts. If you had looked at any of us we could have saved you, we would have loved you, you'd be happy, you'd flash us that special steamy pouty grin, and you'd be thin and sleekly beautiful, swiveling those hips in our direction, and you'd sing us a special song, hugging the microphone close, pretending it was our face. Your face was so special to watch; it was soft and babylike and pouty one minute and then suddenly it would be harder and lusting and would seem to say come here baby I want some lovin, not raunchy or crazy but sweet and tender, it said SEX, baby, I need it. And we'd melt and get all mushy inside and nearly faint and just have to sit down and DIE.

But you never saw me, Elvis, though I knew about you and all your women. There were always women in your life, but you died alone.

Your earliest memories were of your Mama, Gladys. You were the center of her universe, her sun, and she was Mother Earth. There were two smaller stars for her, your Daddy Vernon, and her lord Jesus, but they paled in comparison to your fire; you shone more brightly. She lived for you, she loved you like crazy, double even, to blot out the memory of your dead twin brother, she walked you to school, she doted on you, she paced up and down at night if you sneezed and had a cold, she had premonitions, worrying, she slaved and scrubbed and sweated for you so you wouldn't think you were too poor or lowdown or just plain common trash, and she died trying to make you happy. She was too young to die, wanting to lose those Southern-fried pounds, only forty-six; she had just worked too hard and never let up and took all those diet pills and worried about you all the time, and you were traveling and singing and being a big hit and caused her all the more grief when you weren't at home so much. So. She had hepatitis, and heart disease, and she never told you how sick she felt inside and how scared, she'd never do anything to cause you pain. Six days after she was admitted to the hospital her heart gave up. It was August 14, 1958 and it was the biggest shock of your life. She wanted you to be proud of her, and you WERE and you did love her something powerful, too saintly she was, you bought her Cadillacs she never drove, and a big white house and she still hung out the wash and made the neighbors mad. It wasn't fair you cried how could she die I wanted to give her EVERYTHING. "Oh God, everything I have is gone," you sobbed at her funeral, and it made you crazy, you needed her, she was always there for you, no matter what, even if you were bad and feeling guilty, she loved you. So you learned, at the height of your power, that love and loss are inseparable; and the more you loved her the more it hurt you to lose her, and it made you wary and unsure and you, the King, afraid to really love, even when it was there in front of you.

Priscilla

Joan Blackman

A Fan

No, you never told your Mama when you were bad. You had fun chasing the girls but she wanted you to settle down with a nice one, like Dixie Locke, your High School sweetheart, or Anita Wood, your Memphis steady before you went into the Army. You took Anita roller skating, and to amusement parks, and watched TV together, and you gave her a big ol' diamond ring. But she wasn't the one.

You didn't find the real one till you went as Private Elvis to Germany. Priscilla Beaulieu, Army brat, was not quite 15 when you met her, and she sure caught your eye, she was so young and beautiful, and sure of herself and unlike the older, flashy set of women you'd been hanging out with. Fame and money and Hollywood brought lotsa women, Elvis, and you were guilty as any good ol' boy in—well, indulgence. Yet deep in your heart you wanted a lover, a wife, a mother that would've made your Mama proud, an innocent unspoiled and worshipping woman.

Your Mama would never know about all those movie stars. She heard about Natalie Wood, of course, in 1955, when the two of you tore up the town on that motorcycle. When, in one of these early years in Hollywood, someone asked you about being a sex symbol, you scoffed, "They all think I'm a sex maniac. They're just old types anyway. I'm just natural." Being natural meant being a Southern charmer, and you would just flash that grin and be real polite cause your Mama raised you right and there they were. You had a disarming habit of falling in love with your leading ladies, didn't you. The first was Debra Paget, but she wasn't interested cuz she was dating Howard Hughes at the time, oh well. Juliet Prowse, however, forgot all about her beau Frank Sinatra, when she met you. And then there was Ursula Andress, Deborah Walley, May Ann Mobley, Rita Moreno, Kim Novak, Yvonne Lime, Yvonne Craig, Peggy Lipton, Nancy Sinatra, Donna Douglas, Shelley Fabares, Raquel Welch, and Ann-Margret.

You loved Ann-Margret, it's obvious to anyone who watched the two of you in VIVA LAS VEGAS!—the chemistry is there, the certain gleam in your eyes, I could see it I couldn't STAND IT, the fun you had dancing like crazed banshees, how you unselfishly let the camera upstage your own performance and concentrate on her face, how you were "married" in the movie. I knew you wanted to marry her, for real, and she'd call Graceland even though Priscilla was living there and her codename was Bunny, and poor Priscilla was so jealous. Yet when you insisted that Ann-Margret give up the career she had worked all her life for, she refused, and that ended it. And Priscilla's career was to become Mrs. Elvis P. . . .

And your Mama never knew about those other ladies, either, the ones that came after the stars and the starlets, those German bar girls, or the girls you met on tour, and liked, and needed for a short while, and you DID make them happy, I bet most of them would remember a weekend with you as one of the happiest of their lives, and maybe you gave them a car or a ring, but it didn't matter, it was Taking Care of Business. TCB was as much a part of you as was the memory of your Mama, or the fiance waiting for you at Graceland. "You know, Dee, I've been to bed with no less than a thousand women in my life," you candidly told your step-mother IN 1961. But Priscilla, "This is the one, right here."

You couldn't live without women, Elvis, but did you ever really forgive your Daddy for remarrying Dee Stanley in July, 1960? Luckily, though, this marriage provided you with the three little step-brothers that would become your companions, and more important, with the perfect chaper-ones for Priscilla. So what if Priscilla was ten years younger than you, you persuaded her Daddy to let her visit Graceland at Christmas, 1960, and you convinced him once again that she should live in Memphis, with Vernon and Dee, and finish High School at Immaculate Conception, and you'd marry her someday and love her and take care of her forever. Nobody knew that two months after she moved to your Daddy's, she really moved into your bedroom. You were discreet. We could still hope you'd get tired of her and then you'd see us at your concerts and you'd sing for us and decide that we were the ones. No. You groomed her and she waited. It took you six years, but you finally proposed to her on another Christmas, in 1966, and the wedding was on May 1, 1967. I'll never forget it, nor that exactly nine months later your only child, Lisa Marie Presley, was born. You were so happy, beaming, crazy about that baby. She'd love you like nobody else, she wouldn't ask questions, you were her King and she your little Princess. Five years later, they were both gone, your Queen and your l'il Darlin, but no, Priscilla was never really a Queen, you needed the throne to yourself.

I used to wonder about you and Priscilla and how she felt being stuck in that big ol' mansion with women camped out all the time and trying to sneak in and convince you to marry them and screaming for you all the time and ready to die for you. She was nice and loved you and I bet she just wanted you home most of the time, and be alone together a bit, once

Linda Williams

Anita Wood

Dorothy Harmony

in awhile, and some semblance of a normal relationship. You were gone for 85% of your marriage! You weren't about to change for any woman, not even your wife; you had to be accepted the way you were. But you left her, Elvis, you ASKED FOR IT, yes, I bet deep down you WANTED HER TO LEAVE because you were so afraid of being truly loved like your Mama, you were so afraid you DROVE her away. HOW COULD YOU!!! We all loved you, we longed to touch you, you made us swoon—and the woman YOU chose and trained and bought everything for—cars and horses and a whole ranch even and a pink puttputt motorcycle and jewels and furs—SHE left you. She'd had it! The ultimate and most devastating irony! THE sex symbol, THE voice, THE King, the one WE lived for couldn't live with his own wife, who understood him more completely than any of us (though we wanted to). I couldn't hate Priscilla, I didn't want her to die so I could marry you, but I cried for days after the divorce, you looked so lonely, I felt so betrayed and hurt not just for Priscilla and her broken hopes, and for Lisa Marie's broken home, but for you most of all, Elvis, you ruined it. You had cheated on her for so long. She knew it, but she finally couldn't live with you, locked up in Graceland, unable to see you or travel with you, and she knew about those little black books and the TCBing in Las Vegas and the paternity suits and the damn double standard and it killed you most of all to have her run off with the karate instructor, of all people, even though that didn't last, it was that she dared leave you. And you knew it. You ruined it. You broke each other's hearts.

So the boys tried to cheer you up. Luckily they found Linda Thompson, and aside from Priscilla, she lived with you longer than any woman, and dedicated four years of her life to helping you and loving you and staying awake to watch your breathing when you'd taken too many pills and she was afraid. Oh Elvis we could have saved you. Well, maybe.

Linda was good for you, though, great even, though she was a wee bit flashy, a former beauty queen, model-thin and she loved clothes and

Dolores Hart

Tickle Me

Linda Thompson

Ursula Andress and Elsa Cardenas

Ann-Margret

Hope Lange

jewels—you bought her ¼-million worth—and cars and things. You let her travel with you on the road, unlike Priscilla, she wasn't your wife and had no childen, and at that point in your life you needed someone there all the time, and she was, on call twenty-four hours a day, she knew you. She was smart, too, and spoiled you and wrote you silly notes that your Daddy's secretary swiped: "Baby gullion you are just a little fella. Little fellas need lots of butch, ducklin, and iddytream sure. Sure I said it. Iddytream? Grit. Chock. Chock. Shake. Rattle. Roll. Hmmmmm. . . . Grit. Roll again. Hit. Hit. Pinch. Bite. Bite. Bite. Hurt. Grit. Whew. . . ." In fact her world revolved around you and she was patient when you saw other women like Sheila Ryan and Cybill Shepherd, or hung out with the boys, or stayed high too long, or ate a bit too much. But finally she couldn't stand the constant stream of it, she needed time to herself and you slowly drifted apart. Probably just as well, you were fading, sinking, your body gone soft, your spirit drifting, your strongest loves, your daughter, well she was rarely home, and your music, well it was there, but it too had gone soft, it wasn't the same, it didn't seem to hold you.

Two weeks after Linda left for good, in November 1976, the boys found you Ginger Alden, a beautiful twenty-year-old Priscilla lookalike. She was nice, but too young for you and your needs, but you were scared then, scared of losing your voice and your body and your sex appeal and she was living proof that you still had it, still had something, a certain credibility, living the American Dream, the eternal myth of poor-boy-makes-good and gets the girl of his choice, or the football player and the homecoming queen. . . . You introduced her at shows as "my new girlfriend" and she'd beam at you and flash a happy smile and tell all her friends that you were getting married. But you argued a lot, and she was fast asleep when you went into your bathroom for the last time.

What were you thinking as you fell?

Maybe it was about your fans. We still loved you. We weren't like the rich folk from Hollywood who flashed it all and bled you dry, no limos for us, just the tedium of work and raising a family and struggling and you were there, YOU UNDERSTOOD US, you filled our lives when we were lonely, you knew instinctively how we needed you and what to give us, you were always patient with us, you never gave us up, you knew what

Juliet Prowse

Paradise, Hawaiian Style

Ginger Alden

we thought, how we needed lovin', and you didn't send the dogs on us when we'd crowd around the fence at Graceland and wait for you or maybe climb the fence and pester everyone; and we'd always wait for you, and try to touch you, your face, your clothes, just a bit of something that had touched you would bring magic to our lives, see if you were real, try to believe you saw us.

"I figure I better start worrying when they don't bother me any more," you said about your fans once, long ago. You couldn't go anywhere without being followed, you couldn't take out a date, or go for a walk, or go shopping, no, you had to rent the entire theater or amusement park or golf range and at first it was fun and made you feel powerful and special but then it got worse cuz you couldn't breathe without someone jumping and you forgot what life, what women, what was real outside of TCB. And though you loved us, Elvis, you knew we wanted to hear you, see you though there were so many extra pounds there your face was lost, we looked at you as if you were the same as ever, the same face, the same songs, WE DIDN'T SEE IT. We loved you and we understood. We could have saved you. How could you have been such a baby and so sexually irresistible at the same time? We didn't want to mother you, we wanted our eyes to lock, and you, the King, would make us the new Queen, and sing for us. I only wanted you to sing for me.

No. I bet you forgot all about us. You never even saw my face.

I bet you saw your Mama in that bathroom. I bet you looked up and there she was, smiling, you dropped your book and she said, "Here I am darlin', I'll always be here," and your body started to tingle up from your toes and suddenly you were hot and sweaty and dizzy with joy, and she came closer and stretched out her arms to hold you and you knew this moment had been coming, you were waiting for it, you forgot us all, all those women, those dates, those playmates, those stars, those fans, your friends, your wife, your daughter, they were all gone, and it was suddenly bright white in the room and your Mama was there and you smiled, and sighed and closed your eyes. You saw your Mama.

Yours, with love,
A FAN

A REAL GONE CAT
BY STEPHANIE CHERNIKOWSKI

August 16, 1977. New York City. One of the most unpleasant evenings I have ever spent. I finally had to walk out of the Village Gate. Alex was passed out in the dressing room. He refused to get up to play his second set. Lester was at a table, face buried in folded arms, too drunk to raise the head no doubt heavy with what would become one of his more memorable eulogies. John was wandering around the street unable to remember which way was home. I had managed to see Martha into a cab and had given the cabbie her address. Unable to decide who to tackle next I shrugged them all off and went in search of food.

I had been taken aback when earlier that morning my sister Sandy had called from Texas to announce Elvis had died. Oh, yeah. I didn't even ask how, more puzzled by her calling than affected by her news. Sandy never called. The phones hadn't stopped ringing all day. They were all overreacting. Some fat, middle aged Vegas singer takes a lethal combination of pills and croaks in his crapper, and the entire New York music community goes on a nigh as lethal bender.

I found myself wandering far out of my way to Dave's Luncheonette where, contrary to my usual habits, I ordered a burger, fries, and a coke. Biting into a fry and sipping the coke, I felt the delicate stiffening of warm grease struck by the cold liquid. I smiled at the familiarity of the sensation so many years forgotten, recalling a day nearly twenty years earlier when I had sat silent in Janie Butterfield's '57 Chevy, repeatedly biting fries and sipping cokes, fascinated that I could make physical the deep nausea that I felt. We all wore black. We alternated getting out of the car to play the Jimmy Reed dirges, "Honest I Do" and "Baby, You Don't Have to Go," over and over on the Pig Stand Drive-In's inevitably impeccable juke box. No one spoke. There was nothing to say. He was gone. So what if he were coming to Texas. This is March 25, 1958 and the King is Dead. Elvis had been inducted into the army. They had cut his hair.

Janie was always the hippest kid in the class. She was the first girl to break the skirts-for-girls dress code by wearing Levis to Henry Wadsworth Longfellow Elementary school in the fifth grade. Button fly and shrunk to fit by soaking in the bath tub and worn till dry. Janie was clearly privy to some clandestine connection to cool in the outside world that the rest of the population of Beaumont, Texas neither could have nor wished to know about.

Beaumont, a Gulf Coast town between Houston and the Louisiana border, was the region strapped in by the Bible Belt from which there poured eternal sulfurous gasses. By the sixth grade all children of respectable families (at least those not prohibited by their church) were enrolled in ballroom dancing classes at the Arthur Murray Studios where they could be taught the social graces of the foxtrot, the waltz, and (when living got dangerous) the tango. As the jasmine struggled genteely to mask the refineries' ubiquitous emissions, girls were lined on one side of the room, boys on the other, and the decorous ritual of mating was initiated. Young gentlemen in suits and ties were trained to tap politely on the shoulder of a competitor to vie for the partnership of curly-coiffed cuties in dotted Swiss and Capezio flats with ornamented toes. No surprise that Janie's oracular announcements of a world outside the classroom confines were precious.

The big day came one afternoon in 1955 at Dick Dowling Junior High. The "cool" thing to do was to get a letter from Mom granting permission to leave the school grounds for lunch, officially to go home, but in fact allowing us to gather at the local drive-in for greasy burgers, fries and coffee, infinitely preferable to the institutional pale lunches dished out by the school cafeteria in conformance to the obscure nutritional regulations of the determinedly bland Fifties. Sitting at the counter at the Shamrock Shanty, Janie, in her usual understated manner, mumbled the words none of us even knew we'd been waiting for. "I went to the Louisiana Hayride last night and there was this guy named Elvis Presley. . . ." *Have you heard the news/ there's good rockin' tonight.*

A sure reprieve from being trained to be a Good Citizen—the current fad was to teach future homemakers to cook Frito pies—was rock and roll, "race music" as it was called. Afternoons were commonly spent in some bedroom or another, door closed to deny adult access, listening to Big Joe Turner's "Honey Hush" or the Clovers' "Lovey Dovey" and "Your Cash Ain't Nothin' But Trash," while painting fingernails Fire and Ice red. So the move was clearly to check out this Presley cat with the purchase of a couple of tunes. One spin and b-b-b-babybaby he was in.

The mating ritual that followed was performed with religious devotion. It began with the acquisition of totems from the love object: all available golden-labeled 45 rpm discs. Everyday after school I went

home, sequestered myself in my bedroom and played these records over and over until every word, every phrase, every sigh was indelibly etched into memory so that when in school, away from these precious tokens —these songs he sung to me personally—I could silently conjure any song, slur perfect, while subjected to the tedium of the educational system.

"Stephanie," my Mom would call, "what are you doing?"

"Homework."

"What's that *noise?*"

God bless America and all the ships at sea, I would curse silently. How can she be so stupid? Noise, she says. "I got the record player on. I'm doing my algebra. I can do it with the music in the background," I lied. *Never*, I promised Elvis. Never would he have to share me with dumb algebra.

"Stephanie," my teachers would call, "who is the Secretary of State?"

"I forgot," I silently added, "to remember to forget her." Poetic license. I knew the answer. Social Studies

gone for a change. That sassy devil was back in the morning. Time to button up that pink and grey shirt, comb in those duck tails and boogie on down to the school house. Ah, that hair. B-b-b-babybaby. That for-the-Fifties outrageously long, arrogantly long, defiantly long hair, with that rebellious lock across the forehead, and those deliciously impudent sideburns that would offend—did offend—did drive to pompous indignation every paunchy unattractive-as-Elvis-was-magnificent adult in the United States. In the Age of Conformity at the age of conformity, I adored this man's originality, Elvis was not just beautiful and sexy. He was right.

The next step, cruel though it may be, had to be taken. The timing couldn't have been worse. My boyfriend at the time, Agee Speidel, had been the coveted catch of the ninth grade when he moved to Beaumont that year. As I put on the sterling silver disc engraved with his name and his football letter jacket that night, I vowed it would be the last time I would be burdened with their weight. Besides, I'd had it with all those girls inviting me to their silly teas, pretending to

Maple Leaf Gardens, Toronto, 1957.

was the most boring, with everyone having to read current events clipped the evening before from the *Beaumont Journal*. Dumb Secretaries of State would be gone in a few years, but not Elvis. Elvis would live eternally and I would love him forever.

Then came the search for pictures. Slowly the pictures began edging out the collections of stuffed koala bears and Madame Alexander Little Women dolls. Finally only Gregory, my faithful old stuffed dog, remained to be nestled with, daintily nuzzled and nibbled each night as I fell asleep. With the night light on, my last image was always those heavy lidded eyes fringed with those long, black lashes (little did I imagine they could be mascaraed) gazing down at me; and that sulky mouth, full lips pouting and parted. It was not an option that he could be the idol of other teens with other nagging mothers in other bedrooms in equally boorish towns. Janie and Brenda and Linda might love him too, but he was My Hero.

Well, I woke up this morning and I looked out the door. . . Hold it fellas, that don't mooove. Let's get real real

be my friend just so they could try to get close to him. Let them have him. He was real cute and real nice, but . . . *that don't move.* The alleged Christmas party at Agee's parents' house turned out, as anticipated, to be a surprise birthday party for me, and when Agee handed me a huge aquamarine stuffed poodle with tiny pink flowers at the ear, I handed him his disc. Make mine vinyl, b-b-b-babybaby. Maybe I'd give him a copy of "Heartbreak Hotel" for Christmas, a parting gift—since I hadn't bought him anything yet.

Needless to say when Janie brought the word that the King would come to Houston, that the Pelvis would be made Flesh, we began planning. Janie, Brenda and I were driven to Houston by Janie's dad, fought to get third row seats where we screamed like Maenads at each pivot of thigh and thrust of shoulder. Would that my first physical love affair had been so satisfying as my first rock and roll show.

Elvis was everything we wanted him to be—except audible. They were right. This was jungle music. It did drive kids wild. But they were not the initiates. They could not know what really happened. And the three silent girls sprawled across the back seat of Mr. Butterfield's Oldsmobile heading east on Highway 90 late that night weren't telling.

His second coming had an even more extraordinary touch. I had again gone to Houston, this time with Carolyn Cantella and her cousin, Madeleine Petty. Carolyn's father drove. Back in the car after the show, as if some unspoken message had been transmitted during the performance, I said quietly, Elvis is at the Shamrock Hotel. Let's go get his autograph." Mr. Cantella graciously obliged.

"Where's Elvis," we asked the first bellhop we saw. A room number was tossed back. Up the elevator. Knock on the door. A man who Madeleine later identified as Nick Adams opened the door.

The author in her Beaumont days.

"Is Elvis here?" The door closed. We stood. Did that mean go away? Was this even the right room? Quite virginal, it never occurred to us there might be anything questionable about three girls lurking about the hotel room of a traveling musician. The door opened. Elvis stood before us. He was wearing a brick red brocade smoking jacket and was tinier than I had imagined. Standing to his left I studied his profile, more delicate than photos had promised. We mumbled our requests for autographs. Suddenly I realized he was looking at me, asking my name; and I, relieved to discover I could remember, was answering. For a moment in my relentlessly dissatisfied youth, there was no place else I wanted to be. Dream made flesh. We conversed briefly, received the autographs inscribed to us personally—tomorrow's proof that wishes can be granted—

and turned to go. Before I knew what was happening, Elvis was leaning toward me, kissing me gently and thanking me. I am told he kissed the others. I only knew that Semele must have gone joyful into flames of death upon seeing Zeus in his mortal form. All the way back to Beaumont the others argued with cheerful incessance about the order and placement of kisses and which of them was preferable. Secure in the knowledge that perfection is ineffable, I did not participate.

I placed the appropriate number of bills on Dave's counter beside my now cold, untouched hamburger and went out into the deserted pre-dawn street. *I just had to reach you, baby/Spite of all you put me through/I kept travelin' night and day. . . .* "Bastard," I muttered, realizing he was back, slur perfect, to the beat of my footsteps, "still not rid of ya."

MORE NOTES OF A FAN-ATIC
BY GAY McRAE

ELVIS

He had a smile that could light up the world
Everyone loved Him—every boy and girl.
Into our lives He brought so much pleasure
So much love, there is no way to measure
The feelings we had for Him all our lives
The kind of affection that never dies.

The world has never seen such love for one man
From near and far they came—just to touch His hand.

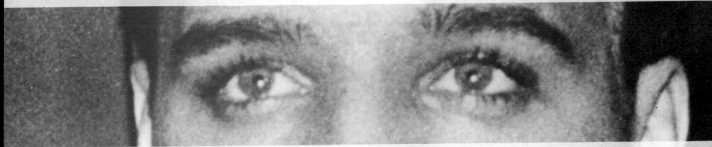

To hear Him sing and oh, to see Him smile
Any fan of His would walk a mile.
Yes, that twinkle in His eyes so blue
Was a taste of Heaven for me and you.

Thank God that I was married (and still am) to Stanley, a man who doesn't feel his manhood threatened by his wife's fascination with an entertainer.

The very first time I saw him he was singing "That's All Right (Mama)" on a flatbed truck at the opening of Katz Drugstore in Memphis' first shopping center. I was standing there with my baby daughter Glenda Gay and my husband.

Elvis had the most perfect features I'd ever seen and the profile of a Greek god statue. I've heard rumors he had a nose job after he made a lot of money. Well, my answer to that is why would any plastic surgeon try to improve upon perfection? At first I thought he had brown eyes, until he looked in my direction (naturally I thought he was looking right at me) and I'll never forget how that surprised me. I still don't know why—but it did. I remember thinking, "My God! He's got blue eyes!" Not only blue but the bluest eyes I had ever seen in my life.

If you ever saw him, you never ever forgot him. He was tall, well built (with a very nice set of shoulders even then), good looking and that "different" voice. I remember thinking "I'm really going to like this guy,"

when we first walked up, but by the time he'd finished, the combination of that voice and those looks had completely destroyed me. Here I was a normal happy housewife with a baby one year old and I was standing there caught up in what was later named "Presley mania." Well, I caught it that night. It's not a disease *but it is incurable.*

Lucky for me, Stanley liked him, too, or we'd both have been miserable. He still doesn't quite understand my total fascination with him, but then it's not an understandable thing. It's something you understand only if you *feel* it.

Once Elvis touched your life, even lightly, it seemed he touched your very soul. That sounds ridiculous to a lot of people but it's normal to an Elvis fan. That's why people didn't just "like" Elvis; when they said they *loved* him, it's because they really did. That was a gift Elvis had, he made you feel you knew him personally. When he was happy, you were happy; when he hurt, you hurt with him. A person could (and still can with me) make an enemy for life just by being critical of Elvis.

We would see Elvis around town, occasionally; we'd be driving along and he'd pull up beside us at a light or pass us on the street. Glenda Gay (my daughter) recognized him on sight and was always looking for him. Once when she was about four, Elvis had moved into Graceland that year (1957) and we were driving out there. Mr. and Mrs. Presley passed us and Glenda Gay spotted them as usual (in the famous pink Cadillac). We caught up with them, then stopped and watched while Vernon pulled up to a 7-11 type store and went in and bought a loaf of bread and came out carrying it in his hand, not in a bag. I thought it was so funny when she said, "Golly, Mom, Elvis' daddy went in the store and bought a loaf of bread—just like regular people!" I explained to her that Gladys was a very down to-earth person from what I'd heard about her and would like fresh bread as well as anyone.

We bought his records, saw his movies, laughed when he laughed in them and cried when he was hurt. When Glenda was three and a half, we took her to see *Love Me Tender* and she was so upset when Elvis was killed in the end. She was really not convinced no matter how much explaining we did that he wasn't really dead until she saw him again in the flesh.

When *Loving You* premiered at the Strand, July 9, 1957 in downtown Memphis, I took Glenda, picked up Mary and her two little girls, and we went. We had read that Elvis might be there a couple of weeks before, but Elvis had just completed *Jailhouse Rock* and he was home for the premiere, however we really didn't expect to see him that day because of a terrible tragedy. Elvis' co-star Judy Tyler and her husband of only four months, George Lafayette, were involved in a two-car

With Judy Tyler.

crash near Billy the Kid, Wyoming, which killed Judy instantly. Her husband died the next day from chest injuries. The twenty-three-year-old driver of the other car was killed. Both Judy and her husband were only twenty-four at the time. Elvis wept when shown a copy of the wire service report, and said he had to go to the funeral even if it meant missing the premiere. He said "All of us boys loved that girl." The funeral was to be held on Tuesday, the day of the premiere.

Elvis did not go to the funeral however. Gladys told the press "The family talked it over and decided it was best if Elvis didn't go." Something was said about Elvis remembering her the way she was but we all thought that was not the real reason. I still believe it was out of total respect for her and her family. Elvis knew—he had to know by now—that some of his fans would stop at nothing to see him. I'll always believe that he was afraid

that Judy and George's double funeral in New York would quickly turn into a three-ring circus if he had gone and he was probably right. I thought it was so sad that he couldn't even go to a funeral of a friend. He said he didn't think he'd be able to stand watching the recently completed movie. I don't know if he ever watched it or how long before he did but I do know that when he was on leave from basic training my sister, Wanda, went to a party he had at Graceland with Barbara Pittman, who recorded for Sam Phillips. Elvis was at the piano at one time singing what they wanted to hear . . . her favorite song was "Young & Beautiful," and Wanda requested he sing it. He looked very sad and said, "Honey, I can't." and she could have bitten her tongue off; for the moment she'd forgotten about Judy, but apparently Elvis had not.

And then in December of 1957, as everyone knows, Elvis was drafted. He was to be inducted January 20, but Elvis was to start working on the movie *King Creole* on January 13th in Hollywood. Paramount had already spent $350,000 in "preparatory investments," so the company wrote the draft board and requested a sixty day delay. But they were told Elvis would have to make the request himself. Later, Elvis wrote saying he was ready to enter immediately but asked for deferment so Paramount "will not lose so much money with everything they have so far." The request was honored with the deferment board voting unanimously. (Quoted from the Memphis *Commercial Appeal*, December 28, 1957). Part of the film was made in New Orleans—and Elvis went into the Army as scheduled—I cried! So did thousands of other fans.

While in basic training at Fort Hood, Texas, he had rented a place nearby for his Mom and Dad. How many young men do you know who would take their parents along while in basic training?

While in Texas, Gladys became very ill. Regardless of how many times you've heard "Elvis flew her home," this is not true. Being a Memphian, we received word immediately in our local newspapers. She came home on a train. His Mom was afraid of planes. She did not even want Elvis to fly. Gladys was admitted to the hospital on Saturday—and her condition worsened. She had "acute severe hepatitis" with evidence of liver damage. Four specialists were aiding the family physician. A seven-day emergency leave was granted to Elvis after his family physician phoned Fort Hood. On Tuesday night, August 12, at 7:45 p.m. Elvis went in to see his Mom at Methodist Hospital in Memphis. Contrary to what most people assume—*she was not in the Baptist Hospital.* When he came out he had tears in his eyes. Friends were at the hospital and he told them, "I nearly went crazy when I put her on the train in Texas. She looked so awful bad then." No visitors were allowed except for the immediate family. When Elvis entered the room, she was heard outside to say, "Oh, my son, my son." That was a "shot in the arm" for Gladys and she seemed to feel better the next day according to our newspapers and her doctors. Elvis

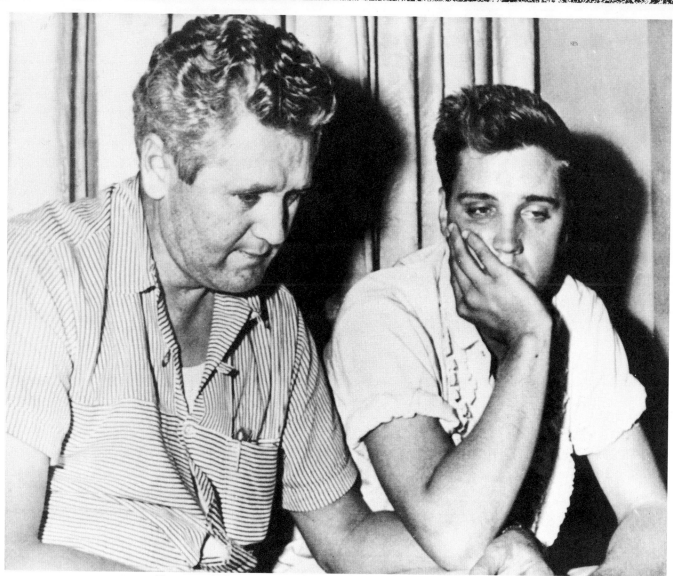
Vernon and Elvis comfort each other at Graceland after Gladys' funeral.

visited with her the next day and night and finally went home to get some rest. Vernon stayed with her. Gladys died with a heart attack at approximately 3:15 a.m. on August 14, 1958. Contrary to the *Elvis* special with Kurt Russell, Elvis was *not* at the hospital: he was at Graceland with his beloved cousin Billy Smith, with whom he'd always been very close. It was Billy who answered the telephone. (I didn't know who answered the phone until Billy told me a couple of years ago.) Billy said they took off in the car and broke speed limits all over town and when they arrived at the hospital Elvis was out of the car almost before it was stopped.

On August 15, Elvis collapsed several times during the funeral services and burial of his mother. At the graveside, Elvis leaned on the casket and said, "Oh God, everything I have is gone. Goodbye, darling, Goodbye, Goodbye." To read it on the front page of the paper on August 16th would break your heart. He loved her so much—he was an only son—but you have only one mother. Services for Gladys Smith Presley were held at National Funeral Home. It was not a private funeral. There was a crowd of approximately 700 people—mostly teenage girls and women packed the chapel and overflowed into the hallways and outside parking lots. The Blackwood Brothers sang at the services. Both Elvis and Vernon were at the point of hysteria throughout the ceremony and Elvis had to be helped in and out of the car at the cemetery. Five policemen stood guard in the chapel—the same number of "fans" had already gathered at the cemetery. Some seemed actually bereaved (and I'm sure some were) but the majority craned their necks for a look at Elvis and chattered. Personally, I think it was a disgrace. Some even had on halter tops and shorts and that sort of attire at the cemetery. Friends called me that night to see how Elvis did and were amazed to learn I didn't go to his mother's funeral as much as I loved Elvis. That's why I didn't go. Because I *did* love him. I did not know Gladys Presley, but I had the greatest admiration for her and I thought she did a terrific job of rearing her son. I had seen her happy and smiling—I wanted to keep that picture in my mind. I would not have dreamed of being there; I considered it an intrusion on his privacy. I always saw him laughing and happy. Why should I want to go there and see him broken to pieces? I knew how much he loved her. How do you think he felt seeing people craning their necks to gawk at him at a time like that? I heard (or read) Elvis saw some of the half dressed girls at the cemetery and remarked that he was really disappointed in them. I was ashamed at them.

Gladys Presley died at age forty-six, not forty-two as the papers said. That's how the story started when Elvis died that he died at the same age as his mother. Her obituary read forty-two. I suppose that's because she was a few years older than Vernon and so they let people think they were the same age, but you can subtract the birthdate from the death date on her gravestone and see that she was forty-six years old at

the time. I never heard anything but good things about Gladys Presley. She was a great lady. But give 'em time—there'll be some dirt out on her if they have to make it up and if it puts a dollar in their pockets it will come to pass.

After Gladys' funeral and a few days to recuperate, Elvis had to return to service and the next month he left for Germany. We were not to see him again for a year and a half. It seemed like ten.

Elvis was a model soldier and came home radiant and smiling—with the Colonel right behind him. He came into Union Train Station in March of 1960. We still had a little snow on the ground. He was in a dress uniform and when he stepped off that train he was happy to be home and it showed. He shook hands, hugged Gary Pepper, his wheelchair-bound fan club president, shook hands, kissed a few and was whisked away in a squad car to head for Graceland. There were thousands at the train station. The King had returned and all was right with the world.

Things went back to normal—normally Elvis!

Then in 1961, Elvis did a benefit show in Memphis. I was going. It was Saturday and cold weather but today I was going to see Elvis on stage again. I couldn't believe it. My childhood friend, Charlotte Roberts, had purchased the tickets for the price of $3. There were no reserved seats—can you imagine that today! The reason? The show was for charity. Elvis was appearing at two shows, at 2 and 8:30 p.m. We were going to the afternoon show. It was his first public appearance since 1957. Every penny was to go to charity: there was a $100-a-plate luncheon for Elvis, at 12:30 p.m. at the Claridge Hotel. Gov. Buford Ellington and Memphis Mayor Henry Loeb were there and George Jessel was M.C.

George Marek, William Bullock, John Burgess, Jr., all top brass from RCA, were on hand to pay tribute to Elvis. There was a press session at 1:45 p.m. in the hotel Empire Room; hence the 1961 Press Conference. Most Elvis fans own a bootleg tape or record (or both) of this.

Brother Dave Gardner, my favorite comedian, was on the bill, as were Nip Nelson, an impressionist; an acrobatic act; a tap dancer; the now legendary Boots Randolph; Floyd Cramer; and Larry Owens and his orchestra.

Elvis was twenty-six. By now I was twenty-eight years old. I had a daughter who was seven and a half and a son who was just past two. I considered myself a settled down, very much in love, mature young lady. I couldn't wait to see Elvis! I was ecstatic!

I knew exactly what I'd do! Sit there and watch him and oooh and aah just like everyone else, but I really hoped all those screaming yelling teenagers would act their age and let us *hear* him as well as see him. I'd seen films of the screaming crowds (from Tupelo for instance) and I couldn't believe the way some of them acted. It was absolutely ridiculous, and so childish, I thought.

We sat through the various introductions and entertainment and waited and waited—then finally the King made his grand (royal) entrance. To say that pandemonium broke out would be like comparing Hurricane Camille to a thundershower. I thought my eardrums would burst! I'm at a loss as how to describe the situation—it was a fairy tale come true to me. It was like a dream, but I knew that it was impossible for all that yelling to wake anyone up. I couldn't stand it! I put both my hands over my ears and felt a vibration; that's when I realized that I was screaming too! He was totally "with it." He couldn't have done anything wrong if he had wanted to and he didn't want to. He was absolutely brilliant!! He rocked and rolled and the building did too! If you've never seen Elvis on stage you truly don't know what you've missed. He is indescribable. He catches an audience and holds it in the palm of his hand like no one you have ever seen. He has a style that is pure magic and it's all his. He hasn't copied from anyone. He has the instinct of a genius about what to say or do next. He's cute, he's beautiful and he's sexy—and he *knows* it. By now he has to know or he'd be a complete fool—but part of his charm and sexiness is that he never, never *acts* like he knows it. He sang it hard, soft, rock, blues, ballad, gospel and he could do all equally well. He can sing high and he can sing low, he can reach up and hit a note that's unbelievable. He can turn a tune a 1000 different ways. I still say "if he ain't got it—you don't need it!!"

It was August 16, 1977, and all was right with my world. Only a few more days and Elvis would be at the Mid-South Coliseum. Everyone was excited about it.

I was an affiliate broker for Matlock Realty Company and my office was only a couple of miles away. I'd never really had a job. I didn't think anyone else would take as good care of my children as I would and I stayed home with them. But now, they had grown up and I was selling real estate part time and loving it. I went into my office, made a few calls, and sat and talked awhile and had a restless feeling and decided to come home. It was approximately 2:00 p.m. I usually had the car radio on. That day I didn't. I stopped by Barbara Moore's house, a co-worker who lived a block or so from the office. She always had the TV on with her soap operas going—that day she didn't. I visited about half an hour and came home. It was then approximately 3 p.m.

We are creatures of habit. I walked through the back door into my kitchen, reached over and turned the radio on. I always did that. I heard these words, "He is still in the emergency room at the Baptist Hospital—we still have no word yet as to his condition" and I thought who could that be? Then he finished with "Please stop calling the hospital and the stations, the telephone company has reported that calls are coming in from every place in the world and all Memphis lines are tied up. We repeat, please quit tying up all the phone lines! Steve is there now and we will let you know as soon as we have any word." I went to

pieces—now I knew who it was. Only Elvis, only my beautiful, talented, beloved Elvis. It *had* to be him. President Kennedy was assassinated, Martin Luther King was assassinated right here in Memphis, but nobody, no, nobody had ever tied up all our lines. Only Elvis Presley could do that.

I knew it, I expected it, and yet I couldn't believe it. Not Elvis, why Elvis, dear God, do you know how many people all over the world *love* that man? How many people's lives revolve around him, actually worship the ground he walks on? I looked up through my tears and the sun shone brightly through the yellow kitchen curtains; and I thought how *can* it? I didn't see how the sun could continue to shine with him gone. It seemed to me the world ought to stop turning. My phone started ringing, "I'm sorry. I know how much you loved him." I took it off the hook. I couldn't talk about it, didn't want to try. I only wanted to be left alone. Within an hour, people had come in—once the report was confirmed I think I must have been in shock. I was numb. I talked to people, I didn't know what I said. I refused to talk on the phone. Stanley and Glenn answered the phone. By now, they were home from work and had it back on the hook. They would explain that I didn't want to talk about it, both knowing if I got on the phone and people started to sympathize with me I would go to pieces again.

I stayed awake almost all night. I cried as millions did until I thought there couldn't be any more tears. No one at my office expected me in. I didn't even have to call. We all loved Elvis at my office, but I was *The* Elvis fan—the fanatic as some would say. The others could still manage to take care of business. I couldn't. I didn't even try because I knew I couldn't.

For months I think I was in a state of shock and disbelief. I had friends who loved him as much as I did. We tried to comfort each other. I have a cousin in Texas, raised near Tupelo, who worshipped Elvis. I sent her a flower from his funeral because I knew what it would do for her. Ever since she was twelve years old, we'd talk Elvis when we got together. We wrote and we called each other until our phone bills were tremendous. I wonder if the phone company has any ideas of how many calls Elvis is responsible for today?

I knew the people who lived around Elvis were having to adjust to this life without him. I wondered how they could cope with it. I had seen Elvis many times, gotten to talk to him a second or two and I felt like the world had ended. Then I thought of Vernon and Lisa and all the people who really *knew* him—those who lived at Graceland and loved him. My heart broke for them. I could only think that if I feel so completely destroyed by his death, my God, what are those people going through? I couldn't imagine how they could hurt any worse than I did, but you know they did. I prayed God would comfort them for their grief must have been indescribable.

I thought of Red West, Sonny West and Dave

Hebler and wondered how they felt, if they felt guilty, if they were hurting—and I hoped they were. I hoped they were perfectly miserable. I *despised* them. I knew that was a sin but we can't help how we feel, can we? I saw Sonny and Dave on TV and heard Sonny West talk about drugs and how they tried to "help" Elvis and I didn't believe a word of it. As Sonny said, "We tried to help him, man, we tried." I thought "you lying rat, if he had *any,* you were probably partly responsible for bringing them in." I think we all despised Sonny for that interview. A few months ago, a friend called me to say she'd just had a long distance call from Los Angeles relaying that Sonny West had been arrested for drugs. "Vengeance is mine" saith the Lord; but I must admit when I picked up the newspaper and read it for myself, two days later, I loved it! It was true!!

Now if that had been Elvis who'd done it, it would have made headlines, but this was a small item on page two. "Former Elvis Aide Indicted for Drugs" and a small article about how this house was being raided by the authorities for drugs and who should just happen to come up with a nice amount of cocaine on him? That's right—the fine, upstanding "friend" of Elvis— Sonny West. He was arrested for "possession with intent to sell." I have not seen the results yet. He was out on bail, of course, but I sincerely wish they could put him in. He made the statement on TV "Nobody is out of the reach of drugs." Right, and as long as there are people like that in possession of them, nobody will be. It still amazes me that an Elvis fan would put one thin dime into the West's and Hebler's pockets by buying the book. I would not. I saw Elvis fans pick the book up, tear pages in it and put it back on the shelf at K-Mart. I heard Elvis fans went into stores and book shops and glued the pages together. I think it better to leave it untouched on the shelf and act as if it didn't exist, but people angered over someone they love will do strange things and nothing can upset an Elvis fan like trash in print about him.

You think you have accepted the fact that he is gone but you realize you have not when you see his name carved on that long cold marker. That's when it hits you, the cold hard facts of life, that you will have that empty space there in your heart forever because it was the one that Elvis occupied. It's one that nothing nor anyone else can ever fill. And so you don't dwell on it, you think about the good times, the times you saw him happy and smiling; the September in 1954 when you first saw him, the concerts, the times he rode his horse across the front lawn of Graceland, the coveted autographs you were lucky enough to get, the time he pulled up beside you at a stoplight in his purple car in the 50's, and you almost wrecked the car, and he sped off laughing. You think about how that smile he had could light up the world and you know that you only have to look around you and you'll see so many others who feel the same way . . . Somehow you feel sorry for those who don't because then you know they never loved, admired or appreciated him like you did, and *you* know what they have missed, but they don't. You've seen him smile, you've touched those hands— that were as soft as a baby's—as he handed you an autograph, you've stood close enough to see that absolutely flawless complexion he had that would be the envy of any woman and you know that you have something that no one can take away from you. . . MEMORIES . . . and a love in your heart that will live forever, because the legacy he left his fans was love and nothing has ever been found to equal that. And so with all these thoughts you know that you can cope— because even though you may have tears in your eyes, you've got a song in your heart.

ELVIS IN HOLLYWOOD BY BILL REED

"I feel like a bird who's been let out of his cage and wants to fly a little. I want to flap my wings. I want to feel sure I'm free again. I never know what I want to do, but I sure want to do something that has nothing to do with this (movie) business."

—Elvis Presley

When Elvis Presley went to Hollywood in 1956 to make *Love Me Tender*, he and his aides checked in at the Beverly Wilshire Hotel for an unusually lengthy stay. For earlier West Coast recording sessions with RCA, Elvis had touched down briefly at places like the Knickerbocker and Roosevelt hotels, where his visits always triggered pandemonium. At the Beverly Wilshire it was more apparent than ever that hotel living in Hollywood would never cut it on a long term basis. Still, from April of '56 until the autumn of the following year Elvis and his down home crew mostly camped out there—even though the scene in the hotel's lobby constituted a *fanatical* obstacle course.

The novelty of whooping it up (with room service yet!) still hadn't worn off. Elvis, Alan Fortas, Red West, and others of Elvis' aides and cronies were still humorously getting off on the attention and pranks of the almost exclusively female horde of lurking, pouncing Presley fans who had to be literally—as they say—beaten off with a stick.

Even if Elvis *could* have engaged in normal rounds of partygoing and nightlife he probably wouldn't have. For the innate country boy in him caused him to feel generally uncomfortable around most of the Hollywood "types" he met during the day while making movies. In fact, almost immediately after his first lengthy exposure to the movie capital, he put it down publicly. At a press conference back home in Memphis during a break in the filming of *Love Me Tender* he spoke very bitterly of Hollywood, stating that he'd never want to live there permanently. In so many words he expressed the opinion that he wasn't *ever* going to let the bright-lights-big-city atmosphere of tinsel town cause him to forget that when all was said and done his heart belonged to Memphis, Tennessee. A little more than a year later, though, Elvis' heart would belong to Uncle Sam. He entered the Army in March, 1958, and for the next two years the theoretical and practical problems of "going Hollywood" were temporarily defused.

When Elvis was mustered out of the service in 1960 he immediately went back to making movies. His first post-Army film, naturally enough, was *G.I. Blues*, and perhaps the only person who *wasn't* surprised at how successful it was (even more so than *Love Me Tender*)

was Colonel Tom Parker. If ever there was any doubt that Elvis Presley was a long-range movie phenomenon, *G.I. Blues* effectively dispelled it. For the foreseeable future, Elvis would be spending as much time, if not more so, in the movie capital as back home at Graceland. Hotel living this time around was obviously out of the question.

The year of *G.I. Blues*, 1960, Elvis and his entourage (not yet known as the "Memphis Mafia," but beginning to be called El's Angels) moved into the first of four rented homes they would occupy throughout most of the 1960's. All were located either in or near Beverly Hills or Bel Air. (When Elvis married he finally bought a house in Los Angeles' exclusive Truesdale Estates section.) The first house was at 565 Perugia Way, adjacent to the Bel Air Country Club golf course. One of Elvis' neighbors was another early rock and roller (of sorts)—Pat Boone. Also living nearby was "Mrs. Minniver," Greer Garson. The house was a pseudo-oriental affair, built in a semi-circle around a garden and a waterfall. The first thing Elvis did when he moved in was to rip out the garden, replace it with a "rec" room, which he then proceeded to fill up with pool tables, a jukebox and other leisure time accoutrements. (Since Elvis couldn't go out for fun and games it's little wonder he made adequate provisions for "r and r" right off the bat.)

By the time Elvis moved into the Perugia way compound, the potential for precipitating a riot should he go out in public was even greater than during the earlier years. Not only were restaurants and nightclubs totally out of bounds, but so too was movie going, one of Elvis' favorite pastimes.

In an early fan magazine interview, Elvis said, "I go to the movies. I'm a movie fan. Me and the boys take off at any time to take in a movie, there isn't a weekend we don't take in two. We go to any movie house. I've seen some movies a half-a-dozen times when it's got something to say by way of interesting acting."

By 1960, though, the possibility of visiting just "any movie house" was an utter impossiblity. But like the mountain and Mohammed, if Elvis couldn't go to the movies, the movies would have to come to Elvis.

Private home screenings in Hollywood are nothing unusual. Most of that town's successful industry officials and celebrities enjoyed home movie viewing. But Elvis, of course, really outdid himself. Just as in Memphis where he rented the Memphian Theatre for all-night movie parties on a fairly regular basis, similarly in Hollywood most of Elvis' nights at home with friends and employees included the showing of at least

Opposite: Finale of *It Happened At The World's Fair*, with Joan O'Brien.

one movie. (This at a time before home video when showing films was a moderately complex and cumbersome affair.)

Some of the films cropping up most frequently at these movie parties were Elvis' personal favorites. These included: *To Kill a Mockingbird, Lawrence of Arabia, Diamonds Are Forever, Straw Dogs, Rebel Without a Cause, The Godfather*—and later a special favorite for which Elvis shared his enthusiasm with Richard Nixon, *Patton*. Most of these titles are on the downbeat/fantastical/violent side, but they constitute a fairly erudite selection. Surprisingly though, the film Elvis showed most frequently was Blake Edwards' amiable knockabout comedy, *The Party*. The reason being that, wonder of wonders, Elvis' favorite movie performer wasn't Clint Eastwood, James Dean or Spencer Tracy (all of whom he appreciated unceasingly) BUT, *The Party*'s star, Peter Sellers. (It seems like an unlikely choice even after you think about it for a while.) Elvis was also fond of Edwards and Sellers' *A Shot in the Dark*.

To underscore just how much of a film fan Elvis was, many times during his Las Vegas shows he would often veer off into lengthy and uncannily accurate renderings of scenes from favorite films. One that cropped up often was Marlon Brando's "Don Corleone" death scene from *The Godfather*.

Sometimes upwards of a hundred people were invited to Elvis' "at-homes," which generally were highlighted by the showing of a film or two. The evening didn't officially begin until the host had made his entrance, with guests tending to hold themselves in a kind of pre-party holding pattern until then. Finally, at least at the Perugia Way house, the walls would literally part—Red Sea fashion—to reveal Elvis elaborately costumed. After surveying the room momentarily, Elvis would slowly enter into the goings-on. It was a show biz "entrance" in every sense of the word.

Invariably the males in the room were outnumbered by the females, many of whom were part of a whole elaborate pecking order of sexual liaisons to be gone through before (at some later date) finally getting to bed down with Presley himself. In the early Hollywood years, the parties never approached being wild or orgiastic—in keeping with Elvis' proprietous self-image. Generally on hand too for these often large but always casual affairs was Elvis' current girlfriend, who as likely as not turned out to be his on-screen love interest of the film he was working on at the time.

During the years prior to Elvis' marriage to Priscilla in 1967 Elvis was publicly reported as being romantically involved with a lengthy list of stars and starlets—this was near the end of the era of that happy breed. Gossip columnists' tongues wagged over Elvis pitching woo with such of his co-stars as: Tuesday Weld (*Wild in the Country*); Ursula Andress (*Fun in Acapulco*); Yvonne Craig (*Kissin' Cousins, It Happened at the World's Fair*) and Ann-Margret (*Viva Las Vegas*). There was also Nancy Sinatra from *Speedway*. The mind reels over what Papa Frank might've thought about Elvis as a prospective son-in-law. (Ironically Nancy Sinatra ended up wedding early Elvis clone, singer Tommy Sands.)

Elvis also dated Natalie Wood (one of the few of his girlfriends honored with an invite to Graceland), Roger Corman starlet, Yvonne Lime and Raquel Welch, whose first movie part was a walk-on in Elvis' *Roustabout*.

And there was the one that got away, Debra Paget, Elvis' *amour* in *Love Me Tender*. Small wonder she tried to (and successfully) elude her co-star's advances. For she just happened to be dating an even more powerful king from another domain at the time—Howard Hughes. (The potential combo of Presley and Hughes surely constituting two-thirds of the equivalent of a grand slam in the game of romantic triangles.)

Throughout the early sixties the parties continued, and up until the time of *Kissin' Cousins* (1964), Elvis was reported to still have been enthused by film work. He was quite proud of his straight acting role in Don Siegel's *Flaming Star* (1960), and he was also pleased by the job he'd done in *King Creole* (originally intended for James Dean), the last film he completed before entering the service. *Wild in the Country* (1961) also finds an Elvis still trying to hone his acting skills. However, even then, three full years before the disastrous *Kissin' Cousins*, there were apparently already some doubts as to whether Elvis would be allowed to carry on as a "serious" actor.

Phillip Dunne, the director of *Wild in the Country*, recalls in his autobiography, *Take Two*, the various ways in which front office intervention helped botch this project, with its script by prominent playwright Clifford Odets. 20th-Century-Fox, for example, insisted that songs be inserted into the plot, no matter how unnecessary they were for plot development. Part way through the film's shooting a rushed schedule was instituted, at which time the film's budget was also suddenly slashed. All of this wreaked havoc on a film that Dunne (and Presley) hoped would help establish Presley once and for all as a respectable straight actor. (Even with all the tampering Elvis' acting skills still manage to come across in the film.)

Most of Elvis' films during the next three years following *Wild in the Country*, including *Kid Galahad*, *Girls! Girls! Girls!* and *Follow That Dream*, were nothing to write home about. For sheer tattiness, though, none of them could compare with the crucial *Kissin' Cousins* (1964), produced by that cut-rate movie expert, Sam (*Rock Around the Clock*) Katzman.

Colonel Parker linked up with Katzman after he'd observed the impressive grosses for the producer's film of the life story of Hank Williams. (Elvis had once considered playing the lead in this film, *Your Cheatin' Heart*, which ended up being one of the better grossing films of 1964.) Watching the success of Katzman's country music bio, Parker for the first time became intrigued with the potential bottom line profits if he placed Elvis

Opposite: Filming *Blue Hawaii*.
Opposite, from top left: *Viva Las Vegas*. Natalie Wood. *Flaming Star*. *Fun In Acapulco*.

before the cameras in the same kind of quickie venture as was Katzman's stock-in-trade. And so he hired on the "B" movie producer to oversee Presley's next picture.

Every movie of Elvis' prior to *Kissin' Cousins* had been a quality affair, typified by relatively lengthy shooting schedules and fairly generous budgets. Suddenly, with this new approach, Elvis' films began costing one-third to one-fourth of what they had before. *Kissin' Cousins*, for example, had a shooting schedule of only seventeen days—about the amount of time it takes to make a run of the mill made-for-TV movie.

It didn't take long for Elvis to realize what was happening; and after their friend's death many of those closest to Elvis have noted that his single greatest disappointment in life was that he didn't get a chance to prove himself as an actor.

Apparently though Elvis didn't entirely give in to the Colonel without a struggle, for all the while he was appearing in the post-*Kissin' Cousins* embarrassments he was taking at least tentative steps to get himself back on the right track. To exactly what extent Elvis went with these efforts are facets of The Elvis Presley Story already lost to the dim recesses of Hollywood lore. In later years Elvis is said to have been seriously interested in being a part of at least two more "respectable" film projects, *Midnight Cowboy* and *A Star is Born*. (In the years before the three-pictures-a-year routine set in Elvis was sought out for and/or wanted roles in such prestige projects as *How the West Was Won* and *West Side Story*. His first movie *was* to have been the "classy" *The Rainmaker*, with Katherine Hepburn and Burt Lancaster; and almost immediately upon arriving in Hollywood for *Love Me Tender* there was talk of a film bio of the life of James Dean, to star Elvis.)

With the exception of Elvis' last two films, which were concert movies, seldom did films numbers 14-31 ever deviate fom the formula hit on with *Kissin' Cousins*, i.e. exotic locale, curvaceous cuties literally draped over the sets, an inane action-filled script and a neat LP's worth of songs. (Elvis' excellent 15th film, *Viva Las Vegas* though released after *Kissin' Cousins*, was actually shot prior to it.)

It is almost a cliche today to speak of how bad Elvis' later films were, but even *while* they were being turned out strong reaction had set in against them. Newspaper reviews when they appeared at all were nearly uniformly damning; and even *Elvis Monthly* had stopped running articles about their idol's films, stating that they were "puppet shows for not overbright children."

No one is entirely certain how much money these "puppet shows" brought in, but some estimates place the *profits* at over $200,000,000. (Elvis also co-owned the music publishing rights of his films.) Only when audience interest in these affairs dropped off with *Charro* and *Change of Habit* was the decision made to stop grinding them out.

In the Elvis memorial issue of *Rolling Stone* Magazine, Don Siegel, the director of *Flaming Star* (which some consider Elvis' best film) related the obstacle course he had to run in order to get a quality film made. Recalled Siegel, "I found him very sensitive and very good, with the exception that he was very unsure of himself. Very insecure. He felt he could have done better things. And his advisors—namely the Colonel were very much against doing this kind of (straight) role. They tried to get him to sing throughout the picture. (Note: The film ended up with only a title tune over the credits.) Obviously they didn't want him to get off a winning horse. But when I was able to calm him down, I thought he gave a beautiful performance."

In the same issue of *Rolling Stone*, Norman Taurog, the director of *nine* Presley features, echoed Siegel's sentiments by saying that he felt Elvis "never reached his peak." Taurog passed away in 1979, and with his death went a treasure trove of Elvis' oral history. To term Taurog a "director," though, is a bit of a misnomer, for by the time he came on the scene the part he played in the making of the films was more akin to that of a traffic cop and/or camp counselor. Yes, to allay the boredom of the daily moviemaking grind (and of the films themselves) Elvis and his retinue regularly engaged in Katzanjammer hi-jinks such as cherry bomb throwing, karate antics, water bombs, shaving cream battles and chasing one another around the set with Bic lighters which had the tips cut off them, altering them into miniature flame throwers. (To underscore his impatience with the shabby film projects Elvis once sardonically remarked, "Hey, there are some pretty funny things in this script. I'm going to have to read it some day.")

Although Elvis worked on heavily guarded closed sets, sometimes important visitors were allowed to watch the filming of his pictures. "El's Angels" were probably on their best behavior when such visiting *non*-show business royalty as the kings and queens of Nepal and Thailand and princesses from Denmark, Norway and Sweden dropped by

The recollections of writer George Kirgo, the author (with Theodore Flicker) of *Spinout* (1966)—one of the better of the quickies—points up the jerrybuilt, assemblyline aspect of Elvis' later films. The writing team had originally been assigned to concoct a feature for Sonny and Cher. Just as Kirgo and Flicker got to work writing the film, they received a call from MGM, their producers, requesting that they write something for Elvis instead. Kirgo still doesn't know why the Bonos' movie was cancelled, but he recalls, "We finished the script and turned it in and a few days later we were called into a meeting with Colonel Parker. He *loved* the script— except for one thing. 'Put a dog in it,' he said. And so we went back and put a dog in it. Then a few days later we got a call from MGM back on the East Coast telling us to put a race car in it." (Initially, you see, *Spinout* wasn't a racing picture at all.)

Opposite: With Yvonne Craig and Cynthia Pepper in *Kissin' Cousins*.

Kirgo also remembers the film's first three distinctly non-auto working titles. At first it was called *Always At Midnight*. Then it was known as *Never Say Yes*, which was *then* slightly adjusted to *Never Say No*. None of these titles were Kirgo and Flicker's; but the final one of *Spinout* was Kirgo's. "It was left over," he explains, "from an earlier race car picture I'd written for Howard Hawks, who nixed it at the last minute in favor of *Red Line 7,000*."

Kirgo never actually met Elvis until the final day of the film's shooting. "The producers asked Ted Flicker and myself if we'd like to meet Elvis. Naturally we said yes, and we went on to the set. It was a very brief meeting. He was very polite, and thanked us for the script. He said it was very good. Then he reached over to a stack of the most hideous . . . most horrible fake oil paintings of himself I've ever seen. Ghastly! Then he signed one and handed it to me." And that was the extent of meetings between the star and his screenwriters. All of five minutes; and at the *end* of the shooting.

By the time of *Spinout* in 1966 Elvis and his retainers had been leading an increasingly nomadic existence in the film community. In 1963, it was decided that the Perugia Way house just wasn't large enough so Elvis and his crew pulled up stakes and moved to a nearby baronial white elephant of a Hollywood-style mansion located at 1059 Bellagio Road in Bel Air. It came complete with a tennis-court-sized marble entrance hall and a bowling alley in the basement. The problem was it was *too* big and just plain creepy—almost immediately the outfit moved back into the old Perugia Way house, where they remained until 1965. After that it was onward to a low-slung modern house at 10050 Rocca Place situated in a cul-de-sac in Stone Canyon near the Bel Air Hotel. This was the house where Elvis and Priscilla would spend the first few months of their married life together before Elvis made the decision to plunk down the money and *buy* his first West Coast house.

The home he bought at 1174 Hillcrest Road was an elaborate multi-level pseudo-French regency affair, with four huge bedrooms, six bathrooms and the requisite Olympic size swimming pool. This new acquisition was only six years old, and so the $400,000 purchase price was considered a "steal"—especially since it was located in the exclusive Truesdale Estates section. High on an uppermost hill, the house was surrounded by cypress trees and commanded a sweeping view of the Los Angeles area. Here in keeping with his new image as a married man, Elvis cut back his "staff" considerably with only Richard Davis and Joe Esposito (from the inner circle) staying on at the Hillcrest address.

Elvis' Hollywood lifestyle had remained more or less the same at all of his "western Gracelands"—only the personnel changed from time to time, with the one constant being Elvis' semi-legendary and highly destructive alcoholic chimpanzee, Scatter. (Elvis bought him after seeing him on a TV show.) The TV was on constantly, the movie screenings and dates with co-stars continued, and Sunday touch football games became an institution at De Neve Park in Bel Air.

This weekend pastime of Elvis and his pals came on like an early version of TV celebrity sports shows. With a rag tag football crew consisting of, among others, Ty Hardin, Ricky Nelson, Kent McCord, Gary Lockwood, Dean Torrance (of Jan and Dean), Max Baer, Jr. and Robert Conrad (reportedly Pat Boone even showed up on occasion but his wife Shirley would anxiously come to fetch him before the game was over), the football games offered up not just Elvis for all the world to see, but an impressive array of TV's leading men and rock and roll stars. Small wonder then that after a few years the citizens of Bel Air politely requested that Elvis kindly take his game elsewhere, for the ensuing traffic jams and general chaos that usually occurred proved too much for the sedate community.

Favorite activities included filling up the swimming pool with flash bulbs and shooting at them (a sure sign of boredom if there ever was one) and the famed aimless late night rides through the hills of Bel Air and up and down the Sunset Strip with no goal at hand—with Elvis often leading the pack in his Cadillac with its forty coats of diamond and fish scale paint, 24k. gold trim, gold lame drapes, refrigerator, hi-fi, TV and gold-record bedecked ceiling.

But when he could flee the film capitol, Elvis would always kick back at Graceland. The move to Memphis usually consisted of a caravan led by Elvis in his customized mobile home, followed by a flotilla of the faithful in the various of the swank autos he'd purchased for them. And when his movie career bottomed out and his stage activities took an upswing in the late sixties, most of Elvis' time on the West Coast was spent in Palm Springs, rather than Hollywood—which suited him just fine.

Relaxing at the Holmby Hills mansion.

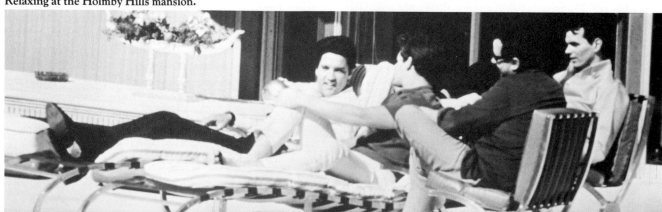

Girls! Girls! Girls!

Loving You.

IF ELVIS HAD LIVED BY LENNY KAYE

There was a stillness that made the room seem even quieter than it was. At first he thought it was the ringing in his ears, and then he realized it was a softer silence than he had ever known, a celestial peace that called to him with a promise of eternal harmony.

His eyes were closed, and yet all around him was light, bright and beaming and dazzling in its radiance. He felt weightless, able to float, and when he let go it was almost as if he actually did rise into the air, an ethereal mist borne aloft on wispy currents of air.

He could look down and see himself if he liked, lying on the brown carpeted bathroom floor. Beyond sadness or joy, he viewed himself objectively, a mirror instead of the mirror's reflection, observing the form as the bodily shell it was, drawing on the serenity of all experience, the dispassion of knowledge.

It had taken much abuse, that body had, and it bore the marks of a life fully lived at the edge. Perhaps too fully. The flesh was padded, and though the sleek and angular lines that marked its classic shape were still

visible, their effect was dulled, as if in disguise. Lines of care etched the features, imprinting the rigors of a struggle waged implacably, like a river slowly wearing away a mountain range.

He couldn't stay long now. Already he could hear the seductive chorus of infinity calling him home; the promise of a muchly deserved rest.

But. Had he done all he could? Was the story that was his story engraved to a just conclusion? He had it all, they'd said. Maybe he'd believed them. But did he believe himself?

He considered, and in the consideration, was decided.

The carpet hurt his cheek. How could a carpet hurt my cheek? he thought. Then he remembered the yawning inkhole that had suddenly opened in front of him as he'd padded into the bathroom after he groggily got up from a nap and. . . .

He shook his head, trying to clear the cobwebs from behind his eyes. My Lord! I've passed out before, he thought, a trifle embarrassed by the memory, but this one takes the cake.

He felt cold sweat all over his body, chilling him. He tried to raise up but a sudden pressure in his chest forced him back down. His heart beat wildly. He felt a twinge of fear.

If my fans could only see me now, he thought ruefully, and suddenly he caught a flicker of memory as it rushed past him, a body sprawled on the floor of a carpeted bathroom, seen for what it really was.

He lay back down on the floor, catching his breath, slowing his body and pulse rate as they'd taught him at karate practice, trying to draw all his energies into his body. God knew he needed them now.

It seemed like hours, but in reality it was only minutes later when he could hear a sharp knocking at the door.

"Elvis? Honey? Are you in there? I'm worried about you . . . are you all right?"

He waited a moment. Once again, at the far corner of his consciousness, he remembered a dream he might have once had, of hovering above himself, and a balance wheel that turned slowly around, spinning out one lucky number after another.

"I'm here, Ginger" he said, not without some difficulty. "You better go get the doctor . . . but I think I'll

be okay. Just hurry."

Exhausted and dizzy with the effort, he slumped back down to the floor.

It was the best suite in Memphis' Baptist Hospital, one he had been in many times before. They had tried to make it comfortable for him, shielding the windows with aluminum foil, turning the air conditioning on high, emptying the entire sixteenth floor so he might have privacy, but it was still a hospital. Elvis looked up at the intravenous feeder attached to his right arm, shrugged, and for the thousandth time that day, grinned sheepishly and derisively at himself.

A close call, that's what the doctors were calling it. Irregular heartbeat, respiratory failure, a deep mistreatment of his God-given body and talent. Look at himself: bloated and fat and uncaring. All for what?

Because he was bored.

A pretty small word, that. Bored waiting for a train. Bored on line at unemployment. Bored by an assembly line job.

But who wouldn't have wanted *his* boredom, the twenty-four hour taken-for-granted glory that comes to a very few of a lifetime's worth of humans. Everything was his, and relentlessly, even methodically, he'd worked his way through each of life's pleasures and pains.

There were the houses and the cars and all the material comforts. Unlimited food (and he'd sure enjoyed that one, especially those cheeseburgers!). Girls galore, and clothes, and . . . you name it, he'd had it. Or given it away. Paradise on a whim.

And, he frowned, there were other things to temper the balance sheet. The twin brother who'd died at birth who he'd never have a chance to know. The loss of his Mom, just as he was starting to make life easier for her. Priscilla, whom he'd loved since he first caught her eye when he was a soldier in Germany, and who now belonged to another. And his little girl. When would he be able to hear her call him Daddy again?

The good, the bad, and now, the ugly. This was it, he thought. When you hit bottom, there's no place to crawl but up.

There was a knock at the door. It cracked open

Vernon.

"I know, Daddy," sighed Elvis. "And the worst thing of all is that I can't blame it on anyone or anything than myself."

"Now Elvis," cried Ginger. "Don't go talking like that. I love you; your daddy loves you; people the world over love you!"

Elvis looked up at her, and when he spoke it was not only to his father and girlfriend, but also a much deeper vision that he could only catch from the corner of his eye, at the outer range of sight, a mote that vanished when he tried to gaze at it directly. A mirror, and yet he was the mirror's reflection and the silvered glass itself, endlessly repeating as he watched himself on the floor watch himself in the mirror watch himself on the floor, till he knew not where one began and the other left off.

"I know that everyone loves me," said Elvis, care-

slightly, poking in a tousled mass of reddish-brown hair. The girl's eyes looked as if she'd been crying, mascara staining her cheeks, skin taut with exhaustion.

"Elvis, are you up?" she asked timidly.

"Yes, darlin' ," said Elvis. "Come on in. And bring my dad in with you."

Ginger Alden turned back to the hall, whispered something, and then together, she and Vernon Presley came into the room, standing on the right side of Elvis' bed, where each reached down to take his hand, gently stroking it, warming him with their touch.

"Oh, honey," said Ginger, her voice breaking. "We were so worried. We thought we'd lost you." She reached out and touched his cheek, a livid bruise shining from where it had struck the floor.

"The doctors said that if they'd got there fifteen minutes later, you would've been a goner, boy," said

fully choosing his words. "But it's time that *I* learned how to love me. If I want to live," and a decision passed through his remembrance, "then I must learn to honor that which I am."

Ginger and Vernon looked at each other, at first in wonderment, then in happy understanding.

The time is the end of 1981. It's been a good year for Elvis Presley. Returning from his first-ever tour of the United Kingdom, where ecstatic crowds of the faithful trailed him from city to city ("A Presley Pilgrimage!" screamed the English press), he was given a surprise greeting by President Ronald Reagan when he stepped off the Concorde at New York's Kennedy airport.

Standing on the podium as the President made a few introductory remarks, Elvis reflected just how far he had come since that fateful day when his life had hung by a thread and he'd held the scissors.

Joe Teodores

At least he'd made good on his promise to his father and Ginger. After the wedding, and it was a quiet one, held in the back garden at Graceland, he'd taken a long vacation to get his health back. Along with a nutritionist and a physical therapist, the family had gone to a small Mexican fishing village on the west coast, where Elvis concentrated on remaking his once-proud body into the strong physical extension it had once been, flushing it of the cycle of drugs that had converted his waking hours into their own.

It was slow going at first, but after the third month he felt he'd turned the corner. He couldn't remember the last time he'd ever enjoyed daylight, he admitted to himself, and he took long runs along the beach, filling his lungs with healing draughts of sea breezes. The guns and jewelry that had once provided amusement for his waking hours seemed hard and cold to him now, their fascinations a world and a lifetime away.

When he returned to Memphis, arriving one surreptitious night just after his forty-third birthday, he was very cautious about plunging into music. He'd never written many songs, proud of his ability to pick a hit, but now he retired into the Graceland basement, where he'd had an eight-track studio installed, and alone with his guitar for the first time in many years, he began to strum it.

The chords came easily, but now he began to hear them form into patterns, suggest melodies, intimate phrases. Some nights he'd just lose himself in a wash of sound, playing until he realized that he'd been going on and on for hours, moving through whole symphonies in his mind.

He wrote down particularly agreeable sounds on scraps of paper, hummed bars of lyrics, smiled in amazement as they became snippets of song. When he had about twelve or fourteen of them, he called up his old friend and guitarist Scotty Moore, who owned a recording studio in nearby Nashville. Together, much as they had in early 1954, they began to try and find a sound that this new, more mature Elvis was hearing, bringing it into focus with a deft, enthusiastic touch. They laid the tracks down with a few select players, and nervously awaited the response.

The resultant album, *Elvis Sings Elvis*, brought him even further back than the famed 1968 television special. Hailed by both critics—"It is an inspiration to see a figure of such stature as Elvis Presley reclaim his artistic birthright" opined *Billboard*—and acclaimed by the public, the album hit the charts and stayed there, number one throughout the closing years of the seventies.

"I feel like I'm just beginning," Elvis proclaimed, paying a surprise visit to the Grand Ole Opry before setting off on a national tour. The shows provided even more of a surprise. Instead of the sumptuous elegance of his previous extravaganzas, with many-pieced bands and even string sections, the new Elvis borrowed a young rockabilly combo called the Tiger Cats (formerly of Lubbock, Texas) to back him. Amped up, driven to

electric frenzy, Elvis worked the crowds like a man possessed. Where before he had been content to toss scarves to the audience, now he virtually leaped among them, risking life and limb.

There were a few serious films, ones in which he had to stretch himself as an actor, not merely play himself. The best of these, a remake of the classic *Sunset Boulevard* with himself in the starring role, garnered him an Academy Award nomination. He also lured director Sergio Leone out of retirement to make a memorable martial arts film, with Elvis' brooding presence creating a new cinematic cult. Colonel Parker tried to steer him toward the safer family comedies of the sixties, but after the box office returns came in, he merely shrugged, smiled, and began thinking of a new level of licensing rights.

Elvis' follow-up album, *I'm My Own Man Now*, only confirmed the fact that he was undergoing a major rejuvenation, especially when the hit single, "It's A Country Kind Of Country" slid easily into double platinum status. Still, he never forgot to count his blessings; a gospel song always rounded off each side of his records, and during the live show, there was always a moment when he would ask the audience to bow their heads, and remember what good could be found in their lives, and live by that.

"And so, knowing a little something about entertainment myself. . . ." The crowd laughed appreciatively, and Elvis suddenly snapped out of his reverie. The President seemed about to be winding up his speech.

"I'd like to present the man who—truly—needs no introduction. A man who is the symbol of America the world over. Who has come to represent the struggle and promise that fulfills the American dream."

The President waves his hand toward Elvis, and the huge crowd explodes into shouts of delirious joy.

"On behalf of the people of the United States, and music lovers everywhere, I would like to present you, Elvis Aron Presley, with the Congressional Medal of Honor, the highest decoration of this great land, for one who has given service above and beyond the call of duty."

Eyes smarting, Elvis felt the medal being pinned to his lapel. The President clapped him on the back, then stepped aside leaving him alone before the microphone.

"I hardly know what to say," he stammered, feeling the rustic nostalgia of a country boy in him, the bare earth under his feet that had never quite deserted a seeming man.

"I'm just happy that I was given a second chance," he mumbled. The assembled multitudes were watching him, waiting on his every word. What could he tell them that would make them understand just why he'd found his way back to them?

He opened his mouth, and as if bidden, out came song:

Wise men say / Only fools rush in. . . .

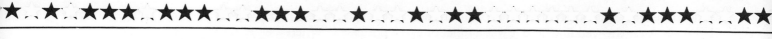

GRACELAND UBER ALLES
BY LESTER BANGS

Remember that Bob Dylan song that went, *I went to see the gypsy/Playin' at a big hotel. . . ?* A lot of people said that was supposed to be about Bob going to see Elvis do his rubberromp thang onstage in Vegas. What people were not prepared for was that Bob himself would take up permanent residence in said hotel so soon thereafter. He and Elvis took out adjacent suites, in fact, and late-nites they'd sit up shooting out TV sets, popping Dexamyls and Percodans and discussing the state of the cosmos, this cosmos, *their* cosmos. Times bein' what they were, it far greater befitted a Prophet's dignity to go into retirement, if not some Cloisters. No good could come of anything brewing without. The Beatles they were particularly disappointed in, all for different reasons, of course. One night Bob tried to think of some defense for John.

"At least he's makin' a fool of himself."

"Yeah," droned Elvis, a little too far on the nod to totally hold up his end of their mutual Query and Quest just now. "Go take a look't Li'l Richard."

"Hmm, I see what you mean."

"Don't work. Nuthin' does. 'Cept shootin' the toobs, goin' out'n the back yard'n blowin' up stuff. Since rock 'n' roll stop bein' fun . . . 'sss tha only pleassshhh lef' in life."

"Yeh, I finished off a delivery truck fulla Mark IVs just Thursdey."

"Thass right." Elvis seemed on the verge of snoring. But Bob was gettin' himself all exercised, irritable in front and workin' on it, chewing his gums off obsessive-likely.

"Hell man, I seen a few o' them dumb movies of yours, an' you know what? *They* were more fun than any of this shit!"

Elvis' head twitched, causing his cowlick to stand out even more—*Jesus*, thought Bob, *at the rate he's goin' pretty soon he'd be reject for the cast of* Andy of Mayberry;—but Elvis was sliding cross a Butchwax oil slick back towards consciousness as the chemicals commingling in his body shifted slightly, striking off each other. Suddenly he sat up and took a huge swig of Pepsi from a half-gallon bottle on the stand by his Pasha's Throne. He perched there a minute more, legs drawn up, looking back at Bob who thought him too far gone to hector through slit ole Southern eyelids sly as a flop-house desk-clerk. *He thank he so aw-fuckin-mighty, jus' cause he can geeze up a clutch o' crank an' then cram all them damn words into them stupid songs. Aw right, smart boy, you know what the words "Don't tamper with the U.S. male" mean?* The session boys in Nashville had told Elvis how they all sat there smokin' cigarettes, drinkin' beer and laughin' at him while Bob kept flicking through the door of the next room after each take, emerging twenty minutes or two hours later with the next one.

"I'm talkin' about people like Jeff Beck and Cream and Led Zeppelin!" Dylan ranted on, oblivious to whether he had an audience or not. "Who the fuck do they think they are, calling all that shit 'progressive? Playin' ole blues songs, AN' ALL OF EM PLAYIN' THE SAME ONES!!!, handin' em down to kids so pompous like they just got a deed to 'Rock Me Baby' from outer space! *I* sang Blind Lemon too, *and* Blind Willie, Blind Boy Fuller, Blind Boy Grunt, all them old blind coons you didn' hafta pay no royalties to!"

"Yeh, but you was singin' to *caw-lehdge stuh-dints*," Elvis said, pronouncing the last two words with a little biting twist Bob didn't hear the sneer in, "it was their fuckin' *dooo*-ty to not only *know about* all them coons, but *listen to* and even *like* 'em."

"But you sang Crudup and all that shit. You musta liked 'em too."

"I didn't *like* 'em, I *lived with* 'em," Elvis said incredulously, as if telling a retarded child the most basic facts of functioning human life. "Don't 'magine yawlz *git* too many them Ethiopians up Minnesota way, do ya?"

"You're not even *listening* to me! *Everybody* starts out singin' that shit, but these guys are acting like this was some wild new idea was *just thought of* and all by themselves. It's just a big *ego* trip!"

Look who's talkin', thought Elvis, but he agreed.

"And *none* of 'em can write songs, which is why they're doin' those 90-minute solos in the first place! And the reason they can't write songs is because they're all fuckin' *guitar players*, and guitar players are all *morons*! Would *you* wanna hang out with your session-men?"

"Hell, why not? I'm hangin' out with you, ain't I?"

"Yeah, but how come nobody can write no fuckin *songs* no more?"

"Nothin' to say, I guess . . . I dunno, never wrote one in m' life. Seemed like a hard way to go when y'can jus' yap 'em out instead."

"All right, so *I've* got writer's block and just keep rewritin' the same song lyin' about how wonderful my marriage is! That's *my* problem! Van Morrison has it too! I spent *all those years* teaching *all those assholes* how it's done, and now can a *one* of 'em stand up and maybe pay me back a little, give me some *clue* life still exists on Earth? No! They're all junked out, or like me they got married and moved to the country, so now they're 'mellowing out,' and what a lot of horse manure THAT is!!, or they've lost their politics, or Found God—IT'S ALWAYS SOME COMPLETE BULLSHIT—so now the guitar players've taken over the world, and hell mosta them were only hot back in 1965 when they were down on Carnaby Street doin' all that speed, plus now they're all junkies, so there's NO SOUL in ANY of their playing, just these big loud cement solos that go on and on and on and on!"

"You know what I think you oughta do, Bob? Now listen to me. Y'gittin' y'self all het up over nuthin'. Take some Quays, you just' got speed-froth, and if you'll quiet down for *just a minute*, I'll tell ya. . ."

Bob was broaching apoplexy—all that would come out of his mouth were little bullets of saliva. His eyes bugged out of his head and he gaped showing teeth at Elvis, looking more insane than The King had ever seen him, and that was goin' some. But The King was cool. About everything, which was why he was where he was now. Whereas Bob wasn't happy less he'd connected for some whole *new* way of makin' himself miserable with all them damn *words*, which of course were the problem in the first place.

"Aww-*raht!*", Elvis announced. "Y'know, I never tole ya cuz I never tell nobody nuthin' about their music 'cause nuthin' ever sounds any good to me an' hasn't since oh 'bout halfway through m'army stretch when Jerry Lee an' Carl an' all them boys'd went down too an' there was nuthin' on the radio but white boys imitatin' *white* boys. That Beatles shit, I was polite to 'em but it was a lotta nuthin', folks jus' needed somethin' an' they wuz cute . . . but I'll tell ya, I *do* like this new album o' yours!"

"You *do?*"

"Yup. Whutchew feelin' guilty cuz it's a *movie soun'-track?* Howya think *I* feel? Ain't listen t'a one of 'em yet, ain't even *counted*. Forgot ever'thing 'bout the movies too, allus jus' drivin' a car, kissin' a gurl, drivin' a car, kissin' a gurl, and then once in a while I gotta punch somebody . . . but anyway this 'un soun's real nice, no shit. You play sum *good* country, boy, when you stop *tryin'* to. Whut'sa matter with instrumentals? They stop ya thinkin' an' that's the only time music flows. You're constipated, man! But not on this album."

"But it's got *five versions* of the *same song!* Or maybe it's four, it's like you about your movies, I just did it to be doin' somethin' besides rottin' away in Woodstock or New York City and there's only one *real* song on it, 'Knockin' On Heaven's Door,' and *that's* only 'cause, pal, my guns ARE in the ground!"

"Naw, that one was awright, sounds like you might gitcherself few cover versions there, but I still say ain't nothin' wrong with instrumental music or music where

nothin's goin' on, hell nuthin' *ever* goin' on on *any* o' my tracks, but y'know, people like trank music, they need a little soothin' out insteada all this rantin' ravin' holy rollin' y'awl specialized in till y'ran outa gas an' I would too if I wuz carryin' on like that an' never knowin' what a word of it meant."

"No, that's not true. I knew what 'To Ramona' meant. Forget just now, but. . . ."

"Well, now, lissen, that's okay, don't matter either way cuz *other folks* knew what they meant or thought they did or took dope an' put their meanin's in 'em, but, y'know it's true I don't get out much but I did go down 'n' pick up my Federal Narcotics badge from the Prez an' I tell ya times have *de-finitely* changed! People don' wanna hear 'bout how bad it is for the niggers or the commies or the this or that or 'speshly *you*, cuz frankly pal they got problems enough o' they *own!* You followin' me? They 'preciate a spot o' *coolin' out!* None a my fans minds that nuthin' happens in my music, fact they like it better that way—lissen, if I did the Sun sessions now nobody'd wanna know, all that crazy shit's what they'll pay any amount o' money, go anyplace, do anything t'escape from. But I stood up there enough nights mumblin' 'My Way' lookin' out at

'em an' thinkin' about it that I think I done got it figgered out—meanin' them, me, the world, ever'thing. What's happ'nin' kid is folks *want* nuthin' to be goin' on, whether it's in music, sports, whatever they useta get a big kick out of but ain't kickin' so hard now, they don' wan' it to, they wan' nuthin' so they can *relax* inside it! Which is what *I* give 'em! You follow me! Hell, do a album with *twelve* versions o' the same fuckin' song, I liked that Billy the Kid song jus' *cause* it was so nuthin', you obviously didn't give a shit about the words, rhyme it jus' a *little* different each time . . . look, I dunno how else to tell ya, but YOU'RE LUCKY. *Because* nuthin's on your mind! If you put out *Highway 61 Revisited* today, it'd make folks *nervous* 'n' they'd stay away from it like it was the door to a malaria ward! They're *paranoid!* Don' *wanna* put meanin's in no more, fraid o' what they might find out they really truly *meant!* After all, ya know what I mean? Jus' cool 'em out, boy, an' you'll be surprised at first but you'll see soon enough that if you cool 'em, they'll cool you, then vice an' versa again, an' it jus' keeps on goin' forever, so ever'thang gon' be *fine*, after all, jus' getcherself a mint julep an' then go right back to that porch an' *keep* settin' there! I tell ya, it's nirvana!"

"Yeah, hmmm, maybe you're right . . . some of that does seem to make a lot of sense. They want Valium I'll give 'em Valium, an' maybe I'll even steal a page from *your* book an' tour again but take it to *Vegas* an' declare protest songs in Vegas with arrangements that sound like a lounge band in the Catskills is actually 'The Sound of the Future, so ya better get used to it!' An'

then glower at 'em that special way way I worked up that warns 'em this is me talkin' so they better mind or I'll get cranky an' bring down a plague of locusts or some such. I'll pass myself off as *history*, the Smithsonian, the Spirit of America, last chance for a glance at what the frontier mighta once looked like! An' for something like that they'll *pay*! Hey, thanks Elvis, I think tonight you mighta given me a whole new lease on life! Hell, I was swimmin' upstream an' never knew it!"

"Why shore. Y'awl welcum, it's nuthin', really, see, there I go again, that's why they can scalpt tickets fer one o' my shows for upwards of $200 sometimes, 'cause they know *I deliver*. Nuthin', jus' like I promised. Sheeit, boy, you gotta big enough ego, big as they come cept for me, after all you been thu an' dun already you don' hafta do nuthin' but *make a point a doin' nuthin'*. Let 'em know they're damn fuckin' lucky to get to pay $200 just to stare at you pretendin' to sing for two hours. They *know* you're not singing well as you do, way back in their heart of hearts, you ain't even really strictly *there* at all, your mind's wanderin' all over the place daydreamin' while you're wanderin' all roun' the stage or hell just stand stone still like Abe Lincoln an' don't move all night! They'd *really* appreciate that, even more I betcha! 'Cuz take it from The Champ Now 'n' Forever: the more absent you get, the more thems cums flowin' in cryin' out like sex-starved ole maids justa shake, shv'rin an-a hollerin' away at a backwoods revival meetin'! They gotta get it out somehow, and it might as well be you."

"That's for *damn sure*. Yeah . . . maybe I'll put out a album with a whole buncha versions of one song an' one'll be about the *weather* the day I cut it: 'Tempertures dropped slightly in the early morning *hours*/slight gusts from the *south*. . .'"

"There you go! Elton John, watch out—ole Bob's headin' back for *Number One!*"

They lapsed into silence, each not pondering his own situation to the best of his abilities. Bob was fired with this new vision of his future, Elvis had totally turned his head around, he could go on forever like this! The King himself, meanwhile, was kicked back with the chair on ex-treeem ree-cline again, eyes closed, pretending to nod while he pondered Bob's situation. The truth was that while much of what he'd said was true, he'd also known all along that it was the sort of advice that Bob constitutionally would be totally incapable of following if he worked at it a million years, and he never worked a day in his life anyway or even found out how people do it so that's out too. The truth was that when it came right down to it, Bob was just like all the rest—oh, he mighta been more talented, a little or maybe even a lot, once maybe, but he's been sittin' down there in the same boat with all those other depressed singer-songwriters catch cold jus' from contemplatin' their bellybutton the wrong way. The truth was that they were all stray golden boys who'd gotten off the ponderosa somehow and were gonna just spend the rest of their lives chasin' their own egos like a foxtail while wanderin' all over the map and never have the slightest idea where they're at or what's really goin' on. He, Elvis, was the Only One who knew what was goin' on—well, maybe the Colonel, but Elvis really knew that the Colonel didn't know because Elvis wasn't the dumb shacktrash the Colonel'd mistook him for in the first place. He'd got outa the army after servin' his regular time jus' like anybody else whereas the Colonel was sentenced to stay there his whole fuckin' life fore an' aft. The Colonel in this respect was somewhat like Bob, shared his deficiencies: always had to be *doin'* somethin'. If they ain't gotta itch to scratch they'll go hunt up a mosquito an' pay it to sting 'em. 'Cause that's just their nature and people never really change, ever, they just talk about it a lot while getting older and slower. The truth was that the talk was designed to keep a permanent screen of static hissing so's to get up a camouflage they'll never quite hafta see through to just exactly how old and slow they really are this very second, and the pondering of the knowledge beyond that could only grind on down heavier and dimmer and that ain't a pretty thing to contemplate. So they distract themselves with bullshit, invent excuses to worry, then invent new words to modernize 'n' customize 'em, words like "neuroses," and by the time they call 'em that they're just where they always wanted to be: permanently out of touch. With themselves, that is: *of course* they yak around with each other, that's what it's all about; why be bored sitting around workin' up one dull homely "neuroses" when you can be *actively collaborating* with your neighbor to jam your two l'il "neuroses" together jus' like two gitar players git together. Who knows what emerge, maybe a whole new strain o' "neuroses" make ya both rich or the two of y'can take 'em out the whole mess an' collar a few friends hell make it a party at-home or drag the whole stew all over town till y'all done mounted a Colossus of Neuroses or Tower of Babel of Neuroses that will stand forever and pilgrims come from far afoot to stand and gaze on up in awe.

The truth was that the likes of Bob and the Colonel would never be happy and Elvis would always be happy for a very simple reason: that while they kept thrashing and twitching this way and that in pursuit of always something brand-new to do do do, Elvis was in fact himself the only person that had ever lived in the entire world and therefore of course there truly was nothing to do and no reason to do it no rhyme or reason no words no meaning no day or night or sun or rain or this or that or you or I. He had it licked: he had beaten God, forget the devil. But then, he wondered how it must feel to God to now be beaten. *Well, guess there's jus' some questions ain't got no answers*, he thought to himself, *That's life*, shrugging and then drifting away once more and givin' a few flecks of his will and desire into it too for which he would not ask one red cent this time cause he was in too good a mood and remote was something that you could never get too much of.

A-Z LIFE/MUSIC/

Bob Abel
Documentary film maker, co-director of *Elvis on Tour* (1972).

Jean and Julian Aberbach
Brother music publishers, who founded Hill and Range which became the repository of Elvis' catalogue. The Aberbach Brothers worked along with Colonel Parker. Over the years, their company was managed by Freddie Bienstock and later, Lamar Fike.

"A Big Hunk O' Love"
(Sid Wyche – Aaron Schroeder)
Swinging, prototypical rock n' roll recorded June, 1958 at RCA Studios in Nashville; released in 1959 as a single and on *50,000,000 Elvis Fans Can't Be Wrong*; performed live at *"Aloha"* show (1973) and released on album; a staple of Elvis' road show, also performed in *Elvis On Tour* film (1972).

Lee Ablerson
The designer of the TCB/TLC chains, partner in Sol Schwartz's Beverly Hills outlet.

"A Boy Like Me, A Girl Like You"
(Sid Tepper – Roy C. Bennett)
Recorded March of 1962 for the film *Girls! Girls! Girls!*; released on album in November, 1962.

Johnny Ace
R & B composer and musician who died in a game of Russian Roulette on Christmas Eve in 1954, a legendary figure in the annals of rhythm and blues. Most renowned for his song "Pledging My Love", which was the B-side of Elvis' last single released before he died. It soared on the charts following the news of his death.

"Adam And Evil"
(Fred Wise – Randy Starr)
The "snake charmer" number, a medium rocker recorded in Hollywood in February of 1966 for the film *Spinout*; released in October of 1966 on soundtrack album.

Faye Adams
R & B singer whose 1933 hit "Shake A Hand" was a favorite of Elvis'. He finally recorded the song in 1975.

Jack Adams
Mississippi rancher, whose property became the Circle C Range when Elvis bought it in 1967.

Julie Adams
"Vera Radford," sexy proprietress of the dude ranch in *Tickle Me* (1964).

Nick Adams
One of Elvis' earliest Hollywood pals, who met Elvis during *Love Me Tender* and became "Johnny Yuma" in *The Rebel* on television. Together, they rode motorcycles and remained close until Nick's death in 1968 from an overdose of pills. Adams died on February 7, 1968, the same day Lisa Marie Presley was born.

A Date With Elvis
1959. RCA Victor. LP
(LPM-2011).
Side 1: "Blue Moon Of Kentucky"; "Young And Beautiful"; "(You're So Square) Baby I Don't Care"; "Milkcow Blues Boogie"; "Baby Let's Play House."
Side 2: "Good Rockin' Tonight"; "Is It So Strange"; "We're Gonna Move"; "I Want To Be Free"; "I Forgot To Remember To Forget."

Pierre Adidge
Co-director of *Elvis On Tour* (1972).

Ronnie Lee Adkins
One of the three arrested at Forest Hill Cemetery after Elvis was interred (August 29, 1977). The incident, widely reported, involved two other men, Raymond Green and Bruce Nelson. As macabre as it sounds, they were suspected of trying to steal Elvis' body and ransom it, but the charges were dismissed.

"A Dog's Life"
(Sid Wayne – Ben Wiseman)
Recorded in July of 1965 for the film *Paradise – Hawaiian Style*; released on soundtrack album in June of 1966.

Brother Adolph
The octogenarian monk, inti-mate of Yogananda, with whom Elvis sought spiritual counsel at a Self Realization Fellowship in Pacific Palisades in the 1960's.

"A Fool Such As I"
(Bill Trader)
Hank Snow's 1952 hit, recorded by Elvis at RCA's Nashville Studio in June of 1958; released in 1959 as a single and included on *50,000,000 Elvis Fans Can't Be Wrong*; performed at the benefit performance in Hawaii for the U.S.S. Arizona, 1961.

"After Loving You"
(E. Miller – J. Lantz)
Soulful, heavily produced number from the second round of Memphis sessions, recorded at American Studios in February of 1969; released in May of 1969 on *From Elvis In Memphis*.

"A House That Has Everything"
(Arnold – Morrow – Martin)
Recorded in January of 1967 at RCA's Nashville Studio, for the film *Clambake*; released on the soundtrack LP in November, 1967.

"Ain't That Loving You Baby"
(Clyde Otis – Ivory Joe Hunter)
Vintage rocker recorded in June of 1958 at RCA's Nashville Studio; not released until September of 1964 when RCA issued it as a single, the flip-side of "Ask Me." Also released on *Elvis Gold Records, Volume 4* in 1968.

Airport Inn
Local Memphis night club that booked C & W acts during Elvis' early days, when he performed after the release of his first Sun singles in 1955. It was here that Oscar "The Baron" Davis was supposed to have seen Elvis perform and relay the news of his "find" back to his boss, Colonel Thomas A. Parker.

Aladdin Hotel
Las Vegas hotel where Elvis was married to Priscilla on April 30, 1981 and the site of the press reception.

Ginger Alden
Elvis' last girlfriend and, many

FILMS/PEOPLE/PLACES/THINGS

say, his bride-to-be before he died. She was nineteen when he met her, a former Miss Memphis Traffic Safety, who became a companion during his last year and discovered his body on his bathroom floor on the morning of his death. Their relationship was a source of great speculation among friends, family and fans alike. After the death, Ginger claimed that Elvis was planning to marry her on Christmas Day of 1977 (apparently he had given her a diamond engagement ring). Since the death, many reports have disputed her claim. In *The Truth About Elvis*, for instance, Larry Geller reveals that Elvis was convinced that the marriage was a misguided idea, though he *had* been seriously considering it. Ginger has remained a sore spot with many. Her appearance in the movie *The Living Legend*, an endeavor that seemed exploitative to many fans, further irritated many of Elvis' friends.

Jo Alden

Ginger's mother, who filed a $40,000 lawsuit against the Presley estate after Elvis died, claiming that Elvis orally agreed to pay the mortgage on her home and provide improvements in return for letting Ginger travel with him on tour. The case is pending, but it did little to improve her daughter's image with Elvis' fans.

Terry Alden

Ginger's older sister, whom Elvis first noticed on a Memphis television program. When George Klein introduced the Alden Sisters to Elvis in Las Vegas, it was assumed that Elvis and Terry would pair up. Instead, Elvis favored Ginger.

Walter Alden

Ginger's father. He had the distinction of inducting Elvis into the Army in March of 1958, an irony that did not go unnoticed by Elvis.

Muhammed Ali

"The Greatest." Elvis' boxing idol and personal friend; a frequent visitor backstage in Las Vegas. Elvis once presented him with a royal boxing robe, which Ali wore to his first Norton fight. (Norton then broke Ali's jaw.)

Aliases

Elvis was known to have traveled incognito on several occasions. He often used the names John Carpenter or John Burrows (or Burroughs). The latter name was used when he went to Washington to meet President Nixon. He also disguised himself at times. On one occasion in Las Vegas, he was said to have walked around the casino in flowing robes, a turban and a beard!

"A Little Bit Of Green"

(Arnold – Morrow – Martin) Recorded in January of 1969 at American Studios, Memphis; released in November, 1969, on *From Memphis To Vegas/From Vegas To Memphis*.

"A Little Less Conversation"

(Davis – Strange) From *Live A Little, Love A Little* (1968), a Mac Davis – Billy Strange number recorded in March of 1968 at MGM Sound Studio, Hollywood; released as a single in September, 1968, the flip of "Almost In Love." Later, it appeared on the Camden RCA LP *Almost In Love*.

All About Elvis

Bootleg novelty album in two volumes, including humorous and satirical material on Elvis by many artists.
Volume One: "United Press News – Comments About Elvis"; "Dear Elvis" (Parts I & II); "Hey Mr. Presley"; "My Boy Elvis"; "I'm Lonesome for Elvis"; "Elwood Pretzel Fan Club" (Parts I & II); "All About Elvis" (Parts I & II); "Oh Elvis"; "Elvis Presley For President"; "I'm In Love With Elvis Presley"; "I Wanna Spend X-Mas With Elvis."
Volume Two: "All American Boy"; "Dear Elvis" (Parts I & II); "My Boy Elvis"; "Hey Mr. Presley"; "Bye Bye Elvis"; "Dear 53310761"; "Gonna Get Even With Elvis' Sergeant"; "Elvis And Me."

All About Elvis, Volume 1

33⅓ Bootleg LP
Side 1: "United Press News – Comments About Elvis"; "Dear Elvis, Part 1"; "Dear Elvis, Part 2"; "Hey, Mr. Presley"; "My Boy Elvis"; "I'm Lonesome For Elvis"; "Bye Bye Elvis"; "Marching Elvis."
Side 2: "Elwood Pretzel Fan Club, Part 1"; "Elwood Pretzel Fan Club, Part 2"; "All About Elvis, Part 1"; "All About Elvis, Part 2"; "Oh Elvis"; "Elvis Presley For President"; "I Wanna Spend X-Mas With Elvis."

All About Elvis, Volume 2

33⅓ Bootleg LP
Side 1: "All American Boy"; "Dear Elvis, Part 1"; "Dear Elvis, Part 2"; "Elvis Blues"; "All About Elvis, Part 1"; "All About Elvis, Part 2."
Side 2: "My Boy Elvis"; "Hey, Mr. Presley"; "Bye Bye Elvis"; "Dear 53310761"; "Gonna Get Even With Elvis' Sergeant"; "Elvis And Me."

Woody Allen

One of Elvis' favorite comic actors and writers.

"All I Needed Was The Rain"

(Fred Wise – Ben Weisman)
Mellow Blues number recorded in October of 1967 in Hollywood, used in connection with the *1968 TV Special;* released in 1969 on the LP *Elvis Sings Flaming Star.*

"All Shook Up"

(Otis Blackwell – Elvis Presley)
Otis' classic, recorded in January of 1957 at Radio Recorders, in Hollywood (with Scotty, Bill, D.J., Dudley Brooke on piano, and the Jordanaires); first released as a single in March of 1957 (flip-side of "That's When Your Heartaches Begin") and on the LP *Elvis' Golden Records* in 1958. Since then, it became a staple of his live appearances: on *"Elvis"* (1968), on *From Memphis to Vegas* (1969), on *Elvis In Person* (1970), on *Elvis As Recorded At Madison Square Garden* (1972), and on many bootleg releases.

"All That I Am"

(Sid Tepper – Roy C. Bennett)
Romantic ballad recorded in February of 1966 in Hollywood for the film *Spinout;* released in October of 1966 as single (flip-side of "Spinout") and as soundtrack LP.

All-Time Christmas Favorites

1976. Collector's Edition. LP (CE-505).
Side 1a: "Ding-a-ling the Christmas Bell"; "Frosty The Snow-

man"; "A Wistle A Wisker Away"; "Rudolph The Red Nosed Raindeer"; "Soon It Will Be Christmas." (All songs by Lynn Anderson.)
Side 1b: "Christmas in My Home Town"; "Little Drummer Boy"; "Deck the Halls"; "O Holy Night"; "Silent Night." (All songs by Charlie Pride.)
Side 2a: "Jingle Bells"; "Gounod's Ave Maria"; "The Best Gift"; "The Christmas Song"; "Sleep in Heavenly Peace." (All songs by Barbra Streisand.)
Side 2b: "The Christmas Song"; "Mistletoe and Holly"; "I'll Be Home For Christmas"; "The First Noel"; "Silent Night." (All songs by Frank Sinatra.)
Side 3a: "Sleigh Ride"; "Christmas Holiday"; "Winter Wonderland"; "Mary's Little Boy Child"; "Silver Bells." (All songs by Andy Williams.)
Side 3b: "It Must Be Getting Close To Christmas"; "Have Yourself A Merry Christmas"; "Blue Christmas"; "The Christmas"; "Pretty Paper." (All songs by Glen Campbell.)
Side 4a: "I'm Dreaming of a White Christmas"; "It's a Marshmellow World in the Winter"; "Silver Bells"; "Walking in a Winter Wonderland"; "Silent Night." (All songs by Dean Martin.)
Side 4b: "Come All Ye Faithful"; "Noel"; "I'll Be Home For Christmas"; "Silver Bells"; "Walking in a Winter Wonderland." (All songs by Elvis Presley.)
Side 5a: "Away in the Manger"; "Silent Night"; "O Little Town of Bethlehem"; "Joy to the World"; "It Came Upon a Midnight Clear." (All songs by Tammy Wynette.)
Side 5b: "Walkin' in a Winter Wonderland"; "Sleigh Ride"; "I'm Dreaming of a White Xmas"; "Silver Bells"; "Blue Christmas."
(All songs by Johnny Mathis.)
Note: All information on this album has been reprinted exactly as it appeared on the record (including numerous errors).

"Almost"

(Florence Kaye – Ben Weisman)
Heavily orchestrated ballad recorded in October of 1968 in Hollywood; released in April of 1970 on the RCA Camden LP *Let's Be Friends.*

"Almost Always True"

(Fred Wise – Ben Weisman)
Love song, half-crooned with a note of mockery in Elvis' voice. Recorded in April of 1961 in Hollywood for the film *Blue Hawaii;* released in October of 1961 on the soundtrack. Also on bootleg LP *Behind Closed Doors.*

Almost In Love

1970. RCA Camden. LP (CAS-2440).
Side 1: "Almost In Love"; "Long Legged Girl"; "Edge Of Reality"; "My Little Friend"; "A Little Less Conversation."
Side 2: "Rubberneckin'"; "Clean Up Your Own Backyard"; "U.S. Male"; "Charro"; "Stay Away, Joe."

Almost In Love

1973. RCA Camden. LP (CAS-2440).
Side 1: "Almost In Love"; "Long Legged Girl"; "Edge Of Reality"; "My Little Friend"; "A Little Less Conversation."
Side 2: "Rubberneckin'"; "Clean Up Your Own Backyard"; "U.S. Male"; "Charro"; "Stay Away."

"Aloha From Hawaii"

The television special in January of 1973 beamed via satellite throughout the world, and source of the double album. Many consider it to be Elvis' peak before a slow decline following the divorce. The show was seen by more than 1½ billion people.

Aloha From Hawaii Via Satellite

1973. RCA. EP (DTFO-2006).
Side 1: "Something"; "You Gave Me A Mountain"; "I Can't Stop Loving You."
Side 2: "My Way"; "What Now My Love"; "I'm So Lonesome I Could Cry."

Aloha From Hawaii Via Satellite

1973. RCA. LP (VPSX-6089).
Side 1: "Introduction: Also Sprach Zarathustra"; "See See Rider"; "Burning Love"; "Something"; "You Gave Me A Mountain"; "Steamroller."
Side 2: "My Way"; "Love Me"; "Johnny B. Goode"; "It's Over"; "Blue Suede Shoes"; "I'm So Lonesome I Could Cry"; "I Can't Stop Loving You"; "Hound Dog."
Side 3: "What Now My Love"; "Fever"; "Welcome To My World"; "Suspicious Minds"; "Introductions By Elvis."
Side 4: "I'll Remember You"; "Medley"; "Long Tall Sally/Whole Lotta Shakin' Goin On"; "An American Trilogy"; "A Big Hunk O' Love"; "Can't Help Falling In Love."

"Aloha Oe"

(Traditional – Adapted by Elvis Presley)
Traditional Hawaiian song recorded in March-April of 1961 in Hollywood for the film *Blue Hawaii;* released in October of 1961 on soundtrack LP.

Also Sprach Zarathustra

The symphonic piece by Richard Strauss used to open Elvis' shows, better known as the

sunrise sequence from the film *2001: A Space Odyssey.*

Alternate Takes

Many different versions of Elvis' recordings have been issued. Sometimes they got onto a disc by mistake, and sometimes they were specially released. Following is a list of studio songs, and all the many different versions of hits sung at each concert. For instance, songs like "Hound Dog" were sung at most shows, and many versions are available on disc. Many songs were also issued with a different mix, such as one stereo channel missing, or beginnings or endings faded out. In 1979, RCA began to issue songs with the overdubbing stripped off, and in 1981, with new backings.

a) Alternate takes
   A Cane And A High-Starched Collar
   A Dog's Life
   After Loving You
   Are You Sincere
   Big Boots
   Big Boss Man
   Blue Suede Shoes
   Can't Help Falling In Love
   Datin'
   Doncha Think It's Time
   Don't Leave Me Now
   Fame And Fortune
   Follow That Dream
   Frankfurt Special
   Guadalajara
   Guitar Man (2)
   I Love You Because
   I Want You I Need You I Love You
   I Was Born About 10,000 Years Ago
   If I Can Dream
   I'm Falling In Love Tonight
   I'm Left, You're Right, She's Gone
   It Hurts Me
   It's Still Here
   Just Call Me Lonesome
   Let Yourself Go
   Love Letters
   Lover Doll
   Old Shep
   Roustabout
   Stay Away Joe
   She Thinks I Still Care
   Shippin' Around
   Such A Night
   Thanks To The Rolling Sea
   They Remind Me Too Much Of You
   Wild In The Country
   Also, "Tonight's All Right For Love" was a slightly different tune to "Tonight Is So Right For Love," and "He Is My Everything" is the same tune as "There Goes My Everything."

b) Different Mixes, etc.
   A Little Less Conversation
   Ask Me
   Baby I Don't Care
   Baby Let's Play House

Blue Moon Of Kentucky
Dixieland Rock
Don't Think Twice, It's
  Alright
Faded Love
Flaming Star
Funny How Time Slips Away
Good Rockin Tonight
Heart Of Rome
I Don't Care If The Sun Don't
  Shine
I Want You I Need You I
  Love You
I Feel That I've Known You
  Forever
I'm Left You're Right She's
  Gone
I'm Yours
Is It So Strange
It Hurts Me
It's Only Love
Kiss Me Quick
Life
Long Legged Girl
Long Lonely Highway
Make The World Go Away
Merry Christmas Baby
Milkcow Blues
Mystery Train
Poor Boy
Suspicion
That's All Right
Tonight's All Right For Love
We're Gonna Move
Whole Lotta Shakin' Goin' On
Wild In The Country
You'll Think Of Me
You're A Heartbreaker
Young And Beautiful

c) Backings Removed

Find Out What's Happening
For The Heart
Girl Of Mine
Green Green Grass Of Home
I Can Help
I Got A Feelin' In My Body
I'll Never Fall In Love
  Again
It's Midnight
My Boy
Never Again
She Thinks I Still Care
She Wears My Ring
Solitaire
Spanish Eyes
Take Good Care Of Her
There's A Honky Tonk Angel
Thinking About You
Waydown
Your Love's Been A Long
  Time Coming

d) New Backing

After Loving You
Cleanup Your Own Backyard
Faded Love
Guitar Man
I'm Movin' On
Just Call Me Lonesome
Loving Arms
She Thinks I Still Care
Too Much Monkey Business
You Asked Me To
The above lists are not exhaustive, and no doubt RCA will continue to release alternate takes, etc.

"Always Elvis"
Colonel Parker's first convention at the Las Vegas Hilton, September 1-10, 1978. Both Priscilla and Vernon appeared as special guests (a statue of Elvis was unveiled during ceremonies). Also present was Henri Lewin, the hotel's President, and Barron Hilton, the hotel's owner, both of whom were prime sponsors of Elvis' Las Vegas bookings over the years. It also became the Colonel's marketing-promotion slogan.

"Always Elvis"
The white wine marketed by the Italian firm of Frantenac, authorized by Colonel Parker and Factors, Inc. for distribution and sale in the U.S. Ironically, Elvis never drank wine.

"Always Late (With Your Kisses)"
A Lefty Frizzell tune recorded by Elvis for Sun Records sometime in 1954, never released.

"Always On My Mind"
(Wayne Carson – Mark James – Johnny Christopher)
Recorded in March of 1972 at MGM Recording Studios, Los Angeles; released as a single in November of 1972, the flip-side of "Separate Ways"; and on the Camden RCA LP *Separate Ways* (1973).

"Amazing Grace"
(Traditional – adapted by Elvis Presley)
Elvis at his inspirational best, backed by the Nashville Edition, The Imperials and others. Recorded in March of 1971 at RCA's Nashville Studio; released in April of 1972 on the LP *He Touched Me*.

"Amen"
(John W. Pate, Sr. – Curtis Mayfield)
Chorus used as part of a medley in live performances at the end of "I Got A Woman." It can be heard on the LP *Elvis Recorded Live Onstage In Memphis* (1974).

"America (The Beautiful)"
(Track arranged by Elvis Presley)
Elvis pays homage to Uncle Sam and the Bicentennial; recorded in concert around 1976-77; released as a single in November of 1977, with "My Way" on the flip-side.

"A Mess Of Blues"
(Doc Pomus – Mort Shuman)
Elvis' first recording sessions back from the Army produced this one, recorded at RCA's Nashville Studios in March of 1960; released as a single in July, 1960 (the flip-side of "It's Now Or Never"). Later, on the LP's *Elvis Gold Records, Vol. 4* (1968) and *Elvis: Worldwide 50 Gold Award Hits, Vol. 1* (1970).

Amigos
Vocal backing for the soundtrack LP *Fun In Acapulco* (1963) who also appeared in the film. They also worked with the Jordanaires in 1962 on *Girls! Girls! Girls!*.

"Am I Ready"
(Sid Tepper – Roy C. Bennett)
Typical Elvis film ballad with the Jordanaires and in Hollywood for the film *Spinout*; released in October of 1966 on the soundtrack LP.

Amory, Mississippi
The concert in 1955 played by three of Sun's biggest stars (Elvis, Johnny Cash and Carl Perkins). Legend has it that Carl Perkins penned the words of his rockabilly masterpiece "Blue Suede Shoes" there, though he received the inspiration at the Roadside Inn.

"An American Trilogy"
(traditional – arranged by Mickey Newbury)
This song, a combination of "Dixie"; "All My Trials" and "The Battle Hymn Of The Republic" was instituted by Elvis as a special segment of his rock show. It became one of his many dramatic trademarks. First recorded live onstage at the Las Vegas Hilton in 1972 (released in May as a single), it was subsequently recorded and released on live LP's: *Madison Square Garden* (1972), *Aloha From Hawaii* (1973), *Live Onstage In Memphis* (1974).

"And I Love You So"
(Don McLean)
A hit for Bobby Goldsboro and Perry Como, Elvis recorded this in May of 1975 in Hollywood; it was released in 1975 on the LP *Today*.

Ursula Andress
The curvaceous "Margarita Dauphine," the hotel social director in *Fun In Acapulco* (1963).

"And The Grass Won't Pay No Mind"
(Neil Diamond)
A Diamond love tune done forcefully and tastefully by Elvis, recorded in February of 1969 at American Studios in Memphis; released that year on the LP *From Memphis To Vegas/ From Vegas To Memphis*.

"An Evening Prayer"
(CM Battersby – Charles H. Gabriel)
Another inspirational tune recorded in May of 1971 at RCA Studio in Nashville; released in April of 1972 on the LP *He Touched Me*.

"Angel"
(Sid Tepper – Roy C. Bennett)

Movie ballad with the Jordanaires recorded in July of 1961 at RCA Studio in Nashville for the film *Follow That Dream*; released by RCA as an EP in April of 1962.

"Animal Instinct"
(Bill Grant – Bernie Baum – Florence Kaye)
A throwaway cut from *Harum Scarum*, recorded in February of 1965 in Hollywood; released in October of that year on the soundtrack LP.

The Anita Kerr Singers
The vocal group who overdubbed vocals to "Tomorrow Night," LaVern Baker's hit of 1948 that Elvis recorded for Sam Phillips in July of 1954. RCA, which received the master, never released the song until 1965, when it appeared on the LP *Elvis For Everyone* with its new backing.

Paul Anka
Composer/singer/musician, a teen heart-throb of the late fifties and early sixties, who penned such classics as "Diana" and wrote the English words for "My Way" for Frank Sinatra. Elvis adopted the song as well, recording it in 1973. By the end of his life, it became as much his trademark as Sinatra's.

Ann-Margret
"Rusty Martin," Elvis' co-star in *Viva, Las Vegas* and one of his all-time favorite leading ladies. Also a source of serious romantic interest in the period before his marriage and a close friend to the end.

Michael Ansara
"Prince Dragna" in *Harum Scarum* (1965).

"Any Day Now"
(Bob Hillard – Burt Bacharach)
Sharply arranged and potent version of a Chuck Jackson oldie via American Studios in Memphis, recorded in February of 1969, complete with the Memphis Strings; released as a single in April of 1969, the flip-side of "In The Ghetto." Later released on the LP *From Elvis In Memphis* (1969), and *Elvis: The Other Sides – Worldwide Gold Award Hits, Volume 2* (1970).

"Anyone (Could Fall In Love With You)"
(Bennie Benjamin – Sol Marcus – A. Dejesus)
A ballad recorded for the film *Kissin' Cousins* in Hollywood, in October of 1963, but deleted from the film; it was released on the soundtrack LP in March of 1964.

"Anyplace Is Paradise"
(Joe Thomas)

Offbeat Elvis heavy breather, cut at Radio Recorders in Hollywood in September of 1956; released in November of 1956 on *Elvis*, the second RCA LP.

"Anything That's Part of You"
(Don Robertson)
A slow, sad weeper with Elvis in full-throated sincerity and a fine tinkling Floyd Cramer piano. Recorded in October of 1961 at RCA's Nashville Studio; released in March of 1962 as the flip-side of "Good Luck Charm" and on the LP *Elvis' Golden Records, Volume III* (1963).

"Any Way You Want Me (That's How I'll Be)"
(Aaron Schroeder – Cliff Owens)
The ballad that Elvis cut the same day as "Hound Dog" and "Don't Be Cruel" – July 2, 1965, in RCA's New York Studio; released as a single in October of 1956, the flip-side of "Love Me Tender"; and on the LP *Elvis' Golden Records* (1958), later *Elvis: Worldwide 50 Gold Award Hits, Volume 1*.

Anyway You Want Me
1956. RCA Victor. EP (EPA-965).
Side 1: "Anyway You Want Me"; "I'm Left, You're Right, She's Gone."
Side 2: "I Don't Care If The Sun Don't Shine"; "Mystery Train."

"Appreciation"
Ann-Margret number from *Viva Las Vegas* (1964), unreleased on the soundtrack LP.

"Are You Lonesome Tonight"
(Roy Turk – Lou Handman)
Al Jolson wowed audiences with this tune before Jaye P. Morgan made it a hit in 1959. Elvis, of course, made it a sentimental smash after his discharge from the Army and it became a solid staple in his repertoire ever since. Recorded on April 4, 1960 at RCA's Nashville Studio, (along with "It's Now Or Never,"), it had a talk-sing passage in the middle that melted millions of female hearts. Released as a single in November of 1960 (flip-side of "I Gotta Know" – it was #1 for six weeks). Released on the LP *Elvis' Golden Records, Volume III* (1963), *A Legendary Performer, Volume I* (1974), *Worldwide 50 Gold Hits, Volume I* (1970); performed live on *From Memphis to Vegas* (1969) and *Elvis In Person At The International Hotel* (1970), and *A Legendary Performer, Volume I* (1974). Also bootlegged frequently. The last live version appeared on the LP *Elvis In Concert* (1977).

"Are You Sincere"
(Wayne Walker)
Old fashioned ballad recorded at Elvis' home in Palm Springs on September 24, 1973, backed by the vocal group Voice; released as a single in September of 1973 (flip-side of "For Ol' Times Sake"), and on the LP *Raised on Rock* in November.

Eddy Arnold
C & W legend, part of Col. Parker's stable of talent from 1945-1953, Grand Ole Opry Star. Elvis recorded several of his hits: "It's A Sin"; "I'll Hold You In My Heart"; "I Really Don't Want To Know"; and "You Don't Know Me." Elected to the Country Music Hall of Fame in 1966.

Edward L. Ashley
The land developer from Grace Valley, California who claimed he had been severely beaten during an Elvis engagement at the Sahara Tahoe on May 20, 1974, and sued Elvis and the hotel for $6,610,000 in damages. Outcome still pending.

"Ask Me"
(Modungo – Giant – Baum – Kaye)
A recycled Italian love ballad, with organ, drums, piano, guitar, the Jordanaires, and new lyrics. Recorded in January of 1964 at RCA Studios in Nashville; released as a single in September of 1964 (the flip of "Ain't That Loving You"), later appeared on the LP *Elvis' Gold Records, Volume 4* (1968).

"As Long As I Have You"
(Fred Wise – Ben Weisman)
Fine ballad from *King Creole*, recorded in January of 1958 in Hollywood; released in August of 1958 on the soundtrack LP.

"A Thing Called Love"
(Jerry "Reed" Hubbard)
Recorded at RCA's Nashville Studio in May of 1971; released in April of 1972 on the inspirational LP *He Touched Me*.

Chet Atkins
Session guitarist and producer who played along with Scotty Moore on numerous early recordings by Elvis at RCA's Nashville Studio in 1955-56, among them "Heartbreak Hotel," "I Got A Woman," and "I Want You, I Need You, I Love You." He later took over A & R for RCA in Nashville, becoming a key figure in sponsoring the production of country music. In 1968, he became Vice President and was eventually elected to the Country Music Hall of Fame. Working with the Colonel and Steve Sholes, he "produced" Elvis until 1966, when Felton Jarvis took over.

A Touch of Gold
1959. RCA Victor. EP (EPA-5088).
Side 1: "Hard Headed Woman"; "Good Rockin' Tonight."
Side 2: "Don't"; "I Beg Of You."

A Touch of Gold Volume II
1959. RCA Victor. EP (EPA-5101).
Side 1: "Wear My Ring Around Your Neck"; "Treat Me Nice."
Side 2: "One Night"; "That's All Right."

A Touch of Gold Volume 3
1959. RCA Victor. EP (EPA-5141).
Side 1: "All Shook Up"; "Don't Ask Me Why."
Side 2: "Too Much"; "Blue Moon Of Kentucky."

Larry Auerbach
Elvis' agent at the William Morris Agency.

Gene Autry
Singer, composer, radio star, millionaire, and the first "cowboy" to make musical films. Autry, among his many accomplishments in the entertainment and business fields, recorded several songs which Elvis later used, such as "Frankie And Johnny," "The Yellow Rose Of Texas," "Blue Hawaii," "Blueberry Hill," "I'll Never Let You Go (Littl' Darlin')" and "Here Comes Santa Claus."

Avon Theater
One of the many Memphis movie theaters to house Elvis and his friends for all night movie marathons. 124 West Broadway, West Memphis.

Awards
Few other entertainers, if any, have ever won as many awards as did Elvis. They range from scrolls, certificates, and so on, given by both fans and the press, to the N.A.R.A.A. award in 1971. Since he shot to fame, Elvis regularly won everything from music polls to polls such as the "Most Handsome Man." He won the "World's Outstanding Musical Personality" and "World Male Singer" polls in the *New Musical Express* more times than anyone else ever did, or probably will. RCA gave him an award in 1961 for selling seventy-six million discs, and it was already out of date as he'd already sold another million or more! Elvis also received certificates to thank him for giving his services free at benefit performances such as the Hawaii 1961 concert, and for helping the Narcotic's Officers Association. Regularly the mayor of a city or the governor of a state would issue a proclamation for an "Elvis Presley Day." One such proclamation was made by the Governor of Georgia, Jimmy Carter, in 1973; and more recently, many cities have issued proclamations to mark January 8th as "Elvis Presley Day." The International Hotel in Las Vegas awarded Elvis a $10,000 gold and diamond belt in 1970 for bringing in unprecedented business. Some of the trophies Elvis won in *NME* polls were taken to him personally. Todd Slaughter presented him with one such trophy in Las Vegas in 1972, and in 1976 Todd took a "Getaway" trophy to Las Vegas for Elvis. The N.A.R.A.S. (National Academy of Recording Arts and Sciences) Award must have particularly pleased Elvis. Only about five people before had ever received one of the gold and ebony plaques. The inscription on it read, "To Elvis Presley in recognition of your artistic creativity and your influence in the field of recorded music upon a generation of performers and listeners whose lives and musical horizons have been enriched and expanded by your unique contribution." Elvis was proud of all his trophies and awards, and often showed people round his huge trophy room at Graceland. (see also Gold Discs and Honors).

"A Whistling Tune"
(Hal David – Sherman Edwards)
Recorded in November of 1961, in Hollywood, for the film *Kid Galahad*; released in September of 1962 on soundtrack album.

"A World Of Our Own"
(Bill Grant – Bernie Baum – Florence Kaye)
Recorded in October of 1962 in Hollywood for the film *It Happened At The World's Fair*; released in March of 1973 on the soundtrack album.

Hoyt Axton
Son of Mae Axton, singer-composer who wrote "Never Been To Spain," (first recorded by Three Dog Night in 1971), which Elvis incorporated into his show and recorded.

Mae Boren Axton
Mother of Hoyt Axton, the folk-singer-composer and a good friend to Elvis in the early days. Co-author of "Heartbreak Hotel."

Rick Ayers
Elvis' part-time beautician (when Larry Geller wasn't around).

Baba
Elvis and Priscilla's collie dog.

"Baby, Baby, Baby"
Stella Steven's number from *Girls! Girls! Girls!* (1962).

"(You're So Square) Baby, I Don't Care"
(Jerry Leiber – Mike Stoller)
Cleverly phrased Leiber – Stoller rocker, fueling the "generation gap." Recorded on May 2, 1957 at MGM Studios in Culver City, with the old crew – Scotty, Bill, D.J., the Jordanaires – and Dudley on piano – the same day as "Jailhouse Rock"; released on the EP soundtrack *Jailhouse Rock* in October, 1957. Then, in 1959, on the LP *A Date With Elvis* (supposedly remixed). Later, on *Elvis – The Other Sides: Worldwide Gold Award Hits, Vol. II* (1971).

"Baby, If You'll Give Me All of Your Love"
(Joy Byers)
Elvis' pattering at breakneck pace, backed up by the Jordanaires. Recorded on June 26, 1966, in Hollywood for the film *Double Trouble* (along with eight others!); released on a soundtrack LP in June, 1967. Later, on the Pickwick LP *Mahalo From Elvis* (1978).

"Baby Let's Play House"
(Arthur Gunter)
A pure delight, with Elvis getting all tangled up in the "babys" at the end, chuckling. An early Sun classic recorded by Sam Phillips in February of 1955; with D.J., Scotty and Bill. Released as a single by Sun in April of 1955 and by RCA in November of 1955 (flip-side of "I'm Left, You're Right, She's Gone"); it was the first Elvis record to hit the national charts. Released on *A Date With Elvis* LP (1959), and *The Sun Sessions* (1976).

"Baby What You Want Me To Do"
(Jimmy Reed)
Lead-in for his 1968 NBC show "*Elvis,*" was recorded in June of 1968 at the Burbank Studios. Only a portion of the song was heard on the show that aired at Christmas and the subsequent LP *Elvis – TV Special* (1968). Complete version was released on the LP *Elvis: A Legendary Performer Vol. 2* (1976).

Burt Bacharach
Composer of movie themes and pop songs, Bacharach is more noted for hit songs (with lyricist Hal David) like "Raindrops Keep Falling On My Head,"and for marrying (and divorcing) Angie Dickinson. He also co-wrote "Any Day Now" with Bob Hillard, which Elvis put to tape in 1969.

"Bad Moon Rising"
When Elvis discovered "Proud Mary" he went off on a Creedence Clearwater Revival kick. Although he played other John Fogerty songs privately, he incorporated "Bad Moon Rising" into his stage repertoire but never recorded it.

Herbert Baer
The first Elvis impersonator to legally change his name to "Elvis Presley," which he did in 1978, setting a precedent.

Max Baer, Jr.
Actor, later director (he played Jethro in *The Beverly Hillbillies*) and a friend of Elvis' during the 1960's, who played in Elvis' Bel Air football games.

Tammy Baiter
One of the girls seriously injured by the car driven by Treatice Whaler III, the demented eighteen-year-old driving his car down Elvis Presley Boulevard on the morning of August 18, 1977. She had travelled to Graceland from St. Clair, Missouri upon news of Elvis' death and was standing on the median strip with her two friends when struck by the car. She suffered serious injuries to the pelvis.

Bill Baize
Occasional soloist with the Stamps Quartet.

LaVern Baker
Atlantic R & B singer of the 1950's, and early 1960's, who recorded two songs Elvis later recorded: "Saved" and "See See Rider." Her 1955 hit "Tweedle Dee" was another song he liked and sang but never recorded.

Ina Balin
"Tracy," Elvis' faithful love in *Charro!* (1969).

George Ball
Graceland security guard and co-author, with Harold Lloyd, of *The Gates of Graceland*.

Caroline Ballard
Daughter of James Ballard, Elvis' childhood friend in Tupelo.

Reverend James Ballard
The pastor of the First Assembly of God Church in Tupelo during Elvis' youth.

Jim Ballard
Mayor of Tupelo who presented Elvis with the key to the city when he returned in 1957 to perform at the Mississippi-Alabama State Fair.

Baptist Memorial Hospital
(899 Madison Avenue, Memphis)
The scene of the happiest and saddest moments in the Elvis Presley story: the birth of his daughter Lisa Marie (February 1, 1968), various hospitalizations during the seventies for health and drug-related reasons (October, 1973, January-February 1975, August-September 1975), the convalescence of Vernon Presley after his first heart attack (February 1, 1975) and the place where his body was brought for unsuccessful revival attempts on the day of his death (August 16, 1977). Also, the scene of his autopsy.

Brigitte Bardot
On September 11, 1958, during the press conference at the Military Ocean Terminal in Brooklyn, Elvis revealed he would have liked to meet "Miss Bardot" while serving in Europe. The news was accordingly flashed across the globe to ascertain the French actress' reaction. To the disappointment of those titillated by the possibility of their meeting, Miss Bardot wasn't interested.

Duke Bardwell
Bass guitar on tour and sessions, 1974–75.

"Barefoot Ballad"
(Dolores Fuller – Lee Morris)
Elvis hooting a hillbilly number for *Kissin' Cousins*, recorded October 11, 1963 in Hollywood; released in March of 1964 on soundtrack LP.

Rona Barrett
Hollywood gossip columnist and "investigative reporter" who broke the news of Elvis' impending marriage and, to the Colonel's delight, erroneously reported the wedding to be taking place in Palm Springs rather than Las Vegas.

George Barris
Renowned auto customizer who received several assignments from Elvis over the years, among them the tour bus used briefly in the 1970's.

James and Annette Baxter
Co-authors of a ground-breaking article entitled "The Man in the Blue Suede Shoes," published in *Harpers* in January of 1958. What was so noteworthy about the piece was that it was the first to take Elvis seriously as a socio-cultural phenomenon that reflected great meaning about the symbols and myths of America and the southern identity, a theme which would be explored brilliantly by Greil Marcus in his book *Mystery Train* (1976).

"Beachboy Blues"
(Sid Tepper – Roy C. Bennett)
Certainly no blues in a musical sense, a bit of show fluff for *Blue Hawaii* in the form of minor celluloid rock n' roll. Recorded in April of 1961 in Hollywood; released in October, 1961, on the soundtrack LP (a slower version appears in the film).

"Beach Shack"
(Grant – Baum – Kaye)
Slightly calypso bit of nonsense with plenty of Jordanaires – bongo drums too! Recorded in February of 1966 in Hollywood for *Spinout*; released in October, 1966, on soundtrack LP. Elvis did eight other songs the same day. . . .

Lonnie Beale
Elvis' character in *Tickle Me* (1965).

Beale Street
The legendary Memphis street down by the Mississippi where the honky-tonks and hookers abounded, called "The Home of the Blues" – Memphis' 42nd Street. Elvis sometimes went there after school to take in the sights at Lansky Brothers.

Orville Bean
The Tupelo dairy farmer who loaned Vernon enough money to build his shotgun house in 1934.

The Beatles
All of the Beatles, particularly John Lennon, have admitted to being greatly influenced by Elvis. Indeed, they were the second major musical phenomenon to rival Elvis and they visited him in August of 1965 at his Bel Air home. Eventually, Elvis performed and recorded "Hey Jude" and "Yesterday."

Joseph P. Beaulieu
Priscilla's stepfather, who adopted her after his marriage to her mother, Ann (following the death of her natural father at the age of four). At the time Elvis met Priscilla in 1958, Beaulieu was an Air Force Major stationed in Wiesbaden. It was Major Beaulieu who gave his permission for Priscilla to move to Graceland at Elvis' request in 1960. During the early sixties, Major Beaulieu was transferred to Travis Air Force Base in California, where the Beaulieus lived. The family also included Michelle, a younger sister, and younger brothers, Jeff, Danny and twins Timothy and Thomas.

Michelle Beaulieu
Priscilla's younger sister, close friend, and Matron of Honor at her wedding. Presently working for Jerry Schilling Management in Los Angeles.

"Because of Love"
(Ruth Batchelor – Bob Roberts) Typical movie ballad with light orchestral touch, Recorded in March of 1962 in Hollywood for *Girls! Girls! Girls!*; released on soundtrack LP in March.

Joyce Becker
Elvis' girlfriend in Hawaii for his brief stay during the making of *Blue Hawaii*.

"Beginner's Luck"
(Sid Tepper – Roy C. Bennett) Elvis crooned this ballad for *Frankie and Johnny*, recorded at United Artists in May of 1965; released in April of 1966 on the soundtrack LP.

Bel Air Club
Memphis nightclub where, in 1954, Elvis played with the Starlight Wranglers and Doug Poindexter.

Bill Belew
Hollywood costume designer par excellence, who created the sensational black leather outfit Elvis wore for the 1968 Christmas special, the series of karate gis and jumpsuits for the Las Vegas engagements, and the eagle outfit for "*Aloha*."

Benefit Performances
Elvis gave several charity shows. In February, 1960, he gave two shows in Memphis, benefitting local charities and his Under-Privileged Children's project in Tupelo. A month later, on March 25th, he gave a show in Honolulu, Hawaii, to benefit the USS Arizona Memorial Fund; and in January, 1973, he returned to Hawaii, to do the "*Aloha From Hawaii*" satellite show, on the 14th, to aid the Kui Lee Cancer Drive. In May, 1975, Elvis gave a benefit show in Jackson, Mississippi, to help recent tornado victims. (See also Elvis Presley Foundation for Under-Privileged Children).

The Benevolent Con Man
The title of Colonel Parker's alleged autobiography which he began in 1956 and most recently tried to sell advertising space in. He is reportedly waiting for the most financially auspicious moment to publish it.

Francis Ford Benjamin
"The Duke of Paducah," famous comedian at the Grand Ole Opry who, with Oscar Davis, scouted talent for Colonel Parker and helped bring Elvis to the Colonel's attention in 1955.

Pandro S. Berman
Produced *Jailhouse Rock* (1958).

Judd Bernard and Irving Winkler
Produced *Double Trouble* (1967).

Chuck Berry
One of the founding fathers of rock n' roll, whom Elvis admired greatly. Over the years, he recorded many of Chuck Berry's most famous hits, among them "Johnny B. Goode," "Memphis, Tennessee," and "The Promised Land."

"Beyond the Bend"
(Fred Wise – Ben Weisman – Dolores Fuller) Bouncy filler for *It Happened at the World's Fair*, recorded in Hollywood in October of 1962; released in March of 1963 on the soundtrack LP.

B.F. Wood Music Company
Elvis' publishing firm in Great Britain.

Freddie Bienstock
The manager of Hill and Range in Nashville for twelve years (1956–1968), who collected songs for Elvis' records.

"Big Boots"
(Sid Wayne – Sherman Edwards) The children's lullaby that surprised everyone – Elvis singing to a baby. Recorded in April, 1960, in Hollywood for *G.I. Blues;* released in October, 1960 on the soundtrack LP. Later, on the LP *Elvis Sings For Children (And Grownups Too)* (1978).

"Big Boss Man"
(Luther Dixon – Jimmy Reed – Jerry Smith). The kind of R & B that Elvis was born to attack – lowdown, with harmonica. Recorded in September of 1967 at RCA's Nashville Studio, with Scotty and Jerry Reed on guitars. Released as a single in October of 1967 (with "You Don't Know Me" as its flip) and re-recorded on June 30, 1968 at Burbank Studios for release on the LP *Elvis – TV Special* (1968).

Big Bunny
Hugh Hefner's private DC-9 jet which he provided for Elvis' 1974 tour, complete with bunnies.

"Big D Jamboree"
The Dallas, Texas concert where Bob Neal and Colonel Parker first met and discussed Elvis' career on June 24, 1955.

"Big Love, Big Heartache"
(Dolores Fuller – Lee Morris – Sonny Hendrix) A dramatic ballad, one of the better tunes of *Roustabout*. Recorded in January of 1964 in Hollywood; released in October of 1964 on the soundtrack LP.

***Billboard* Magazine**
The monthly publication that has, since its inception in 1894, come to be regarded as the "Bible" of popular music. When Elvis was voted eighth most Promising Artist of 1954, he received the attention of Colonel Parker.

"The Billy Goat Song"
Jesse Presley, Elvis' grandfather, released this single in the late 1950's on the Legacy label.

Steve Binder
The young, talented director of Elvis' 1968 *Christmas Special*. The live opening segment signaled, for many, the beginning of his "comeback."

Bio Sciences Laboratories
The medical research lab in Los Angeles entrusted with the analysis of Elvis' body tissue following the autopsy. They found traces of eleven different drugs, some of which were narcotics and amphetamines.

Birthday
Elvis Aron Presley was born on January 8, 1935, in East Tupelo, Mississippi.

Birthplace
East Tupelo, Mississippi, about 104 miles southeast of Memphis. Elvis was born in the two-room shack built by his father and grandfather. It is now a State Historical Monument, and is visited by thousands of fans each year. It has been refurnished in the style of the 1930's. The birthplace is part of the Elvis Presley Park, a large area with facilities for children and teenagers. There's a club house, swimming pool, etc. The Elvis Memorial Chapel stands close by the birthplace. The Old Saltillo Road, on which the birthplace stands, is now called Elvis Presley Drive, and the entire area is called Presley Heights. Elvis lived in other homes in Tupelo before moving to Memphis in September, 1948, but he kept up friendships with many friends in Tupelo, and made visits there, his last one being in July, 1977. (see also E.P. Foundation).

Olivia Bis
Beverly Hills area designer who became Priscilla's partner in their boutique, *Bis and Beau*.

Bis and Beau
Priscilla's short-lived clothing boutique in Beverly Hills.

"Bitter They Are, The Harder They Fall"
(Larry Gatlin) Nearing the end in February of 1976, Elvis recorded this Gatlin ballad, one of his favorites, in the Graceland den. Although

Elvis was deteriorating, the song stands. It was released in May of 1976 on the LP *From Elvis Presley Boulevard, Memphis, Tennessee.*

Bill Bixby
One of Elvis' Hollywood acquaintances and co-stars in several films: as the arrogant playboy James Jamison III in *Clambake* (1967); and again as a playboy – this time Kenny Dow, Elvis' manager in *Speedway* (1968).

Bill Black
Elvis' bassist until 1959, through the early years at Sun and RCA and on the road. Played the upright bass on virtually all of his early bits, and, later, bass guitar. Formed the Bill Black combo in 1959 and died in 1968.

Joan Blackman
Elvis' sweetheart "Maile" in *Blue Hawaii* (1960), and a brief romantic interest during and after the filming. Also his co-star in *Kid Galahad* (1962), Elvis' boxing flick.

Melissa Blackwood
Another eighteen-year-old Memphis belle who entered Elvis' life after his divorce, before Linda – a brief romantic fling.

The Blackwood Brothers
Famous gospel quartet from Mississippi admired by Elvis during his youth and the founders of the 'family gospel quartet.' The group was led by James Blackwood and included R.W. Blackwood, Bill Lyles and William Show. In 1954, after R.W. Blackwood was killed in a plane crash, they were joined by Cecil Blackwood, who had been performing with a younger Blackwood Brothers quartet. Elvis was asked to fill Cecil's place – to him, it was the opportunity of a lifetime – but by then, he was already recording for Sam Phillips. The Blackwood Brothers sang two songs at Gladys Presley's funeral on August 16, 1958: "Precious Memories" and "Rock Of Ages."

Hal Blaine
Session drummer on *Elvis*, the 1968 TV Special.

Nicky Blair
"Shorty," Elvis' mechanic in *Viva Las Vegas* (1964).

Governor Ray Blanton
Governor of Tennessee at the time of Elvis' death, who attended funeral services and ordered a day of mourning in the State.

Bloch Arena
Where Elvis performed a benefit

concert for the Memorial Fund of the USS Arizona in 1961. This Hawaiian appearance, at Pearl Harbor, was Elvis' last public personal appearance until his Las Vegas opening in 1969.

The Blossoms
Vocal back-ups on "Elvis," 1968 TV Special. They included Darlene Love, Jean King and Fanita James.

"Blueberry Hill"
(Al Lewis – Larry Stock – Vincent Rose)
Fats Domino's 1956 hit recorded by Elvis, Scotty, D.J., Bill and Dudley Brooks on piano. Recorded in January of 1957 at Radio Recorders in Hollywood; released in July of 1957 on the LP soundtrack *Loving You*. A live version appears on *Elvis Recorded Live Onstage In Memphis* (1974).

"Blue Christmas"
(Billy Hayes – Jay Johnson)
One of the gems on Elvis' first Christmas album, which established a tradition in his career. "I'll have a blue Christmas without you," he says, and croons a lilting tune. Recorded at Radio Recorders in Hollywood in September of 1957, Elvis was clearly striving hard for both legitimacy and mainstream commercial acceptance. It appeared on *Elvis' Christmas Album* (1957) and was released on the '68 Christmas Special – "Elvis" TV Special. Released as a single in 1964, the flip-side of "Wooden Heart." Later, on the LP *Elvis – A Legendary Performer, Vol. 2* (1976).

"Blue Eyes Crying In the Rain"
(Leon Rose)
Another sad ballad evocative of Elvis' own personal despair at the very end. Recorded at Graceland, in February of 1976; released in May of 1976 on the LP *From Elvis Presley Boulevard, Memphis, Tennessee*.

"Blue Guitar"
(Sheb Wooley)
Song recorded by Wooley and later Red Foley. Elvis recorded a version at Sun in 1955 which has never been released.

Blue Hawaii
Started April 3, 1961
A Hal Wallis Production
A Paramount Picture
Cast
Chad Gates: Elvis Presley; Maile Duval: Joan Blackman; Sarah Lee Gates: Angela Lansbury; Abigail Prentace: Nancy Walters; Fred Gates: Roland Winters; Jack Kelman: John Archer; Mr. Chapman: Howard McNear; Mrs. Manaka: Flora Hayes; Mr. Duval:

Gregory Gay; Mr. Garvey: Steve Brodie; Mrs. Garvey: Iris Adrian; Patsy: Darlene Tompkins; Sandy: Pamela Austin; Beverly: Christian Key; Ellie: Jenny Maxwell; Ito O'Hara: Frank Atienza; Carl: Lani Kai; Wrine: Jose de Varga; Wes: Ralph Hanalie.
Credits
Directed by Norman Taurog
Screenplay by Hal Kanter
Technicolor and Panavision
Songs
"Blue Hawaii"; "Almost Always True"; "Aloha-Oe"; "No More"; "Can't Help Falling In Love"; "Rock-a-hula Baby"; "Moonlight Swim"; "Ku-U-I-Po" (Hawaiian Sweetheart); "Ito Eats"; "Slicin' Sand"; "Hawaiian Sunset"; "Beach Boy Blues"; "Island Of Love"; "Hawaiian Wedding Song"; "Stepping Out Of Line" (cut); "Playing With Fire" (Unreleased cut).
Running Time: 101 Minutes
Previously Titled:
1. *Hawaiian Beach Boy*
2. *Beach Boy Blues*

"Blue Hawaii"
(Leo Robin – Ralph Rainger)
Written in 1937, recorded by Billy Vaughn in 1959, and turned into the title song for the 1961 film of the same name, the song blended Hawaiian guitars, Elvis' baritone, and the Jordanaires. Recorded in April of 1961 in Hollywood; released in October of 1961 on the soundtrack LP. Later, on the LP's *Elvis – A Legendary Performer, Vol. 2* (1976) and *Mahalo From Elvis* (1978).

Blue Hawaii
1961. RCA Victor. LP. (LPM/LSP-2426).
Side 1: "Blue Hawaii"; "Almost Always True"; "Aloha Oe"; "No More"; "Can't Help Falling In Love"; "Rock-A-Hula Baby"; "Moonlight Swim."
Side 2: "Ku-U-I-Po"; "Ito Eats"; "Slicin' Island"; "Hawaiian Sunset"; "Beach Boy Blues"; "Island Of Love"; "Hawaiian Wedding Song."

"Blue Moon"
(Lorenz Hart – Richard Rodgers)
Elvis' rendition of a 1949 Mel Torme hit, recorded by Sam Phillips at Sun Studio in Memphis, July, 1954. If nothing else, the *selection* of the song at that stage reveals a great deal about his musical predilection and tastes – it was recorded at the same session as "That's All Right (Mama)." Released as a single by RCA in September of 1956, the flip of "Just Because", and in April on the LP *Elvis Presley*. Re-released on the 1976 LP *The Sun Sessions*.

Blue Moon Boys
The name used by Elvis, Scotty and Bill while touring in 1955.

"Blue Moon Of Kentucky"
(Bill Monroe)
The bluegrass number Elvis recorded with Scotty Moore and Bill Black at his first commercial recording session between July 6–5, 1954, at Sun Studio in Memphis with Sam Phillips. It was released that month on the flip-side of "That's All Right (Mama)" and performed throughout the first circuits of Elvis' career – on the *Louisiana Hayride*, and on flatbed trucks and in auditoriums. The first RCA release was in September of 1959 on the LP *A Date With Elvis*.

"Blue Suede Shoes"
(Carl Perkins)
Perkins' rockabilly classic. Fast, driving, with Elvis slamming out the lyrics – always one of Elvis' personal favorites which he used to open his Las Vegas show in July–August of 1969. Recorded on January 30, 1956 at RCA's New York Studio with Scotty Moore, D.G. Fontana, Bill Black and Shorty Long on piano. Released in March of 1956 as a single, the flipside of "Tutti Frutti;" and on the LP *Elvis Presley* in April. Re-done for the *G.I. Blues* soundtrack LP in 1960. Live versions appear on *From Memphis to Vegas* (1969), *Elvis In Person at the International Hotel, Las Vegas, Nevada* (1970) and *Aloha From Hawaii* (1973).

Ed Bond
One of the artists touring with Elvis in 1955, during his Sun days.

Books
Elvis became an avid reader during the 1960's and when he went back on the road he travelled with a portable bookcase that contained over 200 volumes of his favorite and newest books. Larry Geller was constantly bringing him new works and Elvis frequently gave copies of his favorites to friends and associates. Over the years, he read widely in religion, philosophy, psychology, medicine, biography, and other areas. Aside from the Bible and the dictionary, which he read often, the books most commonly associated with him over the years were: *The Prophet* by Kahlil Gibran; *The Impersonal Life* by Joseph Benner; *Autobiography of a Yogi* by Paramahansa Yogananda; *The Infinite Way*, by Joel Goldsmith; *The Mystical Christ*, by Manley Palmer Hall; *The Life and Teachings of the Master of the Far East* by Baird Spalding; *The Inner Life By Leadbetter; The First and Last

Freedom by Krishnamurti; and Cheiro's *Book of Numbers*. He was fascinated by the Dead Sea Scrolls, the Hebrew Cabala, the works of Albert Pike, Madame Blavatsky, May Heindel, mystics Corine Heline and Nicholas Roerich and Alice Bailey's book *Esoteric Healing*. The book he took to the bathroom on the day of his death was *The Force of Jesus* by Frank Adams.

Pat Boone
Singer and evangelist, and because of his lily-white image, one of Elvis' biggest rivals in 1956. In reality, they were good friends.

Bootlegs
Ever since the early 1970's, an ever-growing succession of Elvis bootleg records has been issued. Material found on such discs ranges from early and later live concerts, early TV shows, outtakes and alternate takes, and so on. The quality varies from excellent to very poor; it's a case of buyer, beware. Since bootlegs are illegal, the people hawking them have to do so under cover most of the time, and many such people have been caught and faced the consequences. Bootlegging will probably be with us for a long time to come. In this book, the more prominent bootleg LP's are listed individually.

Boppin' Hillbilly
Another nickname for the "Hillbilly Cat."

Ernest Borgnine
Oscar winner for *Marty* in 1955 who later played Quint McHale in *McHale's Navy*, Borgnine met Elvis and the Colonel in 1956 during the filming of *Love Me Tender*. They became good friends in the following years.

"Bosom Of Abraham"
(William Johnson – George McFadden – Ted Brooks) Well-known spiritual of medium tempo and short length, blending voice with the Imperials. Recorded in June of 1971 at RCA Nashville Studio; released as a single in March of 1972 as the flip side of "He Touched Me" and on the LP *He Touched Me* that year. Never released live but featured as a rehearsal scene in the film *Elvis on Tour* (1972).

"Bossa Nova Baby"
(Jerry Leiber – Mike Stoller) Elvis in a rocking groove with trumpets and the Jordanaires yelling in chorus. Recorded in Hollywood in January of 1963 for *Fun in Acapulco*; released as a single in October of 1963 as the flip side of "Witchcraft" and on the soundtrack LP.

Ralph Boucher
Worked with Alan Fortas to look after Circle G Ranch.

Carol Bourtierre
One of the stewardesses on the *Lisa Marie.*

Milton Bowers
Chairman of the Memphis Draft Board in 1957–58 and the man who delivered the news on December 20, 1957 that Uncle Sam wanted Elvis.

Boxcar Enterprises
Colonel Parker's management/ merchandising company operating to promote Elvis products, which includes the Presley estate and Tom Diskin.

Rube Boyce
The Coach of the football team at Humes High School during Elvis' years. Elvis went out for the team in 1951. Coach Boyce, as he later revealed, wasn't thrilled with Elvis' appearance.

Virginia "Billie" Boyd
Custodian of the grounds and the shotgun shack where Elvis was born in Tupelo, which has become a museum called Elvis Presley Park.

C. W. Bradley
Pastor of the Whitehaven Church of Christ, and one of the eulogizers at Elvis' funeral.

Harold Bradley
Session guitarist, in 1966, Nashville.

General Omar N. Bradley
Five Star General who was one of Elvis' military heroes. Elvis once visited him in Beverly Hills and presented him with a gold TCB chain.

Neville Brand
"Mike Gavin," the man who killed Elvis in *Love Me Tender.*

Marlon Brando
Another of Elvis' favorite actors and important early influences on his "style." Elvis studied many of his early performances particularly in *The Wild One* and *On the Waterfront.*

"Bridge Over Troubled Water"
(Paul Simon) Dramatic rendition of Simon & Garfunkel's 1970 hit, performed in the film *That's The Way It Is* (1970) and released on the soundtrack LP that year. The recording, made at RCA Nashville Studio in June, is different from the rehearsal scene in the film; but the climax, complete with the massed voices of the Imperials supplemented by several other vocalists, emphasizes the beauty and power of Elvis' voice and his obvious affinity for the lyric.

David Briggs
Session organist in Nashville in 1966 who accompanied Elvis in scores of recording sessions. He later became Linda Thompson's boyfriend after she split from Elvis in 1976, (before she started seeing Bruce Jenner).

Delta Mae Briggs
Elvis' paternal aunt, who was invited to become a permanent member of Graceland after her husband, Pat Briggs, died.

Brightest Stars of Christmas, The
1974. RCA. LP (DLPI-0086). Side 1: "We Wish You A Merry Christmas" (Eugene Ormandy & the Philadelphia Orchestra); "Here Comes Santa Claus" (Elvis Presley); "Winter Wonderland" (Danny Davis & the Nashville Bros.); "Home For The Holidays" (Perry Como); "Medley: It Came Upon A Midnight Clear/The First Noel/Away In A Manger." Side 2: "Jingle Bells" (Julie Andrews); "Joy To The World" (Ed Ames); "Sleigh Ride" (Arthur Fiedler and The Boston Pops); "Christmas In My Home Town" (Charlie Pride); "Hark! The Herald Angels Sing" (Robert Shaw Chorale); "Silent Night" (Sergio Franchi).

T. C. Brindley
Principal of L.C. Humes High during Elvis' years.

"Bringing It Back"
(G. Gordon) One of the tunes haphazardly selected for the *Today* LP, recorded in Hollywood in May of 1975; released in June of 1975.

"Britches"
(Sid Wayne – Sherman Edwards) A tune recorded in August of 1960 for *Flaming Star* but unused in any film and unre-

leased until *Elvis – A Legendary Performer Vol. 3* in 1973.

Robert Brock
Los Angeles attorney who represented Priscilla during her divorce proceedings in 1973.

Charles Bronson
"Lew Nyack," the trainer of *Kid Galahad* (1962). Reportedly, they kept their distance from each other. Years later, Elvis would become affected by his performance in *Death Wish.*

Dudley Brooks
Piano session man in 1957 on songs like "Blueberry Hill" and "All Shook Up."

Stan Brossette
Press agent who worked with Colonel Parker promoting Elvis' movies over the years.

Aubrey Brown
The other gas station attendant floored by Elvis in the "Ed Hopper" fracas on October 18, 1956.

James Brown
Popular black entertainer from Macon, Georgia. Considered one of the most dynamic R & B/soul performers of all time, he recorded hits like "I Feel Good". Brown admired Elvis and attended his funeral.

Jim Brown
Elvis' football idol, who became a friend in Hollywood after his career as fullback with the Cleveland Browns.

Roy Brown
R & B composer/performer who penned "Good Rockin' Tonight" in 1947 (one of Elvis' favorites). Elvis saw Brown play the song in high school and later saw Brown perform in Memphis clubs in the years after his graduation, before cutting his first records at Sun.

Tony Brown
Pianist for the group Voice, who replaced David Briggs when Briggs returned to Nashville in 1974.

Tony Brown
Glenn Hordin's replacement in Elvis' touring band, 1974–1977.

Cathy Jo Brownlee
Another of Elvis' young Memphis girlfriends after his divorce, and before Linda Thompson.

"Brown Suede Combat Boots"
Phil Silver's parody of "Hound Dog" from the episode about Elvin Pelvin on the *Phil Silvers Show.*

Boudleaux Bryant
Composer and musician who, with his wife Felicia, wrote many classics for the Everly Brothers, like "Bye Bye Love" and "Bird Dog." Also a classical violinist who could play a mean country fiddle, Bryant was a friend of Chet Atkins. Together, they wrote "How's The World Treating You," which Elvis recorded for RCA in September of 1956.

Margit Buergin
The pretty, seventeen-year-old Elvis dated briefly in Germany before meeting Priscilla.

Burbank Sessions, Volume One, The
Two-volume bootleg released in November of 1978. Contains the entire live concert by Elvis at the NBC Studios in Burbank, California on June 27, 1968. Side 1: Dialogue; "That's All Right"; "Heartbreak Hotel"; "Love Me"; "Baby, What You Want Me To Do"; Dialogue; "Lawdy, Miss Clawdy." Side 2: "Are You Lonesome Tonight"; "When My Blue Moon Turns To Gold Again"; "Blue Christmas"; "Tryin' To Get To You"; "One Night" (two versions); "Memories." Side 3: Dialogue; "Heartbreak Hotel"; "Baby What You Want Me To Do"; "Blue Suede Shoes"; "One Night." Side 4: "Love Me"; Dialogue; "Tryin' To Get To You"; "Lawdy, Miss Clawdy"; Dialogue; "Santa Claus Is Back In Town"; "Blue Christmas"; "Tiger Man"; "When My Blue Moon Turns To Gold Again"; "Memories."

Burbank Sessions, Volume Two, The
Two-record bootleg album released in November of 1978 on the German Audifon label. This album contains the entire live show that Elvis gave on June 29, 1968 in the NBC Studios in Burbank, California. Side 1: Intro and Dialogue; "Heartbreak Hotel/One Night"; "Medley: Heartbreak Hotel/ Hound Dog/All Shook Up"; "Can't Help Falling In Love"; "Jailhouse Rock"; "Don't Be Cruel"; "Blue Suede Shoes." Side 2: "Love Me Tender"; Dia-

logue; "Trouble"; Dialogue; "Baby, What You Want Me To Do"; "If I Can Dream."
Side 3: Intro and Dialogue; "Medley: Heartbreak Hotel/ Hound Dog/All Shook Up"; "Can't Help Falling In Love"; "Jailhouse Rock"; "Don't Be Cruel"; "Blue Suede Shoes"; "Love Me Tender"
Side 4: Dialogue; "Trouble No. 1"; Dialogue; "Trouble/Guitar Man"; Dialogue; "Trouble/Guitar Man"; Dialogue; "If I Can Dream."

Burke's Florist
One of the Memphis florist shops patronized by Elvis over the years, at 1609 Elvis Presley Boulevard.

Johnny Burnette
A singer with Scotty Moore and Bill Black before Elvis sang with them, and an early friend of Elvis'. Before his death, Burnette wrote the classic oldie "You're Sixteen" and "The Fool," which Elvis recorded on *Elvis Country* in 1971.

"Burning Love"
(Dennis Linde)
A heavy Ronnie Tutt beat, a variety of guitars (James Burton and John Wilkinson) and a heavily echoed, powerful Elvis made this the first brash single from Elvis in many years. Recorded in March of 1972 at MGM Recording Studio, Los Angeles, it was released in August of 1972 as a single—with "It's A Matter Of Time" as the flip side. (It reached #2 on *Billboard*'s Hot 100 Chart and remained for 15 weeks at a time when Elvis needed a solid single.) The song was hopped up and performed in rehearsal in *Elvis on Tour* (1972) and later performed and released on *Aloha From Hawaii* (1973).

Burning Love (And Hits From His Movies Vol. 2)
1972. RCA/Camden. LP (CAS-2595).
Side 1: "Burning Love"; "Tender Feeling"; "Am I Ready"; "Tonight Is So Right For Love"; "Guadalahara."
Side 2: "It's A Matter Of Time"; "No More"; "Santa Lucia"; "We'll Be Together"; "I Love Only One Girl."

James Burton
Elvis' lead guitarist, 1969–1977, on tour and in countless recording sessions. A versatile session musician, who played with Rick Nelson before he joined Elvis.

Pacer Burton
Elvis' character in *Flaming Star* (1960).

"By and By"
(Traditional—Arranged and Adapted by Elvis Presley)
A rousing spiritual with piano, guitar, banging tambourine and the Imperial Quartet, recorded May 27, 1966 at RCA Nashville Studio for the majestic LP *How Great Thou Art*; released in March of 1967.

Bye Bye Birdie
Broadway musical from 1960–1962 and later film written by Charles Strauss and Michael Stewart about the induction of a rock n' roll singer named Conrad Birdie into the Army. Based on *guess who?* The film in 1963 starred Dick Van Dyke, Janet Leigh, Jesse Pearson, and made a star out of Ann-Margret, who would play opposite Elvis the following year in *Viva Las Vegas*.

Sheila Ryan Caan
Another beautiful actress-model and Playboy cover who travelled with Elvis briefly during his relationship with Linda Thompson. She later married actor James Caan.

Cadillac Club
Well known New Orleans night spot where Elvis tried to play in 1954, only to be turned away by owner Lois Brown because his records were relatively unknown outside of Memphis.

Cadillac Elvis
Bootleg LP including interviews and a pastiche of studio and live recordings, most from the early seventies: "Polk Salad Annie" (January, 1970), "Heartbreak Hotel" (February, 1972), "Rags To Riches," "The Lady Loves Me" (Ann-Margret duet from *Viva Las Vegas*), "That's All Right (Mama)" (June, 1968), "Blue Suede Shoes" (August, 1972), "All Shook Up" (August, 1972), "Shake A Hand" (July, 1975), "Young And Beautiful," "Happy Birthday," "Mickey Mouse March" (May, 1970), "I Want You, I Need You, I Love You," "Hound Dog," (July, 1956), "Blueberry Hill" (July, 1975) and "Lawdy, Miss Clawdy" (March, 1974).

Charles E. Calhoun
(Jesse Stone) 1950's R & B composer, wrote "Shake, Rattle and Roll," which Elvis recorded in 1956.

Camden
The RCA subsidiary label used for Elvis' discount albums between 1969–1973, on which ten LPs were released. (The label was named after Camden, New Jersey, the site of an RCA East Coast pressing plant.) The albums were: *Elvis Sings Flaming Star* (1969), *Let's Be Friends* (1970), *Elvis' Christmas Album* (1970), *Almost In Love* (1970),

You'll Never Walk Alone (1971), *C'mon Everbody* (1971), *I Got Lucky* (1971) *Elvis Sings Hits From His Movies, Volume 1* (1972) and *Volume 2* (1972), *Separate Ways* (1973). In 1975, RCA sold rights to the Camden LPs to Pickwick Records, which changed several covers and reissued them.

Glen Campbell
Another long-time friend who also played guitar on several of Elvis' movie soundtracks and spent time with him while performing in Las Vegas over the years. In 1969, Elvis recorded Campbell's hit "Gentle On My Mind."

"A Cane And A High Starched Collar"
(Sid Tepper—Roy C. Bennett)
C & W song recorded for *Flaming Star*, with accordian and guitar and the rowdy cast answering Elvis' verses about his case against marriage. Never released on disc until January of 1976, when it was included on the LP *Elvis—A Legendary Performer, Volume 2*.

"Can't Help Falling In Love"
(Hugo Peretti—Luigi Creatore—George Weiss)
One of Elvis' greatest all-time love songs, rendered in his sexiest low register—a song originally recorded for *Blue Hawaii* in April of 1961, in Hollywood; released in October of 1961 on the soundtrack LP. Eventually, it became the finale of his road shows, after which he would make his exit. Performed live and released on "*Elvis (NBC TV Special)*" (1968), *From Memphis To Vegas* (1969), *Elvis As Recorded At Madison Square Garden* (1972), *Elvis In Person At The International Hotel, Las Vegas, Nevada* (1970), *Aloha From Hawaii* (1973) and *Elvis Recorded Live Onstage In Memphis* (1974). The song was also performed in the film *That's The Way It Is* (1970) but not released on the soundtrack LP.

Capricorn
Elvis' astrological sign.

Elsa Cardenas
"Dolores Gomez," the stunning lady bullfighter in *Fun In Acapulco* (1963).

Cardiac Arrhythmia
Listed as the official cause of Elvis' death by Dr. Jerry Francisco, Shelby County Coroner, on August 16, 1977—the irregular heart beat resulting from hypertension and other factors. The finding has caused much controversy since the death following revelations of Elvis' drug problem.

Michelle Carey
The starlet pursuing Elvis in *Live A Little, Love A Little* (1968).

Richard Carlson
"Bishop Finley" in *Change of Habit* (1969).

"Carny Town"
(Fred Wise—Randy Starr)
A tinny piano and a honk n' roll type atmosphere—but strictly a movie novelty tune. Recorded in Hollywood, in January of 1964 for the film *Roustabout*; released on the soundtrack LP in October of 1964.

John Carpenter
Young filmmaker who directed the Dick Clark production of *Elvis*, the ABC-TV movie of 1978 starring Kurt Russell.

Dr. John Carpenter
Elvis' character in *Change of Habit* (1969).

Ross Carpenter
Elvis' character in *Girls! Girls! Girls!* (1962).

Jerry Carrigan
Session drummer in Nashville, 1970–1971.

Cars
Elvis loved cars and vehicles of all sorts and learned to drive in his teens. His first pink Cadillac was one of his favorites, and one of his best-known. It is still housed at the back of Graceland. Over the years he bought many more Cadillacs in all colors, and Lincoln Continentals were another car he loved. In the early 1960's he had a Cadillac customized by George Barris of Hollywood. It was sprayed gold, gold trim, and fitted inside with a gold TV, and all sorts of other gadgets, and decorated with replicas of gold records. Elvis drove this car for only a short while, then gave it to RCA, who toured it all over the USA and then to Australia for charity. It is now in the Country Music Hall of Fame at Nashville, and attracts many fans. Another special car Elvis owned was his six-door Mercedes, seen briefly in *Elvis On Tour*. He kept it at Los Angeles airport and rented it out to celebrities. It had a plaque inside saying "Specially made for Elvis Presley." It was also used while Elvis was in Las Vegas. He was given a BMW sports car while in Germany and he once owned a three-wheeler car in the 1950's. Elvis also favored the Italian handmade Stutz cars, owning several of them. He also had George Barris customize a touring bus for him because he didn't like flying, and it was all fitted out in plush red, and used

for the long journeys from Memphis to Hollywood. Motorcycles were another form of transport Elvis loved. He favored huge Harley-Davidsons, and also bought some Triumph Bonnevilles. In 1975, he bought three bright red Super-cycles, three-wheelers, halfway between a car and a motorbike. Elvis was an excellent driver, fast and skillful, but he was also chauffered much of the time. He often rode his motorbikes without a crash helmet, preferring his yachting cap. Go carts, golf carts, a stately black Rolls Royce and a zingy yellow Pantera sports car: Elvis enjoyed them all.

Billy Carter
The former President's brother, who visited Elvis at Graceland in 1976.

Jimmy Carter
While Elvis shied away from political endorsements (not wanting to alienate fans), it was well known that he was proud of the former President's Southern origins and was photographed with him during his campaign for the Presidency. Carter's tribute to Elvis after his death was both gracious and moving: "Elvis Presley's death deprives our country of a part of itself. His music and personality, fusing the styles of white country and black rhythm and blues, permanently changed the face of American popular music. His following was immense and he was a symbol to the people of the world over of the vitality, rebelliousness, and good humor of this country."

June Carter
Country singer, former wife of Carl Smith, presently married to Johnny Cash. She was a part of Colonel Parker's talent stable in 1955 and toured briefly with Elvis during that period. It was Elvis who introduced June Carter to her future husband, then a fellow recording artist at Sun Records.

The Carter Sisters
Another of the country acts popular in the 1950's who appeared with Elvis during his tours of the South and Southwest.

Enrico Caruso
Elvis' prototypical operatic hero.

Johnny Cash
C & W Composer—musician—performer from Kinsland, Arkansas, who recorded on the Sun label in 1955 during Elvis' first year. They toured together that year throughout the Southwest and remained friends

(Elvis introduced Cash to June Carter, his future wife). The two, along with Carl Perkins and Jerry Lee Lewis, were a part of the fabled Million Dollar Session at Sun Records on December 4, 1956. Elvis loved many Cash recordings over the years and sang them privately for enjoyment. He also performed "Folsom Prison Blues" and "I Walk The Line," but never recorded them.

"Casual Love Affair"
At Elvis' second visit to the Memphis Recording Service at 706 Union Avenue, he recorded this song on a ten-inch acetate for $4 and met Sam Phillips. On that same day, January 4, 1954, he also recorded "I'll Never Stand In Your Way." Sam was impressed, but it would be another six months before his first formal commercial recording session at Sun Records.

"Catchin On Fast"
(Bill Grant—Bernie Baum—Florence Kaye)
A dance quickie for the film *Kissin' Cousins* (Elvis singing about being taught how to kiss). Recorded in October of 1963 in Hollywood; released in March of 1964 on the soundtrack LP.

Fort Chaffee
The Arkansas Army base where Elvis had his hair cut and sideburns shaved after his induction.

Chai
The Jewish symbol of life. Elvis wore a gold Chai around his neck.

"Chain Gang"
Sam Cooke's 1960 classic was a long-time Elvis favorite. In later years, Elvis had fun performing the song, using vocal arrangements with the Stamps and the Sweet Inspirations, but never recorded it.

Change Of Habit
Started March, 1969
A Universal International Production
Cast
Dr. John Carpenter: Elvis; Sister Michelle: Mary Tyler Moore; Sister Irene: Barbara McNair; Sister Barbara: Jane Elliott; Mother Joseph: Leora Dana; Lt. Moretti: Edward Asner; The Banker: Robert Emhardt; Father Gibbons: Regis Toomey; Rose: Doro Merande; Lily: Ruth McDevitt; Bishop Finley: Richard Carlson; Julio Hernandez: Nefti Millet; Desiree: Laura Figueroa; Amanda: Lorena Kirk; Miss Parker: Virginia Vincent; Colom: David Renard; Hawk: Ji-Tu Cumbuka

Credits
Produced by Joe Connelly
Directed by William Graham
Technicolor
Songs
"Change Of Habit"; "Have A Happy"; "Rubberneckin"; "Let Us Pray"; "Lawdy Miss Clawdy" (inst. by El)

"Change Of Habit"
(Florence Kaye—Ben Weisman) Recorded at MCA Studio in Hollywood in March of 1969, as the title song for the film. It had Elvis shouting against a noisy bass and drum backing with a muted message in the lyric. Released in April of 1970 on the RCA-Camden LP *Let's Be Friends.*

Charro
Started July 22, 1968
A National General Production
A National General Picture
Cast
Jess Wade: Elvis Presley; Tracy: Ina Blain; Vince: Victor French; Sara Ramsey: Barbara Werle; Billy Roy: Solomon Sturges; Opie Keetch: Paul Brinegar; Gunner: James Sikking; Heff: Harry Landers; Lt. Rivera: Tony Young; Sherriff Ramsey: James Almanzar; Mody: Charles H. Gray; Lige: Rodd Radwing; Martin Tilford: Garry Walberg; Gabe: Duane Grey; Henry Carter: J. Edward McKinley; Jerome Selby: John Pickard; Will Joslyn: Robert Luster; Christa: Christa Lang; Barman (Harvey): Robert Karnes; Marcie: Lynn Kellogg

"Charro"
(Scott Davis—Strange)
Strings, castinets, indian drums, swooning girls—Elvis singing the theme song to the film, a dramatic western. Recorded in Hollywood in July of 1968—one

of the last few recorded songs before the great Memphis sessions of 1969. Released as a single in 1969—the flip-side of "Memories"; and in November of 1970 on the RCA-Camden LP *Almost In Love.*

Cheiro's *Book Of Numbers*
The well-known work on numerology, the science of numbers, which Elvis frequently consulted. Of his many favorite books; a constant companion.

Chenault's
Popular Memphis restaurant at 1402 Bellevue Boulevard, where Elvis threw practice for his friends during the 1960's.

"Chesay"
(Fred Karger—Ben Weisman—Sid Wayne)
A gypsy style number from *Frankie and Johnny*, with accordian—not much to offer. Recorded in May of 1965 at United Artists Recording Studio in Los Angeles; released in April of 1966 on the soundtrack LP.

Chess Records
Legendary Chicago R & B record company founded by Leonard and Phil Chess. Between 1947 and 1969, the Chess brothers recorded and distributed records by black R & B artists like Chuck Berry and Muddy Waters, among many others. Originally, Sam Phillips sold the master tapes of his recordings with the Great Bluesmen of the Deep South like Howling Wolf Burnett to Chess Records, (at one time he tried unloading his entire catalogue of artists, including Elvis, on them; they refused). Eventually, with Elvis' success and the money from his contract in 1955, Phillips released his own artist on his own label.

Captain Hubert Childress
Elvis' company commander while stationed at Friedberg.

Gene Christman
Studio drummer on Elvis' Memphis sessions, 1969.

Christmas With Elvis
1958. RCA Victor. EP (EPA-4340).
Side 1: "White Christmas"; "Here Comes Santa Claus."
Side 2: "Oh Little Town Of Bethlehem"; "Silent Night."

Johnny Christopher
Session guitarist, Memphis, 1973.

Charles Church
Owner of the law enforcement accessories shop in Whitehaven and the indoor shooting range patronized by Elvis over the years. Also the man entrusted with the installation of Elvis'

multi-camera closed circuit video monitoring system at Graceland.

Church of the Immaculate Conception
The parochial school where Elvis had Priscilla enrolled after she first moved to Memphis (which greatly pleased her parents.)

"Cilla"
Like "Beau," another of Priscilla's nicknames.

"Cindy, Cindy"
(Florence Kaye – Ben Weisman – Dolores Fuller)
Elementary old-style rocker with horns featured and an excellent guitar break hidden beneath the brass. Certainly not a top notch selection for Elvis during that dynamite period of June, 1970. Recorded at RCA Nashville Studio; released in May of 1971 on the LP *Love Letters From Elvis.*

Circle G Ranch
163-acre ranch that Elvis bought for riding horses, located about four miles west of Highway 51, across the Mississippi State Line. Alan Fortas became the custodian of the ranch until it was eventually sold. Elvis paid $300,000 for the ranch.

"City By Night"
(Bill Grant – Bernie Baum – Florence Kaye)
Bluesy trumpets and the Jordanaires back Elvis on this number for *Double Trouble.* Recorded in Hollywood in June of 1966; released in June of 1967 on the soundtrack LP.

Clambake
Started March 6, 1967
J. Levy, A. Gardner, A. Laven Production
An United Artists' Picture
Cast
Scott Heyward: Elvis Presley; Dianne Carter: Shelly Fabares; Tom Wilson: Will Hutchins; James Jamison III: Bill Bixby; Duster Heyward: James Gregory; Sam Burton: Gary Merrill; Ellie: Amanda Harley; Sally: Suzie Kaye; Gloria: Angelique Pettyjohn; Gigi: Olga Kaye; Olive: Arlene Charles; Mr. Hathaway: Jack Good; Doorman: Hal Peary; Race Announcer: Sam Riddle; Cigarette Girl: Sue England; Lisa: Lisa Slagle; Bartender: Lee Krieger; Crewman: Melvin Allen; Waiter: Herb Barnett; Bell Hop: Steve Cory; Barasch: Robert Lieb; Ice Cream Vendor: Red West

"Clambake"
(Ben Weisman – Sid Wayne)
Peculiar, up-tempo groover for the film, a typical Weisman-Wayne production with "Oh,

yeahs," subdued Jordanaires and very little continuity, even for an Elvis film number. Recorded in February of 1967 at RCA Nashville Studio; released in November of 1967 on the soundtrack LP.

Clambake
1967. RCA Victor. LP (LPM/LSP-0000).
Side 1: "Guitar Man"; "Clambake"; "Who Needs Money"; "A House That Has Everything"; "Confidence"; "Hey, Hey, Hey."
Side 2: "You Don't Know Me"; "The Girl I Never Loved"; "How Can You Lose What You Never Had"; "Big Boss Man"; "Singing Tree";
"Just Call Me Lonesome."

Albert Clark
Elvis' trusted gardener/groundskeeper, and Mr. Fix-it at Graceland – the man entrusted with everything from mowing the lawns to repairing the music gate.

Dick Clark
One of Rock's pre-eminent figures, Philadelphia DJ, father and host of "American Bandstand," and a great supporter of Elvis' career over the years. He conducted several phone interviews with Elvis from Germany, 1958–60. He also produced the made-for-television film of *Elvis* in 1979, starring Kurt Russell and Season Hubley.

The Claude Thompson Dancers
The dance company on the 1968 NBC–TV special, "*Elvis.*"

"Clean Up Your Own Backyard"
(Scott Davis Strange)
Elvis almost talks the lyrics in the tradition of "U.S. Male." From "*The Trouble With Girls*". Recorded in October of 1968 in Hollywood; released as a single in June of 1959 – the flip-side of "The Fair Is Moving On." Later released in November of 1970 on the RCA Camden LP *Almost In Love.*

Governor Frank G. Clement
In 1953, as Governor of Tennessee, he made Thomas A. Parker an honorary "Colonel." Parker received another commission from Louisiana Governor Jimmy Davis.

Jack Clement
"Cowboy Jack," Sam Phillip's protege, singer, musician, arranger, producer, engineer at Sun Records during the Golden Days. Clement, who produced recordings by Jerry Lee Lewis, Carl Perkins and Johnny Cash, was one of the lesser known but key figures in the Memphis music scene of the 1950's.

Clothes
Elvis was always a trend-setter on and off stage in what he wore. His first great interest in clothes was inspired by the colorful garments he saw in Lansky Brothers' store on Beale St., in Memphis. In the 50's, he loved to wear pink and black outfits, and brightly-colored velvet shirts. His most famous 50's outfit was the $10,000 Gold Suit, worn with a fancy white shirt and gold shoes. When in 1958 he went into the US army, he looked really trim and handsome in the various uniforms he wore, particularly his dress uniform. In the early 60's, Elvis went for smart suits offscreen, often coupled with ruffled white shirts for special occasions, although he didn't like ties much. Onscreen, he wore some colorful outfits: the all-white suit with red cumberbund and lei from *Blue Hawaii;* the Sy Devore-designed smart suits of *It Happened at the World's Fair;* Spanish costumes from *Fun in Acapulco;* riverboat gear for the period film *Frankie and Johnny;* even Arabian robes in *Harum Scarum!* In 1968, Elvis chose a black leather outfit by Bill Belew for his sensational TV special, and both the suit and show were a hit with the fans.

The return to live appearances gave birth to the jumpsuit, which appeared in all colors and all sorts of designs over the years, with capes being added for a short time between 1971–73. Off-stage in the 1970's, Elvis' dress was often very colorful, with caped coats, long leather coats, and puff-sleeved

shirts. Photos often showed him in his karate *gi,* or tracksuits. Elvis loved hats, too. In the 60's, he wore a pork pie hat sometimes, and his beloved yachting cap (even though he only owned a speedboat). During concerts, Elvis would invariably wear any hat given to him, and he was given hundreds, ranging from the summer festival boaters to fireman's helmets with flashing lights on top! Elvis had a walk-in wardrobe at Graceland, filled with outfits, including some from his films, but he gave away many items of clothing to friends and fans, and many more items to be raffled off for good causes or to fans. He gave away thousands of his silk scarves to fans at concerts, and in 1971, he gave away a large chunk of his wardrobe to RCA, to be cut up and put into envelopes for distribution with the "*50 Gold Award Hits Vol. 2*" LP set. Many of Elvis' outfits are stored now at Graceland, but the "*Aloha From Hawaii*" jumpsuit from 1973 is on show at the Las Vegas Hilton.

"C'mon Everybody"
(Joy Byers)
A rocker from *Viva Las Vegas* with a catchy bit of drum work between verses – lively, ripping, plenty of rhythm – one of the better rockers from his 1960's film scores (in the movie, he duets with Ann-Margret). Recorded in July of 1963 in Hollywood; released in July of 1964 on the RCA EP soundtrack.

C'mon Everybody
1971. RCA/Camden. LP (CAL-2518).
Side 1: "C'mon Everybody"; "Angel"; "Easy Come, Easy Go"; "A Whistling Tune"; Follow That Dream."
Side 2: "King Of The Whole Wide World"; "I'll Take Love"; "Today, Tomorrow And Forever"; "I'm Not The Marrying Kind"; "This Is Living."

Mrs. Marion Cocke
Elvis' personal nurse during the later years, author of the book *I Called Him Babe.* She met Elvis at Baptist Memorial during his stay in 1975.

Tommy Cogbill
Guitarist, bassist, producer, and sessionman for Elvis' records.

"Cold, Cold Icy Fingers"
One of the songs performed at Elvis' high school talent show during his senior year. The other song was "Old Shep."

The Colonel's Army
The name given to Tom Parker's crew of assistants, who worked on the promotion and business

end of Elvis' life. They were Jim O'Brien, George Parkhill, Tom Diskin, and Gabe Tucker.

Colonel John Burrows
One of Vernon Presley's pseudonyms over the years.

Colonel Midnight
Vernon Presley's horse, a gift from Elvis.

"Color My Rainbow"
Recording made in 1973 – unreleased because of incomplete vocal track.

"Come Along"
(David Hess)
Elvis doing New Orleans-style music hall show jazz for *Frankie and Johnnie.* Recorded in May of 1965 at United Artists Recording Studio in Los Angeles; released in April of 1966 on the soundtrack LP.

The "Comeback"
Applied to Elvis' return to live performance in 1969, but generally accepted as the period 1969–1972, which began with Elvis' hugely successful Christmas television special of 1968, his stunning Las Vegas opening of 1969, the release of the album *From Elvis in Memphis,* which included hits like "In The Ghetto" and "'If I Can Dream," and several subsequent years of touring with a multi-million dollar road show, and the resulting documentary films.

"Come Out, Come Out"
Recording made in 1969, unreleased because of incomplete vocals.

"Come What May"
(Table Porter)
A missed rocker, confusing because it's hard to follow Elvis. A kicking guitar, drums and hand-clapping, the Imperial Quartet and a Boots Randolph sax solo. Recorded in May of 1966 at RCA Nashville Studio; released as a single in June of 1966 – the flipside of "Love Letters."

Concerts West
The touring apparatus behind Elvis, 1970–1976, headed by Jerry Weintraub and Tom Heulett.

"Confidence"
(Sid Tepper – Roy C. Bennett)
A sort of rewrite of Sinatra's "High Hopes" for the film *Clambake* – a family entertainment number with a gang of kids. Recorded in February of 1967 at RCA Nashville Studio; released in November of 1967 on the soundtrack LP. Later, on the Camden-RCA LP *Elvis Sings From His Movies, Vol. 1* (1972).

Robert Conrad
Popular actor who played James West in *The Wild, Wild West* and enjoyed Elvis' rough and tumble Bel Air football games during the 1960's. He later befriended Red West and helped Red land supporting roles on his TV series "Baa Baa Black Sheep" after 1976.

Freddie de Cordova
Director of *Frankie and Johnny* (1966).

"Cotton Candy Land"
(Ruth Batchelor – Bob Roberts)
Elvis phrasing a song for the child in us, for *It Happened At the World's Fair.* Recorded in Hollywood in October of 1962; released on the soundtrack LP in March of 1963. It was later released on *Elvis Sings for Children and Grown-ups Too!* (1978).

"Could I Fall In Love"
(Randy Starr)
Floyd Cramer piano, soft-voiced Jordanaires, acoustic guitar and violin fill-in produce the background for this ballad (the duet on portions of the song is by Charlie Hodge). Recorded for *Double Trouble* in Hollywood on June 26, 1966 (along with *all* of the film's eight other tunes). Released in June, 1967 on the soundtrack LP.

Country Memories
1978. RCA Record Club. LP (R-244069).
Side 1: "I'll Hold You In My Heart"; "Welcome To My World"; "It Keeps Right On A-Hurtin'"; "Release Me"; "Make The World Go Away."
Side 2: "Snowbird"; "Early Morning Rain"; "I'm So Lonesome I Could Cry"; "Funny How Time Slips Away"; "I'm Moving On."
Side 3: "Help Me Make It Through The Night"; "You Don't Know Me"; "How Great Thou Art"; "I Washed My Hands In Muddy Water"; "I Forgot To Remember To Forget."
Side 4: "Your Cheatin' Heart"; "Baby Let's Play House"; "Whole Lotta Shakin' Goin' On"; "Gentle On My Mind"; "For The Good Times."

Country Music In The Modern Era 1940's–1970's
New World Records. 1976. LP (NW-207).
Side 1: "Bouquet Of Roses" (Eddy Arnold); "Never No More Blues" (Lefty Frizzell); "Much Too Young To Die" (Ray Price); "Squid Jiggin' Ground" (Hank Snow); "There's Poison In Your Heart" (Kitty Wells); "Try Me One More Time" (Ernest Tubb);

"Love Letters In The Sand" (Patsy Cline); "Jean's Song" (Chet Atkins); "Mystery Train" (Elvis Presley).
Side 2: "Little Ole You (Jim Reeves); "Jimmy Martinez" (Marty Robbins); "I'm A Honky-Tonk Girl" (Loretta Lynn); "Lorena" (Johnny Cash); "Don't Let Her Know" (Buck Owens); "All I Love Is You" (Roger Miller); "Sing A Sad Song" (Merle Haggard); "Coat Of Many Colors" (Dolly Parton); "Help Me Make It Through The Night" (Kris Kristofferson).

Yvonne Craig
Co-star in several of Elvis' movies: as "Dorothy" in *It Happened At The World's Fair* (1963); as "Azalea" in *Kissin' Cousins* (1964).

Floyd Cramer
Well-known piano session player who first met Elvis on the "Louisiana Hayride" in December of 1955. Cramer joined Shorty Long and Dudley Brooks in forming the distinctive piano styles on Elvis' early RCA hits (Cramer played on "Heartbreak Hotel"). He later played piano on many albums and movie soundtracks during the 1960's.

"Crawfish"
(Fred Wise – Ben Weisman)
Hot New Orleans R & B for *King Creole,* and the first instance of Elvis using a female vocalist (Kitty White, who sang almost one word and nothing else throughout: *Crawfish!*). Recorded in Hollywood in January of 1958; released in August of 1958 on the soundtrack LP. Later, on the LP *Elvis – The Other Sides – Worldwide Gold Award Hits, Volume 2* (1972).

Christina Crawford
"Monica George" in *Wild in the Country* (1961), she was really Joan Crawford's adopted daughter, who later wrote the best-seller *Mommie Dearest.* Elvis reputedly had a run-in with Miss Crawford at a Hollywood party when she threw water in his face.

Donna Lee Crayle
Leader of the movement among Elvis' fans to persuade Congress to declare Elvis' birthday a national day of recognition.

"Crazy"
One of the many nicknames for Elvis by his entourage. Others were "Boss," "Chief," "Big E."

Credence Clearwater Revival
Elvis loved the sound and style

of this popular rock group of the 1960's and 1970's. While Credence originated out of the San Francisco area, they had an uncanny ability, through the spare musical styles and the rasping, powerful voice of leader John Fogerty, to capture the spirit of the South in songs like "Born On The Bayou" and "Proud Mary," which Elvis recorded and performed in the early seventies.

Charlie Crosby
One of the paramedics from Unit 6 of the Memphis Fire Department called by Joe Esposito to try to save Elvis' life on August 16, 1977.

Gary Crosby
"Andy," Elvis' crony in *Girl Happy* (1965).

"Cross My Heart And Hope To Die"
(Sid Wayne – Ben Weisman)
Sax and piano introduction to a slinky-voiced Elvis – but a minor film number nonetheless. Recorded in July of 1964 in Hollywood for the film *Girl Happy;* released in April of 1965 on the soundtrack LP.

Crosstown Theater
One of several local movie houses in Memphis rented for Elvis' all-night movie sessions with friends.

Crown Electric Company
Elvis' first employer out of high school, where he worked as truck driver at $1.25 an hour until meeting Sam Phillips in 1954. Located at 353 Poplar Avenue.

Arthur "Big Boy" Crudup
Black R & B composer-singer who influenced Elvis' early style. Elvis listened to Crudup's Chess recordings of songs like "My Baby Left Me," "That's All Right (Mama)" and "So Glad

You're Mine"; all of which he recorded. "That's All Right (Mama)" was his breakthrough single for Sun Records in 1954. Though Elvis never met Crudup, he reportedly helped finance his recordings for Fine Records.

"Crying"
Unreleased Roy Orbison tune recorded by Elvis in 1976.

"Crying Heart Blue"
Unreleased song recorded at Sun sometime between July, 1954 and June, 1955.

"Crying In The Chapel"
(Darell Glenn)
Elvis at his very best, turning a minor hit by the Orioles featuring Sonny Till (1953) and later Adam Wade (1965) into a breathtakingly beautiful pop song — simple, sentimental, and transcendentally Elvis, backed by the Jordanaires. Recorded at RCA Nashville Studio in October of 1960; not released until April of 1965 when it appeared as a single with "I Believe In The Man In The Sky" as its flip-side. Later, it appeared on the LP *How Great Thou Art* (1967). Also on *Elvis: Worldwide 50 Gold Award Hits, Volume 1* (1970).

"Crying Time"
(Buck Owens)
Song recorded by Owens in 1964, later a hit for Ray Charles (1966) which Elvis performs in *That's The Way It Is* (1970) but which was not released in the soundtrack LP.

"Cultural Phenomenon of Elvis Presley: The Making of a Folk Hero"
The first formally accredited university level course on Elvis taught at the University of Tennessee in 1980.

Jack Cummings and George Sidney
Produced *Viva Las Vegas* (1964).

Lloyd Cupas
"Cowboy." C & W performer on the tour bill with Elvis in 1955 (Elvis headlined), who later died in a plane crash in March of 1963.

Current Audio Magazine — Elvis: His First And Only Press Conference
1972. Current Audio Magazine. LP (CM); Vol. 1 No. 1 August/September 1972.
Side 1: "Mick Jagger Speaks"; "Manson Will Escape"; "Robert Klein"; "Teddy Kennedy"; "Angela Davis"; "Monty Python's Flying Circus"; "Spam."

Side 2: "Elvis Presley"; "The Killer Was A Narc"; "Bella Abzug Loses"; "Scoop's Column"; "Nader Group Hits Vegas"; "Crime Watch"; "Sensuous You."

Tony Curtis
One of Elvis' early movie idols, whose ducktail he would try to emulate

Michael Curtiz
Famed Hollywood director, responsible for such classics as *Casablanca*, who coaxed and drove Elvis to give one of his finest performances in *King Creole*.

"Dainty Little Moonbeams"
Leiber — Stoller tune from *Girls! Girls! Girls!*. Elvis sang a short part of the song which was added to the title tune of the film, but the track was never released by itself.

Dance Party
Teen program on WHBQ in Memphis during the 1950's hosted by Wink Martindale, on which Elvis appeared in 1957.

"Danny"
(Fred Wise — Ben Weisman).
One of the tunes created for *King Creole* that never made it into the movie or album. A short, bluesy track, recorded in January of 1958 in Hollywood, it wasn't released for twenty years, until *Elvis: A Legendary Performer, Volume 3* (1978).

"Danny Boy"
(Fred E. Weatherly)
The old Irish air written in 1913 and recorded scores of times was one of the songs Elvis loved to play at the piano at home for friends, or to exercise his pipes. Elvis never recorded it until February of 1976, in Memphis, when health and drug problems were seriously impairing him. Still, it rings true (appropriately, it was recorded in the Graceland den). Released in May of 1976 on the LP *From Elvis Presley Boulevard, Memphis, Tennessee*.

Ken Darby
Composer — singer and conductor — arranger. Leader of several vocal back-up groups during the 1940's and 1950's, such as The King's Men and The Ken Darby Singers. Musical Director of *Love Me Tender* (1956), for which he wrote "Love Me Tender," "Poor Boy," "We're Gonna Move" and "Let Me" (Elvis received co-authorship with Vera Motson, Darby's wife, because of publishing-copyright problems between BMI and ASCAP). The Ken Darby Trio

also provided vocal backings for the recordings.

Ken Darby's trio
Background singers on "Love Me Tender."

"Datin'"
(Fred Wise — Randy Starr)
Bouncy, beaty and very pedestrian number form *Paradise Hawaiian Style* (in the film, Elvis duets with Donna Butterworth; on the record, he sings alone). Recorded in July of 1965 at Paramount Recording Studio, in Hollywood; released in June of 1966 on the soundtrack LP.

Elwood Davis
Pilot of Elvis' Convair 880.

Mac Davis
Texas-born composer — singer — actor who saw Elvis perform in 1955 and later wrote "In The Ghetto," one of his monumental single hits of the 1960's. Also composed "Clean Up Your Own Backyard," "Charro," "A Little Less Conversation," "Don't Cry Daddy," "Nothingville," and "Memories," all of which Elvis recorded.

Oscar Davis
"The Baron." One of Colonel Parker's promotion assistants in the early years, who alerted the Colonel to Elvis' talent.

Richard Davis
Elvis' personal valet during the sixties from 1963–1969, until Elvis' stepbrother, Rick Stanley, took the position.

Sammy Davis, Jr
A Presley admirer and friend who appeared with Elvis on the *Sinatra Special* and often spoke of Elvis' unique gifts as an entertainer.

Annette Day
The pretty young English girl who got Elvis in *Double Trouble* (1967).

Dealer's Prevue
1957. RCA Victor. EP (SDS 7-2).
Side 1: "Loving You" (Elvis Presley); "Teddy Bear" (Elvis Presley); "Now Stop" (Martha Carson); "Just Whistle Or Call" (Martha Carson).
Side 2: "The Wife" (Lou Monte); "Musica Bella" (Lou Monte); "Mailman, Bring Me No More Blues" (Herb Jeffries); "So Shy" (Herb Jeffries).

Dealer's Prevue
1957. RCA Victor. EP (SDS 57-39).
Side 1: "The Old Rugged Cross" (Stuart Hamblen); "Old Time Religion (Stuart Hamblen); "Jail-

house Rock" (Elvis Presley); "Treat Me Nice" (Elvis Presley); "Till The Last Leaf Shall Fall" (Statesmen Quartet); "Every Hour And Every Day" (Statesmen Quartet).
Side 2: "A Slip Of The Lip" (Kathy Barr); "Welcome Mat" (Kathy Barr); "Just Born" (Perry Como); "Ivy Rose" (Perry Como); "Sayonara" (Eddie Fisher); "That's The Way It Goes" (Eddie Fisher).

James Dean
Another early idol of the Fifties generation and one of Elvis' favorite actors, originally slated to play in *King Creole* before his death.

Joan Deary
Steve Sholes' assistant at RCA during the early days; later worked with Harry Jenkins at RCA handling Elvis; presently in charge of A & R catalogue for Elvis at RCA.

Mike Deasy
Session guitarist on Elvis' TV Special 1968.

Death
To millions of fans, the mention of August 16, 1977 brings back memories of the worst day of their lives. When it was announced that Elvis had died at age forty-two of a heart attack at his Graceland Mansion in Memphis, it was the signal for millions and millions of tears to flow, and the news was a shock to fans and non-fans alike. Tributes began to flow in, from the humblest fan to the President of the United States, and many people realized just how much they admired Elvis, and joined the ranks of the fans. On the blacker side, there were lurid media stories revealed by so-called friends, and a massive souvenir market opened up, much of it insulting to Elvis' memory. The trauma of Elvis' passing is still being felt today, and for many fans, their lives will never be the same. The loss of the King left a gap that will never be filled. His death was a major tragedy and a major news story of the 20th century.

Dolores Del Rio
"Neddy Biston," Elvis' Indian mother in *Flaming Star* (1961).

Terry Dene and the Dene-Agers
Well known British Elvis impersonator during the 1950's.

Jim Denny
Opry booking agent during the 1950's, who booked Elvis' first appearance in 1954, and nearly broke Elvis' heart by telling him to go back to driving a truck.

Jackie DeShannon
Pop composer-singer who Elvis dated for a period in Hollywood during the mid-sixties.

"(You're The) Devil In Disguise"
Bill Giant—Bernie Baum—Florence Kaye)
A good, solid rendition of a teasing rocker, which fluctuates from a slow, lilting *You walk like an angel, talk . . . like an angel* to the ripping *You're the Devil in Disguise . . .* With the Jordanaires, it was recorded in May of 1963 in RCA Nashville Studio; released as a single in June of 1963, with a flip side of "Please Don't Drag That String Around." Later released on the LP's *Elvis' Gold Records, Vol. 4* (1968) and *Elvis: Worldwide Gold Award Hits, Vol. 1* (1970).

Sy Devore
The Hollywood "celebrity" tailor who created many of Elvis' suits and outfits over the years.

Neil Diamond
Brooklyn born composer-singer-actor. Elvis recorded two Diamond songs: the 1969 hit "Sweet Caroline" and "And The Grass Won't Pay No Mind."

Bo Diddley
(*aka* Elias McDaniels). Legendary R & B guitarist singer of the 1950's and 1960's and Chess recording artist. Because Elvis once saw Bo Diddley perform at New York's Apollo Theater in 1956, there has been speculation that Elvis copied his gyrations and hip-swiveling stage style from Diddley. In actuality, Elvis had been grinding and pumping his songs since late 1954.

"Didja Ever"
(Sid Wayne—Sherman Edwards).
From the finale of *G.I. Blues*, with Elvis asking "*Didja evah* git one of them days, boys" and the entire audience responding. (On the record, it's the Jordanaires). Recorded in April of 1960 in Hollywood; released in October of 1960 on the soundtrack LP.

Dolores Dinning
Back-up singer, who often teamed with Millie Kirkham on Elvis' records.

"Dirty, Dirty Feeling"
(Jerry Leiber—Mike Stoller)
Uptempo complaint about Elvis having a "dirty, dirty" feeling because his girl friend has left him. Hank Garland on guitar along with Scotty, Bob Moore, D.J. and Floyd Cramer's piano. Recorded in April of 1960 at RCA Nashville Studio; released that same month on the LP *Elvis Is Back!*

Tom Diskin
Colonel Tom Parker's brother-in-law and assistant.

"Dixie"
The traditional song that became the first part of Elvis' American Trilogy, his tribute to America arranged by Mickey Newbury.

"Dixieland Rock"
(Claude Demetrius—Fred Wise)
Elvis' swinging blend of jazz and rock from *King Creole*—a real show stopper. Recorded in January of 1958 in Hollywood (the film version is different and the recorded version has a shortened introduction). Released in August of 1958 on the soundtrack LP.

Willie Dixon
Famed Chicago bluesman of the 1930's and 1940's. Wrote "Big Boss Man," "My Babe" and "Doncha Think It's Time," all recorded by Elvis.

Dodge'ems
The bumper cars Elvis loved to ride with his friends at Liberty-land in Memphis.

"Dodger"
Elvis' nickname for his grandmother, Minnie Mae Presley.

"Doin' The Best I Can"
(Doc Pomus—Mort Schuman)
A mood piece from *G.I. Blues*, with Elvis curling his voice smoothly up from bass register to a dramatic crescendo. Recorded in Hollywood in April of 1960; released in October of 1960 on the soundtrack LP.

Kitty Dolan
The Las Vegas showgirl Elvis dated in 1956 while appearing at the Frontiere Hotel.

"Dominick"
The song Elvis sang to the bull in *Stay Away, Joe* (1968) never released by RCA on the soundtrack LP.

Domino
The horse Elvis gave to Priscilla during their riding craze.

"Doncha' Think It's Time"
(Clyde Otis—Willie Dixon)
One of the lesser R & B ballad/slow rockers from 1958, a slapping calypso beat with the Jordanaires and guitar work by Scotty and H.J. Timbrell. Recorded on February 1, 1958 at Radio Recorders in Hollywood; released as a single in April of 1958 as the flip-side of "Wear My Ring Around Your Neck." Later, on the LPs *50,000,000 Elvis Fans Can't Be Wrong, Elvis' Gold Records, Volume 2* (1969), and *Elvis: The Other Sides—Worldwide Gold Award Hits, Volume 2* (1971).

"Do Not Disturb"
(Bill Grant—Bernie Baum—Florence Kaye)
A romantic girl-chasing ballad from *Girl Happy*—mushy and mellow. Recorded in July of 1964 in Hollywood; released in April of 1965 on the soundtrack LP.

"Don't"
(Jerry Leiber—Mike Stoller)
Low, tender, sincere and lovely—a harbinger of things to come. Classic backing by the Jordanaires helped Elvis showcase his pipes on this slow one. Recorded in September of 1957 at Radio Recorders in Hollywood; released in January of 1958 as a single with "I Beg Of You" as its flip-side (it entered the Hot 100 Chart *as* number one); later released on the LP *50,000,000 Elvis Fans Can't Be Wrong* (1959) and on *Elvis: Worldwide 50 Gold Award Hits, Volume One* (1970).

"Don't Ask Me Why"
(Fred Wise—Ben Weisman)
A tender love ballad from *King Creole*. Recorded in January of 1958 in Hollywood; released in June of 1958 as a single—the flip-side of "Hard Headed Woman." Later released on the soundtrack LP.

"Don't Be Cruel"
(Otis Blackwell—Elvis Presley)
The Blackwell classic of 1956, turned into one of the biggest selling singles of all time. From the first strains of Bill Black's double bass, the song never quits. The Jordanaires make their debut and establish a glorious tradition of background bop singing. Recorded on July 2, 1956 at RCA New York Studio; released as a single that same month—the flip-side of "Hound Dog." Performed on *The Ed Sullivan Show*, January 6, 1957. Concert versions of the song

appear live in a medley with "Teddy Bear" on *Elvis As Recorded At Madison Square Garden* (1972) and *Elvis in Concert*, (1977). Released on the LP *Elvis' Golden Records* (1958). Re-released on *Worldwide 50 Gold Award Hits, Volume One* (1970).

"Don't Cry Daddy"
(Scott Davis)
Somewhat saccharine weeper about a mother who has died, leaving a child and father behind, but Elvis' sincerity and time make this one haunting nonetheless. A simple, effective background with a duet on the last bars with Ronnie Milsap. Recorded in January of 1969 at American Studios in Memphis; released as a single in November with "Rubberneck" as the flip. Later, on the LP *Elvis: Worldwide 50 Gold Award Hits, Vol. 1* (1970).

Don't Knock Elvis
1959 novelty record by Felton Jarvis on Viva Records (Jarvis would become Elvis' producer in 1966).

"Don't Leave Me Now"
(Aaron Schroeder—Ben Weisman)
A quickie from *Loving You*—a simple ditty that many say never satisfied Elvis, either on screen or on record. Recorded in February of 1957.

"Don't Think Twice, It's All Right"
(Bob Dylan)
Legend has it that this song was an impromptu take—Elvis was singing to James Burton's picking of the Dylan classic during a recording session and the engineer flipped the switch. True or not: it's one of two Dylan songs Elvis *ever* released, a twangy, hurried version, more country than folksy. Recorded in May of 1971 at RCA Nashville Studio; released in July of 1973 on the LP *Elvis*. Later, on *Our Memories of Elvis, Volume 2* (1979).

Thomas A. Dorsey
Chicago-born singer-songwriter-musician-bandleader who composed jazz, blues, and gospel songs. He wrote "Peace In The Valley" and "Take My Hand, Precious Lord," both of which Elvis recorded.

"Do The Clam"
(Bill Grant—Bernie Baum—Florence Kaye)
The big dance number fom *Girl Happy*, with the Jordanaires, Carol Lombard Trio, and the Jubilee Four substituted for the bunch of groovers in the film.

Many critics point to this number as the nadir of his film career. Recorded in Hollywood in June of 1965; released in April of 1965 on the soundtrack LP.

"Do The Vega"
(Bill Grant – Bernie Baum – Florence Kaye)
A mother dance number with instructions about said dance. Jerky high tone against a Latin touch with the Jubilee Four pitching in. Recorded in Hollywood in July of 1963 for *Viva Las Vegas*; not released until November of 1968, when it appeared on *Singer Presents Elvis Singing Flaming Star And Others*.

Double Dynamite
1975. RCA/Camden-Pickwick. LP (DL 2-5001).
Side 1: "Burning Love"; "I'll Be There"; "Fools Fall In Love"; "Follow That Dream"; "You'll Never Walk Alone."
Side 2: "Flaming Star"; "Yellow Rose Of Texas/The Eyes Of Texas"; "Old Shep"; "Mama."
Side 3: "Rubberneckin' "; "U.S. Male"; "Frankie & Johnny"; "If You Think I Don't Need You"; "Easy Come, Easy Go."
Side 4: "Separate Ways"; "Peace In The Valley"; "Big Boss Man"; "It's A Matter Of Time."

Double Trouble
Started June 19, 1966
An MGM Production
Cast
Guy Lambert: Elvis Presley;
Jill Conway: Annette Day;

Gerald Waverly: John Williams;
Calire Dunham: Yvonne Romain;
The Wiere Bros.: Themselves;
Archie Brown: Chips Rafferty;
Arthur Babcock: Norman Rossington;
Georgie: Monty Landis;
Morley: Michael Murphy;
Insp. De Groote: Leon Askin;
Iceman: John Anderson;
Captain Roach: Stanley Adams;
Frenchman: Maurice Marsac;
Mate: Walter Burke;
Gerda: Helene Winston;
The G. Men: Themselves.
Credits
Produced by Judd Bernard and Irwin Winkler
Directed by Norman Taurog
Screenplay by Jo Heims
Technical Advisor: Colonel Tom Parker
Panavision and Metrocolor
'U' certificate.

"Double Trouble"
(Doc Pomus – Marty Schuman)
Big band treatment of the title song for the film, filled in by the Jordanaires. Recorded on June 26, 1966 in Hollywood; released in June of 1967 on the soundtrack LP.

Double Trouble
1967. RCA Victor. LP (LPM/LSP-3787).
Side 1: "Double Trouble"; "Baby If You'll Give Me All Your Love"; "Could I Fall In Love"; "Long Legged Girl"; "City By Night"; "Old MacDonald."
Side 2: "I Love Only One Girl"; "There Is So Much World To See"; "It Won't Be Long"; "Never Ending"; "What Now, What Next, Where To."

Donna Douglas
"Frankie" in *Frankie and Johnny* (1966) who became famous playing Elly Mae Clampett on *The Beverly Hillbillies* on television. She and Elvis became good friends and had many interests in common: meditation, yoga, religion, philosophy.

Gordon Douglas
Director of *Follow That Dream* (1962).

"Down By the Riverside and When the Saints Go Marching In"
(Trad. – Arranged by Bill Giant – Bernie Baum – Florence Kaye)
New Orleans swing-style music hall number from *Frankie and Johnny*, one segueing into another. Plenty of energy and voices and color. Recorded at United Artists Recording Studio in Los Angeles; released in April of 1966 on the soundtrack LP.

"Down In The Alley"
(Jesse Stone and the Clovers)
A heavy beater for the film *Spinout*, with Elvis adding plenty of "yeahs" and "alrights." Recorded in May of 1966 at RCA Nashville Studio; released in October of 1966 on the soundtrack LP.

"Down The Line"
One of Elvis' unreleased Sun recordings of 1955, penned by Sam Phillips. Jerry Lee Lewis later released the song.

"Do You Know Who I Am"
(Bobby Russell)
Dark, moody atmosphere – a dispirited love song and something of a departure: this signaled a change (during the Memphis sessions) from the mellow smooth love ballads of the films to soulful ballads of personal meaning and feeling. With the Memphis Strings and vocal support from the Blossoms. Recorded in February of 1969 at American Studios in Memphis; released in November of 1969 on the LP *From Memphis To Vegas/From Vegas To Memphis.*

Peter Drake
"Sneaky Pete" – pioneer C & W steel guitarist famous for his 1964 hit "Forever," who played steel guitar on Elvis recordings like "Guitar Man" and "Big Boss Man."

Dr. Strangelove
Elvis loved Stanley Kubrick's 1964 film, a black comedy about nuclear war, because of the performances by Peter Sellers and George C. Scott, two of his favorite performers.

"Drums Of The Islands"
(Sid Tepper – Roy C. Bennett)
A Hawaiian drum number from *Paradise Hawaiian Style* backed by the Jordanaires, a rather monotonous adaptation of "Bula Lei," played in the film. Recorded in July of 1965, at Paramount Recording Studio in Hollywood; released in June of 1966 on the album soundtrack.

Mrs. Dubrovner
Presley's landlady at 462 Alabama Street in Memphis, where they lived in 1953.

Steve Dunleavy
The Australian reporter-columnist imported by Rupert Murdoch, publisher of the *National Star* to write for his American papers. Dunleavy became the writer behind *Elvis: What Happened?*, who shocked Americans after Elvis' death by referring to him as "white trash." Presently city-editor for *The New York Post*.

Phillip Dunne
Director of *Wild In the Country* (1961).

Al Dvorin
Produced and emceed the benefit concert for the Memorial Fund of the USS Arizona on March 25, 1961. Also conducted the orchestra in Joe Guercio's absence during the seventies, and announced Elvis' performance at Mid-South Coliseum on March 24, 1974.

Ronald Dwyer
Los Angeles attorney hired to defend Elvis from a $4 million lawsuit brought against him in 1973, in which four disgruntled "fans" – Robert and Kenneth MacKenzie, Marcelo Elias and Marlo Martinez – claimed that they were attacked by Elvis' bodyguards. The suit was dismissed.

Bob Dylan
Elvis considered Dylan's vocal style alien and unappealing, but he admired his lyric genius. The one Dylan song he recorded, "Tomorrow Is A Long Time" in 1966 – he found irresistable; the other – "Don't Think Twice, It's All Right" in 1971 – was an impromptu idea during a recording session.

Eagle's Nest
Ballroom on Lamar Avenue in Memphis, site of one of Elvis' first singing jobs after the release of "That's All Right (Mama)."

"Early Morning Rain"
(Gordon Lightfoot)
A countrified version, Nashville-style, with harmonica by Charlie McCoy and vocal backing by the Nashville Edition. Elvis is indistinct and seems oddly unsuited to this popular song, but he gives it his best. Recorded in March of 1971 at RCA Nashville Studio; released in February of 1972 on the LP *Elvis Now*. A live version appears on the LP *Elvis In Concert* (1977).

"Earth Boy"
(Sid Tepper – Roy C. Bennett)
The Chinese "junk" number from *Girls! Girls! Girls!*. Sung to the kiddies (their voices were left off the recording). Recorded in March of 1962 in Hollywood; released in November of 1962 on the soundtrack LP.

Earth News
1977. Earth News. LP (August 22–29).
Side 1: "1956 Elvis Interview"; "Blue Suede Shoes" (from the Dorsey Brothers Stage Show), "1956 Elvis Interview"; "Don't Be Cruel" (from the Ed Sullivan Show); "Heartbreak Hotel" (from Dorsey Show); "1956 Elvis Interview"; "Jay Thompson's Elvis Interview"; "Elvis Sails Interview"; "Dick Clark/Elvis Phone Call"; "The Truth About Me."
Side 2: "1956 Elvis Interview"; "1961 Elvis Interview"; "Red West Interview"; "The Truth About Me"; "In the Ghetto"; "Steve Bender Interview"; "Hound Dog"; "Willie Mae Thornton Interview"; "Medley: Hey Mr. Presley/I Dreamed I Was Elvis/My Baby's Crazy About Elvis/Elvis Presley for President."

East Bottom
The rich farmland where Vernon Presley hoed cotton, corn and peas as a sharecropper.

East Heights Garden Club
Organization behind the restoration of Elvis' Tupelo birthplace, which was turned into a historical monument in June of 1971.

East Tupelo
Small neighborhood community, pop. 5800, where Vernon and Gladys Presley lived, worked and built the shotgun shack where Elvis was born.

East Tupelo Consolidated School
Elvis' elementary school.

Clint Eastwood
Elvis' favorite action-movie star, whose police character, "Dirty Harry," became a model for his own occasional police shenanigans.

Easy Come, Easy Go
Started September 12, 1966
A Hal Wallis Production
A Paramount Picture ☞
Cast
Ted Jackson: Elvis Presley;
Whitehead: Mickey Elley;
Tompkins: Reed Morgan;
Schwartz: Sandy Kenyon;
Jo Symington: Dodie Marshall;
Judd Whitman: Pat Harrington;
Dina Bishop: Pat Priest;
Vicki: Elaine Beckett;
Mary: Shari Nims;
Gil Corey: Skip Ward;
Cooper: Ed Griffith;
Captain Jack: Frank McHugh;
Madame Neherina: Elsa
Lanchester.
Credits
Directed by John Rich
Screenplay by Allen Weiss and
Anthony Lawrence
Songs
"Easy Come, Easy Go"; "The Love Machine"; "You Gotta Stop"; "Sing You Children"; "Yoga Is As Yoga Does"; "I'll Take Love"; "Wheel Of Fortune" (cut & unreleased).
Previously titled:
A Girl In Every Port
Easy Does It
Nice And Easy
Port Of Call

"Easy Come, Easy Go"
(Sid Wayne—Ben Weisman)
Typical 1967 film title song with Elvis making the most of a corny rocker, shouting "Alright!" after the guitar-drum break. Along with *all* of the other six film tunes, it was recorded on September 26, 1966 at Paramount Recording Studio in Hollywood; released in May of 1967 on the soundtrack EP. Later on the Camden RCA LP *C'mon Everybody* (1971) and the Pickwick LP *Double Dynamite* (1975).

Easy Come, Easy Go
1967. RCA Victor. EP (EPA-4387).
Side 1: "Easy Come, Easy Go"; "The Love Machine"; "Yoga Is As Yoga Does."
Side 2: "You Gotta Stop"; "Sing You Children"; "I'll Take Love."

"(Such An) Easy Question"
(Otis Blackwell – Winfield Scott)
A slow/medium ballad – light, pleasant, but a lesser effort. Recorded in March of 1963 at RCA Nashville Studio; released in June of 1962 on the LP *Pot Luck*.

"Echoes Of Love"
(Robert McMains)
Sad ballad, beautifully sung. Recorded in May of 1963 at RCA Nashville Studio; released in March of 1964 on the soundtrack LP *Kissin' Cousins* (it wasn't in the film).

Barbara Eden
Popular American TV star who played "Rosalyn Pierce" in *Flaming Star* (1960).

"Edge Of Reality"
(Bill Grant – Bernie Baum – Florence Kaye)
A ballad, European in flavor, with deep-toned strings, and staccato vocal backing. From the film *Live A Little, Love A Little*. Recorded March 11, 1968 at MGM Sound Studio in Hollywood; released as a single – the flip-side of "If I Can Dream," in November of 1968. Later, on the RCA-Camden LP *Almost In Love* (1973).

Mike Edwards
Elvis' character in *It Happened At The World's Fair* (1963).

Richard Egan
Elvis' brother, "Vance Reno," in *Love Me Tender* (1956) and a loyal Elvis fan over the years.

Buford Ellington
Governor of Tennessee who made Elvis an honorary Colonel when Elvis appeared by special invitation before the General Assembly of the Legislature of Tennessee on March 8, 1961.

Maurice Elliot
The official at Baptist Memorial Hospital at the time of Elvis' death and autopsy who handled the press.

Ellis Auditorium
The site of Elvis' last live appearance until the Great Comeback. The Concert took place in Memphis on February 25, 1961.

"El Paso"
(Marty Robbins)
One of Elvis' favorite C & W standards – a song he sang occasionally but never recorded.

"El Toro"
(Bill Grant – Bernie Baum – Florence Kaye)
From *Fun In Acapulco* (what else?), with Elvis singing dramatically about the matador and the famous bull, El Toro. Lots of Mex flavor, not much else. Recorded in January of 1963 in Hollywood; released in November of 1963 on the soundtrack LP.

"Elvin Pelvin"
Tom Gibson's satirical take-off on Elvis, performed on *The Phil Silvers Show* in 1958.

Elvis
1979
Dick Clark Motion Pictures Inc.
Credits
Executive Producer: Dick Clark; Produced and written by: Anthony Lawrence; Directed by: John Carpenter; Director of Photography: Don Morgan.
Cast
Elvis Presley: Kurt Russell; Gladys Presley: Shelly Winters; Vernon Presley: Bing Russell; Red West: Robert Gray; Priscilla Presley: Season Hubley; Col. Tom Parker: Pat Hingle; D.J. Fontanna: Ed Begley, Jr.; Scotty Moore: James Canning; Sam Phillips: Charlie Cyphers; Jim Denny: Peter Hobbs; Sonny West: Les Lannom; Bill Black: Elliott Street; Ed Sullivan: Will Jordan; Joe Esposito: Joe Mantegna; Hank Snow: Galen Thompson; Marion Keisker: Ellen Travolta; Natalie Wood: Abi Young; Charlie Hodge: Charlie Hodge; Lisa Marie Presley: Felicia Fenske; Elvis as a Boy: Randy Gray.
Songs: recorded by Ronnie McDowell and produced by Felton Jarvis: "Mystery Train"; "Good Rockin' Tonight"; "Old Shep"; "My Happiness"; "That's All Right (Mama)"; "Blue Moon Of Kentucky"; "Lawdy Miss Clawdy"; "Tutti Frutti"; "Long Tall Sally"; "Heartbreak Hotel"; "Rip It Up"; "Are You Lonesome Tonight"; "A Fool Such As I"; "Crying In The Chapel"; "Pledging My Love"; "Bosom Of Abraham"; "Suspicious Minds"; "Until It's Time For You To Go"; "Separate Ways"; "Sweet Caroline"; "Blue Suede Shoes"; "Dixie/Battle Hymn Of The Republic"; "Unchained Melody"; "Oh Lord, My God."
The film premiered in America on February 11, 1979, on ABC-TV against *Gone With The Wind* (on CBS) and *One Flew Over The Cuckoo's Nest* (on NBC). *Elvis* received the highest share of the ratings.

Elvis
1956. RCA Victor. LP (LPM-1382).
Side 1: "Rip It Up"; "Love Me"; "When My Blue Moon Turns To Gold Again"; "Long Tall Sally"; "First In Line"; "Paralyzed."
Side 2: "So Glad You're Mine"; "Old Shep"; "Reddy Teddy"; "Anyplace Is Paradise"; "How's the World Treating You"; "How Do You Think I Feel."

Elvis, Volume One
1956. RCA Victor. EP (EPA-992).
Side 1: "Rip It Up"; "Love Me."
Side 2: "When My Blue Moon Turns To Gold Again"; "Paralyzed."

Elvis, Volume Two
1956. RCA Victor. EP (EPA-993).
Side 1: "So Glad You're Mine"; "Old Shep."
Side 2: "Reddy Teddy"; "Anyplace Is Paradise."

"Elvis" (From His NBC-TV Special)
1968. RCA. LP (LPM-4088).
Side 1: "Trouble/Guitar Man"; "Lawdy Miss Clawdy/Baby What Do You Want Me To Do"; "Medley: Heartbreak Hotel/Hound Dog/All Shook Up/Can't Help Falling In Love/Jailhouse Rock"; "Love Me Tender."
Side 2: "Where Could I Go But To The Lord/Up Above My Head/Saved"; "Blue Christmas"; "One Night"; "Memories"; "Medley: Nothingville/Big Boss Man/Guitar Man/Little Egypt/Trouble/Guitar Man"; "If I Can Dream."

Elvis
1973. RCA Victor. LP (DLP2-0056e).
Side 1: "Hound Dog"; "I Want You, I Need You, I Love You"; "All Shook Up"; "Don't"; "I Beg Of You."
Side 2: "A Big Hunk O'Love"; "Love Me"; "Stuck On You"; "Good Luck Charm"; "Return To Sender."
Side 3: "Don't Be Cruel"; "Loving You"; "Jailhouse Rock"; "Can't Help Falling In Love"; "I Got Stung."
Side 4: "Teddy Bear"; "Love Me Tender"; "Hard Headed Woman"; "It's Now Or Never"; "Surrender."

Elvis (Including "Fool")
1973. RCA. LP (APL1-0283).
Side 1: "Fool"; "Where Do I Go From Here"; "Love Me, Love The Life I Lead"; "It's Still Here"; "It's Impossible."
Side 2: "For Lovin' Me"; "Padre"; "I'll Take You Home Again Kathleen"; "I Will Be True"; "Don't Think Twice, It's All Right."

Elvis
33⅓ LP Bootleg.
Side 1: "Change Of Habit"; "Rubberneckin'"; "Spring Fever"; "Girl Happy"; "Shake, Rattle And Roll" (*Dorsey Show*, 1956); "Party"; "Happy Ending."
Side 2: "Kiss Me Quick"; "Suspicion"; "Let Me"; "Departure From The U.S.A."; "Arrival In Germany, 1958"; "Arrival In The U.S.A., 1959"; "Love Me Tender" (last verse).

Elvis
33⅓ LP Bootleg.
Sides 1 and 2: Same as the Australian *Fool* LP.

Elvis
33⅓ LP Bootleg.
Side 1: Same as Elvis side on *Good Rocking Tonight*.
Side 2: "Teen Parade"; "Teddy Bear"; "Got A Lot O'Livin To Do"; "Treat Me Nice"; "Jailhouse Rock"; "1958 Interviews."

Elvis – A Canadian Tribute
1978. RCA. LP (KKL 1-7065).
Side 1: "Intro . . . Jailhouse Rock"; "Intro . . . Teddy Bear"; "Loving You"; "Until It's Time For You To Go"; "Early Morning Rain"; "Vancouver Press Conference (1957)."
Side 2: "I'm Movin' On"; "Snowbird"; "For Lovin' Me"; "Put Your Hand In The Hand"; "Little Darlin'"; "My Way."

Elvis – A Collectors Edition
This is a five album set which includes the following LP's, all of which follow in this text.
Elvis. RCA (DPL2-0056e) Double LP.
Elvis Forever. RCA (KSL 2-7031) Double LP.
Elvis In Hollywood. RCA (KSL 1-7053).

Elvis (Volume One) – A Legendary Performer
1974. RCA. LP (CPL1-0341).
Side 1: "That's All Right"; "I Love You Because" (unreleased version); "Heartbreak Hotel"; "Don't Be Cruel"; "Love Me" (unreleased live version); "Trying To Get To You" (unreleased live version).
Side 2: "Love Me Tender"; "Peace In The Valley"; "A Fool Such As I"; "Tonight's All Right For Love" (unreleased in English speaking countries); "Are You Lonesome Tonight" (unreleased

live version); "Can't Help Falling In Love."

Elvis (Volume Two)—A Legendary Performer

1976. RCA. LP (CPL 1-1349). Side 1: "Harbor Lights"; "Jay Thompson Interviews Elvis (1956)"; "I Want You, I Need You, I Love You" (unreleased alternate take); "Blue Suede Shoes"; "Blue Christmas"; "Jailhouse Rock"; "It's Now Or Never." Side 2: "A Cane And A High Starched Collar"; "Presentation Of Awards To Elvis"; "Blue Hawaii" (unreleased version); "Such a Night" (with false starts); "Baby What Do You Want Me To Do" (unreleased live version); "How Great Thou Art"; "If I Can Dream."

Elvis (Volume Three)—A Legendary Performer

1978. RCA. LP (CPL 1-1378). Side 1: "Hound Dog"; "1956 (TV Guide) Interview"; "Danny"; "Fame And Fortune" (unreleased

alternate take); "Frankfurt Special" (unreleased alternate take); "Britches"; "Crying In The Chapel." Side 2: "Surrender"; "Guadalajara" (unreleased alternate take); "It Hurts Me" (unreleased version); "Let Yourself Go" (unreleased version); "In The Ghetto"; "Let It Be Me" (unreleased live version).

"Elvis: Aloha From Hawaii"

Concert broadcast via Intelsat TV satellite on January 14, 1975 from the Honolulu International Center Arena and viewed by over one billion people in over forty countries. The proceeds from the gate were donated to the Kuiokolani Lee Cancer Fund. The U.S. edition of the broadcast (April 4, 1973) included an additional three songs, taped after the audience left the Arena: "Blue Hawaii," "Hawaiian Wedding Song," and "Early Morning Rain." (Two songs, "Ku-u-i-po" and "No More" were also taped but not used in

that broadcast.) The songs in the telecasts were: "Also Sprach Zarathustra," "Blue Suede Shoes," "See See Rider," "I'm So Lonesome I Could Cry," "Burning Love," "I Can't Stop Loving You," "Something," "Hound Dog," "You Gave Me A Mountain," "I'll Remember You," "Steamroller Blues," "Long Tall Sally," "What Now My Love," "Whole Lotta Shakin' Goin' On," "Fever," "American Trilogy," "Welcome To My World," "A Big Hunk O'Love," "Suspicious Minds," "Can't Help Falling In Love," "Blue Hawaii" (USA); "Love Me," "Hawaiian Wedding Song" (USA), "Johnny B. Goode," "Early Morning Rain" (USA), "It's Over."

Elvis Aron Presley

8-album set. RCA. LP (CPL8-3699, 1-8). Released August 16, 1980 to mark the 25th anniversary of Elvis on RCA Records. An early live performance: "Heartbreak Hotel," "Long Tall Sally," "Blue Suede

Shoes," "Money Honey" (all from 1956, Las Vegas); "An Elvis Monologue" (1962); An early benefit performance: "Heartbreak Hotel," "All Shook Up," "A Fool Such As I," "I Got A Woman," "Love Me," "Such A Night," "Reconsider Baby," "I Need Your Love Tonight," "That's All Right," "Don't Be Cruel," "One Night," "Are You Lonesome Tonight," "It's Now Or Never," "Swing Down Sweet Chariot," "Hound Dog" (all from Hawaii, 1961); Collector's gold from the movie years: "They Remind Me Too Much Of You," "Tonight Is So Right For Love," "Follow That Dream," "Wild In The Country," "Datin'," "Shoppin' Around," "Can't Help Falling In Love," "A Dog's Life," "I'm Falling In Love Tonight," "Thanks To The Rolling Sea" (all alternate takes); The TV Specials: "Jailhouse Rock" (1968), "Suspicious Minds" (1973), "Lawdy Miss Clawdy," "Baby What You Want Me To Do" (1968), "Blue Christmas" (1968).

"Lord You Gave Me A Mountain" (1973); "Welcome To My World" (1977); "I'll Remember You" (1973); "My Way"; The Las Vegas Years: "Polk Salad Annie," "You've Lost That Lovin' Feeling," "Sweet Caroline," "Kentucky Rain," "Are You Lonesome Tonight," "My Babe," "In The Ghetto," "American Trilogy," "Little Sister – Get Back," "Yesterday" (all unreleased versions); Lost singles: "I'm Leaving," "The First Time Ever I Saw Your Face," "Hi Heel Sneakers," "Softly As I Leave You," "Unchained Melody," "Fool," "Rags To Riches," "It's Only Love," "America (The Beautiful)"; Elvis at the piano: "It's Still Here" (longer version), "I'll Take You Home Again Kathleen," "Beyond The Reef," "I'll Still Be True"; The Concert Years: "2001: Space Odyssey," "See See Rider," "I Got A Woman – Amen," "Love Me," "If You Love Me Let Me Know," "Love Me Tender," "All Shook Up," "Teddy Bear – Don't Be Cruel," "Hound Dog," "The Wonder of You," "Burning Love," "Johnny Be Good," "Long Live Rock & Roll," "T-R-O-U-B-L-E," "Why Me Lord?," "How Great Thou Art," "Let Me Be There," "American Trilogy," "Funny How Time Slips Away," "Little Darlin'," "Mystery Train – Tiger Man," "Can't Help Falling In Love" (1975 concert).

Elvis As Recorded At Madison Square Garden
1972. RCA. LP (LSP-4776).
Side 1: "Introduction: Also Sprach Zarathustra"; "That's All Right"; "Proud Mary"; "Never Been To Spain"; "You Don't Have To Say You Love Me"; "You've Lost That Lovin' Feelin'"; "Polk Salad Annie"; "Love Me"; "All Shook Up"; "Heartbreak Hotel"; "Medley: Teddy Bear/Don't Be Cruel"; "Love Me Tender."
Side 2: "The Impossible Dream"; "Introductions By Elvis"; "Hound Dog"; "Suspicious Minds"; "For The Good Times"; "American Trilogy"; "Funny How Time Slips Away"; "I Can't Stop Loving You"; "Can't Help Falling In Love"; "Exit Music."

Elvis: A Way Of Life, Volume One
10″ LP Bootleg.
Side 1: "Party"; "Shake, Rattle And Roll" (Dorsey Show); "I Got A Woman" (Dorsey Show); "Girl Happy"; "Spring Fever"; "Happy Ending."
Side 2: "That's The Way It Is" (rehearsals).

Elvis Back In Memphis
1970. RCA. LP (LSP-4429).
Side 1: "Inherit The Wind"; "This Is My Story"; "Stranger In My Own Home Town"; "A Little Bit Of Green"; "And The Grass Won't Pay No Mind."
Side 2: "Do You Know Who I Am"; "From A Jack To A King"; "The Fair Is Moving On"; "You'll Think Of Me"; "Without Love."

Elvis By Request
1961. RCA Victor. EP (LPC-128).
Side 1: "Flaming Star"; "Summer Kisses, Winter Tears."
Side 2: "Are You Lonesome Tonight"; "It's Now Or Never."

Elvis' Christmas Album
1957. RCA Victor. LP (LOC-1035).
Side 1: "Santa Claus Is Back In Town"; "White Christmas"; "Here Comes Santa Claus"; "I'll Be Home For Christmas"; "Blue Christmas"; "Santa Bring My Baby Back."
Side 2: "Oh Little Town Of Bethlehem"; "Silent Night"; "Peace In The Valley"; "I Believe"; "Take My Hand, Precious Lord"; "It Is No Secret."

Elvis' Christmas Album
1970. RCA Camden. LP (CAL-2428).
Side 1: "Blue Christmas"; "Silent Night"; "White Christmas"; "Santa Claus Is Back In Town"; "I'll Be Home For Christmas."
Side 2: "If Every Day Was Like Christmas"; "Here Comes Santa Claus"; "Oh Little Town Of Bethlehem"; "Santa Bring My Baby Back"; "Mama Liked The Roses."

Elvis Commemorative Album
1978. RCA. LP (DPL 2-0056e).
Note: This double album set is a repackaging of Elvis (Brookfield Records). For complete details of the contents, see that listing.

Elvis Country ("I'm 10,000 Years Old")
RCA. 1971. LP (LSP-4460).
Side 1: "Snowbird"; "Tomorrow Never Comes"; "Little Cabin On The Hill"; "Whole Lotta Shakin' Goin' On"; "Funny How Time Slips Away"; "I Really Don't Want To Know."
Side 2: "There Goes My Everything"; "It's Your Baby, You Rock It"; "The Fool"; "Faded Love"; "I Washed My Hands In Muddy Water"; "Make The World Go Away."
Note: Excerpts from the title song "I Was Born About 10,000 Years Ago" are heard following each track on this LP. The song can be heard in its entirety on the LP Elvis Now.

Elvis' Country Memories
Bootleg.
Two-record album only available to RCA Record Club members. RCA R244069.
Side 1: "I'll Hold You In My Heart (Till I Can Hold You In My Arms)"; "Welcome To My World" (live); "It Keeps Right On A-Hurtin' "; "Release Me (And Let Me Love Again)"; "Make The World Go Away."
Side 2: "Snowbird"; "Early Mornin' Rain"; "I'm So Lonesome I Could Cry" (live); "Funny How Time Slips Away"; "I'm Movin' On."
Side 3: "Help Me Make It Through The Night"; "You Don't Know Me"; "How Great Thou Art"; "I Washed My Hands In Muddy Water"; "I Forgot To Remember To Forget."
Side 4: "Your Cheatin' Heart"; "Baby Let's Play House"; "Whole Lotta Shakin' Goin' On"; "Gentle On My Mind"; "For The Good Times" (live).

Elvis – Dorsey Shows
33⅓ LP Bootleg.
Side 1: "Blue Suede Shoes"; "Heartbreak Hotel"; "Tutti Frutti"; "I Was The One"; "Shake, Rattle And Roll"; "I Got A Woman."
Side 2: "Baby, Let's Play House"; "Tutti Frutti"; "Blue Suede Shoes"; "Heartbreak Hotel"; "Money Honey"; "Heartbreak Hotel."

Elvis Forever
1974. RCA. LP (KSL2-7031).
Side 1: "Treat Me Nice"; "I Need Your Love Tonight"; "That's When Your Heartaches Begin"; "G.I. Blues"; "Blue Hawaii"; "Easy Come, Easy Go."
Side 2: "Suspicion"; "Puppet On A String"; "Heartbreak Hotel"; "One Night"; "Memories"; "Blue Suede Shoes."
Side 3: "Are You Lonesome To-night"; "Hi Heel Sneakers"; "Old Shep"; "Rip It Up"; "Such A Night"; "A Fool Such As I."
Side 4: "Tutti Frutti"; "In The Ghetto"; "Wear My Ring Around Your Neck"; "Wooden Heart"; "Crying In The Chapel"; "Don't Cry Daddy."

Elvis For Everyone
1965. RCA Victor. LP (LPM/LSP-3450).
Side 1: "Your Cheatin' Heart"; "Summer Kisses, Winter Tears"; "Finders Keepers, Losers Weepers"; "In My Way"; "Tomorrow Night"; "Memphis Tennessee."
Side 2: "For The Millionth And The Last Time"; "Forget Me Never"; "Sound Advice"; "Santa Lucia"; "I Met Her Today"; "When It Rains It Really Pours."

Elvis' 40 Greatest Hits
Bestselling British LP, released on the Arcade Label.

Elvis' Gold Records Volume 2 (50,000,000 Elvis Fans Can't Be Wrong)
1959. RCA Victor. LP (LPM-2075).
Side 1: "I Need Your Love Tonight"; "Don't"; "Wear My Ring Around Your Neck"; "My Wish Came True"; "I Got Stung."
Side 2: "A Big Hunk O' Love"; "I Beg Of You"; "A Fool Such As I"; "Doncha' Think It's Time."

Elvis' Gold Records Volume 4
1968. RCA Victor. LP (LPM/LPS-3921).
Side 1: "Love Letters"; "Witchcraft"; "It Hurts Me"; "What'd I Say"; "Please Don't Drag That String Around"; "Indescribably Blue."
Side 2: "Devil In Disguise"; "Lonely Man"; "A Mess Of Blues"; "Ask Me"; "Ain't That Loving You Baby"; "Just Tell Her Jim Said Hello."

Elvis' Golden Records
1958. RCA Victor. LP (LPM-1707).
Side 1: "Hound Dog"; "Loving You"; "All Shook Up"; "Heartbreak Hotel"; "Jailhouse Rock"; "Love Me"; "Too Much."
Side 2: "Don't Be Cruel"; "That's When Your Heartaches Begin;" "Teddy Bear"; "Love Me Tender"; "Treat Me Nice"; "Anyway You Want Me"; "I Want You, I Need You, I Love You."

Elvis' Golden Records Volume 3
1963. RCA Victor. LP (LPM/LPS-2765).
Side 1: "It's Now Or Never"; "Stuck On You"; "Fame And Fortune"; "I Gotta Know"; "Surrender"; "I Feel So Bad."
Side 2: "Are You Lonesome Tonight"; "His Latest Flame"; "Little Sister"; "Good Luck Charm"; "Anything That's Part Of You"; "She's Not You."

"Elvis Has Left The Building"
J.D. Sumner's 1977 tribute recording on RCA Records.

"Elvis In Concert"
CBS-TV Special that aired on October 3, 1977 – Elvis' last. It included performances from his final concert tour: Omaha, Nebraska, on June 19, 1977; Rapid City, South Dakota on June 21, 1977.

Elvis In Concert
1977. RCA. LP (APL2-2587).
Side 1: "Elvis' Fans' Comments/ Opening Riff"; "Also Sprach Zarathustra (theme from 2001: A Space Odyssey/Opening Riff (reprise)"; "See See Rider"; "That's All Right"; "Are You Lonesome Tonight"; "Medley";

"Teddy Bear/Don't Be Cruel"; "Elvis' Fans' Comments"; "You Gave Me A Mountain"; "Jailhouse Rock."
Side 2: "Elvis' Fans' Comments"; "How Great Thou Art"; "Elvis' Fans' Comments"; "I Really Don't Want To Know"; "Elvis Introduces His Father"; "Closing Riff"; "Special Message From Elvis' Father, Vernon Presley."
Side 3: Medley: "I Got A Woman/Amen"; "Elvis Talks"; "Love Me"; "If You Love Me (Let Me Know)"; Medley: "O Sole Mio—Sherrill Nielsen Solo/It's Now Or Never"; "Trying To Get To You."
Side 4: "Hawaiian Wedding Song"; "Fairytale"; "Little Sister"; "Early Morning Rain"; "What I'd Say"; "Johnny B. Goode"; "And I Love You So."

Elvis In Hollywood
1976. RCA. LP (DPL2-0168).
Side 1: "Jailhouse Rock"; "Rock-A-Hula Baby"; "G.I. Blues"; "Kissin' Cousins"; "Wild In The Country."
Side 2: "King Creole"; "Blue Hawaii"; "Fun In Acapulco"; "Follow That Dream"; "Girls! Girls! Girls!"
Side 3: "Viva Las Vegas"; "Bossa Nova Baby"; "Flaming Star"; "Girl Happy"; "Frankie And Johnny."
Side 4: "Roustabout"; "Spinout"; "Double Trouble"; "Charro"; "They Remind Me Too Much of You."

Elvis In Person At The International Hotel
1970. RCA. LP (LPS-4428).
Side 1: "Blue Suede Shoes"; "Johnny B. Goode"; "All Shook Up"; "Are You Lonesome Tonight"; "Hound Dog"; "I Can't Stop Loving You"; "My Babe."
Side 2: Medley: "Mystery Train/Tiger Man"; "Words"; "In The Ghetto"; "Suspicious Minds"; "Can't Help Falling In Love."

Elvis Is Back
1960. RCA Victor. LP (LPM/LPS-2231).
Side 1: "Make Me Know It"; "Fever"; "The Girl Of My Best Friend"; "I Will Be Home Again"; "Dirty, Dirty Feeling"; "Thrill Of Your Love."
Side 2: "Soldier Boy"; "Such A Night"; "It Feels So Right"; "The Girl Next Door"; "Like A Baby"; "Reconsider, Baby."

Elvis King Of Las Vegas Live
33⅓ LP Bootleg.
Sides 1 and 2: *That's The Way It Is* soundtrack.

Elvis Live On Stage, Hilton Hotel, 1972
33⅓ LP Bootleg.
Side 1: "Theme, *2001*"; "See See

Rider"; "You Don't Have To Say You Love Me"; "Polk Salad Annie"; "You've Lost That Loving Feeling."
Side 2: "What Now, My Love"; "Fever"; "Introductions/Love Me"; "Blue Suede Shoes"; "All Shook Up"; "Heartbreak Hotel"; "I'll Remember You."

Elvis Lives
Short-lived Broadway show of 1978, starring Larry Seth.

Elvis Memories
1978. ABC Radio. LP (ASP-1003).
Side 1: "Memories"; "Elvis Memories (Jingle/Logo)"; "That's All Right"; "Good Rockin' Tonight"; "Mystery Train"; "I Want You, I Need You, I Love You"; "Heartbreak Hotel."
Side 2: "Burning Love"; "Rip It Up"; "Follow That Dream"; "Loving You"; "Love Me Tender"; "Hound Dog"; "Don't Be Cruel"; "Way Down"; "Moody Blue"; "Devil In Disguise"; "Suspicion."
Side 3: "Elvis Memories (Jingle/Logo)"; "His Latest Flame"; "All Shook Up"; "Teddy Bear"; "Jailhouse Rock"; "It's Now Or Never"; "Elvis Memories (Jingle/Logo)"; "I Got Stung"; "One Night"; "Wear My Ring Around Your Neck"; "Stuck On You."
Side 4: "Elvis Memories (Jingle/Logo)"; "My Wish Came True"; "Good Luck Charm"; "The Grass Won't Pay No Mind"; "Fame And Fortune"; "Kentucky Rain"; "In The Ghetto."
Side 5: "Viva Las Vegas"; "Don't Cry Daddy"; "Separate Ways"; "You Don't Have To Say You Love Me"; "Elvis Memories (Jingle/Logo)"; "Blue Christmas"; "Are You Lonesome Tonight"; "Can't Help Falling In Love."
Side 6: "Elvis Memories (Jingle/Logo)"; "My Way"; "How Great Thou Art"; "Crying In The Chapel"; "If I Can Dream"; "The Wonder Of You"; "Memories."

Elvis' Midget Fan Club
One of Col. Parker's more celebrated publicity stunts of 1957, when he hired a troupe of midgets to parade in Hollywood.

The Elvis Monthly
British fan magazine founded by the late Albert Hand in 1959 and distributed by the Elvis Presley Fan Club, worldwide.

Elvis Now
1972. RCA. LP (LSP-4671).
Side 1: "Help Me Make It Through The Night"; "Miracle Of The Rosary"; "Hey Jude"; "Put Your Hand In The Hand"; "Until It's Time For You To Go."
Side 2: "We Can Make The Morning"; "Early Morning Rain";

"Sylvia"; "Fools Rush In"; "I Was Born About Ten Thousand Years Ago."

Elvisology
The study of the life, times, music and phenomenon of Elvis Presley.

Elvis On Stage In The U.S.A.
33⅓ LP Bootleg
Sides 1 and 2: The same as *The Monologue* LP minus the monologue.

Elvis On Tour
Started March, 1972
A Metro Goldwyn Mayer Presentation
Produced by Pierre Adidge
Directed by Robert Abel
Associate Producer: Sidney Levin
Metrocolor
Musicians
Lead Guitar: James Burton; Guitar and Vocal: Charlie Hodge; Drums: Ronnie Tutt; Piano: Glen Hardin; Bass: Jerry Scheff; Rhythm Guitar: John Wilkinson; Orchestra Conducted by Joe Guercio.
Backup Vocalists: The Sweet Inspirations, J.D. Sumner and the Stamps Quartet, Kathy Westmoreland.
Elvis' Assistants: Vernon Presley, Joe Esposito, Jerry Schilling, Sonny West, Red West, James Caughley, Lamar Fike, Marvin Gamble.
Running Time: 93 minutes.
Previously titled: *Standing Room Only*.
Songs
On Stage – April 1972
"Johnny B. Goode"; "See See Rider"; "Polk Salad Annie"; "Proud Mary"; "Never Been To Spain"; "Burning Love"; "Don't Be Cruel" (TV Film); "Reddy Teddy" (TV Film); "Love Me Tender"; "Bridge Over Troubled Water"; "Funny How Time Slips Away"; "An American Trilogy"; "I Got A Woman"; "Big Hunk Of Love"; "You Gave Me A Mountain"; "Sweet Sweet Spirit"; "Lawdy Miss Clawdy"; "Can't Help Fallin' In Love."
Off Stage
"Separate Ways"; "For The Good Times"; "The Lighthouse"; "Lead Me, Guide Me"; "Bosom Of Abraham"; "I John."

Elvis On Tour went further behind the screens than did *That's The Way It Is*, and Elvis was more involved in the film. He gave a long tape interview in September, 1972 to producers Pierre Adidge and Bob Abel and parts of the tape were used in the film, for instance, at the start, where Elvis spoke about his father's scepticism of Elvis' becoming a guitar player, and

where he also talks about his early movements onstage and his Gospel singing.
The film began very excitingly with Elvis singing "Johnny B. Goode" over the credits, and this opening sequence is the best in any Elvis film, using the multiple image effect. Elvis is filmed arriving at the auditoriums, waiting nervously backstage (surrounded by aides and his father), and then appearing onstage to rapturous welcomes. The multiple-image effect is used throughout the film, to great effect, though mesmerizing in such songs as "Polk Salad Annie," with its stunning karate ending. Part of several concerts are shown, interspersed with rare footage of the first *Ed Sullivan Show*, Army induction, Elvis in his gold suit, and other clips and stills. The audience can never anticipate what's coming next; the film reflected a real Elvis concert – unpredictable and exciting.
Two of the best segments showed Elvis in the L.A. studios recording "Separate Ways," and then driving to his jet plane with J.D. Sumner and the Stamps and Charlie Hodge. Elvis is seen being driven to and from concerts, running the gauntlet of fans as he exits and enters hotels and concert halls. He's seen rehearsing, teasing fans, an giving some outstanding performances of songs like "Bridge Over Troubled Water," "American Trilogy," "Lord You Gave Me A Mountain," "Lawdy Miss Clawdy," and so on. Two very telling scenes are when he's riding in a car. A faraway look comes on his face as he smiles at some remembrance, and when the cameras stayed on his face while listening to the Stamps do "Sweet Sweet Spirit."
In between shots of Elvis singing and kissing his fans in "Love Me Tender," many "kissing" scenes from previous MGM movies were edited in, and this made for a very entertaining segment. There were scenes of preparations for concerts by the stage crew, and of fans arriving excitedly at concerts and waiting for Elvis to arrive onstage. The inevitable fan interviews were included, but they fitted in more smoothly than in *TTWII*. A travelogue of where the tour had taken Elvis to (in April, 1972) was shown while the original *Mystery Train* record was played. Graceland was shown in all its beauty; the music gates swing enticingly open and Vernon Presley rode a horse with the house in the background. There was a tantalizing glimpse

Elvis on tour.

of the Trophy room and a few of the Gold Discs, as Vernon told about the wild fans. Shots of Elvis Presley Boulevard segue into a great clip of the June '72 press conference. A highlight sequence showed Elvis on his plane with the mayor of Roanoke, and then meeting fans at the airport.

Elvis was seen in several jumpsuits of deep red, white, and light and dark blue. The outfits were studded and spangled, and had matching capes. He looked a little heavier than in *TTWII*, but with just as magnetic a personality.

A lot of action is packed into the film, along with nostalgia and good music. Like the Elvis shows themselves, it had to finish; and the end of the film shows Elvis running offstage after "Can't Help Falling In Love" and into a waiting limousine, which carries him swiftly and safely away from the seething thousands beyond the footlights. As the closing credits roll, "Memories" is the perfect background music to the travelling and backstage scenes being shown. As the film fades, there's a reprise of the shot of Elvis in the car, smiling at some distant memory.

On Tour is a marvellous film, capturing Elvis doing what he did best; singing for his fans. Like *TTWII*, it will always be a cherished, favorite movie and a fitting memorial to the King.

Elvis Presley
1956. RCA Victor. EP (EPA-747).

Side 1: "Blue Suede Shoes"; "Tutti Frutti."
Side 2: "I Got A Woman"; "Just Because."

Elvis Presley
1956. RCA Victor. EP (EPA-830).
Side 1: "Shake, Rattle And Roll"; "I Love You Because."
Side 2: "Blue Moon"; "Lawdy, Miss Clawdy."

Elvis Presley
1956. RCA Victor. EP (EPB-1254).
Side 1: "Blue Suede Shoes"; "I'm Counting On You."
Side 2: "I Got A Woman"; "One-Sided Love Affair."
Side 3: "Tutti Frutti"; "Tryin' To Get To You."
Side 4: "I'm Gonna Sit Right Down And Cry"; "I'll Never Let You Go."

Elvis Presley
1956. RCA Victor. LP (LPM-1254).
Side 1: "Blue Suede Shoes"; "I'm Counting On You"; "I Got A Woman"; "One-Sided Love Affair"; "I Love You Because"; "Just Because."
Side 2: "Tutti Frutti"; "Tryin' To Get To You"; "I'm Gonna Sit Right Down And Cry"; "I'll Never Let You Go"; "Blue Moon"; "Money Honey."

Elvis Presley
1956. RCA Victor. EP (SPD-22).
Side 1: "Blue Suede Shoes"; "I'm Counting On You."
Side 2: "I Got A Woman"; "One-Sided Love Affair."
Side 3: "Tutti Frutti"; "Tryin' To Get To You."
Side 4: "I'm Gonna Sit Right Down And Cry"; "I'll Never Let You Go."

Elvis Presley
1956. RCA Victor. EP (SPD-23).
Side 1: "Blue Suede Shoes"; "I'm Counting On You."
Side 2: "I Got A Woman"; "One-Sided Love Affair."
Side 3: "I'm Gonna Sit Right Down And Cry"; "I'll Never Let You Go."
Side 4: "Tutti Frutti"; "Tryin' To Get To You."
Side 5: "Don't Be Cruel"; "I Want You, I Need You, I Love You."
Side 6: "Hound Dog"; "My Baby Left Me."

Elvis Presley
45 EPA Bootleg
"I Don't Care If The Sun Don't Shine"; "I'll Never Let You Go"; "My Baby Is Gone"; "Blue Moon Of Kentucky."

Elvis Presley Boulevard
Ten-mile stretch of US Highway 51 South that passes Graceland, named in honor of Memphis' favorite son in 1971.

Elvis Presley Center Courts, Inc.
The aborted racketball franchise entered into by Elvis, with Joe Esposito, Dr. Nick and Mike McMahon before Elvis died—disbanded when Elvis pulled out of the deal.

Elvis Presley Chapel
The chapel built on Elvis Presley Park, dedicated on August 17, 1979.

"Elvis Presley Day"
Elvis has been honored by statewide decrees of official recognition. The first was September 26, 1956, in Mississippi, on the occasion of Elvis' return to Tupelo and his appearance at the Mississippi-Alabama Fair (he donated $10,000 to the city). The second day was September 29, 1967, in Tennessee (proclaimed by Gov. Buford Ellington). Portland, Oregon honored him on November 11, 1970; and on January 8, 1974, he was honored in Georgia by then Governor Jimmy Carter.

Elvis Presley Drive
The street in Tupelo, Mississippi, where Elvis was born.

Elvis Presley Enterprises
The company originally formed by Bob Neal with Elvis when Neal managed Elvis in 1954. Later, it became the name of the company used to market Elvis products with Special Products, Inc. Finally, it was the name

Elvis gave to his football team in the early 1960's, which played in Memphis and Hollywood.

Elvis Presley Foundation For Under-Privileged Children
In 1956, plans were laid for a Youth Center and Park to be built around the area of Elvis' birthplace in Tupelo. Elvis himself wanted the young people of Tupelo to benefit from a better environment than he himself had. Fans were able to send in donations, and Elvis did a show in Tupelo in September, 1956, and donated his fee to the project. He continued to take an interest in the Project, and asked that part of his 1961 Memphis Charity Concert proceeds be given to the Youth Center. A club house was built, as were a swimming pool (rectangular shaped, not guitar shaped as originally planned), a play area, and a baseball field (now called Presley Field). Elvis visited Tupelo from time to time to check on the project, and was reported to be not entirely pleased with the little that had been done with all the money

Elvis Presley Is Alive And Well And Singing In Las Vegas
33⅓ LP Bootleg.
Side 1: "Big Boss Man"; "If You Love Me Let Me Know"; "Until It's Time For You To Go"; "If You Talk In Your Sleep"; "Hawaiian Wedding Song"; "Early Morning Rain"; "Softly As I Leave You"; "Amen"; "How Great Thou Art."
Side 2: "T-R-O-U-B-L-E"; "And I Love You So"; "Green Green Grass Of Home"; "Fairytale"; "Happy Birthday"; "James Burton"; "Glenn D. Hardin Solo"; "Young And Beautiful"; "It's Now Or Never"; "Burning Love."

Elvis Presley Music, Inc.
A subsidiary of Hill and Range and a BMI affiliate—used to market Elvis' music.

Elvis Presley National Fan Club
The first, founded in 1957, with 250,000 members. Within two years, it would grow to millions across the globe.

Elvis Presley Park
Park created by the City of Tupelo around Elvis' birthplace in 1979. It included a chapel and a community swimming pool.

The Elvis Presley Story
Twelve hour radio documentary written by Jerry Hopkins, produced by Ron Jacobs and broadcast in 1971.

Elvis Presley Story, The
1975. Watermark. LP (EPS 1A-13B). By Watermark Inc.
Side 1: "Introduction: Medley Of Elvis Hits"; "Old Shep"; "Jesus Knows What I Need" (comparison of versions by the Statesmen Quartet and by Elvis).
Side 2: "That's All Right" (Arthur Crudup); "Hound Dog" (Willie Mae Thorton); "Early FIfties Medley: Harbor Lights (Sammy Kaye)/Rag Mop (Ames Bros.)/Tennessee Waltz (Patti Page)/Cry Of The Wild Goose (Frankie Lane)/You Belong To Me (Jo Stafford)/My Heart Cries For You (Guy Mitchell)/Come-On-A-My House (Rosemary Clooney)/Cry (Johnnie Ray)"; "Working On The Building" (comparisons of Elvis' and the Blackwood Bros. versions).
Side 3: "That's All Right"; "Blue Moon Of Kentucky"; "Good Rockin' Tonight"; "You're A Heartbreaker"; "Just Because."
Side 4: "Milkcow Blues Boogie"; "The Truth About Me"; "Baby Let's Play House"; "I'm Left, You're Right, She's Gone"; "Blue Moon"; "I Forgot To Remember To Forget"; "Mystery Train."
Side 5: "Heartbreak Hotel"; "I Was The One"; "Heartbreak Hotel" (Stan Freberg); "Medley: Reddy Teddy/Blueberry Hill/Money Honey/Rip It Up/I Got A Woman/Lawdy Miss Clawdy/Long Tall Sally/Shake, Rattle And Roll/Tutti Frutti"; "Blue Suede Shoes"; "I Want You, I Need You, I Love You."
Side 6: "Hound Dog"; "Don't Be Cruel"; "Love Me"; "Love Me Tender"; "One-Sided Love Affair"; "Too Much."
Side 7: "All Shook Up"; "Loving You"; "Teddy Bear"; "Got A Lot Of Living To Do"; "Peace In The Valley."
Side 8: "Medley Of Songs About Elvis"; "Party"; "Jailhouse Rock"; "Baby I Don't Care"; "Oh Little Town Of Bethlehem"; "Blue Christmas"; "Don't."
Side 9: "King Creole"; "Dear 53310761" (Thirteens); "Won't You Wear My Ring Around Your Neck"; "Hard Headed Woman"; "If We Never Meet Again"; "Elvis Sails Interview."
Side 10: "Trouble"; "I Got Stung"; "A Fool Such As I"; "My Wish Came True"; "A Big Hunk O' Love"; "I Will Be Home Again."
Side 11: "I'm Hanging Up My Rifle" (Bill [Bobby Bare] Parsons); "Dirty, Dirty Feeling"; "Stuck On You"; "It's Now Or Never"; "Fever"; "G.I. Blues."
Side 12: "Wooden Heart"; "Flaming Star"; "Are You Lonesome Tonight"; "I Slipped, I Stumbled, I Fell"; "His Hand In Mine"; "Surrender"; "I'm Coming Home."
Side 13: "Medley Of Elvis' Film Songs"; "Blue Hawaii"; "I Feel So Bad"; "Can't Help Falling In Love"; "Good Luck Charm"; "Return To Sender."
Side 14: "One Broken Heart For Sale"; "Medley: Elvis' Film Songs"; "Bossa Nova Baby"; "Happy Ending"; "Memphis, Tennessee"; "Fun In Acapulco."
Side 15: "Devil In Disguise"; "Santa Lucia"; "What'd I Say"; "Crying In The Chapel"; "Ain't That Loving You Baby"; "Your Cheatin' Heart."
Side 16: "Little Egypt"; "Medley Of Silly Elvis Film Songs"; "Down By The Riverside/When The Saints Go Marching In"; "Puppet On A String"; "Do The Clam"; "When It Rains It Really Pours."
Side 17: "Old MacDonald"; "Long Lonely Highway"; "Down In The Alley"; "Tomorrow Is A Long Time"; "Paradise Hawaiian Style."
Side 18: "If Everyday Was Like Christmas"; "There Ain't Nothing Like A Song"; "He's Your Uncle, Not Your Dad"; "Big Boss Man"; "How Great Thou Art."
Side 19: "Guitar Man"; "U.S. Male"; "A Little Less Conversation"; "Memories"; "Yellow Rose Of Texas/The Eyes Of Texas"; "If I Can Dream."
Side 20: "Songs From The NBC-TV *Special*"; "Only The Strong Survive"; "Gentle On My Mind"; "In The Ghetto."
Side 21: "Songs from *Elvis Live At The International Hotel, Las Vegas, Nevada* LP"; "Don't Cry Daddy"; "Kentucky Rain."
Side 22: "Songs From *On Stage* LP"; "You've Lost That Lovin' Feeling"; "The Wonder Of You"; "The Next Step Is Love."
Side 23: "Patch It Up"; "Bridge Over Troubled Water"; "Rags To Riches"; "There Goes My Everything"; "Whole Lotta Shakin' Goin' On"; "I'm Leavin'."
Side 24: "Help Me Make It Through The Night"; "American Trilogy"; "Don't Think Twice"; "Also Sprach Zarathustra/See See Rider"; "Hound Dog"; "Burning Love"; "It's A Matter Of Time."
Side 25: "Separate Ways"; "My Way"; "I'm So Lonesome I Could Cry"; "Raised On Rock"; "Talk About The Good Times"; "Steamroller Blues."
Side 26: "Medley Of Elvis Hits"; "I've Got A Thing About You Baby"; "Help Me"; "Promised Land."

Elvis Presley Story, The
1977. Watermark. LP (EPS 1A-13B). By Watermark Inc.
Note: Only the beginning and ending of this show was changed to reflect Elvis' death. The remainder of the program is unchanged in this reissue.

Side 1: "Introduction: Medley Of Elvis' Hits"; "Old Shep"; "Jesus Knows What I Need" (comparison of versions by the Statesmen Quartet and by Elvis).
Side 2: "That's All Right" (Arthur Crudup); "Hound Dog" (Willie Mae Thornton); "Early Fifties Medley: Harbor Lights (Sammy Kaye)/Rag Mop (Ames Bros.)/Tennessee Waltz (Patti Page)/Cry Of The Wild Goose (Frankie Lane)/You Belong To Me (Jo Stafford)/My Heart Cries For You (Guy Mitchell)/Come-On-A-My House (Rosemary Clooney)/Cry (Johnnie Ray)"; "Working On The Building" (comparisons of Elvis' and the Blackwood Bros.' versions).
Side 3: "That's All Right"; "Blue Moon Of Kentucky"; "Good Rockin' Tonight"; "You're A Heartbreaker"; "Just Because."
Side 4: "Milkcow Blues Boogie"; "The Truth About Me"; "Baby Let's Play House"; "I'm Left, You're Right, She's Gone"; "Blue Moon"; "I Forgot To Remember To Forget"; "Mystery Train."
Side 5: "Heartbreak Hotel"; "I Was The One"; "Heartbreak Hotel" (Stan Freberg); "Medley: Reddy Teddy/Blueberry Hill/Money Honey/Rip It Up/I Got A Woman/Lawdy Miss Clawdy/Long Tall Sally/Shake, Rattle And Roll/Tutti Frutti"; "Blue Suede Shoes"; "I Want You, I Need You, I Love You."
Side 6: "Hound Dog"; "Don't Be Cruel"; "Love Me"; "Love Me Tender"; "One-Sided Love Affair"; "Too Much."
Side 7: "All Shook Up"; "Loving You"; "Teddy Bear"; "Got A Lot Of Living To Do"; "Peace In The Valley."
Side 8: "Medley Of Songs About Elvis"; "Party"; "Jailhouse Rock"; "Baby I Don't Care"; "Oh Little Town Of Bethlehem"; "Blue Christmas"; "Don't."
Side 9: "King Creole"; "Dear 53310761" (Thirteen); "Won't You Wear My Ring Around Your Neck"; "Hard Headed Woman"; "If We Never Meet Again"; "Elvis Sails Interview."
Side 10: "Trouble"; "I Got Stung"; "A Fool Such As I"; "My Wish Came True"; " Big Hunk O' Love"; "I Will Be Home Again."
Side 11: "I'm Hanging' Up My Rifle" (Bill [Bobby Bare] Parsons); "Dirty, Dirty Feeling"; "Stuck On You"; "It's Now Or Never"; "Fever"; "G.I. Blues."
Side 12: "Wooden Heart"; "Flaming Star"; "Are You Lonesome Tonight"; "I Slipped, I Stumbled, I Fell"; "His Hand In Mine"; "Surrender"; "I'm Coming Home."
Side 13: "Medley Of Elvis' Film Songs"; "Blue Hawaii"; "I Feel So Bad"; "Can't Help Falling In Love"; "Good Luck Charm"; "Return To Sender."
Side 14: "One Broken Heart For Sale"; "Medley: Elvis' Film Songs"; "Bossa Nova Baby"; "Happy Ending"; "Memphis, Tennessee"; "Fun In Acapulco."
Side 15: "Devil In Disguise"; "Santa Lucia"; "What'd I Say"; "Crying In The Chapel"; "Ain't That Loving You Baby"; "Your Cheatin' Heart."
Side 16: "Little Egypt"; "Medley of Silly Elvis Film Songs"; "Down By The Riverside/When The Saints Go Marching In"; "Puppet On A String"; "Do The Clam"; "When It Rains It Really Pours."
Side 17: "Old MacDonald"; "Long Lonely Highway"; "Down In The Alley"; "Tomorrow Is A Long Time."
Side 18: "If Everyday Was Like Christmas"; "There Ain't Nothing Like A Song"; "He's Your Uncle, Not Your Dad"; "Big Boss Man"; "How Great Thou Art."
Side 19: "Guitar Man"; "U.S. Male"; "A Little Less Conversation"; "Memories"; "Yellow Rose Of Texas/The Eyes Of Texas"; "If I Can Dream."
Side 20: "Songs From the NBC-TV *Special*"; "Only The Strong Survive"; "Gentle On My Mind"; "In The Ghetto."
Side 21: "Songs From *Elvis Live At The International Hotel, Las Vegas, Nevada* LP"; "Don't Cry Daddy"; "Kentucky Rain."
Side 22: "Songs From *On Stage* LP"; "You've Lost That Lovin' Feeling"; "The Wonder Of You"; "The Next Step Is Love."
Side 23: "Patch It Up"; "Bridge Over Troubled Water"; "Rags To Riches"; "There Goes My Everything"; "Whole Lotta Shakin' Goin' On"; "I'm Leavin'."
Side 24: "Help Me Make It Through The Night"; "American Trilogy"; "Don't Think Twice"; "Also Sprach Zarathustra/See See Rider"; "Hound Dog"; "Burning Love"; "It's A Matter Of Time."
Side 25: "Separate Ways"; "My Way"; "I'm So Lonesome I Could Cry"; "Raised On Rock"; "Talk About The Good Times"; "Steamroller Blues."
Side 26: "Medley Of Elvis' Hits"; "I've Got A Thing About You Baby"; "Medley of Elvis' Hits through 1977."

Elvis Presley Story, The
1977. RCA. LP (DML5-0263). By Candlelite Music Inc.
Side 1: "It's Now Or Never"; "Treat Me Nice"; "For The Good Times"; "I Got Stung"; "Ask Me"; "Return To Sender."
Side 2: "The Wonder Of You"; "Hound Dog"; "Make The World Go Away"; "His Latest Flame"; "Loving You."

Side 3: "One Night"; "You Don't Know Me"; "Blue Christmas"; "Good Luck Charm"; "Blue Suede Shoes"; "Surrender."
Side 4: "In The Ghetto"; "Too Much"; "Help Me Make It Through The Night"; "I Was The One"; "Love Me"; "Little Sister."
Side 5: "Can't Help Falling In Love"; "Trouble"; "Memories"; "Wear My Ring Around Your Neck"; "Blue Hawaii"; "Burning Love."
Side 6: "Love Me Tender"; "Stuck On You"; "Funny How Time Slips Away"; "All Shook Up"; "Puppet On A String"; "Jailhouse Rock."
Side 7: "Heartbreak Hotel"; "I Just Can't Help Believin'"; "I Beg Of You"; "Don't Cry Daddy"; "Hard Headed Woman"; "Are You Lonesome Tonight."
Side 8: "Teddy Bear"; "Hawaiian Wedding Song"; "A Big Hunk Of Love"; "I'm Yours"; "A Fool Such As I"; "Don't."
Side 9: "I Want You, I Need You, I Love You"; "Kissin' Cousins"; "I Can't Stop Loving You"; "Devil In Disguise"; "Suspicion"; "Don't Be Cruel."
Side 10: "She's Not You"; "From A Jack To A King"; "I Need Your Love Tonight"; "Wooden Heart"; "Have I Told You Lately That I Love You"; "You Don't Have To Say You Love Me."

Elvis Presley: The Best Years
33⅓ LP Bootleg.
Same LP as *I Wanna Be A Rock 'n' Roll Star.*

Elvis Presley Youth Center
The complex in Tupelo, Mississippi that developed from the benefit money donated by Elvis from his 1957 return to Tupelo, which eventually grew into a shrine and national landmark.

Elvis Presley Youth Foundation
Charity created by Elvis in 1958 for underprivileged children in Memphis. He was its largest contributor.

Elvis Recorded Live On Stage In Memphis
1974. RCA. LP (CPL1-0606).
Side 1: "See See Rider"; "I Got A Woman"; "Love Me"; "Tryin' To Get To You"; "Medley: Long Tall Sally/Whole Lotta Shakin' Goin' On/Your Mama Don't Dance/Flip, Flop And Fly"; "Jailhouse Rock/Hound Dog"; "Why Me"; "How Great Thou Art."
Side 2: "Medley: Blueberry Hill/I Can't Stop Loving You"; "Help Me"; "American Trilogy"; "Let Me Be There"; "My Baby Left Me"; "Lawdy Miss Clawdy"; "Can't Help Falling In Love"; "Closing Vamp."

Elvis Remembered
1979. Creative Radio. LP (CRS

1A-3B).
Side 1: "Heartbreak Hotel"; "Medley: Your Cheating Heart/When The Saints Go Marching In/Won't You Wear My Ring Around Your Neck"; "Medley: Hound Dog/King Creole/Don't Be Cruel/Teddy Bear/Blue Suede Shoes/ Reconsider, Baby/Hard Headed Woman/Loving You"; "All Shook Up"; "That's All Right"; "I Really Don't Want To Know"; "Hound Dog"; "Make The World Go Away."
Side 2: "Jailhouse Rock"; "I Forgot To Remember To Forget"; "Money Honey"; "Are You Sincere"; "You Gave Me A Mountain"; "Such A Night"; "Fame And Fortune."
Side 3: "Medley: I Got Stung/A Big Hunk O' Love/One Broken Heart For Sale/Return To Sender/Surrender/Down By The Riverside"; "Treat Me Nice"; "I Can't Stop Loving You"; "I Got

A Woman/Amen" (unreleased version); "I Want You, I Need You, I Love You."
Side 4: "In The Ghetto"; "It's Now Or Never"; "I Beg Of You"; "She Wears My Ring"; "Wear My Ring Around Your Neck"; "Where Did They Go Lord."
Side 5: "Love Me Tender"; "I Can Help"; "A Fool Such As I"; "Crying In The Chapel"; "If I Can Dream"; "Suspicious Minds."
Side 6: "See See Rider" (unreleased version); "Hurt" (unreleased version); "There Goes My Everything"; "Green, Green Grass Of Home"; "There's A Honky-Tonk Angel (Who'll Take Me Back In)"; "Memories."

Elvis Rock'n Blues
33⅓ LP Bootleg.
Side 1: "A Mess Of Blues"; "When It Rains, It Really Pours"; "Shake A Hand"; "Reconsider, Baby"; "Stranger In My

Own Hometown."
Side 2: "High-Heel Sneakers"; "Wearing That Loved-One Look"; "Promised Land"; "T-R-O-U-B-L-E"; "Burning Love"; "Big Hunk O' Love."

Elvis Sails
1958. RCA Victor. EP (EPA-4325).
Side 1: "Press Interviews With Elvis Presley."
Side 2: "Elvis Presley's Newsreel Interview"; "Pat Hernon Interviews Elvis In The Library Of The U.S.S. Randall At Sailing."

Elvis Sings Christmas Songs
1957. RCA Victor. EP (EPA-4108).
Side 1: "Santa Bring My Baby Back"; "Blue Christmas."
Side 2: "Santa Claus Is Back In Town"; "I'll Be Home For Christmas."

Elvis Sings Flaming Star
1969. RCA Camden. LP (CAS-2304).
Side 1: "Flaming Star"; "Wonderful World"; "Night Life"; "All I Needed Was The Rain"; "Too Much Monkey Business."
Side 2: "Yellow Rose Of Texas/The Eyes Of Texas"; "She's A Machine"; "Do The Vega"; "Tiger Man."

Elvis Sings For Children And Grownups Too!
1978. RCA Victor. LP (CPL1-2901).
Side 1: "Teddy Bear"; "Wooden Heart"; "Five Sleepyheads"; "Puppet On A String"; "Angel"; "Old Macdonald."
Side 2: "How Would You Like To Be"; "Cotton Candy Land"; "Old Shep"; "Big Boots"; "Have A Happy."

Elvis Sings From His Movies Volume 1
1972. RCA (RCA Camden). LP (CAS-2304).
Side 1: "Down By The Riverside/When The Saints Go Marching In"; "They Remind Me Too Much Of You"; "Confidence"; "Frankie And Johnnie"; "Guitar Man."
Side 2: "Long Legged Girl"; "You Don't Know Me"; "How Would You Like To Be"; "Big Boss Man"; "Old Macdonald."

Elvis Sings The Wonderful World Of Christmas
1971. RCA. LP (LSP-4579).
Side 1: "O Come, All Ye Faithful"; "The First Noel"; "On A Snowy Christmas Night"; "Winter Wonderland"; "The Wonderful World Of Christmas"; "It Won't Seem Like Christmas (Without You)."
Side 2: "I'll Be Home On Christmas Day"; "If I Get Home

On Christmas Day"; "Holly Leaves And Christmas Trees"; "Merry Christmas Baby"; "Silver Bells."

Elvis Special, Volume 1

10″ 33⅓ LP Bootleg.
Side 1: "Ed Sullivan Introducing Elvis"; "Peace In The Valley"; "Ed Sullivan Says Farewell To Elvis"; "Army Interview."
Side 2: "Earthboy"; " 'Aloha' Press Conference"; "Johnny B. Goode"; "Happy Birthday."

Elvis Special, Volume 2

33⅓ LP Bootleg.
Side 1: "Peace In The Valley" (live); "Uncle Tom's Cabin Interview"; "Little Darlin' "; "Uncle Penn."
Side 2: "Separate Ways" (alternate take); "Burning Love"; "Ready Teddy"; "Twelfth Of Never."

"Elvis' Summer Festival"

The annual Las Vegas Elvis extravaganza, held in August at the International and then the Hilton, which would be decorated with banners and souvenirs for the fans gathering from all over the world.

Elvis Talks Back

33⅓ LP Bootleg.
Side 1: "Interview, 1957."
Side 2: "Herman's Hermits Interview Elvis"; "Colonel Parker Interview, 1965"; " 'Charro!' Interview."

Elvis Today

1975. RCA. LP (APL1-1039).
Side 1: "T-R-O-U-B-L-E"; "And I Love You So"; "Susan When She Tried"; "Woman Without Love"; "Shake A Hand."
Side 2: "Pieces Of My Life"; "Fairytale"; "I Can Help"; "Bringing It Back"; "Green Grass Of Home."

Elvis' Unique Record Club

Club founded by Paul Lichter, author of *Elvis In Hollywood* and *The Boy Who Dared To Rock*, which specializes in buying and trading rare Elvis records and memorabilia.

Elvis: What Happened?

"The bodyguard book" by Red West, Jimmy West and David Hebler, as told to Steve Dunleavy (Ballantine, 1977) written the final year of Elvis' life, and published only fifteen days before his death. The book provides the first "inside" look at Elvis' life and exposed his "Dark" side, revealing his drug use, and many of his most selfish, insensitive moments, which shocked fans throughout the world. Four years later, because of its controversy, sensationalized (exploitative) tone, and its detrimental effect of Elvis and his public image, it

remains a source of bitterness among Elvis' family, friends, associates and fans.

Bobby Emmons

A sessionman on many Elvis records (organ–keyboards), formerly with Bill Black's combo.

Leif Erickson

"Joe Lean," the badman at the root of all of the evil in *Roustabout* (1964).

Elie Erzer

Hollywood hairdresser who became involved with Priscilla Presley after Mike Stone, before she started seeing Michael Edwards.

Joe Esposito

Elvis' personal bookkeeper, the foreman of his road show and his number one aide and most trusted friend. He and Elvis met in the service, in Germany, and Joe remained with him until the very end, through every crisis, and past the death, as the most trusted employee of the Presley estate. Later, he became road manager of the Bee Gees.

Joseph Evans

Memphis judge who was responsible for the legal affairs of Elvis' estate after the death.

Vince Everett

Elvis' character in *Jailhouse Rock* (1957).

"Everybody Come Aboard"

(Bill Grant–Bernie Baum–Florence Kaye)
The jazzy finale of *Frankie and Johnny*. Recorded in May of 1965 at United Artists Recording Studio in Los Angeles; released in April of 1965 on the soundtrack LP.

E-Z Country Programming No. 2

1956. RCA Victor. LP.
Side 1: (G70L-0108) "When You Said Goodbye" (Eddy Arnold); "Hi De Ank Tum" (Nick, Rita & Ruby); "Mystery Train" (Elvis Presley); "Honey" (Chet Atkins); "These Hands" (Hank Snow); "The Last Frontier" (Sons of the Pioneers).
Side 2: (G70L-0109) "I Forgot To Remember To Forget"; "I Wore Dark Glasses" (Anita Carter); "Rock-A-Bye" (Skeeter Bonn); "Love And Marriage" (Homer & Jethro); "Love Or Spite" (Hank Locklin); "Handful Of Sunshine" (Stuart Hamblen).

E-Z Country Programming No. 3

1956. RCA Victor. LP.
Side 1: (G80L-0199) "Heartbreak Hotel" (Elvis Presley); "I'm Moving In" (Hank Snow); "If It Ain't On The Menu" (Hankshaw Hawkins); "The Poor People Of

Paris" (Chet Atkins); "I Want To Be Loved" (Jack & Johnny & Ruby Wells); "That's A Sad Affair" (Jim Reeves).
Side 2: (G80L-0200) "Do You Know Where God Lives" (Eddy Arnold); "If You Were Mine" (Jim Reeves); "The Little White Duck" (Dorothy Olsen); "Borrowing" (Hawkshaw Hawkins); "What Would You Do" (Porter Wagoner); "I Was The One" (Elvis Presley).

E-Z Pop Programming No. 5

1956. RCA Victor. LP.
Side 1: (F70P-9681) "Dungaree Doll" (Eddie Fisher); "Stolen Love" (Dinah Shore); "Take My Hand (Show Me The Way)" (Rhythmettes); "Not One Goodbye" (Jaye P. Morgan); "Don't Go To Strangers" (Vaughn Monroe); "The Rock And Roll Waltz" (Kay Starr); "I Forgot To Remember To Forget" (Elvis Presley); "The Little Laplander" (Henri Rene)."
Side 2: (F70P-9682) "The Large, Large House" (Mike Pedicin); "All At Once You Love Her" (Perry Como); "When You Said Goodbye" (Eddy Arnold); "My Bewildered Heart" (Jaye P. Morgan); "Mystery Train" (Elvis Presley;); "That's All There Is To That" (Dinah Shore); "Jean's Song" (Chet Atkins); "Everybody's Got A Home But Me" (Eddie Fisher).

E-Z Pop Programming No. 6

1956. RCA Victor. LP.
Side 1: (G70L-0197) "Lipstick And Candy And Rubbersole Shoes" (Julius La Rosa); "Mr. Wonderful" (Teddi King); "The Bitter With The Sweet" (Bill Eckstein); "Forever Darling" (Ames Bros.); "Sweet Lips" (Jaye P. Morgan); "Do You Know Where God Lives" (Eddy Arnold).
Side 2: (G70L-0198) "Grapevine" (Billy Eckstine); "The Poor People Of Paris" (Chet Atkins); "Juke Box Baby" (Perry Como); "Little White Duck" (Dorothy Olsen); "I Was The One" (Elvis Presley); "Hot Dog Rock And Roll" (The Singing Dogs).

Shelly Fabares

Close friend and romantic co-star in several of Elvis' films: as Valerie in *Girl Happy* (1965); as rich girl "Cynthia Foxhugh" in *Spinout* (1966); and as husband-chasing "Diane Carter" in *Clambake* (1967). According to many, Shelley was Elvis' favorite co-star. Once, during the filming of *Spinout*, they held a kissing embrace for three minutes after the director called out to cut the scene.

The Face of Jesus

The spiritual work by Frank

Adams given to Elvis by Larry Geller, the book he was reading when he died.

Factors, Inc.

Harry Geissler's Delaware merchandising firm designated by Col. Parker to pump out the authorized line of Elvis "souvenirs" after the death.

Eddie Fadal

A friend of Elvis' and the Colonel's, who lived in Houston, Texas. Elvis visited there while stationed at Killeen in 1958 and ate chili and sang a few songs. In 1977, Fadal released a bootleg record of some of the tapes he made called *Forever Young, Forever Beautiful* on Memphis Flash Records. ☞

"Faded Love"

(Bob Wills–John Wills)
A magnificent R & B driver with a sizzling Burton guitar solo, with Elvis pouring himself with abandon into the sad lyric. Recorded in June of 1970 at RCA Nashville Studio; released in February of 1971 on the LP *Elvis Country*.

"Fairytale"

(Anita Pointer–Bonnie Pointer)
The Pointer Sisters contributed this one, done steadily but without gusto by an obviously disinterested Elvis. Recorded in May of 1975 in Hollywood; released that same month on the LP *Elvis Today*.

"Fame And Fortune"

(Fred Wise–Ben Weisman)
A slow ballad performed with true emotion, a lament about the worthlessness of fame without love (something Elvis came to know intimately). Backed nicely by the Jordanaires. Recorded in March of 1960 at RCA Nashville Studio; released as a single in April of 1960–the flip-side of "Stuck On You." Later, on the LP *Elvis: The Other Sides–Worldwide Gold Award Hits, Volume 2* (1971).

Fan Clubs

In the past 25 years, thousands of Elvis fan clubs have been formed, all over the world. All sizes, from a handful of members to thousands upon thousands. Many clubs have closed; a handful have got stronger over the years. The biggest and best fan club in the world is the British one. It was formed in August 1957 by Jeanne Saword and Dug Surtees. In 1962, Albert Hand took over, and in 1967, the present leader, Todd Slaughter, became Secretary. Membership averaged some 12,000 until 1977, when the tragic death of Elvis jumped the membership up to over 30,000. From the start, the club maintained contact with Elvis and his management, and soon after Elvis' death, Col. Parker made the club the World-wide Elvis Fan Club. The club keeps members informed of anything to do with Elvis' memory, has an active travel service, and holds annual conventions for raising money for charity. (See conventions.) Local film/Disco events are also popular. Listed below are addresses of some of the Fan Clubs and Societies, etc.:

WORLDWIDE ELVIS PRESLEY FAN CLUB
P.O. Box 4, Leicester, England. Secretary: Todd Slaughter.
ELVIS MONTHLY
41–47 Derby Road, Heanor, Derby. DE7 7QH, England.
ELVIS PRESLEY FAN CLUB TRAVEL SERVICE
P.O. Box 29, Felixstowe, Suffolk, England. Travel boss: David Wade.
*TRENDS * VINTAGE ELVIS CLUB*
10 Chapel St., Barwell, Leicester, England. Ian Bailey or John Huckle.
ELVIS IS KING
59 Cambridge Rd., New Silksworth, Sunderland, Wyne & Wear, SR3 2DQ, England. President: David Trotter.
TODAY TOMORROW AND FOREVER FAN CLUB
"Graceland," 3 Lower Quay St., Gloucester, GL1 2JX, England. Presidents: Diana and Ray Hill.
THE NEVER ENDING ELVIS FAN CLUB
Low St., Thomastown, Co. Kilkenny, Ireland.
ELVIS CRUSADERS
22 Cherry Tree Rd., Charing Heath, Ashford, Kent, England. President: Val Quinn.
ELVIS PRESLEY MEMORIES APPRECIATION CLUB
2 Osward Place, Edmonton, London, N.9, England. President: Hazel Tomlin.
HELMUT RADERMACHER
2 Vorsitzender der Elvis Presley Gesellshaft e.V., Postfach 1264, 8430 Newmarkt 1, Germany.
ELVIS PRESLEY FAN CLUB OF NORWAY
P.O. Box 52, 1470 Lorenskog, Norway. Presidents: Mona and Pal Granlund.
BLUE HAWAIIANS FOR ELVIS
P.O. Box 69834, Los Angeles, California 90069, USA. President: Sue Wiegert.
C.E.F.C. (Completely Elvis Fan Club)
P.O. Box 8206, Van Nuys, California, 91409, USA.
ELVIS UNIQUE RECORD CLUB
P.O. Box 339, Huntingdon Valley, Pennsylvania 19006, USA. President: Paul Lichter.
HOUSE OF ELVIS
5404 Hillside Drive, Kansas City, Missouri 64151, USA. President: Sean Shaver.
The above are only a small selection of the clubs operating. In the U.K. too, there are fifty branches of the main fan club.

Glenda Farrell
"Ma Tatum" in *Kissin' Cousins* (1964).

"Farther Along"
(Traditional sacred – arranged and adapted by Elvis Presley) Spiritual done quietly, backed by tinkling piano, mellow guitar, and a chorus of the Imperials. Recorded in May of 1966 at RCA Nashville Studio; released in March of 1967 on the LP *How Great Thou Art*.

Frank Faylen
Character actor with whom Elvis made his screen test for Hal Wallis on April 1, 1956, doing a scene for *The Rainmaker.*

Charlie Feathers
Mississippi-born singer-composer who recorded for Sun Records briefly after Elvis' departure to RCA, who co-authored "I Forgot To Remember To Forget" with Stan Kessler.

Features
Height: Elvis was just over six feet tall.
Weight: Elvis weighed around 180 lbs. normally, but his weight went up to well over 260 lbs. in his last few years.
Eyes: Elvis' eyes were smoky blue, with long lashes.
Hair: Natural color was dark blond, but he began to dye his hair around the time he made *Loving You*, and in almost all his films his hair is black. It was left its natural color for *Follow That Dream* and *Kid Galahad* in 1961. In the '50's, Elvis had long sideburns that disappeared when he went into the army, and only reappeared again around 1967. In the '70's, he grew his hair a little longer, but never overly long or untidy.
Chest side: 39", normal; 41" expanded.
Neck Size: 15½–16".
Overall figure: Elvis was well-proportioned, with broad shoulders, and was a most impressive-looking man, and in his fans' eyes, the most handsome man ever.
He had a short scar over his left eye.

"Fever"
(John Davenport – Eddie Cooley) Elvis scored mightily with Peggy Lee's 1958 hit. Elvis' version is slow, breathy, with a softly beating drum and plenty of vocal sizzle. Recorded in April of 1960 at RCA Nashville Studio; released the same month on the LP *Elvis Is Back*. Performed live and released on the LP *Aloha From Hawaii Via Satellite* (1973).

Arthur Fiedler
Conductor of the Boston Pops from 1929–1979 who expressed the desire for Elvis to perform with his orchestra and record an album for RCA.

Lamar Fike
Originally a fan of Elvis' from Texas during the earliest days of his fame, Lamar became a trusted employee who stayed until the very end, working at Hill and Range in Nashville. Because of his ballooning weight and good humor, Fike became the court jester of the "Memphis Mafia" over the years. He later collaborated with writer Albert Goldman on the biography *Elvis* (McGraw Hill, 1981).

Films Never Made
Over the years there were dozens of films offered to Elvis that were turned down because: 1) The Colonel couldn't get his price, 2) The part was deemed to be "bad" for Elvis' public image, or 3) Elvis wasn't interested or he was but he was frightened about taking the job. Some of the films were turkeys, but some were offers for roles in quality movies that may well have challenged Elvis as a "serious" actor for the first time in his life. Who knows what would have happened? The most interesting possibilities were the lead in *West Side Story*; the lead in *Thunder Road* (which went to Robert Mitchum); the role of "Chance Wayne" in the film version of Tennessee Williams' *Sweet Bird of Youth* (to Paul Newman); the role of Hank Williams in the film biography *Your Cheatin' Heart* (to George Hamilton); and the role of the fading rock star in the Barbra Streisand – Jon Peters remake of *A Star Is Born*. It is also known that Elvis was interested in playing the part of "Don Corleone" in *The Godfather*. Elvis was also interested in producing his own film and commissioned Rick Husky, a TV writer and friend of Jerry Schilling, to do a screenplay for an "Action" film, but nothing ever came of it. There have also been reports of a screenplay commissioned by Elvis tentatively entitled *Billy Easter*, which would have been a straight dramatic film. But try to imagine Elvis as "Joe Buck," the hustler in John Schlesinger's *Midnight Cowboy* (another he was offered). Pretty interesting speculation. . . .

"Finders Keepers Losers Weepers"
(Dory Jones – Ollie Jones) A rocker in the "Return To Sender" idiom with enthusiastic backing by the Jordanaires almost drowning Elvis out, but he wobbles happily away. Recorded in May of 1963 at RCA Nashville Studio; released in July of 1965 on the LP *Elvis For Everyone*.

"Find Out What's Happening"
(Jerry Crutchfield) A low-grade rocker reminiscent of scores of the more forgettable tunes from Elvis' films. Recorded at Stax Recording Studio in Memphis in July of 1973. Released in November of 1973 on the LP *Raised On Rock*.

John Finlator
Deputy U.S. Narcotics Director, who first refused Elvis his badge as a Federal Narcotics Agent when Elvis visited Washington in 1972.

First Assembly of God Church
The small, rickety church attended by the Presleys in East Tupelo, where Elvis first heard and sang gospel music.

"First In Line"
(Aaron Schroeder – Ben Weisman) One of the most unusual and obscure of Elvis' early RCA recordings. A stark recording with vocals by the Jordanaires. An oddly melancholic song for that period, both in vocal texture and arrangement. Recorded in September of 1956 at Radio Recorders in Hollywood; released in November of 1956 on the LP *Elvis*.

First Years, The
1978. LP. HALW (00001). Side 1: "Scotty Moore Talks

Flaming Star.

About Elvis."
Side 2: "Good Rockin' Tonight";
"Baby Let's Play House"; "Blue
Moon Of Kentucky"; "I Got A
Woman"; "That's All Right."
Listed are the proper titles. On
this LP only "Baby Let's Play
House" and "Blue Moon Of
Kentucky" were correct. The
others were "There's Good
Rockin' Tonight," "I've Got A
Woman" and "That's All Right
Little Mama."

Danny Fisher
Elvis' character in *King Creole*
(1958).

"Five Sleepy Heads"
(Sid Tepper – Roy C. Bennett)
A short children's lullaby com-
missioned for *Speedway*.
Recorded in June of 1967 in
Hollywood; released in June of
1968 on the soundtrack LP.

Flaming Star
Started August 8, 1960. A 20th
Century-Fox Production.
Cast
Pacer: Elvis Presley; Roslyn
Pierce: Barbara Eden; Clint:
Steve Forrest; Neddy Burton:
Dolores Del Rio; Pa Burton:
John McIntire; Buffalo Horn:
Rudolph Acosta; Dred Pierce:
Karl Swenson; Doc Phillips:
Ford Rainey; Angus Pierce:
Richard Jaeckel; Dorothy
Howard: Anne Benton; Tom
Howard: L.Q. Jones; Will
Howard: Douglas Dick; Jute:
Tom Reese; Ph'sha Knay:
Marian Goldina; Ben Ford:
Monte Burkhart; Hornsby: Ted
Jacques; Indian Brave: Rodd
Redwing; Two Moons: Perry
Lopez.

"Flaming Star"
(Sid Wayne – Sherman Edwards)
The title tune to the film with
Elvis trying his best to make
something out of nothing. Re-
corded in August of 1960 in
Hollywood; released in April of
1961 on the EP *Elvis By
Request*. Later, on the Camden-
RCA LP *Elvis Sings Flaming
Star* (1969).

"Flip Flop And Fly"
(Joe Turner – Charles Calhoun)
The rocking companion to
"Shake, Rattle And Roll" per-
formed in medley in February of
1956 on the *Dorsey Show*. Later
performed and recorded on
March 20, 1974 at Mid-South
Coliseum in Memphis and
released on the live LP *Elvis
Recorded Live On Stage In
Memphis* (1974).

Red Foley
One of the legendary figures of
country music – a member of the
Country Music Hall of Fame
who performed at the Grand Ole
Opry and influenced Elvis' early
musical taste. "Old Shep," "Peace

In The Valley," and "Shake A Hand" were all Foley hits before Elvis recorded them.

Follow That Dream
Started July 3, 1961
A Mirisch Company Production
A United Artists Release
Cast
Toby Kwimper: Elvis Presley;
Pop Kwimper: Arthur O'Connell;
Holly Jones: Anne Helm; Alicia Claypoole: Joanna Moore; Carmine: Jack Kruschen; Nick: Simon Oakland; Endicott: Herbert Rudley; H. Arthur King: Alan Hewitt; George: Howard McNear; Eddy and Teddy Bascombe: Gavin and Robin Koon; The Governor: Harry Holcombe; Ariadne Pennington: Pam Ogles; The Judge: Roland Winters
Credits
Produced by Kavid Weisbart
Directed by Gordon Douglas
Screenplay by Charles Lederer
Art Direction by Mal Bert
Music by Hans J. Salter
Based on a story by Richard Powell
Songs
"What A Wonderful Life"; "I'm Not The Marrying Kind"; "Sound Advice"; "Follow That Dream"; "On Top Of Old Smokey" (unreleased)
Running time: 109 minutes
Previously titled: *Here Come The Kwimpers; What A Wonderful Life; Pioneer Go Home.*

Credits
Produced by David Weisbart
Directed by Don Siegel
Screenplay by Clair Huffaker and Nunnally Johnson
Based on a Novel by Clair Huffaker.
Music by Cyril J. Mockridge
Conducted by Lionel Newman
Art Direction by Duncan Cramer and Walter M. Symonds
Assistant Director: Joseph E. Rickards
Costumes Designed by Adele Balkan
Hair Styles by Helen Turpin, C.H.S.
Second Unit Director: Richard Talmadge
Sound by E. Clayton Ward and Warren B. Deaplain
Orchestration by Edward B. Powell
Dances Staged by Josephine Earl
Vocal Arrangements to Elvis Presley's songs by the Jordanaires
Color by De Luxe
Songs
"Flaming Star"; "A Cane And A High Starched Collar"; "Britches" (cut) (unreleased); "Summer Kisses, Winter Tears"
Previously titled:
Flaming Arrow/Lance

*Black Star
Brother Of Flaming Lance*

"Follow That Dream"
(Fred Wise—Ben Weisman)
The rocking title tune to the film, high-pitched, energetic but marginal. Recorded in July of 1961 at RCA Nashville Studio; released in April of 1962 on the soundtrack LP.

Follow That Dream
1962. RCA Victor. EP (EPA-4368).
Side 1: "Follow That Dream"; "Angel."
Side 2: "What A Wonderful Life"; "I'm Not The Marryin' Kind."

"Folsom Prison Blues"
(Johnny Cash)
Elvis never recorded a version of this 1955 classic by Johnny Cash, his old colleague at Sun Records, but he did sing it, sometimes in concert. A version appears on the bootleg LP *From Hollywood To Vegas.*

D.J. Fontanna
Elvis' drummer from the days of the "Louisiana Hayride" in 1954 to his induction into the Army in 1958, backing him on all of the RCA early hits. Later worked on soundtrack LPs and played on the *1968 Christmas Television Special*, in the live segment.

"Fool"
(Carl Sigman—James Last)
The Stamps and Joe Guercio's strings pile on the dramatics on the "Lost Love" plea, which Elvis never brings to full throttle. Recorded in March of 1972 at MGM Recording Studio in Los Angeles; released in April of 1973 as a single, with the strong flip-side of "Steamroller Blues." Later, on the LP *Elvis* (1973).

"Fools Fall In Love"
(Jerry Leiber—Mike Stoller)
The same formula as "Come What May," but faster, with the Imperials. An old hit by the Drifters. Recorded in May of 1966 at RCA Nashville Studio; released as a single in January of 1967—the flip-side of "Indescribably Blue." Later, on the RCA-Camden LP *I Got Lucky* (1971) and the Pickwick LP *Double Dynamite* (1975).

"Fools Rush In (Where Angels Fear To Tread)"
(Johnny Mercer—Rube Bloom)
Glenn Miller made it famous in 1940, then Rick Nelson did it in 1963. Elvis' version is not unlike Nelson's, right down to the James Burton guitar solo (Burton, a member of Rick Nelson's band, had played on the '63 disc as well). Recorded in May of 1971 at RCA Nashville Studio; released in February

1971, on the LP *Elvis Now.*

William Foote
The hypnotist who tried working with Elvis in 1976 to help him learn relaxation and pain relief. Foote later told his story to the *National Enquirer.*

Buzzie Forbess
One of Elvis' friends at L.C. Humes High.

Forest Hill Cemetery
1661 Elvis Presley Boulevard. Gladys Presley was buried there on August 6, 1977. Her body was placed with Elvis' in a family mausoleum on August 18, 1977. Because of fans and an attempt at stealing the body, both were moved to the Meditation Gardens at Graceland on October 2, 1977.

Forever Young, Forever Beautiful
33⅓ LP. Bootleg.
Released by Memphis Flash Records in August of 1977. Consists of a number of songs of Elvis taped by Eddie Fadal in his Houston, Texas home, in 1958. Some songs were sung with records, some with Anita Wood and some with Elvis playing the piano. Songs included are: "Happy, Happy Birthday Baby"; "Who's Sorry Now"; "I Understand"; "I Can't Help It (If I'm Still In Love With You)"; "Baby, Don't Ya Know"; "Tomorrow Night"; "Little Darlin'"; "Tumbling Tumbleweeds"; "Just A Closer Walk With Thee."

"Forget Me Never"
(Fred Wise—Ben Weisman)
Recorded for *Wild In The Country* but never used in the film, this is a simple ballad with a C & W flavor accompanied by a lone acoustic guitar. Elvis lilts over the lyric, making it lovely. Recorded in November of 1960, in Hollywood; not released until July of 1965, when RCA found a place for it on the LP *Elvis For Everyone.*

"(That's What You Get) For Lovin' Me"
(Gordon Lightfoot)
Countrified rendition of a Lightfoot song done previously by Waylon Jennings and Peter, Paul, and Mary. Charlie McCoy harmonica and vocal backup by the Nashville Edition. Elvis makes the most out of the mean lyric: *I've had a hundred just like you and I'll have a thousand before I'm through. . . .* Recorded on March 15, 1971 at RCA Nashville Studio; not released until July of 1973, on the LP *Elvis.*

For LP Fans Only
1979. RCA Victor. LP. (LPM-1990).
Side 1: "That's All Right";

"Lawdy Miss Clawdy"; "Mystery Train"; "Playing For Keeps"; "Poor Boy."
Side 2: "My Baby Left Me"; "I Was The One"; "Shake, Rattle And Roll"; "I'm Left, You're Right, She's Gone"; "You're A Heartbreaker."

"For Ol' Times Sake"
(Tony Joe White)
A disorganized melody against a soft acoustic guitar with Elvis waxing sentimental. Recorded in July of 1973 at Stax Recording Studio in Memphis; released as the flip-side of the single "Raised On Rock" in September of 1973. Later on the LP *Raised On Rock* (1973).

Steve Forrest
"Clint Burton," Elvis' (Pace Burton's) brother in *Flaming Star* (1961).

Alan Fortas
One of the early Memphis buddies, placed on the payroll in 1957 as companion-bodyguard, but absent from the "Memphis Mafia" in the later sixties. Alan took care of the Circle G Ranch and kept Elvis' fleet of cars in running condition.

"For The Good Times"
(Kris Kristofferson)
Elvis did a studio version of Kris' plaintive country number in March of 1972 at MGM Recording Studio in Los Angeles, that was never released. He performed it live at the famous Madison Square Garden gig in June of 1972, done stylishly with gentle Burton guitar work and the Stamps coming up behind—a starkly sad number injected into the Garden festivities. Also, in the *On Tour* movie, Elvis is shown warbling a verse or two with the boys in the car, coming away from a performance. He obviously liked this one. Released in June of 1972, on the live LP *Elvis As Recorded At Madison Square Garden.*

"For The Heart"
(Denis Linde)
This song typifies where Elvis' musical tastes took him—a nakedly emotional, autobiographical selection, recorded in the Graceland den, with Elvis far from top vocal form but making the most out of the lyric. Recorded in February of 1976; released in March of 1976, as the flip-side of the single "Hurt." Later, on the LP *From Elvis Presley Boulevard, Memphis, Tennessee.*

"For The Millionth And Last Time"
(Sid Tepper—Roy C. Bennett)
A pleasant, mainstream ballad with a Latin flavor, and a mellow Floyd Cramer piano. Recorded

in October of 1961 at RCA Nashville Studio; not released until July of 1965, when it appeared on the potpourri LP *Elvis For Everyone.*

Fort Hood, Texas
The place of Elvis' basic training in the spring of 1958 after his induction, where his parents moved and his mother became fatally ill.

"Fort Lauderdale Chamber Of Commerce"
(Sid Tepper – Roy C. Bennett) Typical film fare: a zany piano and a slow calypso beat, an attempt at clever lyrics for girl chasing in *Girl Happy.* Recorded in July of 1964 in Hollywood; released in April of 1965 on the soundtrack LP.

"Fountain Of Love"
(Bill Grant – Jeff Lewis) Schmaltzy, slightly up tempo and a Spanish flair. Elvis is mixed faintly back instead of dominant. Recorded in March of 1962 at RCA Nashville Studio; released in June of 1962 on the LP *Pot Luck.*

Redd Fox
Well-known black comedian and personal friend of Elvis who attended Elvis' wedding reception at the Aladdin Hotel.

"Frankfurt Special"
(Sid Wayne – Sherman Edwards) The swinging train scene from *G.I. Blues,* with Elvis imitating the sound of the train and the Jords replying *OOOOO-OOOOH!* A hot-time instrumental beat of guitars and some wonderful rapid-fire phrasing by Elvis. Recorded in June of 1960 in Hollywood; released in October of 1960 on the soundtrack LP.

Dr. Jerry Fransisco
The Shelby County Coroner at the time of Elvis' death, who performed the three hour autopsy and has stood in the center of controversy and allegations about a possible cover-up regarding the true causes of Elvis' death.

Frankie And Johnny
A United Artists Release
Cast
Johnny: Elvis Presley; Frankie: Donna Douglas; Nellie Bly: Nancy Novack; Clint Braden: Anthony Eisley; Mitzi: Sue Ane Langdom; Cully: Harry Morgan; Peg: Audrey Christe; Blackie: Robert Strauss; Wilbur: Jerome Cowen.
Credits
Produced by Edward Small
Directed by Fred de Cordova
Screenplay by Alex Gottlieb
Story by Nat Perrin
Technicolor

Associate Producer: Alex Gottlieb
Music by Fred Karger
Songs
"Everybody Come Aboard"; "Frankie And Johnny"; "Come Along"; "Petunia, The Gardeners Daughter"; "Chesay"; "What Every Woman Lives For"; "Look Out, Broadway"; "Beginner's Luck"; "Down By The Riverside/When The Saints"; "Shout It Out"; "Hard Luck"; "Please Don't Stop Loving Me"
Running time: 87 minutes

"Frankie And Johnny"
(Alex Gottlieb – Fred Karger – Ben Weisman) The jazzy title tune to the film, a remake of a standard – stagey and filled with choruses. In the film, the music was intercut with dance routines and contained the voices of Donna Douglas and Sue Ane Langdon. The record version is shorter, with unbilled female voices. Recorded in May of 1965 at United Artists Recording Studio in Los Angeles. Released in March of 1966 as a single, with "Please Don't Stop Loving Me" as the flip. Later, on the soundtrack LP (1966) and on the Camden LP *Elvis Sings Hits From His Movies Volume 1* (1972).

Frankie And Johnny
1966. RCA Victor. LP (LPM/LSP-3553).
Side 1: "Frankie And Johnny"; "Come Along"; "Petunia, The Gardener's Daughter"; "Chesay"; "What Every Woman Lives For"; "Look Out Broadway."
Side 2: "Beginner's Luck"; "Down By The Riverside/When The Saints Go Marching In"; "Shout It Out"; "Hard Luck"; "Please Don't Stop Loving Me"; "Everybody Come Aboard."

Frankie And Johnny
1976. RCA Camden-Pickwick. LP (ACL-7007).
Side 1: "Frankie And Johnny"; "Come Along"; "What Every Woman Lives For"; "Hard Luck"; "Please Don't Stop Loving Me."
Side 2: "Down By The Riverside And When The Saints Go Marching In"; "Petunia, The Gardener's Daughter"; "Beginner's Luck"; "Shout It Out."
Note: Because RCA had deleted the original LP, Pickwick was given permission to reissue in 1976. The cover was totally changed; the "*and*" in the title was changed to an ampersand, and three of the original tunes were dropped: "Chesay," "Everybody Come Aboard" and "Look Out Broadway."

Dallas Frazier
C & W singer-composer who

recorded three songs later covered by Elvis: "There Goes My Everything," "True Love Travels On A Gravel Road," and "Wearin' That Loved On Look."

Alan Freed
WINS disc-jockey in New York who became the patron saint of rock n' roll during the early years (many say he was the first to use the phrase). In 1956, he broke "Heartbreak Hotel" on his show in New York.

Joann Freeman
"Cathy Lean," daughter of vindictive Leif Erickson in *Roustabout* (1964).

Friedberg
Elvis' base in Germany. ☞

"From A Jack To A King"
(Ned Miller) C & W selection from the first Memphis session, 1969. Blossoms, Memphis Strings, and a fairly routine arrangement – one of the lesser cuts from a glorious sequence of sessions. Recorded in January, 1969 at American Studios in Memphis; released in November of 1969 on the LP *From Memphis To Vegas/From Vegas To Memphis.*

From Elvis In Memphis
1969. RCA. LP (LSP-4155). Side 1: "Wearin' That Loved On Look"; "Only The Strong Survive"; "I'll Hold You In My Arms (Till I Can Hold You In My Heart)"; "Long Black

Limousine"; "It Keeps Right On A-Hurtin' "; "I'm Moving On."
Side 2: "Power Of My Love"; "Gentle On My Mind"; "After Loving You"; "True Love Travels On A Gravel Road"; "Any Day Now"; "In The Ghetto."

From Elvis Presley Boulevard, Memphis, Tennessee
1976. RCA. LP (APL1-1506).
Side 1. "Hurt"; "Never Again"; "Blue Eyes Crying In The Rain"; "Danny Boy"; "The Last Farewell."
Side 2. "For The Heart"; "Bitter They Are, Harder They Fall"; "Solitaire"; "Love Coming Down"; "I'll Never Fall In Love Again."

From Elvis With Love
1978. RCA Record Club. LP (R234340). Songs with *"Love"* in the title—
Side 1: "Love Me Tender"; "Can't Help Falling In Love"; "The Next Step Is Love"; "I Need Your Love Tonight"; "I Can't Stop Loving You."
Side 2: "I Want You, I Need You, I Love You"; "I Love You Because"; "Love Letters"; "A Thing Called Love"; "A Big Hunk O' Love."
Side 3: "Love Me"; "Without Love"; "Faded Love (alternate version)"; "Loving You"; "You've Lost That Lovin' Feeling."
Side 4: "Have I Told You Lately That I Love You"; "You Don't Have To Say That You Love Me"; "True Love"; "Ain't That Loving You Baby"; "Please Don't Stop Loving Me."

From Hollywood To Vegas
33⅓ LP Bootleg.
Released on Brookfield label, featuring "live" Las Vegas songs and unreleased movie material.
Side 1: "Loving You"; "Husky Dusky Day"; "On Top Of Old Smokey"; "Dainty Little Moonbeams"; "Girls! Girls! Girls!"; "Auralee"; "Signs Of The Zodiac"; "Folsom Prison Blues" (Vegas); "I Walk The Line" (Vegas); "Oh Happy Day" (Vegas).
Side 2: "I Need Your Loving Every Day" (Vegas); "I Ain't About To Sing" (Vegas); "I Got A Woman" (Vegas); "Amen" (Vegas); "Crying Time" (Vegas); "Lovely Mamie"; "Long Tall Sally"; "Flip, Flop, And Fly" (Vegas); "My Boy" (Vegas); "Hound Dog" (Vegas).

From Las Vegas . . . To Niagara Falls
33⅓ bootleg two-record album released on the Brookfield label. Songs are from the Las Vegas dinner show on September 3, 1973, and from the Niagara Falls concert on June 24, 1974.
Side 1: "See See Rider"; "I Got A Woman"; "Amen"; "Love Me";

"Steamroller Blues"; "You Gave Me A Mountain"; "Trouble."
Side 2: "Love Me Tender"; "Fever"; "Suspicious Minds"; "My Boy"; "I Can't Stop Loving You"; "Teddy Bear"; "Don't Be Cruel"; "The First Time Ever I Saw Your Face"; "Can't Help Falling In Love."
Side 3: "See See Rider"; "I Got A Woman"; "Love Me"; "Tryin' To Get To You"; "All Shook Up"; "Love Me Tender"; "Hound Dog"; "Fever"; "Polk Salad Annie."
Side 4: "Why Me? Lord"; "Suspicious Minds"; "I Can't Stop Loving You"; "Help Me"; "An American Trilogy"; "Let Me Be There"; "Funny How Time Slips Away"; "Big Boss Man"; "Teddy Bear"; "Don't Be Cruel"; "Can't Help Falling In Love."

From Memphis To Vegas/ From Vegas To Memphis
1969. RCA. LP (LSP-6020).
Side 1: "Blue Suede Shoes"; "Johnny B Goode"; "All Shook Up"; "Are You Lonesome Tonight"; "Hound Dog"; "I Can't Stop Loving You"; "My Babe."
Side 2: "Medley: Mystery Train/Tiger Man"; "Words"; "In The Ghetto"; "Suspicious Minds"; "Can't Help Falling In Love."
Side 3: "Inherit The Wind"; "This Is My Story"; "Stranger In My Own Home Town"; "A Little Bit Of Green"; "And The Grass Won't Pay No Mind."
Side 4: "Do You Know Who I Am"; "From A Jack To A King"; "The Fair Is Moving On"; "You'll Think Of Me"; "Without Love (There Is Nothing)."

Bootleg
From Memphis To Vegas/From Vegas To Memphis
RCA LSP-6020. 33⅓ LP, released in November of 1969. Sides 1 and 2 were recorded "live" in Las Vegas and Sides 3 and 4 were recorded in the Memphis Studio. Originally released as two separate albums in November of 1970:
Elvis—Back In Memphis and *Elvis In Person At The International Hotel, Las Vegas, Nevada.*
Side 1: "Blue Suede Shoes"; "Johnny B. Goode"; "All Shook Up"; "Are You Lonesome Tonight"; "Hound Dog"; "I Can't Stop Loving You"; "My Babe."
Side 2: Medley: "Mystery Train," "Tiger Man"; "Words"; "In The Ghetto"; "Suspicious Minds"; "Can't Help Falling In Love."
Side 3: "Inherit The Wind"; "This Is The Story"; "Stranger In My Own Home Town"; "A Little Bit Of Green"; "And The Grass Won't Pay No Mind."
Side 4: "Do You Know Who I Am"; "From A Jack To A King"; "The Fair's Moving On"; "You'll

Think Of Me"; "Without Love (There Is Nothing)."

From The Dark, To The Light!
33⅓ LP Bootleg.
Side 1: "That's The Way It Is."
Side 2: "Elvis On Tour" (The King On Tour).

From The Waist Up
33⅓ bootleg album released on the Golden Archives label. All songs were performed on the *Ed Sullivan Show.*
Side 1: "Don't Be Cruel" (9/9/56); "Love Me Tender" (9/9/56); "Hound Dog" (9/9/56); "Don't Be Cruel" (10/28/56); "Love Me Tender" (10/28/56); "Hound Dog" (10/28/56).
Side 2: "Hound Dog" (1/6/57); "Love Me Tender" (1/6/57); "Heartbreak Hotel" (1/6/57); "Don't Be Cruel" (1/6/57); "Peace In The Valley" (1/6/57); "Too Much" (1/6/57); "When My Blue Moon Turns To Gold Again" (1/6/57).

Frontier Hotel
Elvis' first Las Vegas performance, on April 23, 1956—where, legend has it, he bombed. He would return thirteen years later to more favorable circumstances.

Alf and Jeanette Fruchter
Jewish family who lived upstairs from the Presleys when they resided at 464 Alabama Street in 1954.

Candy Jo Fuller
C & W singer who has claimed to be Elvis' illegitimate daughter. The claim started with her mother, Terri Taylor, who has stated that she and Elvis knew each other (carnally) in the 1950's. Thus, they also assert that Candy's son, Michael, is Elvis' grandson.

Funeral
On August 18, 1977, funeral services were held for Elvis at Graceland. About 200 people attended. Vernon and Lisa led the mourners, and Priscilla, Linda Thompson and Ginger Alden were there. There were few show business celebrities, despite the Memphis paper stating that people like John Wayne and Burt Reynolds had attended. But Ann-Margret and her husband Roger Smith were there, looking very grief-stricken. The TV preacher, Rex Humbard, who Elvis had admired, gave the eulogy. Kathy Westmoreland sang "My Heavenly Father," a song she'd often sung for Elvis onstage. The services began about 2 p.m., and at about 4 p.m. a long line of white cadillacs and other cars began the slow journey along Elvis Presley Boulevard to Forest Hill Cemetery. A white

Cadillac hearse carried the casket of Elvis. Thousands of fans and onlookers lined the boulevard; some estimates put the number of people there at about 100,000. Over 3,000 floral tributes were sent, covering the lawns of the cemetery, and in all forms, such as hound-dogs, guitars, crosses, broken hearts, and so on. There was a short service in the Mausoleum before the casket was placed in the private crypt. Many of Elvis' closest friends acted as bearers. Memphis TV covered the funeral "Live" and it was given prominent coverage on all news programs and in the press all over the world. On the following day, the flowers were given to thousands of fans who visited the mausoleum (Elvis and his mother were moved from the mausoleum on October 2, and buried in the Meditation Garden at Graceland).

Fun In Acapulco
A Hal Wallis Production
A Paramount Picture
Cast
Mike Windgren: Elvis Presley; Marguarita Cauphine: Ursula Andress; Dolores Gomez: Elsa Cardenas; Maximillian: Paul Lukas; Raoul Almeido: Larry Domasin; Moreno: Alejandro Rey; Jose: Robert Carricart; Janie Harkins: Teri Hope; Mr. Harkins: Charles Evans; Hotel Manager: Alberto Morin; Desk Clerk: Francisco Ortega; Bellboy: Robert De Anda; Telegraph Clerk: Linda Rivera; First Girl: Darlene Tomkins; Second Girl: Linda Rand; Musician: Eddie Cano; Musician: Carlos Mejia; Musician: Leon Cardenas; Musician: Fred Aguirre; Photographer: Tom Hernandez; Secretary: Adele Palacios

Credits
Assoc. Producer: Paul Nathan
Directed by Richard Thorpe
Unit Managers: Richard Blaydon and William Gray
Second Unit and Assist. Director: Michael Moore
Hairstyle Supervision by Nellie Manley
Musical numbers staged by Charles O'Curran
Music Scored and Conducted by Joseph J. Lilley
Special Photographic Effects by Paul K. Lapae
Sound Recording by Hugo Crenzback and Charles Grenzbach
Vocal Accompaniment by The Jordanaires and The Four Amigos
Art Direction by Hal Pereira and Walter Tyler
Screenplay by Alan Weiss
Technicolor
Technical Advisor: Col. Tom

Parker

Songs
"Fun In Acapulco"; "Vino, Dinero Y Amor"; "Mexico"; "El Toro"; "Marguarita"; "The Bullfighter Was A Lady"; "There's No Room To Rhumba In A Sports Car"; "I Think I'm Gonna Like It Here"; "Bossa Nova Baby"; "You Can't Say No In Acapulco"; "Guadalajara"
Running Time: 97 minutes
Previous Titles: *Holiday In Acapulco*

"Fun In Acapulco"
(Ben Weisman – Sid Wayne)
Film title song, a gradual, waking effect bringing in the Jordanaires and then Elvis. Recorded in January of 1963 in Hollywood; released in November of 1963 on the soundtrack LP. ☞

Fun In Acapulco
1963. RCA Victor. LP (LPM/LSP-2756).
Side 1: "Fun In Acapulco"; "Vino, Dinero Y Amor"; "Mexico"; "El Toro"; "Marguarita"; "The Lady Was A Bullfighter"; "No Room To Rhumba In A Sports Car."
Side 2: "I Think I'm Gonna Like It Here"; "Bossa Nova Baby"; "You Can't Say No In Acapulco"; "Guadalajara"; "Love Me Tonight"; "Slowly But Surely."

"Funny How Time Slips Away"
(Willie Nelson)
A fine, almost haunting rendition of a sad song, performed softly and with great impact, though the cut is a bit over produced. Complete with strings and the Imperials and Jordanaires mixed way in the background. A live recording was originally recorded in August of 1969 but was not released. It was then recorded in June of 1970 at RCA Nashville Studio; released in February of 1971 on the LP *Elvis Country*. A superlative version was recorded at Madison Square Garden on June 10, 1972, and released on the LP *Elvis As Recorded At Madison Square Garden* (1972). Another excellent performance is featured in the *On Tour* film.

Kathy Gabriel
One of Elvis' showgirl flames during his engagement at the Frontiere Hotel in Las Vegas, in 1956.

Marvin "Gee Gee" Gambil
Elvis' personal chauffeur for many years, who married Elvis' cousin Patsy Presley (Vester's daughter).

Patsy Presley Gambil
Elvis' cousin and a long-time secretary at Graceland. She married Elvis' chauffeur, Marvin "Gee Gee" Gambil.

"Brother" David Gardner
Comedian and personal friend who occasionally opened Elvis' shows in Jackie Kahane's place.

Hank Garland
Guitarist who worked with Elvis from 1958–1966, after Scotty Moore left.

Chad Gates
Elvis' character in *Blue Hawaii* (1961).

Larry Gatlin
One of Elvis' favorite country composers, who gave Elvis songs like "Bigger They Are, The Harder They Fall."

Gatorade
Elvis' favorite thirst-quencher onstage (he kept it in an ice bucket, along with his ever-present Mountain Valley water).

Harry Geisler
"The Bear," owner of Factors, Inc., the promotion-merchandising firm authorized by Col. Parker to market Elvis' face and name after the death.

Larry Geller
Elvis' beautician and close companion over many years, also his "spiritual advisor." Authored *The Truth About Elvis* with Jess Stearn after Elvis died.

"Gentle On My Mind"
(John Hartford)
Heavy-handed rendition of a Glen Campbell hit from the Memphis sessions, 1969. Elvis leans on the lyrics and personalizes this one nicely. Recorded at American Studios in January; released in May of 1969 on the LP *From Elvis In Memphis*.

"Gently"
(Murray Wizell – Edward Lishona)
Delicate, unassuming ballad done with a light touch, backed by the Jordanaires. Recorded in March of 1961 at RCA Nashville Studio; released in June of 1961 on the LP *Something For Everybody*.

"Get Back"
(Lennon-McCartney)
Another of Elvis' favorite Beatles tunes, never recorded but sometimes performed live, in a medley with "Little Sister."

Getlo
Elvis' chow, suffered from kidney problems; Elvis tried to save its life at enormous expense, but it died.

Dr. Elias Ghanem
Las Vegas physician of Pakistani descent treating many showbusiness people over the years, allegedly involved in abetting Elvis' habit for narcotic prescription drugs.

G.I. Blues
Started: April 26, 1960
A Paramount Picture
Cast
Tulsa McLean: Elvis Presley; Lili: Juliet Prowse; Cooky: Robert Ives; Tina: Leticia Roman; Rick: James Douglas; Marla: Sigrid Maier; Sgt. McGraw: Arch Johnson
Credits
A Hal Wallis Production
Directed by Norman Taurog
Written by Edmund Beloin and Henry Carson
Assistant Director: Michael Moore
Associate Producer: Paul Nathan
Technicolor and Vistavision
Songs
"G.I. Blues"; "Blue Suede Shoes"; "Tonight Is So Right For Love"; "Frankfurt Special"; "Wooden Heart"; "Pocketful Of Rainbows"; "Didja Ever?"; "What's She Really Like?"; "Shoppin' Around"; "Big Boots"; "Doin' The Best I Can"
Running Time: 104 minutes
Also Titled: *Cafe Europa* for European release

"G.I. Blues"
(Sid Tepper – Roy C. Bennett)
Pounding Army marching number, the title tune from the film, complete with drill sergeant shouting "Hup! Hup!" as Elvis segues into the melody. Recorded in April of 1960 in Hollywood; released in October of 1960 on the soundtrack LP.

G.I. Blues
1960. RCA Victor. LP (LPM/LSP-2256).
Side 1: "Tonight Is So Right For Love"; "What's She Really Like"; "Frankfurt Special"; "Wooden Heart"; "G.I. Blues."
Side 2: "Pocket Full Of Rainbows"; "Shoppin' Around"; "Big Boots"; "Didja' Ever"; "Blue Suede Shoes"; "Doin' The Best I Can."

Kahlil Gibran
Lebanese poet, artist, and philosopher whose works, particularly *The Prophet*, greatly influenced Elvis' thought.

Gifts
Generosity was part of Elvis' nature; it had little to do with his being able to afford to give to people less fortunate than himself. As a child, he was said to have given what little he had in the way of toys to other children. Since Elvis disliked publicity, there must have been thousands of gifts that have

A gift for a fan.

never been disclosed, but sometimes the fans or press did find out about the gifts. Cars by the dozen were given to relatives and friends, and even strangers. In 1975, Elvis gave a car to a black lady he saw admiring his car in a showroom; and he added a large check for some clothes to go with the car. Denver police friends received cars as gifts, and then he gave another to a radio announcer who reported the gifts, and said he wouldn't mind a car too. His nurse, Marion Cocke, received a car from Elvis in 1975; he pointed it out to her from the hospital window. Any time anybody in Elvis' family or circle of friends and musicians needed anything, Elvis came through; naturally he was taken advantage of in some cases. He paid hospital and medical bills, bought houses, gave checks, and so on. If he read in the paper of a needy cause or person, he helped out. He gave buses to the Stamps, and to country singer T.G. Shepard. Girlfriends, musicians, and friends all received rings and other expensive jewelry. He even gave the Colonel a plane once! Every Christmas, Elvis would sign up to fifty checks for Memphis charities, and over the years, he must have given millions of dollars to all manner of charities and churches. Fans too, were lucky recipients of gifts from Elvis. Fan-friend Gary Pepper received a car one Christmas, other fans visiting Graceland were given items of Elvis' clothing. From the stage, Elvis gave thousands of scarves to fans, and even on occasion capes, guitars and expensive rings. There seemed to be no end to Elvis' generosity, but the greatest gift that Elvis gave to the world was himself and his music, and in these instances he gave until he could give no more. Now fans try to follow his example, and work in

his name to help less fortunate people.

Homer "Gil" Gilliland
The hairdresser who took Larry Geller's place in 1967 (after Elvis became "disillusioned" with Larry's spiritual pursuits) and worked for Elvis until Geller's return in the early 1970's.

Girl Happy
An MGM Picture
Cast
Rusty Wells: Elvis Presley; Valerie: Shelley Fabares; Big Frank: Harold J. Stone; Andy: Gary Crosby; Wilbur: Joby Baker; Sunny Daze: Nita Talbot; Deena: Mary Ann Mobley; Romano: Fabrizio Mioni; Doc: Jimmy Hawkins; Sgt. Benson: Jackie Coogan; Brentwood Van Durgenfield: Peter Brooks; Mr. Penchill: John Fielder; Betsy: Chris Noel; Laurie: Lyn Edginton; Bobbie: Pamela Currad; Nancy: Gale Gilmore; Linda: Rusty Allen

Credits
Produced by Joe Pasternak
Directed by Boris Segal
Written by Harvey Bullock and R.S. Allen
Music by George Stoll
Vocal backgrounds by The Jordanaires
Art Director: George W. Davis and Addison Hehr
Assistant Director: Jack Aldworth
Technical Advisor: Colonel Tom Parker
Make-up Supervisor: William Tuttle
Hair Styles by Sydney Guilaroff
Recording Supervisor: Franklin Milton
Panavision and Metrocolor
Songs
"Girl Happy"; "Spring Fever"; "Fort Lauderdale Chamber Of Commerce"; "Startin' Tonight"; "Wolf Call"; "Do Not Disturb"; "Cross My Heart And Hope To Die"; "The Meanest Girl In Town"; "Do The Clam"; "Puppet On A String"; "I've Got To Find

My Baby"; "Read All About It" (Nita Talbot/Shelley Fabares)
Running Time: 96 minutes
Previously titled: *The Only Way To Love; Girl Crazy*

"Girl Happy"
(Doc Pomus — Norman Meade)
Thumping title tune to the film, carefree, corny and oddly infectious. Recorded in June of 1964 in Hollywood; released in April of 1965 on the soundtrack LP.

Girl Happy
1965. RCA Victor. LP (LPM/LSP-3338).
Side 1: "Girl Happy"; "Spring Fever"; "Fort Lauderdale Chamber Of Commerce"; "Startin' Tonight"; "Wolf Call;" "Do Not Disturb."
Side 2: "Cross My Heart and Hope To Die"; "The Meanest Girl In Town"; "Do The Clam";; "Puppet On A String"; "I've Got To Find My Baby"; "You'll Be Gone."

"Girl of Mine"
(Reed — Mason)
A midnight mood track with a catchy chorus coupled with a tranquil 1960's approach to an Elvis ballad. Country flavor but a lesser effort. Recorded in July of 1973 at Stax Recording Studio in Memphis; released in November of 1973 on the LP *Raised On Rock.*

Girls! Girls! Girls!
Started: March, 1962
A Paramount Picture
Cast
Ross Carpenter: Elvis Presley; Robin Gantner: Stella Stevens; Laurel Dodge: Laurel Goodwin; Wesley Johnson: Jeremy Slate; Chen Yung: Guy Lee; Kin Yung: Benson Fong; Mme. Yung: Beulah Quo; Alexander Stavros: Frank Puglia; Mama Stavros: Lili Valenty; Loona and Linda Stavros: Barbara and Betty Beall; Arthur Morgan: Nestor Paiva; Mrs. Morgan: Ann McCrea; Mai Tung: Ginny Tiu.
Credits
Producer: Hal Wallis
Director: Norman Taurog
Screenplay by Edward Anhalt and Allan Weiss
Songs
"Girls! Girls! Girls!"; "I Don't Wanna Be Tied"; "I Don't Want To"; "We'll Be Together"; "A Boy Like Me, A Girl Like You"; "Earth Boy"; "Return To Sender"; "Because of Love"; "Thanks To The Rolling Sea"; "Song Of The Shrimp"; "The Walls Have Ears"; "We're Coming In Loaded"; "Plantation Rock" (cut) (unreleased); "Twist Me Loose" (cut) (unreleased); "A Potpourri" (cut) (unreleased); "Baby, Baby, Baby" (Stella Stevens); "Never Let Me Go" (Stella Stevens); "The Nearness

Of You" (Stella Stevens); "Mama" (cut)
Previously titled:
Cumba Ya Ya, Jambalaya

"Girls! Girls! Girls!"
(Jerry Lieber — Mike Stoller)
It's hard to believe this is by the same guys who wrote "Jailhouse Rock." Not a particularly bright rocker for the title tune of the film — the high points are one of the Jordanaires burping in the background and a hot sax break. Recorded in March of 1962 in Hollywood; released in November of 1962 on the soundtrack LP.

Girls! Girls! Girls!
1962. RCA Victor. LP (LPM/LSP 2621).
Side 1: "Girls! Girls! Girls!"; "I Don't Want To Be Tied"; "Where Do You Come From"; "I Don't Want To"; "We'll Be Together"; "A Boy Like Me, A Girl Like You"; "Earth Boy."
Side 2: "Return To Sender"; "Because of Love"; "Thanks To The Rolling Sea"; "Song Of The Shrimp"; "The Walls Have Ears"; "We're Coming In Loaded."

"The Girl Next Door"
(Bill Rice — Thomas Wayne)
Mixed-up lyrics, a steady beat, and Elvis hopping: *The girl next door went a-walking, she found a boy she liked. Do-wha-Do,* the Jordanaires respond. Recorded in April of 1960 at RCA Nashville Studio; released that same month on the LP *Elvis Is Back!* This is a song that, if nothing else, illustrates how quickly the Colonel wanted "Product" from Elvis after his discharge.

"Give Me The Right"
(Fred Wise — Norman Blagman)
Elvis half sings, half growls his way through this strongly worded plea for love and respect: *Give me the right to love you tonight, the tears that I cry over you, give me the right.* Recorded in March of 1961 at RCA Nashville Studio; released in June of 1961 on the LP *Something For Everybody.*

Gladys Music
One of Elvis' music publishing companies, named for his mother.

Cliff Gleaves
One of Elvis' companions of the early days, who accompanied Elvis to Germany but was not a part of the "Memphis Mafia" of the sixties. Gleaves also accompanied Elvis on his furlough to Paris in 1959.

"Go East, Young Man"
(Bill Grant — Bernie Baum — Florence Kaye)
Awkward ballad from *Harum Scarum* — Elvis in great voice

but the song never takes flight. Recorded in February of 1965 in Hollywood; released in October of 1965 on the soundtrack LP.

"Goin' Home"
(Joy Byers)
Drums, Indian chants and Elvis singing about the proud desert land and how he's coming home to stay. Minor fare from *Speedway*. Recorded in October of 1967 in Hollywood; released in June of 1968 on the soundtrack LP.

Gold Cadillac
The famous 1960 Cadillac Sedan limousine customized by George Barris for Elvis. The headlight rims were plated with twenty-four karat gold, and the exterior was painted with forty coats of diamond-pearl dust made of crushed diamonds and mixed with fish scales and rubbed to an incredible luster. The interior was designed like the lounge of a yacht, complete with every imaginable luxury. Total cost: $100,000. The car, however, attracted *too* much attention (people tried to break off pieces!) so Elvis got rid of it. The Colonel sent it on a cross-country publicity tour – it ended up in the Country Music Hall of Fame in Nashville. Check it out if you're ever there.

Gold Records
The number of Elvis' Gold Records has long been a source of disagreement among Elvis' followers because of changing criteria over the years. The standard was any single or Extended Play that sold over a million *units* would become gold, but LPs must generate over $1 million in *sales* to qualify. Starting in 1975, however, the standard for the LP was dropped to 500,000 *units*. The Elvis records that definitely qualify are:

Singles:
1956:
"Heartbreak Hotel," "I Was The One," "I Want You, I Need You, I Love You," "Don't Be Cruel," "Hound Dog," "Love Me Tender," "Any Way You Want Me."
1957:
"Too Much," "Playing For Keeps," "All Shook Up," "That's When Your Heartaches Begin," "Teddy Bear," "Loving You," "Jailhouse Rock," "Treat Me Nice," "Don't," "I Beg Of You."
1958:
"Wear My Ring Around Your Neck," "Hard Headed Woman," "I Got Stung," "One Night."
1959:
"A Fool Such As I," "I Need Your Love Tonight," "A Big Hunk O' Love."
1960:
"Stuck On You," "It's Now Or

Never," "A Mess Of Blues," "Are You Lonesome Tonight," "I Got To Know," "Wooden Heart."
1961:
"Surrender," "I Feel So Bad," "Little Sister," "His Latest Flame," "Can't Help Falling In Love," "Rock-A-Hula Baby."
1962:
"Good Luck Charm," "Anything That's Part Of You," "She's Not You," "Return To Sender," "Where Do You Come From."
1963:
"One Broken Heart For Sale," "(You're The) Devil In Disguise."
1964:
"Kissin' Cousins," "Viva Las Vegas," "Ain't That Loving You Baby," "Blue Christmas."
1965:
"Crying In The Chapel," "I'm Yours," "Puppet On A String."
1966:
"Tell Me Why," "Frankie And Johnny," "Love Letters," "Spinout," "All That I Am," "If Every Day Was Like Christmas."
1967:
"Indescribably Blue," "Big Boss Man."
1968:
"Guitar Man," "Stay Away," "We, All Call On Him," "Let Yourself Go," "Almost In Love," "If I Can Dream."
1969:
"Charro," "His Hand In Mine," "In The Ghetto," "Clean Up Your Own Backyard," "Suspicious Minds," "Don't Cry, Daddy."
1970:
"Kentucky Rain," "The Wonder Of You," "Mama Liked The Roses," "I've Lost You," "You Don't Have To Say You Love Me," "Patch It Up," "I Really Don't Want To Know."
1971:
"Where Did They Go Lord," "Only Believe," "I'm Leavin'," "It's Only Love."
1972:
"An American Trilogy," "Burning Love," "Separate Ways."
1973:
"Raised On Rock."
1974:
"Take Good Care Of Her," "It's Midnight."
1975:
"My Boy," "T-R-O-U-B-L-E."
1976:
"Hurt."
1977:
"Way Down," "My Way."

Long Playing Albums (LP's):
Elvis Presley, Elvis (1956); *Loving You, Elvis' Christmas Album* (1957); *King Creole, Elvis' Golden Records* (1958); *50,000,000 Elvis Fans Can't Be Wrong, Elvis' Gold Records, Volume 2* (1959); *Elvis Is Back, G.I. Blues, His Hand In Mine* (1960); *Something For Everybody, Blue Hawaii* (1961); *Pot*

Luck, Girls! Girls! Girls! (1962); *Elvis' Golden Records, Volume 3, Fun In Acapulco* (1963); *Kissin' Cousins, Roustabout* (1964); *Girl Happy, Elvis For Everyone* (1965); *Paradise Hawaiian Style* (1966); *How Great Thou Art* (1967); *Elvis-TV Special* (1968); *Elvis Sings Flaming Star, From Elvis In Memphis*, (1969); *On Stage, February, 1970, Elvis: Worldwide 50 Gold Award Hits, Volume 1, Elvis, That's The Way It Is* (1970); *Elvis Country, Elvis Sings The Wonderful World of Christmas* (1971); *Elvis As Recorded At Madison Square Garden* (1972); *Elvis: Aloha From Hawaii Via Satellite, Elvis (TV Mail Order)* (1973); *Elvis – A Legendary Performer, Volume One* (1974); *Promised land, Pure Gold* (1975); *Elvis – A Legendary Performer, Volume Two, From Elvis Presley Boulevard, Memphis, Tennessee* (1976); *Welcome To My World, Moody Blue, Elvis In Concert* (1977).

Extended Play (EP's):
Jailhouse Rock (1957).

Billy Goldenberg
The musical director for Elvis' smash *Christmas Show* in 1968.

"Golden Coins"
(Bill Grant – Bernie Baum – Florence Kaye)
Elvis as Sheik, from *Harum Scarum*, crooning away, complete with mandolines. Recorded in February of 1965 in Hollywood; released in October of 1965 on the soundtrack LP.

"Gone"
(Smokey Rogers)
Elvis recorded this song while at Sun in 1955 (it was a hit for Ferlin Husky in 1957) but the song was never released.

"Gonna Get Back Home Somehow"
(Doc Pomus – Mort Schuman)
A frantic beater with a few pauses, but Elvis, in full voice, overtakes it. Recorded in March of 1962 at RCA Nashville Studio; released in June of 1962 on the LP *Pot Luck*.

"Good Luck Charm"
(Aaron Schroeder – Wally Gold)
Elvis' #1 hit in 1962, a tuneful arrangement in the sexy style of "All Shook Up." Classic Jordanaires. Lots of *Uh-huhs* and *A-hems* and *O-yeas*. Always a fun record. Recorded in October of 1961 at RCA Nashville Studio; released as a single in March of 1962 with "Anything That's Part Of You" as the flip. Later released on the LP *Elvis' Golden Records Volume III* (1963) and *Worldwide 50 Gold Award Hits, Volume I* (1970).

"Good Rockin' Tonight"
(Roy Brown)
The quintessential invitation to rock, Elvis-style. The song he sang with a guitar all over Memphis, on flat-bed trucks and in dance hall auditoriums throughout the South. Recorded by Sam Phillips with plenty of *echo* reverb for his Sun label in September of 1954; released as a Sun single that month, (Elvis' second) with "I Don't Care If The Sun Don't Shine" on the flip. Rereleased as a single by RCA in November of 1955 and on the EP *A Touch of Gold, Volume 1* (1961). Remixed slightly for later RCA album releases, like *A Date With Elvis* (1959) and *The Sun Sessions* (1976).

Good Rockin' Tonight
33⅓ LP Bootleg.
Side 1: "Good Rockin' Tonight"; "My Baby Is Gone"; "I Don't Care If The Sun Don't Shine"; "Blue Moon Of Kentucky"; "I'll Never Let You Go"; "Mystery Train"; "I Forgot To Remember To Forget."
Side 2: Unreleased track by Jerry Lee Lewis, Warren Smith and Billy Lee Riley.

Good Rockin' Tonight
33⅓ bootleg LP released in 1974 on the Bobcat Label (Bobcat LP-100).
Featured various unreleased Sun recordings.
Side one features cuts by Elvis, with Sam Phillips and Elvis talking between cuts, and side two featured cuts by Jerry Lee Lewis, Billy Lee Riley and Warren Smith.
Side 1: "Good Rockin' Tonight"; "My Baby Is Gone"; "I Don't Care If The Sun Don't Shine"; "Blue Moon Of Kentucky"; "I'll Never Let You Go (Little Darlin')"; "Mystery Train"; "I Forgot To Remember To Forget."
Side 2: "The Return Of Jerry Lee (break-in)"; "Savin' It All For You" (Warren Smith); "Milkshake Mademoiselle" (Jerry Lee Lewis); "Jerry And The Lord" (studio discussion); "Great Balls Of Fire" (Jerry Lee Lewis); "Rock With Me Baby" (Billy Riley); "Trouble Bound" (Billy Riley).

"Good Time Charlie's Got The Blues"
(Danny O'Keefe)
The Danny O'Keefe hit recycled, Memphis style. Recorded in December of 1973 at Stax Studio, in Memphis; released in March of 1974 on the LP *Good Times*.

Good Times
1974. RCA. LP (CPL1-0475).
Side 1: "Take Good Care Of Her"; "Loving Arms"; "I Got A Feelin' In My Body"; "If That

Isn't Love"; "She Wears My Ring."
Side 2: "I've Got A Thing About You Baby"; "My Boy"; "Spanish Eyes"; "Talk About The Good Times"; "Good Time Charlie's Got The Blues."

Laurel Goodwin
"Laurel Dodge," Elvis' love interest in *Girls! Girls! Girls!* (1962).

Emory Gordy
Session bassist, Los Angeles, 1972

Got A Lot O' Livin' To Do
33⅓ LP Bootleg.
Side 1: "Jailhouse Rock" (soundtrack); "Dick Clark interviews."
Side 2: "Loving You" (soundtrack); "Vancouver, Canada, excerpts (live performance and short interviews).

"Got A Lot Of Livin' To Do"
(Aaron Schroeder – Ben Weisman)
Fast, furious, and wild – from *Loving You*, one of Elvis' finest moments. Recorded in January of 1957 at Radio Recorders, in Hollywood; released in July of 1957 on the LP *Loving You*. Believe it or not, the film version is *slower*.

"Got My Mojo Working"
(Preston Foster)
Old Muddy Waters – a loose, enjoyable rocker, with Elvis gulping in the old style before *She belongs to me* and chuckling at the ending. Recorded in June of 1970 at RCA Nashville Studio; released in May of 1971 on the LP *Love Letters From Elvis*.

Jack Gould
The New York Times television critic who panned Elvis' first appearance and uttered the words: "Mr. Presley has no singing ability."

Robert Goulet
Elvis' *least* favorite singer, whose image he reportedly blew out on TV screens with any handy firearms.

Graceland
Elvis' Memphis estate from March of 1957 until his death (374 Elvis Presley Boulevard, Memphis, Tennessee). Elvis bought the home and the thirteen-acre property from Mrs. Ruth Brown Moore for $100,000. The two-story, twenty-three room mansion had been built in the 1940's by her husband, Dr. Thomas Moore and was named "Graceland" after Grace Toof, Mrs. Moore's aunt (the mansion was being used as a church at the time Elvis purchased it). Over the years, the

interior was enlarged at Elvis' whim (he created music rooms, wardrobe rooms) and was decorated by the various women who lived with him there: Gladys Presley, Dee Presley, Priscilla Presley, and Linda Thompson. Elvis had his wrought-iron music gates installed soon after purchase, as well as a swimming pool. The walls were also raised and trees planted for privacy. Elvis also used the mansion for recording late in his career.

Graceland Fan Club of Memphis
Club founded and headed by Harold Lloyd, Elvis' cousin and a former gateskeeper at Graceland.

Grammy Awards
Despite innumerable gold award records and the worldwide adoration of millions, Elvis only

won three awards from the National Academy of Recording Arts and Sciences, all for gospels. They are: "Best Sacred Performance" in 1967 for *How Great Thou Art*; "Best Inspirational Performance" in 1972 for *He Touched Me*; and, in 1974, another "Best Inspirational Performance for *How Great Thou Art*.

Grand Ole Opry
The Mecca of Country Music, in Nashville, where Elvis first appeared on September 25, 1954, introduced by Hank Snow, and performed both sides of his single.

Grand Ole Opry
From 1942–1974, the country music show broadcast on WSM from the Ryman Auditorium in Nashville was the Mecca of Country Music. Elvis appeared

on the show on September 25, 1954 and performed his first two Sun recordings "That's All Right (Mama)" and "Blue Moon Of Kentucky"; after which Jim Denny, the Opry booking agent told Elvis to go back to driving a truck.

Currie Grant
An officer with the Army Special Services who introduced Priscilla Beaulieu to Elvis at a party in Elvis' house on Goethestrasse, in Bad Nauheim.

Great Country/Western Hits
1956. RCA Victor. EP (SPD-26).
Side 1: "Bouquet Of Roses"; "Molly Darling" (Eddy Arnold).
Side 2: "Alabama Jubilee"; "Unchained Melody" (Chet Atkins).
Side 3: "The Banana Boat Song"; "Slow Poison" (Johnnie and Jack).

Side 4: "I'm My Own Grandpaw"; "Cigarettes, Whisky And Wild, Wild Women" (Homer And Jethro).
Side 5: "Looking Back To See"; "Draggin' Main Street" (Jim Reeves).
Side 6: "Blue Moon Of Kentucky"; "Love Me Tender" (Elvis Presley).
Side 7: "According To My Heart"; "Am I Losing You" (Jim Reeves).
Side 8: "I Don't Hurt Anymore"; "I'm Moving On" (Hank Snow).
Side 9: "Cool Water"; "The Everlasting Hills Of Oklahoma" (Sons of the Pioneers).
Side 10: "Company's Coming"; "A Satisfied Mind" (Porter Wagoner).
Side 11: "Seeing Her Only Reminded Me Of You"; "Eat, Drink, And Be Merry" (Porter Wagoner).
Side 12: "I Wonder When We'll Ever Know"; "Red River Valley" (Sons of the Pioneers).
Side 13: "Old Doc Brown"; "Grandfather's Clock" (Hank Snow).
Side 14: "Yonder Comes A Sucker"; "Waitin' For A Train" (Jim Reeves).
Side 15: "Mystery Train"; "Milkcow Boogie Blues" (Elvis Presley).
Side 16: 'Down Yonder"; "Aloha Oe" (Del Wood).
Side 17: "Slow Poke"; "Over The Waves" (Homer and Jethro).
Side 18: "Love, Love, Love"; "We Live In Two Different Worlds" (Johnnie and Jack).
Side 19: "San Antonio Rose"; "Arkansas Traveler" (Chet Atkins).
Side 20: "The Cattle Call"; "I Wouldn't Know Where To Begin (Eddy Arnold).

Greatest Show On Earth, The
1978. RCA Special Products. LP (DML1–0348). — By Candlelite Music Inc.
Side 1: "I'll Remember You"; "Without Love"; "Gentle On My Mind"; "It's Impossible"; "What Now My Love."
Side 2: "Until It's Time For You To Go"; "Early Morning Rain"; "Something"; "The First Time Ever I Saw Your Face"; "The Impossible Dream."

Jeannie Green
Back-up vocals on the Memphis sessions, 1969; in Nashville, 1970–71; in Memphis, 1973.

"Green, Green Grass of Home"
(Claude Putnam, Jr.)
Elvis flipped when he heard Tom Jones' 1966 version while riding cross-country. He vowed to record it, but never got around to it until 1975. Recorded in

May of 1975 in Hollywood; released in May of 1975 on the LP *Today*; remixed for *Our Memories of Elvis, Volume 2* (1979).

Bob Greene
Las Vegas columnist who was the first to report that Elvis had a "drug problem" when Sonny West, after his termination as Elvis' bodyguard in July of 1976, revealed to him that Elvis used cocaine.

Earl Greenwood
One of Elvis' Army friends who *didn't* become part of the "Memphis Mafia."

Steve Gregson
Elvis' character in *Speedway* (1968).

Dick Grob
Ex-Palm Springs policeman and ex-fighter pilot who became Elvis' chief of security at home and on tour.

"Guadalajara"
(Pepe Guizar)
Elvis crooning in Spanish, with organized vocal chaos in the background from the Amigos. From *Fun In Acapulco*. Recorded in January of 1963 in Hollywood; released in November of 1963 on the soundtrack LP. Later, on the Camden LP, *Burning Love and Hits From His Movies, Volume 2* (1972).

Joe Guercio
Arranger and Las Vegas bandleader who worked with Elvis during the period 1969–1976.

"Guitar Man"
(Jerry "Reed" Hubbard)
A talking–fast–blues about a jobless country picker, with Jerry "Reed" providing the licks himself. Recorded in September of 1967 at RCA Nashville Studio; released as a single with "High-Heel Sneaker" as its flip. Three different segments of the song were used on the 1968 TV Special *Elvis* and released on the LP–longer, faster, with Elvis shouting hoarsely against the big NBC orchestra. Another verse was used for continuity and new lyrics penned for the finale of the show.

The Guitar That Changed The World
Scotty Moore's tribute album to Elvis (Epic Records, 1964).

Walter Gulick
Elvis' character in *Kid Galahad* (1962).

Merle Haggard
C & W composer/singer — another one of Elvis' favorites, whose tribute recording "From Graceland To The Promised Land" became a Southern folk anthem about Elvis after his death.

Walter Hale
Elvis' character in *The Trouble With Girls* (1969).

Stuart Hamblen
Country and gospel singer-composer prominent during the 1950's, who wrote "It's No Secret" and "Known Only To Him," both of which were covered by Elvis.

Roy Hamilton
Popular balladeer of the 1950's whose dramatic style Elvis greatly admired. Elvis recorded several of his hits over the years: "You'll Never Walk Alone," "I'm Gonna Sit Right Down And Cry," "Unchained Melody," "Without A Song," "Pledging My Love."

Albert Hand
Founder and editor of *Elvis Monthly*, the British newsletter of the "worldwide" Elvis fan club. Hand, who died in 1972, was a great authority on Elvis and compiled the first "A–Z" in the early sixties.

Rev. James Hanill
The Presley's pastor at the First Assembly of God Church on McLemore St., in Memphis, who eulogized Gladys Presley at Forest Lawn in 1958.

"Happy Ending"
(Ben Weisman – Sid Wayne)
The finale of *It Happened At The World's Fair*, another swinger in the mold of "Beyond The Bend" with tricky phrasing. Recorded in October of 1962 in Hollywood; released in March of 1963 on the soundtrack LP.

Bill Harbach
Co-producer of Elvis' last TV special, on CBS, from Rapid City, South Dakota.

"Harbor Lights"
(Jimmy Kennedy – Hugh Williams)
There is confusion about the original recording of this song, a popular tune of 1950 recorded by Sammy Kaye, Guy Lombardo and Bing Crosby. Most discographic authorities trace it to Elvis' very first recording session at Sun Records in July of 1954 (presumably, like "Without You," it was one of the songs Sam Phillips wasn't thrilled about). It surfaced as a monaural track on the 1976 LP *Elvis: A Legendary Performer, Volume 2* and remains a valuable artifact.

"Hard Headed Woman"
(Claude De Metrius)
One of Elvis' most rapid-fire deliveries ever to be recorded — nasty, furious, and fun — heard, unfortunately, offstage in the film *King Creole*. Recorded in January of 1958 in Hollywood; released as a single in June of 1958, with "Don't Ask Me Why" as its flip, and later on the soundtrack LP. Also released on *Worldwide 50 Gold Award Hits, Volume 1* (1970).

"Hard Knocks"
(Joy Byers)
A short rocker from *Roustabout* with Jordanaires and a throbbing drum beat. Recorded in January of 1964 in Hollywood; released in October of 1964 on the soundtrack LP.

"Hard Luck"
(Ben Weisman – Sid Wayne)
Sad, bluesy ballad from *Frankie and Johnny*. Recorded in May of 1965 at United Artists Recording Studio in Los Angeles; released in April of 1965 on the soundtrack LP.

Glen Hardin
Piano player for Elvis' band from the days of the first Vegas engagements, on the road, until 1976, when he joined Emmylou Harris.

Murray Harman
Drummer and percussionist who played with Elvis in 1960.

Dotty Harmony
Las Vegas entertainer who dated Elvis and accompanied him to his Army examination in 1957.

Louis Harris
One of Elvis' Memphis boys before his Army days, who did not figure prominently in his life after his discharge.

George Harrison
Elvis loved the former Beatles song, "Something," performing it live and recording it in 1973. Like the other Beatles, Harrison also loved Elvis, visiting him backstage in 1972 and several other times in Las Vegas.

Dolores Hart
The sweet young singer (Susan Jessup) in *Loving You* (1957), who established the traditional type of "good girl" who ends up with Elvis in many of his subsequent movies. She also appeared as Nellie, the pretty waitress in *King Creole* (1958).

"Harum Holiday"
(Peter Andreoli – Vince Pancia, Jr.)
Off-beat ballad from one of Elvis' corniest movies, *Harum Scarum*. Still, Elvis fills the lyrics with muscle and tries his

best. Recorded in February of 1965 in Hollywood; released in October of 1965 on the soundtrack LP.

Harum Scarum
Started: 1965.
A Four Leaf Production
Presented by MGM
Cast
Johnny Tyrone: Elvis Presley; Princess Shalimar: Mary Ann Mobley; Aishah: Fran Jeffries; Prince Dragman: Michael Ansarra; Zacha: J. Novello; King Toranshah: Philip Reed; Sinin: Theo Marcuse; Baba: Billy Barta; Mokar: Dick Harvey; Julna: Jack Constanza; Captain Herat: Larry Chance; Leilah: Barbara Werle; Emerald: Brenda Benet; Amethyst: Wilda Taylor; Sari: Vicki Malkin; Mustapha: Ryck Rydon; Scarred Bedouin: Richard Reeves; Yussef: Jerry Rousso
Credits
Produced by Sam Katzman
Directed by Gene Nelson
Written by Gerald Grayson Adams
Music Scored by Fred Karger
Backing by The Jordanaires
Choreography by Earl Barton
Metrocolor and Panavision
Songs
"Harum Holiday"; "My Desert Serenade"; "Go East, Young Man"; "Mirage"; "Kismet"; "Shake That Tambourine"; "Hey Little Girl"; "Golden Coins"; "So Close, Yet So Far"; "Animal Instinct" (cut in most prints); "Wisdom Of The Ages" (cut in most prints).

Harum Scarum
1965. RCA Victor. LP (LPM/LSP – 3468).
Side 1: "Harum Holiday"; "My Desert Serenade"; "Go East, Young Man"; "Mirage"; "Kismet"; "Shake That Tambourine."
Side 2: "Hey Little Girl"; "Golden Coins"; "So Close, Yet So Far"; "Animal Instinct"; "Wisdom Of The Ages."

"Have A Happy"
(Ben Weisman – Florence Kaye – Dolores Fuller)
Stale, left-over from *Change of Habit*, notable only because it ended Elvis' contractual obligations to sing poor songs for worse films (to think that the previous month he'd recorded "Kentucky Rain!"). Recorded in March of 1969 at MCA Studio in Hollywood; released in April of 1970 on the RCA Camden LP *Let's Be Friends*.

"Have I Told You Lately That I Love You"
(Scott Weisman)
An old ballad done with great style at medium tempo with a

slapping guitar. Recorded in January of 1957 at Radio Recorders in Hollywood; released in July of 1957 on the soundtrack LP, *Loving You*, though it didn't appear in the film.

"Hawaiian Sunset"
(Sid Tepper – Roy C. Bennett)
One of the better film ballads, from *Blue Hawaii*. Lovely, slow, with soft Hawaiian guitars, sung in a tender voice. Recorded in April of 1961 in Hollywood; released in October of 1961 on the soundtrack LP.

"Hawaiian Wedding Song"
(Al Hoffman – Dick Manning – C.E. King)
Elvis singing while floating down the river to be married at the end of *Blue Hawaii*, looking saintly, and covered with leis. Recorded in April of 1961 in Hollywood; released in October of 1961 on the soundtrack LP. A live version appears on *Elvis In Concert* (1977).

Hoyt Hawkins
Baritone with the Jordanaires.

Lowell Hays
Another Memphis jeweler fortunate enough to be around during Elvis' sprees, selling him close to a million dollars of merchandise over the years. He even accompanied Elvis on tour with his wares, in case Elvis got in the "mood."

"He Is My Everything"
(Dallas Frazier)
Country spiritual rewritten by Dallas from his "There Goes My Everything," done hymn style. Recorded in June of 1971 at RCA Nashville Studio; released in April of 1972 on the LP *He Touched Me*.

"He Touched Me"
(William J. Gaither)
A lovely spiritual hymn with the Imperials, displaying warmth and great fervor – exactly the kind of gospel Elvis loved to sing around the piano for relaxation in private. Recorded in May of 1971 at RCA Nashville Studio; first released as a single in March of 1972 with "The Bosom Of Abraham" as the flipside. Later, on the LP *He Touched Me* (1972).

He Touched Me.
1972. RCA. LP (LSP-4690).
Side 1: "He Touched Me"; "I've Got Confidence"; "Amazing Grace"; "Seeing Is Believing"; "He Is My Everything"; "Bosom Of Abraham."
Side 2: "An Evening Prayer"; "Lead Me, Guide Me"; "There Is No God But God"; "A Thing Called Love"; "I, John"; "Reach Out To Jesus."

He Walks Beside Me
1978. RCA Victor. LP (AFL1-2772).
Side 1: "He Is My Everything"; "Miracle Of The Rosary"; "Where Did They Go Lord"; "Somebody Bigger Than You and I"; "An Evening Prayer"; "The Impossible Dream."
Side 2: "If I Can Dream"; "Padre"; "Known Only To Him"; "Who Am I"; "How Great Thou Art."
Note: This LP contains the previously unreleased "If I Can Dream" and "The Impossible Dream."

Barbara Hearn
Elvis' first "public" girlfriend back home in Memphis when the press began to focus intensely on his life; many say the first girl to date Elvis after Dixie Locke.

"Heart of Rome"
(G. Stephens – A. Blaikley – K. Howard)
Heavily romantic production with Italian lilt despite horns and Spanish flavored guitars. Sentimental and a bit excessive, even for the man who sang "It's Now Or Never." Recorded in June of 1970 at RCA Nashville Studio; released in June of 1971, as the B-side of "I'm Leaving." Also on the LP *Love Letters From Elvis* (1971).

David Hebler
Personal bodyguard for several years during the seventies, fired along with Red and Sonny West, co-author of *Elvis: What Happened?*

"He'll Have To Go"
(Joe Allison – Audrey Allison)
One of the last songs Elvis ever recorded, on October 31, 1976. It was released in July, 1977 on the *Moody Blue* LP.

Anne Helm
The nubile nineteen-year-old adopted by Elvis' family in *Follow That Dream* (1962), who gets him in the end.

"Help Me"
(Larry Gatlin)
A country weeper by one of Elvis' favorite young composers. Recorded in December of 1973 at Stax Studios in Memphis; released in May of 1974 as a single, with "If You Talk In Your Sleep" as its B-side. Later, on the LP *Promised Land* (1975).

"Help Me Make It Through The Night"
(Kris Kristofferson)
A crowded production of Kris' classic, too busy and gussied up with the Imperials. Elvis' low tones are perfect but the treatment should have been stark. Recorded in May of 1971 at RCA Nashville Studio; released in February of 1972 on the LP *Elvis Now*; later, on the LP *Welcome To My World* (1977).

"Here Comes Santa Claus (Right Down Santa Claus Lane)"
(Gene Autry – Haldeman – Melka)
Christmas fare for the kiddies, from Elvis' first "Christmas

Session" for RCA. The beginning of a tradition. Recorded at Radio Recorders in Hollywood in September of 1957; released in November of 1957 on the LP *Elvis' Christmas Album.*

"He's Your Uncle, Not Your Dad"

(Sid Wayne – Ben Weisman)
A song about Uncle Sam from *Speedway*, a big marching production with trumpets and drums and a male chorus. Recorded in June of 1967 in Hollywood; released in June of 1968 on the soundtrack LP.

Jake Hess

One of Elvis' favorite gospel singers and boyhood idols, leader of the Statesmen Quartet (who recorded "How Great Thou Art" with Elvis). He performed "Known Only To Him" at Elvis' funeral.

"Hey, Hey, Hey"

(Joy Byers)
Fluffy, repetitive groover from *Clambake*. Recorded in February of 1967 at RCA Nashville Studio; released in November of 1967 on the soundtrack LP.

"Hey Jude"

(John Lennon – Paul McCartney)
Elvis' interpretation begins thinly and builds to a climax with his band, a horn section, and the voices of Jeannie Green and Mary and Ginger Holladay. A song he enjoyed performing live during the first years in Las Vegas. Recorded in January of 1969 at American Studios in Memphis; not released until 1972, when it appeared on the LP *Elvis Now.*

"Hey Little Girl"

(Joy Byers)
A *Harum Scarum* rocker, a typical film groover with quick drumming and instrumental breaks. Recorded in February of 1965 in Hollywood; released in October of 1965 on the soundtrack LP.

Scott Heyward

Elvis' character in *Clambake* (1967).

The Hickory Log

The small roadside cafe on Elvis Presley Boulevard that has become a gathering place for Elvis' fans visiting Graceland. Owned by Bonnie and Hobert Burnette.

Milo High

The pilot of the *Lisa Marie*.

"High Heel Sneakers"

(Robert Higgenbotham)
Elvis' update of a hit for Tammy Tucker, Jerry Lee Lewis, and Stevie Wonder; bluesier with a hand-clapping, driving bass sound, a Charlie McCoy

harmonica and wailing, shouting vocals. Low-down but dated. Recorded in September of 1967 at RCA Nashville Studio; released in January of 1968 as the B-side of the single "Guitar Man."

Hillbilly Cat

One of the show names and nicknames of Elvis' early touring years, because R & B was called "cat music."

The Hillbilly Cat

45 EPA Bootleg.
"Jailhouse Rock" (soundtrack); "The Truth About Me"; "The Lady Loves Me"; "Tryin' To Get To You."

The Hillbilly Cat "Live"

Double 33⅓ LP Bootleg.
Side 1. "That's All Right"; "I Got A Woman"; "Tiger Man"; "Love Me Tender"; "I've Lost You"; "I Just Can't Help Believin'."
Side 2: "You've Lost That Loving Feeling"; "Polk Salad Annie"; "Introductions/Johnny B. Goode"; "Wonder Of You"; "Heartbreak Hotel"; "One Night."
Side 3: "All Shook Up"; "Blue Suede Shoes"; "Whole Lotta Shakin' Goin' On"; "Hound Dog"; "Bridge Over Troubled Water"; "Suspicious Minds"; "Release Me"; "Can't Help Falling In Love."
Side 4: (Bonus songs) "I Got A Woman"; ""Ave Maria"; "Polk Salad Annie"; "Heartbreak Hotel"; "One Night"; "Hound Dog"; "When The Snow Falls On The Roses."

The Hillbilly Cat, 1954–1974, Volume 1.

33⅓ LP Bootleg.
Side 1: September 9, 1956: "Don't Be Cruel"; "Love Me Tender"; "Ready Teddy"; "Hound Dog"; October 28, 1956: "Don't Be Cruel"; "Love Me Tender"; "Love Me"; "Hound Dog."
Side 2: "Rags To Riches"; "First Time Ever I Saw Your Face"; "It's Only Love"; "The Sound Of Your Cry"; "Come What May"; "Where Did They Go, Lord"; "Let Me."

Hillbilly Cat "Live," The

A 1970 bootleg double LP featuring songs from Elvis' 1969 Las Vegas shows.
Side 1: "That's All Right"; "I Got A Woman"; "Tiger Man"; "Love Me Tender"; "I've Lost You"; "I Just Can't Help Believin'."
Side 2: "You've Lost That Loving Feeling"; "Polk Salad Annie"; "Johnny B. Goode"; "The Wonder Of You"; "Heartbreak Hotel"; "One Night."
Side 3: "All Shook Up"; "Blue Suede Shoes"; "Whole Lotta Shakin' Goin' On"; "Hound Dog"; "Bridge Over Troubled Water";

"Suspicious Minds"; "Release Me"; "Can't Help Falling In Love."
Side 4: "I Got A Woman"; "Ave Maria"; "Polk Salad Annie"; "Heartbreak Hotel"; "One Night"; "Hound Dog"; "When The Snow Falls On The Roses."

Hillbilly Cat 1954–1974, The, Volume 1

Bootleg LP, released on the Brookfield label, featuring songs from Elvis' appearances on *The Ed Sullivan Show* and some unreleased RCA material.
Side 1: "Don't Be Cruel" (*Ed Sullivan Show*, 9/9/56); "Love Me Tender" (*Ed Sullivan Show*, 9/9/56); "Ready Teddy" (*Ed Sullivan Show*, 9/9/56); "Hound Dog" (*Ed Sullivan Show*, 9/9/56); "Don't Be Cruel" (*Ed Sullivan Show*, 10/28/56); "Love Me Tender" (*Ed Sullivan Show*, 10/28/56); "Love Me" (*Ed Sullivan Show*, 10/28/56).
Side 2: "Rags To Riches"; "First Time Ever I Saw Your Face"; "It's Only Love"; "The Sound Of Your Cry"; "Come What May"; "Where Did They Go, Lord"; "Let Me."

Hi-Lo

Publishing company owned by Sam Phillips, the repository of the Sun catalogue until it was purchased by the Aberbach Brothers for Hill and Range in 1955.

Edward Hinton

Session lead guitarist in Nashville, 1970–71.

"His Hand In Mine"

(Mosie Lister)
Classic spiritual from the first gospel LP, the title tune, and one of his personal favorites. Deep-voiced, clear and moving. Recorded in October of 1960 at RCA Nashville Studio; released in December of 1960 on the LP *His Hand In Mine.*

His Hand In Mine

1966. RCA Victor. LP (LPM/LSP-2328).
Side 1: "His Hand In Mine"; "I'm Gonna Walk Dem Golden Stairs"; "In My Father's House"; "Milky White Way Know Only To Him"; "I Believe In The Man In The Sky."
Side 2: "Joshua Fit The Battle"; "Jesus Knows What I Need"; "Swing Down Sweet Chariot"; "Mansion Over The Hilltop"; "If We Never Meet Again"; "Working On The Building."

His Songs Of Inspiration

1977. RCA Special Products. LP (DML1–0264).
Side 1: "Crying In The Chapel"; "Put Your Hand In The Hand"; "I Believe"; "How Great Thou Art"; "If I Can Dream."
Side 2: "Peace In The Valley";

"Amazing Grace"; "An American Trilogy"; "Follow That Dream"; "You'll Never Walk Alone."

"Heartbreak Hotel"

(Mae Axton – Tommy Durden – Elvis Presley)
Elvis' first national #1 hit for RCA, and the record that metamorphosed him into a myth at the age of 21 and cast his fate to the winds of history. Dramatic, sexy and explosive with a wrenching bluesy guitar break by Scotty Moore and piano by Floyd Cramer. Recorded with plenty of echo at Elvis' first RCA session in Nashville on January 10, 1956 (the first cut was "I Got A Woman"); released as a single in February of 1956 with "I Was The One" as its flipside. Later, on the EP *Heartbreak Hotel* (May, 1956) and the LP *Elvis' Golden Records* (1958), *Worldwide 50 Gold Award Hits, Volume 1* (1970), and *A Legendary Performer, Volume 1 1(1974).* Performed live, as part of a medley for "*Elvis: NBC-TV Special*" (1968). Elvis first performed the song on national television on the *Dorsey* Shows, on January 28, 1956, which has been extensively bootlegged.

Heartbreak Hotel

1956. RCA Victor. EP (EPA-821).
Side 1: "Heartbreak Hotel"; "I Was The One."
Side 2: "Money Honey"; "I Forgot To Remember To Forget."

Hill and Range

Elvis' music publishing concern in Nashville, run for many years by Lamar Fike.

"(Marie's The Name) His Latest Flame"

(Doc Pomus – Mort Schuman)
Bouncy single, a speeded-up "Good Luck Charm" without the Jords, with tuned-down rhythm guitar. Recorded in June of 1961 at RCA Nashville Studio; released as a single in August of 1961 as the flip-side of "Little Sister." Later, released on the LP *Elvis' Golden Records Volume 3* (1963) and *Worldwide Gold Award Hits, Volume 2* (1971).

HMV

"His Master's Voice," the subsidiary of British Decca, which released Elvis records in the British Isles until 1958.

Hobbies

Elvis had a wide range of interests. He enjoyed listening to records and watching TV, especially football games. He enjoyed playing the piano and had a music room at Graceland. He played a variety of sports. In the '60's, he had a football team called the "Elvis Presley Enterprisers," who regularly

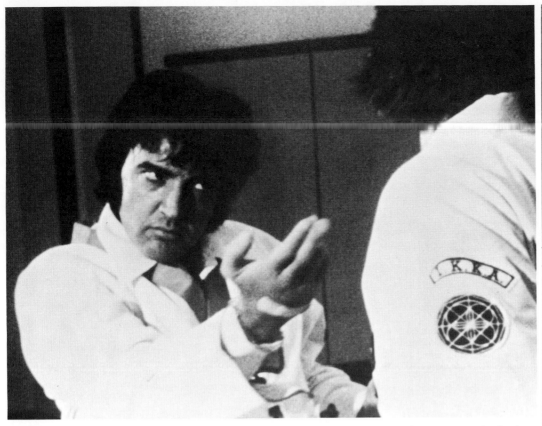

worked out in Hollywood against the other stars' teams, with Elvis cheered on by fans. He boxed a little – Red West was a sparring partner – and went waterskiing on McKellar Lake in Memphis. He had a speedboat on the lake, too. In the '60's, he bought about seventeen horses and liked to ride them around his Graceland grounds, or at the Circle G ranch he bought in Mississippi. His favorite horse was a palomino, "Rising Sun," and he had a Tennessee Walker horse called "Bear." Priscilla had a horse named "Domino." Motorcycling was another interest, along with driving his many cars, go-carts and other vehicles. He had a gun collection at Graceland that included many valuable old pieces. In the '70's, he became interested in racquetball, and had a court built at Graceland. Karate, of course, was his best known interest. He took it up in the army, and got his first-degree black belt in 1960, when he was back home. He continued to learn as much about the art of karate as he could, gradually working his way up to 8th-degree black belt in 1974. He studied under various instructors, the best known being Ed Parker, who taught the kenpo style, and Kang Rhee of Memphis, who taught the psayu style. Elvis began his own style of karate called the TCB style, and worked on a documentary

about it in 1974. He lost interest in karate as his health declined.

Because he couldn't walk about in public, Elvis had to resort to hiring theatres, etc., after closing time. He often hired the Rainbow Skating Rink in Memphis for skating parties in the '50's and early '60's and Libertyland Theme Park (originally the Fairgrounds). In particular, he loved to ride the Dodgems (fender bender) and the Switchback (Zippin Pippin). Fans and friends alike would be invited to Elvis' frequent midnight movies at the Memphian or other cinemas. He'd only watch films he liked, often taking one off after the first reel, and showing others over and over.

Charlie Hodge
Elvis' musical buddy, close companion, and on-stage valet over the years, responsible for draping his capes, handling the scarves, and handing him ice water and Gatorade. Probably the most loyal, adoring member of Elvis' inner circle, he and Elvis met on the USS General Randall. Elvis asked him to work for him after his discharge. Charlie played rhythm guitar on several albums and onstage, and roomed at Graceland in the apartments above the garage. One of the three witnesses to Elvis' will.

Dr. Lester Hoffman
Elvis' Memphis dentist, whom

he visited with Ginger the final night of his life.

Mary and Ginger Holladay
Back-up vocals on the Memphis Sessions, 1969, and later in Hollywood, 1975.

Buddy Holly
Rock n' roll composer-singer – one of the great originals – from Lubbock, Texas, who opened a show for Elvis at the Cotton Club in 1955 and later recorded several of his hits: "Good Rockin' Tonight," "Love Me," "Blue Suede Shoes," and "Ready Teddy." Although Elvis never recorded any Holly originals, he admired him and was saddened by the tragedy of his death in 1959.

"Holly Leaves and Christmas Trees"
(West – Spreen)
Red West's Christmas tune, beautifully produced with bells, strings, and vocals by Cathy Westmoreland and the Imperials. Recorded in May of 1971 at RCA Nashville Studio; released in October of 1971 on the LP *The Wonderful World of Christmas*.

"Home Is Where The Heart Is"
(Sherman Edwards – Hal David)
Nice Ballad from *Kid Galahad*, decent lyrics and production. Recorded in Hollywood in November of 1961; released in September of 1962 on the soundtrack EP.

Honors
On March 8, 1961, Elvis was made an honorary Tennessee Colonel at a ceremony in Nashville, attended by Governor Ellington. He was made a blood brother of the Los Angeles Tribal Indian Community, in recognition for his portrayal of a man of Indian blood in *Flaming Star*. He was made a sheriff in Shelby County, Tennessee, which gave him the right to carry a gun. The Hawaiians honored him for raising so much cash for the Arizona Memorial Fund, and the Kui Lee Cancer Fund. In January, 1971, he was honored at a ceremony in Memphis, making him one of the "10 Outstanding Young Men of America," the honor being accorded to him by the Jaycees. Also, in 1971, Memphis honored its best-known citizen by naming a twelve-mile stretch of Highway 51 South, which ran past Graceland, "Elvis Presley Boulevard." His greatest honor, perhaps, came posthumously, when President Carter issued a statement from the White House, after Elvis' death. The statement said: "Elvis Presley's death deprives our country of a part of itself. He was unique, irreplacable. More than twenty years ago, he burst upon the scene with an impact that was unprecedented and will probably never be equaled. His music and personality, fusing the styles of white country and black rhythm and blues, permanently changed the face of American popular culture. His following was immense, and he was a symbol to people the world over of the vitality, rebelliousness and good humor of his country."

Many more honors have been given and are still being given to Elvis, such as the Chapel in Tupelo, the various statues, and the buildings and roads named after him. (See also Awards, Memorials.)

E. Gregory Hookstratten
Beverly Hills attorney and the Presley lawyer over a period of years – and, allegedly, a key figure in the drawing up of the Presley will, in handling the patrimony suits and in Elvis' divorce proceedings.

Arthur Hooten
One of the Memphis boys from the fifties, who was not a part of the "Memphis Mafia" of later years.

Jerry Hopkins
Journalist, contributing editor of *Rolling Stone*, and author of *Elvis* and *The Final Years*, two authoritative biographical works.

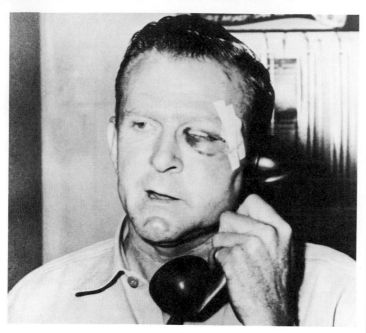

Ed Hopper 👆
The gas station manager
Elvis punched on October 18,
1956 in Memphis. Elvis was
called into court to give his side
of the story (a crowd had formed
because of Elvis, which had
angered Hopper, who then
slapped Elvis). Hopper was
fined, Elvis was cleared, and the
event was recorded for posterity
by the national press.

"Hot Dog"
(Jerry Leiber – Mike Stoller)
One of the more disjointed
numbers from *Loving You*,
though as frantic as the big hits.
Recorded in February of 1957;
released in July of 1957 on the
soundtrack LP.

"Hound Dog"
(Jerry Leiber – Mike Stoller)
Elvis took thirty-one takes of
this until he was satisfied, and
what emerged – the slashing
guitar of Scotty Moore, the
machine gun snare drum of D.J.
Fontanna, the background
vocalizing by the Jordan-
aires – comprised an explosive
rock n' roll anthem. The emotional texture of the lyrics as
shout-sung by Elvis, sneering
and uncompromising, defined a
generation of young Americans.
Recorded on July 2, 1956 at the
RCA studio in New York; released as a single that same
month, with "Don't Be Cruel" as
its flip-side. Performed on television on *The Berle Show* (June
5, 1956), *The Allen Show* (July 1,
1956), and on all three of the
Sullivan shows (September 9,
October 28, and January 6, 1957
– cut-off from the waist down
by the cameras). Released on the
LP *Elvis' Golden Records* (1958),
*Worldwide 50 Gold Awards
Hits, Volume One* (1970). Live

versions were performed and
released on the following LP's:
"Elvis" (NBC TV Special) (1968),
*From Memphis To Vegas/From
Vegas To Memphis* (1969), *Elvis
In Person* (1970), *Elvis As Re-
corded At Madison Square Gar-
den* (1972), *Aloha From Hawaii
Via Satellite (1973)* and *Elvis
Recorded Live On Stage In
Memphis* (1974). Also frequently
bootlegged over the years.

"House Of Sand"
(Bill Grant – Bernie Baum –
Florence Kaye)
One of the forgettable numbers
from *Paradise Hawaiian Style*,
with Elvis sounding as bored
as he probably was. Recorded
in July of 1965 in Paramount
Studios in Hollywood; released
in June of 1966 on the soundtrack LP.

Edwin Howard
Memphis Press-Scimitar
reporter, the very first to interview Elvis in July of 1954.

**"How Can You Lose What You
Never Had"**
(Ben Weisman – Sid Wayne)
From *Clambake*, a bluesy beater
and not very interesting, except
for Elvis holding the "lose" note
at the end with characteristic
vibrato and power. Recorded
in February of 1967 at RCA
Nashville Studio; released in
November of 1967 on the soundtrack LP.

"How Do You Think I Feel"
(Cindy Walker – Webb Pierce)
Spare oldie with Elvis rolling his
voice, testing his chops. Typical
Scotty Moore guitar. A light-
hearted tune. Recorded in
September of 1956 at Radio
Recorders in Hollywood; re-
leased in November of 1956 on
the LP *Elvis*.

Bones Howe
Record producer who worked
with Elvis in the late 1950's and
early 1960's and also produced
the '68 Christmas TV special.

"How Great Thou Art"
(Stuart K. Hine)
What can be said about this one
except "How Great Thou Art?"
Nearly every notable singer of
"sacred" music has recorded it,
but Elvis' rendition was monumental – gentle, deep, mellow,
richly evocative, and building
up to a stunning climax. The
production, though complex,
seems effortless, with a tinkling
Floyd Cramer piano and the Jordanaires and Imperials taking
a verse. Worth more than the
words of 10,000 screaming evan-
gelists, and it reputedly brought
tears to the eyes of the recording technicians. Recorded in
May of 1966 at RCA Nashville
Studio; released in March of
1967 on the LP of the same
name. Recorded live and
released on the following LPs:
*Elvis: Recorded Live On Stage
In Memphis* (1974) and *Elvis In
Concert* (1977). Appropriately,
the song was performed at his
funeral by Cathy Westmoreland
and the Sweet Inspirations,
along with the Stamps Quartet.

How Great Thou Art
1967. RCA Victor. LP
(LPM/LSP-3758).
Side 1: "How Great Thou Art";
"In The Garden"; "Somebody
Bigger Than You And I";
"Farther Along"; "Stand By
Me"; "Without Him."
Side 2: "So High"; "Where Could
I Go But To The Lord"; "By
And By"; "If The Lord Wasn't
Walking By My Side"; "Run On";
"Where No One Stands Alone";
"Crying In The Chapel."

**"How's The World Treating
You"**
(Chet Atkins – Boudleaux
Bryant)
A mournful oldie in the vein of
"Blue Moon," but with less echo.
Recorded at Radio Recorders in
Hollywood in September of
1956; released in November of
1956 on the LP *Elvis*.

"How The Web Is Woven"
(Clive Westlake – David Most)
Very controlled ballad featured
in the rehearsal segment of
"That's The Way It Is" (1970)
with Elvis accompanying himself on piano. On record, he fills
in every word but never has a
chance to unwind, constrained,
it seems, by the tempo. Recorded in June of 1970 at RCA Nashville Studio; released in
December of 1970 on the soundtrack LP.

"How Would You Like To Be"
(Ben Raleigh – Mark Barmon)

From *It Happened At The
World's Fair*: Elvis singing to
cute little Vicky Tiu, entreating
her to dance. Recorded in Hollywood in October of 1962;
released in March of 1963 on the
soundtrack LP.

Tom Huelett
The concert promoter who
formed Concerts West with
Jerry Weintraub and made the
deal with the Colonel to mount
Elvis' road show, 1970–1976.

Pete Hullin
Session piano player, Memphis,
1973.

Rex Humbard
Well known television
evangelist, and one of the eulogizers at Elvis' funeral.

L.C. Humes High School
Elvis' high school in North
Memphis, which he attended
from 1949–1953.

"Hurt"
(Jimmie Craine – Al Jacobs)
A poignant recording for Elvis
fans, made in the Graceland den;
country and plaintive. Recorded
in February of 1976; released as
a single in March of 1976, with
"For The Heart" as the B-side.
Later released on the LP *From
Elvis Presley Boulevard,
Memphis, Tennessee* (1976).

Rick Husky
An acquaintance of Jerry
Schilling and television writer-
producer who wrote a treatment
for an "action" karate film that
Elvis wanted to make himself in
1974. Nothing ever came of it.

"Husky Dusky Day"
Elvis duet with Hope Lange
from *Wild In The Country*
(1961), the ditty they sang in the
car. RCA never released the
song, but a good version
appears on the bootleg LP *The
Eternal Elvis*.

Will Hutchins
Veteran character actor who
played "Lt. Tracy Richards" in
Spinout (1966), and "Tom
Wilson" of *Clambake* (1967).

Dale Hutchinson
Produced *That's The Way It Is*
(1970).

Joe Hyams
Reporter for the New York
Herald Tribune, whose 1957
interview with Elvis, excerpted
in *Time*, was the first to reveal
the loneliness and personal dis-
location which developed as a
result of his meteoric success.

"I Beg Of You"
(Rose Marie McCoy – Kelly
Owens)
Smooth mover with Elvis in
vocal control and the Jor-
danaires perfectly filled in.
Recorded at Radio Recorders in

Hollywood on February 23, 1957; released as the B-side of the single "Don't" in January of 1958. Later, on the LP *50,000,000 Elvis Fans Can't Be Wrong* (1959). Later, on the LP *Elvis: Worldwide 50 Gold Award Hits, Volume I* (1970).

"I Believe"
(Ervin Drake – Jimmy Shirl – Al Stillman – Irvin Graham)
Well-performed standard hymn with the Jordanaires, for Elvis' first gospel EP on RCA. Recorded at Radio Recorders in Hollywood in January of 1957; released in March of 1957 on the EP *Peace In The Valley*. Later, on the LPs *Elvis' Christmas Album*, (1957), and *You'll Never Walk Alone* (1971).

"I Believe In The Man In The Sky"
(Richard Howard)
First-class spiritual opened by a four-line verse by the Jordanaires before Elvis bursts through. Recorded in October of 1960 at RCA Nashville Studio; released on the LP *His Hand In Mine*, Elvis' first gospel album after the army. Later, in 1965, released as the B-side of "Crying in the Chapel."

"I Can Help"
(Billy Swan)
Controlled rendition of Swan's song, with Voice and the Holladay sisters. Recorded in May of 1975 in Hollywood; released in May of 1975 on the LP *Today*.

"I Can't Stop Loving You"
(Don Gibson)
Ray Charles immortalized this song in 1962, but Elvis' version, cut live, is emotional and very soulful, with bravura backup by the Sweet Inspirations and a gospel style climax. Recorded August 25, 1969 at the International Hotel in Las Vegas; released in November of 1969 on the LP *From Memphis To Vegas/From Vegas To Memphis*. Additional concert versions appear on *Elvis In Person* (1970), *Elvis As Recorded At Madison Square Garden* (1972), *Aloha From Hawaii Via Satellite* (1973), *Elvis Recorded Live Onstage In Memphis* (1974) and *Welcome To My World* (1977).

"I Don't Care If The Sun Don't Shine"
(Mack David)
From Elvis' second Sun Session, a fast tempo ballad with a laughing-voiced Elvis giving his all. Recorded in September of 1954 at Sun Studio in Memphis; released that month as the B-side of "Good Rockin' Tonight" and in November of 1955 by

RCA. Also, on the RCA EP *Anyway You Want Me* (1956). Remixed for the LP *The Sun Sessions* (1976).

"I Don't Wanna Be Tied"
(Bill Grant – Bernie Baum – Florence Kaye)
Elvis gets as raucous as possible for this medium tempo number from *Girls! Girls! Girls!*, but still can't save the horrendous lyrics. Recorded in March of 1962 in Hollywood; released in November of 1962 on the soundtrack LP.

"I Don't Want To"
(Janice Torre – Fred Spielman)
Nice ballad, the best track for *Girls! Girls! Girls!*. Recorded in Hollywood in March of 1962; released in November of 1962 on the soundtrack LP.

"I Feel So Bad"
(Chuck Wills)
Bluesy, but delivered at a furious pace with great flourish by Elvis and superb drumming by D.J. Fontana. Recorded in March of 1961 at RCA Nashville Studio; released in May of 1961 as a single, with "Wild In The Country" as the flip. Later, on the LP *Worldwide 50 Gold Award Hits, Vol. 1.* (1970).

"I Feel That I've Known You Better"
(Doc Pomus – Alan Jeffries)
Medium-tempo number that heats up at the end. Recorded in March of 1962 at RCA Nashville Studio; released in June of 1962 on the LP *Pot Luck*. Later, on the EP *Tickle Me* (1965).

"If Every Day Was Like Christmas"
(Red West)
Slow Christmas ballad by Red given serious treatment by Elvis, who sings quietly and deeply until the Jords and the Imperials chime in. Recorded on June 11, 1966 at the RCA Nashville Studio; released as a single in November of 1966 with "How Would You Like To Be" on the B-side. Later released on the Camden LP *Elvis' Christmas Album* (1970).

"If I Can Dream"
(Earl Brown)
Earl Brown created this song for Elvis' 1968 NBC television special, because Elvis and Steve Binder, the director, wanted something topical and current. It worked: the song is a dramatic plea for harmony in a time of strife. Trumpets, organ, drums, double bass, and vocals by the Blossoms cannot subdue the raw emotion in Elvis' voice. Recorded in June of 1968 at Burbank Studios; released in November of 1968 as a single, with "Edge Of Reality" as the

flip. Later, on the LP *Elvis TV Special* (1968). An alternate take was released on the LP *He Walks Beside Me* (1978).

"If I Get Home On Christmas Day"
(McCauley)
Girls and soaring strings don't help this Christmas special which seems forced even for Elvis. Recorded in May of 1971 at the RCA Nashville Studio; released in October of 1971 on the LP *Elvis Sings The Wonderful World Of Christmas*.

"If I'm A Fool (For Loving You)"
(Stanley Kessler)
Wistful, minor ballad rendered more authentic by Elvis' hoarse-voiced approach. Recorded in February of 1969 at American Studios in Memphis; released in April of 1970 on the Camden LP *Let's Be Friends* (a good indication that this ballad wasn't considered top notch was that, unlike most from those dynamic Memphis sessions of 1969, it was shunted off to a Camden LP).

"If I Were You"
(Gerald Nelson)
Country-flavored lyrics and style but overproduced with strings. Recorded in June of 1970 at RCA Nashville Studio; released in May of 1971 on the LP *Love Letters From Elvis*.

"I Forgot To Remember To Forget"
(Charlie Feathers – Stanley Kessler)
Elvis' "cute" song from the Sun sessions, pure and unrestrained with a nice edge in his voice. Recorded in July of 1955 (the sixth session with Sam Phillips); released in August of 1955 by Sun as the B-side of "Mystery Train" and in November by RCA (the same single). Later, in May of 1956, on the *Heartbreak Hotel* EP and on the 1959 LP *A Date With Elvis*. Remixed for *The Sun Sessions* (1976).

"If That Isn't Love"
(Dottie Rambo)
Torchy tune but pedestrian production. Recorded in December of 1973 at Stax Studio in Memphis; released in March of 1974 on the LP *Good Times*.

"If The Lord Wasn't Walking By My Side"
(Henry Slaughter)
Gospel gem with Elvis singing half a line and the Jords and Imperials completing it, with moving piano and organ accompaniment by; Floyd Cramer and David Briggs, respectively. Recorded in May of 1966 at RCA Nashville Studio; released in March of 1967 on the LP *How Great Thou Art*.

"If We Never Meet Again"
(A.E. Brumley)
A real tearjerker despite the hackneyed lyrics. One of Elvis' saddest songs, recorded in October of 1960 during the gospel sessions at RCA Nashville Studio; released in December of 1960 on the LP *His Hand In Mine*.

"If You Don't Come Back"
(Jerry Leiber – Mike Stoller)
Very idiosyncratic rocker in that Elvis takes second place to James Burton's wah-wah and the voices of K. Westmoreland, Jeannie Green and the Holladay girls. Recorded in July, 1973 at Stax Recording Studio in Memphis; released in November of 1973 on the LP *Raised On Rock*.

"If You Don't Think I Need You"
(Red West – Joe Cooper)
Slightly disjointed swinger from *Viva Las Vegas* with Elvis straining to overtake the music. Recorded in July of 1963 in Hollywood; released in June of 1964 on the soundtrack EP.

"If You Love Me (Let Me Know)"
(John Rostill)
This former hit by Olivia Newton-John was among the last three songs ever recorded by Elvis, a country-flavored tune that he took on the road toward the end of his career. Done with twangy James Burton guitar and the incredible *basso profundo* voice of J.D. Sumner on the chorus. Recorded on April 25, 1977; released in July of 1977 on the LP *Moody Blue*. A live version was performed and recorded on Elvis' last TV special on CBS and appears on *Elvis In Concert*.

"If You Talk In Your Sleep"
(Red West – Johnny Christopher)
Recorded in December of 1973 at Stax Studio in Memphis; released in May of 1974 as the flip-side of "Help Me." Later, on the LP *Promised Land*.

"I Got A Feelin' In My Body"
(Dennis Linde)
Recorded in December of 1973 at Stax Studio in Memphis; released in March of 1974 on the LP *Good Times*.

"I Got A Woman"
(Ray Charles)
Ray's classic was the first song ever recorded by Elvis for RCA, a powerful, pounding, rollicking rendition until the slowdown at the end. Elvis loved this one. Recorded on January 10, 1956 at RCA Nashville Studio; released in September 1956 as the flip-side of "I'm Counting On You"

and in March on the EP *Elvis Presley (Blue Suede Shoes)*. Released on the LP *Elvis Presley* (1956). Performed live on the *"Dorsey shows,"* February 11, 1956. Elvis put together a soulful live version of the song for his road shows. Concert versions appear on the LP *Elvis Recorded Live On Stage In Memphis* (1974), intercut with a gospel chorus of "Amen," and later on *Elvis In Concert* (1977).

"I Got Lucky"
(Fred Wise – Ben Weisman – Dolores Fuller)
A laughing number from *Kid Galahad*. Recorded in November of 1961 in Hollywood; released in September of 1962 on the soundtrack EP. Re-released on the Camden LP *I Got Lucky* (1971).

I Got Lucky
1971. RCA Camden. LP (CAL-2533).
Side 1: "I Got Lucky"; "What A Wonderful Life"; "I Need Somebody To Lean On"; "Yoga Is As Yoga Does"; "Ridin' The Rainbow."
Side 2: "Fools Fall In Love"; "The Love Machine"; "Home Is Where The Heart Is"; "You Gotta Stop"; "If You Think I Don't Need You."

"I Got Stung"
(Aaron Schroeder – David Hill)
Unrelenting rhythm makes this a foot tapper, though not one of the more thrilling movers from the early RCA days. Recorded in June of 1958 at the RCA Nashville Studio; released as a single in November of 1958, with "One Night" as the B-side. Released on the LP *50,000,000 Elvis Fans Can't Be Wrong* (1959) and on *Worldwide 50 Gold Award Hits, Volume One* (1970).

"I Gotta Know"
(Paul Evans – Matt Williams)
A mellow rocker that glides along like a plane coming to rest. Recorded in April of 1960 at RCA Nashville Studio; released in November of 1960 as the B-side of "Are You Lonesome Tonight." On the LP *Elvis' Golden Records, Volume III* (1963).

"I John"
(Johnson – McFadden – Brooks)
Outstanding gospel with beautifully organized backings by the Imperials – fast, full of fervor, with shouts of "Hallelujah" from Millie Kirkham and June Page. Recorded in June of 1971 at RCA Nashville Studio; released in April of 1972 on the LP *He Touched Me*. Also seen in a rehearsal segment in the documentary *Elvis On Tour* (1972).

"I Just Can't Help Believing"
(Barry Mann – Cynthia Weil)

An interesting number from *That's The Way It Is*, shown in progression from rehearsal to performance. Sung plaintively, dramatically, complete with string and brass by Joe Guercio and blended background by the Imperials and the Sweet Inspirations. Recorded on August 13, 1970 at the International Hotel in Las Vegas; released in December of 1970 on the soundtrack LP.

"I'll Be Back"
(Sid Wayne – Ben Weisman)
From *Spinout* and sung right at the camera, a low-pitched, effervescent "fun song." Recorded in February of 1966 in Hollywood; released in October of 1966 on the soundtrack LP.

"I'll Be Home For Christmas"
(Kent – Gannon – Ram)
From RCA's first "Christmas session," a lovely, mournful and mellow number with tasteful piano by Floyd Cramer. Recorded in September of 1957 at Radio Recorders in Hollywood; released in November of 1957 on the LP *Elvis' Christmas Album*.

"I'll Be Home On Christmas Day"
(Michael Jarrett)
Another Christmas ballad, very well produced with real emotional texture. Recorded in May of 1971 at RCA Nashville Studio; released in October of 1971 on the LP *Elvis Sings The Wonderful World Of Christmas*.

"I'll Be There (If You Ever Want Me)"
(Gobbard – Price – Bobby Darin)
A nice blend of guitar by Reggie Young, but organ by Glen Spreen and the Memphis Strings do little to rescue this nondescript number from the first Memphis session, a leftover from the Camden catalogue. Recorded in January of 1969 at American Studios in Memphis; released in April of 1970 on the Camden LP *Let's Be Friends*.

"I'll Hold You In My Heart (Till I Can Hold You In My Arms)"
(Eddy Arnold – Hal Horton – Tommy Dilbeck)
Elvis accompanying himself on piano on this Memphis workout as he uses his voice skillfully, singing soulfully and high. Recorded at American Studios in Memphis in January of 1969; released in May of 1969 on the LP *From Elvis in Memphis*.

"I'll Never Fall In Love Again"
(Donegan – Currie)
From the Graceland den, the romantic pop song made popular by Tom Jones in 1966. All in all, a lackluster cut – Elvis

was obviously bored. Recorded in February of 1976 in Memphis; released in May of 1976 on the LP *From Elvis Presley Boulevard, Memphis Tennessee*. Remixed for *Our Memories Of Elvis* (1979).

"I'll Never Know"
(Fred Karger – Sid Wayne – Ben Weisman)
Simple ballad with nicely orchestrated strings, though not among Elvis' finest. Recorded in June of 1970 at RCA Nashville Studio; released in May of 1971 on the Camden LP *Love Letters From Elvis*.

"I'll Never Let You Go (Little Darlin')"
(Jimmy Wakely)
Medium ballad with tempo change at the middle eight and Elvis dueting with himself. From the early Sun days. Recorded in January of 1955 at Sun Studio in Memphis; RCA first released in March of 1956, on the LP *Elvis Presley*. Remixed for the LP *The Sun Sessions* (1976).

"I'll Remember You"
(Kuiokalini Lee)
Smooth, romantic ballad from *Spinout*, backed by the Jordanaires and the Imperials. Recorded in June of 1966 at RCA Nashville Studio; released in October of 1966 on the soundtrack LP. Because the proceeds from the gate at Elvis' 1973 Honolulu performance went to Kuiokalini Lee's posthumous cancer research fund, the song was performed and released on *Aloha From Hawaii Via Satellite* (1973).

"I'll Take Love"
(Dolores Fuller – Mark Barker)
Brassy, Latin American sound from *Easy Come, Easy Go*, as Elvis sings about preferring love to fame and fortune. A brisk number that Elvis lets rip. Recorded at Paramount Recording Studio in Hollywood in September of 1966; released in May of 1967 on the soundtrack EP. Later, on the Camden LP *C'mon Everybody* (1971).

"I'll Take You Home Again Kathleen"
(Adapted by E. Presley)
Like "Danny Boy," this was another one Elvis loved to croon in private at the piano. Of course, Sherill Neilson, the great Irish tenor with Voice, was also an inspiration here, but the recording of this song was an afterthought, with Elvis accompanying himself on piano. Unfortunately, the strings, overdubbed later, intrude on the mood of the song. Recorded in May of 1971 at RCA Nashville

Studio; released in July of 1973 on the LP *Elvis*.

"I Love Only One Girl"
(Sid Tepper – Roy C. Bennett)
A bit of lighthearted fluffery from *Double Trouble*, semi-humorous (he loves only one girl – in *every* town) with the Jordanaires. Recorded in June of 1966 in Hollywood; released in June of 1967 on the soundtrack LP.

"I Love You Because"
(Leon Payne)
This was the first commercial recording at Sun Records in July 5, 1954, an elementary ballad that was recorded in four takes. Sam Phillips spliced takes four and two together to make a disjointed version, which RCA (after buying Elvis' contract) later released on the LP *Elvis* in March of 1956. Years later, Scotty Moore revealed in an interview that the first, unabridged take had never been released. RCA then released take one in 1974, twenty years after its original recording, on the LP *A Legendary Performer, Volume One*.

"I'm Comin' Home"
(Charlie Rich)
Despite a fine guitar by Hank Garland and a nice honky tonk piano by Floyd Cramer, this isn't a particularly memorable cut, although Elvis negotiates the tricky phrasing well. Recorded in March of 1961 at RCA Nashville Studio; released in June of 1961 on the LP *Something for Everybody*.

"I'm Counting On You"
(Don Robertson)
From Elvis' first RCA session, an echoey rendition with lead by Scotty Moore. Recorded on January 11, 1956 at RCA Nashville Studio; released in March of 1956 on the EP and LP *Elvis Presley*. Later, in September, released as a single, with "I Got A Woman" as the B-side. Oddly, it was one of the few Elvis singles of that period that did not perform well.

"I Met Her Today"
(Don Robertson – Hal Blair)
Mellow C & W ballad, sung high and sad-voiced, with Jordanaires. Recorded in October of 1961 at RCA Nashville Studio; not released until July of 1965, when it appeared on the *Elvis For Everyone* LP.

"I'm Falling In Love Tonight"
(Don Robertson)
A song for young lovers from *It Happened At The World's Fair*: just Elvis, piano and organ. A favorite among Elvis fans. Recorded in Hollywood in October of 1962; released in

March of 1962 on the soundtrack LP.

"I'm Gonna Sit Right Down And Cry (Over You)"
(Thomas Briggs)
Another cut from the early RCA days, a lesser known and successful number with a chunky beat and Elvis in top vocal form. This cut always drew the distinction of being a novelty among Elvis fans—an overlooked gem. Recorded on January 31, 1956 (the same day as "Tutti Frutti"!) at RCA New York Studio; released in March of 1956 on the EP and LP *Elvis Presley*. In September it was released as the B-side of "I'll Never Let You Go."

"I'm Gonna Walk Dem Golden Stairs"
(Adapted by Elvis Presley)
A rocking spiritual put together by Elvis, which works like gangbusters. Recorded in October of 1960 at RCA Nashville Studio; released in December of 1960 on the LP *His Hand In Mine*.

"I Miss You"
(Donnie Sumner)
A quiet ballad penned by one of the members of the vocal group Voice then singing with Elvis, with a rippling piano. Not much vocal presence, however. Recorded in September of 1973 at Elvis' home in Palm Springs; released in November of 1973 on the LP *Raised On Rock*.

Imitators and Impersonators
Both before and since Elvis' death, there have been scores of Elvis imitators and impersonators around the world, some quite talented and successful, others abysmally bad. Elvis often remarked that it was a compliment to be imitated. Many of them began making a bundle after his death. In the United States, the most well-known are: Morris Bates, Jim E. Curtin, Bill Haney, Johnny Harra, Denis Wise (who had plastic surgery to look like Elvis), Alan Meyer (the former NASA engineer known simply as "Alan," who is among the most successful and talented), Johnny Risk and Ricky Saucedo (who played Elvis in the short-lived Broadway show *The Living Legend* in 1978). The British impersonators include Heathcliffe, Rupert, and Tony Lamtic. Freddie Starr has also been well received in Britain for his imitations, as well as Shaky Stevens, who played the "middle" Elvis in the London stage musical.

"I'm Leavin' "
(Michael Jarrett—Sonny Charles)
A masterly single backed by the Imperials, with Elvis singing about "feeling fast vibrations and living from day to day." The few lyrics are sung in a deliberately high, uncertain voice. Recorded in May of 1971 at RCA Nashville Studio; released in July of 1971 with "Heart Of Rome" as the flip-side. Unreleased on LP to date.

"I'm Left, You're Right, She's Gone"
(Stanley Kessler—Taylor)
Elvis basking in his Sun glory, overflowing with energy and hopping all over the place in the phrases with a brilliant Scotty Moore guitar. Rockabilly! Recorded by Sam Phillips at Sun Records in July of 1955; released in May of 1955 with "Baby, Let's Play House" as the B-side. RCA released the same single in November of 1955 and included it on the EP *Anyway You Want Me* (1956). Remixed with more reverberation for the LP *The Sun Sessions* (1976).

"I'm Movin' On "
(Clarence E. "Hank" Snow)
Elvis chose not to flat-out rock this C & W tune by his former colleague at Jamboree Attractions and did it country (unlike Ray Charles, who souped it up in 1959), but only on the vocal passages—the instrumental breaks at the end pick up nicely. Vocals by Mary and Ginger Holladay with Jeannie Green. An interesting song from the "Memphis Sessions," recorded in January of 1969 at American Studios; released in May of 1969 on the LP *From Elvis In Memphis*.

"I'm Not The Marrying Kind" (Hal David—Sherman Edwards)
An "image number" from *Follow That Dream* delivered briskly, with a tempo change in the middle eight. Recorded in July of 1961 at RCA Nashville Studio; released in April of 1962 on the EP *Follow That Dream*.

The Imperial Quartet
Famous gospel group backing Elvis on *How Great Thou Art* and other albums. They included Jake Hess, Jim Murray, Gary McSpadden, and Arnold Morales.

Imperial Suite
Elvis' Las Vegas home, on the thirtieth floor of the Hilton, and the scene of many parties over the years.

The Impersonal Life, by Joseph Benner
One of Elvis' favorite and most quoted books. Given to him by Larry Geller, Elvis claims it changed his life.

"I'm So Lonesome I Could Cry"
(Hank Williams)
Elvis always referred to this classic as "the saddest song I've ever heard" and he was fond of performing it on tour. Performed with real down-home verve on January 14, 1973 at H.I.C. Arena in Honolulu; released in February, 1973 on the LP *Aloha From Hawaii Via Satellite*.

"I'm Yours"
(Don Robertson—Hal Blair)
Similar to "Ask Me" but without the Jordanaires, this was an unusually slow, straight-from-the-heart love song. Recorded in June of 1961 at RCA Nashville Studio; released in June of 1962 on the LP *Pot Luck*.

"Indescribably Blue"
(Darrell Glenn)
Plenty of schmaltz: mandolin, organ, guitars, piano, but it's all carefully woven. Elvis curls his voice nicely up from the bass tones to overtake the Jords and Imperials and really makes this one his own. Recorded in June of 1966 at RCA Nashville Studio; released in January of 1967 as a single with "Fools Fall In Love" as the B-side. Later, on the LP *Elvis' Gold Records, Volume 4* (1968).

"I Need Somebody To Lean On"
(Doc Pomus—Mort Schuman)
A fine ballad from *Viva Las Vegas* wherein Elvis, walking through a dimly lit, deserted night club, sings of his loneliness. Recorded in Hollywood in July of 1963; released in June of 1964 on the soundtrack EP.

"I Need Your Love Tonight"
(Sid Wayne—Bix Reichner)
Nicely arranged and presented pop song with high beat from the early RCA days. Recorded in June of 1958 at RCA Nashville Studio; released in March of 1959 as the flip-side of "A Fool Such As I." Released on the LP *50,000,000 Elvis Fans Can't Be Wrong* (1969). Later, on *The Other Sides: Worldwide Gold Award Hits, Volume 2* (1971).

"I Need You So"
(Ivory Joe Hunter)
A lesser number from *Loving You*, with difficult phrasing and unsteady instrumental at points and Elvis singing over the top of a steady drum beat. Recorded in February of 1957 at Radio Recorders in Hollywood; released in July of 1957 on the LP *Loving You.*

"Inherit The Wind"
(Eddie Rabbitt)
Good blending of guitars by Reggie Young and Tommy Cogbill; the Memphis Strings are acceptably unobtrusive. Uptempo chorus by the Blossoms. A good track from the "Memphis sessions." Recorded in January of 1969 at American Studios; released in November of 1969 on the LP *From Memphis To Vegas/From Vegas To Memphis*.

Ink Spots
Elvis loved this 1950's quartet. In fact, the acetates he made for his mother at the Memphis Recording Service were hits by the group: "My Happiness" and "That's When Your Heartaches Begin."

"In My Father's House (Are Many Mansions)"
(Aileene Hanks)
A lovely hymn done straight with a stark vocal backing by the Jordanaires and an incredible bass line sung by Hugh Jarrett. Recorded in October of 1960 at RCA Nashville Studio; released in December of 1960 on the LP *His Hand In Mine*.

"In My Way"
(Fred Wise—Ben Weisman)
Elvis and an acoustic guitar—sincere, delicate, but nothing spectacular as far as Elvis ballads go. Recorded in October of 1960 at RCA Nashville Studio; not released until July of 1965, on the LP *Elvis For Everyone*.

International Hotel
Elvis' first Las Vegas engagement was here, in the 2000-seat Showroom International, on July 31, 1969.

175

"In The Garden"
(C.A. Miles)
Light spiritual with viola and a subdued Floyd Cramer piano – The Jords and Stamps drown Elvis in places – but it works. Recorded in May of 1965 at RCA Nashville Studio; released in March of 1967 on the LP *How Great Thou Art*.

"In The Ghetto"
(Mac Davis)
The most emotionally moving release by Elvis of the sixties (or perhaps, his career); a searing, touching ballad of black urban despair which gave Elvis his first smash single in a long time and put Mac Davis on the map. Every word is phrased with uncanny feeling. The recording, with the Memphis Strings, is a bit overproduced, but no matter. Recorded in January of 1969 at American Studios in Memphis; released as a single in April of 1969 with "Any Day Now" on the flip-side. Later on the LP *From Elvis In Memphis* (1969). Live versions appear on *From Memphis To Vegas/From Vegas To Memphis (1969)*, *Elvis In Person* (1970); and it is also collected on *Worldwide 50 Gold Award Hits, Volume One* (1970).

"In Your Arms"
(Aaron Schroeder – Wally Gold)
Elvis powerhouses this one, with the Jordanaires and a sax break by Boots Randolph. Recorded in March of 1961 at RCA Nashville Studio; released in June of 1961 on the LP *Something For Everybody*.

"I Really Don't Want To Know"
(Don Robertson – Howard Barnes)
Sad lyrics suit Elvis well, with country piano by David Briggs and blues guitar by James Burton blending nicely. Recorded in June of 1970 at RCA Nashville Studio; released as a single in December of 1970, with "There Goes My Everything" on the flip. Later, on the LP *Elvis Country*.

John Ireland
"Phil May," the wealthy lawyer of *Wild In The Country* (1961).

Bob Isenberg
Bit actor who played in Elvis films like *Easy Come, Easy Go* (1966) and worked for Colonel Parker at times.

"Is It So Strange"
(Faron Young)
An oldie with Scotty and Bill and D.J. from the early RCA days, but a song that never got the play that the hits of the period did. A straightforward tune, not especially notable. Recorded in January of 1957 at

Radio Recorders in Hollywood; released in April of 1957 on the EP *Just For You*. Later, on the LPs *A Date With Elvis* (1959) and *Separate Ways* (1973).

"Island Of Love (Kauai)"
(Sid Tepper – Roy C. Bennett)
Compact, tender ballad from *Blue Hawaii*, a bit kooky without being slushy. Recorded in Hollywood in April of 1961; released in May of 1961 on the soundtrack LP.

"I Slipped, I Stumbled, I Fell"
(Fred Wise – Ben Wiseman)
From *Wild In The Country*, performed while driving a truck, a medium tempo ballad that swings a bit more on the record (though you miss Elvis revving the engine to accentuate the beat), and belted out with typical Elvis verve. Recorded in November of 1960 in Hollywood; released in June of 1961 on the LP *Something For Everybody*. Later, on the Camden LP *Separate Ways* (1973).

"It Ain't No Big Thing (But It's Growing)"
(Merritt – Joy – Hall)
Lesser C & W effort, Nashville style. Recorded in June of 1970 at RCA Nashville Studio; released in May of 1971 on the LP *Love Letters From Elvis*.

"It Feels So Right"
(Fred Wise – Ben Weisman)
Elvis chose a highly strained vocal style for this one, a raspy approach quite different from his velvet tunes. From Elvis' first session back from the army. Recorded in March of 1960 at RCA Nashville Studio; released in April of 1960 on the LP *Elvis Is Back*.

It Happened At The World's Fair
Started: 1963
An MGM Film
Cast
Mike Edwards: Elvis Presley; Diane Warren: Joan O'Brien; Danny Burke: Gary Lockwood; Sun-Lin: Vicky Tiu; Nurse Supervisor: Edith Atwater; Ling: Kam Tong; Dorothy: Yvonne Craig
Credits
Produced by Ted Richmond
Directed by Norman Taurog
Written by Si Rose and Seaman Jacobs
Music Score by Leith Stevens
Director of Photography: Joseph Ruttenberg, A.S.C.
Art Direction by George W. Davis and Preston Ames
Technical Advisor: Col. Tom Parker
Assistant Director: Al Jennings
Hair Styles by Sydney Guilaroff
Recording Supervisor: Franklin Milton

Vocal Backgrounds by The Jordanaires and The Mello Men
Musical Numbers staged by Jack Baker
In Panavision and Metrocolor
Songs
"Beyond The Bend"; "Relax"; "Take Me To The Fair"; "They Remind Me Too Much of You"; "One Broken Heart For Sale"; "I'm Falling In Love Tonight"; "Cotton Candy"; "A World Of Our Own"; "How Would You Like To Be"; "Happy Ending"
Previously titled: *Take Me (Out) To the World's Fair*

It Happened At The World's Fair
1963. RCA Victor. LP (LPM/LSP-2697).
Side 1: "Beyond The Bend"; "Relax"; "Take Me To The Fair"; "They Remind Me Too Much Of You"; "One Broken Heart For Sale."
Side 2: "I'm Falling In Love Tonight"; "Cotton Candy Land"; "A World Of Our Own"; "How Would You Like To Be."

"I Think I'm Gonna Like It Here"
(Don Robertson)
A tuneful bit from *Fun In Acapulco*. Recorded in Hollywood, in January of 1963; released in November of 1963 on the soundtrack LP.

"It Hurts Me"
(Joy Byers)
A throwback to the early RCA days and discs. This blends a Floyd Cramer piano with The Jordanaires as Elvis sings about how it hurts him to see the way another man is treating a girl whom Elvis loves (and emphasizing how true *he* would be if he had someone like her). Recorded in January of 1964 at RCA Nashville Studio; released in February of 1964 as the B-side of the single "Kissin' Cousins." Later, on the LP *The Other Sides – Worldwide Gold Award Hits, Vol. 2* (1971).

"It Keeps Right On A-Hurtin'"
(Johnny Tillotson)
A superior performance of a run-of-the-mill C & W hit, from the second group of Memphis sessions. Recorded in February of 1969 at American Studios; released in May of 1969 on the LP *From Elvis In Memphis*.

"Ito Eats"
(Sid Tepper – Roy C. Bennett)
The novelty "humor" number for *Blue Hawaii* with a nearly calypso touch. Recorded in April of 1961 on the soundtrack LP.

"It's A Matter Of Time"
(Clive Westlake)
Contemporary ballad with acoustic guitar and J.D. and the

Stamps hooking you in the chorus, but not memorable as Elvis' ballads go. Recorded in March of 1972 at MGM Recording Studio in Los Angeles; released in August of 1972 as the flip-side of "Burning Love." Later, on the Camden LP *Burning Love and Hits From His Movies, Vol. 2* (1972).

"It's A Sin"
(Fred Rose – Zeb Turner)
Simple, effective ballad, solidly delivered by Elvis with minimal backing. Recorded in March of 1961 at RCA Nashville Studio; released in June of 1961 on the LP *Something For Everybody*.

"It's A Wonderful World"
(Sid Tepper – Roy C. Bennett)
From *Roustabout*, an innocuous, pleasant, but weak number. Recorded in January of 1964 in Hollywood; released in October of 1964 on the soundtrack LP.

"It's Carnival Time"
(Ben Weisman – Sid Wayne)
Also from *Roustabout*, a rollicking, fun tune about the fair with smart, showy lyrics done over an imitation Wurlitzer. Recorded in January of 1964 in Hollywood; released in October of 1964 on the soundtrack LP.

"It's Easy For You"
(Webber – Rice)
From the final grouping of songs recorded by Elvis, a mood piece by the team who brought you *Jesus Christ Superstar*. Recorded in October of 1976 in Murfreesboro, Tennessee; released in July of 1977 on the LP *Moody Blue*.

"It's Impossible"
(Wayne Manzanero)
A serenade with sugary arrangement, with a live orchestra and applause dubbed onto the recording. Recorded in February of 1972 at the Hilton Hotel; released in July of 1973 on the LP *Elvis*.

"It's Midnight"
(Billy Edd Wheeler – Jerry Chesnut)
Ballad recorded in December of 1973 at Stax Recording Studio in Memphis; released in October of 1974 as a single, with "The Promised Land" as the B-side. Later, on the LP *Promised Land*.

"It's No Secret (What God Can Do)"
(Stuart Hamblin)
One of the earliest hymns recorded at RCA that really takes flight at the end. Recorded in January of 1957 at Radio Recorders in Hollywood; released in March of 1957 on the EP *Peace In The Valley*.

"It's Now Or Never"
(Aaron Schroeder – Wally Gold)
Elvis' first smash single out of the Army, which locked him forevermore into the tradition of the popular romantic song. A recycling of the Neopolitan operatic "O Sole Mio," Elvis gives it the full treatment: mandolin, Floyd Cramer piano, and Elvis' voice soaring to the peaks of Mount Love. A heart melter, tailor-made for the girls. Recorded in April of 1960 at RCA Nashville Studio; released in July of 1960 as a single with "A Mess Of Blues" as the flip-side. Later on the LP *Elvis' Golden Records, Volume 3* (1963), *Worldwide 50 Gold Award Hits, Vol. 1* (1970). A live version was performed at Elvis' final TV appearance on CBS and released on *Elvis In Concert* (1977).

"It's Only Love"
(Mark James – Steve Tyrell)
A very conscious attempt at a commercial ballad for single release, but the components wander despite a strong rhythm. Recorded in May of 1971 at RCA Nashville Studio; released in September of 1971 as a single, with "The Sound Of Your Cry" as the B-side. Unreleased on any LP to date.

"It's Over"
(Jimmie Rodgers)
Nice Jimmy Rodgers ballad selected for presentation at the 1973 satellite extravaganza, a short, crisp, masterly performance with ringing vocal acrobatics. Recorded on January 14, 1973 at H.I.C. Arena in Hawaii; released in February of 1973 on the LP *Aloha From Hawaii Via Satellite*.

"It's Still Here"
(Ivory Joe Hunter)
Elvis on piano at the end of a recording session performs a falsetto version of this song. A number for the devoted Elvis fan who savors these impromptu moments. Recorded in May of 1971; released in July of 1973 on the LP *Elvis*.

"It's Your Baby, You Rock It"
(Shirl Milete – Dora Fowler)
Country rocker with Charlie McCoy harmonica and lead guitar by James Burton, handled with authority and a sense of fun by Elvis (in fact, he liked this one so much that he incorporated the title into his repertoire of favorite expressions). Recorded in June of 1970 at RCA Nashville Studio; released in February of 1971 on the LP *Elvis Country*.

"It Won't Be Long"
(Sid Wayne – Ben Weisman)

Mid-tempo groover from *Double Trouble*, not especially catchy with Elvis, as usual, trying to make the most of the material's limitations. Recorded in June of 1961 in Hollywood; released in June of 1967 on the soundtrack LP.

"It Won't Seem Like Christmas (Without You)"
(Balthrop)
Uneven, overproduced Christmas number that forces Elvis somewhere into that no man's land between soft and forceful. Recorded in May of 1971 at RCA Nashville Studio; released

Singing "Relax" to Yvonne Craig in *It Happened At The World's Fair*.

in October of 1971 on the LP *Elvis Sings The Wonderful World of Christmas*.

"I've Got A Thing About You Baby"
(Tony Joe White)
Commercial tune by one of Elvis' favorite C & W songsmiths. Recorded in July of 1973 at Stax Recording Studio in Memphis; released in January of 1974 as the B-side of "Take Good Care of Her." Later, on the LP *Good Times*.

"I've Got Confidence"
(Andrae Crouch)

Crouch gospel, done uptempo with the Imperials, a rousing clapper that fades just as the wailing begins. Recorded in May of 1971 at RCA Nashville Studio; released in April of 1972 on the LP *He Touched Me*.

"I've Got To Find My Baby"
(Joe Byers)
A short rocker from *Girl Happy*. Recorded in July of 1964 in Hollywood; released in April of 1965 on the soundtrack LP.

"I've Lost You"
(Ken Howard – Alan Blaikely)
Emotional ballad sung with magnificent quavering *tremolo*. The studio version is tame, refined, and less wrenching. Recorded in June of 1970 at RCA Nashville Studio; released as a single in July of 1970 with "The Next Step Is Love" on the flip-side. A powerful version was included in the film *That's The Way It Is* (1970) and released on the soundtrack LP.

"I Wanna Be A Rock N' Roll Star"
33⅓ LP Bootleg.
Contains most of the releases on the *Please Release Me* LP as

well as "Wild In The Country"; "The Truth About Me"; and "My Baby Is Gone."

"I Want To Be Free"
(Jerry Leiber – Mike Stoller)
A stirring number from *Jailhouse Rock*, reeling and choked with energy (an abbreviated version appears on film). Recorded in May of 1957 at MGM Studios in Culver City, California; released in October of 1957 on the soundtrack EP. Later, on the LPs *A Date With Elvis* (1959) and *Elvis: The Other Sides – Worldwide Gold Award Hits, Volume 2* (1971).

"I Want You, I Need You, I Love You"
(Maurice Mysels – Ira Kosloff)
Elvis' great torch song from the early RCA days, wherein he makes his claim to the title held by Sinatra. Done with much echo and melodrama. Recorded on April 11, 1956 at RCA Nashville Studio. Released in May of 1956 as a single with "My Baby Left Me" as the B-side. Released on the EP *The Real Elvis* (1956) and on the LP *Elvis' Golden Records* (1958). Later, on *Worldwide 50 Gold Award Hits, Vol. One* (1970) and on *A Legendary Performer, Volume 2* (1976). (Another take of the song is included on this LP). Elvis performed the song on July 1, 1956 on the *Steve Allen Show*.

"I Want You With Me"
(Woody Harris)
A 12-bar rocker with Elvis almost drowned out by the background mix – but a battery of drumming and the energy make this reminiscent of those golden RCA days before the Army. Recorded in March of 1961 at RCA Nashville Studio; released in June of 1961 on the *Something for Everybody* LP.

"I Was Born About Ten Thousand Years Ago"
(Adapted by Elvis Presley)
Traditional C & W song arranged by Elvis, talk-sung in parts and scat-sung against the piano at the finale. Recorded in June of 1970 at RCA Nashville Studio; an excerpt of the song first appeared on the LP *Elvis Country* (1971); the full version appears on the *Elvis Now* LP

"I Washed My Hands in Muddy Water"
(Joe Babcock)
C & W standard converted into a frantic rocker with a pounding Jerry Lee style piano by David Briggs, blending horns, a wailing James Burton guitar, and Elvis, who fought to command it all. Recorded in June of 1970 at RCA Nashville Studio; released in February of 1971 on the LP *Elvis Country*.

"I Was The One"

(Aaron Schroeder – Hal Blair – Claude Demetrius)
From Elvis' first RCA sessions, a beautifully executed song with vocal backing by Gordon Stoker and the Speer Brothers – perfect pitch and tempo by everybody. With a nice Floyd Cramer piano. However, this song will be forever overshadowed by the destiny of the song on the A-side. Recorded January 11, 1956, at RCA Nashville Studio; released in February of 1956, as the B-side of "Heartbreak Hotel." Later, in May of 1956, on the EP *Heartbreak Hotel;* released on the LP *For LP Fans Only* (1959) and on *Worldwide 50 Gold Award Hits, Volume One* (1970).

"I Will Be Home Again"

(Benjamin – Laverne – Singer). Elvis sings a full-length duet with Charlie Hodge. Recorded in June of 1960 at RCA Nashville Studio; released in April of 1960 on the LP *Elvis Is Back!.*

"I Will Be True"

(Ivory Joe Hunter). A no-frills ballad in the old style, with effortless vocal gymnastics by Elvis. Recorded in May of 1971 at RCA Nashville Studio; released in July of 1973 on the LP *Elvis.*

"I Won't Have To Cross The Jordan Alone"

Well known gospel that Elvis sang at the Million Dollar Session at Sun Records in 1956.

The Jackie Gleason Stage Show

(Starring Tommy and Jimmy Dorsey)
Elvis' first television show, on which he appeared six times from January to March, 1956. The dates and songs: January 28: "Blue Suede Shoes" and "Heartbreak Hotel"; February 4: "Tutti Frutti" and "I Was The One"; February 11: "Shake, Rattle And Roll," "Flip, Flop And Fly," and "I Got A Woman," February 18: "Baby, Let's Play House" and "Tutti Frutti"; March 17: "Blue Suede Shoes" and "Heartbreak Hotel"; and March 24: "Money Honey" and "Heartbreak Hotel." Originally, Gleason invited Elvis on the show to boost ratings when he had decided that Elvis was "The guitar-playing Marlon Brando."

Lucky Jackson

Elvis character in *Viva Las Vegas,* (1964).

Ted Jackson

Elvis' character in *Easy Come, Easy Go* (1967).

Wayne Jackson

Session horn man, for the sessions in Memphis.

Jailhouse Rock

Started: 1957
An MGM Picture
Cast
Vince Everett: Elvis Presley; Peggy Van Alden: Judy Tyler; Hunk Houghton: Mickey Shaughnessy; Mr. Shores: Vaughan Taylor; Sherry Wilson: Jennifer Holden; Teddy Talbot: Dean Jones; Laury Jackson: Ann Neyland.
Credits
Directed by Richard Thorpe
Produced by Pandro S. Berman
Screenplay by Guy Trosper
An Avon Production
Songs
"Jailhouse Rock"; "Treat Me Nice"; "Young And Beautiful"; "I Wanna Be Free"; "Don't Leave Me Now"; "Baby I Don't Care"; "One More Day" (Mickey Shaughnessy).
Running Time: 97 minutes

"Jailhouse Rock"

(Jerry Leiber – Mike Stoller)
The essence of rock and roll, captured on film and wax for the ages. From the film of the same name, this was one of Elvis' most electrifying song scenes *ever.* The music has the kick of a mule and the vocals are well nigh ineffable – high, uncompromising, angry, violent, sexy, fun, foolish, relentless – everything that rock is, was or is ever likely to be in its purest incarnations. D. J. Fontanna's snare drum was a revelation. Mike Stoller plays piano, and Scotty and Bill rock out. Recorded on May 2, 1957 at MGM Studios in Culver City, California; released in October of 1957 as a single with "Treat Me Nice" on the B-side. Also released on the EP *Jailhouse Rock* in 1957. On the LPs *Elvis' Golden Records* (1958), *Worldwide 50 Gold Award Hits* (1970) and *A Legendary Performer* (1976). Elvis proved he could still whip this song out when he did it on his 1968 television special. Live versions were released on *"Elvis"* (NBC-TV Special) (1968), as part of a medley with "Hound Dog" on *Elvis Recorded Live On Stage in Memphis* (1974) and finally, on *Elvis in Concert* (1977), the last TV special on CBS.

Jailhouse Rock

1957. RCA Victor. EP (EPA-4114).
Side 1: "Jailhouse Rock"; "Young And Beautiful."
Side 2: "I Want To Be Free"; "Don't Leave Me Now"; "Baby I Don't Care."

"Jambalaya (On The Bayou)"

Hank Williams' 1953 classic was a song Elvis loved and performed over the years, although it was never recorded or released.

Hugh Jarrett

Bass player with the Jordanaires.

Felton Jarvis

Nashville producer who worked with Elvis from 1966 to the end, mixing and over-dubbing, and supervising the sound system on tour. Many say Elvis saved Felton's life by paying for his kidney transplant.

Harry Jenkins

RCA vice president "in charge of Elvis Presley."

Mary Jenkins

Elvis' cook at Graceland for many years.

"Jesus Knows What I Want"

(Mosie Lister)
Straightforward hymn done in impeccable style. Recorded in October of 1960 at RCA Nashville Studio; released in December of 1960 on the LP *His Hand In Mine.*

Jewelry

Elvis loved to give and to wear jewelry. He also impulsively gave away much of his own jewelry. When he first hit the big time, he bought himself a diamond horseshoe ring and an initial ring. His friend Judy Spreckles gave him a ring in 1956 that he kept until he became engaged to Priscilla, who used it as an engagement ring. It was a sapphire with four black stars. Onstage, he wore a handful of rings and sometimes told the audience about them. For instance, in Las Vegas in September, 1974, he mentioned that he was wearing the huge diamond ring he'd had for the *"Aloha"* TV show. He said, "It's an 11½-carat diamond, and there are some 16-carat dia-

Stoller, Elvis, Leiber; 1957.

monds all around it." He also mentioned that he was wearing a specially-designed ring that had pear-shaped and oval diamonds in it, and a blue star sapphire and diamond ring that a Japanese fan had given to him. In 1976, he spoke about a black diamond ring he had been trying to obtain for years. There were many more opulent rings over the years. He also liked to wear neck pendants. A special one was his diamond-studded Maltese Cross. He was also proud of the Bicentennial coin necklet Lisa made for him in 1976. Crosses and chokers, ankhs and initial pendants from the Hilton — Elvis wore them all. He had an identity bracelet with his name on it, another with his nickname, "Crazy" on it. All of his friends had similar bracelets with their nicknames. Perhaps the best-known item was his enormous TCB ring. In gold and diamonds supposedly taken from some of his mother's old jewelry, he wore this ring onstage in the mid-'70's, and it can be clearly seen in the *Elvis in Concert* TV special. (Copies can be bought in the Memphis souvenir shops.)

Elton John
British pop pianist-composer-performer was an admirer of Elvis' style over the years and was adored by Lisa Marie Presley. As her birthday present in 1975, Elvis invited John to Graceland.

Johnny
Elvis' character in *Frankie and Johnny* (1966).

"Johnny B. Goode"
(Chuck Berry)
Many thought that Chuck Berry must have written this important rock anthem to symbolize the glory of Elvis: the country boy strumming his guitar in the back woods who one day finds his name in lights. Elvis' version is a rouster, with lickety-split guitar by James Burton and the Imperials chiming in for the choruses. Recorded live at the International Hotel in Las Vegas on August 22, 1969; released in November of 1969 on the LP *From Memphis to Vegas/From Vegas to Memphis*. Other love versions were released on *Elvis In Person* (1970), *Aloha From Hawaii Via Satellite* (1973) and *Elvis In Concert* (1977).

Lyndon Baines Johnson
The first president to meet Elvis (he never met Eisenhower or Kennedy). LBJ visited Elvis on a whim one day on the location of *Spinout* (1966).

Rafer Johnson
Ex-Olympic decathlon champion and actor who played "Davis" in *Wild In The Country* (1961).

Carolyn Jones
The tight-skirted "Ronnie," a girl from the wrong side of the tracks (with the best legs in the State of Maine!) in *King Creole*, (1957).

Sgt. Ira Jones
Elvis' master sergeant while on manoeuvres in Germany.

Tom Jones ☞
Well known singer-entertainer from Wales, who rose to prominence during the late 1960's with a sexy nightclub act in Las Vegas and a TV show. Jones' stage movements, vocal style and popularity with women naturally invited comparison with Elvis, and the two men became friends over the years despite the unmistakable element of competition (they frequented each other's shows and exchanged gifts). It was Jones' recording of Curly Putnam's "Green, Green Grass of Home" in 1966 that deeply moved Elvis, who later recorded it. Elvis also recorded the Jones hits "Without Love" and "I'll Never Fall in Love Again." The two singers undoubtedly shared the same taste in music; Jones, likewise, covered Elvis hits like "Polk Salad Annie," "Proud Mary," and "You've Lost That Lovin' Feelin'."

The Jordanaires
The Jordanaires were a Nashville-based pop-gospel group who began singing with Elvis in 1956. Leader Gordon Stoker and Ben and Brock Speer were on Elvis' first Nashville session on January 10, 1956. The first proper group appearance of the Jordanaires was at the July 2, 1956 New York session that produced "Hound Dog," although they had appeared with him previously on the *Berle* and *Allen* TV shows. They sang on most of Elvis' discs until 1970, and appeared on the *Sullivan* TV shows, and in several movies, like *Loving You*, *King Creole*, and *GI Blues*. They toured with him in the '50's, and backed him on his 1961 benefit show. When Elvis returned to Vegas and began touring again, the group decided to stay in Nashville, where they were in demand as session singers. The Jordanaires' original lineup was Gordon Stoker (lead), Hoyt Hawkings (baritone), Neal Matthews (tenor), and Hugh Jarrett (bass). Ray Walker replaced Jarrett from June 1958 on. The group produced superb spirituals, barbershop quartet, and eventually, rock n' roll. The group was based in Nashville, ☞

originating from Springfield, Missouri. Their distinctive style, evident on hits like "Don't Be Cruel" and "Any Way You Want Me" became a trademark among vocal groups of the time. They have recorded with numerous other artists over the years, among them Marty Robbins and Rick Nelson. Most recently, they provided the authentic vocal backing for Ronnie McDowell's tracks for Dick Clark's production of *"Elvis."* The group still works in Nashville and can be heard on thousands of discs.

"Joshua Fit The Battle"
(Arranged and adapted by E. Presley)
Traditional spiritual delivered at a breathless pace. Recorded in October of 1960 at RCA Nashville Studio; released in December of 1960 on the LP *His Hand In Mine*.

June Juanico
Another reputed romantic interest of 1956, when Elvis played her home town of Biloxi, Mississippi.

Jubilee Four
Another vocal back-up group in *Viva Las Vegas* and *Girl Happy*.

"Judy"
(Teddy Redell)
Silky-smooth ballad with a sweeping feeling. Recorded in March of 1961 at RCA Nashville Studio; released in June of 1961 on the LP *Something For Everybody*.

Jumpsuits
Elvis' famous jumpsuits, designed by Bill Belew and others, became one of his many trademarks. Most were white with designs in gold studs and precious stones. Among those most identifiable were the American eagle (used for *"Aloha From Hawaii"*), Inca Gold Leaf (the final CBS TV special of 1977), Sundial, Burning Flame, Blue Aztec, Mad Tiger, King of Spades, and the Blue Rainbow.

"Just A Little Bit"
(Piney Brown — John Thornton — Earl Washington — Ralph Bass — D. Gordon)
An oldie resuscitated by Elvis and his crew for LP release, for-

merly hits by Roseve Gordon (1960) and Roy Head (1965). Recorded in July of 1973 at Stax Recording Studio in Memphis; released in November of 1973 on the LP *Raised on Rock*.

"Just Because"
(Bob Shelton – Joe Shelton – Sid Robin)
Sun oldie, a rockabilly touch recorded by Elvis, Scotty and Bill, processed by Sam Phillips and sung in a delicious stop/start manner. Recorded in September of 1954 at Sun Studios in Memphis; not released until March of 1956, when RCA included it on the LP *Elvis Presley*, his first. Later, on *The Sun Sessions*, (1976).

"Just Call Me Lonesome"
(Rex Griffin)
C & W touch with Hawaiian guitar from *Clambake*. Minor ballad. Recorded in February of 1967 at RCA Nashville Studio; released in November of 1967 on the soundtrack LP.

"Just For Old Time's Sake"
(Sid Tepper – Roy C. Bennett)
Old "Shep-style" ballad sung simply and with great style. Recorded March 18, 1972 at RCA Nashville Studio; released in June of 1962 on the LP *Pot Luck*.

Just For You
1957. RCA Victor. EP (EPA-4041)
Side 1: "I Need You So"; "Have I Told You Lately That I Love You."
Side 2: "Blueberry Hill"; "Is It So Strange."

"Just Pretend"
(Doug Glett – Guy Fletcher)
Strong ballad supplemented successfully by horns and strings. Recorded in June of 1970 at RCA Nashville Studio; released in December of 1970 on the soundtrack LP for *That's The Way It Is*. The song did not appear in the film.

"Just Tell Her Jim Said Hello"
(Jerry Leiber – Mike Stoller)
Ballad aimed at the teen market, with sad lyrics and Elvis firmly in command. Recorded in March of 1962 at RCA Nashville Studio; released in August of 1962 as the flip-side of "She's Not You"; Later, on *Elvis' Gold Records, Volume Four* (1968), and *The Other Sides: Worldwide Gold Award Hits, Volume Two* (1971).

Jackie Kahane
Elvis' comedian, who often opened his shows in Las Vegas and on tour during the later years. Also, one of the eulogizers at the funeral. Worked with Sophie Tucker and Wayne Newton before Elvis. Kahane was chosen because his jokes weren't "dirty" – they fit Elvis' image, and it was Jackie who delivered the line "Ladies and Gentlemen, Elvis has left the building" at the close of the Elvis Presley show.

Kahunas
Mystical Hawaiian "spiritual gods" and a part of Hawaiian mythology that fascinated Elvis because the Kahuna become, in Polynesian culture, the priests. He called Ed Parker "Kahuna."

Hal Kanter
Director of *Loving You* (1957).

Phil Karlson
Director of *Kid Galahad* (1962).

Sam Katzman
"The King of the Hollywood Quickie." He produced *Kissin' Cousins* (1964), *Harum Scarum* (1965).

Mike Keeton
A Memphis friend who worked for Elvis briefly in 1964. An acquaintance from the Assembly of God Church.

Estes Kefauver
Tennessee senator who inserted a tribute to Elvis in the Congressional Record when Elvis returned home from the Army.

Marion Keisker
Sam Phillips' assistant who met Elvis at the Memphis Record Service and kept mentioning him to her boss as a possible artist. A key figure in the magical process of how Elvis Presley came to the attention of the world.

Jack Kelly
Another undercover, private detective hired by Ed Hookstratten, Elvis' lawyer, to work with Jack O'Grady on the investigation of Elvis' drug sources in 1973.

Caroline Kennedy
The daughter of the late President showed up at Graceland on August 18, 1977, and was led into the wake in the music room because Elvis' family and associates assumed she was there privately. (Reports say her mother, Jacqueline, accompanied her.) However, she was covering the funeral for *Rolling Stone Magazine*, and her report appeared in their special tribute issue on Elvis in August of 1977.

Jerry Kennedy
A captain of the Denver police who once worked on tour with Dick Grob and got to know Elvis because of his endless fascination with law enforcement work. While vacationing in Vail in 1976, Elvis gave him a Lincoln.

"Kentucky Rain"
(Eddie Rabbitt – D. Heard)
A weary search for his girl, with the Memphis Strings simulating rain and the Blossoms providing sweet background, from the second round of Memphis sessions. Recorded in February of 1969 at American Studios; released that same month as a single with "My Little Friend" as the B-side. Later, on *Worldwide Gold Award Hits: Volume One* (1970).

Kirk Kerkorian
Las Vegas bigwig and friend of Colonel Parker, owner of the International Hotel, later the MGM Grand, who supported Elvis by signing him to play Vegas and by lending him his DC-9 jet for touring. Kirk Kerkorian is an Armenian immigrant who dabbled in the fruit growing and auto mechanics fields. Later became one of America's most prominent businessmen by acquiring controlling stock in Western Airlines and taking command of MGM before building the Las Vegas International Hotel and signing stars like Streisand and Elvis to perform for vast amounts of money. Kerkorian and Col. Parker were close at MGM. He eventually sold his hotel, only to take over the MGM Grand.

Stan Kessler
Steel guitarist. Composer of Sun Records during Elvis days, who toured briefly with Elvis. Wrote "Playing For Keeps" and co-wrote several other early recordings: "I'm Left, You're Right, She's Gone" (with Bill Taylor), and (with Charlie Fecthere) "I Forgot To Remember To Forget."

Kid Galahad
A United Artists Release 👉
Started: October 31, 1961
Cast
Walter Gulick: Elvis Presley; Willy Grogan: Gig Young; Dolly Fletcher: Lola Albright; Rose Grogan: Joan Blackman; Lew Nyack: Charles Bronson; Lieberman: Ned Glass;

Maynard: Robert Emhardt; Otto Danzig: David Lewis; Joie Shakes: Michael Dante; Zimmerman: Judson Pratt; Sperling: George Mitchell; Marvin: Richard Devon.
Credits
Producer: David Weisbart
Director: Phil Karlson
Screenplay by William Fay
Based on a Story by Francis Wallace
A Four Leaf Production
A Mirisch Co. Production
Color—Deluxe
Music by Jeff Alexander
Technical Advisor: Mushy Callahan
Songs
"King Of The Whole Wide World"; "This is Living"; "Riding The Rainbow"; "Home Is Where The Heart Is"; "I Got Lucky"; "A Whistling Tune"; "Love Is For Lovers" (cut)
  L. Albright
Running Time: 97 minutes

Kid Galahad
1962. RCA Victor. EP (EPA-4371).
Side 1. "King Of The Whole Wide World"; "This Is Living"; "Riding The Rainbow."
Side 2: "Home Is Where The Heart Is"; "I Got Lucky"; "A Whistling Tune."

Killeem, Texas
Where Elvis lived with his parents in a small house while stationed at Fort Hood during his basic training in the summer of 1958. It was at Killeem that Gladys Presley became gravely ill with hepatitis.

B.B. King
Mississippi-born blues guitarist, singer and composer who recorded on the Sun label before Elvis and played the Beele Street clubs, influencing Elvis during his high school years.

King Creole
Started: January 13, 1958
A Paramount Picture
Cast
Danny Fisher: Elvis Presley; Ronnie: Carolyn Jones; Nellie: Dolores Hart; Mr. Fisher: Dean Jagger; "Forty" Nina: Lilliane Montevecchi; Maxie Fields: Walter Matthau; Mimi Fisher: Jan Shepard; Charles LeGrand: Paul Stewart; Shark: Vic Morrow; Sal: Brian Hutton
Credits
A Hal Wallis Production
Directed by Michael Curtiz
Screenplay by Herbert Baker and Michael Vincente Gazzo
From a book by Harold Robbins
Technical Advisor: Col. T. Parker
Songs
"As Long As I Have You"; "Crawfish"; "King Creole"; "Don't Ask Me Why"; "New Orleans";

"Love Doll"; "Hard-Headed Woman"; "Trouble"; "Steadfast, Loyal And True"; "Young Dreams"; "Danny" (cut) (unreleased); "Dixieland Rock"; "Banana" (Lilliane Montevecchi);
Running Time: 116 minutes
Previously Titled:
Sing You Sinners

"King Creole"
(Jerry Leiber – Mike Stoller) Difficult phrasing pulled off magnificently, with Elvis playing guitar – from the film. Recorded in January of 1958 in Hollywood; released in August of 1958 on the sound track LP, and in October on the EP. Later, on the LP *The Other Sides: Worldwide Gold Award Hits, Volume II*, (1971).

King Creole
1958. RCA Victor. LP (LPM-1884).
Side 1: "King Creole"; "As Long As I Have You"; "Hard Headed Woman"; "Trouble"; "Dixieland Rock."
Side 2: "Don't Ask Me Why"; "Lover Doll"; "Crawfish"; "Young Dreams"; "Steadfast, Loyal And True"; "New Orleans."

King Creole
1958. RCA Victor. EP (EPA-4319).
Side 1: "King Creole"; "New Orleans."
Side 2: "As Long As I Have You"; "Lover Doll."

King Creole Volume Two
1958. RCA Victor. EP (EPA-4321).
Side 1: "Trouble"; "Young Dreams."
Side 2: "Crawfish"; "Dixieland Rock."

King Creole
33⅓ LP Bootleg.
Side 1: "King Creole"; "As Long As I Have You"; "Hard-Headed

Woman"; "Trouble"; "Dixieland Rock."
Side 2: "Don't Ask Me Why"; "Lover Doll"; "Crawfish"; "Young Dreams"; "Steadfast, Loyal And True"; "New Orleans."

The King Goes Wild
33⅓ LP Bootleg.
Side 1: September 9, 1956 – "Don't Be Cruel"; "Love Me Tender"; "Ready Teddy"; "Hound Dog"; October 28, 1956 – "Don't Be Cruel"; "Love Me Tender"; "Love Me"; "Hound Dog."
Side 2: January 6, 1957 – "Hound Dog"; "Love Me Tender"; "Heartbreak Hotel"; "Don't Be Cruel"; "Too Much"; "When My Blue Moon Turns To Gold Again"; "Peace In The Valley."

King Of Rock N' Roll
45 EPA Bootleg.
"Blue Suede Shoes"; "One-Sided Love Affair"; "Hound Dog"; "Ready Teddy"; "Baby, I Don't

181

Care"; "Got A Lot O' Living To Do."

"King Of The Whole Wide World"
Happy-go-lucky rocker from *Kid Galahad* with a Boots Randolph sax break. Recorded in October of 1961 in Hollywood; released in September of 1962 as the soundtrack EP.

"The King Of Western Bop"
Another of Elvis' headlining specials during his earlier years on the road, which illustrated the combining of two styles of music—rhythm and blues with country.

Jimmy Kingsley
Stuntman and bodyguard who was an intermittent part of the "Memphis Mafia" over the years.

Jimmy Kingsley
The reporter on the *Memphis Commercial Appeal* who came from Elvis' neighborhood in North Memphis and saw him socially over the years.

Millie Kirkham
Vocalist backing Elvis on his Christmas album of 1957 and on *Clambake* (1967), later singing with him "live" in Las Vegas. All in all, she sang with him for 15 years.

"Kismet"
(Sid Tepper – Roy C. Bennett). From *Harum Scarum*, one of the more palatable tunes, sung in deep voice. Recorded in February of 1965 in Hollywood; released in October of 1965 as the soundtrack LP.

Kissin' Cousins
A Four Leaf Production
An MGM Picture
Cast
Josh Morgan: Elvis Presley; Jodie Tatum: Elvis Presley; Pappy Tatum: Arthur O'Connell; Ma Tatum: Glenda Farrell; Capt. Robert Salbo: Jack Albertson; Selina Tatum: Pam Austin; Midge: Cynthia Pepper; Azalea Tatum: Yvonne Craig; General Alvin Donford: Donald Woods; Master Sgt. Bailey: Tommy Farrell; Prudy: Beverly Powers; Dixie: Hortense Patra; General's Aide: Robert Stone.

Credits
Produced by Sam Katzman
Directed by Gene Nelson
Music supervised and conducted by Fred Karger
Choreographed by Hal Belfer
Screenplay by Gerald Drayson Adams and Gene Nelson
Story by Gerald Drayson Adams
Assistant Director: Eli Dunn
Recording Supervisor: Franklin Milton
Technical Advisor: Col. Tom Parker

Hair Styles by Sydney Guilaroff
Panavision & Metrocolor
Songs
"Smokey Mountain Boy"; "Once Is Enough"; "Kissin' Cousins"; "One Boy, Two Little Girls"; "Tender Feelings"; "Catchin' On Fast"; "There's Gold In The Mountains"; "Barefoot Ballad"; "Kissin' Cousins" (No. 2); "Pappy, Won't You Please Come Home" (Glenda Farrell); "Anyone Could Fall In Love With You" (cut); "It Hurts Me" (cut)
Running Time: 96 minutes

"Kissin' Cousins"
(Fred Wise – Randy Starr)
The first version of the song is a rocker with a good beat, a sax break and wailing guitars. Recorded in October of 1963 in Hollywood; released in March of 1964 as a single, with "It Hurts Me" on the B-side. Later, on the LP *Worldwide Gold Award Hits, Volume 1*, (1970).

"Kissin' Cousins"
(Number Two) (Bill Giant – Bernie Bloom – Florence Kaye).
The second version is the title song of the film, speeded up, with inferior lyrics to version one. Recorded in October of 1963 in Hollywood; released in March of 1964 on the soundtrack LP.

Kissin' Cousins
1964. RCA Victor. LP (LPM/LSP-2894).
Side 1: "Kissin' Cousins (No. 2)"; "Smokey Mountain Boy"; "There's Gold In The Mountains"; "One Boy, Two Little Girls"; "Catchin' On Fast"; "Tender Feeling."
Side 2: "Anyone (Could Fall In Love With You)"; "Barefoot Ballad"; "Kissin' Cousins"; "Echoes Of Love"; "(It's A) Lonely Highway."

"Kiss Me Quick"
(Doc Pomus – Mort Schuman) Fast tempo, fast cut—with the Jords. Recorded in June of 1961 at RCA Nashville Studio; released in June of 1962 on the LP *Pot Luck.*

George Klein
The president of Elvis' high school class at L.C. Humes High, and an early member of his entourage. In the Sixties, he became a popular disc-jockey at WHBQ in Memphis and remained a loyal friend to the end. Also introduced Elvis to Linda Thompson and Ginger Alden.

"Known Only To Him"
(Stuart Homblen)
Sacred tune with Elvis in his most devout form. Recorded in October of 1960 at RCA Nashville Studio; released in December of 1960 on the LP *His Hand In Mine.*

Larry Krectal
Session bassist on Elvis' television special, (1968).

Kris Kristofferson
Athlete, Rhodes Scholar, boxer, helicopter pilot in Vietnam, author, singer, songwriter, and successful actor, who was one of the songwriters out of the "Nashville Sound" who Elvis came to admire in his later years. Kristofferson ended up with the role originally offered to Elvis in the Streisand-Jon Peters production of *A Star Is Born.* Elvis recorded Kristof-

ferson's "For The Good Times," "Why Me Lord," and "Help Me Make It Through The Night."

"Ku-Li-I-Po" (Hawaiian Sweetheart)
(Hugh Peretti – Luigi Creatore – George Weiss)
One of the prettiest, most pretentious tunes from *Blue Hawaii*, sung slowly with a flourish of guitars at the finale. Recorded in April of 1961 in Hollywood; released in October of 1961 on the soundtrack LP.

Toby Kwimper
Elvis' character in *Follow That Dream* (1967).

Marty Lacker
Elvis' personal secretary and book-keeper from 1960 until 1967 and one of the co-best men at his wedding. Ran a recording studio in Memphis and eventually published the book, *Elvis: Portrait of a Friend*, detailing their relationship.

Patsy Lacker
Marty Lacker's wife, contributed the tart-tongued "Wife was a Four-Letter Word" section of the book, *Elvis: Portrait of a Friend.*

"The Lady Loves Me"
Elvis' humorous duet with Ann-Margret in *Viva Las Vegas* (1964), which was never released for contractual reasons but which appears on the bootleg LP *Viva Las Vegas.*

Elsa Lanchester
Veteran actress of the stage and screen who played "Madame Neherina" in *Easy Come, Easy Go*, (1967).

Angela Lansbury
"Sarah Lee Gates," Elvis' stuffy mother in *Blue Hawaii* (1961).

Jocelyn Lane
Actress who played "Pam," the voluptuous physical education instructress on the dude ranch who slowly melts towards Elvis in *Tickle Me* (1965).

Hope Lange
"Irene Sperry," the psychologist and "older woman" Elvis fell for in *Wild In The Country* (1961).

Lansky Brothers
The clothing store on the corner of Second Street and Beale Street, where Elvis admired the pink sports coats and which provided the threads for his legendary loud outfits as a high school student.

Mario Lanza
Elvis' operatic idol, who made *The Great Caruso* and *One Night Of Love*, two films Elvis enjoyed.

Lao-Tzu
The Chinese mystic who Elvis frequently read during his later years for pearls of wisdom.

"La Paloma"
One of the songs cut from the print of *Blue Hawaii*, unreleased on any record, legitimate or bootleg.

Las Vegas International Hotel (Las Vegas Hilton)
The site of Elvis' stunning return to live performances on July 31, 1969 (Elvis performed in the hotel's 2,600 capacity showroom as the second major act after Barbra Streisand had opened the hotel earlier that month). He received $1 million for a four-week engagement and made two more engagements before Barron Hilton bought the hotel in 1971 and it became part of his worldwide chain. Between 1971-1976, Elvis had thirteen engagements at the Las Vegas Hilton, setting all attendance records.

John Lepley
The DJ on WHHM in Memphis, who, in July of 1954, did for "Blue Moon Of Kentucky" on his country show what Dewey Phillips did for the record's flip-side ("That's All Right Mama") on his WHBQ show *Red Hot and Blue*, by giving the record its first serious exposure. He also booked Elvis' first appearance at the Eagle's Nest.

"Let It Be Me (Je T'Appartiens)"
(Mann Curtis – Gilbert Becaud) Romantic ballad and former hits for the Everly Brothers (1960), The Sweet Inspirations (1967), Glen Campbell and Bobbie Gentry (1969). Charlie Hodge

sings a duet and the Sweet soar in the background (Elvis leaves the crescendo to them). Recorded live at the International Hotel in Las Vegas on February 17, 1970; released in May of 1970 on the LP *Elvis On Stage, February 1970*.

"Let Me"
(Elvis Presley – Vera Motson) The fairground scene from *Love Me Tender*. Pure C & W singing style. Recorded in August of 1956 in Hollywood; released in November of 1956, on the EP *Elvis Presley*.

"Let Me Be There"
(John Rostill) The Olivia Newton-John hit, served up by Elvis and his home-town clan. Recorded live at Mid-South Coliseum in Memphis on March 20, 1974; released in June of 1974 on the LP *Elvis Recorded Live Onstage In Memphis*.

"Let's Be Friends"
(Arnold – Morrow – Martin) Piano, acoustic guitar, and a mellow Elvis in a forgettable tune from *Change of Habit*. Nothing unusual or outstanding. Recorded in March of 1969 at MCA Studio in Hollywood; released in April of 1970 on the Camden LP *Let's Be Friends*.

Let's Be Friends
1970. RCA Camden. LP (CAS-2408).
Side 1: "Stay Away Joe"; "If I'm A Fool (For Loving You)"; "Let's Be Friends"; "Let's Forget About The Stars"; "Mama."
Side 2: "I'll Be There (If Ever You Want Me)"; "Almost"; "Change Of Habit"; "Have A Happy."

"Let's Forget About The Stars"
(A.L. Owens) Another cut-rate, overly-long opus probably left out of *Change Of Habit*. Recorded in March of 1969 at MCA Studio in Hollywood; released in April of 1970 on the Camden LP *Let's Be Friends*.

"Let Us Pray"
(Ben Weisman – Florence Kaye) A "pop" spiritual by a songwriting team for his films. Doesn't work. Recorded in September of 1969; released in March of 1971 on the Camden LP *You'll Never Walk Alone*.

Kui Lee
Hawaiian singer and composer who died of cancer in 1966. Elvis sang his classic song "I'll Remember You" and donated the gate proceeds from the satellite show "Aloha" to the Kui Lee Cancer Fund.

Mike Leech
Bass guitarist for several of

Elvis' recording sessions, including those in Memphis, 1969.

Lance Le Gault
One of the early Elvis cronies and a musician in his own right who became his film double. He can be viewed in a scene in *Kissin' Cousins* (1963), a reverse shot with his face toward the camera instead of Elvis'.

"The Legend Lives"
The short lived Broadway show of 1978, based on Elvis' life and starring impersonator Rick Saucedo. Despite a score by Doc Pomus and others and the added authenticity of Kathy Westmoreland and the Jordanaires onstage, the show lasted a scant two months.

The Legend Lives On
33⅓ LP Bootleg.
Side 1: "Las Vegas, 1969: Elvis Talks About His Career"; "Yesterday/Hey Jude Medley"; "Introduction And Happy Birthday" (James Burton); "In The Ghetto;" "Suspicious Minds."
Side 2: ""What'd I Say"; "Can't Help Falling In Love"; "It's Over" (Vegas, 1972); "A Big Hunk O' Love" (Vegas, 1972); "It's Impossible" (Vegas, 1972); "The Impossible Dream" (Vegas, 1972); "Bridge Over Troubled Water" (studio, January 5, 1970)."

Legendary Concert Performances
1978. RCA Victor Record Club. LP (R-244047).
Side 1: "Blue Suede Shoes"; "Sweet Caroline"; "Burning Love"; "Runaway"; "My Babe."
Side 2: "Johnny B. Goode"; "Yesterday"; "Medley: Mystery Train/Tiger Man"; "You Gave Me A Mountain"; "Never Been To Spain."
Side 3: "C.C. Rider"; "Words"; "Proud Mary"; "Walk A Mile In My Shoes"; "Steamroller Blues."
Side 4: "Polk Salad Annie"; "Something"; "Let It Be Me (Je T'Appartiens)"; "The Impossible Dream"; "My Way."

Jerry Leiber And Mike Stoller
One of rock n' roll's most successful songwriting duos, who penned scores of hits for Elvis and others over the years (Stoller was a fair piano-player, himself, performing with Elvis on the recording and in the film of *Jailhouse Rock*. They also wrote "Trouble," "Love Me," "Hound Dog," "Loving You," "Treat Me Nice," "Girls! Girls! Girls!," "Bossa Nova Baby," "Just Tell Her Jim Said Hello," "Little Egypt," "Hot Dog," "She's Not You," "Dirty, Dirty Feeling," and "(You're So Square) Baby I Don't Care."

Suzanne Leigh
"Judy Hudson," amateur pilot and love interest of *Paradise – Hawaiian Style* (1965).

Last Farewell, The
33⅓ LP Bootleg on E.P. Records containing Elvis' ninety-minute concert at the Market Square Arena in Indianapolis, Indiana (June 26, 1977).
Side 1: "2001 Space Odyssey"; "C.C. Rider"; "I Got A Woman"; "Amen"; "Love Me"; "Fairy Tale."
Side 2: "You Gave Me A Mountain"; "Jailhouse Rock"; "O Sole Mio"; "It's Now Or Never"; "Little Sister"; "Teddy Bear"; "Don't Be Cruel"; "Release Me"; "I Can't Stop Loving You."
Side 3: "Bridge Over Troubled Water"; "Introduction To The Backing Vocals"; "Early Morning Rain"; "What'd I Say"; "Johnny B. Goode"; "TCB Band Theme"; "Blues A La Scheff"; "Two Miles Pike."
Side 4: "I Really Don't Want To Know"; "Bobby's Choice"; "Jazzing In Vegas"; "Hurt"; "Hound Dog"; "Introduction"; "Can't Help Falling In Love"; "Closing Vamp."

Abe Lastfogel
President of the sprawling William Morris Agency over the years and personal friend of Colonel Tom Parker. Lastfogel represented Elvis as his "personal agent."

Lauderdale Courts
The red brick, low rent housing projects run by the Memphis Housing Authority at 185 Winchester Street, where the Presleys moved after 572 Poplar Avenue. They lived in a two bedroom, ground floor apartment.

Charlie Laughton
The famous stage and film actor who was Ed Sullivan's substitute host for Elvis' first appearance on the show – September 9, 1956. (Sullivan had been in an auto accident.)

"Lawdy Miss Clawdy"
(Lloyd Price) Elvis' unique revival of the Lloyd Price hit stands up beautifully today – soulful, funky, with a nice Shorty Long piano touch. From Elvis' second group of RCA sessions. Recorded in February of 1956, at RCA New York Studio; released in August of 1956 as the B-side of "Shake, Rattle And Roll," and on the EP *Shake, Rattle and Roll*. Later, on the LP *For LP Fans Only* (1959). Elvis does a hoarse, loud version of it for his *1968 TV Special*, which appears on *Elvis (NBC-TV Special)* (1968), and another version appears on *Elvis Recorded Live Onstage in Memphis*.

Douglas Lawrence
Produced *Speedway* (1968).

"Lead Me, Guide Me"
(Doris Askers)
Unadorned, straight forward spiritual, nicely colored by Elvis. Seen in rehearsal in the *On Tour* film (1972). Recorded in May of 1971 at RCA Nashville Studio; released in April of 1972 on the LP *He Touched Me*.

Le Disque D'Or
1978. RCA French Import. LP (6886 807).
Side 1: "C'Mon Everybody"; "A Whistling Tune"; "I'll Be There (If You Want Me)"; "I Love Only One Girl"; "Easy Come, Easy Go"; "Santa Lucia."
Side 2: "Tonight Is So Right For Love"; "Guadalajara"; "Angel"; "A Little Less Conversation"; "Follow That Dream"; "Long Legged Girl."

Live Experience In Vegas . . . February, 1971
33⅓ LP Bootleg. Released on the Bonthand label. Made in Canada, although it is stated that it was made in Holland.
Side 1: "That's All Right"; "I Got A Woman"; "Jailhouse Rock"; "Love Me"; "Mystery Train"; "Tiger Man"; "Polk Salad Annie"; "Sweet Caroline"; "You've Lost That Loving Feeling"; "Something."
Side 2: "How Great Thou Art"; "Don't Be Cruel"; "Heartbreak Hotel"; "Blue Suede Shoes"; "Little Sister"; "Get Back"; "Now Or Never"; "Hound Dog"; "The Impossible Dream"; "Johnny B. Goode."

Live Experience In Vegas . . . February 1971
33⅓ LP Bootleg.
Side 1: "That's All Right"; "I Got A Woman"; "Jailhouse Rock"; "Love Me"; "Mystery Train"; "Tiger Man"; "Polk Salad Annie"; "Sweet Caroline"; "You've Lost That Loving Feeling"; "Something"; "Johnny B. Goode."
Side 2: "How Great Thou Art"; "Don't Be Cruel"; "Heartbreak Hotel"; "Blue Suede Shoes"; "Little Sister"; "Get Back"; "Now Or Never"; "Hound Dog"; "The Impossible Dream."

Harold Lloyd
Elvis' cousin and long-time security guard at Graceland, on duty the morning of Elvis' death. Co-author of *The Gates of Graceland*.

Robert Lloyd
Harold's son, and another security guard at Graceland.

"Let Yourself Go"
(Joy Byers)
From *Speedway*, a mid-tempo,

girl-chasing song that is only a cut above the film fare of the 1960's. Recorded in June of 1967 in Hollywood; released in June of 1968 as a single with "Your Time Hasn't Come Yet, Baby." Also, on the soundtrack LP (1968).

Harry Levitch
Memphis jeweler, who, along with Lowell Hays, received an enormous amount of business whenever Elvis was in a generous mood to family, friends and associates. Levitch's jewels became a symbol of life around Elvis over the years.

Levy – Gardner – Levin
Producers of *Clambake* (1967).

Henri Lewin
Hilton Vice-President who negotiated Elvis' Las Vegas performances, 1973–74.

George Lewis
Graceland security guard.

Jerry Lee Lewis
"The Killer." One of the great, originals of rock n' roll and one of Sam Phillips' artists on Sun during and after Elvis, who recorded such classics as the piano-pounding "Whole Lotta Shakin' Goin On." Over the years, his relationship with Elvis was cordial but distant: Jerry Lee, people say, always resented Elvis for stealing his thunder and felt he deserved to be "King." In the early days, he played piano on recordings like "Blueberry Hill."

Paulette Shafer Lewis
A member of the Graceland pool of secretaries, one of the daughters of Paul Shafer of the Malco movie chain in Memphis.

Smiley Lewis
R & B artist of the 1950's who wrote "Blue Monday," "I Hear You Knocking," and "One Night Of Sin," which Elvis recorded and cleaned up as "One Night" in 1956 (it was about an orgy). He later revived the song with great effectiveness on the 1968 NBC Special.

Paul Lichter
Self-proclaimed "Elvisologist" – author of two comprehensive works: *Elvis In Hollywood* and *The Boy Who Dared To Rock: The Definite Elvis*. One of the largest retailers of rare Elvis records and memorabilia and publisher-editor of *The Memphis Flash*.

Frank Lieberman
Entertainment writer for the *Los Angeles Herald Examiner* whose rave review of Elvis' Vegas show in February of 1972 prompted Elvis to give one of his last one-on-one interviews.

"Life"
(Shirl Milete)
The story of earth from formation through decline to the hope of love. Fancy arrangement but doesn't sparkle like a true spiritual. Recorded in June of 1970 at RCA Nashville Studio; released in May of 1971 as a single, with "Only Believe" as the B-side.

"Like A Baby"
(Jesse Stone)
Bluesy and jazzy with Boots Randolph wailing on sax. Recorded in April of 1960 at RCA Nashville Studio; released in April of 1960 on the LP *Elvis Is Back.*

Yvonne Lime
Co-star of *Loving You* and a brief romantic interest in Elvis' life. Before his induction, she visited Graceland and met his family. ☞

Dennis Linde
Composer-guitarist who played bass on several recording sessions of the 1970's and wrote "Burning Love," which Elvis recorded in 1972.

Lisa Marie
The 1.2 million dollar Convair 880 jet Elvis bought in 1975 and named for his daughter. He turned it into his touring plane by making a bedroom in the rear, a conference room, and a lounge, and it required a crew of four. A giant TCB with a gold lightning bolt underneath decor-

ated the tail. The air-call sign was "Hound Dog One." The plane had a range of 3,000 miles. Elvis called it the pride of "Elvis Presley Airways," his fleet of planes. Purchased in 1975 from Nigel Winfield for $1,000,000, Elvis remodeled it into his touring plane for another $750,000.

"Little Cabin On The Hill"
(Bill Monroe – Lester Flatt)
Reminiscent of Dylan's return to C & W basics, with fiddle and all the trimmings of a hoedown, and Elvis' laughter. Recorded in June of 1970 at RCA Nashville Studio; released in February, 1971 on the LP *Elvis Country.*

"Little Darlin' "
(Maurice Williams)
From Elvis' last recording session, April 25, 1977, comes this oldie from the man who wrote "Stay." Released in July of 1977 on the LP *Moody Blue.*

"Little Egypt"
(Jerry Leiber – Mike Stoller)
The "humor" track from *Roustabout* with sax and "strange yick-yicks" in the background. Recorded in January of 1964 on the soundtrack LP. A portion of the song, with a quiet, spoken finish, was included on the *1968 TV Special,* and appears on the LP *Elvis NBC-TV Special* (1968).

"My Little Friend"
(Shirl Milete)

From the Memphis sessions, Elvis reminiscing about his first girl friend. Memphis Strings. Recorded on January 16, 1969, at American Studios; released in February of 1970, as the flip-side of "Kentucky Rain." Later, on the Camden LP *Almost In Love* (1970), reissued on the Pickwick label in 1976.

"Little Sister"
(Doc Pomus – Mort Schuman) Catchy R & B number with excellent vocal treatment by Elvis, bending his voice up and down the scale. Recorded in June of 1961 at RCA Nashville Studio; released in August of 1961 as a single, with "(Marie's the Name) His Latest Flame" as the B-side. The song was performed in the documentary *That's The Way It Is* (1970) but didn't appear on the soundtrack LP. It appeared on the following LPs: *Elvis' Golden Records, Volume 3* (1963), *Worldwide 50 Gold Award Hits, Vol. 1* (1970). A live version was released on *Elvis In Concert* (1977).

Live A Little, Love A Little
Started: March, 1968.
An MGM Film
Cast
Greg Nolan: Elvis Presley; Bernice: Michelle Carey; Mike Lansdown: Don Porter; Penlow: Rudy Vallee; Harry: Dick Sargent; Milkman: Sterling Holloway; Ellen: Celeste Yarnall; Delivery boy: Eddie Hodges; Robbie's mother: Joan Shawlee; Mermaid: Susan Henning
Credits
Produced by Douglas Laurence
Directed by Norman Taurog
Screenplay by Michael A. Hoey and Dan Greenburg
Based on the novel *Kiss My Firm But Pliant Lips* by Dan Greenburg.
Panavision and Metrocolor.
Songs
"Almost In Love"; "A Little Less Conversation"; "Edge Of Reality"; "Wonderful World."
Running time: 89 minutes

Local Board 86
Where Elvis was inducted into the Army in Memphis on the morning of March 24, 1958.

Dixie Locke
Elvis' high school sweetheart and date for the senior prom, a raven-haired little girl who called it quits with Elvis when he began touring with Scotty and Bill in the early days.

Gary Lockwood
"Danny Burke," Elvis' gambling co-pilot in *It Happened At The World's Fair* (1963), and a fellow football player during the 1960's.

Lowes State Theater
Where Elvis worked as an usher in 1950 briefly, until fired for taking a punch at a fellow employee.

Ed Logan
Session hornman, Memphis, 1969.

Rocco Loginestra
President of RCA in the 1970's, and the man presiding over the ever-growing mountain that formed Elvis' catalogue of products.

Carol Lombard Quartet
One of the vocal backup groups on *Viva Las Vegas* and *Girl Happy.*

Guy Lombard
Elvis' character in *Double Trouble* (1967).

Larrie Londin
The drummer who filled in for Ronnie Tutt on Elvis' last few tours.

"Lonely Man"
(Benny Benjamin – Sol Marcus) Soulful ballad recorded for *Wild In The Country* (1961) but cut from the film. Recorded in November of 1960, in Hollywood; released in February of 1961 as a single, the flip-side of "Surrender." Later, on the LP *Elvis' Golden Records, Vol. 4* (1968) and *Worldwide Gold Award Hits, Vol. 2* (1971).

"Lonesome Cowboy"
(Sid Tepper – Roy C. Bennett) Dramatic C & W number from *Loving You* (1957) with vocal tricks. Recorded in February of

Live A Little, Love A Little.

185

1957 in Hollywood; released in July of 1957 on the LP *Loving You*. Also on the EP *Loving You, Volume 2* (1957) and later on the LP *Worldwide Gold Award Hits, Vol. 2* (1971).

Shorty Long
Piano player in several of Elvis' early RCA sessions in 1956.

"Long Black Limousine"
(Vern Stovall – Bobby George) Elvis' interpretation of a C & W weeper about deceased love and the seduction of success. With horns, the Memphis Strings and vocals by the Holladays. Recorded in January of 1969 at American Studios in Memphis; released in May of 1969 on the LP *From Elvis in Memphis*.

"Long Legged Girl (With The Short Dress On)"
(J. Leslie McForland – Winfield Scott)
From *Double Trouble*, 1967, a short rocker with crisp lyrics and clever vocals by the Jords, bringing back memories of the good ole days at RCA. Recorded in June of 1966 in Hollywood; released in May of 1967 as a single, with "That's Someone You Never Forget" on the flipside. Later, on the soundtrack LP *Double Trouble*, the Camden LPs *Almost In Love* (1970, released by Pickwick in 1976), *Elvis Sings Hits From His Movies, Vol. 1* (1971, later released by Pickwick).

"(It's A) Long Lonesome Highway"
(Doc Pomus – Mort Schuman)
From *Tickle Me* (1965), a rocking number sung in Elvis' lowest voice, with the Jordanaires. Recorded in May of 1963 at RCA Nashville Studio; released in March of 1964 on the LP *Kissin' Cousins*.

"Long Tall Sally"
(Enotris Johnson – Richard Penniman – Robert Blackwell) Elvis' version of the Little Richard smash was every bit as fast, furious and naughty. Recorded in September of 1956 at Radio Recorders in Hollywood; released in November of 1956 on the EP *Elvis*. Also on the EP *Strictly Elvis* (1957). Sizzling live versions appear on the LPs *Aloha From Elvis In Hawaii Via Satellite* (1973) and *Elvis Recorded Live Onstage In Memphis* (1974).

"Look Out Broadway"
(Fred Wise – Randy Starr)
Comic music-hall number from *Frankie and Johnny* (1965) with Donna Douglas. Recorded in May of 1965 at United Artists' Recording Studio in Los Angeles; released in April of 1965 on the soundtrack LP.

Jack Lord
One of Elvis' favorite TV stars over the years, and another good friend.

Louisiana Hayride
Saturday night country radio broadcast from Shreveport, Louisiana on KWKH where Elvis appeared regularly from the fall of 1954 (Oct. 16) to December of 1955. His contract paid him eighteen dollars a show (Scotty and Bill made six dollars less). The drummer of the show, D. J. Fontanna, became Elvis' studio drummer in 1955. Elvis also appeared on the *Louisiana Hayride* television show March 5, 1955.

Darlene Love
Former lead singer of the Crystals who joined the Blossoms, who backed Elvis on the *1968 NBC-TV Special* and added her voice to cuts like "Guitar Man."

"Love Coming Down"
(Jerry Chesnut)
A sweet ballad recorded in the Graceland den – a wistful cut. Recorded in February of 1976; released in May of 1976 on the LP *From Elvis Presley Boulevard, Memphis, Tennessee*.

"Love Is For Lovers"
A Ruth Batchelor – Sharon Gilbert tune recorded for *Kid Galahad* but not used in the film or released on record.

"Love Me, Love The Life I Lead"
(Macaulay – Greenaway)
Don't try to change me, Elvis says in this cut. Nondescript, and nothing new, despite being a timely and topical song considering Elvis and Priscilla at the time. Recorded in May of 1971 at RCA Nashville Studio; released in June of 1973 on the LP *Elvis*.

Love Me Tender
A 20th Century Fox Production
Cast
Vance: Richard Egan; Cathy: Debra Paget; Clint: Elvis Presley; Siringo: Robert Middleton; Brett Reno: William Campbell; Mike Gavin: Neville Brand; The Mother: Mildred Dunnock; Major Kincaid: Bruce Bennett; Ray Reno: James Drury; Ed Galt: Russ Conway; Kelso: Ken Clark; Davis: Barry Coe; Fleming: L. Q. Jones; Jethro: Paul Burns; Train Conductor: Jerry Sheldon.
Credits
Produced by David Weisbart
Directed by Robert D. Webb
Screenplay by Robert Buckner
Based on a story by Maurice Geraghty
Music by Lionel Newman
Assistant Director: Stanley Hough

Technical Advisor: Colonel Tom Parker
Hair Styles by Helen Turpin, C.H.S.
Sound by Alfred Bruzlin and Harry M. Leonard, Songs by Elvis Presley and Vera Motson
Songs
"Love Me Tender"; "Poor Boy"; "We're Gonna Move"; "Let Me".
Vocal Supervision by Ken Darby
Orchestration by Edward B. Powell
Running Time: 89 minutes
Previously titled: *The Reno Brothers*

"Love Me Tender"
(Elvis Presley – Vera Motson)
What can one say? From the film of the same name, the quintessential Elvis Presley ballad, backed by Ken Darby's Trio (Darby actually composed the tune, basing it on an actual Civil War ballad called "Aura Lee" but publishing concerns caused him to give writing credit to his wife, Vera Motson, and Elvis). Recorded in August of 1956 in Hollywood; released in October of 1956 as a single, with "Any Way You Want Me" on the flipside. (The film version had one extra verse.) Elvis performed this song on all three appearances on the *Ed Sullivan Show*, on other important TV broadcasts and in documentary films. Elvis actually said he disliked the cut because of flat singing in parts, but there were a million advance orders before its recording! Recorded in August of 1956 in Hollywood; released in October of 1956 as a single, with "Any Way You Want Me" as its flip-side. It appeared on the EP *Love Me Tender* (1956) and on several LPs: *Elvis' Golden Records* (1958), *Worldwide 50 Gold Award Hits, Vol. 1* (1970), *A Legendary Performer, Vol. 1* (1974) and *Pure Gold* (1975). The song was also performed on the *1968 NBC-TV Special* (it appears on the LP *Elvis**TV Special*) and in both concert documentaries, *That's The Way It Is* (1970) and *On Tour* (1972), though these versions were unreleased on record. An additional live version appears on the LP *Elvis As Recorded At Madison Square Garden* (1972).

Love Me Tender
1956. RCA Victor. EP (EPA-4006).
Side 1: "Love Me Tender"; "Let Me."
Side 2: "Poor Boy"; "We're Gonna Move."

"Love Me Tonight"
(Dan Robertson)
Typical El balladeering, with

Jordanaires. Recorded in May of 1963 at RCA Nashville Studio; released in November of 1963 on the soundtrack LP *Fun In Acapulco* (it wasn't performed in the film).

"Lover Doll"
(Sid Wayen – Abner Silver)
The song Elvis sings in *King Creole* (1958) in the five-and-dime to distract the people while Vic Morrow loots the place. Recorded in January of 1958 in Hollywood; released in August of 1958 on the LP *King Creole* (a different version – shorter, minus the Jords – was released on the EP *King Creole, Vol. 1*). Later, on *Worldwide Gold Award Hits, Volume 2* (1971).

"Love Letters"
(Edward Hayman – Victor Young)
The Ketty Lester hit of 1962 revived, as it stands, by Elvis. Elvis' vocals are clear as a bell. Nice Floyd Cramer piano and vocals by the Imperials. Recorded in May of 1966 at RCA Nashville Studio; released in June of 1966 as a single with "Come What May" on the flip-side. Elvis cut another version in June of 1970 at RCA Nashville Studio which substituted quiet strings for the organ and features a stronger, deeper vocal track. It was released on the LP *Love Letters From Elvis* in June of 1971. The original single was also collected on *Elvis' Gold Records, Volume 4* (1968).

Love Letters From Elvis
1971. RCA. LP (LSP-4530).
Side 1: "Love Letters"; "When I'm Over You"; "If I Were You"; "Got My Mojo Working"; "Heart Of Rome."
Side 2: "Only Believe"; "This Is Our Dance"; "Cindy Cindy"; "I'll Never Know"; "It Ain't No Big Thing"; "Life."

"Lovely Mamie"
Short ditty From *Stay Away, Joe* with guitar, never released on record by RCA. It appears on the bootleg LP *From Hollywood To Vegas.*

"The Love Machine"
(Gerald Nelson – Fred Burch – Chuck Taylor)
Relaxed Elvis jumping over the words of this song from *Stay Away, Joe* (1968), but minor film fare. Recorded on September 26, 1966 at Paramount Recording Studio; released in May of 1967 on the RCA soundtrack EP. Later, on the Camden LP *I Got Lucky* (1971).

"Love Me"
(Jerry Leiber – Mike Stoller)
Elvis at his best – heavy feeling, rich tone – a smoldering plea

somewhere between Nashville and the swamps. This cut featured extraordinary vocal range and texture by Elvis and was recorded in the torchy mode of "I Want You, I Need You, I Love You." The fans picked it right off the EP *Elvis: Volume 1* and made it the only song by Elvis never released as a single to reach the top of the singles charts, selling a million. Recorded in September of 1956 at Radio Recorders in Hollywood; released on the EP *Elvis: Volume 1* (1956). Later, on the LPs *Elvis* (1956), *Elvis' Golden Records* (1958), *Worldwide Gold Award Hits, Volume 2* (1971), *Elvis* (1973), *Elvis: A Legendary Performer, Volume 1* (1974). Excellent live versions were performed, with the Stamps Quartet filling in nicely for the Jords, and they appear on the LPs *Elvis As Recorded At Madison Square Garden* (1972), *Elvis: Aloha From Hawaii Via Satellite* (1973) and *Elvis Recorded Live Onstage in Memphis* (1974).

"Love Song Of The Year"
(Chris Christian)
Delicate and attractive but not much to latch onto – awkward lyrics. Recorded in December of 1973 at Stax Studio in Memphis; released in January of 1975 on the LP *Promised Land.*

"Loving Arms"
(Tom Jans)
Well-mounted bluesy ballad. Recorded in December of 1973 at Stax Studio in Memphis; released in March of 1974 on the LP *Good Times.*

Loving You
Started: February 1957
A Paramount Picture
Cast
Deke Rivers: Elvis Presley; Glenda Markle: Lizabeth Scott; Walter "Tex" Warner: Wendell Corey; Carl: James Gleason; Tallman: Ralph Dumke; Skeeter: Paul Smith; Wayne: Ken Becker; Daisy: Jana Lund; and introducing Dolores Hart as Susan Jessup.
Credits
Produced by Hal Wallis
Directed by Hal Kanter
Screenplay by Herbert Baker and Hal Kanter
From a story by Mary Agnes Thompson
Technicolor and Vistavision
Songs
"Lonesome Cowboy"; "Party"; "Teddy Bear"; "Hot Dog"; "Got A Lot Of Livin' To Do"; "Mean Woman Blues"; "Loving You"; "We're Gonna Live It Up"; "Candy Kisses"; "Dancing On A Dare" (cut).
Running time: 101 minutes ☞

Previously titled: *Lonesome Cowboy*

"Loving You"
(Jerry Leiber – Mike Stoller)
The title song of the 1957 film (performed over the credits and on the farm – both versions unavailable on record). Simple, lovely ballad with Floyd Cramer filling in the background which took some forty takes before Elvis was satisfied. Recorded in February of 1957 at Radio Recorders in Hollywood; released in June of 1957 as a single with "(Let Me Be Your) Teddy Bear" on the flip-side. On the EP *Loving You, Volume 1* (1957) and the LPs *Loving You* (1957), *Elvis' Golden Records* (1958), *Worldwide 50 Gold Award Hits, Volume One* (1970), *Pure Gold* (1975) and *Elvis – A Canadian Tribute* (1978).

Loving You Volume 1
1957. RCA Victor. EP (EPA1-1515).
Side 1: "Loving You"; "Party."
Side 2: "Teddy Bear"; "True Love."

Loving You Volume II
1957. RCA Victor. EP (EPA2-1515).
Side 1: "Lonesome Cowboy"; "Hot Dog."
Side 2: "Mean Woman Blues"; "Got A Lot O' Living To Do."

Loving You

1957. RCA Victor. LP
(LPM-1515).

Side 1: "Mean Woman Blues";
"Teddy Bear"; "Loving You";
"Got A Lot O' Living To Do";
"Lonesome Cowboy"; "Hot Dog";
"Party."

Side 2: "Blueberry Hill"; "True
Love"; "Don't Leave Me Now";
"Have I Told You Lately That I
Love You"; "I Need You So."

Loving You

33⅓ LP Bootleg.

Side 1: "All songs from the
Loving You soundtrack."

Side 2: "Loving You"; "Got A
Lot O' Living To Do";
"Crawfish"; "Love Me Tender
(cut version)"; "I Wanna Be
Free"; "Love Me Tender"; "Ready
Teddy (Both from the *Ed Sulli-
van Show*)"; "Love Me"; "Elvis
For The March Of Dimes"; "Blue
Moon Of Kentucky (*Louisiana
Hayride* show)."

Jana Lund

Actress Elvis dated briefly in
1957.

General Douglas MacArthur

One of Elvis' military heroes.

"MacArthur Park"

(Jimmy Webb)
Elvis did a parody of the 1968
Richard Harris hit on the *NBC-
TV Special* in 1968; it never
appeared on the record.

Madison Cadillac

Elvis' favorite car dealership in
Memphis, where, in July of 1975,
he once bought 14 Eldorados.

Madison Square Garden

The site of Elvis' fabled New
York appearances in June of
1972.

The Magical Rockin' Sound Of Elvis Presley

33⅓ LP Bootleg.

Side 1: "First In Line"; "I Got A
Woman"; "Is It So Strange"; "I
Want To Be Free"; "Trouble";
"Lover Doll"; "Crawfish."

Side 2: "I Love You Because"; I
Want You, I Need You, I Love
You"; "Dixieland Rock"; "Don't
Leave Me Now"; "I'm Gonna Sit
Right Down And Cry"; "Young
And Beautiful"; "Anyway You
Want Me."

Magical Rockin' Sound Of Elvis Presley, The

Ten-inch bootleg album on the
Jubilee label in Canada, but
credited to Cambodia.

Side 1: "First In Line"; I Got A
Woman"; "Is It So Strange"; "I
Want To Be Free"; "Trouble";
"Lover Doll"; "Crawfish."

Side 2: "I Love You Because"; "I
Want You, I Need You, I Love
You"; "Dixieland Rock"; "Don't
Leave Me Now"; "I'm Gonna Sit
Right Down And Cry (Over
You)"; "Young And Beautiful";

"Any Way You Want Me (That's How I Will Be)."

Mahalo From Elvis
1978. RCA Camden-Pickwick. LP (ACL-7064).
Side 1: "Blue Hawaii"; "Early Morning Rain"; "Hawaiian Wedding Song"; "Ku-u-i-po"; (The preceding four songs were newly recorded in 1973 for the "*Aloha From Hawaii Via Satellite*" TV Special, and were included in that show but not on the RCA soundtrack of the LP.) "No More"; (Recorded at the same time as the other four songs, but *not* included in the TV show.
Side 2: "Relax"; "Baby, If You'll Give Me All Your Love"; "One Broken Heart For Sale"; "So Close, Yet So Far (From Paradise)"; "Happy Ending."

"Make Me Know It"
(Otis Blackwell)
The first song recorded out of the Army, a passable though gimmicky R & B number. Recorded on March 20, 1960 at RCA Nashville Studio; released in March of 1960 on the LP *Elvis Is Back!*

"Make The World Go Away"
(Hank Cochran)
C & W tune recorded by Eddy Arnold in 1965, rendered by El with flair, embellished by James Burton guitar, and made top-heavy by the addition of strings. Recorded in June of 1970 at RCA Nashville Studio; released in February of 1971 on the LP *Elvis Country.*

"Mama"
(Charles O'Curran – Dudley Brooks)
Recorded for *Girls! Girls! Girls!* but only the Amigos ended up singing it in the film. Latin American touch with insignificant lyrics, grossly overproduced. Recorded in March of 1962 in Hollywood; released eight years later, in April of 1970, on the RCA Camden LP *Let's Be Friends.* Later re-released by Pickwick on *Double Dynamite* (1976).

"Mama, Don't Dance"
(Kenny Loggins – Jim Messina)
Elvis included the Loggins – Messina hit as part of a rocking medley with five other songs, as he segued from "Whole Lotta Shakin'," before going to "Flip, Flop, Fly." Recorded live on March 20, 1974 at Mid-South Coliseum in Memphis; released in June of 1974 on the LP *Elvis Recorded Live On Stage In Memphis.*

"Mama Liked The Roses"
(John Christopher)
Gentle, very sentimental, with a short monologue, church bells chiming and violins. Recorded in January of 1969 at American Studios in Memphis; released in May of 1970 as a single, with "The Wonder Of You" on the flipside. Later on the LP RCA Camden *Elvis' Christmas Album* (1970).

Kal Mann and Bernie Lowe
Songwriting duo who wrote "Teddy Bear" for Elvis.

May Mann
Hollywood reporter who interviewed Elvis over the years and published the book *Elvis and The Colonel.*

Rex Mansfield
One of Elvis' Army buddies in Germany, a fellow karate student and partner.

"Mansion Over The Hilltop"
(Ira Stamhill)
Lovely, western-flavored hymn, backed by Floyd Cramer's ivory keys. Recorded in October of 1960 at RCA Nashville Studio; released in December of 1960 on the LP *His Hand In Mine.*

March Of Dimes Galaxy Of Stars 1957
LP.
Side 1: (GM-8M-0653) "Discs For Dimes"; "Howard Miller" (instructions – not for broadcast); "Eddie Fisher"; "Julie London"; "Denise Lor"; "Jim Lowe"; "Mills Bros."; "Guy Mitchell"; "Vaughn Monroe"; "Elvis Presley"; "Gale Robbins."
Side 2: (GM-8M-0654) "Discs For Dimes"; "Pat Boone"; "Sammy Davis Jr."; "Gogi Grant"; "Bill Hayes"; "Eartha Kitt"; "Ray Price"; "Johnnie Ray"; "Henri Rene"; "Dinah Shore"; "Margaret Whiting"; "Andy Williams."
Each performer gives a statement for the March of Dimes.

March Of Dimes Galaxy Of Stars 1957
LP.
Side 1: (GM-8M-0657) "I Love My Baby" (Jill Corey); "Love Me Tender" (Elvis Presley); "Baby Doll" (Andy Williams).
Side 2: (GM-8M-0658) "Your Love Is My Love" (Alan Dale); "Paper Doll" (Mills Bros.); "Singing The Blues" (Guy Mitchell). In addition to the songs, each performer provided an open-end interview. A guideline script was provided with the LP. These promotional LP's were destroyed in 1957.

"Marguerita"
(Don Robertson)
From *Fun In Acapulco*, the song for Ursula Andress – trumpets, castanets, the whole deal. Recorded in January of 1963; released in November of 1963 on the sountrack LP.

Market Square Arena
The Indiana Hall where, on July 26, 1977, Elvis made his last appearance before an audience.

Marl Metal Products Company
Where Elvis briefly worked a full shift from 11:30 p.m., during high school until he began suffering from fatigue and his mother made him quit.

Elsie Marman
Elvis' music teacher at Humes High.

Dodie Marshall
"Jo Symington," leading love interest in the scuba movie *Easy Come, Easy Go* (1966).

Dean Martin
Elvis told Sam Phillips that Martin was one of his favorite singing stars of the early 1950's.

Grady Martin
Session guitarist with Elvis, 1966-1967 on the *Clambake* LP.

"Mary In The Morning"
(Johnny Cymbal – Michael Rashkow)
Gentle love song, seen in rehearsal from *That's The Way It Is* (1970), with harmonica and acoustic guitar. A skillful rendition. Recorded in August of 1970 at the International Hotel in Las Vegas; released in December of 1970 on the soundtrack LP.

Marlyn Mason
"Charlene" in *The Trouble With Girls (And How To Get Into It)* (1969). ☞

Walter Matthau
The despicable "Maxie Fields" in *King Creole* (1958).

Neal Matthews, Jr.
Second tenor with the Jordanaires.

Diane McBain
"Diana St. Clair," the sexy author in *Spinout* 1966) doing research on *The Perfect American Male.*

Mrs. Janelle McComb
One of Elvis' Tupelo acquaintances, a fan whom Elvis befriended in later years. Also prominent as a force behind the Elvis Presley Chapel.

Charlie McCoy
Bass and harmonica session man 1966-67, and in Nashville, 1970.

Mike McCoy
Elvis' character in *Spinout* (1966).

Ronnie McDowell
Singer who recorded the tribute song "The King Is Gone" and provided Elvis' voice for "*Elvis*," Dick Clark's TV movie starring Kurt Russell.

Bonya McGarrity
One of the secretaries at Graceland.

Mike McGregor
Graceland handyman and stable hand, as well as groundskeeper.

McGuire Air Force Base
The Northern New Jersey air-

189

base opposite Fort Dix where Elvis landed in a blizzard when he returned from Germany on March 3, 1960.

Tulsa McLean
Elvis' character in *G.I. Blues* (1960).

Mike McMahon
Elvis' racquetball partner and one of the people who got him interested in investing in a chain of racquetball clubs with Dr. Nick and Joe Esposito. The corporation, of which he became general manager, was formed in 1975 and was called Presley Center Courts, Inc.

"The Meanest Girl In Town"
(Joe Byers)
From *Girl Happy* (1965) a rocker with sax and a guitar solo and Elvis at his slyest. Recorded in June of 1964 in Hollywood; released in April of 1965 on the soundtrack LP.

"Mean Woman Blues"
(Claude Demetrius)
Fast, straight rocker from *Loving You* (1957), with hand-clapping opening in the film version. Staccato and fun. Recorded in January of 1957 at Radio Recorders in Hollywood; released in July of 1957 on the soundtrack LP. Also on the EP *Loving You, Volume 2* (1957), and later on the LP *Elvis: The Other Sides – Worldwide Gold Award Hits, Vol. 2* (1971).

Meditation Gardens
The fountain and garden Elvis built at the rear of Graceland in 1966. The garden included a statue of Jesus and was designated as a place of prayer and quiet meditation. Today it is the gravesite of Vernon, Gladys and Elvis Presley.

Mello Men
The vocal group that appeared with Elvis in the film *It Happened At The World's Fair* (1963) and sang back-up on "One Broken Heart For Sale."

Memorials
Soon after Elvis' death, many memorials were planned to honor his memory and pay tribute to his contributions to music. In late 1977, a stage musical called *Elvis* took the London stage by storm, later winning an award for Best Musical. The musical was called a celebration of Elvis' music, and the three singers who played Elvis (originally) were Tim Whitnall, Shakin' Stevens, and P. J. Proby. Proby was replaced by Shaun Simon, and then Bogdan Kominowsky.

The City of Tupelo began plans for the Memorial Chapel, and with the help of fans' donations, the chapel was built near Elvis' birthplace and dedicated on August 17, 1979. Tupelo also changed the name of the area in which the birthplace stands to Presley Heights; the Old Saltillo Road to Elvis Presley Drive, and the arterial Highway 78 between Tupelo and Memphis to The Elvis Aron Presley Memorial Highway; it was dedicated in a special ceremony in December, 1977. Elvis' birthplace was also designated as a Mississippi State Historical Monument.

Memphis honored its best-known citizen by placing a large bronze statue of Elvis in Elvis Presley Plaza, just south of the downtown area. The statue was unveiled on August 14, 1980. It was sculpted by Eric Parks. Previous to this, the Las Vegas Hilton had placed a bronze statue near to the entrance of its showroom. It was sculpted by Carl Romanelli, and unveiled by Vernon and Priscilla on September 8, 1978. The showroom was dedicated to Elvis. A jump-suit worn by Elvis on his "*Aloha From Hawaii*" telecast of 1973, plus other mementoes, were also also put on display at the Hilton.

In London, Madame Tussaud's Waxworks made a controversial model of Elvis that met with the fans' disapproval. A second, and only slightly better head was later made.

Sam Phillips renamed his Memphis radio station WLVS, and aired a lot of the King's music. Hollywood made a TV movie called "*Elvis*" with Kurt Russell as Elvis, Season Hubley as Priscilla, and Shelley Winters as Gladys Presley.

No doubt more memorials will be forthcoming; at press time, a statue is planned in Britain.

"Memories"
(Scott Davis – Billy Strange)
From the 1968 NBC-TV *Special*, a smooth slow ballad with repetitive lyrics. The applause was removed for the American release. Recorded in June of 1968 at The Burbank Studios; released in December of 1968 on the LP *Elvis (NBC-TV Special)*. Released as a single in March of 1969, with "Charro" on the flipside.

August 14, 1980: unveiling the bronze statue.

Memories Of Elvis
1978. RCA. LP (DML5-0347). By Candlelite Music Inc.
Side 1: "One Broken Heart For Sale"; "Young And Beautiful"; "A Mess Of Blues"; "The Next Step Is Love"; "I Gotta Know"; "Love Letters."
Side 2: "When My Blue Moon Turns To Gold Again"; "If Every Day Was Like Christmas"; "Steamroller Blues"; "Anyway You Want Me"; "(Such An) Easy Question"; "That's When Your Heartaches Begin."
Side 3: "Kentucky Rain"; "Money Honey"; "My Way"; "Girls! Girls! Girls!"; "Lonely Man"; "U.S. Male."
Side 4: "My Wish Came True"; "Kiss Me Quick"; "As Long As I Have You"; "Bossa Nova Baby"; "I Forgot To Remember To Forget"; "Such A Night."
Side 5: "I Really Don't Want To Know"; "Doncha' Think It's Time"; "His Hand In Mine"; "That's All Right"; "Nothingville Medley"; "Baby I Don't Care."
Side 6: "Playing For Keeps"; "King Of The Whole Wide World"; "Don't Ask Me Why"; "Flaming Star"; "I'm Left, You're Right, She's Gone"; "What'd I Say."
Side 7: "There Goes My Everything"; "Patch It Up"; "Reconsider Baby"; "Good Rockin' Tonight"; "You Gave Me A Mountain"; "Rock-A-Hula Baby."
Side 8: "Mean Woman Blues"; "It Hurts Me"; "Fever"; "I Want To Be Free"; "Viva Las Vegas"; "Old Shep."
Side 9: "Anything That's Part Of You"; "My Baby Left Me"; "Wild In The Country"; "Memphis, Tennessee"; "Don't Leave Me Now"; "I Feel So Bad."
Side 10: "Separate Ways"; "Polk Salad Annie"; "Fame And Fortune"; "Trying To Get To You"; "I've Lost You"; "King Creole."

Memphian Theater
One of the many rented out to Elvis and his entourage for their all-night movie screenings. It was at the Memphian Theater that Elvis met Linda Thompson.

Memphis Fairgrounds
The amusement park in Memphis frequented after hours by Elvis, his entourage, and his family.

Memphis Flash
One of Elvis' early nicknames because of his loud clothes and the title of one of the largest Elvis newsletters, published by Paul Lichter.

"Memphis Mafia"
The sobriquet for the retinue of Elvis' salaried sidekicks, a group whose personnel would change. The group was dubbed by the press after Elvis and the boys were spotted arriving in Las Vegas during the early sixties, all dressed in dark mohair suits with sunglasses. They were also known as "El's Angels" and, later, the TCB group, for Taking Care of Business.

Memphis Recording Service
Sam Phillips' recording shop for the walk-in trade at 706 Union Avenue, where Elvis stopped to record his mother a birthday present one Saturday morning in the summer of 1953. Also the home of Sun Records.

Memphis Strings
Instrumental backing for the Memphis sessions, 1969.

"Memphis, Tennessee"
(Chuck Berry)
Of course, everybody always knew it was only a matter of time before Elvis covered Chuck Berry's 1959 classic (how could he resist a song about his hometown?) but when Elvis' buddy Johnny Rivers had a giant hit with it in 1964, he quickly followed suit with a straight on, rollicking version. Recorded on January 12, 1964 at RCA Nashville Studio; released in July of 1965 on the LP Elvis For Everyone.

"Merry Christmas Baby"
(Lou Baxter – Johnny Moore)
R & B Christmas standard, with Elvis having fun with his musicians and some sizzling licks by James Burton. Recorded in May of 1971 at RCA Nashville Studio; released in October of 1971 on the LP Elvis Sings The Wonderful World of Christmas.

Messerschmidt
Strange, three-wheeled car manufactured in Germany, purchased by Elvis in 1956 as a curiosity (if nothing else, the purchase revealed Elvis' mania for automobiles). On a whim, Elvis swapped the car to Bernard Lansky in return for free run of his clothing shop.

"Mexico"
(Sid Tepper – Roy C. Bennett)
Lively Latin American number from Fun In Acapulco (1963) with El singing about living it up with all the "adorable creatures." Recorded January 20, 1963 in Hollywood; released in November of 1963 on the soundtrack LP.

Dr. David Meyer
The Memphis eye specialist often credited with saving Elvis' eyesight.

Michelob Presents Highlights Of Elvis Memories
1978. ABC. LP (OCC810). By ABC Radio.
Side 1: "Memories"; "Heartbreak Hotel"; "Love Me Tender"; "Hound Dog"; "Don't Be Cruel"; "Jailhouse Rock"; "It's Now Or Never."
Side 2: "Viva Las Vegas"; "Separate Ways"; "You Don't Have To Say You Love Me"; "Are You Lonesome Tonight"; "Can't Help Falling In Love"; "If I Can Dream."

Milam Junior High
Where Elvis was enrolled when the Presleys moved to Tupelo, near Shakerag, in 1947.

Military Ocean Terminal
The point of embarkation from Elvis' trans-Atlantic crossing to Germany, where he held a press conference on September 19, 1958.

"Milkcow Blues Boogie"
(Kokomo Arnold)
Sun rockabilly classic, which starts off with Elvis talking about the old milk cow and saying "Hold it fellers . . . that don't move me. Let's get real, real gone for a change." And that's exactly what Elvis, Scotty and Bill do – with a vengeance. A unique bit of hillbilly boogie. Recorded in December of 1954 at Sun Studios in Memphis; released in January of 1955 as a Sun single with "You're A Heartbreaker" on the flip-side. RCA released its version of the single in November of 1955. Later, on the LPs A Date With Elvis (1959) and The Sun Sessions (1976).

"Milky White Way"
(Arranged and adapted by Elvis Presley)
Sacred standard done easily as a medium rocker. Recorded October 30, 1960 at RCA Nashville Studio; released in December of 1960 on the LP His Hand In Mine.

Bill Miller
The talent broker of the Las Vegas International Hotel in 1969, one of the men instrumental in making the deal which brought Elvis back to the stage.

Mindy Miller
One of Elvis' girlfriends during the period following his breakup with Linda Thompson.

Sandy Miller
An ex-nurse from Denver, Colorado, who became Vernon Presley's girlfriend, nurse and housemate following his separation and divorce from Dee Presley. She lived with Vernon until his death in 1979.

"Million Dollar Session"
The unreleased studio jam recorded by Sam Phillips on December 4, 1956, with Carl Perkins, Johnny Cash, Jerry Lee Lewis, and Elvis. The four Sun recording artists sang and recorded a series of gospel standouts.

Ronnie Milsap
Country-blues singer, back-up vocals for Elvis' recording sessions in Memphis, 1968-69, and one-time house singer at T. J.'s in Memphis, where Elvis held partour.

The Milton Berle Show
Elvis' second live television booking, this time for two appearances. On April 3, 1956, he sang "Heartbreak Hotel," "Money Honey," and "Blue Suede Shoes." One June 5, he sang a furious "Hound Dog" and "I Want You, I Need You, I Love You."

"Mine"
(Sid Tepper – Roy C. Bennett)
Nicely rendered ballad, with backing by the Jords and Floyd Cramer's piano. Recorded on September 11, 1967 at RCA Nashville Studio; released in June of 1968 on the soundtrack LP Speedway (it wasn't in the film).

Wilma Minor
Los Angeles nutritionist whom Elvis visited during his early thirties, in a vain attempt to improve his dietary habits.

"Miracle Of The Rosary"
(Lee Denson)
Prayer converted into a hymn, with an interplay of voices between Elvis and the Imperials. Recorded in May of 1971 at RCA Nashville Studio; released in February of 1972 on Elvis Now. Later, on He Walks Beside Me (1978).

"Mirage"
(Bill Grant – Bernie Baum – Florence Kaye)
Crooning ballad from Harum Scarum (1965), a wobbling, throbbing treatment. Recorded February 24, 1965 in Hollywood; released in October, 1965 on the soundtrack LP.

Mississippi Alabama Fair and Dairy Show
In 1945, Elvis was brought here by his school principal, J. D. Cole, and entered in the talent contest. He sang "Old Shep" and won second prize – five dollars and free admission to the rides. He returned in 1957 to sing and be presented with the key to Tupelo by James P. Coleman, Governor of Mississippi.

Mary Ann Mobley
Hollywood friend of Elvis and co-star in several films; as the sex-pot "Deena" in Girl Happy (1965); as "Princess Shalimar" in Harum Scarum (1965).

Chips Moman
Producer, owner of American

Recording Studio in Memphis, where Elvis made his great comeback LP, *From Elvis in Memphis,* in 1968.

"Money Honey"

(Jesse Stone)
Energetic treatment of the 1953 classic Clyde McPhatter hit, from Elvis' first day at RCA Nashville, January 10, 1956 (recorded right after "Heartbreak Hotel"). Released as a single in September of 1956, with "One-Sided Love Affair" on the flip. Performed on *Stage Show* (March 24, 1956) and on the *Milton Berle Show* (April 3, 1956). Later, on the EP *Heartbreak Hotel* (1956) and on the LP *Elvis Presley* (1956).

The Monologue L.P.

33⅓ LP Bootleg.
Side 1: "The King Talks About His Career"; "Jailhouse Rock"; "Don't Be Cruel"; "Memories"; "Lawdy Miss Clawdy"; "Until It's Time For You To Go"; "Oh Happy Day"; "Sweet Inspirations"; "More."
Side 2: "Hey Jude"; "What Now, My Love"; "Are You Laughing Tonight?"; "I John"; "Baby, What You Want Me To Do"; "I'm Leaving"; "What'd I Say."

Bill Monroe

"The Father of Bluegrass," Country Music Hall of Fame member (1970) who wrote "Blue Moon Of Kentucky" and "Little Cabin On The Hill."

Sonja Montgomery

Back-up vocalist, Nashville, 1971.

"Moody Blue"

(Mark James)
One of the best songs from the Graceland recordings—unusual lyrics and stylishly delivered. Recorded February 4-5 in the Graceland den; released in December of 1976 as a single, with "She Still Thinks I Care" on the flip-side. Later on the LP *Moody Blue* (1977).

Moody Blue

1977. RCA Victor. LP (AFL1-2428).
Side 1: "Unchained Melody"; "If You Love Me (Let Me Know)"; "Little Darlin'"; "He'll Have To Go"; "Let Me Be There."
Side 2: "Way Down"; "Pledging My Love"; "Moody Blue"; "She Thinks I Still Care"; "It's Easy For You."

"Moonlight Swim

(Sylvia Dee—Ben Weisman)
From *Blue Hawaii* (1961), a silky ballad with Hawaiian guitars. Recorded in April of 1961 in Hollywood; released in October of 1961 on the soundtrack LP.

Bob Moore

Bass guitarist with Elvis from

1958-1966, after Bill Black's departure.

Joanna Moore

The seductive researcher "Alicia Claypoole" in *Follow That Dream* (1962) who lures Elvis into the woods for a "word association test."

Mary Tyler Moore

Elvis' co-star in *Change of Habit* (1969) in which she played a nun, Sister Michelle.

Michael Moore

Director of *Paradise—Hawaiian Style* (1965).

Scotty Moore

Elvis' guitarist from the summer of 1954 to 1958, on records, on tour, and in several films. Scotty had been a member of a country band called the Starlight Wranglers along with Bill Black and Doug Poindexter when he met Sam Phillips. Sam suggested that Scotty, Bill and Elvis get together and rehearse a few songs for a possible recording session, which came about the following night, July 5, 1954. Following the release of "That's All Right (Mama)", Scotty served as Elvis' manager (until Bob Neal entered the picture). More importantly, he helped pioneer a whole new direction and style of musicianship called rockabilly, and, with Carl Perkins, Chuck Berry, Buddy Holly, and a few others, became one of the most influential guitarists of his generation. Scotty performed with Elvis in all of his TV appearances and played lead guitar on virtually all of Elvis' recordings until 1958, when he and Bill Black left Elvis after a dispute about their earnings. He appeared with Elvis in the 1957 film *Loving You.* He continued as a studio musician and a producer and appeared on the live segment of the NBC-TV *Special* in 1968.

Rita Moreno

A romantic interest in 1957.

Josh Morgan
One of Elvis' characters in *Kissin' Cousins* (1964).

William L. "Bill" Morris
Another close Presley associate, active in Memphis civic affairs throughout the years, once running for mayor and serving as Sheriff of Memphis, who issued Elvis a permit to carry firearms in the city.

Most Talked About New Personality In The Last Ten Years Of Recorded Music
1956. RCA Victor. EP (EPB-1254).
Side 1: "Blue Suede Shoes"; "I'm Counting On You"; "I Got A Woman."
Side 2: "One-Sided Love Affair"; "I Love You Because"; "Just Because."
Side 3: "Tutti Frutti"; "Tryin' To Get To You"; "I'm Gonna Sit Right Down And Cry."
Side 4: "I'll Never Let You Go"; "Blue Moon"; "Money Honey."

Bitsy Mott
One of Elvis' earliest Memphis buddies to travel the road with him (along with Red West) before his Army days. A distant relative of the Colonel's.

Mountain Valley
Elvis' favorite brand of mineral water.

Mr. Rock And Roll
45 EPA Bootleg.
Side 1: "Fame And Fortune"; "Stuck On You" (From The Frank Sinatra TV Special).
Side 2: "The Truth About Me"; "1972 Press Conference."

"Mr. Songman"
(Donnie Sumner)
A variation on the theme of "Love Song Of The Year" — shallow, but it moves along. Recorded in December of 1973 at Stax Studio in Memphis; released in January of 1975 on the LP *Promised Land*. Also released as a single in April of 1975, with "*T-R-O-U-B-L-E*" on the flip-side.

Larry Muhoberac
Piano player for Elvis' Vegas opening and in subsequent recording sessions.

Dr. Eric Muirhead
Chief of the department of pathology at Baptist Memorial, who directed Elvis' autopsy.

Tony Muscheo
The leader of the Imperials, the outspoken Italian who initiated the changes in the identity of the gospel quartet, making them more modern and upbeat during the period (1968-1971) when they worked for Elvis, from *That's The Way It Is* (1970) and the gospel LP *He Touched Me* (1972).

"My Babe"
(Willie Dixon)
Adaptation of the gospel "This Train," done in Las Vegas in high style (at one point, the song gets away from him). Recorded at the International Hotel of Las Vegas in August of 1969; released in November of 1969 on the LP *From Memphis To Vegas/From Vegas To Memphis*.

"My Baby Left Me"
(Arthur Crudup)
Elvis paying more tribute to "Big Boy" Crudup, this time at RCA New York Studio. A cut that stood the test of time. Recorded on January 30, 1956. Released in May of 1956 as a single, the flip-side of "I Want You, I Need You, I Love You." Released on the EPs *The Real Elvis* and *Elvis Presley* (1956) and the following LPs: *For LP Fans Only* (1959), and *Elvis: The Worldwide Gold Award Hits, Volume 2* (1971). A live version appears on *Elvis Recorded Live Onstage in Memphis* (1974).

"My Boy"
(B. Martin — P. Couleter — C. Francois — Jean-Pierre Boutayre)
A good example of how Elvis personalized a ballad and made it his own — one of the better of the 1970's. Recorded on December 15, 1973 at Stax Studio in Memphis; released in January of 1975 as a single, with "Thinking Of You" on the flip-side. Later, on the LPs *Good Times* (1975) and *Our Memories of Elvis* (1979)

"My Desert Serenade"
(Stanley J. Gelber)
From *Harum Scarum* (1965), Elvis working his voice on a mediocre melody. Recorded on February 24, 1965 in Hollywood; released in October of 1965 on the soundtrack LP.

"My Happiness"
(Betty Peterson — Bornex Bergantine)
The song that was a hit for the Ink Spots in 1953, which Elvis recorded for Gladys at the Memphis Recording Service in the summer of 1953.

"Mystery Train"
(Sam Phillips — Junior Parker)
Elvis' rockabilly-tempo version of Little Junior's blues ranks as one of the most groundbreaking and stirring of his early recordings. With the sound and feeling of the freight yards, Elvis transforms the blues into something purely personal. Recorded in February, 1955 at Sun Studio in Memphis; released in August of 1955 as a single, with "I Forgot To Remember To Forget" on the flip-side. RCA re-issued the same single in November of 1955

as Elvis' first release. Later, on the EP *Anyway You Want Me* (1956) and the following LPs: *For LP Fans Only* (1959) and remixed for *The Sun Sessions* (1976). Elvis performed the song in *That's The Way It Is* (1970) and *Elvis On Tour* (1972). Live versions appear on *From Memphis To Vegas/From Vegas To Memphis* and *Elvis In Person* (1970).

"My Way"
(Paul Anka — Revaux — Francois)
The song that became Sinatra's trademark in 1969 was adopted by Elvis four years later. Most people around Elvis acknowledge that it was the most significant song in his repertoire during the final years of his life; that it was Elvis' way of "spilling the beans" about the glories and the pitfalls of his own life. First recorded on January 14, 1973 at H.I.C. Arena in Honolulu during the broadcast for "*Aloha From Elvis In Hawaii Via Satellite*; released in April of 1973 on the soundtrack LP. Re-released in 1977 as a single, with "America The Beautiful" on the flip-side, and on the LP *Elvis: A Canadian Tribute* (1978). Elvis delivered a poignant rendition of the song on his final CBS-TV special, taped in June of 1977, but the song was not included in the LP *Elvis In Concert* (1977).

"My Wish Came True"
(Ivory Joe Hunter)
An early RCA gem with nicely layered choral backing by the Jordanaires. Recorded on September 5, 1957 at Radio Recorders in Hollywood; not released until July of 1959 (when Elvis was in the Army), when it appeared as a single, with "A Big Hunk O' Love" on the flip. Later, on the LPs *50,000,000 Elvis Fans Can't Be Wrong* (1959), and *Elvis: The Other Sides: Worldwide Gold Award Hits, Volume 2* (1971).

19 Elvis Presley Great Hits
33⅓ LP bootleg album released in England on the Rex label.
Side 1: "I Just Can't Help Believin'"; "Love Me Tender"; "I Gotta Know"; "Surrender"; "Are You Lonesome Tonight"; "Little Sister"; "Good Luck Charm"; "In The Ghetto"; "The Wonder Of You."
Side 2: "Don't Be Cruel"; "One Night"; "It's Now Or Never"; "Jailhouse Rock"; "No More"; "Moonlight Swim"; "King Creole"; "Kiss Me Quick"; "Life"; "(You're The) Devil In Disguise."

1955 Sun Days
Bootleg.
Album featured outtakes by Elvis Presley, Johnny Cash, Charlie Rich, Roy Orbison, Jerry

Lee Lewis, and Carl Perkins on the Sun Records label (Sun 1009), which was planned for release on December 15, 1977 by Shelby Singleton until a lawsuit filed by RCA Victor stopped the release.

Arthur Nadel
Director of *Clambake* (1967).

Joe Namath
One of Elvis' football idols and a frequent visitor to his dressing room in Las Vegas.

The Nashville Outtakes And Early Interviews
33⅓ LP Bootleg.
Side 1: The Same As The "Good Rocking Tonight" LP.
Side 2: The Same As "The Monologue" LP.

Bad Nauheim
Where the Presley contingent stayed during Elvis' hitch in Germany, in a modest house on 14 Goethestrasse. Also where Elvis first met Priscilla and Vernon first met Dee.

Bob Neal
Disc-jockey on WMPS in Memphis, who booked Elvis for the show at the Overton Park Shell and became his manager in 1955 for the brief period before Elvis met Colonel Tom Parker.

Sherill Neilson
Part of Voice, Elvis' vocal back-up group, and one of the greatest Irish tenors in the world.

Gene Nelson
Director of *Harum Scarum* (1965).

Rick Nelson
One of the darlings of Teen America to emerge during Elvis' Army days, star of the family television show *Ozzie and Harriet*, and a great admirer of Elvis. Became a pal of Elvis' during the early sixties, when Elvis was playing football in Bel Air. Elvis' guitarist, James Burton, was once a member of Nelson's band.

"Never Again"
(Billy Edd Wheeler — Jerry Chesnut)
Mournful ballad from the Graceland sessions, February 6-7, 1976. Released in May of 1976 on the LP *From Elvis Presley Boulevard, Memphis, Tennessee*. Later, the song was remixed to showcase more of Elvis' voice on *Our Memories of Elvis* (1979).

"Never Been To Spain"
(Hoyt Axton)
Elvis took this 1971 hit by Three Dog Night and made it seem he was born to sing it. Performed with sexy soulfulness in *Elvis On Tour* (1972) and recorded live at Madison Square Garden, June 10, 1972; released on the

LP *Elvis As Recorded Live at Madison Square Garden* (1972).

"Never Ending"
(Buddy Kaye – Phil Springer)
Torchy, Johnny Mathis-type ballad, rendered with throbbing sincerity by Elvis. Recorded in May 26, 1963 at RCA Nashville Studio; released as a single in July of 1964, with "Such A Night" as the flip. Later, on the LP *Double Trouble* (1967).

"Never Say Yes"
(Doc Pomus – Mort Schuman)
From *Spinout* (1966), a beater without much direction. Recorded in February 21, 1966 in Hollywood; released in October of 1966 as the soundtrack LP.

Mickey Newbury
The singer who helped piece together "An American Trilogy" for Elvis.

"New Orleans"
(Sid Tepper – Roy C. Bennett)
From *King Creole* (1958), a flashy blues with dixieland backing – plenty of pizzazz. Recorded in January of 1958 in Hollywood; released August of 1958 on the soundtrack LP. Also on the EP *King Creole, Vol. 1* (1958) and the LP *Worldwide Gold Award Hits, Vol. 2* (1971).

Wayne Newton
Popular Las Vegas entertainer who befriended Elvis during the early 1970's. Elvis admired Newton's clean image and vocal prowess; Newton bought Elvis' Jet Commander and incorporated several of Elvis' songs into his nightclub act.

"The Next Stop Is Love"
(Paul Evans – Paul Parnes)
From *That's The Way It Is* (1970), a controlled ballad – gentle, unhurried, plaintive. Studio version was recorded June 7, 1970 at RCA Nashville Studio; released in July of 1970 as a single with "I've Lost You" on the flip-side. Later, on the LP *That's The Way It Is* (1970) and *Worldwide Gold Award Hits, Vol. 2* (1971).

Pauline Nicholson
Elvis' housekeeper and cook at Graceland during the later years.

Dean Nichopoulos
Son of "Dr. Nick," and a paid member of the entourage during the final years, whose leg Elvis allegedly tried to heal by the laying on of his hands.

Dr. George Nichopoulos
"Dr. Nick." From 1966 on, he was Elvis' personal physician in Memphis and, later, on the road, a figure of much controversy and condemnation following disclosures of Elvis' drug habits after his death. He was even-

tually reprimanded and barred from practicing following an investigation in 1979-1980 by ABC's *20/20* and the ensuing inquest by the Tennessee Medical Board.

Nicknames
Elvis was given many nicknames. When he first began to tour, the following were popular: "The Bopping Hillbilly," "The Cat," "The Hillbilly Cat," "The Memphis Flash," "Mama Presley's Son," "The King of Western Bop," "The Country Cat," "The Hillbilly Singer," and "The Hillbilly Bopper." Names like "The Hillbilly Cat" stemmed from his fusion of blues and country. After he became famous, more names were added to the list: "Mr. Wiggle & Shake," "Sir Swivelhips," "King of Rhythm," "The Blue Suede Bopper," "The Hip King," "Elvis the Pelvis," and of course, the "King of Rock & Roll." As his appeal widened, names like "King of Pop," and "King Balladeer" cropped up. His friends called him "E" or

"Chief," or "Boss." He didn't like being called "El" and he once told a Las Vegas audience that he hated to be called "Elvy" when he was young, and joked about how Lisa called him "Ailvis!" Fans sometimes called him "E.P." or "Pres." The name by which he is most often called and which is most appropriate is simply "THE KING."

"Night Life"
(Bill Grant – Bernie Baum – Florence Kaye)
From *Viva Las Vegas* (1964), one of the lesser numbers from a solid film and cut from the final print. Recorded July 9, 1963 in Hollywood; released in November of 1968 on the RCA Camden LP *Singer Presents Elvis Singing Flaming Star and Others*.

"Night Rider"
(Doc Pomus – Mort Schuman)
Uptempo swinger from the early 1960's, a brisk cut at a time when Elvis was falling into the hackneyed soundtrack format of filmdom. Recorded March 18,

1962 at RCA Nashville Studio; released in June of 1962 on the LP *Pot Luck.*

Richard Nixon
37th President of the United States, who received Elvis in 1971 and, following its denial by Deputy Director John Finlator, made Elvis a federal narcotics agent. He also received Jerry Schilling and Sonny West.

Sheriff Roy Nixon
Memphis police official who made Elvis a chief deputy. Nixon later became Mayor of Memphis.

"No More"
(Don Robertson – Hal Blair)
One of the better tunes from *Blue Hawaii* (1961). Recorded in April of 1961 in Hollywood; released in October of 1961 on the soundtrack LP. The song was recorded for the U.S. broadcast of "*Aloha From Hawaii*," but did not appear in the broadcast or on the soundtrack LP.

"(There's) No Room To Rhumba In A Sports Car"

(Fred Wise – Dick Manning) From *Fun In Acapulco* (1963) a lighthearted, inane bit of stuff. Recorded on January 20, 1963 in Hollywood; released in November of 1963 on the soundtrack LP.

"Nothingville"

(Scott Davis – Billy Strange) A short production segment from the *1968 NBC-TV Special*, a bluesy workout with harmonica and guitar. Recorded in June of 1968. Recorded June 30, 1968 at Burbank Studios; released in December of 1968 on the LP *Elvis (NBC-TV Special).*

Novelty Discs

Literally hundreds and hundreds of novelty discs about Elvis have been issued, beginning in 1956. Most of them come from the U.S., but the U.K. and other countries have released their share. Most of the discs were not worth the vinyl they were pressed on. Among the best ones were "The All American Boy," by Bill Parsons; "Hey, Mr. Presley" by Pete DeBree; "The King's Country" by Jerry Jaye; "The Old Payola Roll Blues" by Stan Freberg; "The E. P. Express" by Carl Perkins, and "Tupelo Mississippi Flash" by Jerry Reed. Other discs had titles like "I'm In Love With Elvis Presley," "I Wanna Spend Christmas With Elvis," "My Baby's Crazy 'bout Elvis," "Elvis Presley For President," and "Around The World With Elwood Pretzel."

Nudie's ☞

Hollywood costume firm that specialized in extravagant custom-made outfits for the stars. In 1957, Colonel Parker commissioned Nudie's to make Elvis' $10,000 Gold Lame tuxedo, which Elvis wore briefly (on stage and on the cover of the LP *50,000,000 Elvis Fans Can't Be Wrong* in 1959). Elvis later discarded the outfit because it was too hot and cumbersome, and it ended up in the closet of Homer "Gil" Gilliland, one of Elvis' beauticians, as a gift.

"Number Eight"

Elvis' personal number in numerology, to which he attached great significance over the years.

Jim O'Brien

Colonel Parker's long-time, trusted assistant.

Joan O'Brien

"Diane Warren," the pretty nurse who gets Elvis in *It Happened At The World's Fair* (1963).

195

"O Come, All Ye Faithful"
(Arranged and adopted by Elvis Presley)
Piano and the Imperials – a nice interpretation of the Christmas standard. Recorded on May 16, 1971 at RCA Nashville Studio; released in October of 1971 as the LP *Elvis Sings The Wonderful World Of Christmas*.

Arthur O'Connell
Character actor in several Elvis movies: "Pop Kwimper" in *Follow That Dream* (1962); "Pappy Tatum" in *Kissin' Cousins* (1964).

John O'Grady
Hollywood private detective alleged to have investigated Elvis' drug sources and suppliers before he died; and, at Elvis' behest, later tried to negotiate a deal to prevent Red and Sonny West from publishing *Elvis: What Happened?* Originally hired to protect Elvis from paternity suits; O'Grady also investigated his new girlfriends. The investigation into the drug sources was instigated by Col. Parker and Vernon Presley, and led to Priscilla Presley confronting Elvis about his problem in 1975 and suggesting that he be secretly hospitalized.

"Oh Little Town Of Bethlehem"
(Arranged and Adapted by Elvis Presley)
From Elvis' first Christmas session at RCA. Recorded September 7, 1957, at Radio Recorders in Hollywood; released in September of 1957 on the LP *Elvis' Christmas Album* (re-released in later years on the Camden and Pickwick labels).

Old Gold
45 EP Bootleg.
Side 1: "Truth About Me"; "The Lady Loves Me."
Side 2: "My Baby's Gone"; "Jailhouse Rock" (soundtrack).

"Old McDonald"
(Randy Starr)
From *Double Trouble* (1967), with Elvis making animal sounds. Recorded June 26, 1966, in Hollywood; released in June 1967 on the soundtrack LP. Later, on the LP's *Elvis Sings Hits From His Movies* (1972), and *Elvis Sings For Children (And Grownups Too)* (1978).

"Old Shep"
(Red Foley)
The song that won Elvis second prize at the Mississippi-Alabama Fair in 1945 (he later sang it at his senior talent show at Humes High). A song about a boy's love for his dog, with Elvis himself on piano. Recorded on September 2, 1956, at Radio Recorders in Hollywood; released in November of 1956 on the LP

Elvis and on the LP *Elvis, Volume II*. Later, on the LPs *Separate Ways* (1973), *Double Dynamite* (1976) and *Elvis Sings For Children (And Grownups Too)* (1978).

"On A Snowy Christmas Eve"
(Stanley J. Gelber)
Lush Christmas LP filler. Recorded in May of 1971 at RCA Nashville Studio; released in October of 1971 as the LP *Elvis Sings The Wonderful World of Christmas*.

"Once Is Enough"
(Sid Tepper – Roy C. Bennett)
From *Kissin' Cousins* (1964), a cornball rocker. Recorded in October of 1963 in Hollywood; released in March of 1964 as the soundtrack LP.

"One Boy, Two Little Girls"
(Bill Grant – Bernie Baum – Florence Kaye)
From *Kissin' Cousins* (1964), a quiet track without much substance despite chorus, piano, etc. Recorded in October 11, 1963, in Hollywood; released in March of 1964 on the soundtrack LP.

"One Broken Heart For Sale"
(Otis Blackwell – Winfield Scott)
The single from *It Happened At The World's Fair* (1963), with the Mellomen. This version contained an extra verse. Recorded in October of 1962 in Hollywood; released in February of 1963 as a single with "They Remind Me Too Much Of You," on the flip-side. Later, as the LPs *It Happened At The World's Fair* (1963), *Elvis: Worldwide 50 Gold Award Hits, Volume I* (1970), and *Mahalo From Elvis* (1978).

Jimmy O'Neill
One of Elvis' show business friends of the 1960's (O'Neill hosted television's *Shindig* for a time).

"One Night"
(Dave Bartholomew – Pearl King)
Originally titled "One Night Of Sin" (in the 1956 version by Smiley Lewis), this was a song about an orgy. Elvis cleaned up the lyrics, but the energy is raucous and pounding. Recorded February 23, 1957, at Radio Recorders in Hollywood; released in November of 1958 as a single with "I Got Strung" on the flip-side. Later, on the EP *A Touch Of Gold, Volume II* (1958) and the LP *50,000,000 Elvis Fans Can't Be Wrong – Elvis' Gold Records, Volume II* (1959) and *Elvis: The Other Side – Worldwide 50 Gold Award Hits, Volume II* (1971). A sizzling live version was performed on a 1968 NBC television special

and in the 1970 documentary *That's The Way It Is*.

"One-Sided Love Affair"
(Bill Campbell)
More country and western than straight rock n' roll, but a crisp mover from the second RCA grouping. Recorded January 30, 1956 at RCA Nashville Studio; released March 10, 1956 as the EP *Elvis Presley*. Also, on Elvis' first RCA LP, *Elvis Presley* (1956).

"One Track Heart"
(Bill Grant – Bernie Baum – Florence Kaye)
From *Roustabout* (1964), Elvis warning his lover. Recorded in January of 1964 in Hollywood; released in October of 1964 on the soundtrack LP.

"Only Believe"
(Paul Rader)
Religious offering, almost a chant. Not one of Elvis' more distinguished hymns. Recorded in June of 1970 at RCA Nashville Studio; released in May of 1971 as a single, with "Life" on the flip-side. Later, on the LP *Love Letters From Elvis* (1971).

"Only The Strong Survive"
(Jerry Butler – Kenny Gamble – Leon Huff)
A "story" song from the Memphis sessions – a mother's advice to her son. Wonderful backing on the choruses by the Holladay girls. Recorded February 20, 1969 at American Studios; released in May of 1969 on the LP *From Elvis In Memphis*.

On Stage – February, 1970
1970. LP (LSP-4362).
Side 1: "See See Rider"; "Release Me"; "Sweet Caroline"; "Runaway"; "The Wonder Of You."
Side 2: "Polk Salad Annie"; "Yesterday"; "Proud Mary"; "Walk A Mile In My Shoes"; "Let It Be Me (Je T'Appartiens)."

Operation Elvis
The book about Elvis' Army career commissioned by Colonel Parker, published upon his return.

Roy Orbison
Early Sun artist, who wrote "Ooby Dooby" and "Only The Lonely," which he tried unsuccessfully to sell to Elvis in 1960. Orbison and Elvis met briefly during their early days. The two had similar singing styles and admired each other's voices, although they were professionally competitive.

Our Memories Of Elvis
1979. RCA Victor. LP (AQL1-3279).
Side 1: "Are You Sincere" (Unreleased version); "It's Midnight"; "My Boy"; "Girl Of Mine"; "Take Good Care Of Her"; "I'll Never

Fall In Love Again.'
Side 2: "Your Love's Been A Long Time Coming"; "Spanish Eyes"; "Never Again"; "She Thinks I Still Care"; "Solitaire."

Our Memories Of Elvis Volume 2
1979. RCA Victor. LP (AQL1-3448).
Side 1: "I Got A Feelin' In My Body"; "Green Green Grass Of Home"; "For The Heart"; "She Wears My Ring"; "I Can Help."
Side 2: "Way Down"; "There's A Honky Tonk Angel (Who'll Take Me Back In)"; "Find Out What's Happening"; "Thinking About You"; "Don't Think Twice, It's All Right" (Unreleased complete studio jam session).

Overton Park Shell
The all-country music show in 1954 where Elvis made his first big splash in Memphis – his first time on a big stage and the first time his stage movement caused a sensation. Elvis sang "Good Rockin' Tonight," the girls started squirming with delight, and Webb Pierce, the show's upstaged headliner, called Elvis a "sonofabitch."

"Padre"
(Jacques Larue – Paul Francois Webster – Alain Romans)
Latin American offering, complete with guitars, violins, castanets and Elvis straining high. Recorded May 15, 1971 at RCA Nashville Studio; released in July of 1973 on the LP *Elvis*.

June Page
Back-up vocals, Nashville, 1971.

Patti Page
Popular vocalist of the 1950's who recorded "The Tennessee Waltz" in 1950 and captured Elvis' heart as one of his favorite singers.

Debra Paget
Elvis' wife "Cathy" and co-star in *Love Me Tender* (1956) on whom, it has been said, Elvis developed quite a crush (it went unrequited, however).

196

Palm Springs

Elvis honeymooned with Priscilla here in the spring of 1967, although it had long become one of his favorite relaxation spots (with Hawaii). He owned a home on Chino Canyon Road and retired there frequently after his Las Vegas engagements of the seventies. On September 24, 1974, he recorded tracks there for two songs along with the group Voice: "I Miss You" and "Are You Sincere." Col. Parker also resided in Palm Springs, as does Frank Sinatra.

Paradise, Hawaiian Style

Started in 1966
A Hal Wallis Production
A Paramount Picture
Cast
Rick Richards: Elvis Presley; Judy Hudson: Suzanna Leigh; Danny Kohana: James Shigeta; Jan Kohana: Donna Butterworth; Lani Kaimana: Marianna Hill; Pua: Irene Tsu; Joanna: Julie Parrish; Lahua: Londa Wong; Betty Kohana: Jan Shepard; Donald Belden: John Doucette; Moki: Philip Ahn; Mr. Cubberson: Grady Sutton; Andy Lowell: Don Collier; Mrs. Barrington: Doris Packer; Mrs. Belden: Mary Treen; Peggy Holden: Gigi Verone.
Credits
Produced by Hal Wallis
Associate Producer: Paul Nathan
Assistant to Producer: Jack Saper
Directed by Michael Moore
Screenplay by Alan Weiss and Anthony Lawrence
Story by Alan Weiss
Assistant Director: James Rosenberger
Technical Advisors: Howard Anderson and Col. T. Parker
Vocal Support by Mellomen and Jordanaires
Songs
"Paradise, Hawaain Style"; "House Of Sand"; "Queenie Wahine's Papaya"; "You Scratch My Back"; "Drums Of The Island"; "It's A Dog's Life"; "Dating"; "Stop, Where You Are"; "This Is My Heaven"; "Bill Bailey Won't You Please Come Home" (Donna Butterworth); "Sand Castles" (cut); "Now Is The Hour" (cut – unreleased). Running time: 91 minutes Previously titled *Hawaiian/Polynesian Paradise, Isle of Paradise.*

"Paradise, Hawaiian Style"

(Bill Grant – Bernie Baum – Florence Kaye)
The title cut from the 1966 film – pleasant, typically overproduced fare. Recorded July 19, 1965 at Paramount Recording Studio in Hollywood; released in June of 1966 on the soundtrack LP.

Paradise Hawaiian Style

1966. RCA Victor. LP (LPM/LSP-3643).
Side 1: "Paradise Hawaiian Style"; "Queenie Wahine's Papaya"; "Scratch My Back (I'll Scratch Yours)"; "Drums Of The Islands"; "Datin'."
Side 2: "A Dog's Life"; "A House Of Sand"; "Stop Where You Are"; "This Is My Heaven"; "Sand Castles."

"Paralyzed"

(Otis Blackwell – Elvis Presley) Punching rocker from the RCA Golden Days. D. J. Fontana provides some vicious drumming and Elvis' vocal is suitably sullen. Recorded September 1, 1956 at Radio Recorders in Hollywood; released in November of 1956 on the LP *Elvis* (it was released in the U.K. as a single). Later, on the EP *Elvis, Volume 1*, and the LP *Elvis: The Other Sides – Worldwide Gold Award Hits, Volume 2* (1971).

Ed Parker

Hawaiian-born karate expert who personally instructed Elvis in Kempo from 1972 on and became his personal friend and bodyguard, and remained on the payroll until Elvis' death. Parker authored *Inside Elvis* (Ramparts, 1979) following Elvis' death. Ironically, it was through Parker that Elvis met another karate expert, Mike Stone, who fell in love with Priscilla Presley.

Little Junior Parker

R & B artist composer who recorded on the Sun label and co-wrote "Mystery Train" with Sam Phillips and recorded a version of the song before Elvis with his Blue Flames.

Marie Parker

Colonel Tom's wife, by all accounts a supportive, unassuming woman with a sense of humor to match Col. Tom's. Elvis named his daughter "Lisa Marie" in honor of Marie Parker.

Pamela Parker

Another of the Graceland secretaries responsible for Elvis' personal affairs and handling the huge volume of fan mail over the years.

Colonel Tom Parker

"The Colonel." Elvis' manager from 1955 to the present, a legendary figure in American folklore, who has been called everything from Elvis' greatest blessing to his blackest nemesis. Born June 26, 1910 to parents travelling with a carnival in West Virginia, he spent his youth in that rarified world of the Fast Buck. Described variously as a "combination W. C. Fields and P. T. Barnum" (Jerry Hopkins), he was a celebrated practical joker and hardball negotiator – a born gambler and commit at his best when the stakes were the highest. Managed talents like Eddy Arnold before meeting Elvis in 1955. He booked Elvis on several junkets until taking over from Bob Neal.

He negotiated Elvis' first deal with RCA, when they bought Elvis' catalogue from Sam Phillips and Sun Records for $35,000. He then masterminded Elvis' career – contracts, publicity, everything else – through RCA hits, the first television appearance, the first movies, into and out of the Army, the killing seven-year contract with Hal Wallis, the Great Las Vegas Comeback, and he guided Elvis' career through the decline and fall, to the very end, booking him all over the U.S.A. and running Elvis' show like a finely crafted watch piece. Whatever his shortcomings, Tom Parker certainly fulfilled his promise to keep Elvis in the highest tax bracket. Following Elvis' death,

With the Colonel; *Love Me Tender*, 1957.

the Colonel controlled the estate and licensed Elvis' name, continuing to market him. What was his percentage of the Presley millions? Nobody knows for certain, but the common guess is 25%. As expected, Colonel Parker has his share of staunch defenders and committed detractors. He is presently being sued for fraud by the Presley estate in the Memphis Probate Court, a suit which implicates the Colonel and RCA of defrauding Elvis of money rightfully his. Outcome pending . . .

"Party"
(Don Robertson)
From *Loving You* (1957), a rock flavored rendition with furious vocal gymnastics by Elvis (the film contained an extra introductory verse). Recorded in February of 1957 in Hollywood; released in July of 1957 on the soundtrack LP. Also, on the EP *Loving You, Volume 1* (1957). The film version appears on the Australian bootleg LP *Got A Lot Of Livin' To Do.*

Marty Passeta
Director of the smash TV show, *"Elvis: Aloha From Hawaii"* in 1973.

Joe Pasternack
Produced *Girl Happy* 1965) and *Spinout* (1966).

"Patch It Up"
(Eddie Rabbit – Rory Bourke)
Stage rocker from *That's The Way It Is* (1970), first released as a badly mixed single, though all of the elements were abundantly there. Recorded June 8, 1970 at RCA Nashville Studio; released in October of 1970 with "You Don't Have To Say You Love Me" on the flip-side. Later, on *Elvis: The Other Sides – Worldwide Gold Award Hits, Volume 2* (1971). The excellent live version from the film appears on *Elvis – That's The Way It Is* (1970).

Patricia Stevens Finishing School
Where Priscilla studied dance and modelling in Memphis before her marriage to Elvis.

Patton
Elvis was both crazy about the movie, with George C. Scott, and the man, General George S. Patton, whose exploits he studied and admired.

"(There'll Be) Peace In The Valley (For Me)"
(Thomas A. Dorsey)
Elvis' first sacred classic at RCA, with superb support from the Jordanaires. Elvis sang this on *The Sullivan Show* (January 9, 1957) to win over the adults. Recorded January 13, 1957 at Radio Recorders in Hollywood;

released in March of 1957 on the EP *Peace In The Valley.*

Peace In The Valley
1957. RCA Victor. EP (EPA-4054).
Side 1: "Peace In The Valley"; "It Is No Secret."
Side 2: "I Believe"; "Take My Hand Precious Lord."

"Little Richard" Penniman
The craziest, most mobile, most colorful of the early rockers. He escaped the wrath of white America for the havoc he wreaked because, unlike Elvis, he was *black*, and, well, it just wasn't as scandalous for a black man to shake it like that onstage. Little Richard was one of Elvis' favorite singer/songwriters of the early days, and Elvis performed many of his classics: "Tutti Frutti," "Ready Teddy," "Long Tall Sally," "Rip It Up," "Good Golly Miss Molly," and others.

Ann Pennington
One of the glamorous girlfriends to accompany Elvis briefly in the period following his breakup with Linda Thompson.

Gary Pepper
One of the world's most famous Elvis fans, once awarded a car for his devotion. President of the disbanded Elvis Tankers Fan Club, the first in America. Elvis noticed him in his wheelchair outside of Graceland one day and put him on the payroll, coordinating his fan clubs.

Sterling Pepper
Father of Gary Pepper, and a guard at Graceland.

Perfect For Parties Highlighter
EP. RCA SPA-7-37.
Side 1: "Love Me" (Elvis Presley); "Anchors Aweigh" (Tony Cabot); "That's A Puente" (Tito Puente).
Side 2: "Rock Me But Don't Roll Me" (Tony Scott); Happy Face Baby" (The Three Suns); "Prom To Prom" (Dave Pell).

Carl Perkins
Guitarist–composer–singer who first recorded for Flip, a subsidiary of Sun Records, and recorded his own composition of "Blue Suede Shoes" in December of 1955. Along with Scotty Moore, Chuck Berry and a few others, Perkins fathered a new style of guitar playing in pop music. Elvis and Perkins toured occasionally in 1955, and in 1956 Elvis recorded "Blue Suede Shoes" for RCA. The Beatles later recorded several Perkins' compositions which further solidified his reputation as one of the most influential and unique of the great early record-

ing artists of rockabilly – rock n' roll. He later performed with his friend Johnny Cash at concerts and on television.

Gerald Peters
The English sidekick who chauffered Elvis around Los Angeles for a time in the early 1970's.

Pets
Elvis loved the companionship of animals and had a great variety of animals at Graceland over the years. There seems to be no record of his having had a dog or other pet as a boy. After he became famous, he acquired a

terrier-type dog called "Boy," and another dog called "Sweet Pea." Australian fans sent him a kangaroo in 1957, but he had to give this to the Memphis Zoo. After he moved into Graceland, he made sure his mother had a yardful of chickens, and ducks, too. While he was in the Army, someone sent him a pedigree poodle called grandly "Teddy Bear of Zi-pom-pom."

In the early sixties, he acquired perhaps his best-known pet – a chimpanzee called "Scatter." Elvis' boys loved to teach Scatter to drink beer and tease girls, and he was not the best-loved, or in later years, best-tempered chimp. Elvis had several peacocks roaming around the grounds at one time, but he didn't take kindly to their scratching his cars. He had a bowlful of goldfish in his upstairs office, and a parrot for a time. Elvis owned several dogs. Some of the dogs in the helicopter scene in *Paradise Hawaiian*

Style were Elvis' own, including the collie, "Baba." He had a white-haired Pyrennean dog called "Muffin," who was rather vicious. In 1975, he had a young chow called "Getlo," who he brought onstage at the Hilton on one show. Getlo became ill, and despite a small fortune being spent on the dog's veterinary care, he died the same year. There were several cats around Graceland; Lisa had a white long-haired one called "Fluff." Elvis used to joke around in "Fever" onstage sometimes, and after the line *Cats are born to*

give you fever, he'd sometimes change the words to *Be it farenheit or Siamese!* and then say that he was allergic to cats. This may well have been true.

That Elvis owned a stableful of horses is well-known. Around 1967, he began to take a great interest in horses, and with the acquisition of Circle G Ranch, about 15 minutes drive from Graceland over the Mississippi border, his interest increased. The horses he owned around the time of his marriage were: "Rising Sun" (his favorite palomino); "Colonel Midnight" (Vernon's horse); "Domino" (Priscilla's horse); and also "Buckshot," "Keno," "Traveler," "Sheba," "Flaming Star," "Golden Sun," "Mare Ingram," "Lady," "Sundown," "Thundercloud," "Star Trek," "Scout," "Beauty," and "El Poco." He later added a Tennessee Walker, "Bear."

In the early sixties, there were poodles at Graceland, and Priscilla later acquired two or more large poodles. Elvis bought a pair of Great Danes. Priscilla took them to California after the split-up in the marriage. One of them, Brutus, died in supposedly suspicious circumstances, but the other dog, "Snoopy," became Lisa's constant companion. Elvis also gave dogs to friends and girlfriends as gifts.

"Petunia, The Gardener's Daughter"

(Sid Tepper – Roy C. Bennett) Music hall ditty from *Frankie and Johnny* (1966). In the film, Donna Douglas sang the song; on the records, it's mostly Elvis, with a duet at the end. Recorded in May of 1965 at United Artists Recording Studio in Los Angeles; released in April of 1966 on the soundtrack LP.

Dewey Phillips

White disc-jockey who did the *Red Hot and Blue Show* on station WHBQ in Memphis, which first broke "That's All Right (Mama)" in August of 1954. Because of the audience response, Dewey interviewed Elvis on the air that night, prompting Gladys and Vernon Presley to pluck Elvis out of the darkness of the Suzore No. 2 theatre, where he was hiding.

Judd Phillips

Sam Phillips' brother and a noteworthy figure in the Memphis recording scene, having founded Phillips International and recorded artists like Charlie Rich, Karl Mann, and Bill Justis.

Sam Phillips

One of the most influential figures of modern popular music, Sam Phillips was born, in 1935, in Florence, Alabama. His fascination with music had its roots in early childhood, when he heard the "Blues" sitting on the knee of an old black field hand named Silas Payne. His professional career began as an engineer and disc-jockey. He worked stints at several stations in Alabama and Nashville, Tennessee before moving to Memphis in 1946, where he worked at WREC. Eventually, he founded the Memphis Recording Service and before long was recording demos by rhythm and blues artists like Jackie Brentzson and selling the masters to Chess Records in Chicago. He also recorded, among others, B. B. King, Chester "Howlin Wolf" Burnett, Walter Horton, Bobby Bland and Little Junior Parker. In 1952, he founded Sun Records in the same building as the Memphis Recording Service – 706 Union Avenue. Sam Phillips is widely credited with

the saying "If I could find a white man with the negro sound I could make a million dollars" and in 1954 Marion Keisker, a former "Miss Radio" of Memphis who was working as his assistant, brought Elvis Presley to his attention. (Elvis had ventured into the Memphis Recording Service to record a ten-inch acetate for his mother's birthday). Sam had produced artists like the Johnny Burnett Trio and Rufus Thomas, but was far from commercially successful. In July of 1954, he recorded and released Elvis' first record, "That's All Right (Mama)" with its flip-side "Blue Moon Of Kentucky." After the success of this and subsequent releases by Elvis on the Sun label, and after Elvis made the first wave of public appearances on tour and on the *Louisiana Hayride*, Sam Phillips sold Elvis' contract and master tapes to RCA on November 22, 1955 for a total of $35,000. The money allowed Sam to produce artists like Johnny Cash, Roy Orbison, Charlie Feathers, Carl Perkins, Jerry Lee Lewis, and others. His studio became the mecca of a new sound in pop called "Rockabilly," which he helped to shape and define. His production methods were stark, instinctual and distinctive, with echo, clean reverberation and spontaneity. In 1968, he sold his company to Shelby Singleton and later returned to the radio business. Today, he owns WLVS, the station he named in honor of Elvis Presley.

Pickwick

RCA's discount label, which took over Camden's catalogue in 1975 when it went out of business and repackaged and re-released the LP's.

"Pieces Of My Life"

(Troy Seals) Introspective ballad with intense vocalizing and bitter lyrics. Recorded May 12, 1975 in Hollywood; released in May of 1975 on the LP *Today*.

Webb Pierce

Country composer-singer who co-wrote "How Do You Think I Feel" with Wayne Walker, which Elvis recorded in 1956. Pierce was the headliner at the Overton Park Shell in Memphis when Elvis performed there August 10, 1954, and was upstaged by the audience's reaction to Elvis singing "Good Rockin' Tonight." His response that night has become a celebrated anecdote in the annals of Presleyana. "Sonofabitch!" he hissed at Elvis and Dewey Phillips.

Susan Pilkington

Back-up vocals, Memphis, 1973.

Pink Cadillac

When RCA bought Elvis' Sun contract for $35,000, one of the stipulations of the deal allowed Elvis to purchase a car. The Pink Cadillac he bought for his mother in September of 1956 became a metaphor for his new-fangled success and an enduring symbol of his attachment to his mother's memory, for he kept the car in his Graceland garage in mint condition until the day he died.

Barbara Pittman

One of the lesser artists at Sun that Elvis dated briefly in the early days.

"Playing For Keeps"

(Stanley Kessler) Cool, smooth Elvis and hushed Jordanaires from the early days. Recorded September 1, 1956 at Radio Recorders in Hollywood; released as a single in January of 1957 with "Too Much" on the flip-side. Later, on the LP's *For LP Fans Only* (1959) and *Elvis: Worldwide 50 Gold Award Hits, Volume 1* (1970).

"Please Don't Drag That String Around"

(Otis Blackwell – Winfield Scott) A tame, medium rocker – good sound, but without the bite of the earlier stuff. Recorded May 26, 1963 at RCA Nashville Studio; released in June of 1963 as a single, with "(You're The) Devil In Disguise" on the flip-side. Later, on the LPs *Elvis' Gold Records, Volume 4* (1968) and *Elvis: The Other Sides, Worldwide Gold Award Hits, Volume 2* (1971).

"Please Don't Stop Loving Me"

(Joy Byers) From *Frankie and Johnny* (1966), a subdued ballad with mellow piano and Elvis in fine voice. Recorded in May of 1965 at United Artists Recording Studio in Los Angeles; released in March of 1966 as a single, with "Frankie And Johnny" on the flip-side. Later, on the soundtrack LP.

Please Release Me

33⅓ LP Bootleg.
Side 1: "Fame And Fortune" (*Frank Sinatra Show*); "Stuck On You" (*Sinatra Show*); "Teddy Bear" (soundtrack); "Got A Lot O' Livin' To Do" (soundtrack); "Jailhouse Rock" (soundtrack); "A Cane And A High Starched Collar" (soundtrack).
Side 2: "The Lady Loves Me"; "C'mon Everybody"; "Dominique" (soundtrack); "Baby, What You Want Me To Do"; "My Baby Is Gone"; "Interview."

"Pledging My Love"

(Don Robey – Ferdinand Washington) From the Graceland sessions, a ballad with a beat, 1950's style. A nostalgic piece, soulfully done. Originally recorded by Johnny Ace in 1955. Recorded in October of 1976 in Memphis; released as a single in June of 1977, with "Way Down" on the flip-side.

"Pocketful Of Rainbows"

(Fred Wise – Ben Weisman) Warm ballad from *G.I. Blues* (1960), impeccably delivered by Elvis (in the film, Juliet Prowse contributed several lines). Recorded April-June, 1960 in Hollywood; released in October of 1960 on the soundtrack LP.

"Poison Ivy League"

(Bill Grant – Bernie Baum – Florence Kaye) Elvis belting out a rocker from *Roustabout* (1964), with humorous undertones. Recorded January of 1964 in Hollywood; released in October of 1964 on the soundtrack LP.

"Polk Salad Annie"

(Tony Joe White) The big hit of Elvis' 1970 Vegas shows: a kicking, funky bit of Southern stuff that brings out the best in Elvis and his band, making the song reek of the Louisiana swamps. Usually opened with one of Elvis' monologues. Recorded February 18, 1970 at the International Hotel in Las Vegas; released in May of 1970 on the LP *On Stage, February, 1970*. The 1970 documentary *That's The Way It Is* showed three different interpretations of the song at different stages; another version was delivered in *Elvis On Tour* (1972), though these versions weren't released. A fine live version was later released on *Elvis As Recorded At Madison Square Garden* (1972).

"Poor Boy"

(Elvis Presley – Vera Matson) From *Love Me Tender* (1956), Elvis singing about his love for Debra Paget – C & W style, with accordion. The song was actually written by Ken Darby, Vera Motson's husband. Recorded in August of 1956 in Hollywood; released in November of 1956 on the EP *Love Me Tender*. Later, on the LP's *For LP Fans Only* (1959) and *Elvis: The Other Sides – Worldwide Gold Award Hits, Vol. 2* (1971).

Sandy Posey

One of the backup singers at the Memphis sessions at American Studios in January and February of 1969.

Pot Luck

1962. RCA Victor. LP

(LPM/LSP-2523).

Side 1: "Kiss Me Quick"; "Just For Old Times' Sake"; "Gonna Get Back Home Somehow"; "(Such An) Easy Question"; "Steppin' Out Of Line"; "I'm Yours."

Side 2: "Something Blue"; "Suspicion"; "I Feel That I've Known You Forever"; "Night Rider"; "Fountain Of Love"; "That's Someone You Never Forget."

Potomac
FDR's yacht, which Elvis bought and then donated to St. Jude's Hospital in Memphis.

"Power Of My Love"
(Bill Grant – Bernie Baum – Florence Kaye)
From the Memphis sessions, shades of Bo Diddley. Elvis making the most out of mediocre lyrics; the band in fine form and nice singing from Sandy Posey and the Holladay girls. Recorded February 18, 1969 at American Studios; released in May of 1969 on the LP *From Elvis in Memphis.*

"Precious Memories"
(J. B. F. Wright)
The hymn performed at Gladys Presley's funeral by the Blackwood Brothers, said to be her favorite.

Precision Tool Factory
Where Elvis worked following high school graduation in 1953, before his job at Crown Electric Company.

Milton Prell
The principal owner of the Alladin Hotel, whose suite provided the site of Elvis' wedding ceremony on May 1, 1967.

Davada "Dee" Elliot Stanley Presley
Vernon Presley's blonde, blue-eyed second wife. They met in Germany where her husband, Bill Stanley, was a non-commissioned officer at Elvis' base in Freidberg. After she and Vernon fell in love, Dee and Bill Stanley divorced and she married Vernon on July 3, 1960. She moved to Graceland with her three small sons, Billy, Rick, and David, following the marriage. Although there have been reports that Elvis resented his stepmother for trying to take his beloved mother's place, their relations were warm over the years. Her relationship with Vernon Presley, however, was tumultuous. After a period of estrangement, they separated in 1975 and divorced two years later, only days after Elvis' funeral. Dee later chronicled her years with the Presley's in a book – *Elvis: We Love You Tender*, which she wrote with her three sons.

Gladys Love Smith Presley
Elvis' relationship with his beloved mother was known throughout the world as unusually intimate and intense, even for an only child. More than anyone else, Gladys Presley is credited with instilling in Elvis a sense of being as good or better than anybody else, even if the economic circumstances of his life were humble. She was born on April 25, 1912 and married Vernon Elvis Presley in 1933 (she was twenty-one, he only seventeen). Throughout Elvis'

formative years, she was extremely protective of her son, and she worked long hours at her jobs, first as a sewing machine operator in Tupelo, and later as a cafeteria worker and nurse's aide in St. Joseph's Hospital after the family moved to Memphis in 1948. Her relatives and friends in Tupelo and Memphis have remarked that Gladys' overwhelming love for her son was a natural response to the death of Jesse Garon Presley, Elvis' stillborn twin brother, and many have also noted her sense of psychic intuition when it

came to Elvis. Whatever it was, the feeling was more than reciprocated: Elvis' emotional life revolved around his mother, and when he became rich and famous at the age of twenty-one, his true satisfaction evolved from his happiness at being able to ease his mother's life and take care of her. For this reason, her death, from a heart attack triggered by acute hepatitis on August 14, 1958, at the Methodist Hospital in Memphis (while Elvis was undergoing basic training in Killeen, Texas), was all the more cruel and shattering. The body was interred at Forest Hill Cemetery. It is commonly acknowledged by Elvis' friends, family and fans that Gladys Presley's death was the most crucial emotional experience of his life – and, that any true understanding of Elvis' life and personality must be reconciled first and foremost with his relationship to her and the effects of her loss.

Jesse Garon Presley
Elvis' stillborn twin brother, named for Jesse McClowell Presley, buried in an unmarked grave in Priceville Cemetery outside of East Tupelo. Though Elvis' feelings about the loss of his twin brother have seemed overdramatized at times, he did in fact maintain a poignant awareness of how different his life might have been had his twin brother survived childbirth. Elvis was sometimes heard to speak to his brother and often remarked about feeling incomplete, as if a part of himself had been forever lost. He once called his brother his "psychic soulmate."

Jessie D. McClowell Presley (1896-1973)
Vernon Presley's father and Elvis' paternal grandfather, who married Minnie Mae Hood of Fulton, Mississippi in 1913 and fathered five children, among them Vester and Vernon. According to Vernon Presley's conversations about his father in later years, he was a harsh disciplinarian and a poor provider for the family, and left when Vernon was still a boy. By the time Jessie and Minnie May divorced in 1947 (the year before Vernon moved his family to Memphis), they had been separated for many years. He then married Vera Pruitt and lived in northeastern Tennessee until his death in 1973.

Lisa Marie Presley ☞
The birth of Elvis and Priscilla's only child (on February 1, 1968 at Baptist Memorial in Memphis) had been anticipated and awaited by Elvis fans throughout the world as if a royal couple were expecting an heir to the throne. Indeed, upon her twenty-fifth birthday, Lisa Marie, the sole heir to the Presley estate, will inherit a fortune. For the first five years of her life, Lisa lived either at Graceland or at Elvis' house at Palm Springs, and it was a sheltered existence despite her mother's fervent wishes that she lead a "normal" life. When Elvis and Priscilla were divorced in 1973, Priscilla was granted custody of Lisa – Elvis agreed entirely, acknowledging how important that Lisa be with her mother. Priscilla was quite generous with Elvis' visitation privileges and Lisa usually spent part of her summer vacation with Elvis, who adored and doted on his daughter. Still, because she was the most significant person in his life other than his father, he missed her bitterly, and was continually fearful for her safety from potential kidnappers. As Elvis' health and personal problems worsened in his final years, Lisa Marie Presley, was, like his

adoring fans, always a source of joy and pride. Many felt that, despite the trauma of the experience, it was appropriate that Lisa Marie Presley was present at Graceland when her father passed away on August 16, 1977.

Minnie Mae Presley

Elvis' paternal grandmother, another permanent resident of Graceland. Elvis affectionately called her "Dodger." She passed away on May 8, 1980, and many say she was Elvis' greatest fan and staunchest defender, and a feisty, humorous, warm personality. She was also one of the three main beneficiaries of his will.

Priscilla Beaulieu Presley

Elvis' wife and the mother of his only child, Lisa Marie Presley. Priscilla was only fourteen when she met Elvis Presley in Germany in 1959 at a party in Bad Nauheim at the house on Goethestrasse. (They were introduced by Currie Grant, an officer with the special services.) At the time, her father was stationed up in Weisbaden, and when Elvis expressed his desire to date Priscilla, he gave his permission with the provision that they be chaperoned. The two saw each other for the remainder of Elvis' tour in Germany. Priscilla first visited Graceland in 1960, when Elvis invited her for Christmas. The following year, Elvis asked Major Beaulieu if Priscilla could become a permanent resident at Graceland, and Beaulieu con-

sented after Elvis promised, in effect, to become her guardian (he made assurances of her enrollment in school, of providing his father and new stepmother, Dee, as chaperones, and of eventually marrying her). She was enrolled in Immaculate Conception High School in Memphis, graduating in 1963, and then entered the Patricia Stevens Finishing School, studying dance, modeling and design. From 1962 to 1968, from when she was fifteen – twenty-one, Elvis "raised" Priscilla. He was then turning out an average of three films a year. They were married in a small, private ceremony at the Aladdin Hotel on May 1, 1967 by Nevada Supreme Court Judge David Zenoff, in the private suite of Milton Prell, the owner of the

hotel. Joe Esposito and Marty Lacker were co-best men. After the honeymoon in Palm Springs, California, they moved to 1174 Hillcrest Road in Beverly Hills. Their daughter, Lisa Marie, was born nine months to the day after the marriage, on February 1, 1968. Over the next four years, as Elvis made his "Comeback" to live performing in Las Vegas and began touring, and as Priscilla matured, the couple grew estranged for a variety of reasons. When Priscilla became romantically involved with Mike Stone, her private karate instructor, the marriage faltered and she left Elvis on February 23, 1972. Divorce proceedings were instituted by Elvis on January 8, 1973 (his 37th birthday). The divorce was granted by the

a nine-month stretch at Parchman Penitentiary, a period of his life that remained confidential to all except the immediate family until the final year of his life, when it was published by *The Midnight Globe*, much to his unhappiness. (Much about the incident will probably never come to light and remains mysterious. It seems that Orville S. Bean, the farmer who loaned Vernon money, was the man who pressed charges when Vernon took one of his checks for $14 and changed it to $40, an act of obvious financial desperation. Elvis was only three years old at the time and his recollections or feelings about the affair will never be known.)

In 1948, following a long period of scarce employment in Tupelo, Vernon Presley moved his family to Memphis, where he went to work packing crates with paint cans at the United Paint Company. He held the job until Elvis' career exploded in 1956. He devoted himself to his son's personal business affairs. After the death of his wife in 1958, when Vernon accompanied Elvis to Germany, he met and fell in love with Davada "Dee" Stanley, the wife of an army sergeant stationed in Freidberg. When Dee divorced her husband, she married Vernon Presley on July 3, 1960 and Vernon became stepfather to her three sons, Billy, Rick, and David. The marriage lasted seventeen years and fell apart during the tragic years of Elvis' decline, when Vernon began living with a young nurse from Colorado named Sandy Miller, whom he had met in Las Vegas. In 1975, Vernon Presley suffered a serious heart attack, which was no doubt exacerbated by the pressures and pains of Elvis' deterioration. With Elvis' death, many felt it was only a matter of time before Vernon succumbed to the tragedy and passed away himself. He was named executor of Elvis' will in August of 1977 and tried to stay on top of the continuing business affairs of his son's estate until he died on June 26, 1979 in Memphis, reuniting Elvis' friends and family for another solemn funeral at Graceland, where he is buried.

Superior Court of Santa Monica on October 11, 1973. Following the initial settlement, Priscilla brought suit for extrinsic fraud, claiming that Elvis had failed to disclose his true financial assets. The final settlement made her a wealthy woman, and she opened a boutique in Beverly Hills called "Bis & Beau. Although Priscilla had custody of Lisa Marie, Elvis and she remained good friends, and she was generous with Elvis' visitation privileges. Following Elvis' death, Priscilla slowly emerged in public, first as a spokeswoman for Wella Products, and later as one of the hosts of the ABC-TV show

Those Amazing Animals. She presently resides in Los Angeles.

Rosella Presley
Rosie Presley was Elvis' great-grandmother. Very little is known about her, except that she was not married, but had several children.

Sam Presley
Vernon Presley's first cousin who ran a gambling club called the Sage Patch on the Mississippi-Alabama state line with T. B. Richardson. It was Richardson who later signed Elvis to his first Las Vegas appearance at the New Frontier Hotel in 1956.

Vernon Elvis Presley ☞
Elvis' "Daddy," born in 1916 in Fulton Mississippi, died on June 26, 1979, in Memphis, of heart failure following four years of frail health after a major heart attack in 1975. At the age of seventeen, Vernon married the twenty-one year old Gladys Love Smith and settled in East Tupelo, where a dairy farmer named Orville S. Bean loaned him enough money to build the small shotgun shack where Elvis was born on January 8, 1935. Vernon worked as a sharecropper, handyman, and truck-driver until 1938, when he was convicted of forgery and served

Vester Presley
Vernon Presley's brother who married Gladys Smith's sister Cletus and helped to teach Elvis to play his first guitar. Vester later moved to Memphis with his family. When Elvis purchased Graceland, he became famous with Elvis' fans as the guard at

the music gate. He co-authored *A Presley Speaks* in 1978.

Presleyana
Of or having to do with the personal, public, musical or acting career of Elvis Presley, used in connection with those who seek to collect memorabilia.

"Presley Wagon"
The German press designation for Elvis' BMW during his hitch in the Army.

Nashval Lorene Pritchett
Vernon Presley's sister, who became an ordained minister of the Assembly of God Church. Elvis helped her build a church in Walls, Mississippi.

William Earl Pritchett
Nashval's husband, who worked for a time as a guard and groundskeeper of Graceland.

"Promised Land"
(Chuck Berry)
Elvis appropriated Chuck Berry's 1964 classic about a cross-country trip and turned it into a metaphor for his own life on the road. Hot, driving rock (used with great effectiveness on the soundtrack of the 1981 film, *This Is Elvis*). Recorded December 15, 1973 at Stax Studios in Memphis; released in October of 1974 as a single, with "It's Midnight" on the flip-side. Later, on the LP *Promised Land* (1975).

Promised Land
1975. RCA. LP (APL1-0873).
Side 1: "Promised Land"; "There's A Honky Tonk Angel (Who'll Take Me Back In)"; "Help Me"; "Mr. Song-Man"; "Love Song Of The Year."
Side 2: "It's Midnight"; "Your Love's Been A Long Time Coming"; "If You Talk In Your Sleep"; "Thinking About You; "You Asked Me To."

"Proud Mary"
Like "Polk Salad Annie," Elvis picked up Creedence Clearwater Revival's 1969 hit and transformed it into something entirely his own—churning, fun, very Southern. Recorded on February 17, 1970 at the International Hotel in Las Vegas; released in May of 1970 on the LP *On Stage February, 1970*. The song was performed in the 1972 documentary *Elvis On Tour*. Another driving live version was released on *Elvis As Recorded At Madison Square Garden*.

Juliet Prowse
As "Lilli," she was Elvis' leggy, beautiful South African co-star in *G.I. Blues* (1961) and, despite her relationship with Frank Sinatra at the time, she was a serious romantic interest. About her charms, Elvis once remarked: "She has a body that would make a bishop stamp his foot through a stained glass window."

"Puppet On A String"
(Sid Tepper—Roy C. Bennett)
From *Girl Happy* (1965), a straightforward ballad with Elvis in a husky voice, backed-up by the Jordanaires. Recorded July 8, 1964 in Hollywood; released in April of 1965 on the soundtrack LP.

Pure Elvis
1979. RCA. LP (DJL1-3455).
Side 1: "I Got A Feelin' In My Bones"; "For The Heart"; "She Wears My Ring"; "Find Out What's Happening."
Side 2: "I Got A Feelin' In My Body"; "For The Heart"; "She Wears My Ring"; "Find Out What's Happening."

Norbert Putnam
Session bassist, Nashville, 1970-71.

"Put The Blame On Me"
(Fred Wise—Norman Blagman—Kay Twomey)
Well-arranged but nondescript tune. Recorded March 13, 1961 at RCA Nashville Studio; released in June of 1961 on the LP *Something For Everybody*.

"Put Your Hand In The Hand (Of The Man From Galilee)"
(Gene MacLellan)
Elvis couldn't resist this rocking spiritual, which was a big hit for Ocean in 1971. Great fervor in the choruses by the Imperials, along with the voices of Millie Kirkham, June Page, and Sonja Montgomery. Recorded June 8, 1971 at RCA Nashville Studio; released in February of 1972 on the LP *Elvis Now*.

"Queenie Wahine's Papaya"
(Bill Grant—Bernie Baum—Florence Kaye)
From *Paradise Hawaiian Style* (1966), Elvis' duet with little Donna Butterworth (she doesn't sing on the record). Recorded July 19, 1965 at Paramount Recording Studio; released in June of 1966 on the soundtrack LP.

Radio
Soon after he began to tour the U.S.A. in 1954, Elvis appeared on the "Louisiana Hayride" broadcast every Saturday night from Shreveport, Louisiana. On his first appearance, he sang "Blue Moon" and "That's All Right." He soon became a regular, working his way up to a fifteen minute spot on the program. He appeared regularly until the spring of 1956, and he sometimes sang a commercial on the air, which went something like: *You can get 'em pipin' hot after 4 o'clock, Southern-made doughnuts hit the spot!*

It was over Dewey Phillips' *Red Hot & Blue* radio show on WBHQ that Elvis got his first record airplay, and he did quite a few radio interviews in the '50's, being interviewed by DJs in whichever town he was appearing in. The DJs helped Elvis a lot by spinning his discs, apart from a few who refused to.

In the '60's, Elvis and the Colonel made several special programs that went out at Christmas or other special times over hundreds of radio stations. The programs would last some thirty minutes, and Elvis' religious or Christmas songs would be played, with a few commercials slotted in. In the 1967 program, Elvis personally wished the listeners a Merry Christmas. In 1968, the program was used as a build-up to the *TV Special* to be broadcast two days later.

Many special programs about Elvis have been aired over the years, both in the U.K. and the U.S.A. One Christmas in the '60's, the BBC had an all-Elvis program that featured actual soundtrack recordings, instead of records (e.g. "Wooden Heart" with the children singing along). Major series on popular music or film music have usually featured Elvis either in a program himself, or a part-program (e.g. *25 Years of Rock* and *Hollywood And The Stars*). A twelve-part series on Elvis was aired in the early '70's, based on Jerry Hopkins' book, and this was updated to a thirteen-part series in the U.S.A. in the mid-'70's and again revised after Elvis' death and broadcast both here and in the U.K.

DJs have had "Elvis spots" for years; Radio Luxembourg had a fifteen-minute show on Elvis for years, and also "Swoon Club" with Elvis strongly featured. On special occasions, U.S.A. radio stations featured twenty-four hours of Elvis. After Elvis' death, many stations immediately began to program nothing but Elvis, and most stations had tributes of some sort. The tributes have continued, gathering momentum around Elvis' birthday and of course, August 16th. Radio KRLA in Pasadena, California has aired an hour of Elvis every night since August 16, 1977, but the ultimate tribute has to be Sam Phillips', who changed his Memphis radio station identification number to WLVS.

Radio Recorders
Recording studio in Los Angeles used by Elvis for several highly productive sessions in 1956-1958. The first session there, September 5-7, 1957 produced "Treat Me Nice."

"Rag Mop"
One of the unsuccessful tunes Elvis did for Sam Phillips in his studio when Sam invited Elvis to attempt "Without You" in 1954. The song was written by Johnny Lee Wills in 1950.

"Rags To Riches"
(Richard Aeller—Jerry Ross) Elvis erupting at full power after the opening rumble of drums—a stark ballad, uncluttered (a hot for Tony Bennett in 1953). Recorded September 22, 1970 at RCA Nashville Studio; released as a single in March of 1971, with "Where Did They Go, Lord" on the flip-side (unreleased on an album).

Rainbow Rollerdome
2881 Lamar Ave. Well-known Memphis roller rink that Elvis often rented out for all-night skating parties for his friends in the '50's and '60's.

"Raised On Rock"
(Mark James) Strident guitar, thudding bass, and some mean back-up vocals by Misses Westmoreland, Holladay and Holladay, made this song about the "idol" who sang "Hound Dog" attractive but strangely remote. Recorded July 23, 1973 at Stax Recording Studio in Memphis; released in September of 1973 as a single, with "For Ol' Times Sake" on the flip-side. Later, on the LP *Raised On Rock* (1973).

Raised On Rock/For Ol' Times Sake
1973. RCA. LP (APL1-0388). Side 1: "Raised On Rock"; "Are You Sincere"; "Find Out What's Happening"; "I Miss You"; "Girl Of Mine."
Side 2: "For Ol' Times Sake"; "If You Don't Come Back"; "Just A Little Bit"; "Sweet Angeline"; "Three Corn Patches."

USS General Randall
Elvis' troop ship to Bremerhaven, Germany, September 22—October 8, 1958.

Don Randi
Session piano and organ—*"Elvis" TV Special*, 1968.

Bill Randle
Influential disc jockey on WERE in Cleveland during the 1950's who attained notoriety for being one of the first important DJ's to give Elvis records serious airplay north of the Mason-Dixon line in 1955.

Boots Randolph
Saxophonist and Elvis' session man on countless records.

RCA Family Record Center
1962 RCA Victor. EP (PR-121). Side 1: "Good Luck Charm"; (Elvis Presley); "The Way You Look Tonight" (Peter Nero);

"Younger Than Springtime" (Paul Anka); "Frenesi" (Living Strings).
Side 2: "Twistin' The Night Away" (Sam Cooke); "Easy Street" (Al Hirt); "Make Someone Happy" (Perry Como); "Moon River" (Henry Mancini).

RCA Studios in Nashville
The famous recording facilities at 1525 McGavock Street, shared with the Methodist Church, where Elvis recorded "Heartbreak Hotel" and many of his early RCA Golden oldies. He continued to use the studio throughout his career.

"Reach Out To Jesus"
(Ralph Carmichael) Strong piano accompaniment by David Briggs and backing by the Imperials on this gospel. Recorded June 8, 1971 at RCA Nashville Studio; released in April of 1972 on the LP *He Touched Me.*

"Ready Teddy"
(Robert Blackwell—John Marascalo) Elvis slowed down Little Richard's 1956 hit, but the energy pulses. Recorded September 3, 1956 at Radio Recorders in Hollywood; released in November of 1956 on the EP *Elvis, Volume 2.* Also on the LP *Elvis* (1956). On September 9, 1956, Elvis performed the song on his first appearance on the *Ed Sullivan Show* (This early clip was included as documentary footage in *Elvis On Tour* in 1972.)

Real Elvis, The
1956 RCA Victor. EP (EPA-940). Side 1: "Don't Be Cruel"; "I Want You, I Need You, I Love You."
Side 2: "Hound Dog"; "My Baby Left Me."

"Reconsider Baby"
(Lowell Fulson) With a touch of the blues, Elvis growls his way through this one. Boots Randolph shines on the sax break. Recorded April 4, 1960 at RCA Nashville Studio; released in April of 1960 on the LP *Elvis Is Back!*

Record Producers
Steve Sholes was in charge of Elvis' recording sessions when he first moved to RCA, and Chet Atkins also produced some early discs. In 1966, Felton Jarvis joined Elvis and became a more or less permanent record producer and very close friend of Elvis. Felton worked on sessions up until Elvis' last on October 31, 1976, and often accompanied Elvis on his Las Vegas seasons. It was Jarvis who produced the excellent new backings on the "Guitar Man" album issued in

1981. The death of Jarvis in early January 1981 was a tragic loss for the Elvis world. From 1974 on, Elvis was usually listed as "Executive Producer" on albums, e.g. *Having Fun On Stage,* the *Graceland* live album, *Today, From Elvis Presley Boulevard,* and *Elvis In Concert.* Joan Deary did a lot of good work in producing albums released after Elvis' death.

Red, Hot and Blue
Dewey Phillips' famed radio program on WABQ in Memphis from 9 p.m. to midnight was widely listened to by both a white and black audience interested in rhythm and blues. Phillips broke in many artists around the Memphis area on the show and first aired "That's All Right (Mama)" on the evening of July 7, 1954. He interviewed Elvis that same night.

Jerry Reed
Composer—guitarist—performer—actor who wrote "Guitar Man" and "U.S. Male," and "A Thing Called Love" and "Talk About The Good Times," all of which were recorded by Elvis (He played lead guitar on "U.S. Male"). He also recorded an Elvis novelty record called "Tupelo Mississippi Flash" in 1967. Reed also recorded "Big Boss Man," "Ain't That Lovin' You Baby," and "Baby What You Want Me To Do," all covered by Elvis.

Della Reese
One of Elvis' favorite night-club singers.

Reflections
The Elvis newsletter published out of Memphis in 1979 by Charlie Hodge and Dick Grob.

"Relax"
(Sid Tepper—Roy C. Bennett) Elvis sang this song while chasing Yvonne Craig around the room in *It Happened At The World's Fair* (1963). Showy, seductive, and typical. With the Jordanaires. Recorded in October of 1962 in Hollywood; released in March of 1963 on the soundtrack LP. Later, on the Pickwick LP *Mahalo From Elvis* (1978).

"Release Me (And Let Me Love Again)"
(Eddie Miller—W. S. Stevenson) Big-voiced C & W ballad from the Vegas stage, a 1967 hit by Englebert Humperdink. Soulful, schmaltzy, and a bit souped-up, but without the big finale. Recorded on February 18, 1970 at the International Hotel in Las Vegas; released in May of 1970 on the LP *On Stage—February, 1970.* Later, on *Welcome To My World* (1977).

Clint Reno
Elvis' character from *Love Me Tender* (1956).

"Return To Sender"
(Otis Blackwell – Winfield Scott) From *Girls! Girls! Girls!* (1962), a song so commercially sound it was released *before* the film! Elvis is high-pitched, passionate, and obviously in his groove. Recorded in March of 1962 in Hollywood; released in October of 1962 as a single, with "Where Do You Come From" on the flipside. Later, on the 1962 soundtrack LP, and on *Worldwide 50 Gold Award Hits, Volume 1* (1970).

Alejandro Rey
"Mareno," the lifeguard in *Fun In Acapulco*, (1963).

Kang Rhee
"Master Rhee." Elvis' Korean karate instructor in Memphis for many years and another "spiritual" advisor.

Dane Rhudyar
Elvis' personal astrologer, who did his chart.

Charlie Rich
"The Silver Fox." Well-known country composer-performer who recorded for the Sun label. He never achieved fame or fortune like the others, despite his obvious gifts as a singer and composer of songs like "Lonely Weekends." Rich wrote the song "I'm Coming Home," which Elvis recorded in 1961.

John Rich
Director of *Roustabout* (1964), *Easy Come, East Go* (1966).

Rick Richards
Elvis' character in *Paradise, Hawaiian Style*.

Ted Richmond
Produced *It Happened At The World's Fair* (1963).

Don Rickles
One of Elvis' favorite night club comedians.

"Riding The Rainbow"
(Fred Wise – Ben Weisman) Sweet melody, hackneyed lyrics from *Kid Galahad* (1962). With the Jords. Recorded in November of 1961 in Hollywood; released in September of 1962 on the EP *Kid Galahad*. Later on the RCA Camden LP *I Got Lucky* (1971), rereleased by Pickwick.

Billy Riley
Performer and friend from Elvis' Sun days, who often entertained at his private parties in Memphis.

"Rip It Up"
(Robert Blackwell – John Marascalo) Elvis covers the 1956 hit by Little Richard (also recorded by

Bill Haley and The Comets that year). Yes . . . it rocks! With astonishing drumming by D. J. Fontanna, recorded September 3, 1956 at Radio Recorders in Hollywood; released in November of 1956 on the LP *Elvis* and on the EP *Elvis, Volume One*. Later on the LP *Worldwide Gold Award Hits, Volume 2* (1971).

Rising Sun
Elvis' first and most beloved horse when he became a riding nut along with Priscilla in 1967.

Laurence J. Rittenband
Santa Monica Superior Court Judge who granted Elvis his divorce from Priscilla on October 9, 1973.

Geraldo Rivera
Television personality and investigative reporter whose investigations into Elvis' drug abuse and death led to Dr. Nick's troubles with the authorities when they were broadcast on the ABC show *20/20* in 1980.

Deke Rivers
Elvis' character in *Loving You* (1957).

Johnny Rivers
Guitarist-singer and recording artist who did Chuck Berry's "Memphis, Tennessee," and became an intimate song partner of Elvis' during the '60's.

Marty Robbins
Country composer-singer of hits like "El Paso" who toured briefly with Elvis in 1955 and later recorded a version of "That's All Right (Mama)." Elvis admired Robbins over the years and eventually recorded "You Gave Me A Mountain" which he also performed often and considered to be one of the most meaningful numbers in his repertoire.

Dale Robertson
Well-known TV actor who became a personal friend of Elvis when they both promoted Easter Seals over the years.

Don Robertson
Singer-musician-composer who wrote a score of songs for Elvis over the years, among them "I'm Yours" and "They Remind Me Too Much Of You."

Red Robinson
Canadian DJ who narrated the LP *Elvis: A Canadian Tribute* (1979). Robinson's association with Elvis dates back to a 1957 interview conducted in Vancouver, before Elvis performed a concert at Empire Stadium. Robinson released the contents of the interview on a Polydor LP in 1977 entitled *The Elvis Tapes*.

"Rock-A-Hula Baby"
(Fred Wise – Ben Weisman – Dolores Fuller)

From *Blue Hawaii* (1961), one of the big hits – a twisting film rocker, very repetitive, with Elvis' patented growling and slowed-down finish. Recorded in April of 1961 in Hollywood; released in October of 1961 on the soundtrack LP. Also released as a single – the flip-side of "Can't Help Falling In Love." Later on *Worldwide 50 Gold Award Hits, Volume 1* (1970) and *Elvis In Hollywood* (1976).

Rockin' With Elvis New Year's Eve
Double LP Bootleg.
Side 1: "2001 Theme"; "See See Rider"; "I Got A Woman"; "Amen"; "Big Boss Man"; "Love Me"; "Fairytale."
Side 2: "Lord, You Gave Me A Mountain"; "Jailhouse Rock"; "Presentation Of Liberty Bell By Jim Curtin"; "Now Or Never" (With Introduction By Sherril Nielson); "My Way"; "Funny How Time Slips Away"; "Auld Lang Syne"; "Introduction of Vernon And Lisa Presley"; "Blue Suede Shoes"; "Trying To Get To You."
Side 3: "Polk Salad Annie"; "Introduction To Bank"; "Early Morning Rain"; "What'd I Say"; "Johnny B. Goode"; "Ronnie Tutt Drum Solo"; "Jerry Scheff Solo"; "Sonny Brown Piano Solo"; "Love Letters"; "Hail Hail"; "Rock N' Roll"; "Fever"; "Hurt."
Side 4: "Hound Dog"; "Are You Lonesome Tonight"; "Reconsider, Baby"; "Little Sister"; "Unchained Melody"; "Rags To Riches"; "Can't Help Falling In Love"; "Closing Vamp."

Rockin' With Elvis New Year's Eve
33⅓ bootleg double LP released in 1977 on the Spirit of America label (Spirit of America HNY 7677). Includes Elvis' entire concert appearance in Pittsburgh on December 31, 1976.
Side 1: "Also Sprach Zarathustra"; "See See Rider"; "I Got A Woman"; "Amen"; "Big Boss Man"; "Love Me"; "Fairytale."
Side 2: "You Gave Me A Mountain"; "Jailhouse Rock"; "Presentation Of Liberty Bell By Jim Curtin"; "It's Now Or Never" (With Introduction By Sherril Nielson); "My Way"; "Funny How Time Slips Away"; "Auld Lang Syne"; "Introduction To Vernon And Lisa Presley"; "Blue Suede Shoes"; "Trying To Get To You."
Side 3: "Polk Salad Annie"; "Introduction To Band"; "Early Morning Rain"; "What'd I Say"; "Johnny B. Goode"; "Ronnie Tutt Drum Solo"; "Jerry Scheff Solo"; "Sonny Brown Piano Solo"; "Love Letters"; "Hail, Hail

Rock N' Roll"; "Fever"; "Hurt." Side 4; "Hound Dog"; "Are You Lonesome Tonight"; "Reconsider Baby"; "Little Sister"; "Unchained Melody"; "Rags To Riches"; "Can't Help Falling In Love."

Rock My Soul
33⅓ Bootleg.
Sides 1 and 2: *Elvis On Tour* soundtrack.

Rock Rock Rock (All Star Rock – Volume Two)
1972. Original Sound. LP (OSR-11).
Side 1: "American Pie (Don McLean); "Brand New Key" (Melanie); "Let's Stay Together" (Al Green); "Day After Day" (Badfinger); "Never Been To Spain" (Three Dog Night); "Until It's Time For You To Go" (Elvis Presley); "Country Wine" (The Raiders).
Side 2: "The Way Of Love" (Cher); "Hurting Each Other" (The Carpenters); "Joy" (Apollo 100); "My World" (Bee Gees); "Everything I Own" (Bread); "Feelin' Alright" (Joe Cocker); "Down By The Lazy River" (Osmonds).

Charlie Rogers
Elvis' character in *Roustabout* (1964).

Yvonne Romain
"Claire Dunham," the sophisticated playgirl in *Double Trouble* (1967).

Leticia Roman
Actress who was one of Elvis' girlfriends following his discharge from the Army.

Carl Romonelli
Sculptor commissioned by Barron Hilton of the Hilton chain of hotels to do the six-foot bronze statue of Elvis for the lobby of the Las Vegas Hilton, dedicated by Vernon and Priscilla Presley on September 8, 1978.

Nancy Rooks
One of Graceland's cooks and maids.

Roustabout
Started: 1964
A Hal Wallis Production
A Paramount Picture
Cast
Charlie Rogers: Elvis Presley; Maggie Moore: Barbara Stanwyck; Cathy Lean: Joan Freeman; Joe Lean: Leif Erickson; Madame Mijanou: Sue Ann Langdon; Harry Carver: Pat Buttram; Marge: Joan Staley; Arthur Neilsen: Dabbs Greer; Fred: Steve Brodie; College Student: Raquel Welch; Lou: Jack Albertson; Hazel: Jane Dulo.
Credits
Produced by Hal Wallis

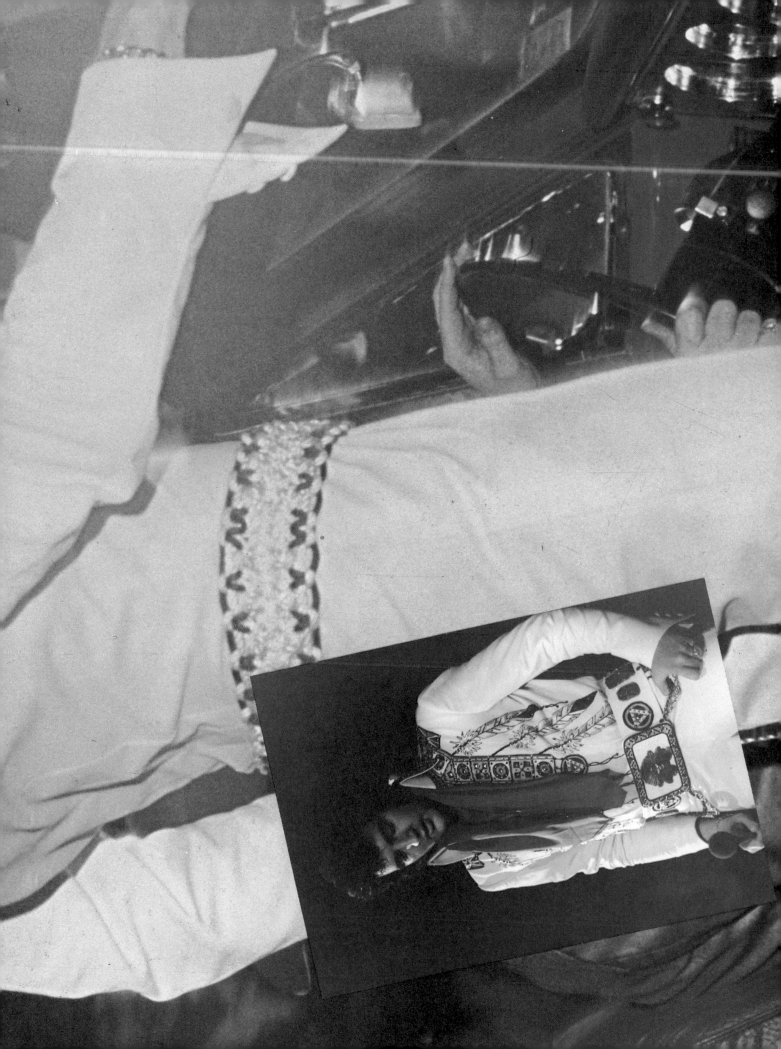

Associate Producer: Paul Nathan
Director: John Rich
Production Manager: Frank Caffey
Unit Production Manager: R. A. Bladon
Screenplay by Alan Weiss
First Assistant Director: D. Michael Moore
Technical Advisor: Col. T. Parker
Music by Joseph J. Lilley
Choreography: Earl Barton
Hair Style Supervisor: Nellie Manley
Technicolor and Techniscope
Songs
"Roustabout"; "Poison Ivy League"; "Wheels On My Heels"; "It's Carnival Time"; "Carnie Town"; "One Track Heart"; "Hard Knocks"; "Little Egypt"; "Big Love, Big Heartache"; "There's A Brand New Day On The Horizon"; "It's A Wonderful World."
Running Time: 101 Minutes.
Previously titled: *Right This Way Folks*

"Roustabout"
(Bill Grant – Bernie Baum – Florence Kaye)
The title tune from the 1964 film, a passable grabber with backing by the Mellomen and Elvis giving it his all. The film piece had more orchestration than the record. Recorded in January of 1964 in Hollywood; released in October of 1964 on the soundtrack LP. Later, on the LP *Elvis In Hollywood* (1976).

Roustabout
1964. RCA Victor. LP (LPM/LSP-2999)
Side 1: "Roustabout"; "Little Egypt"; "Poison Ivy League"; "Hard Knocks"; "It's A Wonderful World"; "Big Love, Big Heartache."
Side 2: "One Track Heart"; "It's Carnival Time"; "Carny Town"; "There's A Brand New Day On The Horizon"; "Wheels On My Heels."

"Rubberneckin'"
(Cory Jones – Bunny Warren)
From *Change Of Habit* (1969), an offbeat, energetic film rocker gussied up with the musicians from the Memphis sessions. Horns, wailing females, and Elvis belting out some lackluster lyrics. Somehow, he makes it all appealing. Recorded January 29, 1969 at American Studios in Memphis; released in November of 1969 as a single, with "Don't Cry Daddy" on the flip-side. Later, on the RCA Camden LPs *Almost In Love* (1970) and *Double Dynamite* (1976).

"Runaway"
(Del Shannon – Max Crook)

Elvis took to Del Shannon's 1961 hit the first year of his Vegas engagements. The results: James Burton doing a 1950's Venture-style lead guitar, the Sweet Inspirations chanting the choruses and Elvis coming the closest of his career to falsetto singing. Recorded August 22, 1969 at the International Hotel in Las Vegas; released in May of 1970 in the LP *On Stage – February, 1970.*

"Run On"
(Arranged and adapted by Elvis Presley)
Elvis, the Jordanaires and the Imperial Quartet. A rousing, up-tempo gospel, nicely put together and beautifully captured by Felton Jarvis in his first session as Elvis' producer. Recorded May 25, 1966 at RCA Nashville Studio; released in March of 1967 on the LP *How Great Thou Art.*

Kurt Russell
The young actor chosen over 700 others to portray Elvis in the 1979 Dick Clark-produced TV movie *Elvis.* Russell delighted Elvis fans by the intensity and authenticity of his performance, and caused a stir by marrying Season Hubley, who portrayed Priscilla Presley in the film. As a child, Russell made his debut in *It Happened At The World's Fair* (1963), by kicking Elvis in the leg, and he went on to star in numerous Disney films.

Leon Russell
Singer, songwriter, arranger, musician who played piano on several soundtracks for Elvis' films during the 1960's. Over the years, Russell has worked with Frank Sinatra, Jerry Lee Lewis, Bob Dylan, Phil Spector, Joe Cocker, and the Rolling Stones, in addition to pursuing a successful career as a solo artist. Elvis admired his style and versatile talents.

Nipsey Russell
Well-known comedian, one of the many to work with Elvis over the years as his opening act.

Ryman Auditorium
The site of the "Grand Ole Opry" broadcast from Nashville, Tennessee from 1942-1974. Elvis performed there on September 25, 1954.

68 Comeback, The
33⅓ bootleg album on the Memphis King label which featured material from Elvis' "comeback" appearance on the 1968 NBC-TV Special *"Elvis"* on December 3, 1968.
Side 1: "Nothingville"; "Guitar Man"; "Let Yourself Go"; "Guitar Man"; "Big Boss Man"; "If I Can Dream"; "Memories"; "Let Yourself Go."
Side 2: "It Hurts Me"; "Trouble"; "Guitar Man"; "Sometimes I Feel Like A Motherless Child"; "Where Could I Go But To The Lord"; "Saved"; "A Little Less Conversation."

Boris Sagal
Director of *Girl Happy* (1965).

"Sand Castles"
(David Hess – Herb Goldberg)
Recorded for *Paradise Hawaiian Style* but not used in the film, a gentle children's lullaby with a fairy tale quality. Recorded July 19, 1965 at Paramount Recording Studio; released in June of 1965 on the soundtrack LP.

Denis Sanders
Director of the documentary *Elvis: That's The Way It Is.*

"Santa Bring My Baby Back (To Me)"
(Aaron Schroeder – Claude DeMetrius)
Swinger from El's first yuletide album – straightforward, fun. Recorded September 7, 1957 at Radio Recorders in Hollywood; released in November of 1957 on the LP *Elvis' Christmas Album.* Also on the EP *Elvis Sings Christmas Songs* (1957).

"Santa Claus Is Back In Town"
(Jerry Leiber – Mike Stoller)
Raucous send-up with Dudley Brooks excelling on piano and Elvis in top R & B voice – the "Jailhouse Rock" of Christmas. Recorded September 7, 1957 at Radio Recorders in Hollywood; released in November of 1957 on the LP *Elvis' Christmas Album.* Also on the EP *Elvis Sings Christmas Songs* (1957). Performed on the 1968 NBC-TV Special.

"Santa Lucia"
(Arranged by Elvis Presley)
From *Viva Las Vegas* (1964), an old Italian folk song done partly in Italian with banjo accompaniment. Ann-Margret humming along in the background. Recorded in July of 1963 in Hollywood; released in July of 1965 on the LP *Burning Love And Hits From His Movies, Volume 2* (1972).

"Saved"
(Jerry Leiber – Mike Stoller)
Gospel-style oldie (a hit for LaVern Baker in 1961) performed with the Blossoms on the *1968 NBC-TV Special.* Recorded June 30, 1968 at the Burbank Studios; released in December of 1968 on the LP *"Elvis" NBC-TV Special.*

Save-On-Records
1956 RCA Victor. EP (SPA 7-27).
Side 1: "Intermezzo" (Frankie Carle); "Moonlight Cocktail" (Al Nevins); "Gonna Sit Right Down And Cry" (Elvis Presley); "Adventure In Time (Sauter-Finegan Orchestra); "Great Gettin' Up Morning" (Harry Belafonte).
Side 2: "Liebestraum" (Rubenstein); "Voi Che Sapete" (Rise

Stevens); "Beethoven: Symphony No. 9" (Arturo Toscanini); "Jalousie" (Arthur Fiedler & Boston Pops); "Symphony Fantastique" (Boston Symphony Orchestra).

Scatter
Elvis' celebrated chimpanzee, who rode in cars, drank bourbon, and pinched girls' behinds.

Jerry Scheff
Elvis' bass guitar player, 1969-1976, on tour and in recording sessions.

Jerry Schilling
A longtime member of the "Memphis Mafia" (1964-1976) and one of Elvis' closest friends over the years (Jerry worked as a bodyguard and in many other areas of Elvis' life). Tall, talented, an ex-athlete and health devotee, he was one of the more articulate and independent members of Elvis' entourage. He managed the Sweet Inspirations for a time and married Myrna Smith before becoming manager of the Beach Boys. Along with Joe Esposito, he was one of the consultants on the 1981 film *This Is Elvis*. Jerry was one of the pall bearers at Elvis' funeral.

Aaron Schroeder
Well-known song-writer who co-composed a score of Elvis songs over the years, among them the hits "I Got Stung" with David Hill, "Stuck On You" with J. Leslie McFarland, "Good Luck Charm" and "It's Now Or Never" with Wally Gold.

Ben Schwalb
Produced *Tickle Me* (1964).

Sol Schwartz
One of Elvis' Beverly Hills jewelers.

Lizabeth Scott
The canny press agent "Glenda Markle" in *Loving You* (1957).

"Scratch My Back (Then I'll Scratch Yours)"
(Bill Grant – Bernie Baum – Florence Kaye)
From *Paradise Hawaiian Style* (1966), Elvis singing to all those pretty wahines. Recorded July 19, 1965 at Paramount Recording Studio; released in June of 1966 on the soundtrack LP.

Scripps Clinic
The San Diego Medical facility used by notables to treat alcohol and drug abuse. Private detective John O'Grady tried to get Priscilla Presley to convince Elvis to go there for his drug problem in 1976, but to no avail.

Mildred Scrivner
Elvis' homeroom teacher at Humes who put Elvis in the school's talent show.

"Seeing Is Believing"
(Red West – Glen Spreen)
Gospel-rocker with an infectious beat, pounding bass, vocal back up by Millie Kirkham, Temple Riser and Ginger Holladay . . . and Elvis singing roughly with gusto. Recorded May 19, 1971 at RCA Nashville Studio; released in April of 1972 on the LP *He Touched Me*.

"See See Rider"
(Ma Rainey – Chuck Willis)
Though songwriter's credit is usually accorded to that matriarch of the blues, Ma Rainey, Big Bill Broonzy was doing this song in the 1920's. Before Elvis fell in love with it, the song had been recorded by Chuck Willis (1957), La Vern Baker (1962), Bobby Powell (1965), Mitch Ryder and the Detroit Wheels (1965) and the Animals (1966). It became a standard for opening his shows after "Also Sprach Zarathustra," and featured rumbling drums by Ronnie Tutt, hot licks by James Burton on lead guitar, and brass arrangements. (Elvis would oftentimes segue into "That's All Right (Mama)". First recorded February 17, 1970 at the International Hotel in Las Vegas on the LP *On Stage, February, 1970*. Performed in *Elvis On Tour* (1972) and on the broadcasts of "Elvis: Aloha From Hawaii" (1973) and *Elvis In Concert* (1977). Released on the LPs *Elvis: Aloha From Hawaii Via Satellite* (1973), *Elvis Recorded Live Onstage In Memphis* (1974) and *Elvis In Concert* (1977).

Peter Sellers
Elvis' favorite comic actor.

"Sentimental Me"
(Jim Morehead – Jimmy Cassin)
Elvis covering the 1950 hit by the Ames Brothers – well produced but strained. Recorded March 13, 1961 at RCA Nashville Studio; released in June of 1961 on the LP *Something For Everybody*. Later, on the RCA Camden LP *Separate Ways* (1973).

"Separate Ways"
(Red West – Richard Mainegra)
Red West's song about Elvis' separation from Priscilla in 1972 (of course, Elvis and Red would one day go their "separate ways" as well). Weak arrangement, syrupy lyrics, but Elvis survives the ordeal, bolstered by the obvious emotion. Charlie Hodge in the background. Recorded March 27, 1972 at MGM Recording Studios in Los Angeles; released as a single in November of 1972 with "Always On My Mind." Performed in *Elvis On Tour* (1972). Later, on the LPs *Separate Ways* (1973) and *Double Dynamite* (1976).

Separate Ways
1973 RCA Camden. LP
(CAS-2611).
Side 1: "Separate Ways"; "Sentimental Me"; "In My Way"; "I Met Her Today"; "What Now, What Next, Where To."
Side 2: "Always On My Mind"; "I Slipped, I Stumbled, I Fell"; "Is It So Strange"; "Forget Me Never", "Old Shep."

Paul Shafer
Presley family friend who arranged midnight movies at the Malco Theatre.

"Shake A Hand"
(Joe Morris)
Elvis covering the former hit by Faye Harris (1953), Red Foley (1953) and Little Richard (1957), done splendidly in a slow, bluesy voice. A strong track. Recorded in May of 1975 in Hollywood; released in June of 1975 on the LP *Today*.

Shakerag
The weathered township of small shacks beyond the Tupelo tracks where the blacks lived during Elvis' youth and where he first heard the blues.

"Shake, Rattle And Roll"
(Charles Calhoun)
Hot stuff, written by Jesse Stone, recorded by Joe Turner in 1954, cleaned up a bit by Bill Haley and the Comets that same year. Elvis' version changed lyrics but comes apart at the seams with vitality. Performed on his third "Stage Show" appearance (February 11, 1956). Recorded February 3, 1956 at RCA Studio in New York; released in September of 1956 as a single, with "Lawdy, Miss Clawdy" on the flip-side. Later, on the EP *Elvis Presley* (1956) and the LP *For LP Fans Only* (1959).

"Shake That Tambourine"
(Bill Grant – Bernie Baum – Florence Kaye)
The "Do The Clam" of *Harum Scarum* (1965). Recorded February 24, 1965 in Hollywood; released in October of 1965 on the soundtrack LP.

Nancy Shap
Wardrobe girl Elvis dated briefly in 1961.

Max Shapiro
Beverly Hills dentist also named in the ABC investigation of Elvis' prescription drug abuse.

Sean Shaver
Photographer who has taken thousands of shots of Elvis over the years and published his work in *The Life Of Elvis Presley* (Timur, 1976).

Arnold Shaw
Producer, music publisher and vice-president of Hill & Range in

Nashville who orchestrated a plan in 1955 to help Elvis get airplay in the north, which ultimately led to his contract with RCA.

Cybill Shepherd
The actress was another Memphis belle who had a brief fling with Elvis after his breakup with Linda Thompson.

T. G. Sheppard
Country singer, RCA promoter and fringe member of Elvis' entourage in the 1970's, who also was one of the people who introduced Linda Thompson to Elvis.

"She's A Machine"
(Joy Byers)
Cut not used in *Easy Come, Easy Go* – and for good reason. Recorded September 26, 1966 at Paramount Recording Studio in Hollywood; released in November of 1968 on the LP *Singer Presents Elvis Singing Flaming Star And Others*.

"She's Not You"
(Doc Pomus – Jerry Leiber – Mike Stoller)
The Elvis his fans loved – warm, romantic, wistful. Recorded March 19, 1962 at RCA Nashville Studio; released in July of 1962 as a single, with "Just Tell Her Jim Said Hello" on the flip-side. Later, on the LP *Elvis' Golden Records, Volume 3* and *Elvis: Worldwide 50 Gold Award Hits, Volume 1* (1970).

"She Thinks I Still Care"
(Dickie Lee)
C & W weeper (a hit for George Jones in 1962) done in a strong voice from the Graceland sessions. The overdubbing was later removed to good effect. Good modern country ballad. Recorded February 2-3, 1976 at 3764 Elvis Presley Boulevard; released in December of 1976 as a single, with "Moody Blue" on the flip-side. Later, on the LPs *Moody Blue* (1977) and *Our Memories of Elvis* (1979).

"She Wears My Ring"
(Boudleaux Bryant – Felice Bryant)
Slow-to-medium ballad with flowing melody and El in good voice. Recorded December 16, 1973 at Stax Studio in Memphis; released in March of 1974 on the LP *Good Times*. Later, Felton Jarvis stripped down the overdubbing for *Our Memories of Elvis* (1979).

James Shigeta
"Danny Kohana," Elvis' Hawaiian buddy in *Paradise Hawaiian Style* (1965).

Steve Sholes
RCA Air man in Nashville responsible for signing Elvis to the label on November 22, 1955

for $35,000. Sholes specialized in attracting and producing RCA's country roster over the years. Along with Chet Atkins, Sholes personally guided many of Elvis' early recording sessions and helped shape his sound and style. He was a genial, dedicated man who was elected to the Country Music Hall of Fame in 1967, the year before his death.

"Shoppin' Around"
(Sid Tepper – Roy C. Bennett – Aaron Schroeder)
The only true rocker from *G. I. Blues* (1960), other than "Frankfurt Special" – an effervescent rockabilly-style number with abrupt starts and stops. Horns are heard in the film version. Recorded April-June of 1960 in Hollywood; released in October of 1960 on the soundtrack LP.

Sammy Shore
The comedian who was originally hired to open Elvis' shows in Las Vegas.

"Shout It Out"
(Bill Grant – Bernie Baum – Florence Kaye)
From *Frankie and Johnny* (1966), ordinary track with El hitting some nice bass notes, but peculiar, awkward changes in tempo. Recorded in May of 1965 at United Artists Recording Studio in Los Angeles; released in April of 1966 on the soundtrack LP.

George Sidney
Director of *Viva Las Vegas* (1964).

Don Siegel
Director of *Flaming Star* (1960).

"Silent Night"
(Joseph Mohr – Franz Gruber)
Not as grandiose as Bing Crosby's 1942 rendition, but celestial nontheless. Recorded September 6, 1957 at Radio Recorders in Hollywood; released November of 1959 on the LP *Elvis' Christmas Album*.

"Silver Bells"
(Ray Evans – Jay Livingston)
Festive and charming, with mellow strings. Recorded May 15, 1971 at RCA Nashville Studio; released in October of 1971 on *Elvis Sings The Wonderful World Of Christmas*.

Frank Sinatra
Always one of Elvis' singing idols, even in the days when Sinatra referred to rock n' rollers as "cretins." On March 26, 1960, only days after his discharge from the Army, Elvis appeared on his *Timex Special* broadcast from The Fountainbleau Hotel in Miami to welcome him home singing "Fame And Fortune" and "Stuck On You," followed by

a duet with Sinatra (Frank tried a few bars of "Love Me Tender," Elvis did "Witchcraft"). During Elvis' Vegas years, the two of them visited and exchanged gifts, and Elvis was friendly with Sinatra's daughter, Nancy.

Nancy Sinatra
Daughter of *You Know Who*, and an early admirer of Elvis who met him at the airport upon his discharge from the Army in 1960, sparking rumors of *You Know What*. Actually, they were good friends over the years and Nancy played "Susan Jacks," the mathematician-bookkeeper of *Speedway* (1968).

Singer Presents Elvis Singing Flaming Star And Others
See *Elvis Sings Flaming Star*, since the contents of both albums are identical.

"Singing Tree'
(Owens – Solberg)
From *Clambake* (1967), Elvis duets with himself. Recorded February 21, 1967 at RCA Nashville Studio; released in November of 1967 on the soundtrack LP.

Shelby Singleton
Record producer who purchased all of the old non-Elvis tapes from Sun Records, only to find recordings from the fabled "Million Dollar Quartet Sessions" of 1954. His attempts to release the material were blocked by legal action by RCA and Sam Phillips.

"Sing You Children"
(Gerald Nelson – Fred Burch)
From *Easy Come, Easy Go* (1967), a strange mixture: a spiritual telling the stories of Joshua and Jonah with Latin American horns, with El adding "Hallelujah!" Recorded September 26, 1966 at Paramount Recording Studio in Hollywood; released in April of 1967 on the EP *Easy Come Easy Go*. Later, on the RCA Camden LP *You'll Never Walk Alone* (1971).

Ray "Chief" Sitton
Another fan-friend from the early days, who was part of Elvis' entourage.

Henry Slaughter
Session organist in 1966, Nashville.

Hank Slemansky
Elvis' first karate instructor in the Army in 1958.

"Slicin' Sand"
(Sid Tepper – Roy C. Bennett)
From *Blue Hawaii* (1961), a fast, pounding number, done almost as a put-on by Elvis. With the Jordanaires. Recorded in April of 1961 in Hollywood; released in October of 1961 on the soundtrack LP.

"Slowly But Surely"
(Sid Wayne – Ben Weisman)
From *Tickle Me* (1965), a good, steady bit of rock n' roll. Recorded May 27, 1963 at RCA Nashville Studio; released in November of 1963 on the soundtrack LP *Fun In Acapulco*.

Beecher Smith III
Vernon Presley's personal attorney who represented Vernon in his divorce settlement with Dee Presley and along with his wife Ann, Charlie Hodge and Ginger Alden, witnessed Elvis' will on March 3, 1977.

Billy Smith
Elvis' favorite cousin, Travis' son, who traveled with Elvis as valet and personal assistant for many years and was always one of Elvis' closest companions. When he married, he settled in Graceland with his wife, Jos, in their trailer quarters at the back of the grounds. Presently active with the Elvis fan clubs and the author of a forthcoming book.

Bobby Smith
Elvis' cousin, another of Travis' sons who worked at the Graceland gate and died in 1968.

Carrol 'junior' Smith
Elvis' cousin (another of Travis' boys) who traveled widely with Elvis during the 1950's with Scotty Moore, Bill Black, D. J. Fontanna and Red West. He died in 1958.

Clettes Smith
Gladys Presley's younger sister, who married Vester Presley, Vernon's brother.

Gary Smith
Co-producer of Elvis' last TV special, on CBS, from Rapid City, South Dakota.

Gene Smith
Elvis' cousin, another of Travis

Smith's sons, who worked as a valet and chauffeur and was one of the pallbearers at his funeral.

John Smith
Elvis' uncle, one of Gladys Presley's brothers, who worked at Graceland before his death in 1968. Along with Vester Presley, it was Johnny Smith who taught Elvis his first guitar chords.

Travis Smith
Elvis' uncle, Gladys' older brother, who worked both at Graceland and at the Circle G Ranch as a security guard and caretaker.

"Smokey Mountain Boy"
(Lenore Rosenblatt – Victor Millrose)
From *Kissin' Cousins* (1964), a marching song with banjo. Recorded October 11, 1963 in Hollywood; released in March of 1964 on the soundtrack LP.

"Smorgasbord"
(Sid Tepper – Roy C. Bennett)
From *Spinout* (1966), brassy, bouncing bit of fluff – Elvis having fun by reversing words at the end. Recorded February 21, 1966 in Hollywood; released in October of 1966 on the soundtrack LP.

Hank Snow
Celebrated Country-Western singer managed by Colonel Parker and booked through Jamboree Attractions. In 1955, Snow helped the Colonel woo Gladys and Vernon Presley's confidence in order to manage Elvis. Elvis and Snow performed on the same bill for a while; though Snow was resentful of the "kid." It didn't take long before Elvis was the top dog in the Colonel's stable of talent.

"Snowbird"
(Gene McLellan)
Elvis loved this song so much – a hit for Anne Murray in 1970 and an instrumental hit for Chet Atkins in 1971 – that he played it over and over again. His version is countrified, but with flowing strings. Still, he comes through clear as a bell. Recorded September 22, 1970 at RCA Nashville Studio; released in February of 1971 on the LP *Elvis Country.*

"So Close, Yet So Far (From Paradise)"
(Joy Byers)
From *Harum Scarum* (1965), the best ballad, with Elvis modulating his voice beautifully. Recorded February 24, 1965 in Hollywood; released in October of 1965 on the soundtrack LP.

"Softly As I Leave You"
(G. Calabrese – A. De Vita – Hal Shaper)

Elvis started doing this song in 1973 by simply speaking the words onstage, which always moved his audiences. Then he sang duets with Sherril Nielson. Finally, he recorded a version of the song at a Las Vegas performance circa in 1976, with Charlie Hodge singing the back-up part. A moving rendition of a 1964 hit by Frank Sinatra. Released as a single in March of 1978, with "Unchained Melody" on the flip-side, and nominated for a Grammy.

"So Glad You're Mine"
(Arthur Crudup)
Once again, Elvis' interpretation of a Big Boy Crudup song of 1946 falls somewhere in-between blues and rock. Great fun, from the Golden Days of RCA. Recorded January 30, 1956 from RCA New York Studio; released in November of 1956 on the LP *Elvis* and on the EP *Elvis, Volume 2.*

"So High"
(Arranged by Elvis Presley)
Soulful, hand-clapping gospel with choruses by the Imperials and the Jordanaires. Recorded May 27, 1966 at RCA Nashville Studio; released in March of 1967 on the LP *How Great Thou Art.*

"Soldier Boy"
(David Jones – Theodore Williams, Jr.)
From Elvis' first session out of the Army, a song for the chicks. Recorded March 20, 1960 at RCA Nashville Studio; released in April of 1960 on the LP *Elvis Is Back.*

Sold Out
33⅓ bootleg album on the E.P. label.
Side 1: "Burning Love"; "Lawdy, Miss Clawdy"; "T-R-O-U-B-L-E"; "I'm Leavin'"; "When The Snow Is On The Roses"; "Need Your Lovin' Every Day"; "Little Sister/Get Back"; "Steamroller Blues"; "Rock Medley"; "Walk The Lonesome Road"; "Help Me Make It Through The Night"; "Faded Love."
Side 2: "Heartbreak Hotel"; "One Night"; Reconsider Baby"; "Mystery Train"; "Tiger Man"; "Jailhouse Rock"; "Teddy Bear/Don't Be Cruel"; "I John"; "Softly As I Leave You"; "It's Now Or Never"; "My Babe"; "Sweet Sweet Spirit"; "I'm Leaving It Up To You"; "I Got A Woman"; "What'd I Say."

"Solitaire"
(Neil Sedaka – Phil Cody)
Elvis covering the 1975 hit by the Carpenters of an old Sedaka tune. A tender, naked ballad from the Graceland sessions. Recorded February 3-4, 1976 at 3764 Elvis Presley Boulevard;

released in May of 1976 on *From Elvis Presley Boulevard, Memphis, Tennessee.* Later, a remixed version appeared on *Our Memories Of Elvis* (1979).

"Somebody Bigger Than You And I"
(Lange – Heath – Burke)
Gospel with Floyd Cramer piano and Elvis in his deepest voice. Listenable track with plenty of color, though one of the lesser cuts on a monumental album. Recorded May 27, 1966 at RCA Nashville Studio; released in April of 1967 on the LP *How Great Thou Art.*

"Something"
(George Harrison)
An oddly dispassionate rendition of a lovely Beatles song – Elvis sounded off-kilter, for some reason. Seen on the *"Aloha"* broadcast. Recorded January 14, 1973 at H.I.C. Arena in Honolulu; released in February of 1973 on the LP *Aloha From Hawaii Via Satellite.*

"Something Blue"
(Paul Evans – Al Byran)
Elvis in low register, but the song itself fails to take off, despite his best attempts. Recorded March 18, 1962 at RCA Nashville Studio; released in June of 1962 on the LP *Pot Luck.*

Something For Everybody
1961 RCA Victor. LP (LPM/LSP-2370).
Side 1: "There's Always Me"; "Give Me The Right"; "It's A Sin"; "Sentimental Me"; "Starting Today"; "Gently."
Side 2: "I'm Comin' Home"; "In Your Arms"; "Put The Blame On Me"; "Judy"; 'I Want You With Me"; "I Slipped, I Stumbled, I Fell."

"Song Of The Shrimp"
(Sid Tepper – Roy C. Bennett)
From *Girls! Girls! Girls!* (1962), Elvis singing sad lines about the shrimp leaving. Sounds silly, but this number was a fave among the fans from the film. Recorded in March of 1962 in Hollywood; released in November of 1962 on the soundtrack LP.

"Sound Advice"
(Bill Grant – Bernie Baum – Florence Kaye)
Pleasant, jog-along tune with guitar backing by Hank Garland. Recorded July 5, 1961 at RCA Nashville Studio; released in July of 1965 on the LP *Elvis For Everyone.*

Sound Of Leadership, The
1956 RCA Victor. EP (SPD-19).
Side 1: "Vesti La Giubba/1907" (Enrico Caruso); "O Sole Mio/1916" (Enrico Caruso).
Side 2: "Ramona/1928" (Gene

Austin); "Marie/1937" (Tommy Dorsey).
Side 3: "Boogie Woogie/1938" (Tommy Dorsey); "Jalousie/1938" (Boston Pops Orchestra).
Side 4: "Beer Barrel Polka/1938" (Will Glahe); "Begin The Beguine/1938" (Artie Shaw).
Side 5: "In The Mood/1939" (Glenn Miller); "Sunrise Serenade/1939" (Glenn Miller)
Side 6: "Blue Danube Waltz/ 1939 (Leopold Stokowski); "Tuxedo Junction/1940" (Glenn Miller).
Side 7: "Star Dust/1940" (Artie Shaw); "Tchaikovsky Piano Concerto/1941" (Freddy Martin).
Side 8: "Chattanooga Choo Choo/1941" (Glenn Miller); "Racing With The Moon/1941" (Vaughn Monroe).
Side 9: "Prisoner Of Love/1946" (Perry Como); "Ballerina/1947" (Vaughn Monroe).
Side 10: "Whiffenpoof Song/1947" (Robert Merrill); "Bouquet Of Roses/1948" (Eddy Arnold).
Side 11: "Be My Love/1950" (Mario Lanza); "Anytime/1951" (Eddie Fisher).
Side 12: "The Loveliest Night Of The Year/1951" (Mario Lanza); "Slow Poke/1951" (Pee Wee King).
Side 13: "Don't Let The Stars Get In Your Eyes/1952" (Perry Como); "You, You, You/1953" (Ames Bros.).
Side 14: "I Need You Now/1954" (Eddie Fisher); "Cherry Pink And Apple Blossom White/1954" (Perez Prado).
Side 15: "Naughty Lady Of Shady Lane/1954" (Ames Bros.); "Rock and Roll Waltz/1955" (Kay Starr).
Side 16: "Hot Diggity/1956" (Perry Como); "Heartbreak Hotel/1956" (Elvis Presley).

"Sound Of Your Cry"
(Bill Grant – Bernie Baum – Florence Kaye)
Elvis leaving before his lady awakes and she cries on learning of his departure – sort of "By The Time I Get To Phoenix." Elvis exploits the lilting lyrics admirably. The end is drawn out and melodramatic. Recorded June 4, 1970 at RCA Nashville Studio; released in September of 1971 as a single, with "It's Only Love" on the flip-side.

Soundtrack Recordings
Many of Elvis' movie songs were different in the movies than on disc, despite RCA's claim of albums being original soundtrack recordings. Listed below are songs that had a very noticeable difference:
"Love Me Tender" – extra verse at end of film. "Loving You" – fast version sung over opening credits. "Got A Lot O' Livin' To Do" – slow ending to first ver-

sion in film. "Party" – extra verse in first version in film. "Don't Leave Me Now" – different styling from first version in film. "Crawfish" – crawfish seller joins in. "Wooden Heart" – children join in. "Pocketful Of Rainbows" – Juliet Prowse joins in. "What's She Really Like" – unaccompanied version in "shower scene." "Jailhouse Rock" – extra voices, etc. "Almost Always True" – Joan Blackman joins in. "Hawaiian Wedding Song" – Joan Blackman joins in. "Sound Advice" – Arthur O'Connell joins in. "This Is Living" – other boxers join in. "Girls! Girls! Girls!" – finale has extra verses, including slow one called "Dainty Little Moonbeams." "Earth Boy" – Chinese lyrics sung by Elvis; Chinese girls join in. "How Would You Like To Be" – Vicky Tiu joins in, plus long instrumental section. "One Broken Heart For Sale" – extra verse. "Mexico" – Mexican boy (Larry Domasin) joins in. "Happy Ending" – Joan O'Brien joins in. "C'mon Everybody" – Ann-Margret joins in. "Spring Fever" – girls in car join in. "Chesay" – Gypsies join in. "Frankie And Johnny" – Production number with all cast, and different words. "Queenie Wahine's Papaya" – Donna Butterworth joins in. "Datin'" – Donna Butterworth joins in. "Scratch My Back" – Marianna Hill joins in. "Drums Of The Island" – Polynesian groups join in, with extra instrumental section (2 versions). "I Love Only One Girl" – Production number with extra instrumental section. "Yoga Is As Yoga Does" – Elsa Lanchester joins in. "Confidence" – children join in; extra instrumental section. "You Don't Know Me" – Different styling and tempo.

"Spanish Eyes"
(Bert Kaempfert – Charles Singleton – William Snyder)
Elvis goes South of the Border again: Latin tempo, lovely lilt, high-spirited voices. Al Martino had a hit with it in 1965. Recorded December 16, 1973 at Stax Studio in Memphis; released in March of 1974 on the LP *Good Times*. Remixed with less overdubbing and cleaner vocals on *Our Memories of Elvis* (1979). Elvis often performed the song live as a duet with Sherril Nielson but it was never recorded live.

Special Palm Sunday Programming
1967 RCA Victor. LP (SP 33-461).
Side 1: "How Great Thou Art"; "In The Garden"; "Somebody Bigger Than You And I"; "Stand By Me."
Side 2: "Without Him"; "Where

Could I Go But To The Lord"; "Where No One Stands Alone"; "Crying In The Chapel"; "How Great Thou Art (excerpt)."

Special Products, Inc.
The Beverly Hills marketing firm of Howard Bell and Hank Saperstein licensed by Colonel Parker to get Elvis' name and face on every conceivable product in 1956-57. By the end of 1957, Saperstein estimated the gross to be $55 million on some 188 Elvis gadgets.

Phil Spector
Legendary producer, considered the most eccentric, most creative techno-genius in rock's history. He is credited with the production technique called "wall of sound" associated with groups like the Crystals and Righteous Brothers. Produced demo records for Elvis over the years and later produced John Lennon.

Speedway
Started: June 15, 1967 ☞
An MGM Picture
Cast
Steve Grayson: Elvis Presley; Susan Jacks: Nancy Sinatra; Kenny Donford: Bill Bixby; R. W. Hepworth: Gale Gordon; Abel Esterlake: William Schallert; Ellie Esterlake: Victoria Meyerink; Paul Dado: Ross Hagen; Birdie Kebner: Carl Ballantine; Juan Medala: Poncie Ponce; The Cook: Harry Wilcox; Billie Joe: Christopher West; Mary Ann: Miss Beverly Hills; Lori: Charlotte Considine.
Credits
Produced by Douglas Laurence
Director: Norman Taurog
Written by Phillip Shuken
Panavision and Metrocolor
Songs
"Speedway"; "There Ain't Nothing Like A Song"; "Your Time Hasn't Come Yet Baby"; "Who Are You"; "He's Your Uncle, Not Your Dad"; "Let Yourself Go"; "Five Sleepy Heads" (cut); "Your Groovy Self" (Nancy Sinatra).
Previously titled: *Pot Luck So I'll Go Quickly*

"Speedway"
(Tom Glazer – Steven Schlake)
Title tune from the 1968 film, a pounder about the race track with motors revving at the fadeout. Recorded June 19, 1967 in Hollywood; released in June of 1968 on the soundtrack LP.

Speedway
1968 RCA Victor. LP (LPM/LSP-3989).
Side 1: "Speedway"; "There Ain't Nothing Like A Song" (Duet with Nancy Sinatra); "Your Time Hasn't Come Yet, Baby"; "Who Are You (Who Am I)"; "He's

Your Uncle, Not Your Dad"; "Let Yourself Go."
Side 2: "Your Groovy Self (Nancy Sinatra solo)"; "Five Sleepy Heads"; "Western Union"; "Mine"; "Goin' Home"; "Suppose."

Spinout
Started: February, 1966.
An MGM Production
Cast
Mike McCoy: Elvis Presley; Cynthia Foxhugh: Shelley Fabares; Diana St. Clare: Diane McBain; Les: Deborah Walley; Susan: Dodie Marshall; Curly: Jack Mullaney; Lt. Tracy Richards: Will Hutchins; Philip Short: Warren Berlinger; Larry: Jimmy Hawkins; Howard Foxhugh: Carl Betz; Bernard Ranley: Cecil Kellaway; Violet Ranley: Una Merkel; Blodgett: Frederic Worlock; Harry: Dave Barry
Credits
Producer: Joe Pasternak
Director: Norman Taurog
Screenplay: Theodore J. Flicker and George Kirgo
Songs
"Stop Look And Listen"; "Adam And Evil"; "All That I Am"; "Never Say Yes"; "Am I Ready"; "Beach Shack"; "Smorgasbord"; "I'll Be Back"; "Spinout"
Previously titled
Never Say Yes/No
Spinout (U.S. Title)
After Midnight
Never At/Always At Midnight
Jim Dandy

"Spinout"
(Sid Wayne — Dolores Fuller)
Title song from the 1966 film, typical swinger with cornball-groovy lyrics about racing and Elvis giving his best shot. Recorded on February 21, 1966 in Hollywood; released in September of 1966 on the soundtrack LP.

Spinout.

Judy Spreckels ☞
One of Elvis' early girlfriends, who accompanied Elvis to the Draft Board the morning of his induction. She was the heiress to a sugar fortune.

Glen Spreen
Session organist in the Memphis sessions, 1969, in Nashville, 1971.

"Spring Fever"
(Bill Grant — Bernie Baum — Florence Kaye)
From *Girl Happy* (1965), a toe-tapper about the joys of living. Not much. Recorded June 8, 1964 in Hollywood; released in April of 1965 on the soundtrack LP.

Sri Daya Mata
Head of the self-realization fellowship center in California and author of *Only Love* (a gift from Priscilla) which became one of Elvis' favorite books. Formerly Fay Wright, Elvis visited her ashram atop Mt. Washington near Los Angeles at Larry Geller's behest.

The Stamps Quartet
Elvis vocal back-up group on tour and on record, 1972-1977; led by J.D. Sumner. They included Donnie Sumner, Bill Blaize, Ed Enoch, Richard Staborn, later joined by Ed Wideman.

"Stand By Me"
(Arranged by Elvis Presley) Slow hymn, simply produced with beautifully restrained

Imperials and Elvis feeling the spirit. Recorded May 26, 1966 at RCA Nashville Studio; released in February of 1967 on the LP *How Great Thou Art*.

Billy Stanley
Presley's stepbrother and personal aide. Co-authored *Elvis: We Loved You Tender*.

David Stanley
Another Presley stepbrother, and a personal bodyguard during Elvis' final years, traveling with him constantly. Co-authored *Elvis: We Loved You Tender*.

Ricky Stanley
One of Elvis' stepbrothers and a personal aide from the period 1969–1972, another of Elvis' most trusted employees until his death. Co-authored *Elvis: We Loved You Tender* and became an ordained minister.

Barbara Stanwyck
"Maggie Moore," the owner of the traveling carnival in ☞ *Roustabout* (1964).

Starlight Wranglers
The C & W Band led by Doug Poindexter that Bill Black and Scotty Moore played with around Memphis before hooking up with Elvis Presley. The other members included Malcolm Yeo on fiddle, Tommy Seals on steel guitar, and Clyde Rush on guitar. Although Elvis is alleged to have appeared with the Wranglers in 1954, there is no record of it; and after the release of "That's All Right (Mama)" in July, Scotty and Bill never went back.

"Starting Today"
(Don Robertson)
Slow ballad with Floyd Cramer on piano and Elvis soft and gentle. Recorded March 13, 1961 at RCA Nashville studio; released in June of 1961 on the LP *Something For Everybody*.

"Startin' Tonight"
(Lenore Rosenblatt – Victor Millrose)
From *Girl Happy* (1965), one minute and fifteen seconds of almost rock and roll. Recorded June 5, 1964 in Hollywood; released in April of 1965 on the soundtrack LP.

Stax Recording Studio
Legendary recording studio in Memphis on McLenore Avenue used by many R & B artists over the years, where the "Memphis Sound" originated. Among the artists who recorded there were the Mar-Keys. Chips Moman, who founded American Recording Studios, was originally a recording technician-producer at Stax. Elvis used the studio in July and December of 1973 for highly productive sessions.

"Stay Away"
(Sid Tepper – Roy C. Bennett)
From *Stay Away, Joe* (1968), a take-off on the melody of "Greensleeves," with uneven orchestration and Elvis in sad, graceful voice. Recorded October 4, 1967 in Hollywood; released as a single in March of 1968, with "U.S. Male" on the flip-side. Later, on the LP *Almost In Love* (1970).

Stay Away, Joe
Started: October 18, 1977
An MGM Picture
Cast
Joe Lightcloud: Elvis Presley; Charlie Lightcloud: Burgess Meredith; Glenda Callaghan: Joan Blondell; Annie Lightcloud: Katy Jurado; Grandpa: Thomas Gomez; Hy Slager: Henry Jones; Bronc Hoverty: L.Q. Jones; Mamie Callaghan: Quentin Dean; Mrs. Hawkins: Anne Seymour; Congressman Morrissey: Douglas Henderson; Lorne Hawkins: Angus Duncan; Frank Hawk: Michael Lane; Mary Lightcloud: Susan Trustman; Hike Bowers: Warren Vanders; Bull Shortgun: Buck Kartalian; Connie Shortgun: Mourishka; Marlen Standing-Rattle: Catlin Wyles; Billie-Joe Hump: Marya Christen; Jackson He-Crow: Del (Sonny) West; Little Deer: Jennifer Peak

Credits
Producer: Douglas Laurence
Director: Peter Tewkesbury
Screenplay by Michael J. Hoey
Based on the novel *Stay Away,
Joe* by Dan Cushman
Photographed by Fred
Koenekamp, A.S.C.
Panavision and Metrocolor
Running Time: 102 minutes
Songs
"All I Needed Was The Rain";
"Stay Away"; "Stay Away, Joe";
"Goin' Home"; "Dominic"
(Unreleased); "Mamie"
(Unreleased)

"Stay Away, Joe'
(Sid Wayne—Ben Weisman)
From the 1968 film of the same
name, a brisk C & W feeling
with harmonica and fiddle and
hooting. Recorded October 4,
1967 in Hollywood; released in
April of 1970 on the RCA
Camden LP *Let's Be Friends.*

"Steadfast, Loyal And True"
(Jerry Lieber—Mike Stoller)
The school song in *King Creole*
(1958) and now the official song
of the International Elvis
Presley Appreciation Society.
No backing in the film, but a
male chorus on the record.
Recorded January of 1958 in
Hollywood; released in August
of 1958 on the soundtrack LP.

"Steamroller Blues"
(James Taylor)
Elvis fell in love with this one as
soon as his stepbrothers played
it for him—he ate it up like a
starving man, and it shows: he
chews on the sly lyrics. With an
outburst of brass and James
Burton cooking on guitar.
Performed live on *"Aloha From
Hawaii"* in 1973. Recorded
January 14, 1973 at H.I.C.
Arena in Hawaii; released in
March of 1973 as a single, with
"Fool" on the flip-side. Later, on
the LP *Aloha From Hawaii Via
Satellite.*

"Steppin' Out Of Line"
(Fred Wise—Ben Weisman—
Dolores Fuller)
Cut from the film *Blue Hawaii*
(1961)—you can see where it was
cut from the print. A "Rock A
Ballad" along the lines of "Rock-
A-Hula Baby," with brisk back-
ing and Elvis' grinding slowed-
down finale. Recorded April of
1961 in Hollywood; released in
June of 1961 on the LP *Pot
Luck.*

The Steve Allen Show
Elvis appeared on this show, his
third, on July 1, 1956 doing "I
Want You, I Need You, I Love
You," and "Hound Dog." He also
performed a comedy skit with
Steve Allen and Imogene
Coca—"Tumbleweed Presley."
"Hound Dog" was performed in

tuxedo tails, singing it to a real
hound dog.

Connie Stevens
Elvis dated this actress-enter-
tainer in the early sixties, while
in Hollywood.

Stella Stevens
"Robin Gantner," the nightclub
singer in love with Elvis in
Girls! Girls! Girls! (1962).

Venetia Stevenson
The actress who was another of
Elvis' highly publicized flames in
1958 (along with Judy Speckels
and Anita Wood).

St. Joseph's Hospital
The Memphis hospital where
Gladys Presley worked as a
nurse's aide from 1949–1950.

Gordon Stoker
First tenor with the Jordanaires,
and leader of the group.

Mike Stoller
One half of one of rock's all-time
greatest songwriting duo (with
Jerry Leiber), who co-wrote
scores of hits for Elvis and
songs for his films. Among them

were "Hound Dog," "King
Creole," "Love Me," and "Jailhouse Rock." He also played
piano on recording sessions for
several of the songs he wrote.

Harold J. Stone
Character actor who played "Big
Frank," Shelley Fabares' heavy
father in *Girl Happy* (1965).

Mike Stone
Formerly Phil Spector's
bodyguard, the Hawaiian-born
karate instructor who fell in love
with Priscilla Presley and lived
with her for three years after her
divorce from Elvis.

"Stop, Look And Listen"
(Joy Byers)
From *Spinout* (1966), electric
organ, yelling Jordanaires, a
battery of drums and a sudden
ending. Elvis lets it rip, but the
song leaves you scratching your
head. Recorded February 21,
1966 in Hollywood; released in
October of 1966 on the soundtrack LP.

"Stop Where You Are"
(Bill Grant—Bernie Baum—

Florence Kaye)
From *Paradise Hawaiian Style*
(1966), the part where Elvis
freezes everybody by shouting
"Stop!" Nice, jumping beat,
mediocre song. The version on
film has longer breaks between
verses. Recorded July 19, 1965
at Paramount Recording Studio
in Hollywood; released in June
of 1966 on the soundtrack LP.

Doug Katz Store
Elvis, Scotty and Bill played at
the opening of their store on
September 9, 1954, at the Airways Shopping Center, on a flat-
bed truck. It was one of their
first public performances as a
group.

Tempest Storm
The stage name of the Las
Vegas burlesque performer Elvis
dated while appearing at the
Frontier Hotel in Las Vegas in
1957.

Al Strada
Personal bodyguard and
security man during the last
period of Elvis' life, often at
Graceland.

Venetia Stevenson.

Billy Strange

Elvis' friend and a composer of music, who scored songs for *Speedway* and *The Trouble With Girls*.

Dr. Strangelove

Because of Peter Sellers' *tour de force* performance as three different characters, this was one of Elvis' favorite movies.

"Stranger In My Hometown"

(Percy Mayfield)
Solid blues, with Elvis giving the band a nice workout, scat-singing at the end. Nasty and fun. Recorded February 17 1969 at American Studios in Memphis; released in November of 1969 on the LP *From Memphis To Vegas/From Vegas To Memphis*.

"Stranger In The Crowd"

(Winfield Scott)
Happy romantic song with soaring strings—a controlled,

complex arrangement with Elvis bursting forth to command it all. Recorded June 5, 1970 at RCA Nashville Studio; released in December of 1970 on the LP *That's The Way It Is* (only a smattering of the song was performed in the 1970 film).

Ron Strauss

The co-pilot of the "Lisa Marie," Elvis' Convair 880 Jet.

Barbra Streisand

An Elvis admirer, who first asked him to play the part of the crumbling rock star in her remake of *A Star Is Born*. No deal was ever made.

Strictly Elvis

1956 RCA Victor. EP (EPA-994). Side 1: "'Long Tall Sally"; "First In Love."
Side 2: "How Do You Think I Feel"; "How's The World Treating You."

"Stuck On You"

(Aaron Schroeder—J. Leslie McFarland)
The first release after his discharge from the army—as infectious as "All Shook Up." Can anyone roll "Grizzly Bear" off their tongue better than Elvis? Doubtful. Recorded March 21, 1960 at RCA Nashville Studio; released in April of 1960 as a single, with "Fame And Fortune" on the flip-side. Later, on *Elvis' Golden Records, Vol. 3* (1963) and *Elvis: Worldwide 50 Gold Award Hits, Vol. 1* (1970).

"Such A Night"

(Lincoln Chase)
An oldie but goodie, via Clyde McPhatter and the Drifters (1954) and Johnny Ray (a risque cut banned in 1954). A delicious, panting bit of nonsense that bounces along—Elvis obviously had fun here. Recorded April 4,

The Ed Sullivan Show

The "Really Big Show" that finally broke Elvis' message to America and heralded his reign. On September 9, 1956, he sang "Don't Be Cruel," "Love Me Tender," "Ready Teddy," and "Hound Dog." On October 28, 1956, it was the same songs only "Love Me Tender" was substituted for "Ready Teddy." And, on January 6, 1957 (two days before his 19th birthday) he sang "Hound Dog," "Love Me Tender," "Heartbreak Hotel," "Don't Be Cruel," "Too Much," "When My Blue Moon Turns To Gold Again," and "Peace In The Valley"—but he was cut off from the waist . And, after his show, Mr. Sullivan told America what a nice boy Elvis really was. He was paid $50,000 for his appearances. Sullivan had stated that he would never book Elvis. It was a moment of great

Elvis, singer Leny Everson and Ed Sullivan, 1957.

personal satisfaction to Col. Parker.

J.D. Sumner
Lead vocals with the Stamps Quartet, who sang on tour and on record with Elvis from 1972–1977. One of Elvis' boyhood gospel idols, and the most celebrated bass voice in gospel music. From 1954–1965, he performed with the Blackwood Brothers.

"Summer Kisses, Winter Dreams"
(Fred Wise – Ben Weisman – Jack Lloyd)
Cut from *Flaming Star* (1961), a subdued, delicate love song about a love long ago (it was to have been about Barbara Eden in the film). A pretty tune, done with feeling and nicely polished. Recorded August 12, 1960 in Hollywood; released in April of 1961 on the EP *Elvis By Request.* Later, on the LP *Elvis For Everyone* (1965).

Sun Sessions, The
1976. RCA. LP (AMP-1675).

Sun Collection, The
1976 RCA English Import. LP (HY-1001). 1960 at RCA Nashville Studio; released in July of 1964 as a single, with "Never Ending" on the flip-side. Released on the LP *Elvis Is Back!* (1960) and another version was included on *Elvis: A Legendary Performer, Vol. 2* (1976)).
Side 1: "That's All Right"; "Blue Moon Of Kentucky"; "I Don't Care If The Sun Don't Shine"; "Good Rockin' Tonight"; "Milkcow Blues Boogie"; "You're A Heartbreaker"; "I'm Left, You're Right, She's Gone"; "Baby Let's Play House."
Side 2: "Mystery Train"; "I Forgot To Remember To Forget"; "I'll Never Let You Go"; "Tryin' To Get To You"; "I Love You Because" (standard version); "Blue Moon"; "Just Because"; "I Love You Because" (Newly discovered track).
Although the English version was actually issued in the U.K. in 1975, it was not widely distributed in the U.S. until 1976.

The Sun Sessions
The generic term for the music Elvis recorded under the aegis of Sam Phillips for Sun between July 1954 and July 1955, which comprised the immortal and incomparable genesis of rockabilly – rock n' roll as it developed. The songs are in order of recording: "That's All Right (Mama)"; "Blue Moon Of Kentucky"; "I Don't Care If The Sun Don't Shine"; "Good Rockin' Tonight"; "Just Because"; "Milkcow Blues Boogie"; "You're

A Heartbreaker"; "I'll Never Let You Go"; "Baby, Let's Play House"; "Mystery Train"; "I'm Left, You're Right, She's Gone"; "I Forgot To Remember To Forget," and "Tryin' To Get To You." Of these songs, RCA would release five at first.

Superstar Outtakes
33⅓ LP Bootleg.
Side 1: "*Steve Allen TV Show, July 1, 1956*"; "I Want You, I Need You, I Love You"; "Hound Dog"; "Comedy Sketch"; "*NBC December 1968 TV Special*"; "Let Yourself Go"; "It Hurts Me."
Side 2: "Las Vegas, August 1969"; "Yesterday/Hey Jude"; "Elvis Talks"; "Introduction Of The Band"; "Happy Birthday, James Burton"; "In The Ghetto"; "Suspicious Minds"; "What'd I Say"; "I Can't Help Falling In Love"; "Bridge Over Troubled Water" (Studio 1970).

"Suppose"
(Dee – Goehring)
Cut from the print of *Speedway* (1968), another love song, with the Jordanaires. Simple, restrained, with Elvis in sweet-high vocal form. Recorded June 19, 1967 in Hollywood; released in June of 1968 on the soundtrack LP *Speedway.*

"Surrender"
(Doc Pomus – Mort Schuman)
Elvis challenges the high notes on this romantic classic, sealing the heights and melting the hearts. A tricky, flashy, above-key rendition based on a 1911 Italian ballad called "Torna A Sorrento." (Following in the footsteps of "It's Now Or Never.") Recorded October 30, 1960 at RCA Nashville Studio; released in February of 1961 as a single with "Lonely Man" on the flip-side. Later, on the LPs *Elvis' Golden Records, Vol. 3* (1963), *Elvis: Worldwide 50 Gold Award Hits, Vol. 1* (1970), and *Elvis – A Legendary Performer, Vol. 3* (1978).

"Susan When She Tried"
(Don Reid)
Uptempo C & W tune, nicely delivered by Elvis and his band. Recorded in May of 1975 in Hollywood; released in June of 1975 on the LP *Today.*

"Suspicion"
(Doc Pomus – Mort Schuman)
Commercial offering that delighted Elvis fans everywhere (so much so that it gave advent to Elvis sound-alike Terry Stafford, who recorded the song in 1964 and made it a smash). The sort of melody that Dean Martin turned out by the carload, but there was Elvis and the Jordanaires pulsing in the background – it was . . . well, different. Re-

corded March 19, 1962 at RCA Nashville Studio; released in June of 1962 on the LP *Pot Luck*. Released in April of 1964 as a single, with "Kiss Me Quick" on the flip-side.

"Suspicious Minds"
(Mark James)
The big hit of the 1969 Vegas engagement – the single that sparked The Great Comeback. Many versions exist: the first was from The Memphis Sessions, recorded in January of 1969 as a single, with "You'll Think Of Me" on the flip-side. This studio version was a splicing of three takes that added horns and overdubbed various "Live" parts from the stage versions for enhanced presence and power. Subsequent live versions were tightly controlled and energetic, with superb ensemble singing, drumming by Ronnie Tutt and guitar work by James Burton. Performed in *That's The Way It Is* (1970), *Elvis On Tour* (1972) and "*Aloha From Hawaii Via Satellite*," the 1973 TV Special. Released on the following LPs: *From Memphis To Vegas/From Vegas To Memphis* (1969); *Elvis: Worldwide 50 Gold Award Hits, Volume 1* (1970); *Elvis In Person* (1970), *Elvis As Recorded At Madison Square Garden* (1972) and *Aloha From Hawaii Via Satellite* (1973).

Billy Swann
Before becoming a recording artist and producer, Swann served a stint as a gatekeeper at Graceland. He also wrote "I Can Help," which Elvis later covered in 1975.

"Sweet Angeline"
(Arnold – Martin – Morrow)
Elvis bids a girl farewell and thanks her for a fine romance. He could tackle songs like this till his blue moon turns to gold again. Sincere, old-fashioned in style, captivatingly Elvis. Nice back-up by Kathy Westmoreland. Recorded in July of 1973 at Stax Recording Studio in Memphis; released in November of 1973 on the LP *Raised on Rock/For Ol' Times Sake.*

"Sweet Caroline"
(Neil Diamond)
Elvis' version of Diamond's 1969 hit was suitably show-biz for the Las Vegas stage: catchy licks by James Burton and Elvis' pipes in excellent form. The songs were performed in the 1970 documentary *That's The Way It Is.* Recorded February 18, 1970 at the International Hotel in Las Vegas; released in May of 1970 on the LP *On Stage – February, 1970.*

The Sweet Inspirations
Elvis' vocal backup group,1968–1977, with J.D. Sumner and the Stamps Quartet. The "Sweets" as Elvis called them, included Myrna Smith, Estelle Brown, Sylvia Stenwell, and Cissy Houston, and were named after their 1968 Atlantic hit, "Sweet Inspiration." They sang with Kathy Westmoreland and have performed with Aretha Franklin and Rickey Nelson, among others.

"Swing Low Sweet Chariot"
(Arranged by Elvis Presley)
A rocking gospel – powerful, fast, soulful – one of the very best. Recorded October 31, 1960 at RCA Nashville Studio; released in December of 1960 on the LP *His Hand In Mine.*

"Sylvia"
(Geoff Stevens – Les Reed)
An odd selection for an uptempo ballad, poorly rhymed (*weeping willow – tears on my pillow*); medieval-sounding intro, awkward arrangement. Recorded June 8, 1970 at RCA Nashville Studio; released in February of 1972 on the LP *Elvis Now.*

"Take Care Of Her"
(Ed Warren – Arthur Kent)
Well sung, medium tempo, C & W ballad with full instrumental backing (which was later stripped away to reveal Elvis' voice). Recorded July 21, 1973 at Stax Recording Studio in Memphis; released in January of 1974 as a single, with "I've Got A Thing About You, Baby" on the flip-side. Later, on the LP *Good Times* (1974). Remixed for *Our Memories Of Elvis* (1979).

"Take Me To The Fair"
(Sid Tepper – Roy C. Bennett)
From *It Happened At The World's Fair* (1963), a nice rendering of a mediocre song. (In the film, Elvis pretends to play a toy ukelele.) With the Mellomen. Recorded in October of 1962 in Hollywood; released in March of 1963 on the soundtrack LP.

"Take My Hand, My Precious Lord"
(Thomas A. Dorsey)
Organ, bass and the Jordanaires back Elvis on this slow, reverent spiritual, a favorite among black congregations in southern Tennessee. Recorded in January of 1957 at Radio Recorders in Hollywood; released in March of 1957 on the EP *Peace In The Valley.* Later, on the LP's *Elvis' Christmas Album* (1957) and *You'll Never Walk Alone* (1971).

"Talk About The Good Times"
(Jerry Hubbard)
The 1970 Jerry Hubbard hit, Elvis style. Recorded December

13, 1973 at Stax Studio in Memphis; released in March of 1974 on the LP *Good Times*.

Jodie Tatum
The blonde Elvis in *Kissin' Cousins* (1964).

Norman Taurog
Hollywood director who handled many of Elvis' films, like *Blue Hawaii, Double Trouble, G.I. Blues, It Happened At The World's Fair, Speedway, Tickle Me*.

Bob Taylor
Session hornman, Memphis, 1969.

Rip Taylor
One of Elvis' favorite Las Vegas comedians. Elvis often caught Taylor's nightclub act during his Las Vegas engagements.

TCB
"Taking Care of Business." The metaphor and logo of Elvis' entourage, called the "TCB" group. It meant, quite simply, doing whatever Elvis wanted, whenever, however he wanted it done.

Vera Tchechowa
The dark, sultry Russian-born film actress Elvis dated briefly in Germany.

"(Let Me Be Your) Teddy Bear"
(Kal Mann – Bernie Lowe) From *Loving You* (1957), the song tailor-made for Elvis' mania for stuffed teddy bears – within months, his house was filled with them. Cute, cuddly rocker, nicely balanced with Elvis in an easy groove. If nothing else, the song sent out a message: come on folks, rock n' roll ain't *that* dangerous! Recorded in February of 1957 in Hollywood; released in June of 1957 as a single, with *Loving You* on the flip-side. Also, on the 1957 EP *Loving You. Vol. 1*. Later, on the LP's *Elvis' Golden Records* (1958), *Elvis: Worldwide Gold Award Hits, Volume 1* (1970), *Elvis As Recorded At Madison Square Garden* (1972), *Elvis In Concert* (1977), *Elvis – A Canadian Tribute* (1978) and *Elvis Sings For Children (And Grown-Ups Too)* (1978).

Tommy Tedesco
Lead guitarist for the album released from *Elvis' Christmas Special* in 1968,

Television
Elvis made his first national television appearance on *The Dorsey Brothers Show* on Saturday, January 28, 1956. He sang "Blue Suede Shoes" and "Heartbreak Hotel," and caused quite a stir among the viewers and critics. He made five more

guest appearances on the show (on the CBS network). On February 4, he sang "Tutti Frutti" and "I Was The One"; on February 11, "Shake Rattle & Roll/Flip Flop Fly" and "I Got A Woman"; on February 18, "Baby Let's Play House" and "Tutti Frutti"; on March 17, "Blue Suede Shoes" and "Heartbreak Hotel"; and on March 24, "Money Honey" and "Heartbreak Hotel." By the time of his 6th appearance, "Heartbreak Hotel" was #1 in the charts and Presley-mania had begun. Elvis' subsequent TV appearances were on *The Milton Berle Show*s of April 3 ("Heartbreak Hotel," "Money Honey," and "Blue Suede Shoes"), and June 5 ("Hound Dog," "I Want You, I Need You, I Love You"), on the NBC network. On *The Steve Allen Show* on NBC of July 1, Elvis sang "Hound Dog," to a real live pooch, and "I Want You, I Need You, I Love You," dressed in evening dress, and appeared as "Tumbleweed Presley" in a comedy skit.

The three much publicized, highly-paid, and top rating CBS *Ed Sullivan Show*s were on September 9 ("Don't Be Cruel," "Love Me Tender," "Ready Teddy," and "Hound Dog"); October 28 (Don't Be Cruel," "Love Me Tender," "Love Me," and "Hound Dog"); and January 6, 1957 ("Hound Dog," "Love Me Tender," "Heartbreak Hotel," "Don't Be Cruel," "Too Much," "When My Blue Moon Turns To Gold Again," and "Peace In The Valley"). Part of the September 9th appearance was seen in *Elvis On Tour*.

Elvis was welcomed back from the army on Frank Sinatra's *Timex Welcome Home Special*, taped March 26th at the Fountainebleau Hotel in Miami Beach and shown over the ABC network May 12 in the USA. He got terrific ratings, of course. None of these early TV shows were seen outside of the USA, so fans in Britain had to be content to read about the wild early appearances, or the new smoother Elvis who sang "Stuck On You" and "Fame And Fortune" on the Sinatra show, and even joined the cast for "It's Nice To Go Travelling," and Frank for "Witchcraft."

There followed a long absence of Elvis from TV screens until 1968. On June 27-30 Elvis was at NBC's Burbank Studios taping his first-ever TV Special, "*Elvis*." One June 27, he did two "sit-down shows," and on June 29, two "stand-up shows," clad in a two-piece black leather suit, with slicked-back hair and long sideburns. he sang abbreviated version of his early hits, and

added several new songs. On June 28 and 30, he worked without an audience on production numbers and a Gospel segment. The show aired December 3, 1968 in the USA and got rave reviews from fans and critics alike, and it gained a gigantic share for NBC in the viewing figures. BBC-2 showed it on December 31, 1969, after many petitions and requests from the fans, some of whom had a private preview of the show at a Leicester convention three months earlier.

"*Elvis*" credits and songs: Executive Producer: Bob Finkel. Producer-Director: Steve Binder. Musical Supervisor: Bones Howe.

Songs: "Trouble"; "Guitar Man"; "Lawdy Miss Clawdy"; "Baby What You Want Me To Do"; "Heartbreak Hotel"; "Hound Dog"; "All Shook Up"; "Can't Help Falling In Love"; "Jailhouse Rock"; "Love Me Tender"; "Are You Lonesome Tonight"; "(Sometimes I Feel Like A Motherless Child" – sung by the Blossoms); "Where Could I Go But To The Lord"; "Up Above My Head"; "Saved"; "Blue Christmas"; "One Night"; "Memories"; "Nothingville"; "Big Boss Man"; "Guitar Man"; "Little Egypt"; "Trouble"; "Guitar Man"; "If I Can Dream." Running time: 50 minutes. Many of the songs were sung at the live shows but cut from the completed Special, e.g. "When My Blue Moon Turns To Gold Again"; "Santa Claus Is Back In Town"; "Love Me"; "That's All Right"; "Blue Suede Shoes"; "Don't Be Cruel"; and "Tryin' To Get To You." The production sequences had "Let Yourself Go" (in a bordello scene vetoed by the Colonel) and "It Hurts Me," with the karate fight. When re-screened in the U.S.A. in August, 1969, the song "Blue Christmas" was replaced by "Tiger Man."

Elvis' next TV special was a real spectacle. Called "*Aloha From Hawaii*," it was done live at the Honolulu International Center, at 12:30 a.m. on Sunday, January 14, 1973 and beamed by the Globcom satellite to the Far East and Australia. A recording of the hour-long show was shown in some European countries in the following days, and a 90-minute version was seen on NBC on April 4 in the U.S.A. Extra songs and scenes of Hawaii were edited into the original show. Elvis topped the ratings once again, both on the live telecast and on the USA showing. He sang well, and looked terrific in a white jump suit with eagle motif. The pro-

ducer was Marty Pasetta. Songs: "See See Rider"; "Burning Love"; "Something"; "Lord You Gave Me A Montain"; "Steamroller Blues"; "My Way"; "Love Me"; "Johnny B. Goode"; "It's Over"; "Blue Suede Shoes"; "I'm So Lonesome I Could Cry"; "I Can't Stop Loving You"; "Hound Dog"; "What Now My Love"; "Fever"; "Welcome To My World"; "Suspicious Minds"; "I'll Remember You"; "Long Tall Sally"; "Whole Lotta Shakin' Goin On"; "American Trilogy"; "A Big Hunk O' Love"; "Can't Help Falling In Love."

After the show, Elvis sang the following songs, seen in the 90-minute U.S.A. broadcast: "Blue Hawaii"; "Ku-U-I-Po"; "No More"; "Hawaiian Wedding Song"; "Early Morning Rain." The show was a benefit for the Kui Lee Cancer Fund; Lee wrote I'll Remember You." It was not seen in the U.K. until the BBC screened it on March 5, 1978, with several cuts.

CBS's *Elvis In Concert* was Elvis' third and final TV Special. It was filmed during the June, 1977 tour, in Omaha, Nebraska, and Rapid City, South Dakota, and shown after Elvis' death. It gained massive ratings when seen in the U.S.A. on October 3, 1977. BBC-1 showed it on June 19, 1978. Unfortunately Elvis looked very ill on this show, and overweight, but he was putting everything into his singing, and his voice was magnificent. Elvis wore a white jumpsuit with gold embroidery. It was, and still is, very upsetting for his fans to watch this show. The show was produced by Gary Smith and Dwight Hemion.

Songs: "See See Rider"; "That's All Right"; "Are You Lonesome Tonight"; "Teddy Bear – Don't Be Cruel"; "Lord You Gave Me A Mountain"; "Jailhouse Rock"; "How Great Thou Art"; "Early Morning Rain"; "I Really Don't Want To Know"; "Hurt"; "Hound Dog"; "My Way"; "Can't Help Falling In Love." The show ended with a special message from Vernon Presley. Running time: 50 minutes.

All of Elvis' specials have been seen on U.S.-TV at least twice. Only the *1968 TV Special* has so far had more than one screening in the U.K. Every Elvis film has been seen many times on American TV, but British viewers have yet to see *Live A Little/Love A Little* or *Easy Come, Easy Go*. All the other films have been screened, some three or four times, and the ITV and BBC have both had "Elvis Seasons." Unfortunately, *That's The Way It Is* has been cut at each screening, particularly in the re-

hearsal scenes. The BBC generally screens films complete, while ITV cuts scenes and songs out.

After Elvis' death, the major U.S. networks all screened tribute programmes. ITV had a tribute program, while the BBC wisely showed *That's The Way It Is.* On October 20, 1977, NBC put together the *"Elvis"* and *"Aloha"* specials to form a 3-hour-long *Memories of Elvis* special, linked by Ann-Margret. This has never been screened in the U.K. It comprised the 90-minute version of *"Aloha"* and the original 50-minute version of the 1968 show with extra songs and production scenes. For the first time, songs cut from the original show such as "Don't Be Cruel," and "Tryin' To Get To You," were seen, and the "It Hurts Me" karate scene. In January, 1978, U.S.-TV had a special tribute to Elvis on his birthday. February 11, 1979 saw the premiere on U.S.-TV of *Elvis,* a 3-hour TV movie with Kurt Russell as Elvis. Russell did a good job, in a movie that was full of mistakes (it was later shown in cinemas in the U.K.). On October 11, 1979, BBC-1 showed Neville Smith's sensitively-written play about August 16, 1977, *Long Distance Information,* and repeated it on October of 1980 as part of a Rock Week that also featured Elvis movies.

In December 1980, both the BBC and ITV screened documentaries about Elvis and his fans. The Beeb's *Elvis Lives* effort on December 17 was generally given the thumbs down, but Yorkshire TV's *Elvis — He Touched Their Lives,* screened December 23, gained the fans' approval. It was an interesting and moving account of the Fan Club's 1980 visit to Memphis and Tupelo, and it was hosted and narrated by David Frost, and included some rare Elvis clips.

Elvis has turned up on dozens of other programs on TV over the years, e.g. *Top of the Pops,* TV commercials for albums, or media commercials, film clips, etc., and in several fascinating documentaries such as *All You Need Is Love* and *Heroes of Rock & Roll.* A clip of him in the Army was even used in the opening credits of a BBC comedy series *Hi-de-Hi!* in 1981!

"Tell Me Why"
(Titus Turner)
Potent, bluesy ballad (originally by Marie Knight in 1956), a gem done in the old Sun style with lots of echo and Elvis jumping all over the words, slurring, twisting and getting raucous. Recorded January 12, 1957 at Radio Recorders in Hollywood; not released until 1965, when it appeared as a single, with "Blue River" on the flip-side. Later, on the LP *Elvis: The Other Sides — Worldwide Gold Award Hirs, Volume 2* (1972).

"Tender Feeling"
(Bill Grant — Bernie Baum — Florence Kaye)
From *Kissin' Cousins* (1964), the melody of "Shenandoah." Acoustic guitars, mandolins, Jordanaires. Recorded October 11, 1963 in Hollywood; released in March, 1964 on the soundtrack LP.

Ten Outstanding Young Men Of America
The award given by the U.S. Jaycees to Elvis on January 9, 1971, which Elvis accepted personally from Jaycee President, Gordon Thomas.

Peter Tewksbury
Director of *Stay Away, Joe* (1968).

"Thanks To The Rolling Sea"
(Bill Grant — Bernie Baum — Florence Kaye)
From *Girls! Girls! Girls!* (1962), one minute and twenty-eight seconds of beating tom-toms and Elvis tearing his way through some forgettable lyrics with the Jordanaires. Recorded in March of 1962 in Hollywood; released in November of 1962 as the soundtrack LP.

"That's All Right (Mama)"
(Arthur Crudup)
One could write a book about this one (ask rock critic Greil Marcus). Indeed, hundreds and hundreds of pages have been written about this moment — how it came about, its significance, its lasting legacy to a generation. Suffice to say here that it sold very respectably on the Sun label despite the scandal of its sounding black; that it was musically unique because it represented an explosive synthesis of country music with R & B. It remained an integral part of Elvis' stage repertoire until the very end and was used to open his shows after the introductory "Also Sprach Zarathustra." Crudup's version was recorded in 1946 (original title: "I Don't Know It"). And let's not forget Dewey Phillips, who broke the record on his *Red Hot and Blue* show on WBHQ on the evening of July 7. Recorded on the evening of July 5, 1954 at Sun by the indomitable Sam C. Phillips; released July 19, 1954 with "Blue Moon Of Kentucky" on the flip-side. (The record sold some 20,000 copies — Marty Robbins' cover of the song that year sold many more.) RCA re-

issued the single in November of 1955. Later, on the LP *For LP Fans Only* (1959), *Elvis As Recorded At Madison Square Garden* (1972), *Elvis – A Legendary Performer, Volume 1* (1974), *Elvis – The Sun Sessions* (1976) and *Elvis In Concert* (1977). In 1972, Sun released a single called "That's All Right (Mama)" without any artist listed on the label. RCA instituted a lawsuit to stop the record (many think it was an outtake from the original Sun sessions). Sun re-released the disc with Jimmy Ellis' name on the label. (Ellis is a well-known Elvis sound-alike). The nature of the record's true origin remains a mystery.

"That's Someone You Never Forget"
(Red West – Elvis Presley)
A tune reputedly penned with Gladys Presley in mind, but who knows? Maybe Red West. Wooshing wind sounds by Elvis and the Jords introduce this soft, evocative tune. Recorded June 25, 1961 at RCA Nashville Studio; released in June of 1972 as a single, with "Long Legged Girl (With The Short Dress On)." Later, on the LP *Pot Luck* (1962).

That's The Way It Is
Started: July, 1970
Stage Act Filmed in Las Vegas August, 1970
Stage Act Filmed in Phoenix September, 1970
An MGM Production
Credits
Director: Denis Sanders
Producer: Dale Hutchinson
Panavision, Metroco or Stereo Sound, 70mm
Musicians
James Burton: Lead Guitar; John Wilkinson: Rhythm Guitar; Charlie Hodge: Rhythm Guitar; Jerry Scheff: Bass; Glen Hardin: Piano; Ronnie Tutt: Drums; Millie Kirkham: Vocal; Imperial Quartet; Sweet Inspirations.
Songs in Rehearsal
"Words;"; "The Next Step Is Love"; "Polk Salad Annie"; "Cryin' Time" (unreleased); "That's Alright"; "Words"; "Little Sister"; "What'd I Say"; "Stranger In The Crowd"; "How The Web Was Woven"; "Just Can't Help Believin'"; "You Don't Have To Say You Love Me"; "Bridge Over Troubled Water"; "Words"; "Loving Feeling"; "Mary In The Morning"; "Polk Salad Annie";
On Stage
"Mystery Train/Tiger Man" (Credits); "That's All Right"; "I've Lost You"; "Patch It Up"; "Love Me Tender"; "Loving Feeling"; "Sweet Caroline"; "Just Can't Help Believin'"; "Tiger Man"; "Bridge Over Troubled Water"; "Heartbreak Hotel"; "One Night"; "Blue Suede Shoes"; "All Shook Up"; "Suspicious Minds"; "Can't Help Fallin'"; "Only Patch It Up," "Just Can't Help Believin'" (stage versions), "You Don't Have To Say You Love Me" are on the actual recordings issued on disc.

That's The Way It Is
1970 RCA. LP (LSP-4445). Side 1: "I Just Can't Help Believin'"; "Twenty Days and Twenty Nights"; "How The Web Was Woven"; "Patch It Up"; "Mary In The Morning"; "You Don't Have To Say You Love Me."
Side 2: "You've Lost That Loving' Feelin'"; "I've Lost You"; "Just Pretend"; "Stranger In The Crowd"; "The Next Step Is Love"; "Bridge Over Troubled Water."

"That's When You're Heart-aches Begin"
(William Raskin – Billy Hill – Fred Fisher)
The 1950 Ink Spots hit that Elvis recorded at the Memphis Recording Service in the summer of 1953 as the second song for his mother's birthday present. (Marion Keisker put part of it on tape and later played it for Sam Phillips.) Elvis recorded the song in January of 1957 at Radio Recorders in Hollywood; it was released in March of 1957 as a single, with "All Shook Up" on the flip-side. Later, on the LPs *Elvis' Golden Records* (1958) and *Elvis: Worldwide 50 Gold Award Hits, Volume One* (1970).

"The Bullfighter Was A Lady"
(Sid Tepper – Roy C. Bennett)
From *Fun In Acapulco* (1963), Elvis' song about Elsa Cardenas. Very Spanish. Recorded January 20, 1963 in Hollywood; released in November of 1963 on the soundtrack LP.

"The Fair Is Moving On"
(Fletcher – Flett)
Elvis tried his best to salvage this one, despite obvious vocal strain and an unimaginative arrangement. Recorded February 21, 1969 at American Studios in Memphis; released in June of 1969 as a single, with "Clean Up Your Own Backyard" on the flip-side. Later, on the LPs *From Memphis To Vegas/From Vegas To Memphis* (1969) and *Elvis – Back To Memphis* (1970).

"The First Noel"
(Arranged and adapted by Elvis Presley)
A traditional Christmas offering, dating back to the seventeenth century. Organ introduction and Elvis breathless with the X-mas Spirit. With the Imperials. Recorded May 16, 1971 at RCA Nashville Studio; released in October of 1971 on the LP *Elvis Sings the Wonderful World of Christmas.*

"The First Time Ever I Saw Your Face"
(Ewan McColl)
Roberta Flack recorded her version of this song *before* Elvis, in 1969 – it was popularized and released as a single as a result of *Play Misty For Me,* the Clint Eastwood film (where Elvis, like many others, first heard it). Elvis' treatment was lush but not epic, competent but not overwhelming. With the Imperials and the Nashville Edition. Recorded March 15, 1971 at RCA Nashville Studio; released in April of 1972 as a single, with "An American Trilogy" on the flip-side.

"The Fool"
(Naomi Ford)
A former hit for Sanford Clark in 1955 and the Gallahads in 1956, this is a rocked-up treatment of a C & W song with a bouncing, bluesy feeling. Elvis suits the song perfectly. Recorded June 4, 1970 at RCA Nashville Studio; released in February of 1971 on the LP *Elvis Country.*

"The Girl I Never Loved"
(Randy Starr)
From *Clambake* (1967), Elvis sings about an unconquered girl friend. Dramatic, heavily orchestrated, with the Jordanaires. Elvis in complete vocal control. Recorded February 27, 1967 at RCA Nashville Studio; released in November of 1967 on the soundtrack LP.

"The Girl Next Door"
(Bill Rice – Thomas Wayne)
"The girl next door went a-walkin', she found a boy she liked . . ."; "Do-*wha*-Do" go the Jordanaires in reply. A lively, hopping bit of teen stuff, but nothing exciting. Recorded April 4, 1960 at RCA Nashville Studio, released in April of 1960 on the LP *Elvis Is Back!* (subsequent pressings listed the song as "The Girl Next Door Went A-Walking").

"The Girl Of My Best Friend"
(Beverly Ross – Sam Bobrick)
Well-performed number with El in his most melancholic tones and the Jords filling in the background. Recorded April 4, 1960 at RCA Nashville Studio; released in April of 1960 at RCA Nashville studio; released in April of 1960 on the LP *Elvis Is Back!* (Ralph Donner had a big hit with the song in 1962.)

"The Impossible Dream (The Quest)"
(Joe Darion – Mitch Leigh)
Elvis took a grand shot at this classic from the Broadway hit *Man of La Mancha* at his Madison Square Garden Concert. His rendition was well put together and stirring enough; the finale is booming and spectacular. One can only speculate how El's voice might have carried in a theater, without mikes, in a Broadway show – he obviously enjoyed this kind of thing. Recorded June 10, 1972 in New York; released in June of 1972 on the LP *Elvis As Recorded At Madison Square Garden.* Later, on the LP *He Walks Beside Me* (1978).

"The Last Farewell"
(Roger Whittaker – R. A. Webster)
Beautiful, touching, haunting ballad from the Graceland sessions. Underrated, unfortunately, but Elvis emotes every word, even if his voice wasn't in top condition. Recorded February 2-3, 1976 in the Graceland music den; released in May of 1976 on the LP *From Elvis Presley Boulevard, Memphis, Tennessee.*

"The Love Machine"
(Gerald Nelson – Fred Burch – Chuck Taylor)
From *Easy Come, Easy Go* (1967), a solid beat with brass, and Elvis jumping on the lyrics. Sounds like fifteen other songs from his movies. Recorded September 26, 1966 at Paramount Recording Studio in Hollywood; released in April of 1967 on the EP *Easy Come, Easy Go.* Later, on the RCA Camden LP *I Got Lucky* (1971).

"The Meanest Girl In Town"
(Joe Byers)
From *Girl Happy* (1965), frantic rocker with growls and "uh-uhs," and a raunchy sax break. Yes, folks, the boy *could* rock n' roll, even on these forgettable movie tracks. Recorded July 8, 1964 in Hollywood; released in April of 1965 on the soundtrack LP.

"The Next Step Is Love"
(Paul Evans – Paul Pernes)
Controlled, mellow ballad, unhurried and plaintive, with overbearing strings. Recorded June 7, 1970 at RCA Nashville Studio; released in July of 1970 as a single, with "I've Lost You" on the flip-side. Part of the song was done in the film *That's The Way It Is* in 1970 and released on the soundtrack LP. The original studio version was later re-released on *Elvis: The Other Sides – Worldwide Gold Award Hits, Volume 2* (1971).

"There Ain't Nothing Like A Song"
(Joy Byers – William Johnston)
From *Speedway* (1968), a speedy tune with Elvis getting lost in the backing and Nancy Sinatra adding a few lines. Recorded June 19, 1967 in Hollywood; released in June of 1968 on the soundtrack LP.

"There Goes My Everything"
(Dallas Frazier)
Former hits for Jack Greene (1966) and Englebert Humperdinck (1967), a popular C & W ballad. Pleasant but unexceptional rendition, including a duet with one of the Imperials. Recorded June 8, 1970 at RCA Nashville studio; released in December of 1970 as a single, with "I Really Don't Want To Know" on the flip side. Later, on the LPs *Elvis Country* (1971) and *Elvis: The Other Sides – Worldwide Gold Award Hits Volume 2* (1970).

"There Is No God But God"
(Bill Kenny)
Elementary arrangement of a powerful spiritual. Recorded June 9, 1971 at RCA Nashville Studio; released in April of 1971 on the LP *He Touched Me*.

"There Is So Much World To See"
(Sid Tepper – Ben Weisman)
From *Double Trouble* (1967), a plodding number in which El gets drowned out by guitar, drums and electric organ. Still, he has a couple of nice moments. Recorded June 26, 1966 in Hollywood; released in June of 1967 on the soundtrack LP.

"There's A Brand New Day On The Horizon"
(Joy Byers)
From *Roustabout* (1964), an inspirational rendition, sung high and with passion. Recorded in January of 1964 in Hollywood; released in October of 1964 on the soundtrack LP.

"There's A Honky Tonk Angel (Who'll Take Me Back In)"
(Troy Deals – Denny Rice)
C & W offering with solid lyrics done in a slow, heartfelt manner by the Boss. A hit for Conway Twitty in 1974. Recorded December 15, 1973 at Stax Studios in Memphis; released in January of 1975 on the LP *Promised Land*. Later remixed with less backing for *Our Memories of Elvis, Volume 2* (1979).

"There's Always Me"
(Don Robertson)
Slow ballad, wth nice Floyd Cramer piano and the Jordanaires. A nice crescendo at the end with Elvis' voice and the band. Recorded March 13, 1961 at RCA Nashville Studio; released in June of 1961 on the LP *Something For Everybody*. Released in August of 1967 as a single, with "Judy" on the flip-side.

"There's Gold In The Mountains"
(Bill Grant – Bernie Baum – Florence Kaye)
From *Kissin' Cousins* (1964), a rocking beat and Elvis singing about the gold and pretty girls. Recorded October 11, 1963 in Hollywood; released in March of 1964 on the soundtrack LP.

The Trouble With Girls And How To Get Into It
Started: October 15, 1968
An MGM Picture
Cast
Walter Hale: Elvis Presley; Nita: Sheree North; Johnny Anthony: Edward Andrews; Charlene: Marylyn Mason; Wilby: Dabney Coleman; Carol: Anissa Jones; Willy: Pepe Brown; Mr. Morality: Vincent Price; Betty Smith: Nicole Jaffe; Clarence: Anthony Teague.

Credits
Producer: Lester Welch
Director: Peter Tewksbury
From a Novel by D. Keene and D. Babcock
Panavision and Metrocolor
Running Time: 104 minutes
Cut to: 79 minutes in Britain
Previously titled: *Chataugua Chataqua*
Have Girls, Will Travel
Songs
"Almost";
"Swing Low Sweet Chariot";
"Clean Up Your Own Backyard."

"The Truth About Me"
The 7-inch, 78 rpm plastic disc attached to an issue of *Teen Parade* Magazine in 1956, in which Elvis talks about his life and his music, and thanks his fans. (See attached copy.)

"The Twelve"
One of Elvis' many pseudonyms for his entourage, named for the twelve disciples of Christ.

"The Walls Have Ears"
(Sid Tepper – Roy C. Bennett)
From *Girls! Girls! Girls!* (1962), Elvis singing to Laurel Godwin while the walls shake with the sound of people shouting and throwing things at him. On the disc, it's only Elvis. Recorded in March of 1962 in Hollywood; released in November of 1962 on the soundtrack LP.

"The Wonder Of You"
(Baker Knight)
From Ray Peterson's 1959 hit, this is Elvis' only "live" single release, a sentimental, old-fashioned sort of song with violins. Recorded February 19, 1970 at the International Hotel in Las Vegas; released in May of 1970 with "Mama Liked The Roses" on the flip-side. Later, released on the LPs *On Stage – February, 1970* and *Elvis: The Other Sides – Worldwide Gold Award Hits, Vol. 2* (1971).

"The Wonderful World Of Christmas"
(Tobias – Frisch)
Title track from the 1971 LP, with bells and the Imperials. Recorded May 16, 1971 at RCA Nashville Studio; released in October of 1971 on the LP *Elvis Sings The Wonderful World Of Christmas.*

"They Remind Me Too Much Of You"
(Don Robertson)
From *It Happened At The World's Fair* (1963), Cramer piano provides lazy mood as Elvis sings straight through like a breath of fresh air. With the Mellomen. Recorded in October of 1962 in Hollywood; released in January of 1963 as a single, with

"One Broken Heart For Sale" on the flip-side, and in March on the soundtrack LP. Later, on *Elvis: The Other Sides—Worldwide Gold Award Hits, Volume 2* (1971) and *Elvis Sings Hits From His Movies, Volume One* (1972), and *Elvis In Hollywood* (1970).

"Thinking About You"
(Tim Baty)
Another underrated cut from the mid-1970's, a sweet, medium-tempo ballad, bittersweet lyrics and beautifully worked out backing by Messrs. Tutt, Burton, Norbert Putnam and David Briggs. Recorded December 12, 1973 at Stax Studio in Memphis; released in January of 1975 as a single, with "My Boy" on the flip-side. Later, on the LP *Promised Land* (1975) and remixed with less backing for *Our Memories Of Elvis, Volume 2* (1979).

This Is Elvis
Released by Warner Brothers, 1981
Written, Produced and Directed by Malcolm Leo and Andrew Solt
Director of Photography: Gil Hubbs
Edited by Bud Friedgen
Original music score by Walter Scharf
Cast
Elvis, age 18: David Scott; Elvis, age 10: Paul Boensch, 3rd; Elvis, age 42: Johnny Hara; Vernon Presley: Lawrence Koller; Priscilla Presley: Rhonda Lyn; Gladys Presley: Debbie Edge; Dewey Phillips: Larry Rasberry; Bluesman: Furry Lewis; Minnie Mae Presley: Liz Robinson; Elvis, age 35: Dana MacKay; Sam Phillips: Knox Phillips; Linda Thompson: Cheryl Needham; Ginger Alden: Andrea Cyrill; Bill Black: Jerry Phillips; Scotty Moore: Emory Smith.
Running Time: 101 minutes

Colonel Parker's authorized version of Elvis' life met with mixed reviews from critic and fan alike. The film was a grabbag of documentary footage that contained some of the most electrifying moments of his career gummed together with home movies and faked interviews, dramatic scenes and newsreels interspersed with the real thing. Hence, while the film couldn't succeed as drama or documentary, it presented a powerful cavalcade of images. The film, many people agree, was neither well made nor truthful (we are often presented with the Elvis Colonel Parker and consultants Joe Esposito and Jerry Schilling would have us see and know), and yet it leaves us with one more artifact of his life to mull over.

Once we get through the scene in which Colonel Parker pretends to receive the news of Elvis' death and the flashback of the young Elvis in Tupelo, the film clips and kinescopes begin; we see Elvis handling his audience with an energy and expertise that takes your breath away. We see thrilling renditions of "Shake, Rattle And Roll" and "Hound Dog," interviews with people cheering Elvis and rock and roll. We see him glow when Ed Sullivan pronounces him a "real, fine, decent boy." Production numbers from films are used effectively, particularly the flamboyant dance routine from *Jailhouse Rock*. Throughout, a "voice" of Elvis is used to narrate his own story. This device, used to lend authenticity to the production, often backfires because of the utter simplemindedness of the comments. "If only I could have seen what was happening to me," Elvis laments at the end of his life, when he is bloated and wasted, "I would have done something about it," and it makes you want to scream.

Still, for the Elvisphile, the gems are fascinating: a sequence from the *1960 Timex TV-Special* with Sinatra, when they trade off "Witchcraft" and "Love Me Tender"; home movies of Elvis, Priscilla, Elvis' retinue clowning around; takes from the *1968 NBC Special*, with Elvis singing "Hound Dog" in black leather; the Vegas opening; snippets from interviews, press conferences, and touring; and a wrenching rendition of "My Way" taken from his final tour. The film concludes with a moving performance of "American Trilogy." It never matters that the whole thing was put together to perpetuate Elvis' myths and legends—the film, if nothing else, is a testament to the fact that, for good of bad, Elvis *was* his myths and legends.

"This Is Living"
(Fred Wise—Ben Weisman)
From *Kid Galahad* (1962), Elvis training in the open air, singing to the boys. Recorded in October of 1961 in Hollywood; released in September of 1962 on the soundtrack EP.

"This Is My Heaven"
(Bill Grant—Bernie Baum—Florence Kaye)
From *Paradise Hawaiian Style* (1966), a mellow Hawaiian ballad with the Jordanaires and the prerequisite Hawaiian guitars. Recorded July 19, 1965 at Paramount Recording Studios in Hollywood; released in June of 1966 on the soundtrack LP.

"This Is Our Dance"
(Les Reed—Geoff Stephens)
A selection for the girls, romantic, with a sing-along quality. Recorded June 6, 1970 at RCA Nashville Studio; released in May of 1971 on the LP *Love Letters From Elvis*.

"This Is The Story"
(Arnold—Morrow—Martin)
Plaintive Elvis sings over the Memphis Strings, organ, and steel guitar. Recorded January 13, 1969 at American Studios in Memphis; released in November of 1969 on the LP *From Memphis To Vegas/From Vegas To Memphis*. Later, on *Elvis—Back In Memphis* (1970).

Rufus Thomas
Reknowned R & B singer from Mississippi who played Elvis' first release as a disc jockey on Station WDIA, Memphis' black station of the 1950's. In 1953, he recorded "Tiger Man (King Of The Jungle)," which Elvis loved and recorded fifteen years later.

Linda Diane Thompson
The former "Miss Tennessee" who became Elvis' live-in, traveling girlfriend and companion in the period after his divorce. They remained together for a period of four years until they drifted apart. A television movie called *Elvis and the Beauty Queen* (1981) was based on their relationship.

Sam Thompson
Linda Thompson's brother, who worked as a personal bodyguard on tour the last few years of Elvis' life.

Willie Mae Thornton
Legendary blues singer who loved Bessie Smith and recorded such classics as "Ball And Chain." In the 1950's she played with Johnny Otis. Willie Mae Thornton laid down the first version of Leiber—Stoller's "Hound Dog" in 1952 for Peacock.

Richard Thorpe
Director of *Jailhouse Rock* (1957) and *Fun In Acapulco* (1963).

"Three Corn Patches"
(Jerry Leiber—Mike Stoller)
Minor stuff from a great duo of songwriters—probably left over from a film. Also covered by T-Bone Walker. Recorded July 21, 1973 at Stax Studio in Memphis; released in November of 1973 on the LP *Raised on Rock/For Ol' Times Sake*.

"Thrill Of Your Love"
(Stanley Kessler)
Elvis' approach to this tune wavers from attack to laying back and the effect is unusual. Beautiful work by his musicians. Recorded April 4, 1960 at RCA Nashville Studio; released in April of 1960 on the LP *Elvis Is Back!*

Vicki Tiu
Little "Sue-Ling" in *It Happened At The World's Fair*, Elvis' most adorable film co-star. ☞

Tickle Me

Started: 1965 ☞
Presented by Allied Artists
Picture Corporation
Released through Warner-Pathe
Cast
Lonnie Beale: Elvis Presley;
Vera Radford: Julie Adams;
Pam Merritt: Jocelyn Lane;
Stanley Potter: Jack Mullaney;
Estelle Penfield: Merry Anders;
Deputy Sturdivant: Bill
Williams; Brad Bentley: Edward
Faulkner; Hilda: Connie
Gilchrist; Barbara: Barbara
Werle; Adolph: John Dennis; Mr.
Dabney: Grady Sutton; Mabel:
Allison Hayes; Ophelia: Inez
Pedroza; Ronnie: Lilyan
Chauvin; Donna: Angela Greene.
Credits
Producer: Ben Schwalb
Director: Norman Taurog
Written by Elwood Ullman and
Edward Bernds
Music Scored and Conducted by
Walter Scharf
Technical Advisor: Col. T.
Parker

Color by De-Luxe
Panavision
Songs
"I Feel That I've Known You
Forever"; "Night Rider"; "Slowly,
But Surely"; "Dirty, Dirty
Feeling"; "Put The Blame On
Me"; "Long, Lonely Highway";
"I'm Yours"; "Such An Easy
Question"; "It Feels So Right."

Tickle Me

1965 RCA Victor. EP
(EPA-4383).
Side 1: "I Feel That I've Known
You Forever"; "Slowly But
Surely."
Side 2: "Night Rider"; "Put The
Blame On Me"; "Dirty, Dirty
Feeling."

"Tiger Man"

(J. H. Lewis – S. Burns)
Rufus Thomas' 1953 Sun release
was always a favorite with
Elvis – a throwback to those
early days of thrashing energy.
Appropriately, Elvis revived the
song for his *1968 NBC-TV
Special* (it was inserted into the
rebroadcast of the show on
August 17, 1969). He later per-
formed the song live, segueing
into the number from "Mystery
Train" in the 1970 documentary
That's The Way It Is, a far
superior edition of the tune that
features some raving guitar
work by James Burton. First
recorded June 27, 1968 at
Burbank Studios; released in
November 1968 on the RCA
Camden LP *Singer Presents
Elvis Singing Flaming Star and
Others*. The "Mystery Train/
Tiger Man" medley was later
recorded on August 26, 1969 at
the International Hotel in Las
Vegas; released in 1969 on the
LP *From Memphis To
Vegas/From Vegas To Memphis*.
Another version appears on the
LP *Elvis In Person* (1970).

H. J. Timbrell

Session guitarist who worked
briefly with Elvis in 1958 on
songs like "Your Cheatin' Heart."

Cal Tajder

Well-known jazz musician who
played on the soundtrack for
Easy Come, Easy Go (1967).

T. J.'s

Popular Memphis nightclub
Elvis rented for parties.

TLC

"Tender Loving Care" – the logo
and metaphor for the women
around Elvis Presley.

To Know Him Is To Love Him

33⅓ bootleg LP released by
Black Belt Records, which
featured songs recorded by
Elvis live in Las Vegas and Lake
Tahoe.
Side 1: "Trouble"; "Raised On
Rock"; "Steamroller Blues";
"Sweet Inspiration"; "Help Me
Make It Through The Night";
"More"; "Suspicious Minds";
"Please Release Me"; "I, John."
Side 2: "Folsom Prison Blues";
"I Walk The Line"; "Until It's
Time For You To Go"; "Fever";
"I'm Leavin'"; "Memphis,
Tennessee" (Pt. 1 And Pt. 2);
Elvis Introduces Bobby Darin;
"Can't Help Falling In Love";
"Closing."

"Today, Tomorrow, And Forever"

(Bill Grant – Bernie Baum – Florence Kaye)
From *Viva Las Vegas* (1964), a tender ballad with simple piano, guitar and subdued Jordanaires in the background. Recorded in July of 1963 in Hollywood; released in June of 1964 on the soundtrack EP. Later, on the RCA Camden LP *C'mon Everybody* (1971).

"Tomorrow Is A Long Time"

(Bob Dylan)
The one Bob Dylan song Elvis couldn't resist – the attraction was to the lyrics, which haunted him. His version was simple, sad, and quite beautiful. Recorded May 26, 1966 at RCA Nashville Studio – the "How Great Thou Art" session; released (inappropriately enough) on the soundtrack LP *Spinout* in October of 1966.

"Tomorrow Never Comes"

(Ernest Tubb – Johnny Bond)
Popular C & W tune recorded by Ernest Tubb (1949), B J. Thomas (1966) and Slim Whitman (1970). The dramatic finale and military beat of the drums all but overpowered Elvis and offer little spontaneity in the texture. Recorded June 7, 1970 at RCA Nashville Studio; released in February of 1971 on the LP *Elvis Country*.

"Tomorrow Night"

(Sam Coslow – Will Grosz)
Off-beat ballad from the early Sun days – a big hit for Lonnie Johnson in 1948 and La Vern Baker in 1954. The actual date of this recording has been hotly debated among Elvis discographers, but the general consensus is that the song was recorded in July of 1955 at Sun Studio and not released until 1965, when RCA added an instrumental track including Chet Atkins and Grady Martin on guitars, Henry Strazelecki on bass, Charlie McCoy on harmonica, Buddy Harman on drums and the Anita Kerr singers. The song was released on the LP *Elvis For Everybody* in July of 1965.

"Tonight Is So Right For Love"

(Sid Wayne – Abner Silver)
From *G.I. Blues* (1960), a tune based on "Bacarolle" by Jacques Offenbach, with Elvis' voice fluctuating skillfully from his normal singing tone to tonsil-splitting power. With the Jordanaires. Recorded April-June 1960 in Hollywood; released in October of 1960 on the soundtrack LP. Later, on the RCA Camden LP *Burning Love and*

Hits From His Movies, Volume 2 (1972).

"Tonight's All Right For Love"

(Sid Wayne – Abner Silver – Joe Lilly)
Because of copyright problems, Elvis was unable to use "Tonight Is So Right For Love" (from *G.I. Blues*) in non-English speaking countries on the European continent. Another version of the song was therefore penned, using similar lyrics but basing the melody on Johann Strauss' "Tales From The Vienna Woods" rather than Offenbach's "Bacarolle." Released in France, Italy, Sweden on the soundtrack LP in 1960, and in Germany as a single (the flip-side of "Wooden Heart"). In the U.S. the song wasn't released until January of 1974, when an edited version appeared on the LP *Elvis – A Legendary Performer, Vol. 1*

Blanchard Toole

Memphis attorney appointed by probate Judge Evans as the guardian of Lisa Marie Presley, who brought suit against Colonel Tom Parker in July of 1981 claiming that the Colonel was no longer entitled to half of Elvis' earnings for life. He also claimed that Parker defrauded the Presley estate of over two million dollars.

"Too Much"

(Bernard Veinman – Lee Rosenberg)
Bass intro by Bill Black works into a solid beat by D. J. Fontanna on this RCA oldie, with Scotty Moore ringing out and Elvis in fine fettle, singing a duet with himself. Performed on Elvis' third time on the *Sullivan Show*, January 6, 1957. Recorded September 2, 1956 at Radio Recorders in Hollywood; released in January of 1957 as a single, with "Playing For Keeps" on the flip-side. Also, on the EP *Touch of Gold, Volume 3* (1957). On the LPs *Elvis' Golden Records* (1958), and *Elvis: Worldwide 50 Gold Award Hits, Vol. 1* (1970).

"Too Much Monkey Business"

(Chuck Berry)
Chuck Berry's 1956 hit, with some light-fingered guitar work and the Jordanaires. Recorded January 15, 1968 at RCA Nashville Studio; released in November of 1968 on the RCA Camden LP *Singer Presents Elvis Singing Flaming Star And Others*.

"Treat Me Nice"

(Jerry Leiber – Mike Stoller)
From *Jailhouse Rock* (1957), an irresistable ditty from the first notes of Dudley Brooks' piano to the finish. Elvis in his huskiest,

sexiest voice and the Jordanaires burping and clapping in the background. Recorded September 5, 1957 at Radio Recorders in Hollywood; released in September of 1957 as a single with "Jailhouse Rock" on the flip-side. Also, on the EP *A Touch Of Gold, Volume 2* (1957). Later, on the LPs *Elvis' Golden Records* (1958) and *Elvis: Worldwide 50 Gold Award Hits, Volume 1* (1970).

Tribute Discs

Many tribute discs and albums of Elvis' songs were issued during the '60's and '70's, but after his death the real flood started. Hundreds of songs were written about him, many almost overnight. Most of the discs were not worthy of him, and appeared to have been written to cash in, and most of the albums of his music were inferior copies of his classic hits. In the U.S.A., a disc called "The King Is Gone" by Ronnie McDowell sold a million, and it was a good song, sincerely sung. In the U.K., a very poor disc by Danny Mirror made its way up the charts. It's title was "I Remember Elvis Presley." However, there were several worthwhile tributes, and these are listed below:

"Loving You" by Donna Fargo. U.S.A. The best tribute of all.
"My Heavenly Father/What Am I Living For" by Kathy Westmoreland. U.S.A.
As mentioned above, "The King Is Gone" by Ronnie McDowell.
"From Graceland To The Promised Land" by Merle Haggard. U.S.A.
From his album, "My Farewell To Elvis," also a fine effort.
"Requiem For Elvis" by Jackie Kahane. U.S.A.
"Candy Bars For Elvis," Barry Tiffins' true story. U.S.A.
"The Day The Beat Stopped" by Ral Donner. U.S.A.
"Elvis Has Left The Building" by J. D. Sumner. U.S.A.
"The Whole World Misses You" by Carl Perkins. U.S.A.
"Just A Country Boy" by Frankie Allen. U.K.
"My Hero" by Jackie Lynton. U.K.
"Salute To Elvis" by Cahir O'Doherty. Ireland.
"Say We're Not Apart" by Trond Granlund. Norway.
The best albums of Elvis music were from Terry Tigre, "To Elvis With Love," U.S.A.; "Elvis, 1935-1977, I've Been Away For A While Now" by Ral Donner, U.S.A.; and two albums from J. D. Sumner and the Stamps, "Elvis' Favorite Gospel Songs," and "Memories Of Our Friend Elvis," both U.S.A.

"Trouble"

(Jerry Leiber – Mike Stoller)
From *King Creole* (1958), another Leiber-Stoller masterpiece with Elvis talking his lines about "I was born standing up and talking back" and then swinging into a dixieland bit and finally ripping furiously to a quick climax. He knocked everybody out by recreating the song for his 1968 NBC-TV *Special* (two versions appear on the LP, vocally so close to the original that it's unbelievable). Recorded in January of 1958 in Hollywood; released in August of 1958 on the soundtrack LP. Also on the EP *King Creole, Volume 2* (1958). Later, on the LP's *Elvis NBC-TV Special* (1968) and *Elvis: The Other Sides – Worldwide Gold Award Hits, Volume 2* (1971).

"T-R-O-U-B-L-E"

(Jerry Chesnut)
A frantic rocker, rattled off admirably by Elvis and backed with flair and excitement by his band. The song demonstrated that Elvis truly liked to rock in the final years. Recorded May 10-11, 1975 in Hollywood; released in May of 1975 as a single, with "Mr. Songman" on the flip-side. Later on the LP *Today* (1975). The eight-disc boxed set *Elvis Aaron Presley* of 1981 contains a nifty live version, recorded in 1975.

Trouble In Vegas

33⅓ bootleg LP.
Side 1: "C'mon Everybody"; "Dominique"; "Memphis, Tennessee" (Las Vegas, 1973); "Hound Dog" (Las Vegas, 1972); "A Big Hunk O' Love" (Las Vegas, 1972); "Got A Lot O' Livin' To Do"; "Treat Me Nice"; 1956 Interview; "Witchcraft" *(The Frank Sinatra-Timex Special)*; "Wild In The Country."
Side 2: "An American Trilogy" (Las Vegas, 1972); "My Baby Is Gone"; "Baby, What You Want Me To Do" (Las Vegas, 1969); "A Cane And A High Starched Collar"; "The Lady Moves Me."

"True Love"

(Cole Porter)
Elvis crooning Cole, with the Jordanaires singing low and sweet – a cover of the 1956 version by Bing Crosby and Grace Kelly in the movie *High Society*. Beautifully performed. Recorded February 23, 1957 at Radio Recorders in Hollywood; released in July of 1957 on the LP *Loving You* and on the EP *Loving You, Volume One*.

"True Love Travels On A Gravel Road"

(Dallas Frazier – Al Owens)
Simple, sad, and very effective

song from the Memphis sessions, with Elvis displaying his range and nice vocal touches by the "girls"—Jeannie Green and the Holladay ladies, Mary and Ginger. Recorded February 17, 1969 at American Studios in Memphis, released in May of 1969 on the LP *From Elvis in Memphis*.

"Tryin' To Get To You"
(Margie Singleton—Rose Marie McCoy)
From the Sun days, a bluesy thing originally recorded in 1954. Elvis' version, like his other Sun tunes, was unique: a hiccoughing, yodelling gem, with verses dragged out and twisted to suit his style and Scotty and Bill on top of every note. Elvis' country roots are also evident in this romantic ballad, as well as his incredible vocal dynamics when he curls his voice low in the refrains. Recorded in July of 1955 at Sun Studio; released by RCA as a single, with "I Love You Because" on the flip-side. Later on the EP *Elvis Presley* (1956) and the LP *Elvis Presley* (1956). A version was recorded for the 1968 NBC-TV *Special* but was not used. Later, on the LP *Elvis—A Legendary Performer, Volume One* (1974). A live version was released on *Elvis Recorded Live On Stage In Memphis* (1974) and on *Elvis In Concert* (1977). The original Sun track was also remixed and released on the LP *The Sun Sessions* (1976).

Ernest Tubb
One of the great country singers who was one of Elvis' favorites as a kid and young man. He has been a member of the Country Music Hall of Fame since 1965. With Johnny Byrd, Tubb composed the song "Tomorrow Never Comes," which Elvis covered in 1970.

Gabe Tucker
Manager, promotion man, one of Colonel Parker's longtime friends and assistants, who co-authored a book with *Houston Post* columnist Marge Crumbaker entitled *Up and Down With Elvis Presley* (Putnam, 1981).

Tupelo Garment Company
Where Gladys Presley worked as a sewing machine operator until 1933 when she left to give birth to her son.

Tupelo Hardware Company
Where Gladys Presley bought Elvis' first guitar in January of 1946 for $12.75, sold by its proprietor, Forrest Bobo. There is some discrepancy between accounts as to whether Elvis originally wanted a bicycle or a .22 rifle; what is certain is that Gladys persuaded him to get the guitar because she feared for his safety with a gun.

Ronnie Tutt
Elvis' drummer, 1969-1976, on tour and in recording sessions.

"Tutti Frutti"
(Richard Penniman—Dorothy La Bostrie)
Elvis took Little Richard's smash head-on; the result was something as crazed, but not as awe-inspiring. Still, loads of fun. Performed twice on the Dorsey Brothers *Stage Show*—February 4 and February 18, 1956. Recorded January 31, 1956 at RCA New York Studio; released in March of 1956 on the LP *Elvis Presley*. Released as a single in September of 1956, with "Blue Suede Shoes" on the flip-side. Also on the EP *Elvis Presley* (1956).

TV Guide Presents Elvis Presley
RCA 8705.
A 45 rpm record considered by many collectors to be the most valuable in the world. Consisting of only one side, it was made in 1956 and sent to radio and television stations:

Band 1: "Pelvis Nickname" (:19);
Band 2: "Adult's Reaction" (:34);
Band 3: "First Public Appearance" (:54);
Band 4: "How Rockin' Motion Started" (:44).
Two special inserts were sent with the record: one suggested questions for the announcer to ask, to match Elvis' responses on the record; the other featured a photo of the September 8-14, 1956 issue of *TV Guide* relating the story of how the interview came to be. *TV Guide Presents Elvis Presley* was recorded by Paul Wilder, a reporter for *TV Guide* in Lakeland, Florida.

TV Guide Presents Elvis
33⅓ LP Bootleg.
Side 1: "Steve Allen TV Show, July 1, 1956" (all songs); *TV Guide* Presents Elvis (interview).
Side 2: "Hy Gardiner Interview, 1956"; *Frank Sinatra Timex Special* (all songs, including "Witchcraft"); "Love Me Tender"; (duet with Sinatra)."

"Tweedle Dee"
(Winfield Scott)
Elvis performed this song, a hit for LaVern Baker in 1954, quite frequently in his early days as a Sun artist. Though Sun or RCA never released any version of the song, several bootleg records contained a version of the song recorded from the *Louisiana Hayride* of 1954.

"Twenty Days And Twenty Nights"
(Ben Weisman—Clive Westlake)
A perfect Elvis ballad—a poignant song of lost love that starts quietly and knocks you out. Strings, acoustic guitar, and light background singing, but all understated for a change—it's Elvis' show. Recorded June 4, 1970 at RCA Nashville Studio; released in December of 1970 on the LP *That's The Way It Is*.

Glenn Tyler
Elvis' character in *Wild In The Country* (1961).

Judy Tyler
"Peggy Van Alden," the record company heroine behind Elvis in *Jailhouse Rock* (1957). She and Elvis became good friends. She died tragically in an automobile accident shortly after the film opened.

Johnny Tyrone
Elvis' character in *Harum Scarum* (1965).

"Unchained Melody"
(Hy Zaret—Alex North)

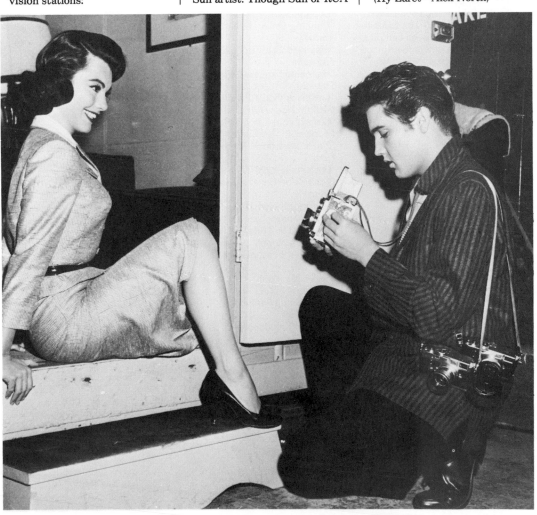

Elvis played and sang this song for twenty-two years before he finally put it on record. It's no small wonder why fans were moved to tears by his interpretation. Many versions of the song were recorded from 1955 on: Lee Baxter (1955), Al Hibbler (1955), Roy Hamilton (1955), June Volli (1955), Vito and the Salutations (1963), The Righteous Brothers (1965) and The Sweet Inspirations (1968). Elvis, during the last year of his life, began playing the song at his concerts, accompanying himself on piano, and it was recorded at the Civic Center of Saginaw, Michigan, on April 25, 1977 – RCA later overdubbed bass, organ and percussion. Released in July of 1977 on the LP *Moody Blue*. Later released as a single in March of 1978, with "Softly As I Leave You" on the flip-side.

United Paint Company
Where Vernon worked packing crates for 83 cents an hour from February 1949 until Elvis became famous.

Unreleased Recordings, etc.
One of the most controversial issues among Elvis fans is the amount of unreleased recordings that might or might not exist. RCA isn't saying. The following list of songs has been compiled from rumors, songs mentioned in many articles, live shows, recording sessions and films. It is comprised of songs that may or may not have been recorded or sung "live" by Elvis, *and should only be regarded as a speculative list.*
a) Pre-Army
"Southern-Made Do-nuts" radio commercial, (1954-5);
"Uncle Penn" (Sun, 1954-5, also sung in San Francisco, 1955);
"Tennessee Saturday Night" (Sun, 1954-5);
"My Happiness/That's When Your Heartaches Begin" (demo disc, private recording 1953);
"Casual Love Affair/I'll Never Stand In Your Way" (demo disc, private recording 1954);
"Night Train To Memphis" (or "Last Train To Memphis," or "Thunderbolt Boogie") (Sun, 1954-5);
"Oakie Boogie" (Sun, 1954-5);
"Satisfied" (Sun, 1954-5);
"Without You" (or "Without Love") (Sun, 1954-5);
"Rag Mop" (Sun, 1954-5);
"Always Late (With Your Kisses)" (Sun, 1954-5);
"Blue Guitar" (Sun, 1954-5);
"Crying Heart Blues" (or "Mean Heart Blues") (Sun, 1954-5);
"Down The Line" (Sun, 1954-5);
"Give Me More More More (Of Your Kisses)" (Sun, 1954-5);
"That's The Stuff (You Gotta

Watch)" (Sun, 1954-5);
"Gone" (Sun, 1954-5);
"Rocking" ("Little Sally") (Sun, 1954-5);
"Long Journey" (Sun, 1954-5);
"Sunshine" (Sun, 1954-5);
"Somethin' Blues" (Sun, 1954-5);
"Fools' Hall Of Fame" (on tour, 1956 or 1957);
"Love Bug Itch" (on tour, 1955);
"Only You" (on tour, 1956);
"Nightmare" (no details known);
"Maybelline" (on tour, 1955);
"Rock The Joint" (*Louisiana Hayride*, 1954-5);
"Rock Around The Clock" (*Louisiana Hayride,* 1954-5, also on tours, 1955);
Million Dollar Quartet Songs (in addition to those already unofficially released at time of going to press); (Sun Studios, December 1956: Elvis, Carl Perkins, Jerry Lee Lewis and Johnny Cash, jam session):
"The Old Rugged Cross"; "I Won't Have To Cross Jordan Alone"; "Island Of Golden Dreams"; "Big Boss Man"; "Blueberry Hill"; "Will The Circle Be Unbroken"; "I Was There When It Happened."
(see also Part f) of Unreleased Recordings).
b) Cut From Films
"We're Gonna Live It Up" (*Loving You*);
"Dancing On A Dare" (*Loving You*);
"Playing With Fire" (*Blue Hawaii*);
"Hawaiian Sunrise" (*Blue Hawaii*);
"I Want A Girl Just Like The Girl" (*Follow That Dream*);
"Let's Live A Little" (*Kid Galahad*);
"Twist Me Loose" (*Girls! Girls! Girls!*);
"Potpourri" (*Girls! Girls! Girls!*);
"You're The Boss" (*Viva Las Vegas*);
"I've Never Had It So Good" (*Roustabout*);
"Now Is The Hour" (*Paradise Hawaiian Style*);
"Wheel Of Fortune" (*Easy Come, Easy Go*);
"Leave My Woman Alone" (*Easy Come Easy Go*);
"I'm Chasing Money" (*Clambake*);
"Chatauqua" (*Trouble With Girls*);
"Rock Of Ages" (*Charro*);
"Ring Of Bright Water" (*Change Of Habit*);
"Whistling Blues" (*G.I. Blues*);
"Malaguene" (*Fun In Acapulco*).
c) Post-Army Studio
"I'd Rather Have Jesus" (1966);
"I Almost Lost My Mind" (1967);
"A Girl's Got A Right To Cry" (1967);
"You Win Again" (1967);
"Girl On My Mind" (1967);
"Birds Fly High" (1967);
"Jelly Roll King" (1967);

"Since I Met You Baby" (1967);
"Little Bitty Baby" (1967);
"Tupelo Mississippi Flash" (1968);
"Baby Let's Play House" (re-recording: 1968);
"Jambalaya" (1968);
"Tiger By The Tail" (1968);
"If I Promise" (1968);
"Remembering" (1968);
"Woman Shy" (1968);
"Love's Gone" (1968);
"I'm Ready For Love" (1968);
"Son Of A Preacher Man" (1969);
"Hooked On A Feeling" (1969);
"A Touch Of Green" (1969, possibly "A Little Bit Of Green");
"Angeline" (1969);
"Come Out Come Out" (1969);
"Poor Man's Gold" (1969);
"Memory Revival" (1969);
"Good, Bad, But Beautiful" (1969 or 1973);
"Funky Feeling" (or "Funny Feeling" or "Funny Fingers" or "Funky Fingers") (1970);
"It's Only Make Believe" (1970);
"Rainy Night In Georgia" (1970);
"Three Good Reasons" (1971);
"Merry Christmas Darling" (1971);
"Silent Night" (re-recording 1971);
"My Garden Of Prayer" (1971);
"Say You Love Me One More Time" (1971);
"It's Not For You" (1971);
"Jody And The Kid" (1971);
"Me And Bobby Magee" (1971);
"Loving Her Was Easier Than Anything I'll Ever Do Again" (1971);
"Blowin' In The Wind" (1971);
"House Of The Rising Sun" (1971);
"It Ain't Me Babe" (1971);
"Mr. Tambourine Man" (1971);
"All I Really Wanna Do" (1971);
"She Belongs To Me" (1971);
"Like A Rolling Stone" (1971);
"Subterranean Homesick Blues" (1971);
"Walking Down The Line" (1971);
"One Too Many Rumors" (1971);
"My Love For You" (1972);
"Color My Rainbow" (1973);
"The Wonders You Perform" (1973);
"Carolyn" (1973);
"A Shoulder To Cry On" (1973);
"Snow Don't Fall" (1973);
"Don't Let The Sunshine Fool You" (1973);
"No Lonesome Tune" (1973);
"A Blues Jam" (1973);
"You Touch Me Softly In The Morning" (1975);
"Neighborhood" (1975);
"Thinking About That Woman" (1975);
"Pearl's A Singer" (1975);
"Dancin' Jones" (1975);
"The Best Thing" (1975);
"Loving You Baby" (1976);
"I Write The Songs" (1976);
"Being King Is A Lonely Life" (or "It's Lonely Being King")

(1976);
"There's A Fire Down Below" (1976);
"McArthur's Park" (1978-9, rumored single);
"Portrait Of My Love" (1978-9, rumored single);
"If You Ever Leave Me" (1976);
"Running Scared" (1976);
"Crying" (1976);
"Feelings" (1976-77);
    Elvis sang many songs – often incomplete – onstage just once or twice:
d) "Live" Songs
"Bad Moon Rising" (1969);
"Land Of 1000 Dances" (1969);
"When The Swallows Come Back To Capistrano" (1969-70);
"It's Crying Time" (1970);
"Cattle Call" (1970);
"Lodi" (early '70's);
"Diana" (early '70's);
"Holly Holy" (1970);
"(I Need You On) The Tips Of My Fingers" (1970);
"You Are My Good Looking Woman" (1970);
"Detroit City" (1970);
"Close To You" (1970);
"Alone Again Naturally" (1972);
"Daddy Don't You Walk So Fast" (1972);
"The Most Beautiful Girl In The World" (1974);
"You're My Reason For Living" (1975);
"Alright OK You Win" (1975);
"Blue Monday" (1975);
"The 12th Of Never" (1970's);
"Lonely Teardrops" (1970's);
"You Can Have Her" (1974);
"What A Friend We Have In Jesus" (1973);
"You Do Something To Me" (1975);
"Aubrey" (1974) (with voice);
"I Couldn't Live Without You" (1974) (with voice);
"Take These Chains From My Heart And Set Me Free" (1976);
"Everybody Loves Somebody" (1970's);
"Jambalaya" (1975);
"It's Over" (Orbison's song) (1976);
"Ave Maria" (1970's);
"Until The Day" (1976).
    Elvis often did these songs at rehearsals:
e) Rehearsal Songs
"Born To Lose" (1969);
"Suzie Q" (1972);
"Love Will Keep Us Together" (1975);
"Portrait Of My Love" (1970's);
"To Spend One Night With You" (1968 TV rehearsal).
    The following songs or parts of songs have been released *unofficially* at the time of going to press:
f) Songs on Bootlegs
"Aura Lee" (Violet) (*The Trouble With Girls*);
"Auld Lang Syne" (live 1976);
"As We Travel Along The Jericho Road";

"And Now Sweetheart You've Done Me Wrong";
"By The Time I Get To Phoenix" (live '70's);
"Blessed Jesus Hold My Hand";
"Crazy Arms";
"Dominic" (Stay Away Joe);
"Don't Forbid Me";
"Folsom Prison Blues" (live, 1969-70);
"Husky Dusty Day" (with Hope Lange) (Wild In The Country);
"Happy Birthday" (live 1970's);
"Happy Happy Birthday Baby" (private recording, 1958);
"I Walk The Line" (live, 1969-70);
"I Need Your Loving Every Day" (on tour);
"I Can't Help It If I'm Still In Love With You" (1958, private);
"I Understand" (1958, private);
"I'm Sorry Dear" (1958, private);
"I'm Leavin' It Up To You" (1970's);
"I Shall Not Be Moved";
"I'm With The Crowd But Oh So Alone";
"I Hear A Sweet Voice Calling";
"I Just Can't Make It By Myself";
"Just A Closer Walk With Thee" (1958, private);
"Just A Little Talk With Jesus";
"Keeper Of The Keys";
"My Baby's Gone" (Sun, 1954-5);
"More" (live, 1970's);
"McArthur's Park" (1968 TV Special);
"Mickey Mouse March" (live, 1975);
"O Happy Day" (live, 1970);
"Plantation Rock" (Girls! Girls! Girls!);
"Signs Of The Zodiac" (with Marylyn Mason in The Trouble With Girls);
"Sweet Inspiration" (live, 1970's);
"Summertime Has Passed And Gone"*;
"The Lady Loves Me" (duet with Ann-Margret in Viva Las Vegas);
"Tweedledee" (Louisiana Hayride, 1954);
"Tiptoe Through The Tulips" (1968 TV Special);
"Tumbling Tumbleweeds" (1958, private);
"The Great Pretender" (live, 1975);
"Witchcraft" (Sinatra's Song) (TV, 1960);
"It's Very Nice To Go Traveling" (TV, 1960);
"When The Snow Is On The Roses" (live, 1970's);
"Who's Sorry Now" (1958, private);
"We Shall Overcome" (live, 1970's);
"Whiffenpoof Song" (The Trouble With Girls);
"Walk That Lonesome Valley"*;
"You Better Run" (live, 1975);
"Yippie-i-o" (song on Steve Allen TV Show) (1956);
*Million Dollar Quartet Songs.

Unreleased Sun Recordings

In addition to the fourteen songs recorded on the Sun Label in 1955 and either released by Sun or RCA (or both), Elvis recorded a number of songs that were never released for artistic or contractual reasons. Speculation is that Sam Phillips still has some in his possession and that Shelby Singleton, who bought Sun in 1968, may have copies. They are: "Uncle Penn," "Tennessee Saturday Night," "Oakie Boogie," "Down The Line," "Blue Guitar," "Always Late With Your Kisses," "Case," "Night Train To Memphis," "Sunshine," and "Crying Heart Blues."

"Until It's Time For You To Go"

(Buffy Sainte-Marie)
Elvis turned Buffy's 1970 version of her own folksy composition into a ballad with piano and strings nicely complemented by the Imperials. The lyrics are stretched and phrased beautifully. Recorded May 17, 1971 at RCA Nashville Studio; released in January of 1971 as a single, with "We Can Make The Morning." Refined in the 1972 documentary Elvis On Tour and later released on the LPs Elvis Now (1972), and Elvis—A Canadian Tribute (1978).

(Untitled)

45 EP Bootleg.
"My Baby Is Gone"; Instrumental version of "I Don't Care"; "Jailhouse Rock"; "Treat Me Nice" (soundtrack); "A Cane And A High Starched Collar"; "Ed Sullivan medley"; "Heartbreak Hotel"; "Love Me Tender"; "Peace In The Valley."

"Up Above My Head"

(W. Earl Brown)
Short gospel track performed on the 1968 NBC-TV Special. (Brown's other composition in the show, "If I Can Dream," had more substance.) Still, a good spiritual. Recorded June 30, 1968 at Burbank Studio; released in December of 1968 on the LP Elvis—(NBC-TV Special).

Upanishads

The sacred book of the Hindus studied by Elvis, from which he derived his belief in reincarnation.

"U.S. Male"

(Jerry Hubbard)
Elvis drawling about his manhood, in a countrified tune backed by Jerry Reed twanging away on guitar and Elvis in a talk-sing voice. Recorded January 17, 1968, at RCA Nashville Studio; released in March of 1968 as a single, with "Stay Away" as the flip-side. Later, on the RCA LP Almost In Love

and the Pickwick LP Double Dynamite (1976).

US53310761

Elvis' serial number in the Army.

Vail, Colorado

Elvis' favorite winter vacation spot, where he enjoyed riding snowmobiles. He celebrated his birthday there in 1976 with his entourage and gave away five cars to police officials, a TV newsman and a local doctor.

Rudy Vallee

Famous megaphone crooner of the 1930's who played "Penlow" in Live A Little, Love A Little (1968).

Vegas EPs

(Two-record set) Bootleg.
Volume 1: "Never Been To Spain"; "Lord, This Time You Gave Me A Mountain"; "Proud Mary"; "Love Me."
Volume 2: "Hound Dog" (blues version); "A Big Hunk O' Love"; "I'm Leavin' It Up To You"; "American Trilogy."

Jimmy Velvet

Singer who toured with Elvis during the 1950's and later recorded for Phillips International. He and Elvis remained good friends over the years.

Venus Room

The nightclub of the New Frontier Hotel in Las Vegas, where Elvis appeared on April 23, 1956 for $17,500 a week on an agreement worked out between the Colonel and Hotel president J. W. Richardson, to which Elvis was supposed to have responded "Good Lord!" Elvis appeared with comedian Shecky Greene and the Freddie Martin Orchestra. Although it is commonly assumed that Elvis "bombed" at his Las Vegas debut, the truth was that the people simply didn't know how to respond; his cool reception was a stark difference from all the screaming in the South. The engagement lasted until the 29th of April.

"Vino, Dinero, Y Amor"

(Wine, Money And Love)
(Sid Tepper—Ray C. Bennett)
From Fun In Acapulco (1963), a fast samba with people yelling and screaming in the background and Elvis going for a characteristic crescendo. With the Amigos. Recorded January 20, 1963 in Hollywood; released in November of 1963 on the soundtrack LP.

Viva Las Vegas

Started: 1964
A Jack Cummings and George Sidney Production
An MGM Picture
Cast
Lucky Jackson: Elvis Presley;

Rusty Martin: Ann-Margret;
Count Elmo Mancini: Cesare Donova; Mr. Martin: William Demarest; Shorty Farnsworth: Nicky Blair.
Credits
Producers: Jack Cummings and George Sidney; Director: George Sidney; Written by Sally Benson; Music by George Stoll; Assistant Director: Milton Feldman; Choreographer: David Winters; Hair Styles by Sydney Guillaroff; Recording Supervisor: Franklin Milton.
"Folies Bergeres" Sequence by arrangement with Hotel Tropicana, Las Vegas
In Panavision and Metrocolor
Songs
"Appreciation" (Ann-Margret); "I Need Somebody To Lean On"; "The Yellow Rose Of Texas"; "Viva Las Vegas"; "The Lady Moves Me" (unreleased); "What'd I Say"; "C'mon Everybody"; "If You Think I Don't Need You"; "Today, Tomorrow and Forever"; "Santa Lucia"; "The Eyes Of Texas"; "The Climb" (Jubilee Four); "The Rival" (Ann-Margret); "Do The Vega" (cut); "You're The Boss" (cut-unreleased).
Running Time: 86 minutes.
Previously Titled:
The Only Game In Town
Viva Las Vegas (U.S. title)
The Lady Loves Me
Mister, Will You Marry Me?

"Viva Las Vegas"

(Doc Pomus—Mort Schuman)
The title tune from the 1964 film—one of the better film numbers. It's fast, corny, remarkably attractive, mean—and it all comes together. The fade-out note that Elvis hits at the finale is one of the most remarkable of his career, a soaring, quasi-operatic scream. Recorded July of 1963 in Hollywood; released in April of 1964 as a single, with "What'd I Say" on the flip-side. Later, on the LPs Elvis: Worldwide 50 Gold Award Hits, Volume 1 (1970) and Elvis In Hollywood. (1976).

Viva Las Vegas

1964 RCA Victor. EP (EPA-4382).
Side 1: "If You Think I Don't Need You"; "I Need Somebody To Lean On."
Side 2: "C'mon Everybody"; "Today, Tomorrow And Forever."

Voice

Another of the vocal and record groups to share the stage with Elvis on tour from 1973–1975, featuring Sherril Nielson, Tim Batey, and Donnie Sumner.

Jess Wade

Elvis' character in Charro (1969).

Jerry Walk
Produced *Wild In The Country* (1961).

"Walk A Mile In My Shoes"
(Joe South)
Along the lines of "Suspicious Minds," another of the stage tunes from the early Las Vegas days. Pleasant tempo, serious lyric, the Sweet Inspirations sounding swell, and Elvis laughing over a flubbed line. Recorded on February 18, 1970 at the International Hotel in Las Vegas; released in May of 1970 on the LP *On Stage—February, 1970.*

Bill Wallace
A Memphis karate champ who served as part-time bodyguard in the TCB entourage.

Deborah Walley
"Les," part of Elvis' musical trio in *Spinout* (1966).

Hal Wallis
One of Hollywood's most prolific producers of "B" action-pictures and the man who gave Elvis his first screen test in 1956. Eventually, a seven-year, non-exclusive contract was signed. Wallis would eventually produce nine Elvis Presley films, which

range from his best, earliest efforts *Loving You* (1957), *King Creole* (1958), to his most ridiculous *Easy Come, Easy Go* (1966). He also produced *G.I. Blues* (1960), *Fun In Acapulco* (1963), *Roustabout* (1964), *Paradise Hawaiian Style* (1965).

Charles M. Warren
Producer of *Charro!* (1969).

"Way Down"
(Layne Martine, Jr.)
Elvis' posthumous single hit in the weeks following his tragic death, a solid, uptempo track with the basso profundo of J. D. Sumner adding a nice touch. Recorded October 29–30, 1976 at Graceland; released in June of 1977 as a single, with "Pledging My Love" as the flip-side. Later, on the LP *Moody Blue* (1977). The song was remixed for the 1979 LP *Our Memories of Elvis, Volume 2.*

WDIA
Memphis' black R & B station which Elvis listened to avidly during and after high school in the 1950's. Rufus Thomas, B. B. King, and Joe Hill Lewis, all Sun artists, had programs on WDIA. On December 22, 1956, the station held a benefit

concert at which Elvis appeared with Little Junior Parker (whose "Mystery Train" he'd recorded in 1955), and B. B. King, among others.

"Wearin' That Loved One Look"
(Dallas Frazier—Al Owens)
A fun song from the Memphis Sessions—a high-voiced, shouting Elvis in a rocking mood with the girls going "shoop shoop." With a biting guitar by Reggie Young and organ by Glen Spreen. Recorded on January 14, 1969 at American Studios; released in May of 1969 on the LP *From Elvis In Memphis.*

"Wear My Ring Around Your Neck"
(Bert Carroll—Russell Moody)
Heavy duty, vintage rocker from the early RCA catalogue. Elvis spinning off lyrics like a madman and D. J. Fontanna drumming like a machine-gun, nearly breaking his sticks. Recorded on February 1, 1958 at Radio Recorders in Hollywood; released as a single in April of 1958 with 'Doncha Think It's Time" on the flip-side. Later, on the EP *A Touch of Gold, Volume 2* (1958), and on the LPs

50,000,000 Elvis Fans Can't Be Wrong, Elvis' Golden Records, Volume 2 (1959) and *Elvis: Worldwide 50 Gold Award Hits, Volume 1* (1970).

Robert D. Webb
Director of *Love Me Tender* (1956).

"We Call On Him"
(Fred Karger—Ben Weisman—Sid Wayne)
Sacred ballad with Elvis in superb control against a perfectly balanced backing. Recorded September 11, 1967 as a single, with "You'll Never Walk Alone" on the flip-side. Later, on the RCA Camden LP *You'll Never Walk Alone* (1971).

"We Can Make The Morning"
(Jay Ramsey)
Carefully blended ballad with guitars, strings and the Imperial Quartet, though Elvis' voice is badly projected in spots. Recorded on May 20, 1971 at RCA Nashville Studio; released in January of 1972 as a single, with "Until It's Time For You To Go" on the flip-side. Later, on the LP *Elvis Now* (1971).

Jerry Weintraub
Rock concert promoter who

Hal Wallis.

formed Concerts West with Tom Huelett and put *The Elvis Presley Show* on the road, 1970–1976.

David Weisbart
The man who produced one of Elvis' all-time favorite films in 1955, *Rebel Without A Cause*. Eventually produced four Elvis Presley films: *Love Me Tender* (1956), *Flaming Star* (1960), *Follow That Dream* (1962) and *Kid Galahad* (1962).

Ben Weisman
One of the most prolific contributors to Elvis' repertoire over the years, having co-written dozens of songs for his films and albums. Among the most successful were "Fame And Fortune," "Follow That Dream," "Easy Come, Easy Go," "Almost Always True," "Rock-a-Hula Baby" and "Hard Luck," all with his partner, Sid Wayne. He also wrote songs with Aaron Schroeder, Dolores Fuller, and others.

Lester Welch
Produced *The Trouble With Girls, And How To Get Into It* (1969).

"Welcome To My World"
(Ray Winkler – John Hathcock) From the *"Aloha" Special* in 1973, Elvis' version of the 1964 hit by Jim Reeves (later recorded by Eddy Arnold in 1971). The song doesn't come across all the way because El was fooling around with the audience. Recorded on January 14, 1973 at the H.I.C. Arena in Hawaii; released in February of 1973 on the LP *Aloha From Hawaii Via Satellite*. Later, on the LP *Welcome To My World* (1977).

Welcome To My World
1977 RCA Victor. LP (ALP1-2274).
Side 1: "Welcome To My World"; "Help Me Make It Through The Night"; "Release Me (And Let Me Love Again)"; "I Really Don't Want To Know"; "For The Good Times."
Side 2: "Make The World Go Away"; "Gentle On My Mind"; "I'm So Lonesome I Could Cry"; "Your Cheatin' Heart"; "I Can't Stop Loving You (Unreleased live version)."

Tuesday Weld
"Noreen," Elvis' sexy cousin in *Wild in the Country* (1961) and a friend of Elvis' for many years.

"We'll Be Together"
(Charles O'Curran – Dudley Brooks) From *Girls! Girls! Girls!* (1962), Elvis singing happily about "being together." A Spanish feeling with the Amigos in the background (only on the record).

Recorded in March of 1962 in Hollywood; released in November of 1962 on the soundtrack LP. Later, on the RCA Camden LP *Burning Love And Hits From His Movies, Volume 2* (1972).

Rusty Wells
Elvis' character in *Girl Happy* (1965).

"We're Coming In Loaded"
(Otis Blackwell – Winfield Scott) From *Girls! Girls! Girls!* (1962), one minute and twenty seconds of energy from Elvis and the Jordanaires. Recorded in March of 1962 in Hollywood; released in November of 1962 on the soundtrack LP.

"We're Gonna Move"
(Vera Matson – Elvis Presley) From *Love Me Tender* (1956), another tune really penned by Ken Darby – C & W type song done in a traditional manner. Recorded in August of 1956 in Hollywood; released in November of 1956 on the EP *Loving You*. Later, on the LPs *A Date With Elvis* (1959) and *Elvis: The Other Sides – Worldwide Gold Award Hits, Volume 2* (1971).

Bobby "Red" West
One of Elvis' oldest and most controversial friends. Red and Elvis met at Humes High, and when Elvis became a recording star and traveled on the road, Red became his first bodyguard. He followed Elvis to Germany during his Army days, and became part of the "Memphis Mafia" upon his release. He became a singer, songwriter, stunt man, karate expert, and actor. Elvis was best man at Red's wedding; Red, on the other hand, was 'snubbed' and not invited to Elvis'. Their relationship had its ups and downs for many years, until Red, after a long period of estrangement and security problems, was fired along with his cousin, Sonny, and Dave Hebler, another bodyguard. The result was their book, *Elvis: What Happened*, published fifteen days before Elvis died – a scandalous, exploitative work but the first "inside" account of Elvis' life and problems, also the first book to confirm the fact of Elvis' drug problems. Following Elvis' death, Red has appeared on several television series in featured roles. He presently resides in Los Angeles with his family.

Delbert "Sonny" West
Red's cousin, a Memphis boy who went to work for Elvis in the early sixties, acted part-time and took care of Elvis' homes in California for a while as a house-sitter. Fired along with Red and David Hebler, he became one of

the co-authors of *Elvis: What Happened*.

Pat Boyd West
One of the Graceland secretaries, who married Red West in 1961.

"Western Union"
(Sid Tepper – Roy C. Bennett) An inferior version of "Return To Sender." Recorded on May 27, 1963 at RCA Nashville Studio; released in June of 1968 on the soundtrack LP *Speedway* (the song wasn't performed in the film).

Kathy Westmoreland
Lead vocalist with the Sweet Inspirations, singing "live" on tour with Elvis and on records, 1969–1977. They dated briefly in 1975, and she sang "My Heavenly Father Watches Over Me" at his funeral.

"What A Wonderful Life"
(Sid Wayne – Jerry Livingston) From *Follow That Dream* (1962), a lighthearted rendition that found favor with Elvis fans everywhere, for its happy-go-lucky quality. Recorded on July 5, 1961 at RCA Nashville Studio; released in April of 1962 on the soundtrack EP. Later, on the RCA Camden LP *I Got Lucky* (1971).

"What'd I Say"
(Ray Charles) From *Viva Las Vegas* (1964), Ray Charles' 1959 R & B classic gets a strong treatment from Elvis (former versions included Jerry Lee Lewis in 1961 and Bobby Darin in 1962). Elvis rocks it, backed by the Carol Lombard Quartet and the Jubilee Four. Recorded in July of 1963 in Hollywood; released in May of 1964 as a single with "Viva Las Vegas" on the flip-side. A snippet was performed in the 1970 documentary *That's The Way It Is*. Later, on the LP *Elvis' Golden records, Volume 4* (1968). A live version was released on *Elvis In Concert* (1977).

"What Every Woman Lives For"
(Doc Pomus – Mort Schuman) From *Frankie and Johnny* (1966), a ballad in which El sings about the "weaker sex." What every woman lives for is to give her love to a man. Recorded in May of 1965 at United Artists Recording Studio in Los Angeles; released in April of 1966 on the soundtrack LP.

"What Now My Love"
(Carl Sigman – Gilbert Becaud – P. Delanoe). Standard ballad performed endlessly in showbiz circles, given serious treatment by Elvis with a crashing finale on the "Aloha"

broadcast. Recorded on January 14, 1973 at H.I.C. arena in Hawaii; released in February of 1973 on the LP *Aloha From Elvis in Hawaii*.

"What Now, What Next, Where To"
(Don Robertson – Hal Blair) Wistful ballad with Floyd Cramer piano and Elvis performing straight from the heart. Recorded May 26, 1963 at RCA Nashville studio; released in June of 1967 on the LP *Double Trouble*. Later, on the RCA Camden LP *Separate Ways*.

"What's She Really Like"
(Sid Wayne – Abner Silver) From *G.I. Blues* (1960), a romantic ballad delivered with great style and flourish by Elvis. Recorded April of 1960 in Hollywood; released in October of 1960 on the soundtrack LP.

"Wheels On My Heels"
(Sid Tepper – Roy C. Bennett) From *Roustabout* (1964), a highway number with a sax break. "Gotta keep r-oo-lin," he sings. Nothing striking but passable. Recorded in January of 1964 in Hollywood; released in October of 1964 on the soundtrack LP.

"When I'm Over You"
(Shirl Milete) High key strings, guitar and girls in the background – Elvis sounds bored by this one; he probably *was*. Recorded on June 7, 1970 at RCA Nashville Studio; released in May of 1971 on the LP *Love Letters From Elvis*.

"When It Rains It Really Pours"
(William Emerson) A great raucous Elvis from the early RCA days – real Blues with piano by Dudley Brooks and ringing guitar by Scotty Moore. Amazingly, the song wasn't released for eight years. Recorded on February 24, 1957 at Radio Recorders in Hollywood; released in July of 1965 on the LP *Elvis For Everyone*.

"When My Blue Moon Turns To Gold Again"
(Wiley Walker – Gene Sullivan) Elvis sings low and throbbing on this C & W rendition from the early days at RCA, done ballad-style with the Jordanaires. Tex Ritter had a big hit with the song in 1949. Recorded on September 2, 1956 at Radio Recorders in Hollywood; released in November of 1956 on the EP *Elvis, Volume 1*. Also on the LP *Elvis* (1956). A version was recorded for the *1968 NBC-TV* telecast, but was not included in the telecast or

the LP release. Later, on the LP *Elvis: The Other Sides—Worldwide 50 Gold Award Hits, Volume 2.*

"Where Could I Go But To The Lord"
(J.B. Coats)
One of Elvis' finest gospel songs. Piano, guitar, and Elvis out in front of the Jordanaires and Imperials. First class. The song was also performed in the *1968 NBC-TV Special,* but the vocal accompaniment is weaker and the orchestra seemed unsuitable. Recorded on May 28, 1968 at RCA Nashville Studio; released in April of 1967 on the LP *How Great Thou Art.* The live version was released on the LP *"Elvis" NBC-TV Special* in 1968.

"Where Did They Go Lord"
(Dallas Frazier—A.L. Owens)
Ballad of lost love belted out powerfully, with the Imperials and the Jordanaires. Recorded on September 22, 1970 at RCA Nashville Studio; released in March of 1971 as a single, with "Rags To Riches" on the flip-side. Later, on the LP *He Walks Beside Me* (1978).

"Where Do I Go From Here"
(Williams)
Confused rendition with erupting choruses. Only two verses of off-balanced lyrics, like the line in the song, this is *A story without meaning.* Recorded on March 27, 1972 at MGM Recording Studio in Los Angeles; released in July of 1973 on the LP *Elvis.*

"Where Do You Come From"
(Ruth Batchelor—Bob Roberts)
From *Girls! Girls! Girls!* (1962), a slow, swooning ballad about a mystical girl. Elvis eats these songs up. Recorded on March of 1962 in Hollywood; released in October of 1962 as a single, with "Return To Sender" as the flip-side. Later, on the 1962 soundtrack LP and *Elvis: Worldwide 50 Gold Award Hits, Volume 1* (1970).

"Where No One Stands Alone"
(Mosie Lister)
Lovely gospel-ballad with piano, organ, Jords, Imperials, and a viola. Elvis is perfect. Recorded on May 26, 1966 at RCA Nashville Studio; released in April of 1967 on the LP *How Great Thou Art.*

WHHM
Memphis' country music station that first aired "Blue Moon Of Kentucky" the country side of Elvis' first record in July of 1954. The cut was first played by DJ "Sleepy-eyed" John Lepley.

Bergen White
Musical arranger who added the orchestration to several of Elvis' songs recorded during the Graceland sessions of February, 1976. The strings and horns heard on "Moody Blue" are examples of his handiwork.

Carrie White
One of Elvis' Hollywood beauticians.

Tony Joe White
C & W composer-singer who gave Elvis "I've Got A Thing About You" and "Polk Salad Annie," which became one of the great hits of his first years in Las Vegas.

"White Christmas"
(Irving Berlin)
From El's first yuletide RCA platter, the largest selling song of all time (the important recordings—Bing Crosby in 1942; Frank Sinatra in 1946, and Ernest Tubb in 1949). Elvis' version is a bit different: more tempo, sweet, simple, less orchestration. Recorded on September 6, 1957 at Radio Recorders in Hollywood; released in November of 1957 on *Elvis' Christmas Album.*

Joe Whitecloud
Elvis' character in *Stay Away, Joe* (1968).

Whitehaven
Suburb in South Memphis where Graceland is located. When Elvis bought his estate on Highway 51 South in March of 1957, it was sparsely populated, but by the time the suburb was formally incorporated into the city of Memphis in 1969, Graceland was ringed by developments and shopping centers. Vernon Presley built a house on Dolan Street in the early 1960's, which bordered Elvis' backyard. Much of Graceland's affairs were conducted with local merchants and Elvis used the football stadium at Whitehaven High for his workouts and games.

Whitehaven Music, Inc.
Another Presley song publishing company.

"Who Am I"
(Charlie 'Rusty' Goodman)
Quiet spiritual with standard backing from the Memphis Sessions. Recorded on February 22, 1969 at American Studios; released in March of 1971 on the LP *You'll Never Walk Alone.* Later, in *He Walks Beside Me* (1978).

"Who Are You (Who Am I)?"
(Sid Wayne—Ben Weisman)
From *Speedway* (1968), a "sophisticated" love song, mixing style and going nowhere.

Highlight is the sax solo. Recorded on June 18, 1967 in Hollywood; released in June of 1968 on the soundtrack LP.

"Whole Lotta Shakin' Goin' On"
(Dave Williams—Sonny David)
Elvis' version in 1970 of Jerry Lee Lewis' 1957 monster rocker is fast and low down, with David Briggs given a little room to step out on the keys but falling far short of the Killer's ivory antics. Recorded on September 22, 1970 at RCA Nashville Studio; released in February of 1971 on the LP *Elvis Country.* Performed in medley with "Long Tall Sally" on the "Aloha" broadcast (June 14, 1973) and released on the LP *Aloha From Hawaii Via Satellite.* Also on the LP *Elvis Recorded Live On Stage in Memphis* (1974).

"Who Needs Money"
(Randy Starr)
From *Clambake* (1967), Elvis' duet with Will Hutchins (it isn't his voice in the film or on the LP—nobody knows who it is). Apart from this lingering mystery, there isn't much to be said about this light-hearted bit. Recorded on February 21, 1967 at RCA Nashville Studio; released in June of 1967 on the soundtrack LP.

"Why Me Lord"
(Kris Kristofferson)
Elvis found the spiritual fervor and soul of Kristofferson's 1971 song irresistible. He performed it live, enlisting the deepest tones of J.D. Sumner for the choruses. Recorded on March 20, 1974 at Mid-South Coliseum in Memphis; released in June of 1974 on the LP *Elvis Recorded Live On Stage In Memphis.*

Bobby Wien
One of Elvis' cousins, who founded the Tennessee Karate Institute with Red West.

Wild In The Country
Started: November 7, 1960
A 20th Century-Fox Production
Cast
Glenn: Elvis Presley; Irene: Hope Lange; Noreen: Tuesday Weld; Betty Lee: Millie Perkins; Davis: Rafer Johnson; Phil Macy: John Ireland; Cliff Macy: Gary Lockwood; Uncle Rolfe: William Mims; Dr. Underwood: Raymond Greenleaf; Monica George: Christina Crawford; Flossie: Robin Raymond; Mrs. Parsons: Doreen Lang; Mr. Parsons: Charle Arnt; Sarah: Ruby Goodwin; Willie Dace: Will Corry; Professor Larson: Alan Napier; Judge Parker: Jason Robards, Sr.; Bartender: Harry Carter; Sam Tyler: Harry

Shannon; Hank Tyler: Bobby West.
Credits
Produced by Jerry Wald
Directed by Phillip Dunne
Screenplay by Clifford Odets
Based on a novel by J.R. Salamanca
Music by Kenyon Hopkins
Associate Producer: Peter Nelson
Assistant Director: Joseph El Rickards
Hair Styles by Helen Turpin, C.H.S.
Orchestration by Edward B. Powell
Color by De Luxe
Songs
"I Slipped, I Stumbled, I Fell"; "In My Way"; "Wild In The Country"; "Lonely Man" (cut); "Forget Me Never" (cut); "Husky, Dusty Day" (Unreleased); *Footnote:* "Forget Me Never" while cut from the movie on a worldwide basis, was still included in the British trailer for *Wild In The Country.*

"Wild In The Country"
(Hugo Peretti—Luigi Creatore—George Weiss)
Sung over the credits of the 1961 film—a quiet ballad—sung with sincerity with the Jordanaires. Recorded in November of 1960 in Hollywood; released in May of 1961 as a single, with "I Feel So Bad" on the flip-side. Later on the LPs *Elvis: The Other Sides—Worldwide Gold Award Hits, Volume 2* (1971) and *Elvis In Hollywood* (1976).

Sharon Wiley
One of Elvis' girlfriends during the mid-1950's.

John Wilkinson
Rhythm guitarist and vocalist for Elvis' Las Vegas opening, and on subsequent tours and albums.

William Morris Agency
Under Abe Lastfogel, the Morris Agency represented Elvis as agents while the Colonel functioned as his "personal manager."

Ernestine Williams
One of the Graceland maids.

Hank Williams
Legendary country-western, composer-performer whose songs Elvis admired. Among the Williams' compositions he performed were "Jumbalaya" and "I'm So Lonesome I Could Cry."

Chuck Willis
Blues singer whose brief career before his death in 1958 produced "See See Rider," which he wrote with Ma Rainey and recorded in 1957. He also wrote "Feel So Bad." Elvis covered both songs very successfully.

Bob Wills
C & W luminary who introduced drums to country music with his Texas Playboys and co-wrote "Faded Love" with his brother John, which Elvis covered brilliantly in 1970.

Mike Windgren
Elvis' character in *Fun in Acapulco* (1965).

Roland Winters
The actor who played "Fred Gates," Elvis' father in *Blue Hawaii* (1961).

"Winter Wonderland"
(Dick Smith—Felix Bernard) X-mas standard rendered admirably, with a slowed down ending and a steel guitar à la Nashville and Elvis in a festive mood. Recorded on May 16, 1971 at RCA Nashville Studio; released in October of 1971 on the LP *Elvis Sings The Wonderful World of Christmas*.

"Widsom Of The Ages"
(Bill Grant—Bernie Baum—Florence Kaye) Recorded for *Harum Scarum* but cut from the print, a strange track with a soft melody that builds to a loud, overbearing climax. Recorded on February 24, 1965 in Hollywood; released in October of 1965 on the soundtrack LP.

"Witchcraft"
(Dave Bartholemew—Pearl King) *Not* Sinatra's famous 1958 hit (by Carolyn Leigh—Cy Coleman) which Elvis toyed with on Sinatra's *Timex TV Special*, May 12, 1960, but something else: a quiet intro that breaks into a swinger with a long sax break. Recorded on May 26, 1963 at RCA Nashville Studio; released in October of 1963 as a single, with "Bossa Nova Baby" on the flip-side. Later, on the LPs *Elvis' Gold Records, Volume 4* (1968) and *Elvis: The Other Sides—Worldwide Gold Award Hits, Volume 2* (1971).

"Without Him"
(Myron R. Lefevre) Lilting spiritual with piano, organ, viola, and a soft, thumping drum; the Jords and Imperials. Gorgeous. Recorded on May 27, 1966 at RCA Nashville Studio; released in April of 1967 on the LP *How Great Thou Art*.

"Without Love (There Is Nothing)"
(Danny Small) From the Memphis sessions, the song popularized in 1957 by Clyde McPhatter, done in grand style with the Memphis Strings and the Blossoms, but with a touch of nostalgia. Recorded on January 21, 1969 at American Studios; released in November of 1969 on *From Memphis To Vegas/From Vegas To Memphis* (1969). Later, on *Elvis—Back in Memphis* (1970).

"Without You"
The simple ballad Sam Phillips asked Elvis to record at Marion Keisker's request in 1953-54. According to Jerry Hopkins, Elvis was awful. Sam asked, "What can you do?" and Elvis replied "I can do anything."

"Wolf Call"
(Bill Grant—Bernie Baum—Florence Kaye) From *Girl Happy* (1965), 1 minute and 25 seconds of nonsense; with . . . you guessed it: a wolf call. Recorded on June 5, 1964 in Hollywood; released in April of 1965 on the soundtrack LP.

"Woman Without Love"
(Jerry Chesnut) Slow ballad, rendered with feeling. Recorded on May 11, 1975 in Hollywood; released in May of 1975 on the LP *Today*.

"Wonderful World"
(Guy Fletcher—Doug Flett) From *Live A Little, Love A Little* (1968), a whistling introduction leads into a lilting melody with Elvis scaling the heights against the strings. Recorded on March 11, 1968 at MGM Sound Studio in Hollywood; released in November of 1968 on the LP *Singer Presents Elvis Singing Flaming Star and Others*.

Anita Wood
One of Elvis' most publicized romances of the 1950's. She was a former WHHM disk jockey, entertainer, and local Memphis TV personality, who met Elvis through Cliff Gleaves in 1958 and dated him for close to a year, until his induction into the Army, sparking rumors of marriage that persisted until 1960. An attractive blonde, her photos appeared everywhere for a time and many fans assumed that Anita was "The Girl He Would Marry Upon His Return." She recorded a record for Sun in 1958 entitled "I'll Wait Forever," which was, of course, a prophetic title, because the marriage was never meant to be. Still, they remained friends over the years.

Bobby Wood
Piano player, song writer and performer, session man on several Elvis records.

Natalie Wood
Elvis' first notable Hollywood romance with this pretty starlet occurred in 1956. She had just completed *Rebel Without A Cause*. When she visited

Memphis in October of that year and went motorcycle riding with Elvis and Nick Adams, the press had a field day: "The Motorcycle Romance" marked the beginning of a long obsession with Elvis' romantic life by the doyennes of gossip journalism in America.

Randy Wood
As head of Dot Records in 1955, he was approached by Sam Phillips with an offer to sell Elvis' contract for $7,500. Wood declined, claiming that Elvis was only "a flash in the pan."

"Wooden Heart"
(Fred Wise – Bert Kaempfert – Kay Twoney)
From *G.I. Blues* (1960), accordion, puppets, kids and Elvis singing engagingly in German. Based on an old German folk song "Mus I Denn Zum Stadtele Naus." Recorded on April 28, 1960 in Hollywood; released in October of 1960 on the soundtrack LP. Single released in the U.K. and West Germany was enormously successful. Later, on the LPs *Elvis: Worldwide 50 Gold Award Hits, Volume 1* (1970) and *Elvis Sings For Children (and Grownups Too)* (1978). ☞

"Words"
(Barry Gibb – Robin Gibb – Maurice Gibb)
Elvis' cover of the 1968 Bee Gee's hit was a stage version marvelously arranged, with exquisite back-up by the Inspirations and the Imperials. Recorded on August 22, 1969 at the International Hotel in Las Vegas; released in November of 1969 in the LP *From Memphis To Vegas/From Vegas To Memphis*. Three snippets of the song were included in *That's The Way It Is* (1970) and not released. Another version was on the LP *Elvis in Person* (1970).

"Working On The Building"
(Hoyle – Bowles)
Swinging gospel with the Jordanaires. Recorded on October 31, 1960 at RCA Nashville Studio; released in December of 1960 on the LP *His Hand In Mine*.

Worldwide 50 Gold Award Hits, Vol. 1
1970 RCA. LP (LPM-6401).
Side 1: "Heartbreak Hotel"; "I Was The One"; "I Want You, I Need You, I Love You"; "Don't Be Cruel"; "Hound Dog"; "Love Me Tender."
Side 2: "Anyway You Want Me"; "Too Much"; "Playing For Keeps"; "All Shook Up"; "That's When Your Heartaches Begin"; "Loving You."
Side 3: "Teddy Bear"; "Jailhouse Rock"; "Treat Me Nice"; "I Beg Of You"; "Don't"; "Wear My Ring Around Your Neck"; "Hard Headed Woman."
Side 4: "I Got Stung"; "A Fool Such As I"; "A Big Hunk O' Love"; "Stuck On You"; "A Mess Of Blues"; "It's Now Or Never."
Side 5: "I Gotta Know"; "Are You Lonesome Tonight"; "Surrender"; "I Feel So Bad"; "Little Sister"; "Can't Help Falling In Love."
Side 6: "Rock-A-Hula Baby"; "Anything That's Part Of You"; "Good Luck Charm"; "She's Not You"; "Return To Sender"; "Where Do You Come From"; "One Broken Heart For Sale."
Side 7: "Devil In Disguise"; "Bossa Nova Baby"; "Kissin' Cousins"; "Viva Las Vegas"; "Ain't That Loving You Baby"; "Wooden Heart."
Side 8: "Crying In The Chapel"; "If I Can Dream"; "In The Ghetto"; "Suspicious Minds"; "Don't Cry Daddy"; "Kentucky Rain"; "Excerpts From 'Elvis Sails'."

Tonight"; "Tell Me Why"; "Please Don't Drag That String Around"; "Young And Beautiful."
Side 4: "Hot Dog"; "New Orleans"; "We're Gonna Move"; "Crawfish"; "King Creole"; "I Believe In The Man In The Sky"; "Dixieland Rock."
Side 5: "The Wonder Of You"; "They Remind Me Too Much Of You"; "Mean Woman Blues"; "Lonely Man"; "Any Day Now"; "Don't Ask Me Why."
Side 6: "His Latest Flame"; "I Really Don't Want To Know"; "Baby I Don't Care"; "I've Lost You"; "Let Me"; "Love Me."
Side 7: "Got A Lot O' Living To Do"; "Fame And Fortune"; "Rip It Up"; "There Goes My Everything"; "Lover Doll"; "One Night."
Side 8: "Just Tell Her Jim Said Hello"; "Ask Me"; "Patch It Up"; "As Long As I Have You"; "You'll Think Of Me"; "Wild In The Country."

consulted through Charlie Hodge.

Becky Yancey
Graceland secretary, author (with Cliff Linedecker) of *My Life With Elvis*, one of the first books published after Elvis' death.

"The Yellow Rose Of Texas/The Eyes Of Texas"
(Fred Wise – Randy Starr – Sinclair)
From *Viva Las Vegas* (1964), Elvis doing the University of Texas Longhorn theme song. What else can you say? Recorded in July of 1963 in Hollywood; released in November of 1968 on the LP *Singer Presents Elvis Singing Flaming Star and Others.*

"Yesterday"
(Paul McCartney – John Lennon)
Fine live rendition of the 1965 Beatles classic, with lively piano by Larry Muhoberac and Elvis displaying fine vocal control and emotional texture. Performed in medley with "Hey Jude."

Worldwide Gold Award Hits Vol. 2 – Elvis, The Other Sides
1971 RCA. LP (LPM-6402).
Side 1: "Puppet On A String"; "Witchcraft"; "Trouble"; "Poor Boy"; "I Want To Be Free"; "Doncha' Think It's Time"; "Young Dreams."
Side 2: "The Next Step Is Love"; "You Don't Have To Say You Love Me"; "Paralyzed"; "My Wish Came True"; "When My Blue Moon Turns To Gold Again"; "Lonesome Cowboy."
Side 3: "My Baby Left Me"; "It Hurts Me"; "I Need Your Love

Worldwide Gold Award Hits, Parts 1 & 2
RCA Record Club. LP (R213690).
Same as contents of *Worldwide 50 Gold Award Hits, Vol. 1*, Sides 1, 2, 3, and 4.
Worldwide Gold Award Hits, Parts 3 & 4
RCA Record Club. LP (R214657).
Same as *Worldwide 50 Gold Award Hits, Vol. 1*, Sides 5, 6, 7 and 8.

Lou Wright
The psychic Elvis periodically

Recorded on August 22, 1969 at the International Hotel in Las Vegas; released in May of 1970 on the LP *On Stage – February, 1970.*

"Yoga Is As Yoga Does"
(Gerald Nelson – Fred Burch)
From *Easy Come, Easy Go* (1967), Elvis' duet with Elsa Lanchester about the disadvantages of yoga – a laugh track with a marching beat and chanting chorus. Recorded on September 26, 1966 at Paramount Recording Studio in Hollywood; released in May of 1967 on the

soundtrack EP. Later, on the RCA Camden LP *I Got Lucky* (1971).

Yogi Paramahansa Yogananda
Well-known guru and founder of the "self-realization fellowship," which interested Elvis for a period. Authored *Autobiography of a Yogi*, one of Elvis' favorite books.

"You Asked Me To"
(Waylon Jennings – Billy Joe Shaver)
Lively uptempo courtly ballad – breezy, with Elvis obviously enjoying himself. Recorded on December 11, 1973 at Stax Studio in Memphis; released in January of 1975 on the LP *Promised Land*.

"You Can't Say No In Acapulco"
(Sid Feller – Dolores Fuller – Lee Morris)
From *Fun In Acapulco* (1963), a nifty production number with Elvis in his showiest form in front of an entire wall of guitars, bass, piano, drums, xylophone, and a choir. Too bad the song itself is so dumb. Recorded on January 20, 1963 in Hollywood; released in November of 1963 on the soundtrack LP.

"You Don't Have To Say You Love Me"
(Vicki Wickham – Simon Napier – Bill P. Donaggio – V. Pallavicini)
From *That's The Way It Is* (1970), Elvis takes a shot at a ballad that never gets off the ground because the horns and strings are too busy fighting it out. Nonetheless, the song was a huge smash when released. Recorded on June 6, 1970 at RCA Nashville Studio (another version was cut in August of 1970 at MGM Recording Studio in Los Angeles); released in October of 1970 as a single, with "Patch It Up" on the flip-side (this studio version was later collected on the LP *Elvis: The Other Sides – Worldwide 50 Gold Award Hits, Volume 2* (1971). Other versions were released on the soundtrack LP *That's The Way It Is* (1970) and (a shorter version) on *Elvis As Recorded At Madison Square Garden* (1972).

"You Don't Know Me"
(Eddy Arnold – Cindy Walker)
From *Clambake* (1967), a fine interpretation of this bit by Eddy Arnold in 1956, Lenny Welch in 1960 and Ray Charles in 1962. Faster in the film – the studio version was more carefully crafted. Recorded on February 21, 1967 at RCA Nashville Studio; released in September of 1967 as a single, with "Big Boss Man" on the flip-

side. Later on the soundtrack LP in 1967 and on the RCA Camden LP *Elvis Sings Hits From His Movies, Volume One*.

"You Gave Me A Mountain"
(Marty Robbins)
This song, recorded by both Marty Robbins and Frankie Laine in 1969, became a metaphor for Elvis' pain in the aftermath of his divorce and the separation from his daughter. He performed it extensively on stage, first in the *Elvis On Tour* documentary of 1972. The first recorded version was for the "*Aloha*" broadcast. Recorded on January 14, 1973 at H.I.C. Arena in Hawaii; released in February of 1973 on the LP *Aloha From Hawaii Via Satellite*. He also performed the song on his final CBS television special in 1977. It appeared on the LP *Elvis In Concert* (1977).

"You Gotta Stop"
(Bill Grant – Baum – Florence Kaye)
From *Easy Come, Easy Go* (1967), a rocker with a big time brass opening that for all of the energy never comes together. Recorded on September 26, 1966 at Paramount Recording Studio in Hollywood; released in April of 1967 on the soundtrack EP. Later, on th RCA Camden LP *I Got Lucky* (1971).

"You'll Be Gone"
(Elvis Presley – Charlie Hodge – Red West)
Brassy Latin American touch, with strong guitar and the Jordanaires. Recorded on March 18, 1962 at RCA Nashville Studio; released in February of 1965 as a single with "Do The Clam" on the flip-side. Later on the soundtrack LP *Girl Happy* (1965).

"You'll Never Walk Alone"
(Richard Rodgers – Oscar Hammerstein)
Elvis' version of this great song from the 1945 musical *Carousel* was based more on Roy Hamilton's 1954 cover than any of the others over the years. Elvis sings it with purity and power, accompanied by the Jordanaires. Full of impact and beauty, to the swelling crescendo and the soft fade. Recorded on September 11, 1967 at RCA Nashville Studio; released in April of 1968 as a single with "We Call On Him" on the flip-side. Later on the RCA Camden label LP *You'll Never Walk Alone* (1971) and the Pickwick LP *Double Dynamite* (1976).

You'll Never Walk Alone
1971 RCA Camden. LP (CALX-2472).
Side 1: "You'll Never Walk Alone"; "Who Am I"; "Let Us Pray"; "Peace In The Valley";

"We Call On Him."
Side 2: "I Believe"; "It Is No Secret"; "Sing You Children"; "Take My Hand Precious Lord."

"You'll Think Of Me"
(Mort Schuman)
From the Memphis Sessions, a solid lyric and an interesting arrangement with subtle tempo changes. Recorded on January 14, 1969 at American Studios, released in September of 1969 as a single, the flip-side of "Suspicious Minds." Later, on the LPs *From Memphis To Vegas/From Vegas To Memphis* (1969) and *Elvis: The Other Sides – Worldwide 50 Gold Award Hits, Volume 2* (1971).

Chip Young
Session guitarist in 1966, Nashville, and again in 1970–71.

Gig Young
The gruff fight promoter "Willy Grogan" in *Kid Galahad* (1962).

Reggie Young
One of Elvis' Memphis session guitarists, formerly of Bill Black's combo.

"Young And Beautiful"
(Aaron Schroeder – Abner Silver)
From *Jailhouse Rock* (1957), the song Elvis sings three times, from rough version to the released record. A fine ballad with Dudley Brooks on piano. Recorded on May 2, 1957 at MGM Studios in Culver City. California; released in October of 1957 on the EP *Jailhouse Rock* (released as a single in Europe with "Lover Doll" on the flip-side). Later, on the LPs *A Date With Elvis* (1959) and *Elvis: The Other Sides – Worldwide 50 Gold Award Hits, Volume 2* (1971).

"Young Dreams"
(Aaron Schroeder – Martin Kalmanoff)
From *King Creole* (1958), a stormy track with first-class singing by Elvis and the band is up to his level of passion. Recorded on January of 1958 in Hollywood; released in August of 1958 on the soundtrack LP. Also on the EP *King Creole, Volume 2* (1958). Later on the LP *Elvis: The Other Sides – Worldwide 50 Gold Award Hits, Volume 2* (1971).

"Your Cheatin' Heart"
(Hank Williams)
Elvis takes Hank Williams' 1952 classic and gives it a touch of the blues, with the Jordanaires. Recorded on February 1, 1958 at Radio Recorders in Hollywood; not released until July of 1965, when it appeared on the LP *Elvis For Everyone*. Later, on the LP *Welcome To My World* (1977).

"You're A Heartbreaker"
(Jack Sallee)
An old C & W standard recorded by Elvis, Scotty and Bill in December of 1954 at the Sun Studio; released in January of 1955 as a single, with "Milkcow Blues Boogie" on the flipside. RCA re-issued the same single in November of 1955. Later, on the LPs *For LP Fans Only* (1959) and *Elvis – The Sun Sessions* (1976).

"Your Groovy Self"
(Lee Hazlewood)
Nancy Sinatra's number from *Speedway* (1968), which appeared on the soundtrack LP.

"Your Love's Been A Long Time Coming"
(Ronny Bourke)
Slow ballad that gets a nice treatment from Elvis, though not particularly memorable. Recorded on December 15, 1973 at Stax Studio in Memphis; released in January of 1975 on the LP *Promised Land*.

"Your Time Hasn't Come Yet Baby"
(Hirschhorn – Kasha)
From *Speedway* (1968), a short track for the children (the Jordanaires join Elvis on the record). Recorded on June 19, 1967 in Hollywood; released June of 1968 as a single, with "Let Yourself Go." Later, on the soundtrack LP *Speedway* (1968).

"You've Lost That Lovin' Feelin'"
(Phil Spector – Barry Mann – Cynthia Weil)
Elvis' version of the Righteous Brothers' 1964 hit is a *tour de force* of vocal style, power, soul, and an instance of his band maximizing his presence. Performed in the 1970 documentary *That's The Way It Is*. Elvis' version at Madison Square Garden on June 10, 1972 was a bit more tentative – he was nervous – but no less powerful. Released on the LP *Elvis As Recorded at Madison Square Garden* (1972).

Sandra Zancan
Las Vegas showgirl who dated Elvis briefly after his divorce, before he met Linda Thompson.

David Zenoff
Supreme Court Judge who performed Elvis and Priscilla's wedding.

Adler, Bill (ed). LOVE LETTERS TO ELVIS. *New York: Today Press, 1978.*

Alicia, Stella H. ELVIS PRESLEY, THE BEATLES. *London: Pendulum Press, 1979.*

Anderson, Clive. "How Elvis Bleached the Blues: Black Roots." LET IT ROCK. *(Special Elvis Issue). December, 1973.*

Aros, Andrew A. ELVIS: HIS FILMS AND RECORDINGS. *California: Applause Publications, 1980.*

Atkins, Chet, with Neely, Bill. COUNTRY GENTLEMAN. *New York: Ballantine Books, 1975.*

Bauman, Kathleen. ONSTAGE WITH ELVIS PRESLEY. *Creative Editions, 1979.*

Barry, Ron. ALL AMERICAN ELVIS. *New Jersey: Maxigraphics, 1976.*

Booth, Stanley. "A Hound Dog, To A Manor Born." ESQUIRE. *February, 1968.*

Bowser, James W. STARRING ELVIS. *New York: Dell Publishing Co., 1977.*

Brooks, Tim, and Marsh, Erle. THE COMPLETE DICTIONARY OF PRIME-TIME NETWORK TV SHOWS, 1946–PRESENT. *New York: Ballantine Books, 1979.*

Canada, Lena. TO ELVIS WITH LOVE. *New York: Everest House, 1978.*

Cash, Johnny. MAN IN BLACK. *New York: Warner Books, 1975.*

Chappel, Steve, and Garafalo, Reebee. ROCK N' ROLL IS HERE TO PAY. *Chicago, Nelson Hall, 1977.*

Charles, Ray, and Ritz, David. BROTHER RAY (RAY CHARLES' OWN STORY). *New York: Dial Press, 1978.*

Christgau, Robert. "Elvis Presley: Aging Rock." ANY OLD WAY YOU CHOOSE IT. *Baltimore: Penguin, 1973.*

Clark, Dick. ROCK, ROLL, AND REMEMBER. *New York: Popular Library, 1978.*

Cocke, Marion J. I CALLED HIM BABE: ELVIS PRESLEY'S NURSE REMEMBERS. *Memphis State University Press, 1979.*

Cohn, Nik. ROCK FROM THE BEGINNING. *New York: Pocket Books, 1970.*

Conolly, Ray. ELVIS COMPLETE. *London: Music Sales, 1974.*

Cortez, Diego. PRIVATE ELVIS. *Stuttgart, West Germany: Fey, 1978.*

Cotten, Lee. ELVIS: HIS LIFE STORY. *1980.*

Crumbaker, Marge, with Tucker, Gabe. UP AND DOWN WITH ELVIS PRESLEY. *New York: G.P. Putnam's Sons, 1981.*

Dalton, David. "Elvis Presley: Wagging His Tail in Las Vegas." THE ROLLING STONE ROCK 'N' ROLL READER. *Ben Fong-Torres (ed). New York: Straight Arrow.*

Dalton, David, and Kaye, Lenny. ROCK 100. *New York: Grosset & Dunlap, 1977.*

Dellar, Fred, and Thompson, Roy. THE ILLUSTRATED ENCYCLOPEDIA OF COUNTRY MUSIC. *New York: Harmony Books, 1977.*

ELVIS: THE OTHER SIDE: WORLD SPIRIT MESSAGES FROM EDIE (SPIRIT GUIDE). *Golden Rainbow Press, 1980.*

ELVIS PRESLEY POSTER BOOK. *New York: Crown Publishers, 1977.*

Escott, Colin and Hawkins, Martin. CATALYST—THE SUN RECORDS STORY. *London: Aquarius Books, 1975.*

—COMPLETE SUN LABEL SESSION FILES. *Self-published.*

Ewen, David. AMERICAN POPULAR SONGS. *New York: Random House, 1966.*

Farren, Mick and Marchbank, Pearce. ELVIS IN HIS OWN WORDS. *New York: Omnibus Press, 1977.*

Friedman, Favius. MEET ELVIS PRESLEY. *New York: Scholastic Books, 1971.*

Gambaccini, Paul. ELVIS ARON PRESLEY: THE MEMORIAL ALBUM 1935–1977. *London: Wise Publications, 1977.*

Gillett, Charlie. THE SOUND OF THE CITY. *New York: Dell Publishing Co., 1972.*

—MAKING TRACKS. *New York: Sunrise Books, 1973.*

Goldman, Albert. ELVIS. *New York: McGraw Hill, 1981.*

Goldrosen, John. THE BUDDY HOLLY STORY.

New York: Quick Fox, 1979.

Graceland Associates. THE LAST VACATION. *1978.*

Gripe, Maria. ELVIS AND HIS FRIENDS. *New York: Delacorte, 1976.*

—ELVIS AND HIS SECRET. *New York: Delacorte, 1976.*

Grissim, John. COUNTRY MUSIC: WHITE MAN'S BLUES. *New York: Paperback Library, 1970.*

Gregory, Neal and Janice. WHEN ELVIS DIED. *Washington: Communications Press, 1981.*

Grossman, Albert. ELVIS. *New York: McGraw Hill, 1981.*

Grove, Martin. THE KING IS DEAD, ELVIS PRESLEY. *New York: Manor Books, 1977.*

—ELVIS: THE LEGEND LIVES. *New York: Manor Books, 1978.*

Guralnick, Peter. FEEL LIKE GOING HOME: PORTRAITS IN BLUES AND ROCK 'N' ROLL. *New York: E.P. Dutton Co., 1971.*

—LOST HIGHWAY: JOURNEYS AND ARRIVALS OF AMERICAN MUSICIANS. *Boston: David R. Godine, 1979.*

Hand, Albert. ELVIS POCKET HANDBOOK. *Derbyshire, England: Albert Hand Publications, Ltd., 1960.*

—ENCYCLOPEDIA. *Derbyshire, England: Albert Hand Publications, Ltd., 1960.*

—ELVIS SPECIAL. *Derbyshire, England: Albert Hand Publications, Ltd., 1962.*

Hanna, David. ELVIS: LONELY STAR AT THE TOP. *New York: Nordon Publications, 1979.*

Harbinson, W.A. THE ILLUSTRATED ELVIS. *New York: Grosset & Dunlap, 1975.*

—THE LIFE AND DEATH OF ELVIS PRESLEY. *London: Michael Joseph, 1978.*

Hardy, Phil and Laing, Dave. THE ENCYCLOPEDIA OF ROCK, VOLS. 1–3. *Frogmore, England: Panther Books, 1976.*

Harms, Valerie. TRYIN' TO GET TO YOU: THE STORY OF ELVIS PRESLEY. *New York: Atheneum, 1979.*

Harper, Betty. ELVIS: NEWLY DISCOVERED DRAWINGS OF ELVIS PRESLEY. *New York: Bantam Books, 1979.*

Harris, Sheldon. BLUES WHO'S WHO. *New Rochelle, New York: Arlington House, 1979.*

Hatcher, Harley. ELVIS, IS THAT YOU? *Great American Books, 1979.*

Heibut, Tony. THE GOSPEL SOUND. *New York: Simon and Schuster, 1976.*

Hemphill, Paul. THE NASHVILLE SOUND. *New York: Ballantine Books, 1970.*

Hill, Ed and Don. WHERE IS ELVIS? *1979.*

Hill, Wanda June. WE REMEMBER ELVIS. *California: Morgan Press, 1978.*

Holzer, Hans. ELVIS PRESLEY SPEAKS. *New York: Manor Books, 1978.*

Hopkins, Jerry. ELVIS. *New York: Simon and Schuster, 1971.*

—THE FINAL YEARS. *New York: St. Martin's Press, 1980.*

Jahn, Mike. ROCK FROM ELVIS PRESLEY TO THE ROLLING STONES. *New York: Quadrangle, 1973.*

James, Anthony. PRESLEY: ENTERTAINER OF THE CENTURY. *New York: Tower Publications, 1977.*

Jenkinson, Phillip and Warner, Alan. CELLULOID ROCK: TWENTY YEARS OF MOVIE ROCK. *London: Lorrimer Publishing, 1974.*

Jones, Peter. ELVIS. *London: Octopus, 1976.*

Jorgensen, Phillip; Rasmussen, Frank; and Mikkelsen, Johnny. ELVIS RECORDING SESSIONS. *Oslo, Norway: Jee Publications, 1977.*

Kelly, Joe. ALL THE KING'S MEN. *Ariel Books, 1979.*

Kinkle, Roger D. THE COMPLETE ENCYCLOPEDIA OF POPULAR MUSIC AND JAZZ, 1900–1950 (4 volumes). *New Rochelle, New York: Arlington House, 1974.*

King, Bernard, and Plehn, Heinz. ELVIS PRESLEY. *London: Music Sales, 1979.*

Lacker, Marty, and Patsy, and Smith, Leslie S. ELVIS: PORTRAIT OF A FRIEND. *Memphis: Wimmer Brothers Books, 1979.*

Lahr, John, and Palmer, Robert. BABY, THAT WAS ROCK N ROLL—THE LEGENDARY LEIBER & STOLLER. *New York: Harcourt Brace Jovanovich, 1978.*

★ ★

Laing, Dave. **BUDDY HOLLY.** New York: Macmillan, 1972.

Landau, Jon. "In Praise of Elvis Presley." IT'S TOO LATE TO STOP NOW. San Francisco: Straight Arrow, 1972.

Langbroek, Hans. **THE HILLBILLY CAT.** Self-published.

Levy, Alan. **OPERATION ELVIS.** 1960.

Lichter, Paul. **ELVIS IN HOLLYWOOD.** New York: Fireside Books, 1975.

—**THE BOY WHO DARED TO ROCK: THE DEFINITIVE ELVIS.** Garden City, New York: Dolphin Books, 1978.

Linedecker, Cliff. **COUNTRY MUSIC STARS AND THE SUPERNATURAL.** New York: Dell Publishing Co., 1979.

Lloyd, Harold and Baugh, George. **THE GRACELAND GATES.** Modern Age Enterprises, 1978.

Logan, Nick and Woffinden, Bob. **THE ILLUSTRATED ENCYCLOPEDIA OF ROCK.** New York: Harmony Books, 1977.

Macken, Bob; Fornatale, Peter; and Ayers, Bill. **THE ROCK MUSIC SOURCE BOOK.** New York: Anchor Books, 1980.

Malone, Bill C. and McCulloh, Judith. **STARS OF COUNTRY MUSIC.** Chicago: University of Illinois Press, 1975.

Mann, May. **ELVIS AND THE COLONEL.** New York: Pocket Books, 1976.

Mann, Richard. **ELVIS.** Van Nuys, California: Bible Voice, Inc., 1977.

Marcus, Greil. "Elvis: Presliad." MYSTERY TRAIN. New York: E.P. Dutton Co., 1976.

Marsh, Dave, and Stein, Kevin. **THE BOOK OF ROCK LISTS.** New York: Dell/Rolling Stone Press, 1981.

Marsh, Dave and Swenson, John (eds). **THE ROLLING STONE RECORD GUIDE.** New York: Rolling Stone Press/ Random House, 1979.

Melly, George. **REVOLT INTO STYLE.**

Miller, Jim (ed). **THE ROLLING STONE ILLUS-TRATED HISTORY OF ROCK 'N' ROLL.** New York: Rolling Stone Press, 1976.

Murray, Albert. **SOUTH TO A VERY OLD PLACE.** New York: McGraw Hill, 1971.

Murrels, Joseph. **THE BOOK OF GOLDEN DISCS.** London: Barrie and Jenkins, 1978.

Nash, Bruce. **THE ELVIS PRESLEY QUIZBOOK.** New York: Warner Books, 1978.

Nite, Norm. **ROCK ON.** New York: T.Y. Crowell, 1974.

—**ROCK ON** (Volume Two). T.Y. Crowell, 1978.

Oakley, Giles. **THE DEVIL'S MUSIC—A HISTORY OF THE BLUES.** New York: Taplinger Publishing.

Osborne, Jerry. **POPULAR AND ROCK RECORDS, 1948-1978.** Phoenix, Arizona: O'Sullivan Woodside and Co., 1978.

—**FIFTY FIVE YEARS OF RECORDED COUNTRY/ WESTERN MUSIC.** Phoenix, Arizona: O'Sullivan Woodside and Co., 1976.

—**RECORD ALBUMS, 1948-1978.** Phoenix, Arizona: O'Sullivan Woodside and Co., 1978.

Osborne, Jerry and Hamilton, Bruce. **PRESLEYANNA: THE COMPLETE ELVIS GUIDE.** Phoenix, Arizona: O'Sullivan Woodside and Co., 1980.

Page, Betty. **I GOT YA, ELVIS, I GOT YA.** Memphis: Pages Publishing, 1977.

Palmer, Robert. **DEEP BLUES.** New York: Viking, 1981.

—**JERRY LEE LEWIS ROCKS!** New York: Delilah Communications, 1981.

Panta, Ilona. **ELVIS PRESLEY: KING OF KINGS.** Exposition, 1979.

Parish, James Robert. **THE ELVIS PRESLEY SCRAP-BOOK.** New York: Ballantine Books, 1975.

Parker, Ed. **INSIDE ELVIS.** California: Rampart House, 1978.

Presley, Dee; and Stanley, Billy, Rick, and David. As told to Martin Torgoff. **ELVIS: WE LOVE YOU TENDER.** New York: Delacorte, 1980.

Presley, Vester, with Bonura, Deda. **A PRESLEY SPEAKS.** Memphis: Wimmer Brothers Books, 1978.

Presley, Vester, and Rooks, Nancy. **THE PRESLEY FAMILY COOKBOOK.** 1980.

Propes, Steve. **THOSE OLDIES BUT GOODIES.** New York: Collier Books, 1973.

—**GOLDEN OLDIES.** Radnor, Pennsylvania: Chilton Book Co., 1974.

—**GOLDEN GOODIES.** Radnor, Pennsylvania: Chilton Book Co., 1975.

Pleasants, Henry. **THE GREAT AMERICAN POPULAR SINGERS.** New York: Simon and Schuster, 1974.

Reed, Bill and Ehrenstein, David. **ROCK ON FILM.** New York: Delilah Communications, 1981.

Reggero, John (introduction by David Stanley). **ELVIS IN CONCERT.** New York: Delta Special/Lorelei, 1979.

Rosenbaum, Helen. **THE ELVIS PRESLEY TRIVIA QUIZBOOK.** New York: Signet Books, 1978.

ROLLING STONE SPECIAL MEMORIAL EDITION. New York: August, 1977.

Roxon, Lillian. **LILLIAN ROXON'S ROCK ENCYCLO-PEDIA.** New York: Grosset & Dunlap, 1969.

Shapiro, Angela and Jerome (eds). **CANDIDLY ELVIS.** Anjie Publishing, 1978.

Shaver, Sean and Noland, Hal. **THE LIFE OF ELVIS PRESLEY.** Memphis: Timur Publishing, 1979.

Shaw, Arnold. **HONKERS AND SHOUTERS.** New York: Collier Books, 1978.

—**THE ROCKIN' FIFTIES.** New York: Hawthorne Books, 1974.

—**THE WORLD OF SOUL.** New York: Paperback Library, 1971.

—**THE ROCK REVOLU-TION.** New York: Paperback Library, 1971.

Shestack, Melvin. **THE COUNTRY MUSIC ENCYCLO-PEDIA.** New York: T.Y. Crowell, 1974.

Slaughter, Todd. **ELVIS PRESLEY.** London: Wyndham, 1977.

Slaughter, Todd (ed). **ELVIS A-Z.** Derbyshire, England: Albert Hand Publications, 1976.

Stambler, Irwin. **ENCYCLO-PEDIA OF POP, ROCK & SOUL.** New York: St. Martin's Press, 1974.

Staten, Vince. **THE REAL ELVIS: GOOD OLD BOY.** Dayton, Ohio: Media Ventures, 1978.

Stearn, Jess with Geller, Larry. **THE TRUTH ABOUT ELVIS.** New York: Jove Books, 1980.

Tathem, Dick. **ELVIS (THE ROCK GREATS).** London, Phoebus, 1976.

Taylor, Paula. **ELVIS PRESLEY.** Creative Editions, 1976.

Tharpe, Jac L. (ed). **ELVIS: IMAGES AND FANCIES.** University Press of Mississippi, 1980.

Thornton, Mary Ann. **EVEN ELVIS.** New Leaf Press, 1979.

Tosches, Nick. **COUNTRY: THE BIGGEST MUSIC IN AMERICA.** New York: Dell Pub-lishing Co., 1977.

Trevena, Nigel. **ELVIS, MAN AND MYTH.** London: Atlantic Books, 1977.

Walker, Robert Matthew. **ELVIS PRESLEY: A STUDY IN MUSIC.** London: Midas Books, 1980.

Wallraf, Rainer, and Plehn, Hans. **ELVIS PRESLEY: AN ILLUSTRATED BIOGRAPHY.** 1980.

Werbin, Stu. "Elvis and the A Bomb." CREEM. March, 1972.

Wertheimer, Alfred. **ELVIS '56: IN THE BEGINNING.** New York: Collier Books, 1979.

West, Joan Buchanan. **ELVIS: HIS LIFE AND TIMES IN POETRY AND LINES.** Exposition, 1979.

West, Red (et al.). As told to Steve Dunleavy. **ELVIS: WHAT HAPPENED?** New York: Ballantine Books, 1977.

Wiegert, Sue. **ELVIS' GOLDEN DECADE.**

—**ELVIS FOREVER.** 1975.

—**FOR THE GOOD TIMES.** 1978.
All privately published.

Worth, Fred L. **THIRTY YEARS OF ROCK 'N' ROLL TRIVIA.** New York: Warner Books, 1980.

Worth, Fred L. and Temerius, Steve. **ALL ABOUT ELVIS.** New York: Bantam Books, 1981.

Yancey, Becky and Linedecker, Cliff. **MY LIFE WITH ELVIS.** New York: St. Martin's Press, 1977.

Zmijewsky, Steven and Boris. **ELVIS: THE FILMS AND CAREER OF ELVIS PRESLEY.** Secaucus, New Jersey: Citadel Press, 1976.

ABOUT THE CONTRIBUTORS

Lester Bangs is a frequent contributor to the *Village Voice, Rolling Stone*, and the *New Musical Express*, among other publications. He is the author of *Blondie* (Delilah, 1980) and a musician-composer.

Stanley Booth is a well-known free lance writer who makes his home in Memphis, Tennessee. Over the years, his articles on music and popular culture have appeared in *Rolling Stone, Esquire, Playboy*, and in many other publications. He is the author of a forthcoming book on the Rolling Stones, to be published by Simon & Schuster in 1982.

Stephanie Chernikowski is a free lance photographer originally from Beaumont, Texas, presently residing in New York's East Village. Her work appears in *New York Rocker*, the *Village Voice, Rolling Stone*, and *The New York Times*.

Lenny Kaye is a musician, composer, and pop music afficionado. He is co-author (with David Dalton) of *Rock 100* (Grosset & Dunlap, 1976) and has published articles on rock music in scores of publications over the years. He was the guitarist in The Patti Smith Group and presently leads his own band, The Lenny Kaye Connection.

Gay McRae is an avid Elvis fan and an American Correspondent of the Worldwide Elvis Fan Club. She contributed the essay "Notes of a Fan-atic" to *Elvis: Images and Fancies* (University Press of Mississippi, 1979), and lives in Memphis, Tennessee, with her husband, Stanley.

Karen Moline is the Managing Editor of Delilah Communications, as well as a free lance writer and editor living in New York.

Glenn O'Brien is a Contributing Editor to *Interview* magazine, where his column on pop music, "Glenn O'Brien's Beat," appears regularly.

Linda Ray Pratt is a professor of English at the University of Lincoln-Nebraska. Her family is from Choctaw County, Mississippi. In 1956 she joined the Northern Mississippi Elvis Presley fan club.

Bill Reed has written extensively on rock music for *Rolling Stone, Fusion* and other journals. He also reviews books and concerts for the *Los Angeles Herald Examiner*. He is the co-author of *Rock on Film* published by Delilah Communications in 1982.

Martin Torgoff is a free lance writer living in New York and the co-author, with Dee Presley and her three sons, of *Elvis: We Love You Tender* (Delacorte, 1980). He is a Contributing Editor to *Interview* magazine and is presently at work on a collection of short stories.

John Walker is a writer and cartoonist living in New York and the author of *Bad Dogs* (Knopf, 1982).

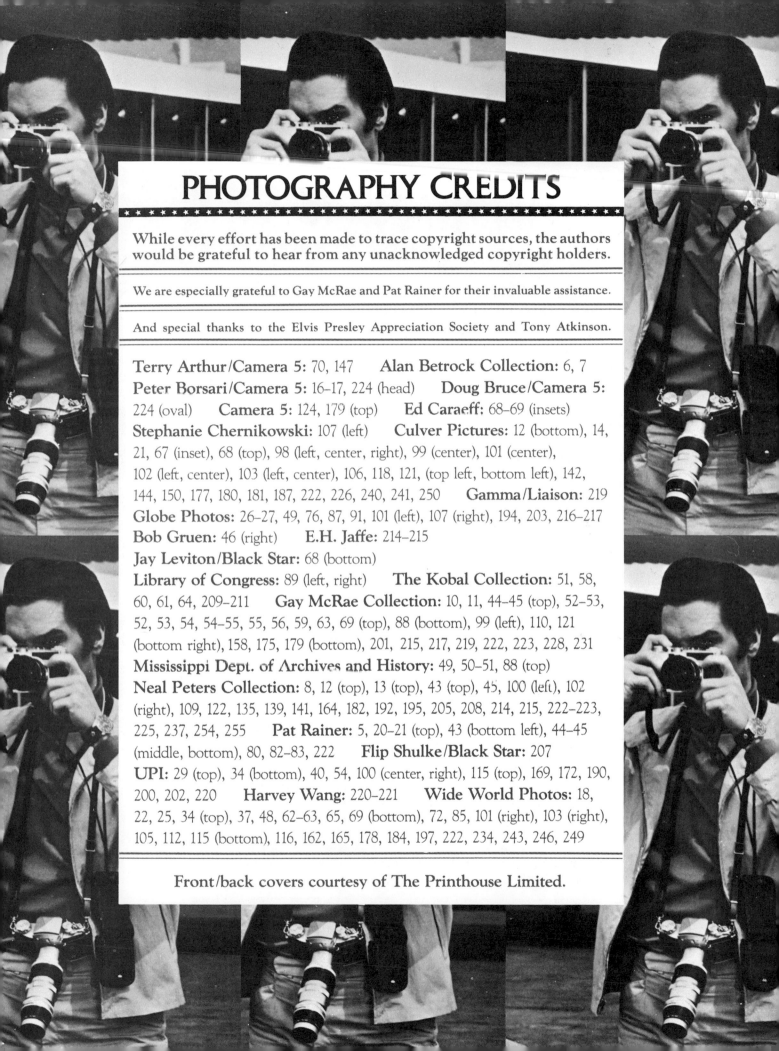

PHOTOGRAPHY CREDITS

★ ★

We are especially grateful to Gay McRae and Pat Rainer for their invaluable assistance.

And special thanks to the Elvis Presley Appreciation Society and Tony Atkinson.

Terry Arthur/Camera 5: 70, 147   **Alan Betrock Collection:** 6, 7
Peter Borsari/Camera 5: 16–17, 224 (head)   **Doug Bruce/Camera 5:** 224 (oval)   **Camera 5:** 124, 179 (top)   **Ed Caraeff:** 68–69 (insets)
Stephanie Chernikowski: 107 (left)   **Culver Pictures:** 12 (bottom), 14, 21, 67 (inset), 68 (top), 98 (left, center, right), 99 (center), 101 (center), 102 (left, center), 103 (left, center), 106, 118, 121, (top left, bottom left), 142, 144, 150, 177, 180, 181, 187, 222, 226, 240, 241, 250   **Gamma/Liaison:** 219
Globe Photos: 26–27, 49, 76, 87, 91, 101 (left), 107 (right), 194, 203, 216–217
Bob Gruen: 46 (right)   **E.H. Jaffe:** 214–215
Jay Leviton/Black Star: 68 (bottom)
Library of Congress: 89 (left, right)   **The Kobal Collection:** 51, 58, 60, 61, 64, 209–211   **Gay McRae Collection:** 10, 11, 44–45 (top), 52–53, 52, 53, 54, 54–55, 55, 56, 59, 63, 69 (top), 88 (bottom), 99 (left), 110, 121 (bottom right), 158, 175, 179 (bottom), 201, 215, 217, 219, 222, 223, 228, 231
Mississippi Dept. of Archives and History: 49, 50–51, 88 (top)
Neal Peters Collection: 8, 12 (top), 13 (top), 43 (top), 45, 100 (left), 102 (right), 109, 122, 135, 139, 141, 164, 182, 192, 195, 205, 208, 214, 215, 222–223, 225, 237, 254, 255   **Pat Rainer:** 5, 20–21 (top), 43 (bottom left), 44–45 (middle, bottom), 80, 82–83, 222   **Flip Shulke/Black Star:** 207
UPI: 29 (top), 34 (bottom), 40, 54, 100 (center, right), 115 (top), 169, 172, 190, 200, 202, 220   **Harvey Wang:** 220–221   **Wide World Photos:** 18, 22, 25, 34 (top), 37, 48, 62–63, 65, 69 (bottom), 72, 85, 101 (right), 103 (right), 105, 112, 115 (bottom), 116, 162, 165, 178, 184, 197, 222, 234, 243, 246, 249

Front/back covers courtesy of The Printhouse Limited.